Theresa Whistler, a granddau... ...
Mare well. Her previous books includ... ...
Poems of Mary Coleridge.

What the critics said:

'... impeccably researched and written, it is difficult to see how this
biography could be bettered, much less replaced.'

London Evening Standard

'This is a very fine, almost exemplary biography ... a work of love and
scholarship.'

The Tablet

'... [Whistler's] portrait of the man is absorbing ...'

The Daily Telegraph

'... plainly a biography was overdue, and, equally plainly, [Whistler]
was the one to write it.'

The Irish Times

'a very intelligent and closely written biography'

Peter Ackroyd, *The Times*

The Life of Walter de la Mare

The Life of
Walter de la Mare

Imagination of the Heart

Theresa Whistler

Duckbacks

Published in 2003 by Duckbacks,
a paperback imprint of Duckworth Publishers
First published in 1993 by
Gerald Duckworth & Co. Ltd.
First Floor, East Wing
90-93 Cowcross Street
London EC1M 6BF
Tel: 020 7490 7300
Fax: 020 7490 0080
Email: inquiries@duckworth-publishers.co.uk
www.ducknet.co.uk

A catalogue record for this book is available
from the British Library

ISBN 0 7156 3216 7

Printed in Great Britain by
BOOKMARQUE Ltd, Croydon, Surrey

Contents

Contents

Part IV. A Citadel More Central

Acknowledgments

My grateful thanks go to all those (too many to list) who have helped me with their letters and memories, and in particular to the de la Mare family who made such a wealth of material available and gave me permission to quote as I needed. I must also thank all those friends who have read the manuscript and advised at various stages.

I owe special gratitude to my former husband, Laurence Whistler, for constant discussions of work in progress during our marriage and for unfailing encouragement since, and also to my children, in particular my daughter Frances for her unstinting professional advice.

I owe a central debt to the generosity of Humphrey Carpenter, who devoted almost as much time to cutting and pulling into shape the first voluminous draft as he would have spent on writing a book of his own. I must also thank Rachel Trickett for generous aid, encouragement and hospitality, and Hugo Brunner for taking so much trouble to place the book.

I thank everyone who has given me kind permission to quote copyright material. Among these, acknowledgments are due to the Society of Authors on behalf of the Katherine Mansfield Estate and to the Executors of the Forrest Reid Estate. I am grateful to Lady Dynevor for permission to reproduce the portrait drawing by William Rothenstein, and to Nicholas and Julian Thompson for use of family photographs from the great store collected by their mother Florence.

To the memory of N.

Prologue

'Biography', it seems to me, is almost as much an umbrella term as 'the novel' – the form any particular one will take depends vitally on the material there to use, and on what stance toward his subject fits the particular biographer.

Sometimes (as in this case) the subject may also present special problems of abundance – a man long-lived, very prolific, sociable and charming, greatly loved and successful in his own day. All this can make him hard to sift, to bring into fresh focus with any justice, nearly forty years after his death – especially years which have seen such a scree-shift in sentiment and in all assumptions, both about poetry and about human purposes.

Add to this in de la Mare's case, that he was conscientious in reply (to a vast post-bag) well beyond the demands of anything charitably reasonable: that he kept all letters received, and that he hoarded also (on principle, as seed-corn) all scraps, notes, revisions, false starts, draft on draft – even his earliest rejection slips.

Faced with such a plethora, the first problem is obviously one of heavy selection – not even just of what to use, or mention, but, more basic still, what of all this even to read thoroughly, much being repetitive.

I have read, and long reflected on, in fact, an enormous amount – all, I think, that is part of his own work – but not by any means all of those stacked files, envelopes, shelves and cupboardsful of peripheral correspondence and business made freely available to me over years and years, mainly by de la Mare's eldest son, Dick. I can never be grateful enough for the patience with which he and his family endured my prolonged munching through this mountain of paper (mostly while staying in the house, too, as Dick was very reluctant to let much of it cross his threshold).

In the later 1950s and 1960s I visited as many as possible of those in de la Mare's wide circle – and several became through this my own dear friends till death – such as Helen Thomas, Sydney Cockerell or Reginald Yarrow, de la Mare's schoolfellow in St Paul's choir. I began

systematically with those nearing ninety, and so worked back, to lose
as few chances as I could by their own departures. Their recollections
and reflections about de la Mare, with my own and those of my close
family, are the staple of this book. I had one great prior advantage by
accident of birth. I inherited a friendship with him already intimate
through three generations by the time I was born, 1927. My mother's
father, Henry Newbolt, had by then been a close friend of de la Mare's
for a quarter century, and in that while multiple bonds of affection had
formed between our families, at all ages, which drew in also
surrounding friends. So I have known personally (some slightly, some
very well indeed and from childhood up) the majority of the principal
figures in de la Mare's story.

It followed naturally that his figure, and his rhymes and poems,
were a live force in my own experience of childhood, and that as I grew
up through the thirties, the war, and into marriage in the fifties with
Laurence Whistler, my sister's widower, de la Mare's books were
keenly discussed as each came out, between us all.

I did not take to it all – sometimes de la Mare prose seemed
exhausting and blood-thinning, sometimes, in verse, the sentiment
dated for me and I grew away – but I remained intently interested, and
what struck root for life did so with central gravitas and penetration –
beyond, I mean, any easy appeal of beauty, verbal music or romance.

It stands time and trouble, it carries the tang of authentic spiritual
experience – however elusive, fantastic, fine-spun and minor-keyed the
stuff in which de la Mare may deal. The outlook communicated (so odd
and sidelong in some respects) proposes enormous horizons to being
alive, as if no human existence, whether narrow or exceptional, could
ever be lived fully enough to exhaust the potential of its given
experience.

In writing his life (a job inordinately interrupted and delayed) I have
kept, throughout, the conviction that I would *not* write yet another
comprehensive biography of someone formerly highly esteemed, now
neglected, who knew everybody worth knowing (and hundreds more)
and whose history (apart from the first hard struggle up into
recognition) took so unexciting and respectable a course. Nothing, to
my mind, is more boring than to read the lists of distinguished
acquaintance and the other paraphernalia of literary success which
take up such wads of the middle and later chapters about writers of
similar fortunes. Instead I must ask the reader to bear with (or shut
this book now) a narrative which indeed I have taken pains to build on
a solid, accurate skeleton of chronological fact, but whose *aim* is
particular.

It springs from a breakfast conversation I had with de la Mare in 1950, at the top of South End House, Twickenham. Up there, the windows looked into the higher branches of his beloved plane tree and we were both much aware of its presence, standing by. I was in my early twenties, de la Mare in his last year or so of full vigour, in his late seventies.

He had been suggesting that imagination comes in several distinct species and mentioned three – first, imagination of the intellect – a third, I think, that day, imagination of the body. But what so pinned my attention that reliable recollecting comes to a halt just there, was the tone of voice in which he proposed the second – imagination of the heart. Obviously, by the way he said it, this was, for him, supreme. So I began to take in the moment around us in the light of that – the small kitchen table spread with a clean newspaper – our enjoyment together of the toast and coffee he had made – the fresh, summer morning light – the exhilarating sense of our height up the great limber tree – and, for me, the massive impression of condensed, acute thoughtfulness which age had by now given to the dark head, turned away from me, towards his thought as he spoke, then swung back, his features creasing into instant humorous affection – delighted to tease, challenge, please, encourage, *test* – and all these at once.

So what I have tried to do is to present that strand or species of the imagination, as he conceived it, and as it was unfolded in his own personality, by the passage of his years. I have wanted to concentrate on the how and why and where and when this central function developed shape and significance, for this individual, between 1873 and 1956.

I have tracked it like a river meandering through his landscape (crowded of course with other features of legitimate, but to me secondary, importance). I have been greatly struck by the way the outfall lies so very close alongside the salient from which it rose in his childhood.

My portrayal of his youth has turned out rather like a row of circumstantial late-nineteenth-century engravings. I have made no attempt to continue the same treatment through his prime and success. I have picked out, instead, to describe (from dozens of perhaps equally flourishing relationships) only those which seemed to give fresh bearings on my theme. So also with his professional, public life. While keeping the general tenor of his doings, I have not dwelt on whatever was, for my purpose, less than revealing. For instance, I have cavalierly left out almost all about his second tour of America, just because the impact of the States on his *imagination*, all took place in the first.

Finally, to highlight what is to me remarkable about his last years, I have again taken a shift in method, trying for something like a series of Impressionist sketches. I wanted, by these, to illustrate the lambent, encouraging quality his old age gave out (not all accounted for by his good fortune, though he *was* very fortunate then, his health apart).

I think his conclusions about the state of old age, and the unusually creative way he lived his own, stem directly from imagination of the heart, put to work on anything that came, till the last day and night, and that this is the final proof of his trust in its touch.

Part I
Industrious Apprentice

1

Origins

Walter de la Mare was born on 25 April 1873 in a small crowded house in Charlton, Woolwich. At that date it was a neighbourhood to give a pungent first taste of the world to any wideawake childhood. Variety lay within easy reach. From the heights of Woolwich Common, London still smoked and glittered apart, along a wide sweep of skyline crests. Woolwich Barracks nearby housed a growing swarm of Royal Artillerymen – figures as gaudy as parrots, who added panache to the local gaieties. Some of the artillery families were neighbours of the Delamares* in the little modern row on the slope of Maryon Road, which had probably been put up to meet the increased military demand in the Crimean War for Woolwich quarters. The row was Charlton's newest approach to Woolwich proper, which overflowed down the side of the Common. Soon both would blend in one. Down on the valley floor beside the river the bold Vanbrugian buildings of the Naval Dockyard rose sheer out of slums – yet another world to themselves. By contrast Charlton itself, a village complete with Jacobean manor-house and squire, was a place of trees and green slopes: feudal Kent, though only a saunter below the Delamares.

In this way, before the precarious balance of both was lost in a welter of mean brick belonging to neither, charms of capital and countryside almost embraced. The Delamares' own house, for instance, enjoyed a minute urban elegance; yet in 1873 its windows still looked across the road at the leafy tops of an old, undisturbed orchard. It was a fringe landscape, and fleeting, pullulating with speculators.†

Before the railway had connected them to London Bridge in 1849, to

---

* The name was usually spelt at the time in this anglicised way. It seems to have been Walter de la Mare himself, as soon as he grew up, who re-adopted the French spelling. he probably felt it was more romantic.

† At first unnumbered, and then numbered 41, the house finally settled down as No 83 Maryon Road in 1874. It was demolished in 1966.

live so far out must have been eccentrically inconvenient for a City
clerk, such as de la Mare's father was. According to family tradition
James Delamare rode to the Bank of England in Threadneedle Street
each day on his mare. But for James the prime requisite was to be close
to his brother Abraham, a clergyman eight years older, to whom he had
clung from motherless boyhood on. They were inseparable. So when
Abraham was given as his first parish a new one carved out of
expanding Woolwich, to Woolwich James had followed, though his own
career in the Bank began at about the same period. Abraham, who
never married, brought with him their ageing father, and a sister to
housekeep. The Ur they all left was the little market town of Romford
in Essex, where their branch of the Huguenot Delamares had
prospered in force from first immigration right down to James's
Regency youth.

In Woolwich James now went on to spend thirteen childless years of
marriage, during the last five of which his wife was ailing, and there he
remained, a solitary widower, more dependent than ever on his
brother's company. After ten years, in 1860, he suddenly married
again. His second bride, Lucy Browning, was twenty-six years
younger, and his devotion to her was correspondingly paternal. Lucy
came from Arrott House in Maryon Road where her widowed mother
and young brothers lived, so it was natural for the couple to choose a
home a few yards away in the brand-new row. It is less clear why they
were never to budge again, for the house was tiny and their family grew
steadily. Decisive no doubt was the fact that only a few steps across
and down Maryon Road stood Abraham's church. They could hardly
live closer, and what could suit James better, since to live next door to
Abraham's actual home (there was no official Rectory till later) was
hardly within his means? Abraham lived in grander style among the
residences of the well-to-do, the Colonels and Generals of the Artillery,
a mile away, close to the crest of the Common. Next best, plainly, was
to cling as close as possible to Abraham's church, where he could be
sure to find him every day.

This church, St Thomas's, loomed like a great Noah's Ark over the
shoals of adjacent roofs – a commonsensical Low Church basilica,
confident enough to dispense with tower or spire. Abraham was no
sooner appointed than he vigorously pushed through its construction.
He remained Rector for more than thirty years and died at work.
James was his churchwarden. They placed a Delamare tomb in the
churchyard, prominent outside the West door. Family names
multiplied rapidly on its sides, and an old servant from Romford days,
who died after working for them sixty-three years, was commemorated

there as if she kept house still in their vault. This pair of brothers had
the patriarchal instinct very strongly, and the seven children Lucy was
to supply were of equal importance to both. Walter John – soon called
Jack (for the little boy detested his first name, as it made him think of
'watery') – was the sixth.

James was by then sixty-one. The Bank had just brought in a new
rule enforcing retirement at sixty-five. He wrote a lament in humorous
verse, but the rule had shaken his security. Soon he would only have a
pension by which to support all this late brood.

Florence, the eldest, and one of the most important figures in Jack's
childhood, was nearly thirteen. Her name is one of half a dozen family
names which de la Mare bestowed on his own children. They come over
and over again in his poems and stories – Herbert, Arthur, Hamilton,
and, more frequently and insistently, Florence, Lucy, and Sophia. Few
writers pluck family names so simply for association's sake.

Flo was gentle and maternal to the younger ones; and Jack became
her favourite. She was patient and domesticated (unlike their mother).
'Never a cross word', according to Poppy, the youngest. Florence was
dark, of middle height and like all the children, taller than their
mother. She had beautiful, deep-set dark eyes, strong features and an
imaginative mind, which a desperately struggling life was not to allow
much scope. Uncle Abraham supplied her with a good education – a
governess shared with the Colonel's daughters next door to him – and
she whiled away hours of her solitary childhood with the Waverley
novels on his study floor.

Solitary for a curious reason. What James and Abraham both lived
for was a civilised, prosaic routine, lit by daylight faith; but to be
happy, each needed children in the house. Abraham took in an
illegitimate daughter of his twin brother, Henry. (Henry was the only
unsteady Huguenot Delamare – a gifted amateur actor, the only
brother with a touch of the romantic temperament.) In addition James
lent him his first child – a rather extreme piece of brotherly sharing,
for Flo was only three. She stayed for twelve years, though she saw her
own family every day or so. The youngest, Poppy, never quite forgave
her mother for agreeing to this arrangement. Furthermore, when Flo
was twelve and Abraham's sister died, Henry's daughter went back to
her own mother, so Flo was left completely alone with her bachelor
uncle. Childhood ended there, and she became in effect lady of the
Rectory, responsible for Uncle Abraham's hospitality. Before she was
fifteen she had become a competent Victorian housewife.

Next to Flo came Arthur, who was eleven when Jack was born. He
was a rebel from the first. Then came Constance, now eight. Ethel Lucy

followed, whose death as a little girl divided the family into two groups
of playfellows. The eldest of the younger group, James Herbert, born in
the year she died, was now three. Last of all, when Jack was two,
would come Ada Mary Frances, known as Poppy – rosy, flaxen and
voluble.

Flo had a dreamy passiveness; Arthur, with his clever wits, a
restless bias towards trouble; and Connie left home very young, set,
against all opposition, on a marriage at sixteen or seventeen to a
good-looking volatile youth, a Bartram. They emigrated at once to New
Zealand and presently lost touch. The younger group of children are
the more interesting. Bert had a dual personality. He was energetically
businesslike from boyhood, yet as a young man his conspicuous points
were remarkably romantic looks and an uncommon flair, like Uncle
Henry, for acting. However, the professional stage was not respectable
– out of the question for a Delamare – and Bert's sober, responsible
side would presently eclipse the other, so that by middle age hardly
anyone could guess such a buried self had ever been (except, one
suspects, Jack). Poppy, the youngest, would manage to keep her
affectionate gusto alive throughout a long hard life. She had much of
her mother's family nature in her, and was certainly born, as she
remained, 'a character'.

Character and energy were unmistakably marked from birth in the
dark sixth baby who came between these two – and in him, these
qualities were well balanced with the dreaming, receptive, passive
powers. Health would vary, sometimes alarmingly, when practical
anxieties and nervous sensibility taxed it, but fundamental stamina
was obviously there from the start – something that has at least as
much bearing on creative attainment as any questions of psychology –
and with it went what de la Mare held in others to be the mark of
genius, 'a sovereign energy of mind'. All his life he repeated with
passionate conviction his credo that a child is born complete, and from
the instant of birth homesick, an exile, though with nothing more yet
than its mother for home.

This mother had style. 'How well I remember,' wrote Flo to Jack in
later years, 'the ceremony observed on the day of your Christening.' He
was a month old that May Sunday afternoon, and Lucy, Flo
remembered, made a decided entrance in a new white tulle bonnet and
veil, sailing up the aisle on James's arm just before the christening to
be 'churched'. 'All of us very smart for the occasion which we much
enjoyed.'[1] Lucy was a tiny upright figure about the size of her Queen,
with whom she had a certain amount in common. Her gaze was very
direct – under a noble brow and brown hair. The eyes were eloquent –

but the jaw, formidable! She would submit outwardly, like other Victorian young women, to male authority, but within reigned absolute independence of spirit – and it often burst out. No wonder the solemn widower James, and the 'dear incumbent' as Abraham was nicknamed, had both been captivated. Lucy brought all they lacked, and more, to warm them and sometimes turn their world upside down – love and salt and laughter, unquenchable verve, hot obstinacy, a sense of duty as exacting as their own, and above all a continual unexpectedness, not capricious but the expression of a thoroughly original heart. Her children and grandchildren treasured anecdotes of her later years that could belong just as well to youth, for she had never been any different. Once, setting out to view a sale of furniture, she walked into the wrong house by mistake. Found by the owners exploring their private domain, she was quite unabashed, merely remarking, 'What beautiful things you have here!' At Edward VII's lying-in-state she knelt down by the bier, holding up the entire shuffling column behind her. Officials trying to hurry her on were put in their place: 'No one is going to prevent me from praying for my King.'

If it was she who lit the drawing-room at Woolwich in the evenings of the sixties and early seventies for James's return from the City, she must be imagined standing at least on a foot-stool to reach, even though the flames were set low. They hissed away on three writhing arms of an imposing gasolier, sprouting from an ornate plaster rose in the middle of the ceiling. The twin dignified rooms on the first floor, even when their triple panelled doors were flung back to combine them, still made only a diminutive chamber. The accent was stylish: the scale tiny – and this went for both, the home itself and its central figure. For Lucy undoubtedly was its centre. James, though he laid down the law, was only its pillar, and Abraham an overshadowing spiritual authority from under whose wings a good deal of Lucy contrived to escape.

As James no doubt foresaw, she would be a first-rate mother. She proved, in fact, the kind that an imaginative child will never cease to recall with regret, delight, amusement: the bond between them at the heart of his gift for the rest of his life. But this bond was particularly potent for de la Mare – more so than his father's death fully accounts for, though this would so soon emphasize it. Probably the reason simply is that the two individuals concerned were each of them, in their own right, very unusual. Lucy de la Mare seems to have had a similar effect in varying degrees on most of her other children, but in her youngest son there was more to stimulate, more to meet, a far subtler personality to captivate and influence. His temperament with its gifts stemmed all from her own Scots line, though the ballast provided by the dependable Delamares was certainly salutary. The Brownings, and behind them the Arrotts of Arbroath, must come into the foreground of this chapter because their influence on de la Mare was something much stronger and more curious than a mere matter of the genes which plainly link his make-up and intelligence to theirs.

The one who mattered most was Lucy's father, Dr Colin Arrott Browning, who ended his career as Superintendent of the Woolwich Naval Dockyard. Alone among Walter de la Mare's forebears he combined dynamic force of personality with the gift of expressing this, at any rate in headlong letters. He was not an artist, but an evangeliser and social reformer, and more of a rocket than a steadily-burning light.

Too poor in boyhood to be given a good education, he had scraped together his naval surgeon's pay until, by a crash course of study ashore, he won a Physician's degree. This was unusual at the time, for most doctors were of Surgeon's rank only. Romantic and impulsive, he searched eight years for his ideal beloved, won a kiss at first encounter, and embarked on a marriage which proved stormy, devoted and badly off, begetting ten children only half of whom survived. He quarrelled rashly with his naval superiors. Yet he carried through a revolution in the conditions for convicts during transportation to labour camps in Van Diemen's Land and other such hells. Previously the convicts, some of whom were guilty of nothing worse than petty theft, had travelled crammed between decks. The Captain took care of crew and navigation only, and the Naval Surgeon had entire charge of the human cargo. His job was to ensure that they arrived alive and caused no uproar on the way. Browning saw things differently, and later published vivid accounts of his reforms in *The Convict Ship* and *England's Exiles*. During his sixth voyage so successful had he become that no lashes were inflicted, and 'not an iron was used nor a convict placed under a sentry'.[2] He denounced corporal punishment as degrading and destroying self-respect, and insisted that petty officers should address prisoners by name, declaring: 'In all cases men should be treated like men. Treat them like slaves and you speedily convert them into slaves.'[3] When he himself fell dangerously ill of blood-poisoning after carrying out a post-mortem between decks, his prisoners became his devoted nurses, and once they presented him with a signed address of gratitude.

He loved to harrow his family with accounts of his perils. To his 'beloved little Lucy', his favourite, he wrote a letter when she was about eight, making the very most of a tense hour, while his ship

wallowed at midnight at the height of a storm in the English Channel –
somewhere off Brighton, where he imagined Lucy tucked up in bed:

> The Ladies have come out of their Cabins so terribly frightened are they
> at the Storm & well they may! for it blows furiously … Were any of the
> poor men to fall from aloft there is no possibility of saving them. One man
> did fall overboard in the great Southern Ocean, but it was not blowing
> such a gale as it does now, & we lowered the boat down, when Mr Wells
> the chief Mate, and four other brave sailors jumped into the boat &
> pulled over the tumbling seas & picked up the poor man Willm. White
> (just as the great Albatrosses were gathering round him to pick his eyes
> out & devour him) & to the joy of us all brought him on board again … I
> hope, dear Lucy, you are asleep & do not hear the wind roar; if you were
> awake I dare say you would think of yr. dear [Papa] especially if you
> knew that I was just off your shore, exposed to the fury of the
> tempestuous winds & rolling sea.[4]

Beside this foreceful Scots temperament, the French blood in de la
Mare was a sober strain. What we notice most about his father's family
is how intensely Huguenot they remained, as late as the Woolwich
generation.

Most refugees react strongly, either by quickly taking the colour of
their new surroundings, shedding their foreign-ness and adapting
their name, or else, in the reverse way, jealously guarding the
traditions of their origin, even marrying where possible among their
own kind. The Delamares from Bolbec in Normandy were obviously of
the latter sort.

The family instinct evidently was to grow in the manner of tough
perennial plants, in clumps. When divided, they re-established
another clump as soon as possible. This cluster instinct was still
strong, as we shall see, in de la Mare's own generation. The marked
persistence of the Huguenot in them owed a good deal to this
solidarity, but also something to a chance peculiarity – the exiled
generations were uncommonly long ones, and therefore uncommonly
few. There was a sequence of long families born to junior sons
themselves born to elderly fathers – evidence incidentally of masculine
stamina. Jean Baptiste de la Mare of Bolbec was only the poet's
great-great-grandfather, though a span of two hundred and sixty-five
years lies between his birth in 1691 and Walter de la Mare's death in
1956. Thus only three complete generations intervene between them –
not much if one is thinking in terms of genes and family psychology:
traditions, recollections passed on, the early setting of habit, prejudice
and taste through what is impressed by the very old on the very young.
Even in looks the French strain kept its stamp unblurred. De la Mare
himself looked strikingly French, and so did his younger son. But one

may search almost in vain down all that sober heredity for the Frenchman's lighter side – for wit, sophistication or imagination.

In fact there could hardly be purer exemplars of the Huguenot ethic than Abraham and James – not grim (in fact particularly affectionate), but strenuous, stable, deeply conscientious. James drew his own portrait in a sedulous, laconic journal, which de la Mare treasured all his life. It ran from 1830 (when James was eighteen) to 1833, and was written in a vellum-bound account book, neatly divided into columns. One was for the Romford weather, and one for the daily mileage of his mare, which was duly totted up at the end of each year. Only once in those three years does he mention a book he has read. Once he made an Aeolian harp. One summer he helped construct a shell grotto. For the rest, all he cares to show of his character is already set – genuine, filial, devout, dull. Yet there may have been some secret current that went underground, as in his son Bert. We know that he wrote other verses besides the ones on his retirement. Of these there survives only 'The Tyrant's Funeral', a set of entirely conventional Augustan stanzas, but de la Mare seems to have known also of some love poems. A late photograph taken when he was dying of cancer shows another aspect, something much more sensitive, and here, if nowhere else, a touching family likeness to his poet son.

*

Up the narrow, neat stairs at the Maryon Road house, above the principal rooms lay two main bedrooms, front and back, quietly elegant, with little basket grates and reeded mantelpieces. One had a small room adjoining, through an arch, which could serve as a dressing-room or hold a cradle. Jack, like the rest of those seven children, was probably born in one or other of these rooms. It was at 4.30, three and a half hours after high tide, in the afternoon of Friday 25 April. One of the first sounds to invade the room would have been the monstrous bellowing and snorting of ocean-going steamers, tugs, military supply-ships and pleasure craft thronging the wide Woolwich reaches of the Thames, barely half a mile away.

Childhood impressions, the matrix of everyone's behaviour, are normally what determine a writer's range, for most impressions that pierce deep enough to affect the springs of creative impulse do so very early. What moved the child will move the heart's imagination to the end. At least this is true of artists whose vision is essentially childlike. It is less so, perhaps, for those in whom it is more active and experimental than contemplative. Then it derives more from boyhood than from childhood and remains boyish, to some extent, throughout adult life. This difference de la Mare explored himself in *Rupert Brooke and the Intellectual Imagination*.

Jack was a particular case. He not only kept, spontaneously, the childlike vision, but also continued deliberately to exercise the special faculties of childhood – day-dreaming, make-believe, questioning that takes nothing for granted. He put a serious value on these ways of exploring life, and used them constantly to establish lines of communication between unconscious powers of the mind and their full articulate recognition. The greater part of all he wrote is either the recreation of experience through the eyes of childhood, or else the absorbed lifelong investigation of how such eyes work. Coleridge rated highly this bent for applying childhood's resources to mature experience.

> To carry on the feelings of childhood into the powers of manhood; to combine the child's sense of wonder and novelty with the appearances, which everyday life, for perhaps forty years, had rendered familiar 'with sun and moon and stars throughout the year, And man and woman'; this is the character and privilege of genius, and one of the marks which distinguish genius from talent.[5]

It is a pity that de la Mare did not leave more records of his own first impressions, for not many more are noted in his books than most people can recall. And it must be admitted that when he recorded them he was apt to overwork details which were far more subtly and vividly conveyed in his talk.

The point is that these details continued to matter to him with a quite unusual intensity, as irreplaceable clues to the centre of his life. Also they were often unusually objective, visualised and particular. He would try every mental dodge to re-enter a world which he had never, as it were, outgrown but which he felt ever-present, just below conscious retrieval. Every stray physical fragment seemed worth the most meticulous salvage operations, for any splinter might provide clues to the whole wonder of their original impact. This was an experiment made when he was nearly sixty:

> Brooding recently on some trifling event in my childhood, I was astonished to discover that at the moment I could recall no more of the interior of the house where it occurred than a glimpse of a table and of the window in one of its rooms. *This* insulated recollection, however, was so intense and definite that it all but amounted to an hallucination.
>
> I let it stay in my mind, so to speak, without stirring, in the faint hope that more would follow. And presently, as if clean out of nowhere, two wooden steps leading out of this room quietly revealed themselves, and

the next moment I was able to explore other rooms in the house, upstairs and down, and so effectively that in a few moments I could recall the position of their doors, windows and fireplaces, together with some of the furniture, the china, the pictures.

And then it was as though a ghost of the mind could draw near within the compass as it were, of the memory itself, and *examine* the pictures – one, I remember, of cattle gathered together under the sullen and lowering clouds of a thunderstorm, another of rocks and pale green trees and coursing water – and the very impress, sealed once on consciousness, was recovered in spite of the experiences amassed in between – even the clear and lively colours of the china figures, and of the Chinese cups and saucers, as they were seen *then*. How strange it seems, then, that among these clear and scattered objects no living figure appears; though other memories vividly reanimate these same remote rooms again.[6]

His earliest detailed memory was of an encounter on Woolwich Common:

I do not see myself, but *am* actually walking – in a vague open place, and to the left of a nursemaid who is propelling an iron-tyred, three-wheeled perambulator. My right hand is resting on the iron support of its handle. In this perambulator, beneath an ample leather apron, reclines – though I can see nothing of her except the frill of a bonnet – an infant sister. This detail is dubious; the vehicle may have been empty; the 'frill' linen. My nurse is talking to a soldier. Not only am I aware that he is a soldier, but also that she should not be thus improving the shining hour. The day is bright, but neither sunny nor hot, and I detect no *colour*, neither the green of the grass, the blue or grey of the sky, that of the wood of the perambulator or my nurse's clothes, nor her attendant swain's artillery blue picked out either with red or yellow. For an artilleryman of some kind he almost certainly was. At this moment I am suddenly startled – alarmed and shattered would be nearer the mark – by an explosive sensation as if icy cold or scalding hot water had been dashed between my shoulderblades. I stare about me in amazement and dismay and see at some little distance men holding shining metal objects. They, I realize, were the origin of the shock. It is a brass band; and it has begun to play. I recollect nothing – and no one – else, am aware of no voices, or of any experience preceding this moment, or following it. And yet its only *once* apparently was this crash of brazen instruments, the sensation of which I attributed (since I did not recognize it as a *sound*) not to my ears but to my spinal column.[7]

Not much later perhaps, on hands and knees he came face to face with a spider:

And though some fifty years have gone by since we met, I can still exchange gaze for gaze with a straddling, hairy, and, as it seemed to me, vilely sagacious spider – its luminous pale yellow little eyes fixed on me from the refuge to which it had scuttled behind the leg of a chair. That

same evening I was reduced to such terror on observing that my younger
sister, in spite of all my anguished entreaties, appeared to have fallen
asleep, that I pushed up one of her eyelids – only to disclose the white
unpupilled sightless ball beneath it![8]

The spider of that memory would reappear in the opening pages of
his novel *The Return*, where Lawford, at the tomb of the Huguenot
suicide, encounters the 'little almost colourless fires' of its eyes in the
sinister crack of the slab: 'It was for the moment an alarming, and yet a
faintly fascinating experience.'[9]

Just that mixture of fear and fascination was to be from the
beginning the impulse that best set his imagination alight. The
spider's eyes in the tomb's crack herald the demonic possession which
issues from it as soon as Lawford falls asleep on the grave. Oddly
enough, even that other unease linked with the spider memory, when
the little boy had pushed up Poppy's sleeping eyelid, leaves its trace on
the same passage. Just as Lawford is surrendering to the sleep during
which his psyche is so horribly invaded, his lids 'presently unsealed a
little, momentarily revealing astonished, aggrieved pupils, and softly,
slowly they again descended'.[10]

*

For James's summer holiday the family always went to Bonchurch or
Ventnor in the Isle of Wight. Lucy, restive at the enforced absence from
the London she loved, and bored with the decorum and palaver of a
family holiday in a furnished house, once pleaded to be left behind.
Could she not have a week in London *on her own*? No doubt there was a
gleam in her eye – so much to do and see, and freedom to taste it alone!
James was predictably scandalized, and Lucy, duly chaperoned and
wreathed around with children, went to Ventnor as she was bid. But
once there, she did at least once assert her independence. James and
Abraham, seeking out a service on the Island where worship was
suitably plain, settled for a Presbyterian chapel, but Lucy went off
defiantly by herself to a service where a Mr Peel actually wore a
surplice. Abraham shook his head over her: 'I am afraid dear Lucy is
getting High Church notions.'

De la Mare kept one recollection of Ventnor which interested him,
because, like the incident of the nursemaid and the artilleryman, a
moral sense gave edge to the scene, as it so often does in childhood –
and nothing makes such amber for a speck of the past as conflict of
feelings at the time. He was watching a group of older children who
had built a sandcastle shutting up a small green frog (or was it a crab?)

in its deepest dungeon, himself as much fascinated as pitying. Every
little boy in his stories has these two selves: one involved; the other
detached, the analyst.

In those brief early holidays he acquired an abiding love of the
seaside – as strong in young manhood and in old age as it was

> when, a child, I was content to rove
> The shingled beach that I was Crusoe of,
> All that I learned there was akin to love.[11]

He cannot have accompanied the family on these expeditions more
than two or three times at most, for in 1877 all such amenities came to
an abrupt end. In January his uncle Abraham, now seventy-three,
collapsed and died of angina while visiting Woolwich workhouse. As
James sat writing the official notification to the parish of the Rector's
death, he must have felt a mortally dismaying chill. His thirty years in
the Bank had ended the previous November. His life-work, and now
his life's prop, had both gone. And then what had appeared to be gout
disclosed itself as cancer of a toe. By October he too was dead.

De la Mare's chief recollection of his father dates from this last
painful illness. Coming in one day, he found 'a beautiful little nest
made of moss containing half a dozen eggs on the bench in the hall. It
had been brought by a friend for my father. I put one of them in my
breeches pocket, and when asked if I had meddled with the eggs, said
No! Facts were against me, especially later in the day when the egg
broke.' Questioned by his father ('What's that then, running down your
leg?') and driven back on Eve's tactics, Jack cried 'Don't beat me. Satan
put it in my pocket, Pa!' Once when he told this story, he added a
further memory. His father had said: 'You know, I'd really better beat
you for this.' De la Mare continued: 'We had one of those old straw
boxes with a thick leather strap round it, and he was going to beat me
with that. I can see my Mother now, standing behind my father in the
doorway with her hand like this' (up to the mouth). 'She was afraid
that my father would really beat me, and, you know, I knew perfectly
well that she was afraid of that, and that he didn't mean to.'[12] The
subtlety and quickness of the child's reaction – he was not yet four –
show (if proof were needed) that those complex, analytical perceptions
of the little boys in his stories had been his own.

Lucy, who had had her life so firmly administered, was suddenly left
alone. She had six children to support, aged from sixteen to two. Of
these Arthur, who had been given an expensive education in Brighton,
was already turning out very difficult, ranging himself against her
authority. During that winter she remained at Charlton collecting her

resources and casting about for somewhere cheaper. There were no other Delamares left to turn to of her husband's generation. Of her own brothers Colin was in India, Herbert, her favourite, was dead, and the youngest, Hamilton, had run wild and vanished.

Lucy had a friend, a Mrs Walstow, who was married to a working man, a mason in the Arsenal, though she herself was of more refined birth. Her sixteen-year-old daughter (christened Martha but known as Pattie) came to live with Lucy and help in the house. She stayed in the family's service and later in Flo's, for the rest of her days.

In November the Bank allotted Lucy an annuity. The sum of £29.11s.2½d. arrived twice a year. It does not sound very much. She also had what Abraham left to James, but his total effects were only four thousand pounds, and of this a portion went to Henry's daughter. James had left only three thousand. With such slender resources, Lucy nevertheless contrived somehow a life that had style and spirit.

She seems to have stayed on at Charlton past Jack's fourth birthday, but by September 1877 another name replaces Delamare in the rate books, and Lucy presumably moved straight to the house where Jack spent the main part of his boyhood. This was 5 Bovill Terrace, Forest Hill,* a few miles to the south-west of Charlton, but still within the outer suburbs of London. It was in the middle of a short terrace, threaded into an enormously long Victorian street. The district was poor, but at that time within easy reach of fields. The house itself, with its round-topped Georgian windows on the main floor and a stuccoed parapet, put quite a pleasant face on things. There was a privet hedge in front, with a scrap of space behind it, and at the back another tiny garden. Once, before the move, Pattie took Jack to see her own home in the Woolwich Arsenal, and he, proud of the pretty strip at his own Charlton home (about twenty feet by twelve) exclaimed 'Oh, Pattie, what a *stinny* garden!' The patch at Bovill Terrace must have looked dismally stinny.

However, there was still good countryside within a child's walk. Above lay Hilly Fields for picnics, and the stream of Ravensbourne flowed through meadows not far off. To this period probably belongs another object of de la Mare's childish fascination, a buried reservoir, which sank into his imagination and emerged years later in the story 'The Vats', where two travellers come across the round stone reservoirs in which Time is stored. Later still, when in old age he wrote his long meditative poem on Time, *Winged Chariot*, he chose this, from among his early memories, to express his first intimations of Eternity somehow indwelling ordinary life:

* Now 61 Bovill Road.

> Yet there was mystery too: those steps of stone –
> In the green paddock where I played alone –
>   Cracked, weed-grown,
> Which often allured my hesitant footsteps down
>
> To an old sun-stained key-holed door that stood,
> The guardian of an inner solitude,
> Whereon I longed but dreaded to intrude;
> Peering and listening as quietly as I could.
>
> There, as I knew, in brooding darkness lay
> The waters of a reservoir. But why –
> In deadly earnest, though I feigned, in play –
> Used I to stone those doors; then run away,
> Listening enthralled in the hot sunny day
>
> To echo and rumour; and that distant sigh,
> As if some friend profaned had made reply, –
>   When merely a child was I?[13]

The Delamare children made the most of whatever country life they could reach, and Jack certainly responded to country sights and sounds with rapture – probably intensified by the very fact that he must seek them, and return from them, along a drab, interminable street. Henry Williamson, describing the suburbs of north-west Kent just before the First World War, spoke of countryside still to be found four miles from London Bridge: partridges in the fields, trout in the watercress beds, roach in the little drinking-ponds for cattle, each with its pair of moorhens. So the Delamare children in their fringe-life knew something of true rural England and lived a life of sharpest contrasts.

It may not be fanciful to trace an effect of this in de la Mare's work. It was always the edges of experience that he liked to probe and extend, and while he was a child he must have been vividly conscious of living physically in a borderland: of that abrupt change where the row of gas lamps ended and the owls began, where on a summer's day he watched the 'wicked fowler' with his tethered birds and tiny cages spread out in the green meadow. His descriptions of nature are never for a moment down to earth. They have at once a peculiar visionary intensity and a marked lack of the true countryman's or naturalist's informed detail. Detail may be there, but as some of de la Mare's earlier admirers felt, it has something in common with Pre-Raphaelite detail: a jewelled, hallucinatory intensity. It is 'inhabited' rather than existing for its own sake. In this he was the very opposite of Hardy (so kindred to him in romantic imagination), and also of naturalists like W.H. Hudson and Gilbert White, whose work he ardently admired. His observation of nature is far nearer to Keats's – another suburb-dweller – and charged with longing. It is even more like Blake's – yet another to whom nature, lying behind black Satanic mills, was the stuff of vision. For these lyric poets the countryside is not the context of daily life but an acute contrast to it: the object of pilgrimage, the type of Paradise. There are things in life which belong only to those who have first taken them for granted, growing up among them; others belong only to those who never did have this chance, and to whom they are always the lure, the sign-post. Nature was this to de la Mare.

Somewhere along these walks, at about six or seven, he first saw a convolvulus, the most regal of all London's wild-flowers. This remained for him the most telling recollection of his whole childhood. He stared in delight into the great pure white trumpet ('colourless' is his curious word for it) and picked it to run home with to his mother. 'But when I came into the house it had wreathed itself into a spiral as if into a shroud. And when I realised it would never more be enticed out of it again, I burst into tears.'[14] That pierced him once and for all with the transience of earthly beauty: the romantic wound, which nothing on earth consoles.

All children are aware to some degree of a pang they cannot name at a sunset, or at some special flower. To personalities for whom the mystical or psychic faculties strongly predominate over the sensuous, such objects of the natural world appear less as bodies than as apparitions. They feel this world primarily as the projection of another. This way of seeing begins in childhood. Blake actually saw angels in the trees, and foretold from a man's face that he would live to be hanged. There are no such psychic stories of de la Mare's childhood, probably because from the beginning he was always impelled to analyse and use his reason on an experience, however overwhelming. He was always most cautious in claiming for himself those psychic experiences which fascinated him from others.

Nor did he give the impression of a dreamy child: rather of the opposite. His powers of attention and his zest seemed to be keyed unusually high. He was never in any way thought odd or precocious. He left on his younger sister the impression of a normally inquisitive, high-spirited, sociable playfellow who was just rather more so than other boys – more inventive, more affectionate at farewells, more in earnest, funnier, quicker than the rest to tire of one game and suggest a better.

*

Soon after the move to Forest Hill he was sent to a dame school kept by a
Mrs Stadden. One of his school-fellows was called Herbert Naughty.
Perhaps the name made an appeal to Jack's dramatic sense. One day
Herbert Naughty was sick in class. 'We watched enthralled, and the
very moment I got home I shared with my mother this wondrous news.
Rather than disappoint her when next day she enquired after little
Herbert, I replied mournfully that he was a little worse. And so, day
after day, until I could bear the strain no longer and had to finish him off.
He had breathed his last, I said, and been buried.'[15] When Mrs Stadden
made an evening call and Lucy condoled with her the cat came out of the
bag and Jack was carried down from bed to face the music.

Lucy kept in the drawing-room at Forest Hill some relics of the graces
of Charlton days. There was a silver teapot for instance, left to her in
her mother's will. When Jack was allowed to handle it, for a treat, and
fell downstairs, he rolled all the way to the bottom clutching it to his
chest to keep it from harm. She also had 'two glass candlesticks hung
about with dangling prisms, which used to quiver gently at the least
disturbance. When the sunbeams traversing the room lit up the marble
chimneyshelf on which they stood, I was captivated by the effect; and
sometimes took one of the pieces of glass off its hook, and holding it up to
my eyes would gaze in rapture at a world of fascinating angles and
abysses decked in all the colours of the rainbow ... One morning, I
remember, though this was strictly forbidden, I pocketed one of these
glass pendants, set out (to show off with it) for my dame school very
early, and arrived to find no one there – not even my reanimated friend
Herbert Naughty. So I sat alone for a while in the small sunny basement
room, practising my magic colours on the map-hung, whitewashed
walls; the lovely silent butterflies of light zigzagging from floor to
ceiling ...'[16]

Cramped as the Forest Hill quarters were, Lucy Delamare still
preserved the better-to-do Victorian's pattern of a sanctum apart for the
adults. The children had their breakfast in the kitchen with Pattie,
while Lucy was served her toast alone with the Tory *Telegraph* and the
Church Times in the drawing-room; and there she formally entertained
her friends over the silver teapot. One, a Miss Catton, the children were
sure wore a wig, for she sported such a mountain of hair. Resolved to
prove the matter, Poppy stood in front and inveigled her into stooping so
that Jack, posted behind her chair, could lean over to look for the tapes.
The observant little boy at these tea-parties early became a connoisseur
of whatever was odd, pitiful, prim, desiccated, hypocritical, eccentric –
or, equally, of whatever was beautiful and spiritually remarkable –
under the bonnets and rustling lavender bodices.

They were mostly feminine callers, no doubt, since Lucy was a widow, and they would have been of small means, preserving appearances, like herself. Some flavour of Lucy's widowhood persists in those many stories and poems preoccupied with old maids and widows in reduced circumstances, like Poor Miss Loo and Miss Duveen. Even Miss Taroone and her servant at Thrae had no masculine company, and a mother only, not parents, set the little boy of this symbolic story on his quest for East Dene. Jack's small world was ruled by petticoat government. Arthur soon faded out of the circle, under a cloud, and so this youngest boy grew up with only Bert and five females.

But if Mrs Delamare had her own sanctum, the children had theirs too, the downstairs nursery-schoolroom at the back, where (short of riot) they were left to their own devices. They organised paper games, collected stamps, played endlessly with putty (storing it for convenience stuck on the underside of the polished table) and cut up a medicine-bottleful of entrancing quicksilver into minute drops with penknives – Bert was especially skilful in nudging the nimble, elusive globules into the outline of a railway engine. They kept white mice in the scullery where there was a big wooden cistern with a fitted top, cleaned twice a year, from which the drinking water was drawn off by a tap. 'Funny bits' were noticed for some time in the water before one of the mice was missed. At one time they also had two white rats which the boys carried up their sleeves, and for a while there was even a pet monkey called Jinnie who stole eggs and sucked them. She remained in the back of Jack's mind for later use. There was also from time to time a dog, but Jack never came to love these much: he preferred the independence of cats. 'I've never really got on *top* of a dog, have you?' was how he put it.

Out of doors the children had stilts, and for other sports they climbed trees and combed hedges for birds' nests. Once Jack killed a sparrow by a fluke shot with catapult and stone – and was instantly transfixed by violent reaction from triumph to remorse. As Poppy grew out of babyhood, they became close allies. Bert kept himself a trifle aloof. But the brothers would combine to victimise the sturdy little girl with cheerful brutality. When they played soldiers she was pushed into the nettles if she refused to be 'other ranks' to their officers. She was coaxed up a tree and then left there: 'It is a lovely night – we'll leave you till morning.' Her dolls were beheaded and buried with ceremony. And so on. Manners were strictly corrected, but the three were left very free from an early age, and Poppy might go anywhere about the streets so long as the boys escorted her.

As one would expect, games of make-believe took prime place. These had what is often enough the mark of creative gifts to come: a wealth of circumstantial detail and observation. The most inventive ideas originated with Jack. Curiously, these games did not dramatise the usual, more glamorous professions – Red Indian, Hunter, Sailor. They played more at Solicitors and Bankers. Out of this last, a lifelong family catchphrase for a cheque arose: 'Here's a piece of paper. If you don't write on it, you won't be able to change it, h'm *h'm*.' 'Solicitors' began after the boys had accompanied Lucy on some visit to her lawyer. At a call of 'Conveyance, please!' an ingenious contraption, a basket operated by a string passed through a ring, carried messages from the one 'desk' to the other, placed in adjacent alcove cupboards, where the legal gentlemen each had a stool and a candle. Poppy, as office boy, answered the door. She remembered that Jack, as clerk and subordinate, was always the first to tire. His moods would change suddenly, and once they heard him begin to whistle the other two would know their game was over.

Poppy was often in doubt whether what Jack told her was fact or fiction. He himself was fairly credulous and set off at Pattie's request, once, on the classic Victorian errand for April Fool's Day, to buy a pint of 'pigeon's milk' at the grocer's. Stories and charades remained lifelong pleasures. There were the traditional fairy tales told by Pattie, and if they were a little gruesome so much the better. Jack's earliest favourite (much like that of the little boy Mamilius in *The Winter's Tale*) began with a house by a churchyard, but significantly both were 'teeny tiny', and so was the woman who lived there. For Jack the minute, the grotesque and the romantic from the start compounded into one spell.

Other lifelong fascinations also sprang first out of listening to grown-up talk. Victorian children were not always psychologically sheltered. Lucy discussed with Jack the case of Constance Kent, the young girl whose priest had persuaded her, after hearing her confession, to acknowledge publicly the murder of her small step-brother. (This priest, Lucy told Jack, had been a distant connection of her family's.) One day, out on a call with her, Jack, aged about five, attentively added the word 'strychnine' to his vocabulary, listening and watching while a suicide was described: 'He thought he was being continually followed … His body was arched up on the bed – like this.'[17] That detail, too, would one day be used in a story, 'The Green Room'.

There were also affairs of the heart and imaginary companions. 'I was no more than 7 years old when (perhaps not for the first time) I fell in love; and the child of my devotion consisted chiefly, I fear (as in maturer glimpses of the divine and the transitory) of day dream.' A poem 'Lucy' tells of 'a birthday maidenhair' given to one of these first loves, an older girl named Lucy Collier. 'A wholly imaginary companion with no less and no more affective sex than an Aunt Sallie ... was a nursery drudge in our young days, dumb, ugly, battered, scorned and reviled.' She was called Tatta and played cards with the family. She was eventually joined by 'Tatta's brother'.

Jack was not at all advanced at lessons, but like all the children, an early and avid reader. One of his memories (from six or seven) was of waking up on Christmas morning to find a book in his stocking with the orange, apple and threepenny bit – a broad, linen picture-book in primary colours and bold type, from which he at once began to spell out the story of Gulliver. It was his first memorable book, and one that was never really superseded. He also loved its crude cuts. In fact, 'serious' art made little impact at all until he was fully mature, long years after poetry and music had captured him.

A series of small threepenny adventure stories was much prized, and when pocket-money ran short the boys clubbed together to present one to Connie for her birthday, borrowing it back again with indecent haste. There were also a number of books in the house they were allowed to browse in, such as *The Cloister and the Hearth*, the novels of Mrs Gaskell and Charlotte Yonge's *Daisy Chain*. Lucy, who loved poetry, introduced Jack to Moore and Hood, which she read aloud. He would also pore over the plates of a large blue book of *Birds of the World*, stormy petrel, tailor bird, swallow ... But the prime nursery favourite (unknown to Lucy who would have confiscated it at once, even though it was Lane's bowdlerized edition) was a volume of the *Arabian Nights* which the children somehow acquired. This made a lasting impression, heightened by secrecy and their tantalising method of reading it, for the book was strictly shared between the three, snatched from hand to hand in mid-sentence, in timed bouts of five or ten minutes.

There was a strong delight in occasions and festivals. Christmas was kept, however hard the times, with stockings, tree, plum puddings and mince-pies – Lucy providing the ceremonial, and their beloved Pattie Walstow from Woolwich the good things. The children's lives revolved in great part around Pattie's spry, neat figure in the kitchen. She wore a high collar, her fuzzy hair fluffed up above it. Her pretty complexion and liveliness made her look younger than her years. She was unselfish, gentle, light-hearted. To a romantic little boy she appeared enchanting. Pattie's big old range had a roasting-jack with a winding clock and a dripping-pan beneath. When the children came home ravenous from school, if a joint was roasting Pattie would open the little door below and supply them with hot bread and dripping. Jack had the instinct for cookery and later would make cakes for visitors, housekeep for himself, and take a feminine pleasure in the arts of housework. His fairy tales are often set in an old-fashioned kitchen, minutely described.

Pattie and Flo each took a share in whatever aspects of mothering bored or defeated Lucy, who was never very practical. In the years between Abraham's death and her own marriage, it was Flo who did the accounts and paid the bills. Yet Lucy remained the chief person in the children's lives, though she never sank her whole life in theirs. She was a great reader, and she had a 'District' among the poor that she visited. Nor was she maternally possessive. Her relationship with Jack, so very close, never encroached on his independence. Tiny, decided, wilful, tender, but unswervingly strong in character, she perhaps managed to supply something out of her own nature that in imaginative Victorian families was more often supplied by the father. She was always surprising them: she made them laugh: she listened and sympathised – and then she swept out of the house on her own affairs.

One aspect of the children's upbringing Lucy did not delegate – morals and religion. She read aloud to them the stories of the Old Testament from a Bible she had thickly scored and annotated on almost every page. De la Mare wrote: 'I was taught to revere the Bible, apart even from its contents, I mean, which I at least *heard* read, whether listening or not – at least five times over. I still, rather furtively, I fear, kiss its covers if it has the mischance to fall on the floor, and I feel uneasy at the sight of any book resting on top of it.'[18] Lucy supplied the rock of conviction on which faith may be founded in childhood for good and all, a long way below the level on which specific religious creeds are either formulated or rejected. The little boy who absorbed through her eyes and company the reconciliation of Joseph with his brethren, the parables of the Gospels and the images of *Pilgrim's Progress*, took in a reassurance about the indestructible value of human life and love, which was more profound and lasting, perhaps, than Lucy's orthodox Victorian teaching.

The Bible became as much a lifelong influence as Lucy would have wished, but not precisely in the way she intended. Its authority became to him the authority of the imagination, not of accepted beliefs. It was a storehouse of poetry, the supreme ensampler of narrative style. The subtle sonorous rhythms of the Authorised Version had a crucial

influence on his own. It was a 'mystery of the spirit'. '... You have only
to read a chapter or two,' he said in old age, 'to see that it could not be of
purely human origin.'[19] He also placed a kind of mystical value on the
biblical mentions of natural things. A lion had more essential lion
about it, he held, in a passage from the psalms, the sun was more
royally the sun. Their biblical images moved him all his life as the
archetypes or paradigms of their natural counterparts. Above all, the
Bible presented to the boy (whose personal intuition led him that way
already) a view of Earth as matter transfused with a spiritual meaning
– so that the whole of it was a parable, and all human fate hung poised
between vast forces of good and evil. This – the sense of a huge
spiritual context – was what 'talked with his expectation and moved
his desire'. Already, by instinct sensing life to be haunted, it was
simple to accept guardian angels and demons as the haunters. Angels
remained part of his imaginative life, used several times as the nucleus
of stories – 'The Trumpet', an early and unpublished one called 'The
Giant', 'The Guardian' – as well as in poems.

When he wrote the opening pages of *Henry Brocken* (a symbolic
traveller in the 'scarce-imaginable regions of romance') he described
Brocken's childhood in words that could have very well fitted his own –
except, as ever, for the isolated setting. 'Well fed, warmly clad, and in
freedom, I grew up almost in solitude between my angels, hearkening
with how simple a curiosity to that everlasting warfare of persuasion
and compulsion, terror and delight.'[20] This warfare, this context –
beyond all human drama and sensuous delight – was what life *was*. He
never tired of questioning the meaning of life and he never found an
answer that satisfied him completely. But he never seriously doubted
(as so many sensitive minds have) that the meaning was there. Except,
that is, during the stressful years between school and marriage, when
that nightmare possibility did haunt and shake him temporarily.

Like other children fond of drama, his religious instruction coloured
much of his rituals and play. He draped the clothes-horse with a sheet
and gathered the family in the parlour for an evening sermon. He was
then about four. (Wilfred Owen as a child did the same.) Jack
announced the text 'God is Love' and, his nerve failing, burst into
tears. That, of course, is a mere social mishap – but he had a more
interesting memory in the same connection. 'I used to debate within
myself whether it was right and proper to pray for the Devil. The
debate, I fancy, remained inconclusive: but the prayers went on.'[21] The
hymn 'Now the Day is Over' formed part of his devotions, and touched,
for life, the nerve of poetry: 'As a child I believe I thought over and
explored every word of it.' With Lucy he very early acquired another

lifelong appetite – that for rambling around any churchyard he chanced to pass on walks to read the inscriptions.

But whether or not one should pray for the Devil, a Roman Catholic (in that Huguenot family) was another matter. The funeral of a Catholic child, which he and Lucy had come upon during some such cemetery ramble, stirred his pity and interest. But, as he reflected to Lucy soberly, perhaps it was just as well it had died so young.

Along with Tatta, Joseph and his Brethren, Gulliver and Sinbad, Jack had for unsubstantial company that uncle, Herbert Browning, whom he had never seen and who had died young. There was perhaps an affinity between this favourite brother of Lucy's and her favourite son. The little boy certainly identified with Herbert. She would tell him all she remembered, 'and however often she repeated her remembrances I was never wearied'. One moonlit night, as a child, Lucy awoke to see Herbert 'rising up in his bed in his nightshirt, a tenpenny nail which he had just pulled from under his pillow in his hand. This he proceeded to hammer into the wall with the back of a hairbrush. "We must be *tidy*, Lucy", he explained.'

Their mother read him the story of the Prodigal Son. When he finds himself at his wit's end, reduced to eating the pigs' husks, she asked, 'What would *you* have done, then, Herbert?' 'I *think*,' was the practical reply, 'I should have killed a pig and had some pork.'

In the days when the Brownings had a house in the Naval Dockyard Herbert possessed a boat, and also some gunpowder. Experimenting with a small brass cannon, he singed off Lucy's eyebrow and badly hurt his thumb. To postpone facing the music he tucked her into the boat and rowed her about the Dockyard for a while.

His resourceful character was appreciated by his stern old father. On one occasion Dr Browning presented Lucy, who was about ten, with a gold half-sovereign for her birthday. Herbert at once suggested she use it on a tour of London with himself as guide. When the truants returned, after dark, to their dismayed family, Herbert rendered his father an account of how he had laid out the money – on the Abbey, the Tower, St Paul's and a bunshop or two. His father was so impressed with his good sense and enterprise that he let him off a thrashing – a real achievement, for it was said of Dr Browning that he treated convicts like his children, but his children like convicts. Herbert continued to inhabit Jack's mind right on into old age, as if he had never died but had been a fellow childhood self.

Lucy was faced with a difficult problem – how to provide a good education for three boys when she could not afford fees. Arthur (fifteen when his father died) must have left his expensive school at Brighton straight away – he may have resented this, and it no doubt helped to unsettle him. Very soon after, he broke adrift from home altogether and began a shiftless career, which led to more than one criminal conviction – probably for forging cheques or suchlike. He ended his life (again at Brighton) as a bookie. Bert and Jack grew to detest and fear his occasional returns and the misery he caused their mother. He developed into a burly, crop-headed, coarse-voiced man. His affronted and alarmed brothers refused to have him in the house at all after they grew up. When Lucy wanted to speak to him, she had to slip away to meet him at Flo's home.

There remained the two younger boys. Bert won a place at Christ's Hospital – then still about as tough a school as it had been in Lamb's time. He was at first so homesick that he wrote a letter home pleading for rescue, and then stood at the school gate looking out for the rescuers who never came. Poppy and Jack tramped up and down stairs at home singing 'O bring my brother back to me, I cannot play alone'. Jack showed promise of a good voice when he joined in the family favourites, such as 'O Ruddier than the Cherry'. Flo had had singing lessons as a girl from a blind lady, Mrs Hitchman, who lived not far from Woolwich and was now engaged to give him coaching, in hopes of a choir-school place at St Paul's Cathedral.

Mrs Hitchman was a purposeful, remarkable woman, and a good friend to Jack, who became devoted to her, though always in awe of her.

Jack's first acute experience of homesickness was connected with this voice-training. He was sent to board for a few days at a girls' school at Shooter's Hill, where Mrs Hitchman probably taught. He remembered all his life the brass pelmet above the white muslin curtains where, in his anguish of heart, he would lean out to watch the railway line and count the signal lights. If there were more green than red, the omens were good for speedy return home. All the same, he kept an affection for The Grange as a house name from this association and it crops up in stories – 'The Almond Tree' and another unpublished, allied novella, of which more later.

The coaching only just succeeded. At the first voice-test at St Paul's he failed, but they gave him another chance. On 21 March 1882, at 2 o'clock, Lucy and he presented themselves again at Choir House, and this time he was accepted. It must have been a great relief to his mother. But for Jack, who was ten when he entered the school, childhood proper was over, to be rivalled by no other experience in life. 'Those happy, unhappy, far-away days seem like mere glimpses of a dragon-fly shimmering and darting ... though at the actual time they more closely resembled, perhaps, a continuous dream broken into bits of vivid awakening.'[22]

In his private thoughts he had already decided against maturity. Comparing the drab routine of adults with the poetry and intensity of his own adventures, he had by now registered a vow not to live beyond forty. And at double that age experience still had not really changed his opinion. Of growing up he wrote to a friend: 'It is a fiasco I am more convinced every day.'[23] The writer of this book once ventured to protest against this wholesale dismissal of adult life. I was only about twenty-one, but he had known me since I was born. 'Take your own case,' he expostulated. '*Look how diluted you are!*' What could one reply to that!

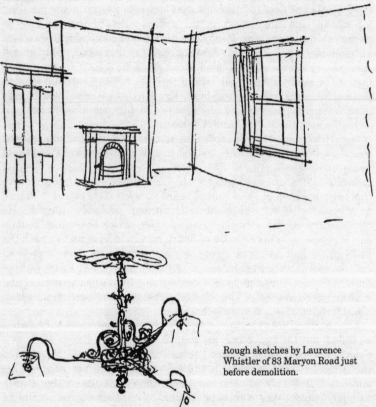

Rough sketches by Laurence Whistler of 83 Maryon Road just before demolition.

2

Schooldays

St Paul's was a place of education that Uncle Abraham would have shunned above any. By the early eighties the Cathedral had become the very fountainhead of 'High Church notions'. Disciples of Pusey and the Tractarians had taken it over just before de la Mare was born, radically reforming its musical and spiritual life after long neglect. By the time he entered the choir they had restored St Paul's to a position of national prestige it had not held since Donne's day. It was a notable revival. Wren's baroque masterpiece had long fallen out of favour, and the vast spaces of the interior had lain almost totally naked and unused, except at the burial of a hero, like the Duke of Wellington, or such annual occasions as the festival of the Charity Children – the ceremony described by Blake in 'Holy Thursday' in *Songs of Innocence* – when, for an hour, the sombre wastes of Portland stone would be banked with thousands of childish faces: Blake's 'Flowers of London Town'.

The empty Cathedral had also become horribly dirty. It was so cold that Sydney Smith declared in the 1830s that to attend service was certain death, and that the sentences of his sermons froze as they came out of his mouth, and thawed in the course of the following summer 'making strange noises and unexpected assertions in various parts of the Church'.[1] The daily services were cut off from the main body of the church by the massive organ screen. Ceremonial was mean and slovenly; the tiny choir, undisciplined, unrehearsed and unpunctual, maundered on to a handful of worshippers. Gladstone seized his chance and fortune helped when the old guard of the Chapter, fossilized in this inertia, happened to die off all together within three years. Gladstone extracted the scholar Richard Church in 1871 from his seclusion in a country parish, and convinced him that his mission was to set St Paul's in order, as the great English Cathedral in the nation's eyes. Dean Church's quietness was deceptive, and he

27

succeeded formidably during the brief period Jack spent trotting about Woolwich and to dame school.

In Canon Gregory (appointed a few years before by Disraeli) Church found an ally who was also a first-rate administrator. Gregory's reputation for forcefulness had made his appointment so unpopular with the old regime that at his installation everyone left straight after Evensong and put out the lights, leaving a single Canon to conduct the ceremony and a verger with a kitchen candlestick. But Gregory was not to be rebuffed so easily. The new team gained a fine New Testament scholar in Lightfoot (followed by Stubbs, a notable historian) while Scott-Holland and Liddon, both appointments of Gladstone's, were magnetic preachers.

All these remarkable High Anglicans became to Jack, at ten, his familiar daily acquaintances. He became a connoisseur of their oratory and foibles. His first earnings were a half-crown tip from an Archbishop (Benson) for carrying his black satin train. Looking back, he liked to think he might perhaps have trebled away, some afternoon, to Cardinal Newman himself, who clinging to his friendship with the Dean, would sometimes creep into the nave, a troubled old exile, to listen wistfully to Evensong.

When de la Mare was twenty-five he wrote portrait sketches of Church and Liddon as he had known them nine years or so before.[2] (Both died the year after he left school). The subject had remained for him a romantic one, every detail sharp, and indeed would remain so all his life. He noted every subtlety of appearance, voice, and mannerism of Dean Church, ending:

> His glance was brief and tranquil and keen ... he had no acquaintance with pretence ... yet I think pity and tenderness were so sharp within him as to be like sorrow ... His solitary purity of heart, his candid and keen understanding, his zeal and his meekness, though you might be afraid to meet his eye and stand abashed in his presence, these entered into your memory like the bleak shining of a star.

The authority of a man so unusual, who walked gently about his cathedral, ruling all with a nod – the 'permanent, acute, venerated conscience of the place', as Scott-Holland described him – gave Choir House a perspective on to a stage of grander spiritual drama than the common run of boarding schools usually affords for imaginative small boys. And this child, brooding in his carved stall, with eye and heart attentive, was clearly not wasting his time there.

Liddon, by the time Jack knew him, had lost the rapt beauty of his youth and had grown plump, stooping, smooth-cheeked, grey and gentle. Jack, like everyone, remembered him best by his voice:

His speech was delicate, as if each word were finely chiselled ... voice mellow ... it rose with a winning break almost to treble, it stirred the echoes like a bugle call ... Sweat dripped from his chin ... the hollow, silent spaces of St Paul's would ring and quaver the melody and ardour of his eloquence, it seemed that a Seraph was crying out above the clouds.

Gregory, the most powerful of the Canons, appealed to boyish interest less exaltedly: a bulky figure with bushy, irascible eyebrows and white hair flowing, afraid of nobody. The Bishop of London was the formidable Temple, but one day when he arrived two minutes late for a service he was due to take and found it already in full swing, all he got from Gregory was: 'When the clock strikes, we begin.'[3] It was Gregory who introduced the custom of performing Bach's St Matthew Passion in Holy Week – the work which made the deepest impression on de la Mare of all he heard and sang in his years there.

Under Stainer, brought in by Liddon to reform the music, and his successor George Martin, the choir had become a great one. Otto Goldsmidt, Jenny Lind's husband, considered it the second choir in Europe after Vienna. The little school itself, founded in the Middle Ages, had not always provided its boys with a regular life or much learning. In Elizabethan London the 'Children of Paul's' were best known as one of the city's regular dramatic companies, and in the early nineteenth century the almoner officially in charge of them would supplement his salary by hiring out the boys to public evening concerts, leaving them to find their way back after midnight as best they could. But in Jack's day the school (as thoroughly reformed as the rest of the Cathedral) had regained a reputation for soundness and care. About thirty-eight choirboys and probationers studied there, under a headmaster in Holy Orders with two or three assistants. The organist and choirmaster ruled the rest of the boys' curriculum. It was a tough school, with long working hours and only five weeks' holiday a year. As there was no second choir, a boy could only snatch the end of Christmas Day in his own home by pelting off after service for a few hours – if he could get there in the time.

There was a good deal of bullying, alarming to this small gentle newcomer of ten (some were only eight). The seniors ranged up to sixteen, and were not segregated by day. One of them took charge of each new probationer, and bellowed and cuffed him into shape; and there was some official fagging. Jack was there a term and a half before he became a full chorister: usually probation took longer. The boys were of mixed class – anyone with a good voice might gain a place if not actually in rags and off the streets. The entry tests officially demanded some knowledge of Latin declensions, the catechism, the Bible and the

Prayer Book, but what counted was 'a pleasing quality and right
production of the vocal scale'.

It is a shock for most little boys to enter for the first time an
exclusively masculine world, and Jack's had been more than usually
petticoat. His first letter shows the strain: a litany of homesickness too
desperately concentrated upon the world he had lost to describe much
of this new one:

                                   Choir House   Dean's Court
                                           June 10th p.m.

Dearest Mother
   I feel very homesick will you or someone come and see me on Thursday
… I am not getting on very well with my lessons I am longing to see you
or someone … mind you write and tell me all about home I have written
to Mrs Hitchman have you seen anything of Uncle Colin I am longing to
see you … I cant come home on Thursday because I shall have bad marks
do someone come and see me … you dont know how I long for home I saw
Herbert this afternoon … I went under the Thames this evening with Mr
Russel it is ofly funny under there. you don't know how I long for home
Mr Bathe is very nice hoping you will excuse the things I have put under
twice and wrong as I feel very confused and giddy
                       I must say goodbye
                   Believe me your darling Boy
                        W. J. De la Mare
           Mind you come or someone on Thursday

However, he was resilient and sociable and soon adapted himself.
Choir House, in Dean's Court, tucked down the canyon of Carter Lane,
a cramped alley just off Ludgate Hill, was a distinctive building, begun
a few years before, in the elaborate Victorian-Renaissance manner –
grey brick with terra-cotta dressings, arabesques of plaster decoration
– with a large text from Galatians along the frieze. Above a
shoulder-high parapet, a wire cage turned the flat roof into the only
playground then available. In Jack's later years there, the school
shared a playing-field at Willesden and would travel there by
Underground, shutting the windows against the sulphurous steam and
passing the ball wildly from hand to hand. Jack rather enjoyed games
and, though not particularly good at them, won two cricket bats. He
remembered collaring a curate and bringing him down in a tackle
when he was fifteen. In later life he was no great enthusiast for
physical exercise.

Choir House inside was a brownish, barish place – pleasantly, not
grimly shabby; ecclesiastical but not oppressively so. In old age, de la
Mare said he could still wander about it all in memory – touch the
round brass door-handle and pass into the dark panelled dining room

with two long side-tables and high table laid across. Next this was a fairly large class-room – shared in his time between two forms – with high-up windows, and the old narrow benches and original oak locker doors from an earlier school-house, in which choristers as far back as the eighteenth century had cut their names – one of the Wesleys among them. A circular iron stair called the Well took Jack clattering upstairs to the small prayer-room, where prayers were said morning and evening, and to the two long, identical dormitories, junior and senior, one above the other, where between each bed a wooden partition ran nearly to the ceiling, affording a little welcome privacy. Above these dormitories the playground commanded a superb view south-west over roof-tops to St Andrews-by-the-Wardrobe, and further, to Big Ben and the Houses of Parliament. On quiet nights Big Ben boomed out – as near by, it seemed, as the bell of St Paul's itself, whose shoulder, over the brief huddle of roofs on the other side of the playground, soared close above them, blazing white when the sun shone.

But playground and dormitory could both hold their terrors. Three or four confirmed bullies used to encourage the juniors to pick on one particular little victim. Jack was himself ill-treated: 'Oh yes, I was bullied all right,' he would say, 'but not as badly as some.' One amusement was a gamed called Sardines in which the small boys were piled criss-cross and the older ones competed to see how many could be cleared at a jump from the lockers. But whatever his fears may have been, Jack had spirit, and also soon took the sensible precaution of banding together with two other boys, so that if one were set on, allies were always at hand.

In old age he thought he owed some of his never-failing pleasure of getting into bed – its bliss of security – to the relief it had brought in these years from the terrors of the school day. Even so he remembered a boy snatched back just as he was getting in between the sheets, to be 'handsomely caned'. The seniors were not the only tyrants to fear. The headmaster was Dr Barff, a Tractarian who had been chosen out by Liddon for his 'deep and simple piety' and 'originality of mind'. From a boy's-eye view Barff's piety was rigid, his temper not only strict but erratic. He took a morbid pleasure in physical punishment and had a curious nature altogether, at once old-maidish and tyrannical. He was expert at needlework and embroidery and kept a grey parrot that talked, but with the boys he was hot-tempered, sarcastic and overbearing. His glance, as he shook hands in the morning, seemed to one to 'hold you guilty until proved innocent'. Punishment for the worst offences was a public beating by the Dean, after which there would be a general souvenir-hunt for scattered twig-ends, but Barff beat much more often. Even after some wretched boy's long hours in school and stall had ended with weary impositions, he would think it well to round off matters with a final birching. And yet when Raffield, the Cathedral carpenter, came to give the boys evening drill, Barff would join in and insist on being whacked with the rest for any mistakes. Liddon was perhaps a little innocent not to suspect a want of perfect psychological balance in the 'originality' of the headmaster's mind. De la Mare, however, never alluded to any memory of homosexuality, either in his own experience or as a topic of talk among his school fellows.

The sole woman on the staff, the Matron, was scarcely more sympathetic than Barff. She fed the boys well – some of the poorer ones better than in their own homes – for it was realised that a good voice must be well nourished. But if anyone begged off a service, a dose of castor oil, whatever the symptoms, was the invariable sequel. After Jack had been at school two years, an epidemic of scarlet fever closed the choir in September, and from then on a regular summer break was arranged. Perhaps to this time, but more probably earlier, belongs his old-age tale of some serious childhood illness when a sheet soaked in disinfectant had been hung over his door. Though it seems improbable, his firm recollection was that the doctor had said in his hearing that he 'would not be coming again' – implying the worst. However that may be, the boy put this interpretation on the matter and began to whistle softly to keep his courage up. The immediate relaxation of the hushed suspense around his bed told him at once that he had made a fatal psychological blunder. No chance now of death-bed solicitude – and he had not yet even opened his eyes!

The school day began with a cold-water wash. Then came prayers at 7.30 with one invariable hymn, unaccompanied, 'Now that the daylight fills the skies' – whether it did or not. Then on with boots and away, whatever the weather, to the Embankment, as far as Waterloo Bridge, whose granite each boy must kick before doubling back to breakfast.

Pea-soup fogs (common when every grate burnt coal at only twenty shillings a ton) allowed the bolder spirits a little straying from the crocodile. Somewhere along these walks Jack saw a face whose beauty he never forgot, a ragged girl picking over a dust-bin 'where there was little enough to pick'. It occurred to him later that Francis Thompson might well have been among those wretched figures he used so often to pass wrapped in their newspapers and inert on the Embankment benches. One memory he mentioned in a late poem, 'The Jacket', was of a suicide's corpse towed behind a police boat, the body swollen, the head lolling out of the water. Subdued, the boys filed back to the breakfast they no longer wanted.

Lessons began at nine, broken off for Cathedral Matins (including all the psalms allotted and twice in the week the Litany as well). After a brief lunch-break they were rehearsed for an hour, with unremitting scales and solfeggi, till Evensong at 3.45. Then came their one hour of freedom. Then six o'clock tea, followed by lessons and preparation until the smaller boys were released to bed after a roll-call at nine. Sunday, naturally, was no leisure day; full choral eucharist, following directly on a full choral matins (the sermon often an hour long), kept them in the Cathedral continuously till one o'clock. Ordination services could last four hours apiece.

Yet, oddly, de la Mare does not seem to have found the long sessions in the Cathedral unbearably tedious. He certainly responded to the fine ceremonial, and in those days of St Paul's glory any small boy privileged to wear the distinctive mortar-board with upsticking tuft could feel himself a personage of genuine importance in the great world.

*

Jack would love in later years to revisit the Cathedral, to sit in the churchyard, or take a friend in to see Donne's effigy. The dying Dean had sat to Nicholas Stone, sculptor, dressed dramatically in his frill-topped shroud. In the little boy, that striking *memento mori* helped form the characteristic bent of his mind. Long hours of enforced passive reverie in such surroundings must have done much to confirm for life his urgent, innate presentiment that human life took meaning from some vast, obscure, unignorable context. This was the mystery which these brooding stones arched over him expressly to illustrate. St Paul's affected not only his spiritual stance and the temper of his imagination. It very likely supplied also some actual materials: oddities of humankind, hag-ridden old cranks, eccentric vergers – some elements of the grandeur of the Cathedral in the story 'All Hallows'; also the germ perhaps of the carved angel of 'The Trumpet', for the heights of the Grinling Gibbons organ case (by his time divided in two and placed along each end of the choir stalls) were peopled with beautiful, remote-eyed angel trumpeters. One might have expected that baroque would be a style quite antipathetic to so gothic a fantasy as de la Mare's; yet in fact the architecture of St Paul's did appeal profoundly to him: perhaps because, in Wren's serene conception, baroque sheds its superbia and the unearthly pierces in – mystery coming foremost by means of the dome. Wren's majestic blue bubble floating over London was for de la Mare supremely important, an icon

– the centre, always, of London – 'now misty with November fog, now sun-becalmed with the radiance of Spring'.[4]

Jack's mother shared all his romantic feeling for the place, and revelled in the ritual, colour, drama so long denied her. She had discovered her spiritual home, and as often as she could she would make the long journey from Forest Hill to bring Poppy and the other children to attend Evensong.

By his own account, personal religious faith (as distinct from a sense of the numinous) meant something real enough to de la Mare in these years. He would look back later with a passionate sense of deprivation to the trust in divine loving-kindness and the poignant sense of grace that he had felt as a chorister. Yet he did once advise a young couple against a choir education for their son if they wanted him to grow up a believer. The preaching, except as a stirring histrionic performance, was always a trial, and it crystallized very early his lifelong hatred of dogma. Yet boys – acute detectives of humbug – respond deeply to the spiritual atmosphere a real sincerity will generate, even if they remain deaf to the arguments advanced; and St Paul's in that fervent era was a place of living conviction. A sacred awe hung murmuring, after the surge of worship led by the boys' voices, in that curious 'still roar or loud whisper', as it was described in Colet's day, which was the nearest the Cathedral's echoes ever came to silence.

To compensate for the rigours, treats, when they came, were satisfactory enough. On Sundays the four canons and eight minor canons resident in Amen Court took turns to invite the boys in pairs round to breakfast. There were hot sausages and eggs. Archdeacon Sinclair would oblige by inserting a whole egg into his mouth; Gregory would lift his beard by the tip to touch his ferocious eyebrows. After lunch Col. Vivian Majendie, Chief Inspector of Explosives, who had attached himself to the school as a kind of universal godfather, came regularly to tell them a story, standing with his back to the lockers. He was by far the most dashing figure in their world – a refreshing change from the clergy with his military bearing, charming manner, and repertoire of dangerous exploits. He brought round a bomb, defused, for the boys to inspect. Fenians had left it in Charing Cross station, disguised ingeniously as a clock. He gave them scientific lectures illustrated with mild but pleasing explosions, and would read aloud the latest number of the *Strand Magazine* in which the adventures of Sherlock Holmes were then appearing. He also read them 'Q's' *Dead Man's Rock*, and *Treasure Island*, which had just appeared.

De la Mare himself came to hold that the influence of such boyhood reading is a tenuous affair. Those very first books at home – *Gulliver's*

Travels and the *Arabian Nights* – counted in his development more
than did most of his schoolboy reading, which consisted largely of the
usual adventure stories: Henty, Kingsley, Marryat, Jules Verne,
Ainsworth and whatever 'penny bloods' the boys could scrounge. He
also delighted in Baron Munchhausen. Imagination, it would seem,
went partly underground for a stage; he showed no great liking for
poetry and no gift yet for it himself. Poe's fiction was certainly a
formative influence, and he began early to learn from him by imitation,
trying out in adolescence a mystery tale (unfinished) involving a
cryptogram. Aged about twelve, he also got hold of some dumpy little
book in a flimsy pink cloth binding, which so shocked him with its
sexual revelations that he tried to burn it, afraid to have it discovered
in his possession. (He remembered it as 'The Mysteries of Paris', but
that is likely to be a slip of memory, for this run-of-the-mill historical
romance by Eugene Sue could scarcely alarm the most prudish soul.)
Whatever the book really was, it refused to burn. In the school grate it
merely charred, do what he would, so he fished it out and dropped it in
the Thames.

He was temperamentally a Puritan. He had fallen easily and
frequently in love as far back as he could remember, and would never
outgrow the same impulsive susceptibility as long as he lived; but, by
all the evidence, physical sex had a minimal importance for him, first
to last. Birth and death were profoundly fascinating mysteries;
sexuality never seems to have been to him a paramount mystery at all.
It was more, one suspects, a disappointing and random conjuring trick
played by the glands on what really mattered: the divining
imagination of the heart. His attitude mirrored Sir Thomas Browne's:

> I could be content that we might procreate like trees, without
> conjunction, or that there were any way to perpetuate the world without
> this triviall and vulgar way of coition. It is the foolishest act a wise man
> commits in all his life, nor is there any thing that will more deject his
> coold imagination, when hee shall consider what an odde and unworthy
> piece of folly hee hath committed; I speake not in prejudice, nor am
> averse from that sweet sexe, but naturally amorous of all that is
> beautifull.[5]

Certainly nothing before Choir House had prepared de la Mare for
schoolboy smut. He referred once in strong terms to 'what a hideous
woe lewd company at its first onset' can be. But the lewdness
mentioned concerns birth facts. There is nothing, no evidence either
way, whether homosexuality also was concerned. Long afterwards he
recalled the 'actual asphalted City spot' on which another boy confided
to him some fact of obstetrics, and the 'very expression on his flushed,

mock-innocent face ... He found me ignorant ... and left me confused.'
At one time when he was about eleven, he wrote that his closest friend,
an older boy, used to win 'covert smiles from a very lovely dark girl of
about seventeen' at the afternoon services. Jack asked him one day on
a walk, 'with a sort of hushed and doubtful joy – "If she asked you go to
in, would you?" – "Wouldn't I just" he said. "And if she asked you to go
into her bedroom?" And he nodded with flashing blue eyes. All *pure*
romance – but I was coldly curious too.'[6] Evidently he was neither a
prig nor at all uninterested. He had, by choir-school days, long
pondered for himself the sexual passages in the Old Testament, finding
them (so he recalled) perfectly natural and acceptable.

My own conclusion about his personal sexuality, based on a long
close friendship (though of course I was two generations younger, and
a woman, so there would be reticences) is that he was definitely no
suppressed homosexual nor crippled unduly by his obvious inhibitions,
but that he was just not highly sexed nor at all exclusively masculine.
By nature he was romantic, fastidious and private, with all such innate
characteristics very much confirmed by his early upbringing. For
Victorian womanhood, all straight sexual advice to boy children was
ruled out, and quite likely (brought up as they both were almost
exclusively by women) even with Bert in their small boyhood there
may well have been a minimum of sibling 'rude' discussion to help
enlighten either. Quite likely these two brothers were not very
different in degree of sexual shyness. In Jack's case the physical
aspects of *anything,* not merely of love, would always be secondary: the
illustration, not the text, of what really absorbed him about it. This is
salient, whether he was concerned with, say, an old house, a dead
mole, a constellation or a teashop. Where passionate sexual love was
concerned, it would seem as if he glanced as cursorily as possible at
such illustrations, and could never quite solve for himself what they
had fundamentally to do with the text. Sex remained for him in some
way obstinately unilluminating – not repellent, perhaps, so much as
discrepant. He thought it a 'bramble',* walked round it and went
another way. This attitude was already fully apparent by adolescence
– I would hazard, innate.

On their Thursday half-holiday, if they were not going home, the
boys were accompanied by a master to a lively range of
entertainments. Even a matinée at a Music Hall or the Royal
Aquarium at Westminster were considered permissible. The Aquarium
was a large building running an almost continuous variety

---

* 'As in 'Sleeping Beauty'; see p.384.

performance from eleven in the morning till eleven at night: Blondin and Ella Zuila wheeling little Lulu on the tightrope, Professor Kennedy the Mesmerist calling for volunteers, a Samson (once there were two, rival and embittered), Succi who fasted forty days, Paula with her crocodiles and snakes. A high diver, tied up in a sack, plunged from the roof into a small tank where he released himself under water, a lady was shot from a gun, and there were performing fleas. Jack revelled in such marvels; his pronounced interest in them, persisting throughout his work, probably originated in these half-holidays. The choirboys also sampled the Lord Mayor's Show, Buffalo Bill Cody and his Indians, Thomas German Reed's Entertainment at St George's Hall (two one-act plays, with a good orchestra) and Barnum's Wild Beast Show. This comprised five circus performances running simultaneously, with Siamese Twins, Giant, Fat Boy, Tattooed Lady, and Dwarf. The last caught Jack's speculative eye and his pity, sowing the seed of his *Memoirs of a Midget*.

The Cathedral itself provided some sideshows. Jack caught sight of Gladstone quite often, calling on his friends in the Chapter. Once, from the depths of a tiny brougham coming out of Charing Cross Station, he felt himself transfixed by his austere stare, from behind the hooked, budgerigar nose – not, the boy thought, with approval.

To one junior at Choir House Jack seemed at this age to have been 'full of fun, always up to larks', though not of the sort that got him into trouble. And kind, too: 'Come downstairs, Yarrow, and let's have a fight,' he suggested but, seeing the little boy's alarm, at once broke off to explain that he was joking. To his fellows he seemed happy, bold, one who enjoyed choir life – an affectionate, squareset, lively companion. But one photograph in the attitude characteristic of his manhood days, his chin propped between fist and second finger, suggests something of the thinker within. Another, reproduced here (though 'official', perhaps marking his promotion to full chorister) shows a more sensitive and delicate child.

His end-of-term reports, some of them kept all his life, were seldom complimentary, except about conduct. Typical comments were: 'Low average', 'work latterly disappointing', or 'still at times very unsatisfactory'. Even by 1887, when he was fourteen and had been at St Paul's four years, he 'shows a want of general information for a boy so high in the school'. Probably those queer nuggets of out-of-the-way fact (the kind one would expect to find in Thomas Browne) which he already delighted to hoard up, did not rank with schoolmasters as 'general information'. As to Classics, the staple fare – the Greek and Roman vision, the great statements of achieved order – they were not for him. His northerly, crepuscular, ramifying intuitions were wholly Romantic. The Classical nymphs and divinities were so much marble to him; he could find no instinctive way into the imaginative source from which they had sprung. Beside the intimate vitality of the elves and fairies, giants and goblins of northern Europe, they seemed to him null. If he made any exception it was for the Naiad, or water nymph, a recurrent symbol in his work for Beauty the tantaliser, the vision that evades. But even she turns up in a guise much nearer to a Hans Anderson creature, or to an Undine, than to the Greek spirit; and such few other nymphs as his poetry introduces are perfunctory stock properties.

He did once say he had taken a 'particular pleasure in Latin verse' while at St Paul's, but of all kinds of poetry the classical seems to have meant least to him throughout life. (In any case, during his early years at school he said that he came to hate all poetry wholesale, from the odious tedium of having verse to write out in punishment as 'lines'.)

All the same what startled him at fourteen into realising with a vital shock that poetry is the communication of *truth* – a moment so crucial he referred to it as 'conversion of the mind' – was not something from Keats or Coleridge but came as a thunderbolt, while he was dismally trying to construe a few lines of the *Iliad*. As he stammered out 'And Achilles ... went out ... black as ... night', insight flashed upon him: 'Why that means black as NIGHT.' Looking back he wrote: 'It was a revelation thus suddenly to have become aware that a fine poem means every single syllable and iota of what it says. As may the Creation itself.'[7] The experience made such an impact that poetry reawoke in him, never again to be less than the pole of his spiritual compass.

For the rest, music, it seems, was the only art that made early appeal. The Bach aria that remained his favourite, 'Have mercy Lord on me', overwhelmed him from the very first time he heard it. No child, he thought, could fail to be moved by its beauty, whether he had musical knowledge or not. 'Apart from any associations,' he wrote, 'I loved it then, I love it now. It seems to me to be a flawless revelation of the human heart and spirit and perhaps the most exquisite fragment in that supreme achievement, the St Matthew Passion.' Bach, Mozart and Handel became his favourite composers from choir days on, and Brahms he also learned to love at St Paul's, where the *Requiem* was part of the repertoire. But musically he was a no better than average performer and never sang solo. His ear was far from faultless; when leader of the Decani side he realised one day that they were off-pitch and passed the word along to 'sing *sharp*' – so disastrously (for it should have been *flat*) that the organist had to call a halt.

*

The person who had far the greatest influence on Jack at St Paul's was the brilliant, dynamic, widely-loved Canon Henry Scott-Holland, appointed after Jack's first year. He was thirty-seven, and very boyish himself. Once a favourite pupil of William Cory, Scott-Holland shared, it seems, that outstanding teacher's gift for arousing the wits and affection of boys. Passionately devout, but never solemn, he would grin openly across at the choirboys if anything ridiculous struck him in a service. He was one of the editors of the *English Hymnal* and took an ardent interest in the singing. His hilarity, gusts of enthusiasm, love of games and sports, and particular pleasure in swimming where the currents were dangerous all made him popular. 'One didn't mind being ignorant or stupid in his company,' de la Mare wrote, 'indeed one stopped being so! Also I can recall his breakfast sausages, certain oyster pâtés at his Christmas Party, and his reading me Browning. He used to run up the western steps of the Cathedral, two (or was it three) at a time in a diagonal bee-line … and wasted no love on Archdeacon Sinclair who wore scent. "Pf," he cried one day on entering the vestry, "that Charwoman again!" '[8]

For the little dark boy with the big head who got poor reports, but was so full of interests and so responsive, Scott-Holland had a specially protective affection. Jack pelted him with questions, and took to him the first poem he could remember attempting. The theme, he recalled, was Pharaoh's rout at the Red Sea, 'in anapaests, I fancy. I confided the MS to a bosom friend. Canon Henry Scott-Holland – a friend to whom a boy could confide all but anything either in head or his heart. That mercurial, that most original countenance! He read it and remarked with an amiable twinkle in the alertest of human eyes that the subject was a familiar one … I was a little daunted by this tepidity, but quickly recovered. That virus is not so easily sterilized.'[9] Scott-Holland was known for 'a certain ruthless incorruptibility of judgment', and his praise for later verses, when it did come, was the more valued.

His letters to the fifteen-year-old de la Mare would begin 'My little son' or 'My own dearest Jack'. Today such tenderness even between men, let alone from man to boy, would instantly be suspect: the Victorians were less inhibited and would have found us crude. Our trumpeted sexual liberation seems to have substituted a new set of hang-ups, equally hobbling to the imagination, and to truth to life, though it is unfashionable for the biographer to say so.

Even so, there was always a recognised risk in such attachments, and they had cost Cory his Eton Master's career. Scott-Holland's own conduct was irreproachable, but his lack of caution or of any self-consciousness let him in for imputations at least once. (They were afterwards withdrawn.)

Scott-Holland not only entertained Jack at No. 1 Amen Court, but took him home in the holidays. In April 1888 he wrote to invite him for the first of several visits. It reads so much like a tender letter to a child that it is a real jolt to realise that Jack was already by then fifteen!

> My little son,
>   This is really my last letter to you! I shall be frightening the Postman ... My sister and I will go to *my home* on Thursday 1 at *Wimbledon*. Now Wimbledon has *beautiful* air – and, after all our plans, we *must* meet. So *please*, ask and beg your good mother to let you come to my home at Wimbledon from *Thursday* to *Saturday* – and you shall trot up and down our wide common: and walk in Richmond Park, & talk to me ...
>   *My Mother* will be very good to you, and tell *your* Mother. So there! ... And I will get you an autograph of Mr Gladstone if only you will do this.
>   Goodbye, dear child, *till Thursday*.
>   *Pray come*.
>   Yr loving
>   H. S. Holland[10]

So Jack came to know Wimbledon Common from Scott-Holland's Italianate villa, a theatrical-looking house at its edge, with a tower, and a dragon for weathervane. The Common (for several years probably the loveliest wild open country he ever saw) became a treasure of de la Mare's boyhood, to which his early stories instinctively homed. He made it the setting of no less than three of these, and of that other, mentioned earlier, with a house called The Grange in it, and never finished – all this in a lifework notably sparse in topographic references. When he was living as a young man in Wandsworth, he would take his sweetheart, whenever he could, not only to walk on nearby Wandsworth and Clapham Commons – tame places by comparison – but right across London to revisit Wimbledon. Here again was 'edge-country': open, rolling, heathy slopes, crested sometimes with a small wood of firs and bracken – green dells, yellow-hammers calling, a solitary pond and a may-tree here and there – now and then a cornfield or a stretch of gleaming grass, but always, along the border, the intermittent twinkle of windows: not the windows of cottages of the countryside, but of well-to-do villas, the urban streets never very far behind them.

Judging by his letters, Jack seemed to Scott-Holland a delicate, vulnerable, gifted little boy. Even allowing for the difference of the paternal Victorian style, Jack seems to have been fixed in his mind's eye as an innocent, and one only too likely to get snuffed out by lack of encouragement. Nevertheless Scott-Holland's affection was saved from sentimentality by something perspicacious and intellectually demanding which would make him later on a wise critic, once he had got over the jolt of finding the child grown into a moody, complex, highly-strung adult.

Probably even now, when his voice was about to break, there was much more of child than adolescent about Jack to any elder's eye. There certainly stuck in Scott-Holland's memory a wistful expression and pale face that Jack's schoolfellows do not seem to have noticed. 'Children are our daylight,' Scott-Holland held; 'we do not get wiser but stupider.' The whole life ahead of this child he had befriended was to be spent eloquently preaching on that text and the turn of phrase itself might well be de la Mare's own.

After his third year at St Paul's there was a welcome change of headmaster. The Rev. William Russell, Barff's second-in-command, saintly, bearded and delightful, came one morning into the schoolroom armed as usual with his unfolded umbrella, and announced his promotion. 'We crowded round him; we cheered; someone cheeked him; he laughed; and never have I heard laughter *merrier* than his.'[11] Under Russell the rigours of Choir House relaxed considerably. He would read stories aloud to the boys, and 'when he talked of anything he had keenly in mind or at heart he would bend himself almost double in his chair; a light came into his blue eyes; he would tug at his beard, and move his long lean fingers with nervous enthusiasm.' He opened Jack's mind to the English poets, even kindled a keenness for algebra and theorems, 'made riders a joy, and Latin verse almost a hobby'. He had a light hand with impositions too and once gave Jack, whose punctuation was never strong, a hundred full stops.

It was Russell who prepared Jack for confirmation. The school custom was for candidates to go to the headmaster for absolution the day before they were confirmed, and Yarrow (that younger boy in whose memory Jack shone with such affection) went up with him to knock on the prayer-room door. After their shriving, Russell talked to them, then blessed them as they knelt side by side, laying his hands on their heads. Yarrow remembered that they were both much moved. Outside afterwards on the stairs Jack, smiling, but with nothing said, put his own hand on Yarrow's head briefly, before the school world closed round them again. The Midget specially mentions her own confirmation in her memoirs, and since the childhood of this *alter ego* includes so many touches from Jack's own, one can read her reaction as his: 'The experience cast a peaceful light into my mind and shook my heart, but it made me for a time a little self-conscious of both my virtue and my sins.'[12]

Towards the end of Jack's schooldays Holman Hunt came one day to sketch the boys at their afternoon practice; he wanted to make studies of their open mouths for his painting 'May Morning on Magdalen Tower'. He invited the boys to see the finished picture when it went on exhibition, but de la Mare had left by then. The figures of the men in the picture are identifiable portraits, but Holman Hunt himself wrote of the boys' faces: 'It was impossible for me to have the opportunity of painting from any of them'; and though Jack fancied that one of the dark choristers in the picture was very like himself, it is unlikely that the painter had intended it.

Not long after came the spring day in 1889 when Jack himself heard 'what was left of an indifferent voice *crack* in the middle of that favourite aria from the Bach Passion music'. He glanced up abashed at Sir George Martin, who was conducting. Their glances met, and Martin just perceptibly shook his head. Jack stopped singing; his choirdays were over. Next term's report, under 'Usefulness', put tersely: 'Voice gone.' The six years in the choir had meant a great deal to him. He held singing to be good both for heart and body ... '*Music*, even if not very closely attended to, is on this earth what the soul can unwittingly breathe, to its infinite benefit.'[13]

He was by now near the top of the school, hard-working and dependable, responsible for the younger choristers, though Martin reported: 'He does not appear to have that influence over the boys which is so necessary in his position.' In fact Jack was not possessed of the upperclass English schoolboy virtue of 'leadership'. He disliked having to give orders, detested the masterful in man or woman, and never achieved the 'presence' of natural authority. All the same he successfully insisted on clean hands among his fags, for he was already fastidious and beginning to be something of a dandy.

At Michaelmas 1889, his final term, when he was sixteen and Senior Boy, the idea came to him and Bouquet, the boy who had sat next to him in choir, to found a Choristers' Journal. Russell gave them every encouragement, though he demurred at the title 'journal'. In fact they began with a weekly which soon slackened to a fortnightly. Even so the editors found that it swallowed all their free time. They wrote most of each number between them, organised competitions, scoured encyclopaedias for replies to queries and for the series called 'Great Little Facts'. They jellygraphed the first issues in the boot room, where they also consumed a roast pheasant which Colonel Majendie contributed to cheer them on. First issued at a penny, the Journal consisted of six sheets closely impurpled on both sides. It was a great success. Russell mused in his preface: 'Who knows that this little world may not be nourishing in it an incipient Sir Walter Scott or a Lord Macaulay.'

In fact Jack's own contributions do not suggest literary genius or even particular promise. They include 'Powder Monkey Bob' (a childish sailor's yarn) and 'A Moonlight Skate' (a thriller). He was probably also the author of an equally childish ghost story, 'A Race for Life', in which the narrator is pursued by a party of spectral Druids 'unrelentlessly'. The whole lively and naive production is worlds away from the sophisticated sixth form of a public school. In later life de la Mare remained loyal to his own innocent, rough, tough, musically expert education, and never much held with the public-school mystique. He watched his grandsons go to Eton with some regret; he thought that public school had a stultifying effect on the imagintion, and that 'the only real education a boy of character gets anyway he gets for himself – and probably in his leisure hours'.

All through the summer of 1889 he was expecting to join his brother Bert in the Bank of England, and a December entry in his diary-notebook wonders whether he will be going there before the month is out. But something intervened, and the Bank plan was abandoned. We do not know why, and when Jack went into Russell's study to say goodbye at Christmas he knew nothing of his next step: 'He talked to me: I felt that things had suddenly become a little different – the World was looming round the corner. He gave me the brown leather Bible, embossed with its cross-swords, and his own personal parting-present, an inkstand. It was not, I think, intended in any way as a portent or an omen. But we should both of us perhaps have felt many misgivings if we could have foreseen how many times its cut-glass bottle was to be filled and to be emptied again in the years that were to follow.'[14]

3

'Floundering in oil'

Colonel Majendie, the Explosives Inspector, always helpful with his City connections in finding the choristers a place in the world, secured one for Jack at the beginning of March 1890, two months after he had left school. One of Majendie's friends was Frank Bliss, father of the composer Arthur Bliss, and at this time a director of the Anglo-American Oil Company, established in London two years before this as the first foreign off-shoot of the American giant, Standard Oil. Bliss interviewed Jack, and accepted him as a junior clerk – one rank above office-boy – in the Statistics Department.

The Bank of England may have had no immediate opening for Jack, but in any case his mother's advisers were persuaded that this new company, fruit of such rapid transatlantic expansion, offered the boy a much brisker start and rosier future than the sleepy Old Lady of Threadneedle Street. Nor would Majendie have realised from talk with Frank Bliss, who was himself cultivated and kindly, how hard and grasping the Company would prove as an employer. In fact well-meaning elders could scarcely have hit upon a more uncongenial career. Had Jack joined Bert in the Bank, he might have found the actual work no less tedious but the day would have been far shorter and the pace, atmosphere and English business traditions would have seemed civilisation itself by comparison. Other imaginative writers, such as Kenneth Grahame and T.S. Eliot, found that life quite supportable – Grahame stayed in the Bank of England thirty years and rose to be its Secretary. He was already working there when Bert began, and at that period it was a very easy-going place. It would have been quite feasible to devote a good part of each day there to study and writing. The Oil offices in Billiter Street, however, were very differently conducted. Big Business, then a new phenomenon, had its first London foothold here. Rockefeller, the Company's head, himself pioneered the whole new conception of organising on a global basis. Oil

44

was far ahead of the other industries, and by the 1870s there were several enterprising companies selling kerosene around the world.

Dock House, Billiter Street, in grandiose Victorian Gothic, was a deceptively old-fashioned setting for so much modern drive. Inside it was cramped, Dickensian and dingy: rooms packed with thirty high-spirited young clerks at massive sloping double-desks, two to each side. To keep them in order, a manager supervised from a dais: a scene much like an overgrown school-class. The manager was liable to challenge anyone leaving the room, and his 'Haven't you anything to do? Very well, get on with it' could not be flouted, or openly resented, for the threat of the sack was real. Rockefeller's, racing to get its hands firmly on a European empire, kept no underling whose pace was slack.

No records of de la Mare's time of service have come to light, but in the usual way he would have begun by addressing envelopes, running errands, taking telegrams to the Post Office, and he would have spent laborious hours copying documents, a job requiring neatness as well as faultless accuracy, for the copying had to be done in special ink which tended to clog the nib, and each clerk sat with a damp sponge in a bowl before him. There were no mechanical aids except a 'ready reckoner'.

Through gradual stages of drudgery a clerk might rise, at about twenty-three or so, to the job of compiling the daily sales sheet, a complex affair. After that, promotion depended on individual talent, and there de la Mare apparently stuck fast. He made himself useful, but comments remembered by a fellow clerk suggest that he was not thought very promising. He was conscientious, however, and by nature neat and painstaking. The endless copying helped to develop the minute fine hand of his adult life. He became adept at quick addition – running up three columns at a time, and scrupulously accurate to the fourth decimal place. When, years later, the first calculating machine was touted to the Company, de la Mare resisted the innovation. He thought it an inaccurate device and proved triumphantly that he could beat it against the clock.

He held that it is always possible to discover *some* interest in a job, however deadly, and he certainly worked hard. The only satisfaction there could be was to set himself a high standard. But it was all against the grain, and gruelling too, for the office day began for him at nine, continuing, with only an hour's break, until six-thirty, often longer. Then came the long journey home, by now out to Wandsworth. (When he was thirteen his mother had moved from Forest Hill to find something smaller now that only three children remained at home, Flo and Connie both being married and Arthur having vanished. First she took a poky Victorian villa on a corner in Lewisham, 57 Brooksbank

Road, near to Flo; but then, at about the time Jack left school, the two households recombined contentedly under one roof at 12 Estcourt Road, near Wandsworth Common.) Although Jack had to start from Wandsworth early and get home late, he was still one of the luckier Oil employees – many came earlier or stayed later, and it was not unusual for some to be slaving away till nine or ten at night.

The pay of a junior clerk, such as de la Mare was, began at ten shillings a week: a half-sovereign almost undetectable in the corner of its envelope. Normally pay went up at the end of the year by half a crown or five shillings. Such rates did not compare badly with those offered in similar companies, but they were not handsome. A general prestige attached to Anglo-American among the young clerks of the City to which neither the pay nor the prospects corresponded, and it was no doubt this popular misconception, fed by adroit American publicity, that had misled Majendie. Writing to Jack a few weeks after he had joined Anglo-American, Majendie urged him to stick the hard work and long hours, as they were 'the signs of a going concern'. He hoped Jack would let them see he was 'real grit', and told him – how far away it must have seemed – that the Choristers' Journal was wilting without him.

Promotion might have come his way had he been a sharp-witted ambitious boy with a salesman's instinct. But he had no push, hated hustle, and was probably not prepared to work abroad, which the sales side of the business would entail. As time went on he came to detest the Company, root and branch, for another reason: the misery of constant moral unease. The more he knew of Anglo-American's business methods, the shabbier they seemed to him. Small companies were everywhere put under pressure and bought up; and to keep the price of kerosene temptingly cheap the safety-point at which vapour ignited was kept as low as the inadequate law permitted, despite terrible accidents. 'Pay no man a profit' was said to be Rockefeller's motto, and in the name of economy any employee might be sacked at short notice even after years of service. So Jack's groove in the Statistical Department, even if hardly bearable, seemed better than sharp-practice in the selling division, and he continued to plod on there for the next eighteen years.

*

If this seems dismally unadventurous, we must remember that it was a period of high unemployment, and he had little by way of qualifications. His musical gifts were too slender to earn him anything, and the rest of his education, though sound, had been brief. That said, he certainly showed more capacity for passive endurance than enterprise. But he was only sixteen and young for his age in many ways – not very independent, closely attached to the warm rule and support of home. Once caught in the daily grind, he had little opportunity to strike out for any alternative; there was never enough money in the family to justify the risk of prolonged unemployment. And when he went into Oil even his true, interior life was only just beginning to reveal its range and needs to him. He had lived till now the child's deep, floating existence, absorbed in perceptions, merely accepting what came from books and learning, without realising at all urgently that in wide, systematic reading lay the key to his powers. He already dreamed of becoming a writer; but it was only dreaming.

It took him no more than the first week or two to realise what a trap had shut on him. Scott-Holland was more sensitive to his frustration and despair then Majendie. He wrote affectionately, trying to keep alive for the boy who was 'cooped up in your barrels of oil, poor dear' a link with the things they had shared together – love of landscape, discussion of ideas and books, and Jack's secret ambition to write. 'What have you been thinking about, I wonder, and have you written anything? or read? I hope the other fellows in the office are decent, and don't talk vilely and coarsely. Cling to pure ways, and thoughts, and don't let standards slip in this matter. It is vital. Dear child – tell me what your *heart* is a-bubble with. Will you? It is generally agog. Tell me how things come to you – or puzzle you; or touch you. Let us help one another.'[1]

Scott-Holland wrote again a month later, enclosing a booklet on purity, anxious for this boy who had no father. But broad talk in the office was probably among the least of Jack's discomforts or temptations. As the months went by, deep into London's airless summer, the struggle to show he was 'real grit' grew no easier. In August, Scott-Holland was writing again with tender concern:

My darling Jack,

I have so often been thinking of you, and of your little soul beating against its narrow bars of Office – and longing for some real work in the world.

Nothing can be done just now – I do not see how you can help going on for a bit in the 'Oil'.

But do not let the ambitions die – and do not think them useless, because just now they are fruitless. Nurse them – and cherish them – and hope ... And do send me anything you write – in prose or verse – and I will try to help you in it ...[2]

We do not know whether Jack took up the offer. Tired out by his long days, he probably had nothing to show.

Someone at the office answered an enquiry from Majendie this month with a satisfactory report on the boy. After this, silence descends on Jack's career, and there is very little to show, from seventeen to nineteen, how his life developed. This is not usually a fallow period, and for luckier boys in their sixth forms it can be one of great intellectual expansion and also a time when the first friendships based on shared ideas are founded. Jack, on the contrary, was more completely on his own than he ever was again. His horizon contracted sharply instead of expanding. He drifted away from his schoolfriends and seems to have made no new intimates. Gradually he dropped even the one or two perceptive friends among his elders outside the family circle. In January 1891 Scott-Holland writes to ask him to look after another St Paul's boy coming into the office. He is still as fond of Jack as ever, and hopes that 'you keep the same as you were'. In May he writes again just as affectionately ('My own dearest Jack') and assures him he is not offended by the gap there has evidently been. Some time before Michaelmas, Jack called on his old headmaster, Russell, who asked him what he had been reading, and when Jack answered 'Locke on the Understanding' Russell's eyebrows went up. He suggested that reading French would be a more profitable amusement. He does not seem to have realised how desperately Jack was seeking a broader base for his intellectual life: how badly he needed to follow his bent. Russell wrote afterwards to Lucy Delamare: 'I felt the happier and more satisfied because he seemed to speak freely and frankly. I hope he will always regard me as his friend.' But Jack seems to have made no further move to preserve these links. There is no mention of his meeting Scott-Holland again in the next four years, and when they did, Jack's tone had altered – 'I saw Canon Scott-Holland last night. I fear that the charm of my boyhood has gone – never mind.'[3] The remark at least shows he had met the dreary knowingness of the world about such friendships and his tone is sour.

It was unlucky that his most encouraging critic should be a cleric. For, at some time between leaving school and when we next find him, at nineteen, beginning to reveal his inner self to any friend, Jack had lost his boyhood faith. He may well have fought shy of intimate talk with Scott-Holland from embarrassment over this, and confused feelings of doubt. Perhaps the loss of belief was in part simply the result of leaving St Paul's. Release from the cathedral discipline may have been at first some relief, but it is very dull to sink from leading Decani in magnificent stalls, to sitting alongside an ordinary parish congregation. No doubt, too, the intellectual climate of the early Nineties, and his own analytical questioning, drifted him still further. At any rate, by the end of these two years he had become curiously, deeply unhappy at his loss of faith. By then, belief had come to seem part of a vanished innocence: yet one more essence of life which growing up had sapped away from the treasure of his childhood.

Meanwhile, though he was unhappy spiritually and isolated, it would be a mistake to picture him as making a gloomy impression on others. A younger clerk and friend, Fred Atha, who shared his desk towards the end of his eighteen years in Oil, just when he had grown to loathe it most, replied, when asked if he had appeared happy, that he 'could not ever imagine him otherwise.' At home, family life was more than ever dear after the bleak routine of the day. The Wandsworth home repeated the familiar childhood pattern: besides his mother, Pattie was once more at hand in the kitchen to cosset everyone. The house, three-storeyed and well-built, was pleasant enough. It had a stair-well down which Bert and Jack, the two City clerks, could pelt any available sister with their pillows, and there were Flo's small children to fool with. Her husband, John Rowley, an engineer, had little luck, and Flo was never without financial worries or anxieties over someone's health. By now she had three children, and a fourth was born soon after the families joined forces again. In time there would be seven of this generation too.

Jack had always been more a child than a brother to Flo. But with his rare sympathies, his understanding of motherhood, and his sense of fun, he was also someone now for her to depend on. His queer fancies and childlike fluency in make-believe became for each of them a chief solace in their drudgery. When the irrepressible young uncle sat on the Rowley children's beds, telling them the next instalment of some interminable fantasy – the favourite was about a tiny race called the Impies who lived in a gold ball on a neighbour's roof – Flo would leave her housework and come to listen.

Jack also kept up the old family custom of small festivals, contributing sixpence a week towards a feast for the children. Once he forgot, and telegraphed to Flo from the City – a matter of another sixpence in the Nineties – 'Spend half a crown on the Feast.' Out of his Oil pay this was reckless generosity. When the occupants of the doll's house were to be married, it was naturally he, with his Cathedral experience, who officiated, afterwards rushing the happy pair round and round the nursery table while Poppy from downstairs loudly played The Wedding March. The clergyman became hilarious when the little girl Ethel finally put them to bed in the big double bed side by side.

But after the long day's grind, and after the children were quiet in bed,

Jack would go up alone to his room. When he opened his books up there his real day's work began. In the shock of finding what meagre prospects faced him he learned the priceless lesson of how to work on his own. He was not very strong, but he had great mental energy, and this, dammed up all day, carried him far into the solitary quiet of the suburban night. Wandsworth Common lay only a street away, and through his window he could smell leaves on the night wind. The common was a confined space compared with Wimbledon – no heath and bracken here – but it was bordered with magnificent black poplars, and these he came to love deeply.

His self-education in these night hours began at the roots, with vocabulary. Words in themselves had fascinated him from childhood. Writing in after years on 'How I Became An Author', he said that to the child whose destiny is to write (particularly verse),

> the sounds of them and the making of those sounds will be his chief decoy
> and enticement. Sound and meaning soon become inseparable and thus
> words themselves become the means of makebelieve – one of the richest
> of human consolations; of silently talking to oneself – one of the closest of
> all human communions ... When I was a child I listened to the sound of
> words – that secret language – no more consciously perhaps, but with no
> less delight than, say, to the running of water over its pebbles.[4]

The stylist, then, had been awake from the very beginning, and now went attentively to school to whatever Victorian prose masters he found on his mother's shelves: Ruskin, Carlyle, Stevenson and Newman (whom he admired at that time as highly as his mother did). These were the models from whom he chose passages to analyse for the skills behind their effects. He also used such humble aids as *A Handy Guide to Correct Pronunciation and Spelling*, and Poppy remembered him seriously tackling a manual of the English language. At about this time too he began to make himself exercise books on waste sheets of paper from the Oil office. The first dated entry is in an alphabetical notebook for November 1892. He has jotted down curiosities of natural history: effects of rain and fine weather on various creatures, attributes of bees and gorillas, and notes on Madame Bovary and arsenic, hellebore and madness. About now, as a result of reading De Quincey, he made one mild experiment – smoking opium in a briar-wood pipe. It was disappointing: the smoke was unpleasant, and he experienced no other effects whatever. In the little notebook he began to make dated observations of the sunrise. Gradually he would elaborate this practice into detailed and highly-wrought passages on the weather, for practice in description and vocabulary. Such new words as he picked up in his day's reading he would set himself to incorporate somehow in the next day's weather-report. Not surprisingly, perhaps, he generally manages to infuse an atmosphere of strangeness into the most commonplace and dreary facts.

With touching readiness to make use of any discipline his narrow experience offered, even the business methods of the office were pressed into service. His systems of annotation and tabulation – analysis of grammar, meanings, effects of sounds, of the incidence of certain consonants and so on, in chosen passages – became in time as minutely methodical and complex as the decimal calculations entered on the reverse side of the sheet. These notebooks were kept up for ten years, an impressive witness to solitary application. There were also such ambitious attempts as a translation of the *Inferno*, with the help of Longfellow, Cary, and Carlyle 'and wholly innocent of Italian'.

His taste formed itself spontaneously along the impulse of his curiosity alone. This gave him, to the end of his life, a distinctively 'unofficial' standpoint from which to appreciate the English writers. Coming to him in his boyhood off Lucy's shelves, or the public library, or in those little volumes of the 'King's Classics' which he gradually acquired from secondhand bookstalls in Holborn during his office lunch break, they sprang on him each their bright, discrete surprise. They never congealed into 'English Literature'. They were to travel into his receptive mind without the academic passport then, and kept this freedom lifelong.

Since no juvenilia apparently survive of those first two and a half years in Oil, it seems likely little was written, for de la Mare hoarded all his life almost every scrap of manuscript – not from vanity, still less systematically, but because anything written down may keep a secret generative power. He earnestly impressed on me once the vital need for such hoarding, when I was an adolescent hoping to become a writer: '*Keep everything.*' The imagination, he pointed out, has the curious capacity to 'fold itself almost into a bud again' and lie dormant in such scraps. No early line was too immature, no scrap of observation too cryptic. All were worth saving because they might one day germinate. He himself was always cropping and recropping – revising, rewriting, even recasting completely, years later.

The first evidence of something of his own after leaving school comes in the autumn of 1893, when he was twenty: not a story or a poem but, rather unexpectedly, a farce. A funny farce too, neat, rollicking, simple, and very actable, written for immediate production; a direct descendant of the charades and improvisations for which he had already made a name for himself at St Paul's. Its title was *A Darling Old Villain* (in later performances: *Wanted An Actor*) and Jack played the old villain. By the February of 1892 he had become a member of the Esperanza Amateur Dramatic Club, joining Bert in his favourite pastime, with results far-reaching indeed. The Esperanza, a humble and lighthearted little society, was a group of young professional people round about Wandsworth, mostly clerks like Jack and Bert themselves, who brought along their sisters – a flourishing and well-organised small company.

Bert was one of its male leads. The brother who had been slightly aloof in the games of the three youngest grew up matter-of-fact, practical, well-informed, but also sufficiently accomplished as an actor to have the two best amateur clubs of the time, the Forbes Robertson and the Irving, both invite him to play for them. He still shared Jack's sensitive, romantic, hollow-cheeked looks. The brothers were sociable, with plenty of friends of their own age as companions, though Jack as yet lacked an intimate. They would go about as a pair, popular, smartly turned out, susceptible to every charming face and devoted to each other.

Among the club's members were the Bedbrook girls, belonging to the large family of a retired rear-admiral, who lived close by in considerably greater style than the de la Mares. They gave big parties and picnics: the house hummed with callers. Some of the girls attended the same school as Poppy, and Bert became attached to serious-minded Violet, known as Lettie. Jack fell in alongside for a while with a pretty and flirtatious younger sister. The Bedbrooks' Saturday 'At Homes' were musical evenings at which Bert was an habitué. Jack's choirboy treble had settled into a pleasant baritone, and Bert soon brought him along too, and he would oblige with 'The Bedouin Love Song', 'droning a bit' as Lettie remembered.

By now he was finding that his personal appearance lent itself strikingly to the Aesthete pose. Men's hair was generally worn short, but he began to leave his wavy, dark locks long enough for errand boys to yell 'Get a hair cut'; and within the next year or two he had an enormously long frock-coat made to his own design (as did the young Max Beerbohm) emulating those of the Mashers, a fashion of coat which reached almost ankle-length by 1895, and was supposed to 'diminish the apparent size of the waist and hips'. No doubt this was Jack's aim, for his figure was always a little stocky, with a faintly nautical roll to his gait, a family way of walking – Bert and Poppy had it too. Jack adopted a flowing cravat with a big knot and floating ends, and added to his height with a top hat. He also took to smoking a cigarette in a long holder. One of the Rowley nephews remembered how particularly nice his young uncle smelt when hugged – not *scented*, but decidedly fragrant from a cherry toothpowder or something of the kind he used.

Conscious of these pleasant personal advantages and very responsive, he flirted mildly, spontaneously, with the greatest enjoyment. Girls found him hopelessly generous, eager for a romantic atmosphere, delighting in a spree. Mrs Bedbrook was a formidable matriarch and tended to cramp the brothers' natural style. The de la Mare family circle was much more free and easy – they liked to laugh: they liked to argue, they were demonstrative; above all they liked to fool. So Bert and Jack much preferred, when possible, to take the Bedbrook girls out – three of them, with another male escort to make up a party of six – to the Crystal Palace. Jack's relish for a show was as strong still as in the days of the choir half-holidays. And Lettie remembered that he never failed to offer some small tribute to his partner on these outings: a box of chocolates or a little bottle of scent – presents he could ill afford. In this cheerful band of young neighbours he never spoke of his private ambitions. And with all his good spirits, he made a modest impression: his gaiety was unassuming. Already he was the one who stirred up conversation in the others, mainly by an irrepressible flow of curious questions. The dark moody side of his character was kept well out of sight. Nor did his aesthete pose ever go further than style of dress: the girls found nothing languid, affected or egotistic about his manners, nor did he ever complain, they said, about his life in Oil. His way of surviving was not to mention it at all. This childlike capacity for flinging himself into the moment, for making instant use of refreshment and relief, was always the secret of his stamina.

With many members of the Esperanza at work in the City all day, performances could not be managed very often, but the club was in brisk demand in parish halls up and down London. The busy season was of course towards Christmas, and by November 1893 Jack had been asked to contribute a new piece to their repertoire – his farce. It was the draw of the evening. The 'darling old villain' of the title is a devoted father who fears the return after years abroad of a nephew likely to steal away the cherished daughter who looks after him. He hits upon a ruse to discredit the suitor: he advertises for an actor to arrive first to impersonate him and offend his daughter in advance. Somebody both obstreperous and wily, who is more than a match for his employer, answers the advertisement. (He was played by Bert.) There is a neat double imbroglio involving the housemaid (Poppy), and a satisfactory volte-face as a finale. The whole thing is neat, endearing, childish, and hearty, only betraying the de la Mare to come by an ear for flavoured dialogue.*

The charming little folded penny programmes – faded yellow, faded pink and green, usually engraved with a vignette of the relevant Parish Church or Hall, their lettering set out with decorative curlicues, advertised seats at sixpence, threepence and a penny. They survive in the de la Mare family papers from five separate hoards – Lettie Bedbrook's and Elfie Ingpen's as well as Jack's, Bert's and Poppy's. For each they were the first mementoes of their courtships. Amateur theatricals, even more than long sea voyages, have always been promoters of love affairs. The late Victorian middle-class society of the suburbs, where young people still conformed to the proprieties of their parents, allowed no other freedom to compare with the fun and of their relaxed Esperanza meetings. There, they were free of all chaperones. The contrast with the other social conventions was very marked indeed: hard to appreciate today.

The company's leading lady, Elfrida Ingpen, known as Elfie, did not appear in Jack's farce, but she must have seen it, the first piece written by any member of the Club. A month later, she and Jack were acting together in another play, popular enough to be repeated. So they had the intimate excitement of shared successes to draw them rapidly together.

A young man of twenty will often fall in love with a woman older and more experienced than himself, and in any case Elfie looked younger than her age. She combined, too, the qualities de la Mare always loved in a woman: something vulnerable and childlike, with a protective maternal gentleness towards the corresponding qualities in him. Her own history, too, and the point at which he entered it, all favoured the attachment. It sprang up promptly and conclusively for both.

The photographs of Elfie from about this time show a definite likeness to the dark-haired, dark-eyed heroines, gentle but spirited, of de la Mare's poems and tales. Probably at this period she answered wonderfully to his private ideal. The pictures also show a sense of personal style: there is something slightly mannish and cavalier about her sense of dress, an appealing mix of the spirited with the shy.

Tenderness, energy, and endurance all show in this portrait; though grief and bitterness had by now coloured her expectations. For Elfie,

* In old age, de la Mare liked to recount that 'my brother and I . once gave an evening performance in the Church Room opposite the Mortuary, in a Whitechapel street in which Jack the Ripper had twice been active in the same night's small hours'. But alas for the pleasantly lurid: de la Mare's memory (though he was vexed by this trick of it) was always apt to concertina the facts. Jack the Ripper's exploits all took place in the autumn of 1888, when Jack the schoolboy was fifteen and presumably asleep in his dormitory.

though she looked much of an age with Jack was in fact thirty, and her extra ten and a half years had not been sunny.

She was the eldest of five. Her parents, Alfred and Constance Emma Ingpen, were second cousins. They set store by the fact they could trace their common genealogy back to Saxon England. Ingpens had lived by farming or the professions. Elfie's people worked in law and came from Hampshire. Alfred was Clerk of the Insolvent Debtors' Court and later Clerk of the Rules. They lived in modest comfort in South London (Lavender Hill) and here Elfie grew up. Alfred Ingpen had been a 'Sunday painter' of some distinction, even exhibiting at the Royal Academy in the 1830s. But children increased, his wife died and the painting stopped. His little dressing-room studio was made over to the handicapped child, the eldest boy, Alfred, nicknamed Dom, born next after Elfie. Dom's fate was her first reason for distrusting life. A careless nursemaid had let him fall out of his baby-carriage. He hit his head, began epileptiform fits and for the rest of his long life depended on his sisters' care. The needlessness of this tragedy was repeated when their mother died from gall-stones, after refusing the operation which was already usually successful in such cases as hers.

Elfie was only twenty-two, and her mother's death left her a heavy responsibility for her father and the younger children, especially Dom. She blamed her mother, and spoke of the consequences for herself with some bitterness when she looked back in later years. Her mother cuts a wan invalidish figure in the little packet of family letters that survive – a contrast to the winning affectionate fun of Alfred, who taught his children to use their eyes and encouraged visits to picture galleries and general sightseeing. His influence developed in Elfie and in Roger, the younger brother, who was her closest ally, sensibilities and interests very attractive to Jack, giving him the first two companions with whom he could really share his own imaginative life. Alfred had sent Roger to Boulogne as a boy, and he became keenly interested in art, both English and continental and a friend of painters and writers. He wrote a book on Belgium and became a Shelley scholar and finally a publisher. Elfie, though with little time ever to give to such things, had a sensitive eye for beauty and a genuine appreciation of poetry and romance; also a definite flair (which she shared with Jack) for picking up good antiques in sales. She inherited also her father's passion for parenthood – another bond with all de la Mares. There was in fact a general affinity and mutual attraction between the two families.

After Mrs Ingpen died a young relation had come to keep house for Elfie, who had already been obliged to take a job. Her father had retired early on a supplemented pension when the office he held was abolished (evidently leaving the family in some difficulty). Elfie went into the Prudential Assurance Company by the time she was nineteen, and with considerable social distress. She was always reluctant to answer her children, they said, when they questioned her about this part of her life. It was still very early for a woman to be so employed; she felt conspicuous in the Prudential and suffered accordingly. Her father died five years after his wife, and from then on she and Roger held the family together.

Besides these many cares Elfie had endured also the death of a young fiancé, probably a childhood acquaintance. She is wearing mourning in most of the early adult photographs.

The sadness and home responsibilities surrounding all these bereavements and troubles had the usual outcome of the period. Elfie's thirties had begun – she was still single. But her appearance and her amateur theatricals prove that she had (at that age at least) kept some self-confidence – a quality she was to lose disastrously in later life. She still had enough to go out and seek a young man for herself.

By the time the Esperanza Club introduced them to the de la Mares, Elfie and Roger had between them run the family home for five years and none of the five siblings had yet left it. Elfie and Roger had formed a close alliance with each other. Roger had grown up into a tall, stooping, delicate-looking, very unworldly young man: absent-minded, gentle and delightful, with great integrity. But his good nature was easy to impose on. He did not act in the Esperanza himself – nobody could be less fond of limelight of any sort – but took a benevolent brotherly interest in the Club, and was on occasion its steward. He soon became the confidant of Jack's private ambitions, and must early on have seen other first attempts besides *A Darling Old Villain*, for only a year and a half after they first met, he was urging Jack to publish. But before this, even before Roger became Jack's intimate, in the spring of 1894 Jack fell flat in love with Elfie.

*

No lack of enterprise here. For all his modesty, there was a strain of the imperious and impetuous in his relations with women. He was as direct in his wooing as a child who has never been snubbed. His mother and Flo and Pattie had never, it seems, foolishly *spoiled* him; yet his upbringing had certainly taught him to expect feminine love and compliance as the natural order of things.

By February 1894 the Esperanza were hoping for another play from their resident author, for a Benefit Night in May. The stage-manager realised that the suggestion would come best from Elfie, and indeed there was no question of Jack's refusing her invitation. The success of his farce had been sweet, encouraging him to try something serious, and he was quick to turn the occasion to personal advantage. He set to work rapidly, and conceived a thorough-going improbable Victorian sentimental piece entitled *Geoffrey*, with a star part for Elfie and another for himself as her lover. Perhaps the personal considerations were rather too pressing; the plot has no shred of originality, nor is it credible. The hero is all noble renunciation and high-souled wistfulness, the heroine a pure, pretty dear, though with rather more genuine life about her. She was called Florence – significantly: no de la Mare heroine was ever awarded the name Florence or Lucy unless the author regarded her with particular affection.

In more than one sense Elfie accepted the role he had created for her. Perhaps she fell in love less headlong than Jack did; certainly hers was a sadder and less hopeful nature, and anyway this was not her first attachment. She was also much less articulate. Yet the attraction was certainly mutual from April 1894 on. Although he was twenty one and she nearly eleven years older, she was pliant and inwardly dependent, and Jack not easy to resist. Mixed with his natural, obvious attractions was a more private quality which the atmosphere of their theatricals would have brought out: something that singled him out from the other young men in their circle, and which Elfie was quick to salute. What is more, she was to keep faith with it through all the grinding disappointments and frustrations that lay ahead.

She believed already in his imagination, which as yet was only throwing up a flickering sheet-lightning of the unusual from a creative gift still well below the horizon. Instinctively (for she was not introspective) Elfie must have realised that in Jack life was offering her what she was extremely unlikely to find again. She believed he had greatness in him. She was the less romantic of the two; yet it was she who made the more total self-surrender.

4

Elfland

Elfie treasured all Jack's love-letters; he only kept a few of hers. What is probably the first of them, written in April 1894, opens with characteristic abruptness. All of them read like a man thinking aloud for a moment, breaking out to talk to himself in random phrases, as if not fully conscious that he is speaking at all. They convey very strongly the pent-up isolation of his inward life, and the uncertainty of who he was, which prompted him to try out now one attitude, now another, in order to discover an identity.

There is no introduction to the first letter, no 'Dear Elfie', and this became characteristic of his love-letters, both now, to her, and later to someone else. It increases the impression they give of addressing an inward companion rather than a correspondent. It is a letter of disturbance and anguish:

> You will read this tomorrow morning and you will be in a matter of fact humour.
> Do you wish to let what we have said tonight be forgotten entirely.
> Was it unwise to have said so much? Can we ever be real friends? are you laughing at it now? are you? or are you real and true and will you be with me and talk with me as tonight. I want you (and yet not *you* but you in the abstract) to be my friend not the cold matter-of-fact lying friend but the real, warm good woman.
> I am only very young – perhaps shall not want you soon – perhaps. I feel sure you will soon despise me, you will tell me when that happens wont you?
> Open, God's truth, between us.
> May it be?
> I shall see you soon.'[1]

Two days later:

> I am very disappointed – I have been looking forward to your letter and now it has come and *you* are not in what you write. Whatever you may

say – nothing will alter my wish for you to be to me as you have promised,
as I know you will be.

I believe in you entirely ...[2]

And he continues to press her ardently. Already by treating her
surrender as a foregone conclusion he had in fact made it one. He
might doubt with a boy's gauche frankness if his own feelings would be
permanent, but he sensed already that he could command hers. And he
had half transmuted the flesh-and-blood woman into a dream figure,
an Idea, a role any real Elfie would scarcely be likely to sustain.

She obeyed his mandate, and that same month, in the little
sitting-room at Wandsworth, or walking the quiet elm- and
poplar-haunted pavements along the edge of the Common, they drew a
step nearer commitment to each other. After they parted, Jack sat up
to write to her in a ferment of conflicting emotions:

> It is over and now it is very late. I am thinking of our talk tonight – it
> seems now as a dream a pleasant dream – and I awake feeling knowing it
> was all true – but, that it was foolish.
>
> That is what you must understand – you must realise how fickle, how
> changeable and faithless I feel myself to be, before I tell you anything
> more. I think of you too highly, far too highly to deceive you, above all
> else I want you to love me as your friend – but even for that I will not lie
> to you.
>
> How sad your life has been how weary you must be, and yet it is better,
> to have had trouble to have felt unhappy far better than not to have felt
> at all – Life is only worth living when one feels and suffers.
>
> It is very good of you to put trust in me as you do; what matters it how
> long we have known one another – we are together now and we can tell
> one another everything.
>
> I am going to be very much to you – I am strong now and I will help you.
>
> It is terrible to think of the future, the past is for ever gone, it is
> terrible to me to think that perhaps a time will come when the shadow of
> darkness will creep between us – shutting you out. Remain with me dear
> – you must be with me –
>
> I want to tell you that though I have written to others in the past the
> thought was with me even as I wrote that it was not to them I was
> writing – I was looking out, longing for that one to come who would give
> me the sympathy that never came.
>
> With you it is different *now* as I write, I am thinking of you
> individually – you only and personally – do you understand me?
>
> I have no real God. What matters it if the wretched physical self of me
> has its way sometimes I can come back to you.
>
> You, Truth, and I – no other –
>
> Only to get away from the wretched overwhelming Doubt: to look a
> little beyond at what comes after.
>
> I love to think of you, I am myself when you are in my thoughts.
>
> Goodnight my dearest one.[3]

Packet after packet of such letters follow, on the same themes – vehement, melancholy, disjointed, self-contradictory, immature; usually brief, often exasperated to downright incoherence by nervous frustration. They are the only intimate record we have of the next five years – a very lopsided one, for it scarcely ever deals in de la Mare's intellectual interests and ideas, only in his emotions. These circle round and round three dominant pains: the loneliness of human life, the dread enigma of death, the ache of lost faith in God. To all three his present romantic love was desperately applied as remedy. Idealizing the beloved, setting her like the figure of Beatrice in the ascendant over her lover, he hoped to find again the lost divine principle in her and somehow, by uniting with such a being, to avoid extinction.

Yet at the very moment that he set Elfie on a pedestal as divine Womanhood the human daily self of him remained very critical. She was to find him a wearing and exacting lover. Besides ideal companion and substitute for God, he required her to be – and this with special emphasis – the ideal mother. Why did he demand so many more of these mother-son relationships than most lives need or ever contain? Whatever the cause, it would hardly seem to be *deprivation*, since his bond with his own mother was unusually strong and markedly happy. Yet, in addition to all the defined roles Elfie must try to fill, he looked to her also to satisfy all that burning, nebulous, nameless restlessness of his nature which had felt itself, from childhood, incurably homesick to be here, alive, at all. It was a very tall order for a woman of thirty-one, herself of simple, straightforward, domestic affection, by nature anxious-minded and insecure. But Elfie met this large demand as best she could. In return, when he was not in Byronic mood, Jack brought into her uncoloured life a magic stimulus it had never known.

His letters to her served two purposes. As well as an outlet for his love, they were the main channel, at first perhaps the only channel, for all his pent-up writer's urge. Often they clearly stem from the same impulse as imaginative work, but an impulse still confused and without definite aim. He falls into a pose, strikes attitudes, luxuriates in the pains of thwarted genius, and is wearisomely over-literary. Yet, having nowhere else to try out his writer's wings, he must stretch them here as best he can, in these tiny freckled grey pages, scribbled under the eye of the manager on his dais in the office. The letters were often folded up without envelope into a minute cocked-hat shape and so stamped and posted in a City lunch hour, to reach Elfie before he got home that night. He knew quite well that she would make allowances and find the real affection under the wrappings of self-torment and rhetoric. He knew he was safe with her – as safe as a little boy in the blessed freedom to behave badly to its mother.

'God is in *you* that is why I love you,' he writes to her in one of these letters.[4] There was never a more reluctant unbeliever. His whole nature craved faith that would relate him to a divine beauty and truth. The letters also harp on his intense preoccupation with what happens after death, a problem always to trouble him, but at this period an obsession like a tooth-ache. To the agnostic, the reasons for living may be obscure, and the struggle to formulate a valid philosophy tormenting, but the question of life after death can quite often remain something hardly bothered about at all. For the young de la Mare, however, such indifference was inconceivable. Wherever he turned, the air was charged with mysterious promptings from regions beyond conscious interpretation; these were what seemed to him the most significant experiences life had to offer, but their whole value and meaning for him depended on whatever next state awaited the soul. When he had written to Elfie, 'Only to get away from the wretched overwhelming Doubt to look a little beyond at what comes after', the Doubt was of course, the horrific possibility of a void, the fear that after all there might be *no* after-life, *no* ultimate world of absolutes to which these clues and hints pointed.

De la Mare was very fond of the ballad of True Thomas, in which the Queen of Elfland (whom Thomas has greeted as the Queen of Heaven) shows him from a hill-top the narrow, briery road of righteousness, and that other 'braid, braid road across the lily leven'. But then she points out a third:

> And see ye not that bonny road
> Which winds about the ferny brae?
> That is the road to fair Elfland
> Where you and I this night maun gae.

That third way, all the more valued for its oblique, secretive windings, was the one that de la Mare 'maun gae'; for him, it was the only reliable path to truth. 'Elfland' in this case (though it does include what is ordinarily suggested by the word) represents the whole field of imagination open to traffic with the unconscious: something dangerous, valid, and not at all the province of whimsy and decoration. He was always groping for the true spiritual interpretation of psychic and imaginary experience. Was it or was it not part of a valid ultimate reality? Knowledge of the state after death could alone give him support for the supreme value he put, instinctively, on the imagination as the one reliable interpreter of life.

He would have agreed with Keats that the imagination may be

compared with Adam's dream: he awoke and found it truth. He felt as strongly as Keats that what the imagination seizes as Beauty *must* be Truth. But he felt it less serenely. In his young days he desperately needed the ratification which only certainty of personal survival could supply.

Christian teachers have always said that there is no alternative to Christianity but pessimism, that if Christian doctrine is not true, life is a tragedy. Thomas Hardy agreed with them, and, because he could not think the doctrine true, he embraced the pessimism with stoic endurance. The young de la Mare was not cast in so heroic a mould. If he could not fully accept the Christian hope, then neither was he fully prepared to face the alternative – at least, not steadily and permanently. Around the age of twenty, just before he met Elfie, he evidently *had* faced it, with its full anguish; but he found no way to come to terms with the pain, and gradually he turned aside from full confrontation. He left the question open, would not commit himself in this life: he would wait till death itself 'brings all to an issue' (as he wrote), preferring to avoid ultimate conclusions, perhaps for fear of being forced upon the intolerable one that the day, 'however used, must be wasted'.[5] For good reasons and bad he had begun as he would go on. At some deep, perhaps unconscious level the young who have great potential talent decide to grapple and later may become great artists – or they take evasive action. De la Mare decided for evasion.

Like Hardy he remained, on the level of human behaviour, deeply attached to the Christian ideals of character, and he lived by their light. He too placed the specifically Christian virtues highest of all, for the sake of their *beauty*: fidelity, compassion, humility, kindness. Also he practised prayer, not only on occasion, but (as he told a close friend, Margaret Newbolt, in his middle years) regularly kneeling down to do so before he slept.

But at the age of twenty-one he was probably at the furthest point from accepting his own dilemma; for at that age reasons for belief are passionately sought, and the young are not yet reconciled to living with disparate, unresolved convictions at different levels of their personality, the compromise of later years. In 1894, the year he fell in love, he was certainly not reconciled. Everything to do with religion bruised and stung him. There is an early letter, delivered by hand, in which he can only protest his pain incoherently, blaming God (illogically enough) for putting him into the tormenting position of having no one to pray to:

> Will it never come, the peace the whole Godlove that is in me, is it always to be hopeless cold dark, a dream that knows no waking a dream that is always a dream.

How I shudder at the endless tomorrows ...

God how I think – curse him – I feeble little thing I hate him Kill me he may torture me – Love me Elfie – good purity love me, he cannot touch me then – he is pity – the Lord has need of me somewhere I will be blind and believe – I will cease to think – and trust It is impossible![6]

And so he goes on, in confused anguish, wondering if he is already mad.

Long-continued intellectual frustration can breed a state of tension resulting in such over-stimulation that it does temporarily resemble insanity. Imagination can become active to the point of frenzy, even though it is quite possible, by fierce control, to keep the outward behaviour normal. Once, in writing of the reticence of private eccentrics, de la Mare said: 'A temporary insanity ... revealing itself in no perceptible symptom, may not perhaps be rare. Whether rare or not, it will probably be endured in silence and never alluded to.'[7] He himself felt very near this condition at times in the 1890s, and again in another prolonged emotional strain at the end of his thirties. He was lucky that with Elfie he need not, in this first onset of such miseries, endure them in silence. She let them wear themselves out upon her. The knowledge that he needed her was all the reassurance she required.

His state of frustration was perhaps due less to uncongenial work alone than to the combination of that with something else which he might have had to endure in any case, that belt of inward fog, common enough for any young artist towards the end of his teens, during which he may feel equally cut off from childhood's kingdom and the creative range lying hidden ahead.

De la Mare did not find it quite possible to keep his promise to himself, made at this time, that he would never come to scorn his adolescent self. When old, he certainly looked back with embarrassment at what he had been as a very young man. Of all the stages of his life, he said he felt it was the most immature, the one he least cared to dwell on in recollection – not at all because he had often been wretched then, but because he had been least *himself* at this stage, least sincere and genuine, most self-conscious, artificial and (so he felt) conceited. It is certainly difficult to connect this self-regarding, melancholic young man, trying out a dying fall in prose music, with either the wise and spirited little boy of former years or the remarkable man to come. No doubt the letters to Elfie, taken alone, are unfair to him. Those to her brother, Roger, of which few survive, are much more spirited, even jaunty, much less self-conscious. They show a keen enjoyment of life whenever there was the merest chink for this and a constant, eager, practical discussion of work in hand. Much later, in 1916, de la Mare wrote in a review, looking back to this stage of life:

'We fight (in youth, chiefly) to master circumstance, to exult over it; we fight also to accommodate ourselves to it. We fight in the solitude of the spirit, without hope of truce or respite, for self-realization; and to win also to some kind of shelter and security from the dangers and disasters that threaten us from without … A poet is born an exile, and an exile he must die … "It is not," in Flecker's words, "the poet's business to save man's soul, but to make it worth saving".'[8]

*

On 28 May 1894, a few weeks after his letters to Elfie had begun, his second play was performed at the Esperanza Benefit Night in Wandsworth. The programme announced in thin gilt:

A Play in One Act
entitled
GEOFFREY
by Jack de la Mare

It was a success; but Jack refused to take pleasure in this. Writing afterwards to Elfie, he was all despairing world-weariness. The fact was that the strain of combining authorship, playing the lead, being stage manager, and being passionately in love, all on top of his City grind, had worn him out completely. In any case the chief purpose of *Geoffrey* for de la Mare had been accomplished long before it reached the stage, and the plaudits of his easily-pleased young neighbours could only show him how slight were its artistic merits. All the same the praise in the local press must have whetted his appetite. *The South London News* spoke of 'a capital performance', and he kept a clipping from some other journal which described *Geoffrey* as 'a homely little drama tinged with a gentle pathos which appeared to offer much delight to a friendly audience'. The drawer closed on the manuscript of the play, but it had helped clear a channel. He began to write more.

When Elfie, soon after *Geoffrey* was over, went off for a short holiday to lodgings in Southwold on the Suffolk coast, he decided to do the same. It was the first of many visits. Since Ventnor days of early childhood, he cannot often have seen the sea. Southwold was within reach of his purse for short visits; a picture-postcard of this period among his papers shows a charmingly sequestered little place, a wide village street, gape-mouthed to the sea below. At first, his visits there alternated, for propriety's sake, with Elfie's; but later, plans were contrived for Poppy or Bert, or Roger Ingpen, to chaperone them, so both could be there together. Such a prospect rocketed Jack's spirits into incoherent nonsense, with solicitous asides – 'You are not tired of me my mother-child are you?'. He promises that they would have 'grand ideas' at Southwold for 'that Phantom play'. His ambitions were still set on dramas, and at some time in the next few years he did write a ghost-play set in a house by the sea (*Mrs Urquhart*, unpublished). But he may merely have been thinking of a part for Elfie, since one of his names for her was 'Phantom'.

By the autumn of 1894 he was writing hard, piling up manuscripts which were shown in utmost privacy to Roger and to Elfie, and probably to nobody else. Elfie had his stories typed at her office, and her brother urged action. 'Roger has been inciting me to sell my pretty thoughts – they are pretty to you and me aren't they?' he wrote to her. 'Shall they go for a fine to get me out of prison? Shall I try?'[9]

Soon he did begin to try, at first getting Elfie to send the manuscripts to editors from her address; he was so morbidly intent on the utmost secrecy and anonymity that he could not bear that a rejection slip should arrive at his own home in his own name. Elfie sent them out under various *noms de plume*.

*

He set out to learn his trade by direct imitation, aiming at a definite contemporary market, and teaching himself every skill he could learn from those successful in it. Like the apprentice artists of earlier centuries, he simply examined his masters and discovered in practice how the trick was done. The influence upon him of writers of the Nineties was thus considerable, and it did not pass; for much that he copied from them he later modified, and made his own, with permanent effect on his style. He was very much a child of his time.

These characteristic Nineties writers put their faith in finding a truer reality in the imagination than could be discovered in the actual. Their generation felt, as Peter Green has written in his life of Kenneth Grahame, that there was 'no longer an incalculable dimension to life … There was no salvation in God, for God was on the side of big business and the Puritans. There was no hope from science, for science ate like an acid into the mystery of life. There was no future in political radicalism, because the one aim of the radicals was to destroy the foundations on which English tradition rested.'[10] Every word of this might have been written about the young de la Mare. 'Big business and the Puritans' were his twin detestations: he called them Mammon and Grundy, and as personified evils they were to figure in his poems and his letters. And as to science eating into the mystery of life, he felt this acutely, until late in his life when science took a new turn, and physicists and astronomers in particular began to open fresh vistas more mysterious than ever. But he was luckier than most of his fellows in two respects: in his strong dose of commonsense and caution, and in the rooted stability of his affections. Happy family love in childhood had given him a base of emotional security. With these advantages, he was less at risk than many of his fellow artists of the Nineties, whom Yeats called 'The Tragic Generation' – those who pursued the private exploration of sensation too far, and shipwrecked, ending in drink, drugs, public disgrace, or suicide.

The mere fact that the century was ending seemed to hypnotise the artistic world. The final decade, it was insisted, was different from all others, and this belief induced a certain feverishness. Yet the temper behind this ferment was not really one of hopeful energy: the mood was unbridled, experimental and yet melancholy. There was a languor, and a void. With all this in the air around him, just at his most impressionable age, and with a personal predicament that he could neither alter, nor escape, nor resign himself to, it was no wonder that this decade of his life confirmed for good and all the direction of his gifts – inward-turning, and aslant at that.

The mental energy corked down by his Oil drudgery might have turned inwards in any circumstances; his would always have been an introspective sensibility. But with such particular need of escape, even in his interior life, one sees him from now on avoid the direct issue, prefer oblique approach, side-step confrontation and self-committal. 'Knight's Move' was the label Henry Newbolt was to give to de la Mare's conversation later on; but he himself had already appropriated the idea. In his diary-notebook he jotted an entry about chess, on his mother's birthday, 12 March 1899: 'That one straight and one slanting is a lovely move in the game of life.'

A weaker nature would have turned away entirely from experience, into the compensation-world of fantasy. Certainly the need for relief played a large part: make-believe, he declared, was always to him 'one of the richest of human consolations',[11] and he saw no reason against indulging it. But the impulse was positive also, and he kept some balance beteeen both aspects. The free play of the imagination might, he asserted, be 'the outcome of a thirst for a reality distinct from the actual'. The dominant impulse in the end for him was the quest for another, richer self, and another, essential reality. But the way to these could not be direct and deliberate; symbol and association were one method, as were reverie, passive contemplation, the glance out of the corner of the eye, the use of faculties uncensored by the conscious intellect. This was all *play*; and play was to him an occupation that mattered – a valid, indeed crucial way of approaching truth for the artist, on no account to be jettisoned when childhood is over.

It was in fact largely through using the very same means to penetrate experience that a child uses – make-believe, day-dream, empathy, free association, chanting words as a spell, giving shape to fears and dreams by figures of grotesquerie – that de la Mare as an artist stamped his name on a whole sphere of the human spirit which had never had such articulate recognition before. Between what childhood grasps by intuition and what maturity recognises in its own experience, there is a gap (much of it lying in the unconscious) which his poems and stories bridge, as no other writer has done. They do reflect what he called 'a Real.'

But he was not one of those Nineties escapists, nostalgic for a Golden Age of childhood, who, like Kenneth Grahame, psychologically needed their own chains. Grahame, after working long years in the Bank of England, broke free in his middle years, just as de la Mare was to do; but at once Grahame's creative impulse faded out. De la Mare, on the other hand, the moment he got free, laid hold on the human condition more and more as time went on, finding that to be alive increased in interest and reward right up to his death. Indeed the function of *refuge* that fantasy had for him at the beginning of his career as a writer, played, if anything, a smaller part in his needs as time went on. He came to use imagination less and less as a lulling and fanciful substitute, more and more as a flexible precision instrument for investigating and interpreting reality.

It is noticeable that the poets of the Nineties formed him much less than did the prose writers. His poetry was a more private and more instinctive gift, and developed later and more slowly. While he was learning its skills, he would experiment with every verse-form he found in his reading, but not much among varied styles. But the ideals of the Nineties, the emphasis on fine writing, ornament, and above all its rich vocabulary, formed his taste in prose-effects to the end of his life. And at first the more exotic and exalted his model, the more he was attracted.

De Quincey, as we have seen, was an early favourite. So was Pater, for whom at first he felt 'infatuation ... much less ... on account of what he said ... than on account of his seductive, his very unusual way of saying it. He breathed an incantation, and from incantations one is apt to waken more coldly disillusioned than is quite fair to the enchanter.'[12] This disillusion had set in by about 1896–7, as a letter to Elfie shows. Pater had begun to pall – he was too thin-blooded.

Manner, however, remained de la Mare's conscious quarry at this age. He fully shared the preoccupation with elaborated form and subtlety common to the Aesthetes, the Symbolists and the Beardsley group alike. He dug up archaisms and whatever was odd, suggestive and little used. At first he also fell into the fashionable traps of languid preciosity and purple-patching. His later prose used vocabulary to less facile effect; yet the magpie habit of word-collecting continued, and in old age he was always pressing young writers to experiment with neologisms. Wilde used exotic catalogues of objects such as precious stones and their colours (in *The Picture of Dorian Gray*, for example) much as they occur in the traveller's tales of Hakluyt and Purchas. De la Mare too developed a lifelong fondness for such cumulative effects; he certainly went direct to the Elizabethan travellers for inspiration, but it is likely that he first acquired the taste as a young man from the writers then around him.

With his willingness to try anything once, he could hardly have escaped a touch of Pan, ubiquitous in the Nineties. The Romantics had used Pan with genuine symbolic truth, but in their descendants he came to be a general convenience for representing almost any anarchic impulse out of the Id — the life-force, sexual corruption, even the downright Satanic (as in Arthur Machen). At the other end of the spectrum comes the wistful, mystical sentimentality of Kenneth Grahame's 'Piper at the Gates of Dawn'. It was at once a cloying and a muddy cult. De la Mare employed Pan rather perfunctorily two or three times in poems between the late Nineties and 1906 (one of them, 'Tears', in *Poems 1906*, beautiful in the old Romantic tradition) and in one very bad story that he did not try to print. But bad as it is it illustrates the energy of his apprenticeship. Not only did he try out Pan in it but the chief character talks the most densely affected sham-Shakespeare prose, and there is also, for good measure, a peppering of enterprising Latinisms — 'circumferent' trees, and 'fluctuant' draperies.

It was also the age of paradox and prose epigram, and these, too, he tried his hand at, But the wit of epigram was not a tool he ever mastered — though he kept a hankering for the form and later published a good many attempts at it in verse, none very good. His gift of subtle and humane humour was really too tangential, too warm and loose-ended for the form.

Of all the fin-de-siecle story-writers, Arthur Machen was perhaps the closest to him, for it was Machen who discovered how to juxtapose the commonplace of modern life with what stirred, romantic and sinister, just below the crust. Machen derived much from Poe, and so

did de la Mare – in his youth luxuriating in the unlikely trappings of
Poe's world, and in his gothic stock-in-trade – skeleton spectre, wail
and shriek: gloom and black velvet hangings. But he outgrew all this,
as his insight deepened. In maturity what he had to say was that
strangeness, the ominous, and the supernatural all may lie in wait in
the most ordinary circumstances; and that 'the least explored' is the
familiar.[13] Horror and haunting remained, but they were to be met in
the busy underground train or in the broad sunlight of an August
cornfield: his message is that they belong to man's inescapable human
condition, his perpetual predicament, not just to agreeable indulgences
in the fantastic from which he is free to retreat to the safety of 'real
life'. In the expression of this conviction in prose, he would learn most,
a few years later, from Henry James. De la Mare indeed was to become
the one considerable prose-writer of the Nineties to continue, right
through the first half of the twentieth century, that decade's particular
spirit of consciously-wrought beauty, curiosity and strangeness, with
at times a shade of morbidity, like the odd flavour of a ripe medlar.

His poetry was another matter, and its roots ran deeper, into an
older tradition. The art of the Nineties was, after all, only one erratic
splinter of the Romantic explosion, and its sole lasting effect on his
poetry was to make him, once and for all, a craftsman in verse who
weighed every nuance of every syllable in conscious choice. Wherever
he is simple, he has concealed his pains to be so. But at its centre, the
Romantic movement stirred more profound feelings in him than did
Lionel Johnson or any other of the Nineties poets from whom he
learned some of his skills. The early Romantics, Coleridge above all,
had deeper, sweeter, sadder things to say to him.

His introduction to Beardsley's work came partly through the
enthusiasm of a friend of Roger's. This was W.J. Horton, whom he
would quite often find spending the night with the Ingpens on visits to
town from his Surrey home. Portfolio open, Horton, a fresh-faced and
rather military-looking man in his early thirties, would be discussing
with Roger the strange symbolic drawings in which he had lately taken
to recording the waking visions which featured so largely in his life.
Soon Beardsley gave Horton encouragement that led to the publication
of some of these in *The Savoy* in 1896. But most of the prolific output of
Horton's working life (twenty-five years of it) was only shown privately
to intimates like Roger Ingpen and W.B. Yeats, both of whom
published selections of it after his premature death – brought on by
malnutrition in his disastrous attempts to find the right frugal diet to
promote spiritual and creative powers.

De la Mare does not seem to have become one of Horton's intimates, but it seems likely he took a close interest in Horton's portfolio, for his novel *The Master*, at which he worked during 1895 – much his most ambitious work so far – is full of descriptions of just such works of art as Horton was attempting in his colour studies. De la Mare and Horton loved to talk, speculating together about possible undeveloped human faculties (a subject which had an irresistible fascination for Horton). Roger Ingpen mentions such discussions arising between them of books of the day – Wells's *The Time Machine* and *The Island of Dr Moreau* and Cesare Lombroso's *The Man of Genius* (1889), a study which argues a close connection between genius and insanity. Lombroso may well have supplied the idea for a story de la Mare wrote a year or so later (one of his first successful attempts) by recording the case of a woman who saw everything in her dreams as tiny. The hero of de la Mare's tale ('A Mote') is a man who has a continuous vision, whenever he shuts or rolls up his eyes, of his own figure in miniature, progressing through fantastic scenes towards a fatal end. The whole question of size in mental visualistion intrigued de la Mare throughout his life; one of his favourite inquisitions of visitors concerned the scale on which they saw things in the mind's eye – was it life-size or minute?

Horton had already got up a magazine he mostly wrote himself, for his Surrey friends and neighbours. Now he and Roger Ingpen and de la Mare, with a few friends of their circle, conceived the notion of another, *The Basilisk*, a collection of drawings, stories and light verse, which apparently never got beyond its first issue, in January 1895. Perhaps it entailed more time and labour than de la Mare could spare. The issue is printed in purple ink, off a manuscript mostly in his handwriting; it looks as if he did all the duplicating himself, perhaps in the Oil office out of hours.

The Basilisk could only belong to the era of Wilde and Beardsley, even though its contributors (apart from Horton himself) were mostly from that very stratum of modest suburban gentility most outraged by the morals of those two. Between its tall, narrow, grey sugar-paper covers all was artifice, fancy and elegant ornament. There are twenty contributions, including drawings by Horton in the Beardsley manner. Indeed Beardsley's influence pervades the letter-press too; but perhaps it had so coloured the outlook of the day that these young contributors would scarcely have recognised the source of it in their own prose. At any rate the contribution on Beardsley, signed 'Lucian Junior', is in fact an attack.

There is also an 'Epistle to O.W.', signed with a crabbed and half-diguised 'J.W.d 1 M.', and very difficult to follow, so mixed are the strong feelings struggling incoherently in it. It opens: 'Most insincere

of wise fools! So you have gathered together another Masterpiece.'
Wilde was at his zenith this January (*An Ideal Husband* opened at the
Haymarket at the beginning of the month, and *The Importance of
Being Earnest* was produced at the St James's in February, just before
the Marquess of Queensberry left his defamatory card); so it seems odd
that the Epistle should speak already so damningly. In fact rumours
about Wilde had been circulating well before the scandal broke, and
there had been hints at strange sins. And indeed de la Mare in his
'Epistle' takes a stronger moral line in January than he would have
been likely to do a few months later, after Wilde's fall. For whatever he
thought of Wilde's homosexuality, 'Mrs Grundy' – hypocritical,
revengeful, and detestably self-righteous – was a spirit he loathed far
more.

'The love that dares not speak its name' never engaged his interest
or sympathy; whereas the psychology and aberrations of murderers
fascinated him all his life, in spite of his hatred of physical cruelty. No
bestial detail about a Burke or Hare found him too squeamish to
ponder the springs of such action. But to sexual psychology and its
complexities, whether homosexual or heterosexual, he turned a
baffling blank of non-interest. Not merely did he dislike the whole
subject (though disgust is certainly present in his Epistle to Wilde), but
he seems also to have found it meaningless and dull. Fantasies of sex
seem to have been the one province of the imagination he found not
worth the slightest investigation. Of course this raises a large
psychological question mark and obviously there was a block.

He also contributed a story to the *Basilisk*. It was called 'Kismet',
and when published later (it was the very first of his tales to get into
print) it was subt-titled 'A Novel in a Nutshell'. It hinges on the kind of
tragic coincidence that Hardy loved; indeed, de la Mare may have
derived the idea from the one in *A Pair of Blue Eyes*, the
railway-platform scene in which Elfride Swancourt's two former
lovers discover they have been travelling together to her funeral, each
to make reparation, and that the same train has been carrying her
coffin. In de la Mare's story a seaman coming home on leave by night
begs a lift from a passing carrier and discovers that he is riding with a
coffin. When he reaches home he climbs a tree to look in at his wife's
lighted window before making himself known – only to see the same
coffin carried to her bedside where she lies stretched and still. At this
shock, he falls and cracks his skull. In effect the story is a good deal
less Hardy-like than this summary might suggest, for it is a Hardy
recipe but used with Grimm's ingredients. There is a complete absence
of human characterisation: the sailor is the merest peg for his fate, like

the hero of a folk tale, and de la Mare still kept, at this stage, a child-like matter-of-factness in handling the properties of violence and horror, a zest for the neatly dramatic, not-too-probable disaster.

'Kismet' is more successful than the fantastic stories he was groping with around this period, but it aims lower, straight at the short-story reader of the day who bought such papers as the *Pall Mall Gazette*, which he was examining with an eye to contribution. More of his real artistic identity began to emerge, even if his footing was for a while uncertain, as soon as he turned off into fantasy. But it was the growth of his poetry in him that was at last to teach him his proper vein in fiction, and at this stage (around 1895) there is little evidence of his writing verse at all, though a poorish love poem had been written to Elfie in 1894. It was on short-story writing that he set all his present hopes of getting published and known.

During 1895 he sent 'The Hangman Luck', another story of the 'Kismet' kind, to W.E. Henley's *New Review*. Henley, the catholic patron of talents as diverse as Yeats, Kenneth Grahame and Kipling, turned it down, and there are two other rejection slips from the same journal. It is a pity de la Mare had nothing to show Henley more characteristic of a new secret persona, 'Walter Ramal', an anagram under whose cover he would begin to write in the next year or two. Any young talent taken up by Henley was fortunate; for one thing, he was very hospitable to anyone he discovered and introduced them to each other. His favour could have shortened by several years de la Mare's social isolation from minds of his own calibre.

In the spring of 1895 the writing that was absorbing all his leisure (we hear no more of him in the Esperanza Club after *Geoffrey*) becomes the major theme of his letters to Elfie, gradually displacing the outpourings of emotion. But meanwhile the rejection slips accumulated. The Decadent *Yellow Book* liked his work as little as the Counter-Decadent *New Review*. A promised holiday with Elfie fell through for want of a chaperone, and he was in despair: 'I am dying in this place of Oil ... How greatly I loathe this hurrying, sordid place.' By the time he got to Southwold for a holiday at last, in March 1895, he was reduced to a wretchedly unstrung, exhausted state. But then he took a walk before breakfast to the old church in the woods and instantly the case was altered: 'You can hardly imagine the pure keen-warm sweet-salt soft fragrant air ... I begin to fancy that, when the senses are alert and strange scenes are presenting themselves, the brain merely acts as a receptacle storing those sensations, ready in due season for use. God grant it.'[14] It is odd to recollect that, in the deadly monotony of his life, he depended on those very occasional, very brief

Southwold outings and on even less frequent visits to country cousins
in the south west, for almost his entire stock of remote horizons,
solitary countrysides, deep woods and lichened, crumbling country
churchyards that throng his poems and stories.

There were occasional journeys elsewhere: once, in the late Nineties,
he and Roger and Elfie got to Lyme Regis, where landslips are
frequent, so that the cottages lean as crookedly as in any fairy story.
He lay on the grassy headland reading Alice Meynell's anthology
Flower of the Mind – by the light of some glow-worms he had gathered.
And once, climbing the dark steep streets, he and Roger looked over a
wall and saw a horny old Gardener still awake, hunting snails by
lantern-light – origin perhaps, of 'Old Shellover'. But Southwold was
his chief provider of Nature. He liked his landlady there, and his little
room full of her peculiar ornaments, alive with colours so ugly he felt
they might justifiably be called wicked. She was very kind to her
delicate-looking lodger, and never in his way; she only charged him
18s 3d for a whole week's board, including a Sunday treat of chicken
and beer for Bert, who came to join him for a little. But when he came
back from one such holiday at the beginning of April 1895, to report at
the Oil office, he was not strong; 'flu had led to bronchial catarrh, and
since the previous autumn there had been some suspicion of heart
trouble – one valve was thought to be weak. Some idea was mooted of
getting him 'a job in the south', or at any rate more in the fresh air.
Nothing came of it; and he refused a further month's sick leave, offered
by the Secretary of Anglo-American.

Then, that same month, a letter arrived with a returned manuscript
from James Payn of the *Cornhill Magazine*. Perhaps intended just as a
polite bromide, at least it offered something more encouraging than
blank dismissal. Roger, evidently, had sent in the manuscript. Payn
wrote: 'Your friend's contribution – if it is really a first attempt – is
very creditable to him. It has considerable dramatic force, but it is
merely a fragment, nor is any reason given for the brutality of the
principal character.'[15] This criticism would fit several abandoned
manuscripts of this period; but if it is really a 'fragment' it might be a
chapter from the first try at a novel, *The Master*. De la Mare's attempts
at 'life blood and bone' – at what he said Kipling had and Pater lacked –
at the moment resulted mainly in portraits of motiveless villainy, like
the random evils of a bad dream: stark and rather morbid
extravaganzas.

Listless, restless, jaded, by May de la Mare dreaded a breakdown. 'Is
a time coming,' he wrote to Elfie, 'when I shall have money and be free
– that is all – only to be away from all that I despise. To shut the paltry

London ghost of me in an Underground Railway Carriage – to go into the green places and be a sheep of God and wisdom. Pooh! When it comes I shall have imprisoned the wrong ghost and go complaining of Hay Fever, dust, nettles and new laid eggs.'[16]

And then at the end of that May 1895, a letter came from the *Sketch*, with a three-guinea cheque – accepting 'Kismet'! De la Mare remembered all his life flying up the narrow staircase, to announce the beginning of his career.

'Walter Ramal'

The small success spurred him on with his very hard and serious efforts over *The Master*, which he finished and then rewrote a few months later, in the autumn of 1895. Uneven and chaotic as it is, it shows him for the first time feeling his way into his true range, and sometimes transcending the melodrama, the stagey trappings, violent deaths, grotesques, and coincidences. But only by flashes, for there is abundance of these things as well. It is full of energetic experiment, hit-or-miss invention, always fertile and quite often absurd, but sometimes striking out a scene of real imagination and suggesting a deeper plane of reference. De la Mare was lucky to have the gift of improvisation, to counterbalance the fastidious conscious craftsman in his nature, which, without this, might well have closed him down calamitously. His first drafts (he said) nearly always came easily: he could develop a written story as instinctively as he would make one up to tell aloud, as he went along. This allowed him a wonderfully unselfconscious freedom of invention in the first untramelled narrative. Till that was all written out, he seemed able to suspend the critical sense, which came into play directly he began revising. Then there set in a merciless, meticulous polishing and discarding. He was never to drop the practice of this improvising faculty. He also believed, from his own experience, that a process of inventive fantasy much like sleep-dreaming goes on all day long, if the mind will but attend to it.

The material he chose for *The Master* could hardly be more Ninetyish. The narrator is a young decadent eccentric, living in picturesque disarray in a wharfside warehouse, while squandering an inheritance. He sits naked over his charcoal stove, studying works of magic and metaphysics, or he plunges out for adventure into a London of vice-haunted strangeness and gloom, a city of sailormen, vagabonds, aesthetes and ascetics, where absinthe is so much in evidence one might suppose it to be Rimbaud's Paris – did not the complete absence of sexual vice indicate a de la Mare district. The Master himself is a

mysterious amoral being, possessed of secret powers, a kind of Nineties
Prospero with a grotesque servant, called Fat Baal, for Caliban. The
studies into which the Master initiates the hero centre round that
preoccupation of the Symbolists, the correspondence of the senses. He
'plays' a picture he has made of the Moonlight Sonata, 'reading' the
white globe in the picture as if it were a score. He calls Beethoven's
music 'pomegranates and apple-blossom' and hands to Robin, the hero,
a selection of scents in little bottles. Some were 'so pungent as almost to
deaden the senses, some apparently had no scent, and some brought one
charming daydreams or fits of horror or pretty visions. There is an
emerald scent, and there a tremulous, and there a sodden.' He shows
Robin carved objects he has made: 'An idiosyncrasy often repeated in
these … as also in some of the pictures, was the prodigious *size* which
many even of the tiniest suggested.'

The Master escorts Robin to his barge on the Thames. Its anteroom is
decorated entirely in black – a device adapted from Poe's *Masque of the
Red Death*. Beyond this lies the picture gallery – the *pièce de résistance*
of the story – whose curious contents are described in detail. The
Master's abstract painting of Nothing, for instance, is a square of plain
vivid blue which, when closely studied, reveals a multitude of eyes.
Yeats's description of Horton's drawings so exactly fits this that de la
Mare's whole story must have its origins in his friendship with Horton.

It is plain that *The Master* engaged him in much more serious and
sustained effort than anything else he had yet done. 'I mean to be an
artist it is my Gospel and Creed,' he wrote to Elfie at about this time,
'and the first Article of the Religion is "Satisfy Thyself" and the second
"Be Thyself" and the third "Failure is Success".'[1]

*

The Master was still occupying him when, in September 1895, there
was house-moving in Wandsworth. The joint household broke up, Flo
and her husband departed for Penge; Jack, Bert and Poppy moved with
their mother just round the corner from Estcourt Road to 15 Gayville
Road, a villa of seven tiny rooms with a pocket-handkerchief of a garden.
There cannot have been much privacy for de la Mare's writing, but here
he toiled through the next four years to satisfy himself – and, more
important, to become himself – once at least with perfect success. For it
was here that 'The Riddle', one of his best and most famous stories, was
written. So were also several of the *Songs of Childhood*.

But at the time of the move, the rejection slips were still arriving at

Elfie's door, for her to carry round reluctantly to the young man whose summer energy was petering out again. He realised, in October 1895, when he had done all he could with *The Master*, that his aim had once more eluded his grasp: 'Well Rosebud here is most of it! My pride is at zero, my humility sits perspiring and stretching its legs in my brains. Do not hurry over it. Disappointment does not spoil for being postponed.'[2] Not even the appearance in print that November of 'The Hangman Luck', accepted by the *Pall Mall Gazette*, raised his spirits. Three days after it was published, he was telling Elfie that 'the imp Suicide' was always with him. He was pining for the sea and the summer – the only liberation the year could be relied on to bring again. Yet his restless, active mind was not really overborne by his life's monotony. In the same letter he exclaimed: 'I am a different being each day, each day my opinions have changed … How excellent a climax is Death when life is pelting through the body. Do you really think men desire eternal life. Is not the very essence of happiness the knowledge that it must soon come to an end.'[3] The notion of death as a fit climax to extreme aliveness, the proper *culmination*, rather than a negator, would occur again in letters he was to write to another woman, almost in the same words, when the emotional tide again ran high.

In another letter to Elfie, in December 1895, he wrote sardonically, and cryptically: 'Arm in Arm! I carry Hymen safely in my pocket. It is a frosty soul and I will introduce him to no one. The gaoler of Cupid.'[4] Whatever this snappishness refers to – perhaps he and Elfie had exchanged rings by now? – it is plain that he regarded marriage less as fulfilment in love than as an institution of Mrs Grundy's. He always had reservations on the subject; once in old age he said: 'I approve of marriage – I think that's the way to put it – but that's no reason why one should disapprove of unmarriage. It seems to me more a question of convention than of ethics or morals.'[5]

What Elfie thought about this, we do not know. But her encouragement and faith in his writing steadily continued, and if he dismissed some of her praise as 'delightful prejudice', it still helped him. Just because she and Roger believed in him so, he could begin to be more shrewdly self-critical. While struggling with *The Master*, he had seen how full it was of 'contrarieties to overcome'. He wrote to Elfie: 'The lesson I have to teach myself is the woodenness of fantastic imaginary folk. Style makes a beautiful book; Blood makes a great book.' In that 'woodenness', he had put his finger on a real weakness he would in time overcome, becoming in maturity a master of 'fantastic, imaginary folk'.

The adolescent thrashing about, only a year earlier than this letter, was turning into an artist with an objective view of himself. By its similar tone, another letter, not dated, belongs here:

> The young man is not dead but sleepeth. I am very tired little woman.
> Smoke and voices and inkpots! If there were some other way than by
> literary work to gain freedom! I love it so well it seems traitorous to
> myself to use it.
>   But freedom must come before peace of mind. Do not think I am not
> full of life …
>   The present is always the best, if we treat it royally.[6]

*

By the end of March 1896 there were two new stories for Elfie to send
out for him, 'and do not let me know whither'. (He preferred to cut out
altogether the agitations of hope before the rejection slips arrived.
These, however, he grimly preserved; he had enough eventually, he
said, to paper a boudoir.)

One of the new tales was a lurid little flesh-creeper called 'A.B.O.' –
capitals standing for 'Abortion' on the lid of a box in which a horrible
creature, a 'missing link' with fawn fur, has been preserved in
suspended animation. It escapes, and its fiendish spirit takes
possession of the unwise Professor who has dug it up. This was de la
Mare's crude first sketch on the theme of possession, which
reappeared, utterly transformed by maturity, in the novel *The Return*,
twelve years later. Elfie tried two magazines with 'A.B.O.' and with
another, 'The Fool's Hostelry', (another in that vein of stark brutality
which was yet wide of all realism, and in which de la Mare was so oddly
persistent through all these apprentice years.)

At last Roger's efforts for him succeeded. The *Cornhill* – a literary
magazine of Roger's publisher employers, Smith, Elder & Co. – acquired
a new editor, St Loe Strachey, and Roger was detailed to help him.
Strachey had a generous and alert eye for new talent. By his own
account he had already accepted more than the *Cornhill* had room for,
when Roger pressed on him, one day, a package by a friend, 'Walter
Ramal', asking him to read it as a personal favour. Reluctantly Strachey
took it home – and was instantly struck by it. Feeling sure that 'a new
planet had swum into [his] ken', he published 'A Mote'. To it, he added a
boldly worded editorial note, for he loved a flourish: 'Those who hold the
doctrine of transmigration will hardly fail, after they have read this
story, to think that the spirit of Edgar Allan Poe is once more abroad.'[7]

What has happened to the hero of 'A Mote', giving him eerie
visionary powers, is nothing magical: he has simply, by accident,
acquired the trick of turning his sight *inward*, rolling up his eyes till
they focus on what happens inside his skull. There he observes a

horrifying world where every thought he has ever harboured, the good and the evil, take appropriate shape, swarming in their thousands round a black mote of a man stalking through their menacing hordes – for the evil outnumber the good – on and on towards a climax which the hero (Uncle of the narrator) attends with mounting horror, for he has recognised that the mote is himself. Throwing away the complications of *The Master*, de la Mare had for the first time hit upon a single coherent theme capable of suggesting other levels of meaning without confusion. *Pilgrim's Progress* (which he placed with *Gulliver* among the 'mines of imagination') perhaps suggested the central idea – his mote, set in a world of expiation and retribution, toils towards judgment through a queer kaleidoscope of changing scenes which lie somewhere near that 'field full of dark mountains' in which the travellers 'stumbled and fell and rose no more'. But this is no Bunyan pilgrimage, morally and spiritually serious – the mood of 'A Mote' is light, and deals in fancy only.

Strachey at the *Cornhill* duly wanted to meet its author, who duly went, but would not allow himself in his report to Elfie to show the encouragement he must have felt. It was always his way, at this stage, to hide from both hope and praise in a moody pose of self-mockery:

> The Interview is ended and I am back in my Tank. Maybe I feel as if I had done myself little service. He was exceedingly pleasant to me, gave me not a little worldly advice and excellent. Also he gave me his hint for a story. Yet dear woman I would prefer to leave it all behind and come back to you.[8]

He felt rather more cheerful the next week, when a cheque arrived for twenty pounds – handsome pay – for 'A Mote' and another story that Strachey had also accepted, 'The Village of Old Age' (a mannered piece, languid to suffocation).

Next April, Strachey would take yet another story, 'The Moon's Miracle'. Strachey thought this the best of the lot, but its central idea – an aerial battle between the 'Moonsmen' and the 'Nightsmen', watched from Wimbledon by a few humans – is less original than the idea in 'A Mote', and has no real development. It is a spirited and highflown exercise in fantastic description, a *tour de force* of the purple patch. It appeared in good company: some other contributors to that number of the *Cornhill* were Leslie Stephen, Walter Besant, Eden Philpotts and Stephen Gwynne.

De la Mare's letters to Elfie all through 1896 are generally briefer, more mannered, more facetious and more cryptic than of old – some of them literally devised as cryptograms – and there is one sad one from her, complaining that she is growing weary and that they do not seem to be able to talk as closely as they had two years before. He would speak of their future together, and of marriage, but evidently with no immediate move in view, and always with a shrug of reluctance about that institution itself.

After staying the night with Roger and her in September 1896 he wrote to thank them for cheering him up – 'and now to the self forever chattering, arguing, analysing, defying, ridiculing, peering, intending, spoiling and ripening, I go back'. A self that was ripening poems now as well as stories. A sonnet follows a few days later, called 'Eve of Sept. 20th' (Elfie's birthday). It is not remarkable as a poem, but throws a thoughtful look at their relationship. He sees its first cause clearly:

> A child who seeks a mother's tenderness
> Was I, thou didst console my misery

And in the concluding lines he accepts that in darkness they will keep side by side, 'with groping hand / Seeking the present safety'. In two years, he had outgrown illusions, and had now some quiet insight into the source of his love.

For his part, he could no longer promise her any very passionate union of spirit. He was only twenty-three, but no longer a boy wildly in love, rather a man measuring himself quietly against the stress of experience, and against the fears of the woman who was, by now, so very dependent on the love and loyalty that the birthday poem promises. Birthdays were becoming sobering milestones for Elfie, at thirty-four; while he (with the odd bent for anticipating that made him, in his middle prime, harp upon approaching old age) seems here in his early twenties to look at his love in middle-aged mood. It is curious how tentative, solemn, even pedestrian his early poems were, those for children aside. All the lyrical ardour, the enchantments of marvel and pining, were to blaze up much later, after actual youth had faded; they would reach their most romantic height when he himself was close on forty.

Meanwhile he chafed to find passion sinking to affectionate habit. The notion of 'dwindling into a husband' filled him with dismay; he wrote to Elfie in October 1896:

We have grown too conventional, you and I ... Someday we shall arrive at politeness. We live too much in the lumber room. We have been introduced to one another. We have inscribed Sanity upon our hearts, have purchased the Domestic Virtues ... All of which things strangle sincerity and send us a begging. It is the squeak of impotence for the knot is clear, who's to cut it?'[9]

But however he might chafe at convention in a letter, his way was not to defy it. The only escape feasible for his temperament was to conform and bear it, leading his real life in secret. Next month he wrote to her: 'My plans are dreams, I live in a world of dreams and shadows real and live enough to me but to others idle silly selfish – we are observed, let us dissemble.'[10] Free-thinking he might be, but how totally un-bohemian he was, now and always. He never achieved, nor attempted, anything whatever through rebellion.

His own birthday next spring, 1897, brought lament, but no wavering: 'Twenty four twenty four tis the gloomy note of a passing bell'[11] but 'I stand whining behind the sun-litten door; someday it will be opened.'[12] In fact 'The Moon's Miracle' was the only story to reach print this year, but he worked on; and now he was beginning to make serious attempts as a poet too – an occupation he kept very private indeed, but there is a rejection slip from the *Pall Mall Gazette* in August 1897 marked 'verse' by him on the back. He went on with his imitations; by now Chaucer had become an enthusiasm, and he said he learned the Prologue to the *Canterbury Tales* by heart on his walks across Clapham Common to catch the City train. Once inside the compartment, it was natural to go on observing his fellow travellers with the same eye, and so he tried his hand at a Chaucerian pastiche – nimble and pleasant enough, but no more – called 'A Suburban Pilgrimage'.

For once, it was events themselves – though nothing more momentous than a duty visit to a country aunt – which slipped really useful material into his hand. When Max Beerbohm came, in 1925, to devise one of his best caricatures, he pictured de la Mare on a hassock, in mute, rapt speculation at the feet of a forbidding elderly lady, sternly absorbed in her knitting, canary cage beside her, in a room with a rectory air. He called it 'Mr Walter de la Mare gaining inspiration for an eerie and lovely story'. One source of such inspiration was surely de la Mare's own Aunt Augusta Michell, his mother's formidable elder sister, married to the mild rector of Dinder, near Wells, of which he was a Prebendary. De la Mare spent some of his office holiday there at midsummer 1897; and his letters, quizzically relishing the rectory blend of tedium and peace, idly begin to spin something much nearer a true de la Mare story than all his deliberate attempts at fine writing had yet achieved.

June 13 Saturday Night 10 o c
Aunts polished footfall is moving nearby. Downstairs a heavy clock ticks insensible minutes forever to a half dozen wigged people of paint ... It is monstrous hot and I must look forward all the morning to a pilgrimage to Wells where the Bishop is going to preach remarkably well.

June 16

... Aunt is an amazing woman ... She reminds me everywhere of Mother
and myself. She is like one of those labyrinthine shell fish without the
fish. She is a dozen notes of interrogation and a full stop ...

Some people are by instinct bird-watchers from childhood, always on
the alert for the turn of a wing. De la Mare was born an
old-lady-watcher. As late as 1955, the year before he died, Aunt
Augusta brushes inconsequently through one of his letters apropos of
nothing in particular:

> There is also an Aunt who gets nearer and nearer – a rather formidable
> lady who once entertained me tête à tête before brilliantly illuminated
> French windows while she gave me details concerning the deathbeds of
> her children. She also, well, insulted two old ladies whom she was
> showing her garden to in a village near Wells. They had lunched with
> her, and their revered husbands were engaged for a while with my
> Archdeacon uncle. In a slightly flattering drawling voice and a graceful
> wave of her hand, she pointed to a little stone bridge over a stream that
> ran through the garden, and remarked 'That little bridge there with the
> willow (or was it ash) is my favourite part of the garden.' And then, after
> a momentary survey of the two old spectacled faces she added 'But I don't
> suppose you can see it and would not care for it if you could, so let's go in.'
> Well, I hadnt a knife handy, or a shotgun, and one mustn't assassinate
> one's maternal aunt in her own garden.[13]

One can trace an echo more than once among his stories of Aunt
Augusta's 'polished footfall', her enigmatic monologue, and the
asperities of her contempt.

From September 1897 there survives, for once, one of Elfie's letters
to de la Mare, written from a holiday alone in Southampton. Its tone
gives a comical jolt of reality to the picture of the couple, when read
beside the one that he was addressing, the very same day, to her. *He*
wrote:

> A young man awoke this morning so heavy and vacant as if his spirits
> had been wandering in the night with lamentation and tears. So might a
> widow feel who turns on her pillow from dreaming of her husband; such
> must be the sentiments of a mother-cat suspicious of a pail and hazy in
> her mathematics ... I will creep into my Johnson and learn 'Sorrow' by
> heart ... All the world is sad because of you and London is yellowly pallid.
> Turn again Queen of Sheba! Pray how many lives has a man got.[14]

She wrote:

> Second Post in and no letter, I feel very much inclined to turn you round,
> but find you would be then looking into the glass and know you would
> feel a sense of satisfaction at the contemplation well perhaps you will be

sorry for I am going for a 16 mile ride this afternoon, and there is no knowing ...
Do write Duckie.[15]

Something eased his heart a little in the winter of 1897; perhaps it was the new secret activity of verse. He had a new scheme – 'a household magazine, remotely after the model of Lewis Carroll's *Rectory Umbrella*'. That is how he describes *The Horn Book*, which ran to five issues, all handsomely bound in little strong shiny leather notebooks, about five by six inches; some olive green, some olive brown, with gilt-edged pages and gilt-lettered title. Small, packed, enticing, they have a more genuinely de la Mare appearance than the modish *Basilisk*, and provided a better platform for his gifts. Here, he had a free hand to arrange all as he pleased, and to write most of the contents himself. Best of all, he had the perfect audience, just enough of a 'public' to provide a stimulus, but without a breath of criticism to chill the most sensitive skin. This was the Rowley family, his nephews and nieces, the children most available to him. A significant situation – childhood always was the key to his poetry, and, in writing for his young Rowleys, he found, by adjusting as he went along to the reception he met, the right pitch for his child-poetry. Aimed so directly at this audience, the poems came directly too. For once, he began with simplicity, and out of his head; not with tortuous industry from approved literary models. Pages of nonsense rhymes and limericks in the *Horn Books*, merge imperceptibly into nonsense poetry, and these into poetry proper. Any little fragment could go in pell-mell, like shells into a homemade grotto:

> The moon most pallid and rare
> A mariner's beacon seems
> And the silent ships of the air
> Sail on to the land of dreams.

There is a patriotic jingle, 'Victoria is My Queen', and a ploughman 'lean and lank stalks on', foreshadowing the personages of *Songs of Childhood*. And, slipped in quietly, comes a little serious verse: a sonnet, 'The Blind Man' (not published in his lifetime), and one poem in curious long experimental lines, almost slackening into biblical prose, dedicated to his mother:

> When the birds sing in the fresh branches, when the Almond Tree
>   is glorious ...
> Thou art with me Mother.

Over the next three or four years the almond tree constantly

haunted his verse and prose as symbol for purity, innocence, promise.
He used it like a private talisman. A bare mention of that tree in
passing gives one story, 'The Almond Tree', its title, symbolising the
tale's final twist, by which all is summed up, to end on a note pregnant
with hope of life out of death. But more of that later.

*

In the next two years, 1898 and 1899, he published nothing; but during
that time he made the essential adjustment of his powers to his range.
He began to 'be himself' and to brave out the fact that the work to
which his deeper instincts led him had no ready-made public at all.
Two of the best poetic stories he would ever write were written then
'The Almond Tree' itself, and 'The Riddle'.

The release into writing poems had much to do with this maturing.
It was in poetic feeling and in truth to life that his earlier stories had
failed, and these two qualities developed together. Poetry was, for him,
the road *into* reality, not aside from it; and the discipline of verse
brought him, for the first time, a much-needed mastery of verbal
economy. A gap in the dated rejection slips suggests he may not even
have sent out much work, quite deliberately keeping to privacy till he
could achieve what he was after.

His self-education in *technique* redoubled in these two years. It was
now directed more to prosody, less to prose construction. Much of the
arcane vocabulary he harvested at this time remained permanently,
sometimes unfortunately, in his usage, such as all these neighbours to
be found in one of his lists: *minatory, minish, minikin*. He made what he
called 'a tabulated analysis in the form of a statistical breakdown of the
use of vowel sounds, consonants, parts of speech, etc … in the works of
Chaucer, Keats, Swinburne, Tennyson and others'.[16] One hardly knows
which to wonder at more: the dry application this bears witness to, or
the fact that it was of any real service to an artist with his fine-spun
impulses. Yet it was. When his ear and his metrical inventiveness were
praised by the critics of his prime, they little guessed what deliberate
drudgery had cultivated these. He seemed to need such a highly conscious and rationalised activity to release music which comes to the
reader as the very breath and modulation of impulse.

The notebooks of quotations he assembled in this pursuit are totally
unlike those of Coleridge or Matthew Arnold, or the allusions to
current reading made by Keats in letters. Scarcely an entry is put
down for the sake of its *content* – that is, for its imagination, felicity,
philosophy, or even just as another nugget of those odd facts he loved to

collect. Instead, they record with avid, energetic austerity, a total absorption in the technician's minutiae. The weather notes come nearest to meditation or the personal.

Once, it is true, a particularly pleasant eerie event did find a space in the diary, and in old age he added some details when telling the story (in the process, as usual, it altered a good deal). The basic event seems to have been that de la Mare and Ethel Rowley (in the middle of a night when his mother was the only other sleeper in the house) heard, independently, a mysterious and delectable singing coming from her room. It was 'slightly lamentable' and 'in a mode', de la Mare remembered (referring to musical technique presumably). His mother was fast asleep at the time, and he later came across a description (in a book about banshees and other such phenomena) of *spectral music* so exactly fitting what he had heard that he passed the book to Ethel without comment, and she spontaneously confirmed that this described just what she had heard herself, that night. 'It is a very delightful mystery,' the diary noted.

In June 1898 de la Mare entered in the diary a draft of a Lullaby: fragile, boyish, with a flavour of Hood, but groping towards the note of *Songs of Childhood*. Later he called it 'Slumbersong'. It would be the very first of his verses to get into print. Meanwhile it went into the third *Horn Book*. There was a fourth by Christmas 1898. These issues show no great advance in power – until suddenly one turns a page and finds 'The Riddle', a masterpiece in its own kind, just casually appearing, when he had written nothing half so good before.

With perfect confidence in what he is doing, the voice of the authentic spell-binder launches the story tranquilly *in medias res*: 'So these seven children, Ann, and Matilda, James, William and Henry, Harriet and Dorothea came to live with their Grandmother.' The voice continues without a word too much, or one false note, at the same pleasantly sure pace, till the enigmatic old lady looks into the chest in which the seven children have vanished one by one, each in turn irresistibly tempted to meddle with its forbidden lid. 'But in her mind was a tangled skein of memories – laughter and tears, and little children now old-fashioned, and the advent of friends, and long farewells. And gossiping fitfully, inarticulately, with herself, the old lady went down again to her window-seat.'

People constantly plagued de la Mare for the meaning of 'The Riddle' (as they did of 'The Listeners', the poem most like it in artistic purpose). Such inquiries he would almost always turn gently aside; his 'riddle' offers no puzzle detachable from the image of the story itself, still less an 'answer'. The story is more like one of those games children play to act out in alternative terms some fear or desire never named and not fully recognised. Once, when he was old, he went so far as to say he had 'a nebulous idea of the clue', and admitted, at any rate, that 'growing up' was the wrong solution. The story meant (so he said on this occasion) that 'the children disappeared', and *that* meant, in effect, the human soul as a child in this world. The old lady is Earth (or Life), who tries to keep them there. Her one edict is that they shall not play with the chest. But they seek it out in their different ways: one as a dreamer, two as lovers, and so on. In other words, it means the childhood soul passing through the knowledge of this world (the old house) and disappearing, none knows where. But Laurence Whistler to whom he gave this explanation, pointed out that the words of the notes he jotted down directly after their conversation are chiefly his own, not de la Mare's. He felt that his own record numbed and defined what de la Mare had left sensitive and vague. Anyway, de la Mare's explanation on this occasion conspicuously omits the most pregnant symbol of all: the chest itself, with its 'darkly smiling' carved heads at the corners, which is older than the old lady herself, older, she says, than *her* grandmother.

Edward Wagenknecht, who was writing an article on 'The Riddle' with reference to allegory in 1949,[17] received only enigmatic replies to his own direct inquiry. All that de la Mare would cede on that occasion was: yes, the children died. Even this, so stated does not quite tally with what he told Whistler. A comment he once made (after telling an anecdote of his own childhood) perhaps throws more light on what was to him the nub of the riddle. Looking back on that bygone day he remarked reflectively: 'I wonder where that little boy is now?' The child-soul – his, or anyone else's – was, to him, a different race of being from the creative maturity which developed from it. He felt that almost as great a gulf lay between the one state and the other as between death and the next life. It is, perhaps, the disappearance of the childhood soul, most precious element of earthly life, not simply physical extinction, that the story tells of.*

Perhaps the message of 'The Riddle' is, in fact, simply that our life poses an insoluble enigma: we are drawn, as if by some more than mortal homing instinct, toward the very death that, so far as Nature knows, annuls us. There was a Saxon king (cited by Bede) who thought the soul in human life resembled the sparrow which flew through one door of his lighted hall and out again into the trackless dark.[19] De la

---

* Forrest Reid, who must have discussed the point with de la Mare, gives yet another interpretation in his critical study of de la Mare's work: that the theme of 'The Riddle' is *'homesickness'* – that fundamental kind, he means, which de la Mare believed involved a child from the moment of birth.[18]

Mare's fable speaks to the imagination in the same terms.

One odd and unique fact about 'The Riddle' is that, when he came to put it in a published collection twenty-five years later, he found nothing to alter. Almost every other manuscript of his whole life was revised over and over, but 'The Riddle' he left just as he wrote it in the *Horn Book* in 1898. One must suppose it came to him complete, and almost involuntarily.

*

The next March (1899), instead of the tiny hand-made office-paper notebooks, he took to making almost daily entries in a large 'Scribbling Diary'. He struggled to catch the kind of visual detail, meticulously exact, that would stimulate his memory to supply the vital envelope of atmosphere and mood:

> Saturday 11th ... A little man with a large round head going bald down the forehead. A pigmy waxed moustache too small for the white upper lip, a round and rather long chin. Pale and hollow between nose and cheeks, and bright colourless, vain eyes. Those eyes he opens wide when he looks and smiles at a woman. A drawling voice and a sneer at the right ['left' crossed out] corner of the mouth. He exaggerates to impress his listeners with his own apathy; finds nothing to be admired, considers discontent a mark of worldly wisdom, is too cynical for self-respect and too dull-witted and purblind to be truly cynical. He could be pertinacious and merciless in revenge, brave at bay, perhaps generous on impulse. A Cornishman, a gentleman, and miserable.

Perhaps he passed this uneasy little man in Gayville Road, his home street; perhaps in a book, perhaps in a dream or a day-dream. A great deal of selection (perhaps unconscious) a continuous transforming process, was at work in all descriptions the diary contains. London, one notices, seems almost entirely dissolved away. He takes pains to be exact and sharp in his metaphors, but those he chooses are always, in kind, romantic. Watching snow, he remarks how the flakes 'tarry ... as if arrested like sheep in apprehension', how the east wind seems to hollow out one's throat down to the chest, 'forming of the mouth as it were a deep goblet of thin cold air'. But most pervasive of all was the curious knack he had by now fully developed, of expanding all his narrow surroundings. This, of course, is common enough in recollections kept from childhood. The first home, revisited in later years, seems bewilderingly shrunk, not only physically but also in its power to rouse the imagination. But de la Mare's knack was not quite this common one. He would take the hum-drum surroundings of his present, adult existence, investing all these with an enlarging and transforming potency. It is consequently disconcerting to visit any of the houses where he lived during the first half of his life, after reading any mention of them in his letters or diaries. He has invented nothing, but he has discovered, selected, bestowed on some detail the startling 'presence' it might have in a Pre-Raphaelite painting, surrounding it with spell-bound solitude, spaciousness and atmosphere, where to any other eye all is bald, banal and poky. He himself was not in the least 'intense' emotionally; but his *attention* had intensity, throughout life. Indeed this quality became more and more pronounced as he grew older. Visitors in his last years were often conscious that they themselves were seeing more while in his company, and for a time after they had left than they would ordinarily notice; commonplace surroundings became quietly remarkable, and their imagination kindled up, forming memories more vivid than usual.

*

By the end of the 1890s much more of his development is revealed in his notebooks and in the *Horn Books* than in the letters to Elfie – many of which, from 1898 on, are no more than a line apiece, making some assignation at Clapham Junction. For it was to the emotion of childhood he was turning now, rather than to the emotion of love, for the catalyst of his gift and his experience. Childhood's second wave was beginning to flow over his daily circumstances now that he found himself, as uncle to Flo's brood, already the companion of a younger generation. He was trying to recreate for them in verse what had been his own chief delights. Scattered through the *Horn Books* are five poems that were to find places in *Songs of Childhood*.

The final volume dated 25 May 1899, and fifth in line, was dedicated to the last of Flo's children, born in January that year. The Rowleys were growing up, and wrote most of this number themselves. Their uncle would not edit for them again, but so well had he brought them up that they continued making family magazines on their own. He himself, with very little poetry to put into this number, contributed family sketches:

P**** [Poppy]: ... How matronly and tersely and positively she talks ... and then she is that boisterous ... She walks a little like a sailor ...
R**** [Roger]: He is never at ease till you are very comfortable; and he is very deft in being thoughtful for you ... You cannot tell what a great deal he knows by just reading the index. And he does you kindnesses so as you cannot even see his shadow ...

There was also a self-portrait:

> J*** talks such a great deal that it is difficult to say if he is a good
> listener. And when he is silent, he will sometimes sit with a singular
> smile at the corners of his mouth – but perhaps he does not mean it. He
> will say pretty things to you, but I don't know why, nor I think does he.
> He also puts his head a [sic] one side when he says How do you do.* I
> fancy he is sometimes different from other people on purpose. He is
> frantic in argument, he will not let you go on any account; and when its
> not things it's words which have many meanings, but only one
> dictionary. Sometimes I think that he would rather be his wrong than
> your right. He has luxuriant hair, a silk cravat and a looking glass. He
> has many moods, he is as changeable as a gilt weathercock; and just
> follows the wind of his thoughts. When he reads in a book, it's like as if
> one could eat with one's eyes.

                                        *

In the summer of 1899, Elfie and he could not wait any longer for the
future to relent. Mrs Grundy had caught up with them, and Jack could
no longer indulge his divided, uncertain feelings about the contract for
life. Elfie was expecting his child.

To what extent they had been lovers – whether on some isolated
occasion the winter before, or whether physical love had been for some
while part of their bond, in despair at the endless postponement of
marriage – must remain pure speculation. If there was ever any
evidence in letters, they destroyed it. As parents, Jack and Elfie kept a
rigid silence on the subject, and kept it lifelong. They always turned
away any talk about their wedding day, lest it lead their children into
matching the date with the birthday that followed.

I would hazard a guess, from all I know of de la Mare, and from his
apparent lack of sexual drive, that some more or less accidental
occasion, probably not often repeated, perhaps never, had led to this
old Victorian situation. A woman closely committed to a man who
wavers and jibs on the question of marriage would naturally, and even
unconsciously, begin to risk more as the months crept despairingly on.
And whatever subconscious forces may have been at work, the
conception of a child would always have brought this particular man to
the sticking point. For to de la Mare there was no 'fact of life' so
all-committing as parenthood.

They were married quite privately in the parish church at Battersea,
on 4 August 1899. The only witness from either family was the relation
who kept house for the Ingpens. De la Mare rented a small villa (at

---

* A gesture he still had when walking forward to shake hands in old age.

that time called 6 Lynton Terrace) which was part of Mackenzie Road, in
the south London suburb of Beckenham. Flo and her family had just
moved there, a little further up, on the opposite side of the street. The
bridegroom's income, at the creeping yearly rise of Oil wages, was still
the merest pittance, and Elfie could no longer earn anything. It must
have been some comfort to have Flo so near, for, to crown all other
distress, there was at first a complete breach between de la Mare and his
beloved mother.

All this was kept out of his diary, which resumed in the autumn with
entries about the character and influence of various flowers, and with
points for an essay on dreams. Next to this comes a prophecy made
with startling confidence, in pencil, on 21 October: 'In a few hours my
little Florence will be born.' And he noted the reference of a quotation
from Isaiah, to bring himself comfort somehow, on this evening of
suspense: 'Shall I bring to the birth, and not cause to bring forth, saith
the Lord: shall I cause to bring forth and shut the womb? saith thy
God.' Underneath, in ink, he added the fulfilment of his prophecy:
'Florence was born at eighteen minutes past ten.'

Since she was a girl – just as he had known she would be – what else
could she be called? No other name could express his tender joy in her;
for her birth was undoubtedly the most momentous event of his life till
now. In his eyes, the bearing of a child was the ultimate poetic
mystery, the supreme bodily experience, which he put far higher than
the act of love. When he was old, he once questioned me – keenly,
closely, enviously – about my feelings when my first child was born,
saying: 'I suppose there's nothing in a man's life to touch that.'

Looking back on that October evening, later on, he wrote 'The
Birthnight: to F':* inventing, or invoking Tennysonian surroundings
most unlike Mackenzie road outside Elfie's bedroom window:

> Dearest, it was a night
> That in its darkness rocked Orion's stars;
> A sighing wind ran faintly white
> Along the willows, and the cedar boughs
> Laid their wide hands in stealthy peace across
> The starry silence of their antique moss:
> No sound save rushing air
> Cold, yet all sweet with Spring,
> And in thy mother's arms, couched weeping there,
>   Thou, lovely thing.

Next day, giving Roger the news, he was ready to set to work harder

---

* Published in *Poems: 1906*.

than ever. Roger was vetting some story for him. 'If you think there is anything in it I could manage perhaps a few more Count's adventures† in the next few weeks, and then might have a try at a book.' Roger's unceasing schemes on his behalf, and his undisapproving support over the marriage, meant a great deal to de la Mare during the break with his own family. (It seems as if Bert de la Mare, too, held aloof, at their mother's side.) Only Roger understood what the baby meant to Jack, and sympathised in all his efforts. He hoped they might (in collaboration) tackle some saleable book.

In November 1899 a kind of desperation seized de la Mare, forcing him to try publication in every direction, and to disregard the wince each rejection of a manuscript cost him – there were at least six in twelve days: the *Pall Mall*, the *Outlook*, the *Speaker*, the *Gentlewoman*, the *Illustrated London News*, the *Century* – wide as the field was, nobody cared for 'Walter Ramal', and all through November the manuscripts homed to Lynton Terrace. Only from the *Pall Mall* came a crumb of comfort:

> I am sorry but your story The Count's Courtship does not suit us. But I cannot return it without saying how excellent we think it in point of style. Had the tale been of a different flavour we should have taken it gladly.[20]

But when he tried again in December with 'The Almond Tree', the difference in flavour did not avail, nor the obvious stride forward in power, subtlety, and human interest. It was 'far too long for our use', and the rejection slips continued. By the next summer, this story alone had returned to him three times.

He was not surprised. He knew it was 'too long and too otherwise' for the conventional editor. But he also knew 'it's about as good as I can do at present – in atmosphere I mean'.[21] When Roger failed with it again soon after, he still refused to let go his modest faith in it, and replied:

> I'm not a bit dejected, old fellow, for I never supposed Smith would care for the story. He bent his eye on the unconventional, and – frowned. I dare say it was painful to him, I am thicker-skinner p'raps. For it's the flavour of the thing I swear by, atmosphere – what you will. If a story has that, and that the glamour of reality – what's else? But the superhuman

† He had created the character of a whimsical and eccentric old Count as a peg for several stories in the past few years, and had hopes that one day a collection might take shape around him. The Count came into 'The Moon's Miracle', and is (rather unconvincingly) the narrator of 'The Almond Tree', and also the hero of a story published much later, 'The Count's Courtship'. But he was one of those 'fantastic imaginary folk' who remained 'wooden', and by 1902 de la Mare had dropped him.

difficulty is to tell the truth – and shame the Public …
    O the graceless guineas! It's not so much *money* I want, but it's lack,
that's the devil. Is there no mad Publisher nowhere?
Every yr affect brother
Jacko[22]

'The Almond Tree' describes through the eyes of a small boy (now recounting these things in later life) his heart's first overwhelming crisis: the foundering of his parents' marriage, resolved in a suicide and a birth. That drama comes to its denouement on a wintry St Valentine's Day, and, in describing the heathland where it is set, the narrator only pauses for half a breath to say: 'I remember on this day to have seen the first fast-sealed buds upon the almond tree.' Nothing more is said on that matter at all. A casual reading might easily miss the tree altogether but for the story's title. Put baldly, the tree of course stands for life's bursting out of death, the secret beckoning of a priceless promise from the margins of a memory which is, in all its central aspects, disastrous. To a child brought up in the suburbs, like de la Mare, the sudden bursting of almond-blossoms from sooty stems, must have been one of the most vivid signs of spring. One thinks also of his habit as a choirboy (noticed by his neighbour in the St Paul's stalls) of underlining biblical passages that had taken root in his imagination: 'And the almond tree shall flourish, and the grasshopper shall be a burden, and desire shall fail: because man goeth to his long home, and the mourners go about the streets.' Ecclesiastes here pins to the almond tree just de la Mare's own talismanic value for it. All the evidence suggests that this biblical imagery was the catalyst for the story, setting the tone of its truth and supplying its 'glamour of reality'.

The Nineties were over, and with them his youth. He stood on the threshold of a new year and a new century, incalculably richer for the child on his arm, but poorer in purse and prospects than ever before.

Somewhere around this time he wrote a poem, not published, which gives a fair picture of the mood in which he embarked on the new chapter that his marriage opened before him. It ends:

Dare not to hope!
Earth hath for thee
And thy poor scope
What victory?
Dare to defeated be![23]

6

Pinker

The next half year – the beginning of 1900 – was a hard one. The baby, loved with equal, uniting, anxious intensity by both parents, can have been their only real refreshment. The break with de la Mare's mother, once healed, would leave no scar, and a strong bond of admiration and affection was later to grow up between her and Elfie, but for most of the first year of the marriage there was only silence.

No manuscripts de la Mare sent out were accepted, and Roger had no better success with a bundle of stories he had been trying to place for him since last October. Yet Roger persevered – and by midsummer hit on what led to rescue. He suggested asking the authors' agent J. B. Pinker, whom he knew personally, to take on de la Mare's work. It was a happy inspiration; soon he could report: 'I have been to Pinker and talked over your work with him … He doesn't take everyone's work, but he will be glad to "handle" yours.'[1]

Roger's tact and affection towards de la Mare were infinitely sensitive; in asking Pinker about his arrangements he had added: 'If you could spare [de la Mare] the humiliation of knowing that his work has been rejected by this or that editor it would be a kindness which I would appreciate.' And: 'If there is a question of any initial fee – please communicate with me.'

The list Roger sent Pinker of manuscripts available shows how hard it can be for a very individual voice to get a first hearing, for it included a number of promising and unusual stories: 'The Riddle', 'The Almond Tree' and an early version of 'An Ideal Craftsman'. The few poems offered are less good; but, perhaps from diffidence at showing verses for children, de la Mare did not include any of these, which were the best pieces so far. As it happened, the very week that Pinker was deliberating over that first sheaf of manuscripts, the *Pall Mall Gazette* independently accepted the verses de la Mare called 'Slumbersong' (though with a request that he improve one couplet).

Pinker accepted the manuscripts sent, reassured Roger that 'unless a client wishes it I never trouble him with details of negotiations except they be pleasant ones,' waived the initial fee ('I think it is nicer for me not to have one')[2] and hinted that it was time he dealt with his author direct. After this, even 'Walter Ramal' could not shelter any longer behind Roger. He wrote to Pinker himself, very diffidently, thanking him for 'his kindness in dealing with what I am afraid is a very obscure person'.[3]

Pinker was both kind and shrewd. His active steady backing, continuing for many many years, did much (particularly over the next two years, 1900–1902) to steer de la Mare through setbacks; and his advice extended well beyond mere matters of business. Above all he was wise enough to sense that this young writer's diffidence might well cripple him, and that warm encouragement would be crucial. He particularly encouraged de la Mare's poetry – which is the more to his credit, as it was bound to put in his own pocket smaller commissions than fiction would. He also took the trouble to send de la Mare's work out to other judges, and to pass on any praise they might bestow.

Summer days of 1900, the child (and with her the return of de la Mare's own tenderest vision of innocence) – encouragement Roger had brought through Pinker, and finally reconciliation with his mother – all this bore fruit in a new wave of child poetry. The very week that Pinker agreed to take him on, de la Mare wrote beguilingly to his mother, who had made some gesture towards him (though evidently not yet towards Elfie). Incidentally a glance at the photograph of the bald ribbon of unprivate back garden he is depicting, will point up what has been said above about de la Mare's 'expansion' when describing meagre environments to make his own 'Real':

July 21st Beckenham

My own dearest,

do not think me a wretch for not coming, but I thought perhaps you would not mind asking Elfie too; still if it would trouble you it does not matter.

Couldn't you come here for two or three days? I really think we could make you comfortable. You can sit in the garden in the quiet o' the evening – hollyhocks, snap-dragons, sweet peas, stocks, mignonette, cherry-pie (tell Bert)! There is a little shady room for a nap and your books, you shall have the paper and the *Church Times* and the *Christian Herald*, go to bed and get up when you like, feel 'eggy' or not as it happens – do just as you please. Baby is very good and just you dearest over again with her little changing face; you shall not be in the least troubled with her. Now come or no, just as you wish; but the view is broad and clear and the air like wine.

Because I don't see you or write – I do not love or think of you less, and

because you don't write to me I know you do not love or think of me less –
it is just our own way, isn't it? Sometimes I fancy I am Herbert and you
are Lucy, and the world of my dearest thoughts is the old salt dockyard;
and then my only ambition is 'to be tidy' – with a great midnight nail.

Some time in the next month, she relented and came. The approach
of Poppy's and Roger's wedding day on 9 August helped to make any
further barrier between the two families absurd to maintain. As if to
seal their renewed intimacy, de la Mare took his mother into his
confidence over the most private of his new ambitions: a *book* of his
poems of childhood. He must have worked on them all the winter that
followed, for on the last day of February 1901 he sent them to Pinker –
forty-two in all.

                                      *

His birthday in April found him in distinctly jauntier spirits than four
years before, when he had bewailed it. Next day, thanking his mother,
he said: 'I will come to take you for a walk soon my dear. Some day the
dukes and so on will turn and say, there's Mr de la Mare our modern
Will Shakespeare. They are so outspoken – dukes and so on.'[4]

A second baby was born that fourth of June 1901, a boy, christened
Richard Herbert Ingpen: another source of anxious joy, another mouth
to feed on the same (or scarcely growing) pittance. Roger was
beginning married life in circumstances even more precarious – he was
out of work. De la Mare wrote in keen sympathy: 'There's nothing ...
cankers one's roots like the doubt of one's mundane bread and cheese. I
do not mean it kills one's spirit – thats [sic] not in money's jurisdiction
at any rate, but it gropes in the belly like a clutching crab, and
sometimes thrusts its foul broad snout among one's thoughts. I know
its habits, I know it well.'[5]

For himself, though not materially better off, he now had hope,
family happiness, and the knowledge of increasing powers. The boyish
posturings of his courtship years had disappeared; his letters are a
mature man's now, and, in spite of his struggles, much more often
cheerful, uncomplaining and humorous. Elfie must have felt a reward
for the strains now upon her through her cares as a housewife in such
poverty (quite apart from the physical drain that her late childbearing
entailed – soon she would have four small children, only one of them
born before her fortieth year). Yet once she had become a mother, and
he a father, she could not fail to see how parenthood brought all the
gift, in which she had so steadfastly believed, to flower.

Meanwhile de la Mare turned once more to another early champion, long neglected: Canon Scott-Holland of St Paul's. He sent him stories and poems, and Scott-Holland wrote back with perspicacity:

> You have got a vivid fancy, quaint, and mystical, and unexpected. But it requires a great deal of control to bring it under, and to make it serve its true literary purpose. It is too wayward. It misses its effect. It scatters itself too loosely. It cannot keep a fixed end before it: or make a clear and prominent impression ...
>
> These fantastic tales are the hardest things in the world to keep sane. And the poems, with antique mystical refrains, are frightfully hard to keep right ... I am sure that you ought to train *down* to a quieter line – before venturing so far afield.[6]

Next month de la Mare told Pinker he was hoping 'in a day or two' to begin a novel – 'It's like presenting Australia with a pair of rabbits, I suppose.'[7] This might mark the beginning of *Henry Brocken*. But he was also around this period at work on a long story, or short novel, so he may have been referring to this. The story, unfinished, untitled, is the one mentioned before which belongs in the same nexus of atmosphere and sentiment from which 'The Almond Tree' and 'The Idealists' sprang. Unequal as it is and at times confusing – de la Mare had no real idea as yet how to sustain a plot at full length – yet the *matter* of it, the history of a small boy's first love for an older cousin, was perfect material for him, and runs close to the *Songs of Childhood* he was absorbed in. The manuscript of this story is almost illegible; at least twice in later years de la Mare hoped to revise it, and grew exasperated when member after member of the home circle, called in to help, could do no better than the defeated typist – all the more annoyed with them because he could not make it out himself!

Some of the child poems focused for him around the child portraits painted by Velasquez. (That abandoned story also alludes to these.) Velasquez treated his child sitters without condescension or sentimentality. They confront the spectator as equals, serious, engrossed by the world of childhood reality which looks out of their grave faces to meet ours on our own level. Velasquez's viewpoint corroborated de la Mare's most central tenet. Late Victorian sentiment and whimsy about childhood does, it must be admitted, flaw some of his work – 'Slumbersong' being a good example. That kind of self-indulgent tenderness led Max Beerbohm to regret disgustedly that the nineteenth century had vanished in a cloud of pinafores. But what de la Mare at his best had to contribute was very different; and the age that had produced Velasquez, Rembrandt and Traherne had insights in this matter far more congenial to him than the Victorian and Edwardian fashions in nursery fancy.

His collection of children's poems just now, in the summer of 1901, came under the favourable eye of Charles Longman, who decided to publish them, and wished to do so in the style of Stevenson's *A Child's Garden of Verses*, ignoring the nursery market and dispensing with the lavish illustration required for that. Longman felt that the poems were over the heads of children themselves. He pointed out to Pinker that some of the rhymes were very faulty. It is in fact a just comment, not a conventional stricture here. Ear for rhythm had developed ahead of competence in rhyming. Andrew Lang, Longman's literary adviser, thought highly of the poems and asked to help with critical suggestions.

De la Mare wrote to Pinker on 17 October 1901:

> Thank you very much for letting me see [Longman's] letter. I accept the 'crudities' in all humility, but I'm afraid the inaccuracies are sometimes intentional – a kind of childish attempt at *essence* of grammar or fact ... I am beginning to fancy it is as absurd to write a 'book for children' as for the 'Selenites'. They differ so decidedly in glory. Let them be birds and then go feeding the linnet on offal and the vulture on groundsel. Isn't that what a book for children seems to imply? If we inserted before 'children' – 'a certain kind of', or 'extraordinary', or 'nice', or 'traditional': that would be safer.

He wrote again the next day:

> I did not wish anything otherwise than as you say [about illustration]. It has always been my opinion that the illustration of such books is a mistake. If there is any true imagination at all in the writing, then pictures only confuse and distract the reader's own constantly fleeting pictures. Even a frontispiece might be dispensed with unless it could be a reproduction – say of a Velasquez or Rembrandt child.
>
> Perhaps the verses are over the heads of *most* children – tho' three children as good as selected them. One could scarcely suppose that 'I met at eve the Prince of Sleep' would take a child's fancy.
>
> It is a lovely riddle – and beyond my answering – what indeed is their philosophy.
>
> The *rhymes* I know are very bad in places, and I should think it a great compliment and privilege to have Andrew Lang's advice on this or any such matter.

The 'three children' were of course the eldest Rowleys, who remembered sitting at a table sorting into little piles their favourites from Uncle Jack's rhymes. Some were familiar to them from the *Horn Books*, but most were new.

Of course this selection committee was an audience already conditioned to the turn of his thought. No need here to create a taste for his own work, as he must do laboriously in the world at large. But gradually it became plain by proof that these poems were not (as many others besides Longman at first expected) above the heads of a variety of children. Many did, and still do, respond intuitively and deeply, far beyond the conscious understanding of their years, to de la Mare's poems. Nor is this confined to children of a cultured background; Glasgow teaching-nuns, London elementary schoolteachers and dockland public librarians reported to him in letters through the years ahead that they found the most unlikely children arrested by the more romantic and least childish of the poems. The verses appeal, also, to what is often a child's innate appetite for metaphysical questionings and the pursuit of enigma.

De la Mare was elated to have won Lang's interest, for Lang, now in his late fifties, had a reputation, not just as editor of the *Blue Fairy Book* and its successors, but as a critic and literary pundit. His social style – the Balliol man, the classical scholar and the writer of ballades on cricket – was one that would neither irritate nor deceive de la Mare, despite his own limited social advantages and unselfconfidence. He got on from the first with such men, and they in turn responded to him at his real value more immediately and percipiently than might have been expected.

Forty-three years later de la Mare was still writing gratefully of Lang as 'uncommonly kind'. When the typescript of *Songs of Childhood* came back speckled with Lang's suggestions he adopted the majority just as they stood. Lang, with real insight, put himself in the poet's shoes and, seeing what he was after, helped him to achieve his own characteristic effects. Many of the poems became not just formally the better for his corrections, but more essentially de la Mare. For instance, he touched 'Neath branches where the blackbird flits' into 'Neath branches that the blackbird frets' – a de la Mare image as well as a corrected rhyme.

But directly Lang got into matters of metre instead of rhyme, de la Mare, on surer ground, usually stuck to his guns. Sometimes he gave his reasons, and they prove that Lang's conservative ear was the one at fault, not his own. Lang would have killed the quality in one of the best poems in the book, 'The Silver Penny', doing away with every one of its checks and sudden brevities, and he put his disapproving crosses by those cunning irregularities which give the life of the storm:

> And all the wild sea-water
> Climbed steep into the boat;
> Back to the shore again
> Sail they will not.

On the other hand, Lang rescued Jinnie in 'The Dwarf' from a sad end
that was quite inappropriate to the rest. 'I don't see the fun of killing
her,' he protested in the margin. 'Marry her to a Prince, just as cheap.'

One of the poems in the book had an odd genealogy. 'Writing must be
far more parasitic than one supposes,' de la Mare remarked, recalling
it. At some time he had come across a sepia drawing by Beardsley,
perhaps when it was first reproduced in the *Studio* in May 1898, or
when reprinted in *The Later Work of Aubrey Beardsley* in 1900.
Composed in five flat washes, it is of a woman, voluminously gowned,
side-saddle on a prancing horse, against a frieze of slender pillar-like
trees; the mystery of the dark avenue and the suggestion of
concentrated reverie in the figure make it a Beardsley from the most
romantic side of his imagination, not the decadent. Under the picture
were printed six bars of Chopin's *Ballade*,[8] whose clip-clop melody had
suggested it. The picture in turn suggested to de la Mare his poem
'Reverie', which begins

> When slim Sophia mounts her horse
> And paces down the avenue
> It seems an inward melody
> She paces to.

Years afterwards, to complete the cycle, Armstrong Gibbs composed a
pavane suggested by the poem.

Though the poems themselves were not to have illustrations,
Longman did want a frontispiece, and de la Mare pressed again for a
Velasquez, saying: 'I think it would give a mood to the book, as it were,
and excuse its being perhaps a little old fashioned.' To Roger he added:
'I don't want anything pretty or "decorative" – but something real and
if possible not of the *novel* childishness or the grotesque. What more
delightful than the Infanta in the Connoisseur!'[9] But Longman was
dubious; de la Mare's approach to childhood was altogether too
unconventionally grave for him, and he wanted a more whimsical
sentiment: 'I have a charming watercolour drawing by Dicky Doyle of
fairies playing under Dock Leaves which seems to me more the sort of
thing if an existing picture is to be utilised. If Mr Ramal cares to call
any day this week I will bring the picture for him to see.'[10] So Mr
Ramal went, and took pleasure in recollecting in old age 'the exact spot
of the Turkey carpet' where he stood in front of his elderly first
publisher. 'I can see his kindly bearded face even now, as he produced
the Dicky Doyle – and, the hole in his carpet. (Publishers do not have
holes in their carpets now; they keep up appearances.)'[11]

Longman not only lent his fairy picture free of charge, but allowed de la Mare to choose his cloth and binding; and the little book came out as enticingly dressed as any young poet could wish – blue and gold with a white spine, octavo, well printed on good paper, price 3/6. Longman also hit upon the title, *Songs of Childhood*, by combining two in a list of de la Mare's suggestions.*

*

Meanwhile Pinker had not neglected the poems for adults. De la Mare was probably lucky that his love of Shakespeare, like his first enthusiasm for pictures, came late and was never an academic study, but made an untutored, direct impact on his own urge to write. Around 1901 he tried a group of verse portraits of Shakespearian characters – in blank verse, which is uncommon in his work. He wrote thirteen, nearly all from the tragedies, three each of these from *Romeo and Juliet* and *Hamlet*, the plays that spoke to him most intimately. These 'Characters' were a leap ahead of anything else he had attempted for adult readers. Imaginative re-creation allowed him a kind of oblique literary criticism – the same impulse that, a year or so later, would lie behind *Henry Brocken*.

The poems illuminate their originals by the curious personal reverie in which he isolated them. It is as if one saw, one by one, these highly-coloured, full-blooded Shakespeare figures pass by as dark trembling reflections through a pool under thick trees. The settings he invents are the symbols for their natures; as he said, 'It seemed impossible to *define* Hamlet – all one outlook of humanity. I could only compare him as it were.'[12] So he saw Macbeth as a 'soul still childish in a withered hell', gazing on the rainy turrets of a storm, 'And all his armour in a haze of blue'. Juliet's nurse in her old age, 'gloomy, vast, glossy, and wise', gossips an evening away with a 'cherried country cousin' in an 'old-world nursery vacant now of children'. He saw Falstaff 'compact of loam', an 'orchard man': 'I could not view his fatness for his soul, / Which peeped like harmless lightnings and was gone.'

Pinker looked for some editor who would print these as a group that might make some mark for an unknown name. He soon decided the very man for this was Henry Newbolt, of the two-year-old *Monthly Review*, who was campaigning for contemporary poetry and was himself a best-selling poet of the day. Newbolt wrote in his memoirs:

* 'Mr Ramal's' nervous instinct for shelter under pseudonyms and disguised addresses made him baulk even at putting his address, 'Mackenzie Road', on the contract when he signed it; was it really necessary, he asked?

> When I agreed to founding *The Monthly Review*, one of my conscious
> motives was a desire to bring about a change in the estimate of Poetry
> then held by the reading public ... In 1900 it was vain to look for poetry in
> the 'serious' reviews ... Papers like the *Spectator* and the *Saturday
> Review* were genuinely interested in verse, but could only afford room for
> a few stanzas at a time. In short, a poet, whatever his quality, could not
> hope to gain a hearing unless he published a volume, and he had little
> chance of his volume being accepted ...[13]

Newbolt carried his policy of giving a poet real scope to bold lengths.
During his four years as editor, he devoted twenty pages of one number
to Binyon's 'Death of Adam', and almost as much to lengthy works by
Meredith, Yeats and a hitherto unpublished Blake. Would he do as
much for someone unknown – literally without a name? It was worth a
try. The little sheaf of typescript was despatched to him, 'Walter
Ramal' being too retiring on this occasion to put more than 'W.R.' at the
foot of the page.

Newbolt's eye, at forty, was alert and experienced. He had a rapid,
versatile, sympathetic mind, crammed with enthusiasms: poetry,
classical scholarship, naval history, education, Liberal politics,
heraldry, church finance. He had practised as a barrister, was a friend
of Rosebery and Asquith and Sir Edward Grey, and had a wide variety
of personal contacts in all these worlds. His judgment was bold and
balanced, and he backed it with uncommon self-confidence. Some
called him sanguine, as he did himself; others found him cocksure. He
pounced on the little package signed 'W.R.', and ever afterwards
considered it the greatest windfall of his career:

> I had no clue whatever to the author's identity. But [the poems] were
> evidently the work of a writer with very unusual powers – probably an
> amateur of genius, for they had a weaker line here and there. I felt sure,
> when my invaluable 'reader', Ella Coltman, sent them into me with a
> note of marked interest, that they were not by any obscure beginner, but
> almost certainly by some well-known writer who had not hitherto
> published verse. I opened *Who's Who* and searched for men of distinction
> with the initials 'W.R.'[14]

After getting disclaimers from Walter Raleigh and Sir William
Richmond – his first guesses, and rather quaint they must have
seemed afterwards – Newbolt appealed to Pinker, who promised to get
the poet to call.

Still disguised as 'Walter Ramal', one day early in February 1902 de
la Mare walked into 50 Albemarle Street, John Murray's publishing
office, where Byron and Walter Scott had first met, and where Newbolt
had a small, high-ceilinged room from which to edit the *Monthly*

Review. His visitor opened the door 'and took my hand', Newbolt wrote, 'with a grip which has never once loosened in the thirty years that followed.'[15] De la Mare, for his part, said: 'I was almost too shy to sigh.'

The man Newbolt rose to meet so eagerly had lost, of late, his Nineties dandy airs, and had cut his hair. At just on thirty, his face now looked rather older than his years, and his manner and dress carried about them something of the business clerk he was – an effect intriguingly at odds with the mobile, imaginative features, now becoming more condensed and impressive in expression. There was nothing of the suburban bourgeois businessman however about the instantaneous *contact* he made of mind with mind, without preliminary small-talk. He did appear very shy, but also as if it were the only natural approach in the world to plunge in at the deep end into ardent discussion. Any topic was welcome, so long as it could at once possess his whole being and his interlocutor's. His way of coming into a room, at the same time diffident and energetic, the slight roll of his walk, the warm grip, the instant effect of his strong personality, raising the pitch – all this had a most sympathetic effect on the man coming forward from behind the editor's desk. Newbolt was so very different in background, temperament, position and appearance, but his imagination and heart were to become intimately congenial to de la Mare's.

Both were generally seen and remembered as short men, though in fact each was of medium height – in de la Mare it was something at once nimble and rather thickset about him, not at all plump, but a sailor-like stockiness, which reduced his inches in the beholder's eye. Newbolt seemed small to quite different effect: he had a bird-boned erect slightness, a silvery fairness, all the expression of his keen features concentrated in the blue eyes, above a prominent nose and a thin, small mouth. De la Mare wrote about Newbolt after he died: 'Any question on the target would at once decoy the lean clear-cut Roman face in your direction, alert as a kestrel – like the figurehead on a vessel voyaging over seas which, however familiar they might be, might also at any moment reveal the unforeseen and the strange. The intent grey-blue eyes pierced into one's own through a remote haze, as it were, of his mind's reverie.'[16] But this is Newbolt seen as the years had mellowed him; the editor of the *Monthly Review* was sharper, very sure of his opinions, and his small mouth could tighten with uncompromising disapproval or a flash of temper. His easy, early success had contributed to his assurance; but this went deeper, and revealed itself gradually as a spiritual quality, a faith in his intuitions which made him prompt to grasp nettles for his friends – and would be decisive for this one's career. His nature rose delightedly to any prospect of battle, competition and risk. As his son-in-law Ralph Furse wrote of him, 'Awkward fences were often cleared, in the manner of the born steeple-chaser, by not noticing they were there.'[17] De la Mare, by contrast, avoided conflicts, totally refused public controversy, had no competitive instinct whatever, and quailed inwardly before risks. His courage was considerable, but it was the courage of the congenitally anxious.

As soon as Newbolt learned – and this was not till de la Mare wrote to him after their first meeting – that 'Walter Ramal' was a pseudonym, he urged him to publish under his real name; he always felt very strongly against anonymity. Undecided, de la Mare appealed to his oldest adviser, and it was Scott-Holland's characteristically staccato burst of support for Newbolt's view which tipped the scale: 'I have no doubt whatever that you ought to write under your own name. It will be infinitely better. You would have to do it if you succeed. Do it now.'[18] So the Shakespeare 'Characters' were published in the *Monthly Review* fully signed, and 'Walter Ramal', who had only just ventured into the bookshops, between the small blue covers of *Songs of Childhood*, was seen no more.

*

Newbolt had been drawn to de la Mare even more strongly as a person than as a poet at their first meeting and he took care to follow up quickly and thoroughly. He longed with proprietary ardour to shower upon his discovery any possible advantages he could share or procure. It was not the condescension of a successful writer to a beginner. Newbolt's head had not been turned by his success; he knew he owed a good deal to the *zeitgeist*, and recognised from the beginning that his own achievement was as nothing beside the promise in his new friend. De la Mare was a kind of marvel to him, and he never ceased to wonder at the luck that brought him 'to knock on my door first'. On occasion, however, he was apt to claim more credit for solo discovery than was strictly accurate – Strachey and Longman and Lang had certainly not been blind; moreover every single opening in the years up till this meeting can be traced back to some personal effort of Roger Ingpen's.

On a spring evening soon after they had met, de la Mare dined for the first time at Newbolt's Kensington house, taking a step into a social ambience totally new to him. When Newbolt remarked that at this time de la Mare 'knew nobody west of S.E.' it was almost literally true. The Newbolts were comfortably off, and entertained a good deal – on a modest scale and outside the fashionable world, but with self-confidence. The poets and artists who came to them were seldom bohemian, more often those who had begun in public schools and would end up as members of the Athenaeum. But it was not a stuffy or pretentious circle. Newbolt's gift for friendship was catholic, open towards new merit and new ideas, and Margaret, his wife, was artistic, musical, keenly interested in science and philosophy. She was a Duckworth, and had rebelled against the very same fond but suffocating family background from which Virginia and Vanessa Stephen would soon flee to Bloomsbury.

Liberated by her marriage, Margaret had expressed her personality in the Earls Terrace drawing-room with a kind of happy austerity leagues away from Victorian overstuffing. She loved its restrained Adam cornices and basket grates and responded by choosing plain white Dresden candlesticks set with blue candles to flank a smallish eagle-crested mirror over the fireplace – a round one to give secrecy to the long room's reflection. Serene grey-green Wilton carpet spread to the incomer's feet (children loved to pretend it was a frosty lawn and scud it surreptitiously into darker tracts with their feet). Typically, it had been made to order, with dark lines spaced along the borders carefully copied by Margaret from some Roman mosaic she had visited and loved. Anything that lay around was there to please her eager painter's eye – perhaps a peacock feather propped on the mantelpiece – but just as likely some plane leaves off the pavement outside. Whatever it was, one could be sure she had come across it out vigorously walking somewhere, and brought it home, passionately absorbed in it, to draw. She had a kind of Tolstoyan energy – physical, mental, spiritual. Over morality, upbringing of children and so on, she was a free spirit, not at all conventional, but neither bohemian nor exhibitionist. She contributed to the household a dash of plain living and high thinking, while Harry Newbolt brought in the hum of action and influence from the world of affairs and politics. Books and poetry were more often discussed than anything else, but in a context, not simply for Art's sake. That context was England.

Public service, patriotism, corporate loyalties, were a sacred flame to Newbolt. His dream of the Good Society had first possessed him as an ambitious boy (of partly Jewish blood) from a gently-bred, but rather narrow, home, when he tasted success at a public school, Clifton. He ever after attached an absurdly inflated glory to the English gentleman's education. However, wise man that he was on other topics, and often a true poet (very far from being a retarded adolescent), he did himself come to regret some of his all-too-quotable verses glorifying the public school ethos. He began to wish he had *not* written 'Play up and play the game' when even a London housemaid, taking his hat at the door, had been known to murmur the line under her breath! But just as strongly as all that was schoolboyish, drumbeating and limited in his idealisms, a genuine dedication, chivalry, good sense, were there too, distilled by a keen and rather austere intelligence. His encouragement proved something precious, even crucial, in a number of remarkable lives, and his company was unusual and distinguished. Hardy, Conrad and Mary Coleridge were some of the imaginative minds who set store by his opinions and conversation, and the public schools neither moulded any of *their* lives, nor irked them in his.

Margaret Newbolt remembered the young stranger, that May evening in 1902, standing by her fireplace in a shy attitude, 'unable to talk at all without asking a diffident question'. He was, she thought, quite unlike anyone else she had ever met, and she was deeply attracted. They sat down four to the oval table often set for twelve. Ella Coltman was present as a matter of course. She was Margaret's elder cousin and closest friend from childhood, and when Margaret married she became an integral part of the marriage itself – as equally indispensable, for the rest of his life, to Harry Newbolt as to Margaret. They shared almost all their multitude of friendships, and their homes, too, for many of those years; and without Ella the Newbolt marriage could not have been so successful. She supplied an extra dimension of romantic affection to their bond, and soothed certain sharp edges by her presence, for both Harry and Margaret were impatient, at any rate in early years. Both had strong personalities, and their moods did not always keep in step. Harry's nickname for Margaret was 'Lad', and if she was absorbed in her own interests, just when he needed feminine sympathy, he could always turn to Ella.

She was herself a strong character, patrician, from proud old Border Country stock, intellectual (though no bluestocking) with an edge to her wits and an insatiable appetite for human affairs. Friendship itself was the art of arts for her, and in exercising it she had, as it were, 'perfect pitch' – tact, discretion and no spinster's egotism. Very good at arranging the practical details of life for others, and always fairly sure what would be best for them, she yet contrived somehow not to be managing – or not often. She was very clear-headed and had no impulse whatever to make trouble. Harry left to her alert literary judgment the first sifting of all contributions to the *Monthly Review*, and he relied on her at every stage of his editing.

Once Margaret, speaking closely of Ella, when she alone of the trio was left, commented: 'You see, *she was married to both of us.*' That, and without a breath of scandal attaching, was the simple fact – and successful (this is the really unusual feature) for close on half a century, till death did them all part, taking first Harry, then very much later the eldest of them, Ella, at the age of ninety. There was so clear a distinction in their own minds, these three, between the private and the furtive, the personally free and the socially guilty, that they were able to live serenely, all mutually in love, without any uneasy stratagems to hide the matter – without doubts, without nerves. Very close friends (as de la Mare was to become) probably never found the question of a *ménage à trois* even cross their minds. Harry, Margaret and Ella were essentially emancipated late Victorians, not at all freakishly displaced permissive moderns. They each held stringent moral and Christian convictions (which included chastity, of course) and I think no hypocrisy was involved, for they felt strongly (given the all-exacting disciplines of trust this three-sided relationship demanded) that to each individual alone belongs the interpretation of St Augustine's dictum: 'Love and do as you please.' What limits they evolved, over the long years, to their bond, they felt to be entirely their own affair, a private adventure in sharing which was for them all, equally, the very centre of life's meaning and happiness.

Newbolt's unusual temperament, of course, was the pivot of this. He had an almost unlimited bent for intimate platonic friendships with intelligent women, and nothing very dominating in his physical masculinity to overbalance the poise of such. But though this affair with Ella too was mostly, probably, in the sphere of the passionately imaginative, physical sex did have a place – not, it would seem, frequent.

Harry's years of intense romance centred more on Ella, it seems from their letters – these years coinciding however with his great fulfilment as a young parent of two much-loved children, experiences he shared, of course, foremost with Margaret. The reliance placed in each other was lived out by these three 'married' ones partly in Ella's separate household in London, but mainly in the Newbolts' home in Wiltshire, and with many holidays together in Europe as well as around England and Scotland. There was a press of literary work always to be shared, and constant hospitality, for they had in common also almost all their very wide circle of friends. The way they loved each other seems to have imposed remarkably little strain on any of them – indeed just the opposite; their triple intimacy provided them all with a wonderful fund of comforting, amused freedom, a secret fortress against anything life could fling. Only perhaps in Ella's frequent spells of ill health can one trace symptoms of psychosomatic stress. She was, after all, the unmarried one, her status as Harry's beloved socially incognito. Being extremely level-headed and collected, Ella would have looked closely at that price, recognised it and paid it gladly, considering it well worth while.

At this first dinner with de la Mare, of the hundreds to follow, her dark, deepset eyes (whose characteristic expression was of intent amusement) would have been snapping with satisfaction. For she was a born collector of uncommon human occasions. De la Mare had no notion of this, of course, but in the minds of each of the other three round the table there was the unanimous conviction that they were entertaining a genius. In the middle of the table Margaret had arranged some sprays of young beech. During dinner, she lifted and laid on the wax-guard of the candle one of the delicate bud-sheaths that had fallen. She remembered the swift, wordless response of the younger man's glance, sharing her pleasure in its beauty: the small, certain shock of the friendship they so easily formed in that instant. She would say that, at the end of an evening of de la Mare's talk, when they all went out to say goodbye on the doorstep, the world seemed transmuted, 'as if turned into spirit', so strong was the effect of sharing for an hour his compelling view of it.

He himself was already quite unable to resist the lure of speculation, and really knew no other form of conversation. He might ask questions at first from shyness, but he kindled instantly to the first answer and was off, pursuing its implications with irrepressible curiosity. A letter of thanks to the Newbolts for some occasion a few months after this first evening, shows the pattern clearly enough set for all the years of conversation that followed: 'I so much enjoyed our talk: but every subject has so keen a scent, one goes breathlessly on, and runs nothing down. Perhaps it would result in a kill otherwise and that's very flat.'[19]

*

Songs of Childhood came out in the early spring of 1902. It sold very slowly, but had better fortune in its judges than many a first volume by a new poet. Scott-Holland wrote in delight, and reviewed the book in the *Christian Commonwealth*, which he edited. Margaret Newbolt went off on her bicycle to ask Mary Coleridge to write an appreciation for the *Monthly Review*. Andrew Lang praised it highly in his monthly causerie 'At the Sign of the Ship' in *Longman's Magazine*. De la Mare remembered to the end the very look (he said) of the printed pages of these reviews, which he slipped into a public library to devour – 'and this not due to inordinate vanity but to the nearness to oneself of one's first book'.[20]

He was also lucky enough to catch the eye of Edward Thomas. Four years later, Thomas wrote to Gordon Bottomley: 'I regret I saw nothing in any except the nonsense pieces in 1902, while I now see that it is poetry.'[21] His review is a beginner's, very fanciful, treating *Songs of Childhood* with six other books of verse as if each poet were one of the doves pulling Venus's car. She is 'more angry with this dove' i.e. Walter Ramal 'than with its yokefellows, because it had put one or two wonderful things in its book and had choked them with unsuccessful verses for children'. Thomas makes Venus quote the whole of 'Lovelocks' as if to illustrate these 'wonderful things', followed by the single comment: 'That, said she, deserves silence from the critics.'[22]

Reviewing *Poems 1906* four years later, Thomas referred back to the *Songs*, as though to make amends, declaring now that some ' ... were perfectly beautiful; all were unusually interesting, because there clearly was a man who wrote so much from his individual heart and brain that every verse was characteristic and his own, just as every nightingale's egg is olive, and not yellow or freckled or blotched.'[23]

Someone sent the book to Katherine Tynan, and de la Mare copied out her reply, which spoke of the *Songs* as 'a string of jewels', which 'might be imagined by a child of Genius'. But the praise he treasured most – so much that the sheet fell apart from being carried around in his pocket book – was a letter from Alice Meynell, who wrote: 'I found so much imagination and fancy in these verses that the book becomes at once one of my treasures. It has a rare and pure quality of magic.'[24] De la Mare replied: 'Will you forgive me ... this simple truth if I say how long and close I have held your work in mind, and so how proud I feel that these little verses have won your praise.'[25] Yet all this did not bring freedom any nearer. The first six months' royalties on *Songs of Childhood* came to just two pounds sixteen shillings and eleven pence.

Undeterred, Pinker began talking of a book of poems for adults. Fifty would be enough, and he asked de la Mare in August 1902 to select them; so there must have been already a fair pile to choose from. He duly sent a collection off; they went to John Murray's, where they passed through Newbolt's hands. He took his time over the manuscript, having no idea what urgent practical hopes rested on his decision, nor how badly the de la Mare household needed whatever mite those poems could bring. During the next year, Jack sometimes had to borrow from Roger, and the smallness of these loans – three pounds, five pounds, which even so Roger could scarcely raise, or Jack quickly repay – tell their own tale.

While waiting for a decision, Jack made, for Newbolt's small daughter Celia (who was earnestly involved in botany, which he disapproved of, in her schoolroom) a slender, tiny manuscript-book, bound in a page of vellum which he clipped at the corners and threaded with green silk ribbon. Into it he copied, in his neatest Oil sales-sheet hand, round-lettered for legibility, a page of poetry, a page of limericks, a Lewis Carroll pastiche ('Amy in Aliceland'), and a story called 'The Earth Child' from the *Horn Books*. For end-piece, he put a poem called 'A Portrait', perhaps originally meant for the Velasquez set, but near enough to Celia's own serious fair-haired looks for a compliment. It began 'Only thy small fair face I see'. Leisure for such delicate and painstaking ways of showing gratitude must have been scarce enough. Yet on another occasion he made her an entire calendar in coloured inks, marking out the dates in neat squares, with a verse to head each month on its separate card, all strung together on scarlet ribbon.

Finally, in December 1902, Newbolt's answer came. He softened it by taking the story 'The Riddle' for the February *Monthly Review*. But he was positive it would be a mistake even to show John Murray himself the collection of poems. Not only (he said) was Murray 'not a poet's man', but the poems themselves (he felt) might well soon be excelled, and some could certainly bear revision. He wanted de la Mare to make his first bow as a serious poet from firmer ground. He would like instead, he said, to print a selection of the best in the *Monthly Review* during 1903. He ended: 'Of course, I shall not be surprised if you decide against this course: I am well aware that these are poems of unusual beauty and that you may find some other publisher to jump at them as they are. I am in any case always yours very sincerely.' But already de la Mare did not dream of opposing Newbolt's judgment.

He switched his energies back to prose, and began another novel. Perhaps it grew partly out of the Shakespeare characters; the underlying impulse is the same, the prose itself verges upon poetry and there is even a figure from Shakespeare – expanded (in the same spirit as the picture he had woven around Juliet's nurse) from the brief volubilities of the Doctor in *Macbeth*, who exclaims over the sleepwalker 'Well, well, well, / ... God forgive us all.'

De la Mare described his enterprise to Newbolt as 'criticism in narrative form'. His hero, Henry Brocken, sets out one day on his prosaic old mare Rosinante, and finds himself soon in the 'Rich, Strange, Scarce-Imaginable Regions of Romance'. His travels and adventures there, among the scenes and characters of favourite books stretching 'from childhood to this side regret', occupied all de la Mare's evenings in 1903 until August. With two small children at home and another on the way, the gaunt Oil office after hours was the quietest place available for writing. A caretaker lived on the premises, so there was no early locking-up; in any case, there were often other late-stayers putting in overtime.

De la Mare often outstayed them all. He shaped the tiny pages of his manuscript out of the backs of the big sales sheets in the office wastepaper baskets. The rambling episodic form of his story no doubt made it easier to pick up the thread after interruptions, and in the constant harassment of household cares and scraping and small debts. As to the latter, he was at present waiting for a cheque from Newbolt for the selection of poems to be put in the *Monthly Review*. When it had not come by mid-July, and the greater part of his rent due at midsummer was still owing, he confided to Roger:

> The fact is this house is quite beyond me, has always been. There's my income (with an average for Literature! included) £157, and my house rent with rates and taxes and gas £43 odd and my fare £8 – of course it's impossible – and if I see no *immediate* prospect of better things at the end of the year I shall move into a flat or lodgings: anything rather than this continual indecent fret to us both. Indeed, looking back we cannot fathom how we have survived so long. I bother you with all this because I would not for the world it should seem I am simply money-witless – an awful malady. I know a shilling so well by *sight* I hope some day to be on nodding terms: friends we can never be.
>
> Ultimate undistractedness I have no doubt of, when, I dare say, these five years will seem the vividest, reallest and even happiest of any. So much for what is my chronic belly-ache.[26]

Henry Brocken is an original and imaginative achievement, though mannered and uneven. The Jane Eyre episode, the visit to Gulliver, and the *Pilgrim's Progress* inn scene, are things which truly penetrate and illuminate their originals, though always at a tangent, and bathed in a romantic afterlight quite de la Mare's own. He takes all kinds of liberties – even daring to scatter an episode about Herrick's girls with lyrics composed by himself. Jane Eyre becomes more intriguing for his romantic vision of her; while Gulliver, a solitary fanatic with his voice of haughty anguish, haranguing the wild horses from the 'brutal and bald order' of his stockaded house, grows into a tragic portrait of Swift himself.

The Bunyan scene at the 'World's End' inn (outcome of various earlier attempts at such hostelry conversation-pieces), though so allusive it is very hard to follow, holds the imagination strongly, and its dark evocative poetry sends one back to Bunyan's own with fresh understanding. Atheist gives his own account of Christian's venture, with, for listeners, some of Bunyan's characters and some extra ones of de la Mare's own invention – Obstinate, Cruelty, Mistrust and Reverie, served by a deaf-mute landlady, a Mrs Nature: 'Her eyes were on all, vaguely dwelling, lightly gone, inscrutable, strangely fascinating. She moved easily and soundlessly (as fat women may).'[27] The company speculates and scoffs, and dissects Christian's character uneasily. Reverie admits: 'I often think of him, in spite of myself. Yet he was a man of little charm. He certainly had a remarkable gift for estranging his friends. He was foe to the most innocent compromise. For myself, I found not much humour in him, no eye for grace or art, and a limited imagination that was yet his absolute master.'[28] Reverie has a sister who lives not far distant, who visits him while Brocken is staying with him, 'delighting us with her wit and spirit and her singing'. Writing to Roger, de la Mare said: 'I rather fancy Poppy is Reverie's sister.'[29] Certainly there was a self of his own in those words of Reverie's about Christian.

In the middle of their talk,

> a stranger softly entered the inn out of the night. His face was of the grey of ashes, and he looked once round on us all with a still, appalling glance that silenced the words on my lips ... He turned his back on us and sipped his drink under the heedless, deep, untroubled gaze of Mrs Nature, and passed out softly and harmlessly as he had come in.
>
> Reverie stood up like a man surprised and ill at ease. He turned to me. 'I know him only by repute, by hearsay,' he said with an effort. 'He is a stranger to us all, indeed, sir – to all.'[30]

Unnamed, an absolute spiritual evil behind the grubby human vices and follies, something on another plane altogether, is marvellously suggested.

Sometimes the essence of the subject is evoked by a piece of pure invention. In the Sleeping Beauty's palace lives a survivor untouched by the spell, a brother of the Princess, the sinister Prince Ennui. 'Was he in very deed,' Brocken wonders, when uneasily accepting his hospitality for the night, 'the incarnation of this solitude, this silence, this lawless abundance? Somewhere, in the green heats of summer, had he come forth, taken shape, exalted himself?'[31] Everything about him, pale yellow and strange as mistletoe, his colourless eyes, his fair hair 'lean on his shoulders', his two stealthy hounds Safte and Sallow, his suave monotonous voice, seem inevitable details, not so much invented as recognised.

So Brocken winds his inconsequent way, with Rosinante for chorus (comic, gaunt, faithful, very much alive), to the further shores of Tragedy. The final episode is so elusive that, though Newbolt thought it the best of all, it is almost impossible to make out what actually happens. Brocken visits Cryseyde, exiled on an island, and finally puts out into the unknown deep.

The novel was de la Mare's most ambitious work so far, and in its course his personal vision matured and extended. When old, he wished he had tried the idea at a later point in his career, when no doubt he would have pruned the flowery style and attempted encounters of a more searching criticism. He stored away with the manuscript a little chart which plots in careful columns the hours of the day and phases of the moon throughout Brocken's travels. Whether made seriously, or half idly borrowing from the disciplines of the office day, it is a very characteristic touch. De la Mare always felt the need to be exact in detail, however airy or romantic the general effect he aimed at. He was vexed to discover (though nobody else remarked on it) that in a later novel, *The Memoirs of a Midget*, he had allowed the moon to set twice in the same night.

He finished *Henry Brocken* at the beginning of August 1903, when the next baby was due. But the baby delayed, and half that month there was a nurse waiting in the house, who had to be paid – a serious matter, delightful as Jack found her 'unique nose' and her fund of reminiscences about her past as a housemaid at Blenheim Palace. (Nurses, like family doctors, were to figure much in his life; he found them a very reassuring race.) He was by this time so hard up that he had to pocket pride and ask Newbolt for payment in advance, once Newbolt had announced that he would be bringing out the poems in October or November. The baby, a girl, christened Lucy Elfrida but known from the start as Jinnie, was born on 30 August.

De la Mare soon afterwards sent, to add to the other manuscripts waiting on Newbolt's desk at Murray's, a new batch of beautiful poems about childhood. Among them was 'Winter', which begins:

> Green Mistletoe!
> Oh, I remember now
> A dell of snow,
> Frost on the bough;
> None there but I:
> Snow, snow, and a wintry sky.[32]

It seems that it was once again the marvel of the birth of a child that had stirred up his gift. Newbolt published all eight poems in the January 1904 issue of the *Monthly Review*.

De la Mare had taken a great stride forward, even since *Songs of Childhood*; his prose and his poetry always reacted upon each other, and the new insights that *Henry Brocken* achieved went hand in hand

with a deeper note in his verse. Once at least early in 1903 he touched
his best as a poet, in verses he first called 'The Lost Playmate', then
'Autumn':

> There is a wind where the rose was;
> Cold rain where sweet grass was;
>   And clouds like sheep
>   Stream o'er the steep
> Grey skies where the lark was.

* * * * *

> Sad winds where your voice was;
> Tears, tears where my heart was;
>   And ever with me
>   Child, ever with me,
> Silence where hope was.[33]

*

Because Roger Ingpen had a friendship with a reader at Constable's,
Henry Brocken went to them first. When they refused it, Pinker sent it
on to John Murray without telling de la Mare, true to his promise to
spare him knowledge of rejections. In consequence de la Mare was
bewildered when he received the news of an acceptance by Murray. He
had to write to Pinker to ask which book it could be. Exhilarated to find
it was *Henry Brocken*, he went off to the Newbolts at Earl's Terrace to
dine and meet Mary Coleridge.

There were only four years for their friendship before she died, but to
the end of his life the mention of two names, hers and Edward
Thomas's, brought a tone into his voice that no others ever did. These
two poets were the pole-stars in his sky, and no other friendships,
however intimate or long, affected him so centrally.

Great-great-neice of Samuel Taylor Coleridge, Mary was by now
forty-two, rich in friends and in achievement of a quiet kind; but she
would still come into a room diffidently, a tall figure, graceful in mood
and movement though dressed without any interest whatever in her
own appearance. Her very blue eyes and full mouth, the gestures of her
beautiful hands as she leaned forward, lost in talk, were expressive of a
hundred volatile moods. 'Animated', de la Mare said, looking back, was
too poor a word to express her effect: 'She *made* life in people.'[34]

Among his new friends she was the one with the most creative
imagination. Her friendship was different from, say, Ella Coltman's
observant, critical relish for all and sundry; in fact she said that things

interested her more than people. But wherever her sympathy was engaged (and it was easily caught), her friends would tease her, because to her all geese became swans. Indeed, while under the spell of her company, people really did reveal themselves as more lovable, romantic and imaginative than they or anyone else had guessed they could be. De la Mare said: 'You know there is one note that will break any glass in a room. Well, she played the note that broke the glass for people.'

She also had what was the cardinal attraction for him in any woman: a child's maturity; and this, no doubt, was due to the fact that, though she was clever, her life-centre was much more her intuition than her intellect. 'If she went into a wood,' de la Mare said, trying to describe this quality, 'she would be ageless, ancient, as she was when a child.'

She shared the same well-to-do, leisured, cultivated background as the Newbolts and Ella Coltman, and lived at home with her father and her one sister, also unmarried. As a child she had watched Browning from behind the legs of her father's piano; as a young woman, free to extend her education all through her twenties, she and Ella had studied Greek under William Cory. Her first novel had been praised by Robert Louis Stevenson; a later one, *The King With Two Faces*, ran into several editions and brought her over nine hundred pounds. She had published a successful volume of essays, and had had her poems criticised in manuscript by Robert Bridges. Only a few of them had been published, and these under a pseudonym; some hundreds more accumulated in private, seen by no one while she lived.

Soon de la Mare began to show her his own, and the criticism she gave him – gentle, erratic, intuitive, unreasoned – was marvellously stimulating to him. She personified to him an imaginative goal in living. Also, she could not only see from within what he wanted to express, but could make it available to him, out of her own inner world. 'Words cannot express how inadequate I find them,' she once exclaimed; but in personal contact the communication did not wholly depend on words. (In fact de la Mare always held that words were a very small part of the actual interchange between friends in a close talk. Much more, he guessed, was really transmitted by a telepathy so common we do not recognise its power.) More than anyone else had ever yet done, perhaps, Mary Coleridge took away his inward isolation – although their meetings were not many in number, and he never got beyond addressing her as 'Miss Coleridge'. In fact he imagined she only looked on him as an acquaintance, and had no idea how she really valued his gift; he would have been astounded to know that she ranked her friendship with him as 'a rather alarming privilege'.

Henry Brocken received some encouraging reviews when Murray brought it out in the early spring of 1904 – particularly one from Francis Thompson: 'The author has much of the poet in his composition, and he succeeds best with the fairy and purely poetic elements,' though Thompson also noticed 'some occasional violences'.[35] Newbolt was enthusiastic, of course, in the *Monthly Review*, and there was a long and favourable notice in the *Times Literary Supplement*. Bruce Richmond, the *Supplement*'s editor, took the trouble, moreover, to rummage around and discover more about this new author – an interest which was to affect de la Mare's career later on.

Newbolt made up for his long delay by bringing out two sizeable collections of de la Mare's poems in the *Monthly* during 1904: the eight 'Memories of Childhood' sent to him after Jinnie's birth, and four sonnets in July. But by then he had already decided that his own Liberal views diverged too far from the Conservatism of John Murray, the *Monthly*'s publisher, and he handed in his resignation. Only one further de la Mare story found a place in the *Monthly* after he had left.

This was a blow; nor did the sales of *Henry Brocken* live up to the reviewers' welcome. When de la Mare wrote in June, with his usual diffident desperation, to enquire whether there might soon be a small cheque from Murray's for the novel, as he was hoping to take a holiday, he learned that on the contrary there was a deficit of £41.19s.3d on costs, and that of this he himself owed Murray's £3.16s.4d for excess proof-corrections – something quite beyond him to pay, even by abandoning the holiday. Not many more than 250 copies had been sold.

There was nothing for it but to try again. But now leisure to write had become a real problem. Petrol was in rising demand in Britain, and the price war between the big oil companies, entailing fluctuations almost daily as they undercut each other, wearily complicated de la Mare's work in office hours on his statistical sheets. The magazine *Black and White* published his short story 'In the Forest' and were so pleased with it that they asked for another; but he had no stocks by him and had to tell Pinker that the moment he had time he would produce something. In this respect he was always confident: that his flow of invention could be relied on. He would talk cheerfully of future production, measuring it directly to time available, just as a cabinet-maker might speak of the delivery of his next consignment.

A little more poetry was trickling into periodicals, but he was afraid that, with Newbolt gone from the *Monthly* and *Henry Brocken* unsuccessful, it would be out of the question now for Murray to take a book of poems. To cap it all, when Longman's royalties for *Songs of Childhood* arrived they came to four shillings. Even this, however, was better than he expected, for he dismally replied: 'I am at a loss who could have bought *Songs of Childhood* this year.'[36]

After the first good fortune that friendship with Newbolt had brought his prospects seemed yet again at a stalemate. Work at the office was growing harder, while at home, with three children growing up fast, the family's needs increased all the time. The trickle of contributions to periodicals failed to build up further; if anything they dwindled again, and their pathetic proceeds, scarcely a pound each, had to be begged for in advance through Pinker, with increasing candour. 'Whatever small sum it may be it would be a convenience just now,' he had to write, and his pride suffered acutely as he did so.

He felt very low about *Henry Brocken* – 'a dismal and complete failure' – and sighed: 'One cherishes absurd hopes on the slenderest of foundations.' While his pen had scratched away at it in the grim nocturnal office, he had half believed that what he was writing might rid him of the detestable Oil life. The three pounds sixteen shillings owing to Murray's sat heavily on his shoulders, and other small relentless sums made their quarterly demands, to be discussed in tones of weary urgency. Elfie was an excellent manager of the household, working tirelessly to preserve whatever small graces of living she could, since they mattered so much to Jack. But she was always tired out, tied by the children, with no energy to go anywhere with him on his rare evenings out. The best pleasures were those the whole family could share together and at no expense. Their suburb had less to offer than Woolwich in the 1870s; yet it was still a long way from the impersonality of its modern counterparts, and there were ways in which de la Mare could recreate for his children the intensity of his own first memories.

Not far west of the little glassed-in nurseryman's shop that they patronised for penny pansy clumps, the real countryside began. At West Wickham there were bluebells. Two stops along the railway, with a picnic basket, they could forget London entirely for a day. Much nearer home, they could still find an old man breaking flints – macadam had not yet reached Mackenzie Road – and the crossing sweepers still worked their pitches. Sometimes past their door came the shambling shabby wonder of a dancing bear; and in May the Jack-in-the-Green, festooned in sprigs and leaves, capered by with his procession as he had done since medieval England.

Newbolt was still hopeful that de la Mare could produce a book of 'adult' poems, and under this encouragement he wrote on, privately making real headway. In the autumn of 1905 he took to dating drafts, in a black notebook. There are a great many entries – quite often two in a day – and here and there one of his best. 'Alone' ('A very old woman lives in yon house') was written now, as well as another from *The Listeners* volume, 'There blooms no bud in May'. One small one waited until 1950 to find a place at last, in *Inward Companion*. Reading it there – 'Here I sit, and glad am I / So to sit contentedly' – one expects it to be a poem of a placid old-age mood, nor would guess it belonged to this early winter of hope deferred. On the pages of the black notebook, the verses are crammed together in tiny writing, sometimes several side by side, as if economy had become an obsession. In fact, de la Mare never came to like the inhibiting self-important look of blank sheets, preferring always to write on the back of an old envelope or the wrapper-band of a packet of new ones.

He was working so late at the office – not reaching home until after nine at night at this period – that most of these 1905 poems must have been composed around midnight. Later on, he would hold that one kind of work all day is a good preparation for another shelf of the mind to come into use at night. But the late hours made prose impossible, and he neither wrote nor published stories for some while after the *Monthly Review* took its final contribution from him.

This story, 'An Ideal Craftsman', was already worlds away from the opiate bookishness of *Henry Brocken*. At last, de la Mare had become skilful enough to bring off successfully a tale of violence and the sordid detail of murder that had always fascinated him, particularly as contrasted with the child's-eye view of the matter. His grasp of child psychology and growing skill in narration make his unemotional small 'craftsman' just credible, and completely absorbing to the imagination, as he helps to string up the corpse of the hated butler to look like a suicide:*

> He skipped hither and thither, now on to, now off the kitchen chair he had pushed nearer; then – having swept back the array of pink-smeared silver candlesticks and snuffers that were in his way – he scrambled up on to the table, and presently, after a few lassoo-like flings of it, he had run the rope and made it fast over one of a few large hooks that curved down from the ceiling ... His mouth was set, his face intent; his soldier

* 'An Ideal Craftsman' had an odd, laborious history before it reached its final form. When Forrest Reid published his full-length critical study of de la Mare's work in 1929, he picked out this tale for special praise, and was keen that it should be collected. De la Mare was by this time dissatisfied with the version that had appeared in the *Monthly Review* but lacked the impulse to alter it. To urge him on, Forrest Reid revised it himself, preparing a new version; and this (as he had known it would) at once set de la Mare correcting the revision. Finally he prepared a new version himself, so heavily revised in places as to be virtually a new story. The manuscript passed to and fro between him and Reid about half-a-dozen times before it came out finally in *On the Edge* (1930).

grandfather's lower lip drawn in under the upper. The more active he was the more completely he became master of the ceremonies, the woman only an insignificant accomplice ...

In November 1905, Roger Ingpen secured for de la Mare, through J. H. Lobban, editor of the *Bookman*, his first assignment as a reviewer. The first parcel was an eclectic assortment of authors: Samuel Smiles, Laurence Housman and A. C. Benson. Smiles was the guide de la Mare chose for a boy named Fred Atha, who around this time began to share his desk in the Oil office, and whose horizons de la Mare set himself to enlarge – very successfully. When Atha first arrived his surreptitious reading (under the eye of the hated managed on his dais) was the *Boy's Own Paper*; de la Mare gave him Smiles's *Self-Help*, and encouraged him to better himself. He would talk to him, describing the London of Johnson and Dickens, recommending biographies and histories, and firing the boy with his own enthusiasms – so much that Fred got into trouble at home for spending his dinner-pennies on the bookstalls in Victoria Street and the Strand. In his first gift to this earnest young disciple, de la Mare wrote on the flyleaf:

> Success awhile the heart beguiles
> But – mingle laughter with your Smiles.

Atha, who would often help de la Mare by running small errands with packages for the post, did not know much about his office neighbour's literary work (de la Mare spoke vaguely of 'little essays') until one day de la Mare remarked: 'Do you want a nice book to read? Well, read one called *Henry Brocken*.' Atha was amazed on reaching the bookshop to find his friend's name on the cover.

Together de la Mare and Atha slaved at the immensely detailed monthly working reports for the New York office, on sheets two feet across and a foot high. They would do half a sheet each, thick with hundreds of figures carried to four points of the decimal, and would check each other's work for mistakes. Atha said he never found any in de la Mare's. The hectograph jellied ink was extremely easy to smudge, and once a jog of Atha's arm spoiled one of de la Mare's. He got no impatient exclamation, only a mild 'Never mind, Fred; I'll stay late and rewrite it'. The hero-worship of the boy and his eagerness to learn were some comfort to de la Mare, and he would take time off whenever possible for murmured discussions and arguments. Atha remembered his impressing one thing upon him: 'Never destroy anyone's belief – you can do harm. Even if he is an atheist, don't break down the principles on which he builds his life. Something may show him later, but don't take away any belief.' Usually de la Mare's advice was much less easy to be certain of. He would argue against whatever point of view was taken up by the boy, till solemn young Fred would become confused and annoyed – because it was plain that today's argument directly controverted yesterday's. Atha would protest: 'What *am* I to believe?' and would get only an ironical smile for answer, which made him doubt he had got a proper grip on anything.

The influence of their murmured discussions remained long after de la Mare had left. Later in life Atha became a lay reader, alongside his profession of chartered accountancy, and he felt he owed the highest things in his experience to the man he called 'Wolter'. Once, thirty years later, the two of them met again and talked of religion. When Atha had set out his ideas on the after-life de la Mare said simply and gently, 'I believe the same' – the first time, Atha thought, that de la Mare had ever agreed with him.

One impression Atha kept vividly: de la Mare's punctiliously formal City dress in those office days: silk hat, tails, and striped trousers. Bert on his visits to the office from the Bank of England wore the same, but it was not customary for Oil employees, and indeed a silk hat was really reserved for ranks higher than de la Mare ever attained. Perhaps his assumption of it was tolerated because of his very long service. Certainly Atha noticed that the usually hectoring office manager treated de la Mare with some respect, and left him alone. The hat was most likely a symbolic gesture of defiant self-respect against his despised Yankee employers.

At last, in November 1905, Newbolt put aside his fears that Murray might refuse the book of adult poems, and urged them strongly upon him as 'the real thing'. Pinker had probably been telling Newbolt more of de la Mare's financial position, for Newbolt now set to work in earnest to find 'some better way of using your brains than in adding up Rockefeller's ill-gotten gains'. He suggested that though it was a precarious security, to become a private secretary seemed the most likely opening. He asked de la Mare outright what was his present salary, and his reply was '£143 a year; which *may* be increased to £160 in January. This, however, is very doubtful.' De la Mare continued:

Anything beyond this sum 'with prospects' would be a greater relief than I can say. It is the future that is so daunting. And only a forlorn hope in writing and a reluctance to surrender 15 years service here kept me from attempting a move before. But things daily grow worse; and to get free of the Company and all its wicked and mean ways would be freedom indeed.[37]

Murray proved more interested in the poems than Newbolt had feared. Just before Christmas 1905 he decided he would publish them; but he would only risk an edition of 500 copies, and he added a cautionary note – no doubt recalling the little bill still unpaid on *Henry Brocken* – that he hoped proof-corrections could be kept to a minimum.

Newbolt had strong ideas about the constitution of the book; all he had himself published in the *Monthly Review* should go in first, and about as much again of new work should follow. De la Mare was pleased at the acceptance, but not so elated as on earlier occasions: ' ... it does in a way *postpone* Henry Brocken's failure doesn't it? And though this is likely to do little better it may possibly repay its cost.'[38]

The only week's holiday de la Mare could afford during 1905 he took in November, and at home. He signed a Christmas ballad for a competition in the *Westminster Gazette* 'F.M.S.', which he told Newbolt was 'For Mercy's Sake'. The prayer succeeded, and he won the prize.

7

Edward Thomas

'It is an abominable experience – fathering books – they are little else but thorns in the flesh from infancy. Whereas children – one enjoys their very few for the flowers between.'[1] So wrote de la Mare to Newbolt, and soon he had a fourfold right to this opinion. By January 1906 he had another son, Colin: the last child, dark and with a strong resemblance to his father. Meanwhile the thornier kind of offspring was being discussed at the Newbolts' at Earl's Terrace. This time there were no Rowley children round a table, sorting rhymes into piles. In their place was 'The Settee', the foursome of the Newbolts and Ella Coltman and Mary Coleridge which had formed, long ago, the habit of meeting weekly over Margaret's blue and white teacups for a 'book talk', to read aloud whatever Mary or Harry had written since the last session. The Settee had borne fruit in four published novels, while Ella particularly, though she did not write herself, was an excellent audience for work in progress. This time the Settee were warmly convinced they were dealing with one of England's lyric geniuses.

Poems 1906 was to be de la Mare's first serious book of poetry, and the Settee, highminded themselves and anxious that he should make his bow as a poet of worth, perhaps selected rather heavily from those poems which consider human life in large general terms, express ideals and use capitalised personifications. Their choice included a good many sonnets, and this verse-form gives his thought a sober, straight-ahead gait which is a little foreign to him. Later, he abandoned sonneteering altogether.

There is a wistful one among these sonnets, 'Winter Coming', which must have sent a pang into Elfie's heart, tender though the tone of its sadness is. It begins: 'O, thou art like an autumn to my days', and ends:

> And all the wonder now hath left my eyes
> And all my heart sinks to remember how
>   Once, once we loved, we who are grown so wise –
>   Youth vanished, winter coming – I and thou![2]

Though he puts himself alongside her in the poem, the physical difference in their ages was growing more marked. In the photographs of a few years on, Elfie comes to look more like a mother to him than a wife.

De la Mare kept a page of Mary Coleridge's notes on the manuscripts of his poems; she loved best the Shakespeare Characters, the childhood poems and a number of the sonnets. ' "Omniscience" I cannot understand, though I have tried again and again. You see I give you just all the worst of my stupidity ... In "Echo" I cannot stand the word "bawled": it makes a most dreadful noise.'[3] She herself suggested the last line of 'England' ('And thine my darkness be'). There was a poem about a robin. De la Mare always saw this little bird as a flitting eerie presence – here 'Perched in his coat of blood'. Mary for once was unperceptive. The very thing that was original in his view of a robin she rejected: ' ... at his heel won't do. One never thinks of a robin's heel ... The thing fascinates me, but it's an elf-robin, none of the robins that I know.'[4] De la Mare laid the poem aside and did not put it in a collection[5] for another twenty-seven years – and then evidently rewritten from the version Mary saw. But he had wisely kept his 'changeling and solitary' view of the bird. And even at the time, he had replied firmly, 'All robins *must* be elf-robins.' When *Poems 1906* came out, Mary was passionately partisan about the book, and sent de la Mare lists of particular favourites half as long as the contents page.

Newbolt's Liberal friends came to power at the close of 1906, and Sir Edward Grey, the closest to him and with a deep love of letters, became Foreign Secretary under Campbell-Bannerman as Prime Minister. Within three months, Newbolt asked de la Mare for details of any commercial qualifications he had, preparing to move Grey in the matter of his plight. De la Mare replied:

> I am 33 in April. During the last eight or nine years I have been engaged on Statistical work – preparing averages and statements of costs. This, I know, means only a very limited and rudimentary commercial knowledge and experience. But here one is simply a cog in a vast mechanical wheel. I think I can say I am quick and accurate at such figuring and *can work hard and protractedly*.
> I don't expect! But if you only knew how much I hope! ...
> Rockefellers dead or dying* make little difference – the whole *organization* is carnivorous.[6]

In July help was enlisted from an old friend of Mary Coleridge's, Mrs

---

* Newbolt had asked if 'this reputed illness of the two Rockefellers' affected his chances.

Wedgwood, whose husband Josiah was a Member of Parliament. They invited de la Mare and the Newbolts to tea on the House of Commons Terrace to meet one Sir Henry Cunningham. He was 'very attentive and interested', de la Mare reported, 'but he saw what I see plainly how rare commercial posts are for not rare qualifications.' By never budging from his department at Oil, de la Mare had gained in fifteen years only the narrowest possible experience of business matters.

Meanwhile Ella Coltman was doing her best to help him in practical ways. She took him and his family under her wing with a crisp, godmotherly thoroughness. She worried about the drains at their house, and their health, and de la Mare's dangerous interests in strange states of mind; she wanted to give him St Augustine's *Confessions* to warn him off astrologers and necromancers. She looked up railway timetables for excursions, which she planned to the last detail. Her sister Anna and a friend shared a holiday cottage, Spyfield Shaws, at Hartfield near Tunbridge Wells, and here, in the summer of 1906, the de la Mare children had their first country holiday. De la Mare spent a brief week with them there, to install the family, and then returned to work, lodging with Roger and going back to see Elfie and the children (when he could afford the fare) at weekends. This became the pattern of the family's holidays for several years. He reported to Ella 'how much I enjoyed my week ... the solitude and silence and the innumerable endless woods'. As usual, he managed to extract what he needed – the forest solitude and the children's joy – from a mass of household frets attendant on the family's now desperate finances.

In the autumn of 1906 they had to abandon the Mackenzie Road house for a cramped slip of a flat in a tiny ugly villa in Samos Road, in the neighbouring suburb of Anerley. Elfie was bravely hopeful about this move in writing to de la Mare, but she was harassed and strained. Meanwhile, as always, she and he fell prey to chronic, wildly exaggerated anxiety whenever any of the children had the smallest ailment. Nor was it a time of peace between the two parents; Elfie clung to de la Mare in whatever storms beset her, large or small, with an anxious intensity that was exhausting to irritable nerves; and he himself cannot have been easy company. She found it more and more impossible not to compare herself distrustfully with women younger than herself, less tired and worn by chores. Nor could de la Mare help responding, on every occasion, to feminine sympathy and grace. He was very attractive, and his intense curiosity about the other person's reactions and secret self opened an immediate door to intimate friendship – especially with women. He himself would remain elusive, but they could not doubt the warmth of his interest in them; and he was the more uninhibited in expressing this, and in making clear his admiration for attractive looks, because there was on his side so little of the physical involved. A man so made may innocently lay siege more directly than one who knows the fundamental attraction to be sexual, and is warier of involvement for that reason. One of de la Mare's temperament cannot see there is any harm in romantic friendship as unhesitating and intense as a child's, and he was always surprised and annoyed when this led to complaints and misunderstandings.

Yet both he and Elfie, in different ways, still strongly supported the other against buffets of fate, and they were deeply united in their passionate devotion to the children. Nor could many husbands have been more domesticated than Jack; he could change a baby's nappies and bake a cake, and took an intimate interest in the home – the arrangement of the furniture, the food, the children's upbringing. This in turn made Elfie the more dependent on his presence, his pleasure, and his interest in every detail. This was what she lived for.

Yet his home could not, in the nature of things, supply him with what he needed so desperately – relaxation and stimulus. Elfie had not the strength of mind to conquer the psychological disadvantage of her age, and she showed jealousy (sometimes reasonable, sometimes silly), so that he grew exasperated. Though their relationship held together till the end, and never lost its note of compassion and protective loyalty, it became over the next years a jarred and unhappy one.

Only a few friends of de la Mare's were perceptive enough to take in Elfie's qualities, and to notice her humour and innocence, and her readiness to fall in with de la Mare's own vision of the passing scene. Her imagination certainly responded to his. In her headlong letters – one day childishly distrustful, the next as childlike in total commitment to de la Mare's hopes and dreams – she put herself on a level with the children, all five of them together looking to their protector; and in his he came to address a composite person – 'Fridy'-and-the-children (sometimes addressed as 'Mr Fives'), an object of devotion for whom, whatever his ruffled temper, no sacrifice was too great.

Alone in London while the family was on holiday, he had more peace for work. 'I wrote nearly *two stories* today,' he told Elfie in September 1906. 'Fancy a baker's dozen in a week, at ten g[uinea]s each – £136.10.0 at the end of October we'll buy a cottage or two, by January a bijou in Park Lane. Won't we be rich! And wretched!'[7] Then in answer to a torrent of fuss from Elfie, on 11 September:

If I could afford it I *would* come down on Saturday – but it's no use wishing. I went into the house last night and I really don't think we shall regret leaving it a bit. It *smells* disastrous; tho' it has only been not *trivially* fortunate. Let the children but be well, we'll easily win through.

Mind *fire*; and Jinny and Colly the wasps ... and please Ma'am there's the hammock; and the temperature's very variable at evening now ... All take care of one another and 'Your very good health Mr Fives!

The slightest relaxing of pressure at the office was enough to send up his spirits and energy – before the family were back he had written four stories, not counting a fairy tale, and a book review, and was jubilant. 'You see we shall float, then we shall swim, and then your poor bard will get cramp and–! I really sometimes smile rather distantly and am afraid so. Still float first ...' This was on the 13th.

This month they began six months in the miserable flat in Samos Road. In Florence's memory, this was the lowest point in all their fortunes. Elfie's health soon gave way. One day while Florence stood drearily humming and buzzing to herself, jogging her lips against the mean glass-panelled door in the passage, the daily maid dismayed her horribly by exclaiming as she came running at the unhappy sound: 'I thought it was your mother dying!' Dick could remember emptying his money-box of pennies for his father when there was nothing else in the house, and de la Mare would go without lunch, getting through his nearly twelve-hour office day on only a piece of chocolate.

But as usual he put a good face on things to Newbolt, to whom he had dedicated *Poems 1906*, only saying that they were glad to leave their old home, and of the book: 'The worst is I am responsible for every inclusion while you and Miss Coleridge have all the secret glory of what has been left out.'[8] Newbolt was now trying to get him a place going as a publisher's reader at Constable's, for two hundred pounds a year. Hope blazed up at Samos Road – like light in a cave, de la Mare said – but for nothing.

Poems 1906 won letters of praise again, from St Loe Strachey, Scott-Holland, and de la Mare's old headmaster, who wrote: 'Your apparent powers take my breath away.' Strong personal support from a number of good judges, long years before the reviewers became generally enthusiastic, must have been a great encouragement, and one that does not always come the way of a struggling beginner. Alice Meynell wrote: 'I cannot think that anything I say in homage is worthy of work so distinguished and so beautiful.'[9] Reviews were mixed – bad, patronising and good. Edward Thomas, however, whose admiration for *Songs of Childhood* had grown since his original notice of it, took this opportunity to strike up an acquaintance.

He wrote to de la Mare in October 1906:

> May I use one of the poems from your new book in my anthology if at the
> last moment I can make room? I thought of 'Keep Innocency'. I like the
> book enormously and one or two papers will be good enough to let me say
> so, though I had not the space I could have wished. I only grumble at
> your 'ev'n' instead of 'even' and so on, especially as it did not seem to be
> needed by the rhythm.[10]

Thomas reviewed the book well in the *Daily Chronicle*, and when de la
Mare thanked him he wrote again on 14 November:

> I was very glad to have your letter this morning. You are the only man I
> do not know who has ever written to me about my reviews and knowing
> your work I cannot but be happy. And yet I feel that even I could do so
> much better – about your book, for example – if only I had time. My
> article was only a hasty review: I had not time to order or make clear the
> thoughts and emotions your 'Poems' suggested. But to have pleased you
> is everything and to talk like this is only vanity.[11]

All de la Mare's side of the prolific correspondence that followed has
vanished. Thomas's wife Helen remembered a day-long bonfire before
Edward left for the front in 1917, in which he destroyed quantities of
private letters, these probably among them.

Thomas was five years younger than de la Mare; he had married
very young and depended on hack-work and journalism for an
exiguous living. He and Helen had two children, and were even worse
off than the de la Mares. At times they existed on kippers and tea. But
Thomas set himself at once to help de la Mare and was as good as his
promise when he said (in a letter) 'no doubt I can do you whatever
service praise may be'.[12] He had made a name for his judgment as a
critic. 'Worth all the rest,' Newbolt said, adding: 'It is a real score to
have pleased him.' Indeed de la Mare's reputation over the next few
years owed its gradual increase as much to Thomas's constant
advocacy, private and public, as to any other kind of help.

Mary Coleridge and Henry Newbolt, meanwhile, were both enjoying
success with new novels, and she wrote to him: 'It makes me sad and
ashamed to think of de la Mare. Why, why, *why* don't they understand.
I felt such dreadful, gentle, mournful discouragement in him, the last
time he came. What can be done?'[13]

*

Edward Thomas took the initiative in friendship, inviting de la Mare
and Elfie for Easter 1907 to his home in Hampshire. But of course they
would not leave the children; and in the end the two men's first

meeting was in the City. De la Mare described the occasion in his
foreword to Thomas's *Collected Poems*. Memory made it 'one still, blue,
darkening summer evening', but it was in fact mid-March. De la Mare
was the first to reach the meeting-place, a 'Mecca' café in St George's
Yard, and (so his memoir related)

> presently out of a neighbouring court echoed that peculiarly leisurely
> footfall ... Gulliver himself could hardly have looked a stranger
> phenomenon in Lilliput than he appeared in Real-Turtle-Soup-Land –
> his clothes, his gait, his face, his bearing. We sat and talked, the dams
> down, in a stale underground city café, until the tactful waitresses piled
> chairs on the marble-topped tables around us as a tacit hint that we
> should soon be outstaying our welcome ...
>
> His face was fair, long and rather narrow, and in its customary gravity
> wore an expression rather distant and detached. There was a glint of
> gold in his sun-baked hair. The eyes, long-lashed and stooping a little
> beneath the full rounded lids, were of a clear, dark blue ... The lips were
> finely lined and wide, the chin square ... The hands that had cradled so
> many wild birds' eggs, and were familiar with every flower in the
> Southern Counties, were powerful and bony; the gestures few; the frame
> vigorous ... His smile could be whimsical, stealthy, sly, ardent, mocking
> or drily ironical; he seldom laughed ... His voice was low and gentle, but
> musical, with a curious sweetness and hollowness when he sang his old
> Welsh songs to his children. I have never heard English used so
> fastidiously and yet so unaffectedly as in his talk. *Style* in talk, indeed, is
> a rare charm; and it was his. You could listen to it for its own sake ...
> Nobody in this world closely resembling him have I ever had the
> happiness to meet.

Thomas sent his own first impressions of de la Mare to Gordon
Bottomley:

> I have made friends with Walter de la Mare. You would like him – a
> subtle, honest person – an accountant in the City (and a clever one, I
> hear) but rather willing to leave it if he saw a way that would not hurt his
> wife and 4 children – 34 years old – handsome like young Dickens but
> short and his eyes too small – finally he has the foible of liking my
> reviews and (I fear) preferring them to my landscapes and people who
> seem to him from a different hand from the Chronicle reviewer's, which
> annoys me.[14]

Meanwhile de la Mare came to know a poet friend of Roger Ingpen's,
living not far from Samos Road, John Freeman, who like himself was
in business – a great deal more successfully than de la Mare. He had
begun as an office-boy at thirteen, and became in time the Secretary of
his insurance company, the Liverpool Victoria. Like de la Mare, he
would come home at the end of an eight- or nine-hour working day in

the City to write verses late into the night. He was also a copious correspondent and very well read. Tall, gangling, ugly, solemn, punctilious, there was in him an endearing quality about these very attributes; Edward Thomas referred to him as 'a kind of angel', and de la Mare, after his death, described even his physical appearance in phrasees that suggest beauty – 'beautiful brows' and ruminative eyes 'of a peculiarly ardent blue'.[15]

Freeman had 'a slow condensed chuckle', sometimes quickeniing into an outright fit of the giggles. He had a taste for literary gossip, and declared that letters should be egotistical and self-revealing, and that 'No man should dare to write below his best'. His own are ceremoniously playful, intelligent, reserved (as de la Mare noted) abaout 'first and last things'. On occasion he was a shrewd critic of de la Mare's work, and in return he relied on his friend's encouragement for his own unobtrusive poetry, which made its way very slowly. Some of Freeman's best work arose out of his love of English trees, and of children – especially (in this last) the mysterious and lovely poem 'The Pigeons'. De la Mare had a disproportionately high opinion of his verse, and championed it on every possible occasion. He was soon pressing it upon Newbolt and Thomas.

He and Freeman saw a good deal of each other, and their friendship lasted warmly till Freeman's early death in 1929. It soon became a friendship that included their families – Freeman had two small daughters – and de la Mare would often walk the few streets between their houses for coffee or 'chop at seven'. The two men came to share many poet friends – Hodgson, Thomas and W. H. Davies among them.

By the spring of 1907 de la Mare had written another of his very best stories of childhood, 'Miss Duveen', and sent it to Newbolt and Ella Coltman to read. The child in it, Arthur, comes very close to de la Mare's own remembered self, with his acute powers of observation and his ambivalent feelings of compassion, detachment, repulsion and curiosity – the same feelings with which Jack had watched the small creature being buried alive in the sandcastle at Ventnor. Miss Duveen, too, is in a way buried alive: that is, she is a spinster a little astray in her wits, with a 'keeper' to fear. Her home has a garden running down to the little river Wandle, directly opposite to the garden of Arthur's grandmother, and Miss Duveen and her tragedy are seen through the small boy's eyes during their surreptitious encounters. She fascinates and embarrasses him; her crooked, disjointed view of life's predicament – which perplexes her as much as it does him – penetrates essential truth now and then, just as the child's does, she from her side of the water, he from his. Just as de la Mare poured into 'The Almond

Tree' the essence of childhood's sense of winter, so into 'Miss Duveen' he distilled the hot, summery inactivity and the scenery characteristic of the Wandsworth edge of London as he had known it. The brook-sized Wandle and its tiny overgrown gardens are all heightened, expanded, pressed full of meaning. He repeated the figure of the eccentric spinster over and over but never caught her more justly, her truth unspoiled here by whimsical over-elaborations. Miss Duveen belongs with the best of her sisters in the poems 'Miss Loo' and the 'very old woman' of 'Alone' from *The Listeners*.

But this kind of psychological interest – the tone and atmosphere which are the essence of such a story – had yet to create its own public. Even the editor of the *Cornhill* (no longer Strachey) replied: 'Attractive as are all things by the river Wandle, I am afraid I must consider … Miss Duveen too painful for my pages.'[16]

At midsummer 1907 the family were thankfully able to leave what de la Mare could now admit was 'the horrible little flat' in Samos Road for a home not a great deal bigger, but much more pleasant, in Worbeck Road, Anerley, a few streets off. It seemed to him 'a friendly little house and squats and looks'.[17] He particularly liked the view through the garden door keyhole, 'like a long little emerald door into fairyland'. It led from a minute room on to a small balcony and a flight of wooden steps above the narrow green bowery garden with ten apple, pear and plum trees in it. At the edge of the grass stood one apple-tree so bountiful that de la Mare gave it a persona in family talk: 'Tom Fifty Puddings.' This garden is 'The Little Green Orchard' of *Peacock Pie*. For some reason the children christened it 'Tim and Bill's Orchard', and for them it was certainly tenanted. De la Mare himself had hopes of a ghost, which on one occasion he seems to have supplied in person. It was a curious incident, and perhaps one seed of his later tale 'The Recluse'. His sister Flo had come alone one evening to call on him at Worbeck Road; the light was shining in the house, but she got no answer. She looked through the letter-box and could see down the passage into the sitting-room. There, plainly visible, was Jack's figure in his armchair, deeply asleep or unconscious. Her knocking did not rouse him, and, disturbed, she hurried home to get help to break in. On her way she met her daughter Ethel, who had been spending the evening with Poppy at the Ingpens' house. Flo told her tale, but Ethel replied that Jack had been the whole evening with them! Then she remembered that he had, at one moment, suddenly declared: 'I can see myself sitting at home', and had gone on to describe the scene Flo had witnessed through the letterbox.

De la Mare stayed by himself in the new home through August 1907,

joining the family at weekends at a Dorking farmhouse, 'Taylors', lent
to them for the holiday by Mrs Josiah Wedgwood. The children had a
time of joy, with a swing in a barn as big as a church and a pond in
which to fish for tench, while their parents wasted it in exchanging
cross and extremely childish letters, de la Mare harping on every detail
that he knew would most inflame Elfie's anxiety (such as his
uncared-for loneliness at home), she fluttering at country noises in the
night, lamenting the milk bills, and finding cause for jealousies. They
even tiffed about which had written most often, at greatest length, and
with least leisure to spare! Between-whiles they made up, promptly
and warmly. And Elfie was as staunch as ever in what really mattered:
'If I were you,' she wrote to him, 'I should be so proud of being seen in
my own company that I am afraid I might come to the same end as the
frog. And I do honestly tell you, you are "not dead" but more alive than
ever you were, for the time is coming near for the great event, and I do
believe that is your restlessness ... Well you will see soon and not be
disappointed.'[18]

During the holiday the de la Mares at 'Taylors' learned, stunned,
what had befallen the Coleridges at Harrogate: Mary had died of
appendicitis. Only two or three weeks earlier she had come out to
Worbeck Road for a long afternoon's talk, and de la Mare had just
lately sent her 'The Almond Tree'. She had reported to a friend: 'I feel
much happier about him. The over-excitement there was in the winter
is almost gone ... His story 'The Almond Tree' is *most* beautiful;
wonderfully beautiful.'

For their part the Newbolts were house-moving from Kensington to
Wiltshire when Mary's death struck. Henry Furse, widowed sculptor
brother of the painter Charles Furse, was making a bust of Margaret;
he had taken a lease of Netherhampton House, close to Wilton and a
few miles west of Salisbury, and now he impulsively invited the
Newbolts to share it with him and his undergraduate son. Equally
impulsively, they accepted, as an experiment – and they stayed there
for the next twenty-seven years.[19]

Newbolt begged de la Mare to write about Mary for the *Guardian*,
feeling he was closer in spirit to her than anyone else; and to many of
Mary's friends his tribute (published in September) did come closest to
her quality: her subtlety, unusualness, and what he called her
'impenetrable innocence' – a sort of transparency behind which a great
deal 'lay not concealed, but too clear and bright, perhaps, for complete
recognition'. But he wrote diffidently, constrained by desperate fears of
seeming to presume, and composed his phrases with elaborate care.[20]

He felt that with Mary Coleridge's death some essential clue to life had been lost, and he wrote to Ella Coltman of his grief and bewilderment:

> I cannot value her friendship now more than I ever did. There was no question of it to me at any time. It was just one of the few precious and unique things life has. I remember her saying that one remembers so strangely the *eyes* of a friend. And hers – who could forget them? ...
> I never can realize death. I simply don't understand it. One *has* to let it pass and take somehow memory for all, instead.[21]

In his tribute he spoke of 'a kind of profound impatience' kindling at the realisation she was gone.

Ella pounced on the influence which had so clogged his style in the tribute. She regretted, with reason, that 'de la M's prose style is not quite as simple and perfect as it was ... the reason is his over-admiration just now for H. James – who has a baneful influence on so many writers *I* think – the clever original writers I mean ... I don't want him to let his style develope along that track – and I think I shall say something some day unless you disagree with me.'[22]

In actual fact de la Mare's admiration for James, even at this date, was something he was in two minds about. In a letter to Ella a few weeks later he was saying:

> I have read the Mirror (of the Sea) – Conrad *is* genius – Nostromo! I don't exactly *like* Henry James, certainly not always – though one almost has to in The Two Magics.* But his inheritance is so enormous. His is a monopoly too of an extraordinary kind: though I don't know one book of his to weigh against a Turgenev.[23]

Admirations often have not the slightest influence on a writer's own work. Conrad, whose fiction de la Mare so ardently loved, had a range too much outside his own to affect it at all, but there are touches of Turgenev in his early simpler fiction, when he is writing directly of human life and love – a quality lost as he grew into the elaborate articulateness he learned from James. He borrowed the long qualifications, the piling of nuance upon nuance, and James's trick of taking a commonplace phrase (or even a cliché) and, with an 'as it were', holding it deliberately to attention. Certainly James's influence worked its way deep, and lasted. It was a pity, as Ella Coltman saw, though the winding, cumulative method showed him the way to bring off stories of great subtlety. More important, he learned to use sinister supernatural effects, as in 'Seaton's Aunt', with James's economy of event. So often in stories of the uncanny the preparation frightens, but

---

* The volume containing 'The Turn of the Screw' and 'Covering End'.

the actual appearance of what horrified in anticipation comes as an anticlimax comparatively bathetic or banal. After de la Mare's enthusiasm for James's novels had palled, he still kept it for 'The Turn of the Screw', 'The Altar of the Dead' and one or two other of James's shorter works which use the supernatural with this fine discretion.

His letters to Ella Coltman and to others around this time make more and more mention of the four children at Worbeck Road. They were gentle, imaginative, delightful; their father might well have invented them. He loved them with an intense solicitude – so much that the Thomases (when later on the families shad outings) would swear that a thermometer was always included in the de la Mare picnic basket, and that Jack, when he was only going out to post a letter, would run upstairs and kiss them all goodbye. When Dick was unwell, his father shared his room. About five o'clock one morning Dick woke him to whisper that he was frightened by a curtain that looked like a polar bear.

> He then went on [de la Mare told Ella], and in the most odd faraway fashion half asleep I conversed with him on sun moon and stars; mathematics, physics, everything that came into his head. It was just as if we were talking across a rather dim river – and I couldn't see his bank![24]

Once, seeking to reassure Dick about the polar bear – this time laired under his bed – he expostulated: 'But Dickie, it isn't a *real* polar bear', to which Dick, who was physically a courageous little boy, replied acutely: 'I know, Daddy – that's the trouble.'

Watching the children now, at what seemed to him the peak of their life, he could only mourn with a kind of incredulity that they would ever grow up. He was telling the elder three of ships and sailors and the perils of the deep, and Florence (eight in 1907) at last asked which was the *safest* of all the things a man might be. ' "O," I said, in one's delicious adult magnanimous way, "to be brave". "No," she said mysteriously, "the safest of all?" And then with extreme and confidential assurance, "Why, to be a poet." '

The safety was not much apparent to her father. Murray's account of *Poems 1906*, when passed on to Pinker in the autumn of 1907, could hardly be worse; they had done no better than *Henry Brocken*. Meanwhile overwork at the Oil office was making new efforts impossible for de la Mare. To Ella he wrote: 'You know how kind it is of you to try and keep the verses alive. But I feel that both books *are* dead and that they are just getting far enough away to enable me to see why and to pretend not to mind.'[25]

*

During 1908 he and Edward Thomas became intimate enough for Thomas to confide his personal problems – his struggle with suicidal depression, and even his brief current infatuation with a girl of seventeen. In de la Mare, on the other hand, there was always an instinct against self-revelation, something (for all his warm loyalties and devoted affections) a little elusive. He was not aware of this himself, and certainly did not intend any reserve towards Thomas. But even for the closest friends there could be a hesitation not easy to define when answering the question: 'Do you know de la Mare very well?' One could know his *company* very well, could love all one knew, and yet feel that he kept some great fastness to one side which it did not occur to him to invite one to visit. 'Reserved' does not describe him at all; he was far too responsive. But some essential solitude, not willed, was one of the terms of his friendship.

At the time that Thomas confided his involvement with the girl, he was at Dunwich, on the coast near de la Mare's beloved Southwold. Dunwich graveyard, dramatically perched above the encroaching tide, and tumbling stray bones daily on to the beach below, figured vividly in Thomas's long letters. Instantly agog (as intended), de la Mare commissioned him to purloin him a skull. He called it Moses, and hoarded it so long, in a decorated box with a moulded lid, that this domestic interment acquired a half-serious importance in his eyes. At eighty-two (the year before he died) he fetched it out to show Laurence Whistler. The box was by then festooned in cobwebs. But when his nurse-companion lifted the lid and Whistler light-heartedly tapped the dark cranium, they were vigorously told off. De la Mare protested that it ought not to have been disturbed – it might crumble to pieces – besides they were wanting in proper respect. In his eyes, it had been decently laid to rest: the box had not been opened for years and years and so on. He was really ruffled, on the edge of anger.

By January 1908 more than a year had elapsed since de la Mare had been brought to Lord Grey's notice. At the time Newbolt had given him *Brocken* and *Poems* for Christmas holiday reading, and these had won him to Newbolt's own high opinion. Since then Grey had made efforts to bring de la Mare to the Prime Minister's notice as a candidate for a Civil List pension. But the wheels turned slowly, and only now with Asquith Prime Minister (instead of Campbell-Bannerman) did Grey's efforts result in a letter to Newbolt from the Prime Minister's office, inviting formal application for a pension. Newbolt was told that his own verdict on de la Mare's ability would suffice without other references. In passing on all this news Newbolt played down de la Mare's chances, for fear of once more raising delusory hopes. He even reported the dampening remark of the Prime Minister's secretary: 'It is not as a rule productive of further good work to pension men while they are young.' Newbolt concluded by asking de la Mare for the personal details required by formal application.[26]

His letter came as a bombshell. De la Mare had not in the least realised Newbolt's objective this past eighteen months. The rough draft of his reply (Newbolt evidently destroyed the actual letter) shows his perturbation – partly a sensitive hesitation over accepting public money, partly a secret worry aroused by the demand for 'personal details':

My dear Newbolt,
    Your letter is a complete surprise to me. It never occurred to me to think when we have talked the matter over together that you had any thought of an application for a pension. I have only continued to hope that it might be possible to obtain a post or apptmt. by your influence where I might still work hard but where the literary side of me might have a little more scope and freedom than in Oil. I feel quite sincerely in compar. with any other that I have done nothing to deserve such recognition; that the little I have done has been only & all through a selfish labour of love. However I feel that I am still not old and ought to be able to win through into quieter waters by writing a little less capriciously and by reviewing and so on. It would be indolence and want of courage not to do so. And yet on the other hand should I be justified in allowing such feelings which are at any rate entirely personal and partly perhaps sentimental to be any obstacle to what would be an immense help and an immense relief of a galling burden to us both and better still of so much service to the children in the future. I am sure you will enter into my thoughts. It would be in a way accepting a gift, acknowledging a claim, receiving payment for what never asked for any except what itself might bring. It seems work and never hint of Finis. You will understand.
    But besides this which I am convinced should not weigh too heavily on my mind, there is one other thing which very probably if told you sooner [sic] have made all this preamble unnecessary. I hoped never to have need to mention it: but in the circumstances feel it obligatory. You know I think of one of my brothers, as good a brother as ever a man had – but I have never spoken of my eldest brother Arthur.
    He long ago gave up our home and we very rarely hear of him. But he has been an utter failure, more than once convicted and an incessant fear and anxiety to my mother from his childhood. My father died when I was three and he fifteen. He was a clever boy and had been given an education even beyond my father's means. My mother was left in much

narrower circumstances with her six children and Arthur the second
eldest. I feel you ought to know this. I am aware how much a matter of
shame this may be considered and how likely seriously to stand in the
way of anything which your efforts have helped to make possible.

I have therefore not yet answered your questions.

And finally I can only say again what perhaps you are tired of hearing
– that it is your kindness and friendship [illeg] the brightest and best
things my books have brought me ... It will remain to the end.[27]

Newbolt replied with his usual warm brisk tact:

Thank you very much for your letter. It cannot have been an easy one to
write, but I am glad to have it, because a confidence of this kind is a step
in friendship, and your friendship I have always desired since I first read
those poems in their anonymous manuscript.

He went on to dismiss any need to bring to official notice what were

mere accidents of birth, and exist in nearly every family. It is the
peculiar good fortune of yours that the failure of one member of it is more
than atoned by the bright name of another. You will leave to your
children 'the purest treasure mortal times afford'.[28]

So would de la Mare please answer the questionnaire after all? And
here Newbolt added that, even if all should prosper, the poems be
approved by the experts, and the many other claimants be set aside, he
had been warned that they could hardly hope for more than fifty
pounds per annum for a man of thirty-five – not enough to get de la
Mare out of Oil. 'I am in despair about this,' Newbolt went on, 'and can
think of nothing to do but to write again and again repeating that I
want, not an addition to your present income, but a substitute for a
good part at any rate of it, which would set you free to earn the rest.'

At the very moment that the case for a pension crystallised, de la
Mare's conditions in the office suddenly grew much worse. Gone some
while already were the days when it had been possible to fit in a little
surreptitious writing during office hours; gone too were the civilised
Frank Bliss and the 'fairly pleasant boss, fairly easy-going' of early
days. A hated man was brought in to overhaul the office routine and to
effect ruthless economies – 'a snuffy little man', as de la Mare
recollected him forty years on, 'made of black bread ... He always used
to keep his head lowered – a bad sign.' To de la Mare's indignation, this
person gave a fortnight's notice to an elderly man who had worked for
the firm for twenty years, one who did his work slowly but got it done.
Moreover these 'American tradesmen', as de la Mare scornfully
referred to them, summed up his own value as that of an employee

from whom they could get the work of two, without effective protest. When they moved to another post the clerk senior to him, who had shared with him the responsibility for the big monthly charts of sales sent to supervisors in America, no one at all replaced him. This was in February 1908, but the fact only transpired when de la Mare was obliged to give some plain reason to the Newbolts why he had to back out of their arrangement for the whole family to holiday in lodgings provided in Netherhampton village at the end of May.

In short he had been edged into a position where he could no longer take *any* break at all. And the work itself, though he minimised its burden ('It is not of course very difficult or complicated,' he told the Newbolts) was in fact involving him in increasing nervous strain, deprived of any colleague to check the infinite number of separate calculations upon which the accuracy of the whole depended. Nor was this all. The preparation of the Trade Fluctuation Charts was now also foisted upon him. Later he told Newbolt that he had been given thirteen of these huge, detailed, complex sheets to compile at short notice. Naturally enough he began to be unwell, and to suffer from eye strain.

Elfie turned to Ella Coltman, hoping she might have some influence on de la Mare's dogged and absurd attempt to plod on under such increasing exploitation. Ella fiercely urged a visit to a doctor, and pointed out: 'It does seem to me madness to go on doing double work at the office without double pay … You did not put forward one single argument to convince me when you tried to defend yourself … You said it was "a gamble" – but I see no stakes to gamble for – You are staking health and life – for *what*? It is a complete puzzle to me what is in your mind … You *know* you cannot go on doing two men's work without breaking down – if the Heads are not even aware how you are working – what advantage has it?'[29] She was writing in April, but not until June did de la Mare put into the Secretary for a rise, in recognition of the extra work. He had carried this by then for three months and more. Nor was it until August that he received the rise requested; and when it came it was a miserly thirteen pounds per annum. In short, a mere five shillings a week more, for double the labour.

He seems to have been simply 'freezing', like a cat in the path of a lorry. He must have seen it was madness (as Ella ruthlessly pointed out), but to risk dismissal by a protest – to be cut loose, without savings, with only the spectre of immediate debt, should he dare to be unemployed even for a few weeks – how could he face this for his family? Unable to meet Ella's arguments at all, he tried to beguile her aside from the practical issues down the escape-tunnel of fancy. 'Time

goes on rather drab and sullenly – and still I keep on asking myself –
isn't it only oneself to blame? I feel sure with a little practice you might
dream out another world – an under-stratum of the real.'[30]

By the end of June he was so run down that he gave in to Ella's
pressure and consulted her doctor. 'He must have been quite convinced
that I was far more mad than ill,' he told her afterwards. 'We had a
most engrossing talk – nearly every comma and capital about me.'[31]
But it is hardly likely that their long talk did not diverge into the
philosophy and speculation with which he loved to ply his doctors all
his life. He treasured a supreme ideal of security: the wise, perfect,
family physician, whose wishfully-drawn father-figure is plain in more
than one of his stories, especially 'Physic'. His doctors are far more
admirable and reassuring confessors than his clergy. One would guess
such a clinging to the doctor for refuge began in the child of three,
sensing, while his father began to die, the ray of comfort in the family's
dread that only the doctor's visits brought. De la Mare certainly had a
much greater interest in his own health than was good for it, but he
was not the ordinary hypochondriac, for the interest was rooted in
intense curiosity far more than in demand for sympathy. In these long,
minutely analytical discussions of symptom and cure he was still
investigating, as ever, the springs of behaviour and the mysterious
relation between spirit and body.

His hypochondria had its endearingly childish side too: his children
noticed that he never could resist sampling anyone else's favourite
nostrum. If anyone in the family was prescribed a tonic, he must at
once bring out a teaspoon for himself, and as soon as he had put his
faith in a favourite medicine he would use it as a panacea for
everything from colds to stomach-aches.

He certainly had, from childhood, exaggerated anxiety about
physical illness in anyone he loved. If his father's painful death, nursed
at home, had entered into some 'granite niche in the undermind', Elfie
was even easier to alarm, perhaps for a similar reason – the untimely
loss of her mother. Probably their children had a great many more
ailments than would normally have come their way, because of this
feverish parental concern. In one letter to Ella, de la Mare mentioned in
a hushed sort of tone 'measles almost at our very door', much as if it
had been the Black Death. On one occasion when Jinnie had
complained of some slight ache, all four children were put to bed, one
after the other, with mounting worry, on the evidence of the
thermometer alone. At last its unvarying answer aroused suspicion,
confirmed by trying it on the aggressively blooming young daily 'help'.
She duly registered the same degree of fever, and so the whole family,

all perfectly well, were got up and dressed again.

But this time it was Newbolt who secured the only effective tonic. His cogent, lawyer-like letter gives little sign of the exultation he was feeling; but probably he was still a little uncertain whether de la Mare – especially in his present state – would really grasp the opportunity offered.

4 July 1908   Netherhampton House
My dear de la Mare,

I have at last received a definite reply from the Prime Minister. Shortly, he thinks that the present is too early a stage for a pension for life: but he offers me a sum of £200 at once to be used at my discretion for setting you free as far as possible for literary work. I must see you at once to discuss the matter, of course: but in the meantime please think of it, and think of it in the light of these special considerations:-

1. The offer is made expressly as a recognition of your service to literature, and in the hope that your future work may 'make it possible to judge whether further recognition is desirable'. It would seem from this that

2. the grant being of the nature of a public honour (though such grants are not, I believe, publicly advertised) it would be very difficult to refuse it: and

3. it is at the same time not easy to see how you could accept it without giving up, or entirely altering, your present position.

4. The practical question therefore is – How can you best secure more time and leisure for writing: by insisting on shorter hours and more help in your work, or by making the bolder venture of resigning and living on the £200 while looking for more suitable employment? You would of course in this latter event begin with a holiday, and then try what can be done in the way of writing for the Times etc.? I imagine the £200 would carry you over a year? and by the end of that you wd have made at any rate something to go on with ...

Let me know ... how the thing looks to you at first sight – so that I may not be quite in the dark – of course you bind yourself to nothing and it is not necessary to make any decision offhand. Meantime I congratulate you very warmly on this recognition of your work in the most difficult quarter of all. It has been critically examined both in the Prime Minister's Office and also by 'independent expert opinion' and I need hardly tell you that the standard is a most exacting one, because the applications are so many, and the money available so inadequate. The sum offered is small, but it is a very large aliquot part of the amount devoted to literature, and you must henceforth regard it as settled, that you are among those few who are capable of serving their country. I hope you will have a happy and adventurous Sunday, walking round your shipyard. Please shew your wife this letter – I have not time to write to her separately – and give her my kindest regards and best wishes.

                              Yours ever,
                              H.N.

Newbolt was right to urge de la Mare quietly. In the end he accepted, without any strong confidence in the future – more in the manner of a limpet thrust from its rock by intolerable pressure. In a note to Elfie he adopted the old melancholy flippancy in which he had told her of his first encouragement by St Loe Strachey: 'It's just his Majesty's nasty German trap. He hates Art. And I suppose he and Asquith are hand in glove together to bring hyacinthine fancies to confusion. O dear.'[32] He accepted, but felt unable to resign from his job until the money was actually forthcoming.

Within a week or two of Newbolt's news, while Elfie was away again with the children at the Coltman cottage, Spyfield, he was quite without money to send her for the week's small bills in the Hartfield shops, until his next Saturday pay-packet came round. He agonised over the never-ending worry and humiliation: 'Oil is just as oily – oilier and oilier, but how dare I leave on nothing fixed.'[33] He was reading *Jude the Obscure* (hardly the book for such spirits) and was haunted by it in his dreams, longing only for the cottage and the forest and the children at the week's end.

Ella urged him to hesitate no more; he seemed to her to be in a lethargy of depression, and no doubt she feared that freedom might come too late to prevent total passive collapse, just when it was vital that he should leap forward into freelance journalism and creative work, seizing every opening. August 1908 dragged by; finally on 7 September de la Mare screwed himself up to ask Newbolt when he would actually receive the grant, so that he could safely hand in his resignation. He felt no exhilaration whatever: 'I shall be glad to go ... very glad, though I fully realise it must be an exchanging of an evil known only too well for an anxiety unknown as yet in full. This feeling of anxiety does rather haunt me: but doubtless a few months' trial will relieve, if not remove it.'

Newbolt replied: 'Plunge and resign', for the money had just reached his bank. He had been given it in trust, to make the best use of it for de la Mare's benefit. He remained undaunted by his very difficult experience only two years before, when he and William Rothenstein had handled a similar trust for Conrad, who had proved extremely prickly, hypersensitive and also erratically apt to divert funds intended for his permanent benefit to meet temporary crises. It had taken all Newbolt's skill to prevent explosions. It is never a light matter to adopt money responsibilities for a friend; the relationship may so easily suffer, but Newbolt had a talent for vicarious responsibility, and kept a clear and straightforward view of his obligations as trustee which avoided embarrassment – setting what he

called the 'mere chink chink' of money in another compartment from
the rest of the friendship.

So, on 15 September 1908, de la Mare did at last hand in his
resignation to Anglo-American Oil, and followed it up by a personal
letter to John Usmar the managing director – intended for a
thunderbolt, and sent first to Newbolt for vetting. It stated his
grievances, for the sake of his successor, and casually flourished the
Prime Minister's 'substantial recognition' almost as an afterthought.
The thunderbolt made very little reverberation; Usmar returned a
mild, brief reply avoiding the whole point at issue, merely saying he
was pleased to hear of de la Mare's improved prospects: 'A company
like ours is a poor place for anyone to be in who is at all ambitious and
it is only on the outside, on the selling division that there are what
might be considered any prospects'[34] – a statement de la Mare took
bitterly from 'the richest monopoly in the world'. But he had the
satisfaction of learning that his successor did reap some benefit from
his protest; Fred Atha, who had shared his desk for six years, took his
place, but with only a reasonable proportion of his work, a second man
being detailed for the rest.

So the door closed on the great waste of eighteen and a half years,
with only a parting gift of silver-plate to show for them. The most
dramatic move of de la Mare's whole career could hardly have taken
place in a flatter mood, and with less stir.

Yet, within, the break was absolute. Directly he had shed the burden
of those endless Oil years, they simply ceased to inhabit his thoughts.
That endless Sahara folded up as if it had never been. In old age, he
once declared that he had never found his Oil life on a single occasion
inspiring the smallest passage or slightest character-sketch in his
writing. It did not enter his dreams, he said, and hardly crossed his
mind again.

8

The Newbolt Circle

It was time, as Newbolt put it, for de la Mare to 'walk around his shipyard'. He had already made some mark by reviews in the *Bookman*; indeed Lobban the editor, on retiring in June 1908, remarked that these had helped to set the paper on an altogether better footing. An article in May on Herrick, written hastily under office pressure, had very much impressed Newbolt and Ella Coltman.* And already in fact his budding career as a critic had taken a fortunate turn by his meeting with Edith Sichel, and, through her, Bruce Richmond.

Edith Sichel, one of Mary Coleridge's closest friends and a fellow-pupil of William Cory, had written to de la Mare about his memorial article on Mary, and invited him to her house. At once, they fell into animated talk on Cory, thought-pictures, and Browning (no favourite of de la Mare's, greatly revered though he was by Mary and all her friends). De la Mare went home and amenably tried *Paracelsus*, but (so he had to report to Ella) 'without the faintest symptom of conversion – two lines of poetry to five pages of verse. Don't tell anyone – they'll all come round to sugary thoughtlessness again in time. And Browning will placidly await Time's leavening. Now, don't *you* think its really "lump" *now*?'[1]

Some thought Edith Sichel alarming, with her handsome, pronounced features, and rather masculine, well-informed mind. De la Mare got on very well with her, finding her deliberately intellectual talk stimulating, and she was extremely helpful to him. They would

---

* The review remained endeared to de la Mare for a misprint in his quotation about the cowslip-picking Maids in 'To Meadows': 'You have beheld how they / With Wicker Arkes did come ...' The maidens on this occasion used 'Wicked Arts' instead. It was not the only time the printers were defeated by his unusual handwriting; later the 'dim-silked musicians' of his poem 'Arabia' made a very lame bow in print as 'demi-skilled'.

141

soon be meeting quite frequently for what they called 'delectable pow-wows' and 'agelong confabs', reading Donne aloud to one another, and eagerly discussing their common critical interests. She had gauged his critical quality in that first argument on Browning, and lost no time in approaching her friend and old colleague Bruce Richmond, with a view to a place for de la Mare on Richmond's regular team of reviewers for the *Times Literary Supplement*. After the fashion of the day, she was 'At Home' once a week to a large salon of the literary – parties not allowed by her to go their own way. She saw to it that, when Richmond and de la Mare attended one of these in June, they had a good opportunity to take each other's measure. The meeting brought reward for both of them.

Richmond has had some disparagement from such writers as Virginia Woolf. But he was an editor of uncommon flair, who secured the best critical minds of the day to write the *Literary Supplement* reviews, and took a very personal interest in the process, often meeting to discuss the article beforehand. Editors at that time exercised anyway a more tutorial authority over their contributors – even the well-known – than is normal today; and Richmond did so particularly. His retentive attention had kept *Henry Brocken* in mind – for its critical insight especially. In taking up de la Mare, as he now did, he clearly felt from the first not that he was giving an unknown pen a chance, but guilty rather that the *TLS* was to benefit at the expense of original creative work that de la Mare should be at instead. Richmond went away from the Sichel tea-table only waiting for the first suitable book to send round; and a fortnight before de la Mare left Oil there arrived the first of many such parcels – *Some 3d Bits* by George Russell (A.E.).*

But journalism (particularly as the *Times Literary Supplement* reviews were unsigned) could only provide bread-and-butter. For reputation de la Mare needed to bring out a full-length work as soon as possible. Edith Sichel urged a biography, and soon, through Roger Ingpen, de la Mare had an agreement with Hutchinson's (where Roger now worked) for sixty to seventy pounds for a life, the subject to be decided later. Much discussion ensued. Friends thought some colourful eccentric would suit him best. Newbolt favoured Thomas Holcroft, an eighteenth-century Quaker jockey who turned actor, wrote fifty plays, and was tried for High Treason; though he hinted that an auobiographical account of de la Mare's own early years 'à la Kipps'

* De la Mare's review of this appeared in mid-September 1908, a fortnight before his piece on *The Potters of Tadcaster*, which he said (in *Private View*, preface, p. xii) was his first contribution to the *TLS*.

was what would really sell. Edward Thomas suggested Beckford, and later Sidney was mooted; but nothing inspired de la Mare, and after six years on the shelf, the agreement was finally cancelled. Instinct had been against it. To the end of his life, he never did write anything biographical at all. The obligations of historical fact hobbled him far too closely.

Instead, now that his great opportunity had come, some totally unforeseen source of energy galvanised the storyteller in him to take it. By mid-October 1908, even before the holiday that Newbolt had suggested could be arranged, the Oil man so lately at the point of prostration was telling Ella: 'First, then, I'm writing the inane adventures of three Monkeys, "Thumb, Thimble & Nod." As this was already begun I thought it best to be finished with it. I rather hate it, but manage to reel out about 2000 words a day. So I am just hoping to have finished the *writing* of it at the end of the month. You will think it horribly childish and dull stuff, and never speak to me again. Next I shall try to turn out one short literary article a week and at least two sets of verses – as nearly all is useless, one must allow for waste.'[2]

His exhaustion all summer up to actual resignation must have been due more to frustration and indecision than to the gruelling work-load itself. He told Newbolt in late October:

> I am just beginning to realise what freedom *begins* to mean. Time, at any rate, passes even more quickly than ever it did, and however one parcels out one's day it is at least 36 hours short. One pines so to dress to the superhuman part of Balzac; to dictate three books at once as, wasn't it?, Napoleon dictated despatches. Time I suppose will bring philosophy, though certainly Time has a curious knack of failing all foresight.[3]

It was as well he could get to work so quickly. Newbolt had paid him the first thirty pounds of the Bounty on 1 October, but only ten days later de la Mare confessed that he could not buy new clothes that he urgently needed nor clear off debts before taking his long-delayed Netherhampton holiday, without another twenty-five pounds at once. It troubled Newbolt to realise for the first time how extreme de la Mare's straits had been, and what a state he would have been in had rescue delayed by even a month. But his capacity for work, and his pace, must have been reassuring. Besides the Monkey story, which had originated in a serial told aloud week by week to the children on Sunday afternoons, by early November he had begun a novel, while the 'at least two-a-week' set of verses that he proposed so matter-of-factly, accumulated punctually: a crop was sent to Edward Thomas by the end of his first month of freedom. What is more, Thomas pronounced them 'up to all but your very best and you ought to send them out with confidence'.[4] Among them came the child-poem 'Nod' that begins:

> Softly along the road of evening,
>   In a twilight dim with rose,
> Wrinkled with age, and drenched with dew,
>   Old Nod, the shepherd, goes.

and ends:

> His are the quiet steeps of dreamland,
>   The waters of no-more-pain,
> His ram's bell rings 'neath an arch of stars,
>   'Rest, rest and rest again.'[5]

That conscious aim at an adult audience, which had perhaps helped to give *Poems 1906* its touch of the didactic, was relaxing. Writing to please himself in his first few weeks of freedom, he was already achieving some of the best poems in the future *Peacock Pie* and *The Listeners*. There was now no such clear division between 'child' and 'adult' poems as there had been with *Songs of Childhood* and *Poems 1906*. There are, in *The Listeners* and *Peacock Pie*, only graver or more playful descriptions of the one vision.

He kept a methodical record this autumn of his daily work, and on most days he turned out between one and two thousand words, as the novel got under way, often writing this on alternate days with the Monkey book – thereby achieving something of his Napoleonic ambition. He also needed to put in a great deal of reading, for reviews of Yeats and John Clare. Toward this, Ella, at first anonymously, made a supremely useful provision. Some months before he left Oil, she had used a small legacy on a life subscription for him at the London Library. It was the freedom of a new world. Even she could hardly guess what it would mean to him, in the next ten years particularly. He not only read omnivorously (probably more in this decade than in all his life hitherto) but the Library reading-room also provided him with a writer's study, free, in central London, peaceful enough even for composing poetry. Yet more, he could share this good fortune, keeping Edward Thomas, in similar need for his own researches, supplied with volumes he was too poor to lay hands on elsewhere.

One day in the autumn of 1908, quite likely at random, de la Mare took down from the Library shelves a volume of *Purchas His Pilgrimes*. He had always loved browsing in travellers' tales, as far back as the *Horn Book* days, and he squirrelled their exotic but circumstantial details for the stimulus and 'body' they gave to his fantasy, just as Coleridge had done. He began *Purchas* at the third chapter of Volume VI, 'The Strange Adventures of Andrew Battell'. That name would have appealed to him for a start, but he incorporated into his Monkey book so much else from the same source – especially in the later chapters – that no other work of his can be so documented.* He took careful notes, and borrowed numbers of decorative details and names that give no hint that they are not original de la Mare. The honeyed Ollaconda trees, the Dondo's magic belt of sorcery, even the Zevvera's or wild horse's tail, even – most de la Marish of them all – 'the old Lord Shillumbansa that feeds a hundred peacocks on his grave' – are all lifted, verbatim, or only very slightly adapted, from Purchas. Many of the actual adventures, too, of the little royal monkey Nod he evolved from incidents related first by that credulous, hardy, imaginative Elizabethen sailor whose account Purchas recorded.

It is curious to see how very little transmutation this material needed to assimilate it to de la Mare's private vision; how Elizabethan, in fact, he was – except, of course, in one very important respect: all elements of barbarity, and with it of primitive black magic, are purged and dissolved into faëry. His northerly imagination also snowed over and frosted the torrid lushness of Battell's forest before he could make it his own. Curiously enough, he never seems to have mentioned that his story had been borrowed from any such source; perhaps in time he himself forgot that material so much to his hand had ever been borrowed at all.

The story he made of it is a symbolic one. Nod's journey throws a shadow of the soul's pilgrimage, and ends on the borders of the fabled Valley of Assassimon, his family's long-lost home. His adventures are picaresque, and end without particular climax, but they take place within a spiritual framework, and one whose philosophy is unusually explicit for de la Mare. At first he nailed down his fantasy with a wealth of circumstantial glosses; some he jettisoned on Newbolt's advice, but he kept those on the names of the two supernatural forces – both feminine, deific beings – that haunt Nod's path: Tishnar is 'that which cannot be told or expressed', and Immanala 'she who preys across the shadow'. The benevolent Tishnar and the menacing spirit-forces are held in apparently equal balance, but de la Mare throws out a hint in the explanatory preface he decided to discard that in the final result, Evil and Loss are only the negative of Good, which is the positive absolute: 'Yet because dark is but day gone, and cruelty

* I owe the discovery of this source to Mr Adrian Green-Armytage.

un-kindness, therefore even the heart-shaking Noomanossi [the last sleep, darkness, change, and the unreturning] is only absent Tishnar.' It seems in this 'theology' (as it were) of the fable, as if de la Mare were trying to give, for children's sake, a consoling view of that problem of immortality and transience which he found for himself so intractable.

Nod and his brothers, the Mulla-Mulgars, are beings half way between humanity and an animal world whose creatures are anyway half-fabulous and dreamlike, akin to the dogs and horses of *Henry Brocken*. The Mulgar brothers reflect, in a kind of loving caricature, man's oddity and his helplessness, his fallibility and his instinct for the divine. They are innocent, wise and absurd, and Nod is a hero children love; but the mannered, brocaded style makes the book outside their scope for most children of today.

The novel de la Mare turned to on alternate days, as the Mulla-Mulgars advanced, was a complete contrast. The loose episodic Monkey story no doubt provided a foil and overflow for the far more concentrated creative effort needed in this. Until it was finished, he simply spoke of it by its hero's name, as 'Lawford'. In the end, he called it *The Return*.

He had to use very careful construction and balance. He had chosen a commonplace, realistic contemporary setting – the most difficult one, for the story stretches belief to the limit. His first task was therefore to make the psychology of the characters so convincing that he could carry the reader with him. But, difficult as this was, his major aim was more ambitious still: not mere credibility, but poetic truth. Here, the sensational and spiritualist element in the story could so very easily have spoiled the far more profound and delicate prime effect of spiritual beauty, which he so much desired.

The Return is the story of a dull middle-aged suburban householder (Lawford) who falls asleep on the tombstone of a Huguenot suicide, and wakes to find that the predatory spirit of the dead man has taken possession of him – not yet completely, but enough to transform his face, so that his own wife thinks him an impostor. He struggles against the possession, and finally conquers, but in the struggle he has awoken to the spiritual vacuum of his former way of life. His intimate experience of the Frenchman's dark, intelligent soul is the making of his own. He has lost his changed face, but he is a changed man for good.

De la Mare's own accounts of his problems in writing the novel differ. To Newbolt he confided that the melodramatic element was a continual hindrance to him: 'I felt very shaky indeed about the novel – the *idea* was sensational and all along it proved rather a burden and a handicap. It may sound like an absurdity; but I kept on rebelling against its sensationalism – I detest it – And now I don't know quite whether to be glad or sorry that it proved too strong for me.'[6] But to Forrest Reid, later on, he spoke of this very thing as deliberately chosen. Reid remembered their discussion of this: 'It was around success,' he said, 'that the conversation ... hovered; and presently there emerged the startling confidence that *The Return* was a bid for it, had been designed deliberately as a sensational story, a "shocker", a thing the public would infallibly rise to, would recognise as its own.'[7]

The two accounts are not really incompatible: de la Mare's response to advice from Strachey or Pinker had often in the past shown a matter-of-fact readiness to produce whatever kind of goods were required. Also he still had that natural predeliction, so strong in his youth, for undertaking a sensational subject when trying stories of real life. The task of subduing such an element to an effect of beauty had always invited him, as it did in 'The Hangman Luck', *The Master*, 'An Ideal Craftsman' and many other early pieces.

But now that his poetic faculty was so much more maturely and seriously engaged, the bias of such material toward a crude effect became a danger he felt far more acutely. To combat it, he used every subtlety of method he had learned from Henry James. But James, whose novels are about social beings, not the soul in solitude, could only teach him to temper the Poe-like element in his material, and could hardly help him make it, as he wished, the vehicle of a profound comment on human identity and responsibility in the face of death, immortality, loss. The Shakespeare plays that had already kindled sparks in his own gift were more use to him here; his main task – just as Shakespeare's had often been – was to transmute melodrama into the poetry of spiritual quest.

A note he wrote in old age suggests how he set about composition:

> Most writers – and probably most painters and musicians – would, I think, agree that, at its most fortunate, a poem, (or a story or a picture) brings its plan with it. Its what and how are part and parcel of itself. The bubble (out of the sediment) resembles a cocoon – a bit odd! But it takes endless pains and labour in the unwinding; and the thread may snap. Fortunately we only so much control our minds as we do our bodies. Best let them work their own way, and trust to Providence. But keep at it.

He always held the conscious mind to be mainly useful as a check, a sieve, an investigator. In what he really valued, he cultivated a receptive passivity, taking his promptings from the unconscious. At the end of his life he was still marvelling at the force and conviction with which characters and stories revealed themselves, detail by irreversible detail, in his mind's eye. They just arrived – down to a particular button, turn of phrase, or gesture. It seems as if this had always been so.

This is linked, perhaps, with that belief of his that in some sense (would we but attend to it) *we are dreaming all day* as well as all night. It is plain, at any rate, that some such process was at work almost continuously in his own case. A tiny detail in *The Return* shows this characteristically passive invention. Miss Sinnet, a minor but very distinct character, is described as a little old lady, but her face, in the draft that Ella first saw, was 'a large quiet one'. That struck Ella as rather odd. When she queried it, de la Mare took out the phrase, yet replied: 'Miss Sinnet *did* have a large quiet face – but it sounds very ugly'[8] – as dispassionately as if he had met her in the street.

The Return cost him great pains and took till Autumn the following year. After it was all done he confessed to Ella: 'I so hated Lawford that if it had not been the madness of wasting so much time I should have liked to destroy it.'[9]

*

At last he could get away to Netherhampton for a break. The Newbolts' new home in Wiltshire lay between the water-meadows and the Downs; there was a large garden and a 'wilderness' of fine trees, and the long low house rambled round a courtyard – part stone, part flint chequer-work, part brick, some of it seventeenth-century. When de la Mare came later on to describe 'Thrae', the most romantic of his symbolic manor-houses, in the introduction to *Come Hither*, it is said to be 'immense', whereas Netherhampton's charms were intimate and nowhere grand; yet some features of this beloved house creep into the details of Thrae: the characteristic Netherhampton croon of the white doves along the roofs, the round bull's-eye window, high up, that so often drew de la Mare to stare out, the porch 'with its slender wooden pillars and a kind of tray above, on which rambled winter jasmine'.

For the little boy in Thrae, the heart of the house is Nahum Taroone's round turret full of books and curios, with windows to the four points of the compass. Hardly less unusual and secretive was the top room in Netherhampton, Newbolt's sanctum, where the two men spent much of the day together working. From the landing, steep twisting stairs of its own mounted to this room, known as the Ark: a long white attic, facing south towards the Downs. A huge transverse beam, a foot high, divided the floor. Two pairs of white rafters supported the roof at intervals. These, and the four deep-set curved-topped windows, with the small round port-hole at the far end, gave the room something of the look of a frigate's gun-deck in Nelson's day. Newbolt worked at a small kitchen table covered with a plain blue cloth and topped by an old-fashioned square sloping writing desk. Beside this stood a capacious accordion file. Methodical and punctual in business and correspondence that mattered, Newbolt would leave trivial and inconvenient letters in this file for a month or two. By then, he held, most had answered themselves. De la Mare admired, but could never bring himself to this ruthless solution; he became a martyr to correspondence throughout the years of his fame.

Newbolt's habit when writing was to break off quite frequently for a spell of musing, pacing up and down out of doors to refresh himself. Usually he made for the 'kitchen garden' – prosaically named but romantic enough in fact for an illuminated missal. Surrounded by a high thatched wall, it was crossed by four grass paths, overhung with cistus and lavender, intersecting at an old stone sundial in the centre. The vegetable plots were hidden behind espaliered fruit trees, hollyhocks and sweet williams. The contemplative, secret effect was of Margaret's devising.

Henry Furse and Newbolt, although they had become warm friends in London, were unlikely men to find sharing one home: a complete contrast in tastes and temperaments. It was only Margaret Newbolt's elastic sympathy with both her Harrys that kept the shared household a successful arrangement for several years. (After that, Furse went back explosively but still affectionate, to Devon, leaving the Newbolts to live on there alone.) Beside Newbolt, parchment-pale and neat, the sculptor was a swashbuckling figure; de la Mare found him a 'ponderous, Henry-the-Eighthly-looking man with dark hair, a short, seamanlike beard, bushy eyebrows and a beautiful arched nose. He is just good English grit right through and what a woman ought to mean by a lover.' Yet Furse's powerful body dwindled below the waist to short legs crippled from birth. A keen foxhunter, his shooting, golf and even, on occasion, salmon fishing were all done of necessity from horseback. Nor had he ever got over the unnecessary tragedy by which, in their first year together, his beautiful wife died of scarlet fever when their only child, Ralph, was born. As time went on he became increasingly manic-depressive. But, at any temporary equilibrium between ebullience and black despair, he would produce, in the studio across the courtyard, work of real gusto and beauty, excelling in heroic studies of animal ferocity – a cock fighting a snake, horses in fierce play, lionesses in whelp or at the kill. De la Mare got on well with him, and Furse admired de la Mare's utterly dissimilar imagination.

Margaret never lost hope that her own faith and Hegelian philosophy, by healing Furse's raging despair of God, might steady his manic-depressive pendulum. Meanwhile it was Ella, always at hand, who dovetailed the joints of this unlikely household tactfully together. In the atmosphere so achieved, Netherhampton became beloved. Its temper was unexacting but industrious: de la Mare found it easy to work there, and delicious to relax.

1909 was a Poe centenary, and Bruce Richmond marked the occasion in the *Times Literary Supplement* by giving de la Mare his first long front-page article. He posted it off in early January to Edith Sichel for her approval. Even over the proofs he hesitated until the last possible moment, and Richmond finally received it covered in alternatives in the very softest blur that pencil affords. But it was a good piece of work, fresh and penetrating at a period when Poe was not very much read:

> It is not only the power of his imagination that ... makes him one of the few masters of the short story. Busy in its service were a logical lucidity, a keenness of intellect, a passion for proportion, for climax and crisis. The masterly combination of these diverse qualities is the secret of his art and its effects. However weird, however distorted, his theme may be – and it was rarely anything else – Poe's presence of mind never fails him. His plot advances, without haste, with the clearest attention to every detail, to its overwhelming conclusion.[10]

As with most creative writers, de la Mare's criticism is a very personal affair, and outstanding only where native sympathy aligns his eye. He sees everything under the same oblique, unusual light that bathes his own creations. Yet the affinities that he discovers, even if unexpected, are never forced or irrelevant, and they are often very revealing. He read thoroughly, and took the greatest pains to be just and accurate. This fidelity, and his absence of conceit, kept his judgement sound, however imaginative his approach. 'Always right down the middle of the road' was Richmond's emphatic approval.[11] The finished articles were invariably as polished a piece of prose as de la Mare (fanatical reviser) could make them.

One curious feature gradually emerges if one reads his reviews in bulk: the self that speaks here on matters of *belief* is distinctly more orthodox and committed than when he discusses faith elsewhere.* Perhaps anonymity made him bolder on such a matter (most of his

* This was noted by Edward Wagenknecht.

reviewing, not only in the *TLS*, was unsigned). Or was it that the critic's standpoint drew out (as later, in time of war, his patriot's standpoint would also do) the side of his character which was most solidly responsible and representative, least singular and eclectic?

Though very ready to praise and encourage beginners, he lacked the bold decisive flair which may make a new reputation at a stroke. No article of his (nor any recommendation, when later he became a publisher's reader) seems to have been the turning-point of anyone's career, though he did certainly praise men like Ralph Hodgson and Frost, justly and perceptively, before the chorus. Moreover writers as little of his own outlook as, say, D.H. Lawrence, became eager over the next few years for the stamp of his public approval. (Although so much of his reviewing was unsigned, his very idiosyncratic style usually made his contributions easy to identify.) His particular gift was for sending a reader back with fresh eyes to a classic – and probably Richmond realised this, as he frequently assigned to de la Mare the collected editions brought out for centenaries.

Poe, of course, had been a rather swamping influence on him in schooldays; he mentioned a first reading as a 'shattering' experience – not an adjective he used glibly. He wrote of Poe again in the 1930s, using this time the old device of the Shakespeare Characters and *Henry Brocken* – 'criticism in narrative form'. In fact the result, 'The Revenant', only later collected as fiction, was first written and delivered as a *lecture*. It is a striking short story. Poe's ghost attends an academic's patronising, prying discourse on him, and confounds the lecturer in an uncomfortable interview after it is over.

Richmond quickly followed up the success of de la Mare's first long *TLS* article with another, this time on Thomas Hardy's selection from the poems of his friend William Barnes. Ella wrote to say that she had never seen Newbolt so delighted with a review of poetry – he kept exclaiming 'I *hope* it is by de la Mare'. From then on, Richmond gave de la Mare the front page whenever he could, and by his own account always reserved for him whatever he thought would specially appeal to him – and that only. Once or twice the importance of the occasion, such as centenaries of Tennyson and Thackeray, led him to break this rule, and then the effort of an uncongenial subject very nearly brought de la Mare to complete stoppage. His whole summer holiday in 1909 was overcast by the Tennyson. He groaned to Ella of the piece he had written: 'It is a *detestable* bit of work – over-fanciful Mr Richmond thinks; so I am studiously hoeing out all the beautiful growths of my Maytime and the result shall be Saharan severity. I don't think I ever was so tired of man or book before. How I would enjoy saying my say!

... I wish AT had expired in 1843 and was Christina Rossetti.'[12] Even when the subject inspired him, reviewing never became easy. To some extent, every page of his prolific journalism was task-work that went against the grain. Looking back when he was old, he would say he had 'often nearly died of quite a short article'.

One of his difficulties was to keep to the length allotted. Richmond was as lenient as he could be, and lesser fry would be chopped about to make room for de la Mare's unbidden paragraphs. If all the same he was forced to amputate de la Mare's piece, Richmond found him unobjecting – the usual case (he commented) with contributors of distinction; generally the smaller the reviewer, the more the fuss.

Once, de la Mare specifically *asked* the *TLS* for a book: J.D. Rockefeller of Anglo-American Oil had brought out his reminiscences. Richmond was willing – 'so long as you tell the truth'. The review that resulted gave de la Mare such fierce pleasure that he republished it half a century later in *Private View* (1953), the only collected volume he made of his criticism, chosen from an output of hundreds of pieces. He really felt he had for once flayed his subject alive. A comic belief, when you read the mild result. Under an attack of such civilised, ironic finesse, one cannot believe the hide of an American oil magnate would register even a pin-prick!

In the summer of 1909 Pinker got de la Mare an introduction to J.A. Spender, editor of the *Westminster Gazette*, which brought out an influential literary supplement on Saturdays. Soon, work for this doubled his reviewing. Once, he was delighted to find that they had sent him a treatise *On the Use of the Sabre in Wartime*; but the office discovered their mistake before he could crystallise his military views. He never came close to Spender, a more formal and conventional editor than Richmond, but he liked and respected him. As a novice, he once asked him for a recipe for composition. Spender pondered and pronounced (to de la Mare's amusement): 'So, I think, to write, as to need no punctuation.'

Edward Thomas's book on Richard Jefferies was published just before de la Mare visited him at Berryfield Cottage, near Petersfield, in January 1909. It won Thomas some warm praise at last; but praise had to be of the right kind. One of his well-wishers roused only indignation. 'Aren't you glad,' he wrote to de la Mare, 'you don't write for a paper that thinks it is doing a kind act by describing you as Mr Edward Thomas a better writer than Richard Jefferies ... God forgive them and preserve me from them.'[13] He could be tart enough to de la Mare himself over some innocent remark that offended his austerely fastidious moral taste. De la Mare came in for a snub for joking about an exasperating old neighbour, a Mr Lintoft, who played the violin appallingly. 'I couldn't make out why you expected me to be amused by the fact that you had a neighbour out of his mind and living alone. I know I am callous about most things that don't concern myself, but not amused: what was your point?'[14] On the other hand the language of his letters shows unconsciously the particular delicacy he felt towards de la Mare. To other male intimates, such as Gordon Bottomley, Thomas would relieve his feelings now and then with a coarse word, but to de la Mare never; he addressed him just as he would a woman.

Harassed as Thomas was in matters of money, means as small as his could provide a much pleasanter life for an artist of his generation than they would today. No struggling young writer now could possibly keep a wife and several children in a house as good as Berryfield Cottage. De la Mare wrote home on his first morning that the country was superb, and the view one of the most haunting and lovely he had seen. True, he was writing from a bedroom so cold that he could hardly hold the pen in his fingers – no Thomas home was luxurious – but it was commodious and well-appointed enough to make 'cottage' a misnomer. It had, in fact, been a small farmhouse, and was tucked away from the village, in an isolated, romantic spot facing rough water-meadows, where a stream ran through meadowsweet and wild forget-me-nots. Beyond, over miles of wooded and pastoral levels, the dolphin lines of the South Downs jostled each other up to Butser Hill. At the back, the house was invaded by noises from the overhanging presence of the woods: foxes' yap and scream, owls by night, loud yaffles by day, roaring weather – for it was a district of gales, turbulent mists and savage winter downpours. Westwards, dense woods covered a dramatic, steep-sided horseshoe of combe, almost a ravine – and surely the origin of that 'unfathomable deep forest' on the border of sleep, in Thomas's poem 'Lights Out'. This was the first really remote deep country that de la Mare had come to know closely: a neighbourhood to nourish poetry, forming even now in Thomas (not yet writing in verse) the impressions from which almost all his own poems would eventually spring. De la Mare's visits here gave him a lifelong love of the South Downs, but it is the precipitous, mysterious *woodland*, close at hand, of the combe itself, which reveals best the bond between him and Thomas. Woods meant more to de la Mare than hills: they were the central enchantment of nature. This was ground that he and Thomas had intimately in common. Walking in those wintry hangers, one can well see why Thomas cared so much for *The Three Mulla-Mulgars*. De la Mare brought some of this story with him on his first visit – enough to convince Thomas that it would be 'a very good thing altogether'.[15] It did, in fact, become one of his prime favourites in all his friend's work.

As to de la Mare's poetry, Thomas would always love the homely and direct enchantments best, and disliked anything that smacked of artifice and deliberate decoration. As de la Mare himself noted, Thomas strongly disliked quaintness in anything. He loved *oldness*, but chiefly as a guarantee of reality – not the antique, the historical, the nostalgic, but oldness as an honourable attribute of simple, useful things, or of folk traditions; proof that they had stood the test of time and trouble. So it was with poetry. There was a realness he looked for, as much in romantic things as elsewhere, and he found it in de la Mare's poems – truth to childhood, truth to the human heart when romance genuinely moves it, and truth to his own vision of Englishness.

Detailed knowledge of England, as Thomas conceived her, was the best thing Thomas was able to give de la Mare, himself largely ignorant of country matters. The teaching took place during daily vigorous rambles throughout what had been the home district of Gilbert White and Cobbett. Thomas liked to avoid the staff of nearby Bedales and similar local intellectuals, and to stop at remote inns or isolated cottages, where, in laconic chat over the bar or the back garden fence, some dying skill or local saga of dreams and ghosts could still be picked up direct from wheelwright, farrier and labourer, unspoiled by the attentions of any earnest theorist or bogus naïf. The store of knowledge and reverie he had laid up in this lonely way fascinated de la Mare, whose own mind supplied in turn, for Thomas, an intensifying medium to look through, something like bottle-glass, that stretched and coloured his view arrestingly.

But there was a cardinal difference in their friendship. Thomas valued equally, as one undivided treasure, de la Mare's company and his verse and prose; but for de la Mare, Thomas was as yet only a poet *in the way he lived his life* – though there, supremely. For all de la Mare's sympathy with his friend's aims in his prose writings (a lot of it prose-poetry), he could not honestly feel as wholehearted an admiration for these pieces as Thomas lavished on his own work, almost in every department. The reason was simply that Thomas had not yet discovered his medium, and scarcely did so before their days for being together were over. When finally the pent-up poetry issued in verse form, the poems were largely made of scenes such as these two men had shared together. Yet even then, after he had these poems to sum up all, de la Mare still wrote of Thomas: 'He meant, beyond most men, infinitely more than his books.'

His personal effect on de la Mare in those country days was

refreshing, humbling and quieting. De la Mare found in his company a quality he called (when pointing it out in the Thomas poems) 'endlessness' – a freedom from the broken-up and intellectualised mental activities of other men. This quality was communicated as much in long friendly silences as by talk, for Thomas fell silent, mostly, while walking, the better to observe, and he liked to be out as much of the day as possible. On a winter visit like this first one, they would light a fire of sticks in a corner of the fields to munch their provisions by – bread and cheese, a few raisins, an apple – all from Thomas's deep jacket pockets, made especially capacious to carry these. They would hold also perhaps a book of poems, for reading aloud, and one of Thomas's beloved clay pipes. He persuaded de la Mare into much more vigorous exercise than was his usual habit, though these walks – five or six miles and back – were still the merest stroll to Thomas's habitual twenty or thirty.

Beside this friend, de la Mare felt a little the Cockney, 'and inky at that' – febrile and bookish. Thomas appeared to him to have a fresher, wiser, more instinctive hold on life; he seemed to bring something of country solitude in at the door with him even when he visited the little urban de la Mare household at Anerley. When de la Mare said that Thomas seemed to want to 'keep living things whole and just themselves rather than to dissect them or huddle them up in categories',[16] one is aware of the implicit self-comparison. But in fact the differing natures of the two were mutually sympathetic and complementary; if Thomas stilled de la Mare's spirit, where he felt his own too shallowly active, then de la Mare's happy good humour in turn soothed Thomas's spasmodic irritability and his bitter melancholy. To himself, Thomas felt not wise but literal and rather matter-of-fact in his approach to external things, 'very much on an everyday ordinary level except when in a mood of exaltation usually connected with nature and solitude. By comparison with others that I know – like de la Mare – I seem essentially like the other men in the train and I should like not to be.'[17] In short, each found the other unusual and superior to himself.

The Thomas family life at Steep was congenial. The day ran to no particular timetable, though the two men usually found it convenient to work in the mornings together. Life was much more rough and ready than at Anerley. Helen Thomas's hospitality was impulsive, bustling and impromptu. She never grew intimate with de la Mare, though she made him welcome now, and turned to him later on for help in the difficult years after Edward's death, when he did much to protect her interests. But she was puzzled by him, and he in his turn shied away from her physical and emotional candour, especially when it came to her books about her life with Edward. She felt they shocked him, as she said they did Frost. In any case the 'David' of her portrait – seen almost entirely as her lover – was not a self of Edward's that de la Mare or Frost would recognise in the Thomas they had known, a man among his men friends, poet among poets.

By now Thomas and de la Mare were in the habit of meeting nearly every week on Thomas's days in London, often still in the St George's café, which was cheap and vegetarian; and sometimes Thomas would spend a night at Anerley – to great welcome from the family and Elfie. To her –and it meant a lot to her – he always extended the same attention and courtesy as to Jack. He took pains to include her, and valued her, as he valued his mother. He soon persuaded de la Mare to join the Square Club, named after the philosopher in *Tom Jones*. It met every month in a central restaurant where, for a shilling a year and 3/6d a dinner, writers of congenial mind could meet and talk. Founded by Edward Garnett (among others), it included in its members, at various times, Chesterton, Masefield, Hudson, Roger Ingpen, J. D. Beresford, Galsworthy and Machen. As time went on, it made a point of contact for a large number of de la Mare's friends, several of them first introduced to him there by Thomas. In his memoirs, Edgar Jepson writes of seeing de la Mare frequently there:

> At the Square Club he did not talk much; he would eat his dinner and survey the gathering with an air of childlike pleasure; then there would sweep across his face, suddenly and for a breath, a look of bewilderment, and you could see him ask himself what the devil he was doing in that galley ... He was uncommonly goodlooking in those days, with dark, wavy hair and one of the finest foreheads I have ever seen, and always he wore the most attractive air of childlike candour.[18]

*

The Mulla-Mulgars began their travels to publishers' offices at John Murray's, and de la Mare now sent a large collection of new poems to Ella and Newbolt for their criticism. Again they advised a division into two books, one for children, to be followed by the rest in another for adults. Many of the latter section already touched the top of de la Mare's powers – 'Music Unheard', 'The Truants', 'All That's Past'. Ella's favourite (it also became one for Thomas) was 'Music Unheard':[19]

> Sweet sounds, begone –
>   Whose music on my ear
> Stirs foolish discontent

Of lingering here;
When, if I crossed
. The crystal verge of death,
Him I should see
Who these sounds murmureth.

Sweet sounds, begone –
Ask not my heart to break
Its bond of bravery for
Sweet quiet's sake;
Lure not my feet
To leave the path they must
Tread on, unfaltering,
Till I sleep in dust.

Sweet sounds, begone!
Though silence brings apace
Deadly disquiet
Of this homeless place;
And all I love
In beauty cries to me,
'We but vain shadows
And reflections be.'

Ella wrote of this poem: 'It brought fresh courage to me when I was needing it – and sounded again that note I told you I recognised and rejoiced in, in the Mulla Mulgars. When Poets (true Poets) preach, they are sure of listeners.'

Among so much in de la Mare's poetry which chooses the minor rather than the major key, it is certainly noticeable how often and straightforwardly he writes of courage. Of all the strenuous virtues, it was the one which most appealed to him, perhaps because (unlike some of the others) its action is entirely liberating and attractive to the sense of wonder. Also because, perhaps, he had needed it so much. Fortitude is the dominant theme of his last long poem, *The Traveller*, just as it had been of the *Mulgars* and of *The Return*.

He was still very glad of advice as a poet, and what he got from Ella, forthright and detailed, stimulated more actual improvements at this period than Newbolt's or Thomas's. She was both quick with the pruning knife and sensitive to unity of feeling. Of 'Martha' she wrote that the ending 'seems a bit banal. I don't think you want to introduce the present there. It spoils to me the picture of the past and the mood. Could you not keep it to the "Once – once upon a time" quite remote and far away.'[20] To this advice, the little poem owed the final lovely stanza by which Martha, and the children listening to her, are

removed even further into the past than they were when we first see
her begin her storytelling in the hazel glen:

> All foredone and forgot;
> And like clouds in the height of the sky,
> Our hearts stood still in the hush
> Of an age gone by.

Pattie (whose real name was Martha) is certainly the original of this
'grave small lovely head' and the slim hands clasped round bended
knees, far back in the Seventies, when she was the family story-teller,
and little Jack and Poppy would loll on their elbows in some nook by
the Ravensbourne, to listen to her through the warm afternoons.

Ella recognised that she had no right to quarrel with what she called
the 'bizarreness' that was so much part of de la Mare's imagination,
just because it was not to her own taste. But he was ready to tone down
an extravagance at her wish. In 'All That's Past' she queried: 'Surely
our dreams in dim Eden are not raved? It seems to me too wild and
restless a word.'[21] And he emended it to: 'Our dreams are tales / Told in
dim Eden / By Eve's nightingales.' She disliked another verb, 'Roams
back the rose'. At first he defended it – 'Roams meant the wild
rose-shoots tangling back across time to the primeval hip!'[22] But the
line was in fact a problem to him, and having removed that 'raves'
further on, he finally plumped for 'roves' here:

> Oh, no man knows
> Through what wild centuries
> Roves back the rose.[23]

Robert Graves said that at his one meeting with de la Mare he had
asked whether he had tried 'all sorts of things to get *roves* right, and
failed and been content with the nearest; and he told me it had been a
nightmare to him and remained unsolved'.[24]

De la Mare sent these poems to Thomas, who also replied with a long
list of preferences and suggestions, but was too tired to make these as
detailed and constructive as Ella's. When he had glanced down his list
of favourites Thomas noticed: 'All those I like best belong rather to
Songs of Childhood than *Poems* don't they? I think they are equal to
the best you have written and ought to be made into a book.' 'Nod', 'Old
Ben', and 'Old Susan' were among his favourites. In the last, he
queried: 'Are you satisfied with "absorbed and sage"?',[25] and de la Mare
took a closer look and altered the expression of the old woman reading
after her day's work, to 'rapt and stern' when

Through her great glasses bent on me,
She'd glance into reality;
And shake her round old silvery head,
With – 'You! – I thought you was in bed!' –
Only to tilt her book again
And rooted in Romance remain.[26]

One of the few pieces that Thomas positively disliked was destined to become one of de la Mare's most anthologised poems, 'Arabia'. De la Mare confessed that it was, for him, 'an ewe lamb'; but to Thomas it probably smacked too much of conscious decoration – something too deliberate, too whimsical.

In the same letter, Thomas confessed to great embarrassment at having just praised Ezra Pound in a review, against his better judgement: 'I began by thinking his work rot but so contemptuously that I seem to have set about altering my view out of pure perversity & desire to be amiable.'[27] In the *English Review* Thomas called Pound 'a great soul' and 'this admirable poet'. According to de la Mare, Thomas told him that at the very moment he heard the envelope containing the favourable review fall to the bottom of the letter-box, he realised that his opinion had completely reversed. Soon after, at a literary party, he saw with horror that Pound was bearing down upon him. He realised he was coming to thank him in person for the appreciation he no longer felt.

Newbolt had sent another twenty pounds of the Bounty in April 1909, with a note to reassure de la Mare that, though the grant (£200 in all) was melting away fast, progress amply justified the outlay. For de la Mare had established himself 'even more successfully than we hoped. The difference between your 'position' now and a year ago is almost impossible to estimate.'[28] Newbolt's steady, sanguine encouragement all through this year was a great help, for Pinker's views were less rosy. Pinker thought – perhaps rightly – that the exotic names in *The Three Mulla-Mulgars* would be a stumbling-block to children, and when it was returned by John Murray (reluctant to risk an advance, after the fate of *Brocken*) he sent it on to Methuen without great hope. Nor was he very optimistic about any of the serious work de la Mare was showing him at present, which included several new stories and a sample of a few thousand words from *The Return*.

De la Mare told Pinker he felt he must aim in this novel at good sales, and in showing it so early he must 'emphasize the fact that I am now ... wholly dependent on writing for a living. And of course reviewing will remain, at least for the present, a more or less fitful and precarious source of income. I must make at least a hundred or a hundred and fifty out of fiction etc.'[29] But Pinker thought the short stories too dark in mood for popularity, and this made de la Mare waver for a while even about *The Return*. He wondered if it would be better to start something entirely fresh, though he was innocently amenable that 'the book need not necessarily end very harrowingly'.[30] He was still so influenced by advice, it is really lucky and commendable that Pinker forbore to discourage, after reading the first sombre chapters. The stories he had disparaged as 'too dark' included 'Miss Duveen' and 'Seaton's Aunt', both of which must rank among de la Mare's finest.

'Seaton's Aunt' appears to have been recently written (probably while de la Mare's mind was playing round the theme of spiritual possession, while he formulated the plot of *The Return*). In this instance the tale tells of the gradual assimilation, by his Aunt, a kind of ghoul, of the soul of the nephew who lives with her. Seaton divines his fate while he is still a lack-lustre and unpopular schoolboy, who cajoles the narrator (a schoolfellow) by an invitation home for the night, into playing the reluctant part of best friend and confidant. The Aunt becomes atrociously actual to the reader, touch by touch. Every detail of her manner and appearance is sharply defined and particular – obsessively so – yet the style somehow conveys at every point that she exists also on another more sinister plane. Long before we have to acknowledge that she knows what goes on in every corner of her house, she seems already somehow physically diffused throughout it. It is a kind of carcase which she animates at will, just as in reverse, sometimes when she is present her face seems vacated, her self elsewhere. The copious meals of lobster mayonnaise and cold game sausage, her Gargantuan appetite and sarcastic geniality, all thicken unease, preluding the active terror of the night. At the narrator's second visit, Seaton is unhopefully engaged to a girl, knowing at heart that he cannot escape his Aunt's power. He bursts out:

'I know that what we see and hear is only the smallest fraction of what is. I know she lives quite out of this. She *talks* to you; but it's all make-believe. It's all a "parlour game". She's not really with you; only pitting her outside wits against yours and enjoying the fooling. She's living on inside, on what you're rotten without ... She's a spider.'[31]

On the third visit, there is no one in the uneasy house but the Aunt alone, the gross spider in the emptied web.

De la Mare never managed a rich prose style to more skilful effect, for even in this story his aim is poetic – and hits the gold. It may be argued that wherever poetry touches evil it must romanticise and so weaken its wickedness, and it is true that in de la Mare's stories he always sacrifices force of moral repulsion to lyrical effect. We are never wholly to reject his monsters and demoniac powers; we keep (as he does) a sneaking romantic respect for them, and a sense that life would be the poorer without them. The Aunt, though gruesome, remains a source of dark and fascinating energy. She is capable of annihilating Seaton, but she does not really *corrupt* him at all. The effect of Quint on the little boy in *The Turn of the Screw* at once points the difference.

*

By July of this year (1909) de la Mare felt secure enough at last to take the first whole month of holiday he had had (he said) since schooldays. The Coltmans arranged for the family to borrow a cottage at West Harting, the other side of Petersfield from the Thomases, with only a pleasant four- or five-mile walk between the two families. Dene Cottage stands away from the other houses of West Harting. It was islanded in a wide green landscape among crying peewits. The eye naturally turns, even before it is caught by the magical line of the downs a mile or two away, to one isolated hill, Tarbury as the de la Mares knew it, Torberry on the Ordnance Map. This rides apart, alongside the downs, like a corvette beside a convoy of big merchantmen. From Dene Cottage its decided shape and its isolation make it much more conspicuous and impressive than its actual height warrants. It was the magnetic, dominant presence in the family's landscape, and, since its foot was only a few hundred yards from their door, it became de la Mare's sanctuary and out-door study. He would retreat to a favourite beech or yew on its flanks to write all morning, and be flagged home for lunch by the family signalling from the upper windows. On fine nights of moon it drew him even more.

Thomas came over frequently to play family cricket, and talk and exchange children for a night. His Mervyn and Bronwen were much of an age with Florence and Dick, and introduced them to country ways. The de la Mare children responded deeply to his charm. He was just his usual, rather grave self with them – not at special pains to amuse them – but he had a kind of austere playfulness they found themselves at ease with. They were a naturally gentle and friendly quartet, free and unselfconscious, though shy in new company, not at all spoilt by their easy-going upbringing. Like the Thomas children, they had their share in any visitor who came, and in return were expected to listen quietly while discussion was going on. Some of their neighbours at Anerley thought their unconventional freedom and comfortable play-clothes 'bohemian'.

De la Mare encouraged their imaginative life in every way. Over the next few years his habit of telling them stories at bedtime, or in his chair after Sunday dinner, developed more than one imaginary companion, as important to their childhoods as Tatta had been to his own. One such was 'Peter'. For this, de la Mare would 'go to sleep' in his armchair after the meal, and then soon the voice of a little boy would begin. Another compelling person, who came through in a similar way, like a spirit possessing a medium, was 'The Waterman', whose business was to go from room to room to say goodnight to the children in their beds and offer them a drink of water. He spoke in a wheedling, drawling, broken English, and in old age, de la Mare could still summon up his tone and accent. He was a good actor as well as inventive, and no one else could transport the children as completely into a world of fantasy. The Waterman was so distinct a character that on one occasion Colin used him for a safe confessor: 'Shall I tell you a secret? Promise you won't tell my Daddy! I smoked a cigarette today.' The Waterman would mention their father in the third person, presently warning them that he was about to come back – which the children of course implored him to prevent. The game hovered on the edge of the alarming and sinister, nicely judged not to overstep that border.

If his children cried (which de la Mare knew they knew he could not bear and therefore used it on him as an unfair weapon), he would sometimes 'cry them down', which they in turn detested. Or he would bawl a phrase out of the Bible at them. But these were only such ruses as one child will use on another. It is characteristic of these parents, and surely de la Mare's idea, that when a cake was discovered with a bite out of it, the method hit on for discovering the culprit was to try out the size of each child's bite on more cakes, and match results. By this test the blame fell (correctly) on Jinnie. Parental authority sat uneasily on de la Mare. Once when Florence was really naughty, he threatened to move her out of her bed and into the next room if she did not stop. She fell silent, but the moment he shut the door she started again. 'I went back,' so he told the story, 'well, frothing at the mouth, and took her without another word into the other room. Then as I went downstairs I had an awful feeling that the next room was like a vault. So I asked Fridy about it. She said, "Well, it *is* a bit cold." So there was nothing for it, I simply had to go up again. I asked, outside the door, "Are you a good girl now?" (hopefully, you know).' But Florence judged his quandary to a nicety. 'I don't *think* so, Daddy.' Game and set to her.[32]

He was not theoretical or systematic over his children's education. Nor did he read aloud to them (as Newbolt and Thomas did to their children). He only made up stories, and Elfie had no time to read or invent. Florence, in fact, learned to read late just because nobody was available to help her. Finally she began upon *The Swiss Family Robinson* for herself. Once literate, their diet was mostly fairy stories; in particular, as Florence remembered, Andrew Lang's 'colour' *Fairy Books*, Grimm, and the *Arabian Nights*. Otherwise, they were a good deal dependent, over the next few years, on the bundles of review copies for their father's omnibus Christmas articles.

In this line of business, de la Mare acquired his particular dislike of E. Nesbit. Indeed he bitterly resented *any* portrayal of children which snipped off the trailing clouds of glory and presented them as little schemers, scoring off their elders. His own four were certainly his most steady human happiness, a fourfold extension of that part of his own experience he prized above all.

They were in this crucial sense the centre of his life. To them, of course, even though he was now at home all day, he seemed preoccupied, absorbed in a world of books and papers beyond their sharing, and they looked to their mother, who held the whole family circle together and sympathised with everyone, as the pivot of their existence. They regarded their father as a Sunday and holiday companion only – enchanting mostly, but sometimes needing to be handled circumspectly.

Much as he watched and studied them, engrossed, he had none of that itch for them to excel which often makes the children of intellectuals precociously sophisticated. He neither wanted them to be exceptionally clever nor thought they were. What he prized, as his anecdotes about them always showed, were the 'morning-new' responses, uninfluenced by adult standards, revealing life from a vantage point more fortunate (he believed) than anything which acquired wisdom can put in its place. But though he was so tender and attached, he was no placid father. When nervously exhausted he could be very irritable, and the children remembered times when he was so on edge and depressed that he would shut himself away in a darkened room. They lived too intimately for the two elder children (at least) to be unaware from an early age of all their parents' anxieties, and of strains between them. Dick and Florence, practical and responsible by nature, developed a protective attitude, particularly towards their mother. They respected her strengths and sympathised with her flutters. Dick, who inherited an Ingpen gift for detail, soon showed a methodical commonsense very unlike his parents. When quite small, he began to keep hens and sold the eggs to the household, with meticulous accountancy. He showed very early a publisher's interest in his father's works, choosing for pastime one convalescent day (aged about eight) to catalogue them bibliographically.

A scheme got on foot in the winter of 1909 among well-wishers in the Newbolt circle, to help with these two children's education. Five donors, sheltering anonymously behind Edith Sichel, approached de la Mare through Newbolt, with a view to paying for a good day school for Dick, whose obvious promise needed more than the retired governess living nearby, shared up till now with Florence. One source of the money offered was the royalties from Edith Sichel's forthcoming book *Gathered Leaves from the Prose of Mary E. Coleridge*, and the fact that such a gift would have pleased Mary helped persuade de la Mare to accept for Dick's sake, though he resisted at first. This enabled Dick to go to the excellent Whitgift School in Croydon, and later the same help was extended to Florence also, for a boarding school.

De la Mare's grant was running out, but he hoped with luck to spin out the forty-five pounds remaining into a second year. He had done better than he expected: his journalism was steadily increasing, and besides the poems that Ella and Thomas saw earlier in the year, he had, by the end of September, half as many again. Edward Garnett, Duckworth's influential reader, had heard about *The Three Mulla-Mulgars*, and intimated that he would like to see it if Methuen's decided not to take it. Even 'The Almond Tree', written so long ago, had at last been accepted – by Ford Maddox Hueffer, for the August number of the *English Review*. Hueffer asked for 'Seaton's Aunt' too, to follow it, but then began to sink into financial troubles and did not in the end publish it. Nor was de la Mare paid for 'The Almond Tree', and he became reluctant to press the matter when he heard that Hueffer was in difficulties. Newbolt was delighted to see 'The Almond Tree' win its place at last. Thomas's comments were more ambiguous; he said it made him feel as if he were 'looking at people through the wrong end of a telescope – they were all so tiny'.[33] He could be curiously unpredictable in his criticism of de la Mare's work; there was no telling what would hit his fancy, or quite why.

De la Mare went to stay with him for two days in the autumn and gave him help with proofs (probably of *Rest and Unrest*). Thomas was always depressed when he had struggled to the end of a book and then found, after all, faults due to haste, and to what he felt as negligence, but could not cure. He supposed that 'at the back of it all is my notebook habit' – his mixing of methods 'of more or less instinctive writing and of slowly adding bits of colour and so on'.[34] These were problems very different from de la Mare's. He *always* worked instinctively; any notes for stories are the briefest peg or kernel, and even these (he said) were only useful if looked over and developed quickly. Otherwise the 'envelope' of imagination evaporates (what the story really is) and so the note made becomes a no longer intelligible hieroglyph, the vital impulse forgotten. The evidence is that he always 'unwound' a book from its kernel *as he went along*, and never constructed plots beforehand. After the exercises of his youth, he dropped altogether the habit of keeping a journal of observations. His scenes of nature betray the opposite weakness to Thomas's: they are so much projections of the inward mood they substantiate that they sometimes scarcely seem external at all.

About the end of September 1909 he finished his novel. He had estimated he could write a full-length work of fiction in nine months, and it had taken him just about that. He sent it straight off to Ella, with the tentative titles of *The Change* or *The Return*. He felt very dubious how she, with her stony objection to all psychological skirmishing among dark states of the soul, would receive a work which combined elements of all her pet dislikes – including Henry James and Poe. But no, she was enthusiastic! So was Newbolt, who said the novel roused his hopes to the highest pitch: 'It seems impossible that a book so original, so breathlessly exciting and so full of deepest truth and beauty, can fail to capture the whole position at once, from the citadel to the outskirts and suburbs, and including the whole garrison of critics and cognoscenti ... Nothing so Shakespearian has ever come my way. Again and again come bits of King Lear and Hamlet, – but bits that didn't happen to occur to W.S.'[35]

The plan the book had 'brought with it' was to unwind its theme a great deal through dialogue, and entirely in Lawford's own presence and consciousness, except for about a dozen lines and a page of epilogue when Mr Bethany the clergyman watches over Lawford's sleep – 'a weary old sentinel on the outskirts of his friend's denuded battlefield'. In the first version, even this was not there, but Ella objected to Mr Bethany dropping out of the story before the end. She rightly held that it was out of character for this faithful comrade to leave Lawford to his lonely struggle against his ghostly antagonist, before he was finally assured he had come through.

The story, told through reverie and speculation, becomes almost too interior; nor does the lavish dialogue counter this insubstantiality, for the main characters, Lawford and his friends Herbert and Grisel, who are brother and sister, might all be inner voices arguing in a single mind. Yet somehow they do live, able closely to concern us for their fate. De la Mare said he had Roger at the back of his mind when drawing the portrait of Herbert, and family tradition among the Newbolts held that Ella had sat for Grisel, but this seems even more tenuous, and life studies were no part of de la Mare's practice. Sheila, Lawford's wife, with her rich voice, unattractive good looks and adroit self-possession, is not a usual de la Mare character at all. At first one might feel sorry for her – commonplace, limited, humourless and set in so dismaying a predicament – but her fundamental lack of charity is exposed at the first threat to 'respectability'. Her personality, seen in such loveless daylight actuality, could scarcely less resemble Elfie's, yet Elfie seems to have taken something in this portrait personally and very much amiss. Perhaps (as all marital disputes have much in common) she fancied she caught some verbal echo from a wrangle of their own. De la Mare told Ella that she pitied Sheila, and thought the book unfair to her, and he went on: 'I simply tire her out in search of reassurance. It's perfectly idiotic.'

Far more important to the book than its characterisation is the passionate questioning all through it of death and the life beyond, which had so haunted de la Mare from childhood. The force, strangeness and beauty of this gives the story a rare quality. Lawford has a startled moment of realisation when repeating a common phrase:

'At death's door ... who was it saying that? Have you ever, Sheila, in a dream or just as one's thoughts go sometimes, seen that door? ... its ruinous stone lintel, carved into lichenous stone heads ... stonily silent in the last thin sunlight, hanging in peace unlatched. Heated, hunted, in agony, – in that cold, green-clad, shadowed porch is haven and sanctuary ... But beyond – O God, beyond!'

This is virtually poetry, and should sound absurd set in a conversation held in a Victorian middle-class suburb. Yet it is not: the reader can accept it, and its ring of authenticity in its context derives from de la Mare's genuine personal experience. He lived in such a suburb and unaffectedly saw life and death from there in such terms – his most commonplace and banal milieu transfigured at every turn, every day, by fundamental mystery and danger. If he did not write a great novel in *The Return*, he certainly sounded a unique 'Qui vive'.

Newbolt felt very happy in all his prophecies by November 1909, for he had on his desk, besides *The Return*, such new poems as 'The Bindweed', 'Where?' and 'The Sleeper', and also one which he had no hesitation in placing straight away among the classics. He wrote to Ella: 'He's never written better – never I think anything so good as 'The Listeners'. It is exquisite in form – free and yet faultless – and, for romance, a great picture and a great poem in one … you might safely print it beside the Ancient Mariner or the Lady of Shalott or St Agnes' Eve: it would only be more obvious how beautiful and original it is.'36 Between them, Newbolt, Ella and Thomas had now seen a substantial part of the poems that made up the volume *The Listeners* three years later – the collection that marks de la Mare out from the lyric poets of a passing fashion – unfashionable as it may be, just now, to make such a claim.

*

By 1910, the first wave of energy which release from Oil brought, had spent itself. After all, he was not young, but on the verge of middle age. He held that 'twentytwo seems generally the middleagedest year of a thoughtful man's life', but by thirty-seven, where he now was, inevitably flatter vistas begin to show ahead. He quailed a bit, recollecting pointedly his childhood vow not to outlive forty. This year he endured bad doubts about his own powers.

Newbolt and Ella did their best to encourage him. Ella wrote that 'every great writer has to create *a taste for himself* in his public … He brings a new dish – and the Public *always* shies off at first. They've learnt slowly to like bananas – So they want only bananas – Then we forced tomatoes on them – Now the Costers' barrows are full of tomatoes. But Mangoes – de la Marish mangoes – no thank you. *But the day will come* when there'll be a boom in mangoes.'37 But meanwhile de la Mare found re-reading *The Return* a grind – 'choke full of crudities and slices of Saharaness'.38 Still, there was a cheering week in April. Duckworth had demurred a good deal over the *Mulgars*, in spite of enthusiasm from Garnett (Methuen had rejected the book). Arnold delayed in similar doubts over *The Return*. Then all at once, both firms decided on acceptance within a day or two of each other.

This month de la Mare mentioned to Pinker writing 'twenty to thirty simple rhymes in a day'. These were probably the ones for a portfolio of child photographs by a Mrs Cadby. The book, arranged as *A Child's Day*, was no more than a jingling and saccharine pot-boiler. Later he came to feel it tawdry, and certainly it is an unworthy successor to *Songs of Childhood*, comparing very poorly with even the *Horn Books*.

He travelled down for a weekend at the brand-new Thomas house at Wick Green, a short way from Berryfield Cottage, up on a plateau and overlooking, from its dramatic brink, sixty miles of the South Downs. The road up to this house from Steep ran along the ridge right round the horseshoe of the wooded combe, tantalisingly close to anyone approaching on foot, but still with the gulf lying between. The Thomas children, drawing level opposite home, would begin to call out for encouragement, and Edward's characteristic 'Coo-ee' would float back to them – later finding its way into a rhyme in *Peacock Pie*:

> Longlegs – he yelled 'Coo-ee!'
> And all across the combe
> Shrill and shrill it rang – rang through
> The clear green gloom ...

By now, Thomas had introduced de la Mare to W. H. Davies, whose poems and *Autobiography of a Super-Tramp* de la Mare had already long admired – enthusiasms pressed on Ella and Newbolt. Ella had been converted completely by the fresh beauty of the poems, but much against her will, for the *Autobiography* shocked her, and she remained a little nonplussed and disturbed that heaven should bestow on a tramp who had lived a sordid life and had, as she said, 'fought society with its own weapons' (i.e. dishonesty), a lyrical gift so radiantly innocent. De la Mare conformed in his personal life to the accepted standards of society, but his moral judgement of any artist took more into account, and he evidently felt Ella's disapproval a touch prim and smug. He himself was very much attracted by Davies's unusual character, his innocent eye, and his far from innocent experience. He delighted in the *Autobiography*, and came to love Davies's talk and outlook, reviewing him several times in print with high praise. They met at the St George's Café on Thomas's Wednesdays in town, and fairly often later on, generally among mutual friends. They never became intimate. This June, 1910, after Davies had come to supper with the de la Mares, de la Mare wrote to Newbolt: 'There never could have been a more delightfully clear view of the world seen by one man, as [sic] his. He told me that he spent nearly the whole of a snowy winter fortnight feeding multitudes of birds – two loaves a day he cut up – until his landlord who had fruit-trees in his garden asked him to leave.'[39] Of the many stories that circulated about Davies's *naiveté*, de la Mare said in a letter in 1945, five years after Davies's death:

I think it is possible to confuse his rare naturalness with just ingenuousness. Anyhow he was a clear-sighted and trenchant critic ... How far he was aware of his own little idiosyncrasies is a nice little question. He had real insight and I rather fancy myself that he may have been amused by the amusement he caused in the more sophisticated. So one hesitates. I expect you have heard (though I cannot myself vouch for this) that one day Harold Monro came to see him when he was living near Leicester Square, and discovered him saw in hand contemplating a rather nice bookcase. He asked what was afoot and was told that Davies thought the book-case too big for his room and intended to saw it in half. Rather shocked at this, H.M. exclaimed that it was a very nice bookcase and that it was a pity to spoil it. '*But*, you see,' retorted Davies, a little ruefully, 'I have bought the saw.'[40]

There are several stories, repeated by such friends of Davies as Osbert Sitwell and William Nicholson, illustrating a fierce jealousy of de la Mare on Davies's part. He certainly felt in competition, and, though ready to acknowledge in de la Mare a wider intellect, believed his own lyric gift had greater directness and was more genuine. He betrayed towards various other poets, Yeats among them, the same jealous ambivalence. Nothing on de la Mare's side shows him aware that Davies was jealous, and indeed one incident would never have happened had he suspected such was the case. Once, in the early years of their acquaintance, when the de la Mares and Ralph Hodgson and Davies were all spending an evening together at the Hootons (friends of Edward and Helen Thomas) Davies, who was still a rather quiet little man in company until warmed up, inquired 'What *is* a limerick?' Everyone began quoting them. De la Mare of course had made a hobby of composing them as far back as *Horn Book* days. All present now agreed to make one up on the spot. Davies's contribution ended:

> He sang one song and he sang no other:
> It's nat-u-ral to love your mother.

Amid the general laughter, de la Mare was heard rallying him: 'Davies, *who writes your poems for you?*'[41]This teasing would have been quite out of character had he suspected it could possibly rankle. Nor did it, probably, on the day in question, while they were in one room together – or ever would have done, perhaps, while de la Mare was present; his modesty and his obvious admiration disarmed Davies, and brought out the side de la Mare was recommending to Naomi Royde-Smith in 1915: 'You ought to have a real talk with him. It's always as fresh and unexpected as a May morning.'[42]

Newbolt wanted de la Mare's new book of adult poems to come out at Methuen in the spring of 1911, and to be followed by a children's volume in the autumn. But these, which gradually crystallised into the two books that made de la Mare's name, *The Listeners* and *Peacock Pie*, were not to the taste of Methuen, nor of Arnold, and it was Constable who finally accepted them. Meanwhile Newbolt dispensed the final fifteen pounds of the Bounty in July 1910, and de la Mare's description of what his help had meant ('a never-failing buttress in the many inevitable hours of worry and anxiety') prompted a reply that shows how accurately Newbolt judged their comparative stature, even while much of de la Mare's best lay in the future, and how little he was deluded by his own success as a poet of the day:

> Don't imagine that any small trouble or time I have spent have been unremunerative. Mr Fondly gets his fun out of eulogising the dead. I out of admiring my contemporaries. To have it once thought that I *helped* one of them – and to an insubstantial person what a massively flattering word is your 'buttress'! But the relentlessly candid friend who dwells within tells me of a time, not 100 years hence, when those who look at your work & mine, & our friendship as it appears in your letters, will say something smiling of the hovels that so often have the air of buttressing the cathedral they lean up against.[43]

Public patronage of the arts does not get a great deal of praise; surely it deserves it at this point in de la Mare's story, when one considers how those two hundred pounds turned the whole course of his career, and when one looks at the quality of the works written in the actual months cushioned by the Bounty cheques – to name *The Return*, 'Seaton's Aunt' and the poem 'The Listeners' alone.

August 1910 at Dene Cottage, West Harting (once more with the Thomases nearby) had the added attraction for the children of a camp of fifteen hundred troops on manoeuvres, with forty guns brushing the dew off the hedges in a 'scout-fight' in the early morning, not fifty yards from the windows, and the camp fires of the friendly Hussars to visit at dusk. It is unusual for de la Mare to lift the incident in a poem directly from life, but the sample of child psychology in 'Dry August Burned' belongs to this holiday. It was Florence, nearly eleven, who 'wept out her heart' to see a harvest hare, limp on the kitchen table in its blood-blubbered fur. Just then the stirring cavalcade of the artillery thudded past the gate. She ran outside to watch the 'sun-tanned soldiery',

> Till dust-white hedge had hidden away –
> Its din into a rumour thinned –
> The laughing, jolting, wild array:
> And then – the wonder and tumult gone –
> Stood nibbling a green leaf, alone,
> Her dark eyes dreaming … She turned, and ran,
> Elf-like into the house again.
> The hare had vanished … 'Mother,' she said,
> Her tear-stained cheek now flushed with red,
> 'Please, may I go and see it skinned?'[44]

De la Mare returned to London having finished, among other holiday tasks, the proofs of *The Return* and *The Three Mulla-Mulgars*, with 'indescribable remorse', lamenting: 'If only I could rewrite both the horrible things – or better still, unwrite them.'[45] Reporting to Ella, he went on to air his latest enthusiasm:

> Do you know anything of a poet named Ralph Hodgson? Or have you seen last week's Saturday Review? If not, you must let me send it to you. It has gone post-haste to H.N. I am very keen to know what he thinks of it – a long poem printed as a Supplement. It's extraordinarily full of beauty, power and originality.[46]

This was 'To Deck a Woman', Hodgson's eloquent polemic against the fashion for wearing birds' plumage on hats and the like. (The change in public opinion and the movement that later brought about the Plumage Act owed something to this poem.) De la Mare's friendship with Hodgson was soon to follow, and blossomed at speed. There is no doubt that he felt more intense admiration for Hodgson's work – so different from his own in its direct approach and generalised emotion – than for any other poetry of his contemporaries. The friendship that resulted, though a good deal less intimate than that with Thomas, remained one of the most prized of his life.

Hodgson, a little his elder and a great deal more experienced, was perhaps the strongest personality of all the poets of their circle. Siegfried Sassoon went so far as to say he gave the impression of a prodigious genius among them – one beside whom de la Mare's more diffident personality paled a little. It was Hodgson who was the natural centre of any group he joined, and who talked most of the time. Not that this was from egotism; he would be extremely interested in what de la Mare or Thomas or anyone else had to say, but the flood of his own ideas would carry him away in reply. His favourite subjects ranged over primitive Man, birds and their species, boxing, billiards, bull-terriers, the America of his footloose youth. It was creative, stimulating talk, full of fascinating information and unusual facts (scientific, or at least purporting to be so), and variegated by anecdotes from Hodgson's rich and wayward personal experience, and descriptions of queer characters he had met in his many careers – which ranged from scene-painting to journalism (he was a reporter at Oscar Wilde's trial) – and experiences at Cruft's dog shows, or as a runaway boy in the boxing fancy. Hodgson's talk, in fact, was perhaps his greatest creative gift – full of intransigent opinions, fervour, poetry and a strong inborn Puritanism – hot, denunciatory and imaginative. 'He would have sent you to the stake,' Sassoon declared. He had a horror of drink and would only touch ginger-beer himself, and he thought dancing immoral. Yet at the same time he disapproved when Helen Thomas's friend, little sparkling Janet Hooton, wore sensible, emancipated suffragette clothes. He tried to reconvert her to silk underwear instead of serge, and had a weakness for the frilly femininity of waitresses. In appearance he was dark, bushy-browed, long-faced, with a long upper lip and deep furrows running down it either side – and often a pipe in the combative mouth. At times a demon of stony, sardonic melancholy seemed to sweep over his features and possess him. He was extremely reticent about his personal affairs, and not even his most intimate friends ever heard much of the lower-middle-class home at Darlington from which he had run away in boyhood – except that he was 'of pure English stock' and took great pride in the fact. Nor would he, in turn, ever question his friends about their private lives. 'Independent as the North Pole' was de la Mare's phrase for him, and of all his circle Hodgson best epitomised what chiefly fascinated de la Mare in life and literature alike: flavour, character, gusto, unexpectedness, a know-ledgeable love of the inexhaustible mysteries of Nature – and all this sun-shot through with idealism and a passion for beauty. Their shared love of these things was what drew de la Mare also to Thomas, but he himself and even Thomas were bookish men, and passive to experience, beside Hodgson. He was a magnet to them both. Davies, it is true, had a correspondingly colourful adventuring quality, but he was limited intellectually within the station from which he had risen. There was nothing naive about Hodgson's potent, ranging mind. Yet he wrote, in all, very little, very seldom, very fastidiously to please himself alone, and sank at last after many years of his odd self-exile from the England he loved into a melancholy fixed foreboding over the nuclear future of mankind.

Newbolt was eager to review *The Return*, and so was Thomas, who wrote to de la Mare warmly enough about it, though discussing the story chiefly on grounds of characterisation. But there is no mistaking the different tone in the letter which followed ten days later, asking for another book to be sent for him to do for the *Bookman* – this time *The Three Mulla-Mulgars*. *The Return* was from the side of de la Mare least congenial to Thomas; he recognised its merits, but it lay outside his personal field of sympathy, whereas the Mulgars lay right at its heart: 'I don't know how to describe my enjoyment. It is beautiful & enchanting all through, & the harmony of the whole makes many & many of the little things wonderful which would have been beautiful even if standing alone ... It is your best book altogether.'[47]

Reviews of *The Return* were mixed, and Newbolt felt disappointed at the book's reception; it was a good deal less than the resounding success he had expected. He put this down, perhaps naively, largely to the fact that it appeared at the same time as Forster's *Howard's End*, which attracted much critical attention.* There was, however, one very favourable review, in the *Saturday Westminster Gazette*, by a young woman, Naomi Royde-Smith, who as its Literary Editor under Spender was now sending de la Mare regular and frequent work. They had in consequence corresponded quite a bit, but had not yet met. Miss Royde-Smith, now in her early thirties, had carved out for herself a position unique at that time. Influential journalism was still an almost exclusively masculine preserve (in spite of George Eliot) and in 1910 no other woman held the literary-editorial chair of a weekly so renowned. A review in the *SWG* carried as much weight as one in the *TLS*. Miss Royde-Smith had risen entirely through her own ability and drive. She had a forceful personality, sharp-tongued and sharp-witted; she was extremely well read, and, while quite able to tackle men on their own terms, she was also fair-haired, feminine and a successful hostess (although not well off). Above all she had a fine literary flair – the same instinct for promise which was so outstanding in Richmond at the *TLS*.

Perhaps she owed her blend of intuition and practical drive, of sensibility and toughness, to the double strand in her heredity, which was both Welsh and downright Yorkshire. Her cultivation she owed entirely to her own reading, after a sound education at Clapham High School. She had gone on to Switzerland, and while still a student, had had to begin to support herself and help her mother. She had learnt early to fight her own battles – and the other side of her nature supplied these with a romantic aura. By the time de la Mare began to receive her brisk editorial postcards (as well as frequent letters in the autumn of 1910 inviting literary discussion) she was already a seasoned reviewer with an easy style, and with a much wider experience of literary society than he had. Yet her article praising *The Return* is a little tentative and constrained, and she felt it inadequate herself. She wrote to apologise: 'Really I had no blame for it – only a kind of awe that made me unable to shout "This is good stuff".'[48] And she spoke of whole pages and passages which seemed 'quite unlike anything else in fiction'. Plainly she was very much impressed, and intent on winning de la Mare's friendship. His replies are courteous, deferring to her wishes and asking her opinion, ready to discuss literary matters; but he did not come to the office, and made no move towards personal acquaintance. By now, he was writing even more for the *Saturday Westminster* than for the *TLS* – at least thirty-two

---

* Forster himself admired *The Return* later on when the award of a prize brought it to his knowledge, and he wrote de la Mare a brief but warm fan-letter.

articles in the three months up to December 1910. Thomas, as usual watching over his interests, however bad his own fortunes, had specifically asked Miss Royde-Smith to 'keep de la Mare in bread and butter', and she was keeping her word.

The stimulating circle of friends was widening rapidly, and by now de la Mare no longer depended chiefly on introductions through the Newbolt household. His journalism, and the increasing reputation *The Return* and the *Mulgars* brought him, made him friends for himself. Among all, Thomas remained the most intimate, the 'friend of friends'. However low his spirits, he had no lowering effect on de la Mare's and always set him at ease within himself. But now an encounter took place very different from all such intimacies; one whose profound effect on de la Mare's life and poetry remains, after all is said, a puzzling affair.

Part II

Romantic Acrobat

9

Naomi Royde-Smith

If a sympathy were going to develop between de la Mare and the Literary Editor of the *Saturday Westminster*, one would have expected much the kind of friendship he had already with Edith Sichel: an attraction of unlike beings, based on common intellectual interests, and unemotional. Instead, his very first meeting with Naomi Royde-Smith in the spring of 1911 shook his life to the core, and set up a ferment in his imagination from which much of his finest lyrical poetry was to spring over the next four years – the peak years.

It is not easy to see why this came about; for the two seem from all evidence now, and appeared to mutual friends at the time, cut from cloth of a completely unlike weave. Their relationship had the tension of something uncharacteristic, certainly on his side, perhaps on hers too.

They met in an upstairs tea-room by the Temple Gardens, one cloudy afternoon as February opened into March. Each came with a strong preconception of the other: both quite wrong. Thomas had for some time intended to make the introduction, but de la Mare had stalled: he had formed an unfavourable picture of Miss Royde-Smith – perhaps partly from Thomas himself, for Naomi at any rate thought Thomas did not like her. De la Mare had pictured the lady editor (so he told her later) as 'of middle height, not a bit slim, with white round hands, O so calm and clever ... I rather hated her.' She for her part had imagined the creator of the spectral Huguenot in 'The Return' as 'a lean ascetic with a high forehead, haunted eyes and a rather quelling power of silence'. Instead, standing between the tall fair Thomas and her assistant in the office, Leonard Henry, also tall and athletic, she took in the impression (she said) of 'a round little man in a round little coat'. At a second glance she decided de la Mare had the face of a Roman Emperor, 'dark, slightly curling hair, brown almost golden eyes and an enchanting smile. His faun's ears stood out a little from the side of his head. His blue serge suit with a round jacket gave him a faintly nautical air and he was far from silent.

'Before I had poured out the first cup of tea,' she recorded, 'he had asked me how old I was and filled my astonished pause with a speculation on the difference between Age and Time. This set us all talking as he meant it should.'[1]

While she poured out the tea, de la Mare in turn was digesting the total reversal of his picture of her – a mental somersault to which his habit of vividly visualising in advance quite often subjected him. (Once, much later on, when a lady was announced with whom he had been corresponding for years, he was so disconcerted by her staggering unlikeness to the figure he had mentally addressed that he was forced to look far out of the window while he rearranged the whole relationship.)

Miss Royde-Smith was just on thirty-three, five years younger than he was. Her remarkable eyes – large, light and bright, very blue – were much on a level with his own. She was strikingly fair, with vigorous wavy gold hair caught back loosely under a little black hat. She dressed stylishly, choosing the sea-greens and blues that best set off her colouring. Her hair, wide brow and speaking eyes made the upper part of her face lovely by any standards. Below came a short, rather blunt nose and a mouth and chin that could look formidable – a fighter's. There was something of the Amazon, all the challenge of a very poised, capable and clever professional woman – and also, for de la Mare, for some reason or other, a kind of glamour of the romantic child, appealing straight to his most secret core, that part of him to which his friends (he would later tell her) were 'near enough, but they don't get *in*'.[2]

Her spell over him was not the most usual one. There are other kinds of magnetism as instant and inexplicable as straightforward sexual attraction, though they are less common. One is spiritual affinity; and this is what these two would assert, over and over, that they had with one another – to the point of shared identity. It seems unlikely that they were right. Each had a romantic imagination, and it was on this level that each answered for a while to something the other had always looked for. In de la Mare the unconscious need, perhaps, was simply for a Muse in human form, for that miraculous imaginative catalyst that a chance encounter with some Beatrice has sometimes brought into the lives of writers. For the kind of romantic artist he was, such a love seems, on the plane of imagination, a destiny, a fulfilment, almost inevitable. But on the plane of actual human relations, in de la Mare's case at least, there is something arbitrary about it, and a bit strained. It does not quite fit.

Naomi on her side felt a great need to be an artist's Muse. She wanted the men she loved to be men of genius; she believed they were, and she felt her destiny was to be a gateway through which such elect spirits could reach their Promised Land. In fact there were many ways in which she was well gifted to help a man's talent to fruition.

From the beginning, their relationship mostly took place, for de la Mare, in 'that other Real' he was always seeking to dream out as a substratum of actuality. He would speak of his first meeting with Naomi as if she had not been there in the flesh but in spiritual essence alone: 'Shall I ever forget the ghost coming in with those amazing straight eyes?'[3] In a very real sense it was her 'ghost' he fell in love with. One cannot think of the two ever marrying, and the long tension of the four years to come, while their relationship was at its emotional height, were humanly speaking very wasteful – destructive of family peace and tormenting to each other. But for de la Mare's flowering as a poet this emotional tension was crucial. And the seven to eight hundred letters he poured out to Naomi reveal, as nothing else does, the world of inner experience peculiar to himself that his art was born from.

In all his other correspondence that survives, he was conspicuously reserved and elusive about his private emotional life. Even the mood he is writing in is usually concealed – in most letters just by reticence on the subject – in the love letters to Elfie by striking poses. The letters to Naomi form his one *journal intime*, the link between emotional experience and its effect, at great remove, in his work.

The actual stuff of the poems is not here – not gold for gold, as the stuff of Keats's poetry is in his letters – for these are not first-class letters. They are monotonous in bulk, too introspective and at times betrayed into whimsy; and he was too uneasy in mind not to strike now and then a false note in protesting his love. Yet here, like loose ore tumbled out of a sack, without inhibition, with the roots and soil of personal, private life still clinging to it, is the actual thought-stuff of feelings and fantasy that filled his mind habitually when he was alone and stirred.

An obscure and secret ground lies between the actual lady editor with Welsh blood (Wales is the 'West Country') who is matter for the biographer, and the voice of all human regret which speaks with such gravitas from the tombstone of the poem called 'An Epitaph':[4]

> Here lies a most beautiful lady,
> Light of step and heart was she;
> I think she was the most beautiful lady
> That ever was in the West Country.

> But beauty vanishes; beauty passes:
> However rare – rare it be;
> And when I crumble, who will remember
> This lady of the West Country?

The letters lie thick across that ground and partly indicate what steps
de la Mare took from one side to the other.

*

The spell was established at first sight – and from the first, de la Mare
spoke of it as one. He really felt under some kind of bewitchment.
Having longed for magic all his life, now, on the edge of middle age and
in very mundane circumstances, he found himself, like Bottom,
suddenly 'translated'. His early romantic wooing of Elfie (high-flown
though the young Nineties aesthete had been) belonged far more to
flesh-and-blood living. Walking together along the Embankment,
leaning over the parapet of a bridge to watch a swan come silently and
suddenly into view beneath, seeing Naomi's face strangely against that
restless background of water, he felt, as never since childhood, the
force of intense wonder and, above all, *recognition* – the actual
palpably haunted by another, deeper kind of existence. Was she really
a witch? Why else should the moment affect him so strangely, so that
imagination kept returning obsessively to question that first meeting?
These thoughts, poured out to her, seem to belong less to the province
of adult masculine sexuality than to sheer romantic fantasy.

That week they talked of *Urn Burial*, and each of them on getting
home took down Sir Thomas Browne from their shelves, and presently
turned from that to poems of their own. Naomi had written verses
since her schooldays, but had not published any. They were not very
good. She read them over now, for de la Mare had asked to see them.
On the other side of London, having read as far as 'St Innocent's
Churchyard', de la Mare put down his *Urn Burial* and began to write.
This new emotion mostly expressed itself obliquely – he did not often
write love poems as self-confessed as this, sent to Naomi at some time
in the next year or two. It has never been published:

> I say I see you; does that tell how much? –
> How that my eyes, past flesh and slender bone,
> Pierce in, and make your very ghost my own?
>
> I say I know you; does that tell how much?
> How that my mind broods on until to me
> No more than one strange burning thought you be?

> I say I love you: O, how could one word
> Tell how the very instant you did come
> Out of life's dark I turned at once straight home.

Most of the other poems escape the personal context by 'knight's move'. One of those he wrote for her two weeks or so after they first met is an example of this – in impulse it is a love-poem, yet human love is scarcely alluded to:

> An apple, a child, dust,
>> When falls the evening rain,
> Wild brier's spicèd leaves,
>> Breathe memories again,
> With further memory fraught,
>> The silver of the may
> Wreathed is with incense for
>> The Judgement Day.*

The images in it in fact had private personal references for them both. 'The Sweetbriar somehow is you,' he wrote; 'its medley of things I can't understand.'[5] And he would sometimes enclose a sprig of it in his letters.

They had shared an apple, too, on the first evening they spent together in her home. Later he called it the magic apple. While they ate they talked of colours, comparing all the blue things of earth that each loved best, sitting alone together after Naomi's other guests had left. Her rooms were in Oakley Street, near the Thames, where she lived with a sister and held a regular 'At Home' to friends who were mostly writers and journalists, on Thursday evenings. De la Mare was soon a regular guest at them, and would stay late, though always rather guiltily, as Friday was Naomi's busiest day of the week, when contributions for the Saturday issue were arranged upon the pages. Those who worked for her learned to be wary on Fridays; storms of nervous exasperation might break on the heads of the careless. She had a fierce temper, but when the typhoon had passed she was quick to make amends, and her assistant would find on her desk a bunch of penitent flowers that Naomi had slipped out to buy. Her masterful relations with younger women had a touch of the romantic and possibly the ambivalent about them, and she always noticed personal looks particularly at a first meeting (with either sex).

De la Mare was soon pressing her constantly for meetings, and between them he would write every day or two, asking to see her

---

* The middle one of three stanzas entitled 'The Hawthorn Hath a Deathly Smell', *The Listeners* (1912).

poems (and in his present state praising them rather extravagantly) or perhaps requesting some particular book to review. They exchanged dreams. For de la Mare these were always as much part of his day-to-day news as a visit to a real place, and he told them well: 'I dreamed once of a sea with three moons aloft, and have often of the clearest, loveliest water – once floods and far across a little cottage under the *blazing* Western sun where I thought some kind of god had hidden a book for me!'[6]

He was possessive, and would have liked to have her time entirely at his disposal. What he wanted to share with her was no more than talk and things of the imagination, but he wanted it with all a lover's total exclusiveness. She called this his Sultanism. It soon galled him to discover how widely her attention was in demand from other admirers. One of the first things she showed him were poems to her by some other man.

The literary competitions she devised in the *Saturday Westminster* for its 'Problems and Prizes' page had become celebrated. Distinguished poets competed: Bridges would send in an entry, and if it won would sometimes leave the prize unclaimed, so that only the editor's staff knew of its authorship. De la Mare could not resist trying his hand with a poem for a contest set on the subject 'The Poet Remonstrates with his Muse'. He initialled his entry 'D.B.' ('Binns' was a nickname Naomi gave him, out of a dream she had had). He left Naomi to guess the author, which she easily did. He kept it back from published collections for seven years, till it appeared at last in *Motley* (1918) along with several others held back for the same reason – that they confess personal passion too plainly. In *Motley* the poem appears just as 'The Remonstrance', and simply for what it is, a love poem; the Muse had dropped out. Yet the two roles, Muse and beloved, were actually much more completely fused in this love-affair than is usual. The vehement letters poured out to the woman he was meeting every few days are just as exclusively concerned with disembodied emotion, lost childhood and the visions of the imagination as these lines are. They are the very terms of his whole concern with her:

> I was at peace until you came
> And set a careless mind aflame.
> I lived in quiet; cold, content;
> All longing in safe banishment,
> Until your ghostly lips and eyes
>   Made wisdom unwise.[7]

Naomi felt bound to mention to the editor of the *Saturday*

Westminster, Spender, that there was one 'real poem' among the entries. Naturally he insisted it should win the prize; in the end Naomi awarded it tied with another (a set of comic verses) because she felt sure de la Mare would not wish to come forward for the money. So, like Bridges, he left the prize unclaimed, and the poem was printed anonymously.

His old preoccupations were at pressure again: the sense of exile, the pang of transience, as sharp as when the little boy's convolvulus had withered in his hand. He wrote to her: 'I wonder if you are haunted to the extremity that I am by this half-peaceful half-fretting sense of the incessant insecurity & fugitiveness of everything. Every moment of the present wears a vaguely surmised suggestion that it is only pretending, that the conspiracy is *just* coming to an end. I always seem to be on the brink of something; & so the future is hateful because it can't possibly come, or if it does, will only lead to other futures that can't. And I long to get things over, to have them safe in memory – beyond the guessings of foreboding and anxiety. Even you are almost best in memory, where I cannot change you, nor you yourself.'[8]

He sent to Naomi at the end of this April (1911) the poems to choose from for a possible new collection – those Ella and Newbolt had already seen, and seven more written for her. It was ironical that just at this moment, when his inspiration was at second Spring, Ella (knowing nothing of these new poems) was complaining to Newbolt that journalism had 'sucked de la Mare dry'. She had looked through a recent batch of verses (probably rhymes for *A Child's Day*) before they went to the publisher and thought most of them 'quite deplorable both to ear and understanding'. Something must be done! She felt he had not done enough yet to qualify for another grant, and how was he in this state to accomplish the 'good big piece of Literary Work' needed for this? She also worried about what she considered 'something a bit Bohemian' in the de la Mare parents, reporting that de la Mare 'dropped out the other day a little tale of Colin, aged 4. 'He was christened last week, rather late, but we hadn't been able to collect the godparents sooner.* When we came out of Church he said to his mother with a sigh of relief 'Oh Mother I'm so glad I was only christened. I was afraid I was going to be married.' That I was aghast at the dilatory Xtening seemed quite funny to Wd1M. And as a family they are quite orthodoxly Church!'[9] De la Mare would have been amused to hear himself described as 'orthodoxly Church'.

Ella prevailed on him to take a week's break at Netherhampton,

---

* Edward Thomas was one of them.

under her vigilant wing. He described it all vividly but moodily in voluminous letters to Naomi. He was not happy, even with such good friends; he would rather have been quite alone for a few days. And he insisted on getting back for the Sunday, a day now set aside whenever possible for Naomi's walking-parties. Elfie stayed at home, of course. Naomi and her friends roamed the woods round Holmbury, near Dorking, where she had a weekend cottage. 'Had I been rich,' de la Mare told her, 'I should have lived a life of lone in a thick wood.'[10] These woods lay not very far from those he had loved at Spyfield. His favourite haunt with Naomi became a great stretch they christened Boundless Wood.

At one of Naomi's parties he met W.H. Hudson, who came with Thomas: a lonely figure 'with the face of an old hawk'.[11] De la Mare felt Hudson had 'changeling blood in him', and had particularly wanted this meeting, which Naomi was glad to arrange for him. But Hudson was a natural solitary, unhappy in a crowd, and de la Mare himself was unwell. 'I was half-blind with neuralgia,' he wrote to Naomi afterwards. 'I remember Mr Hudson was trying to say things that couldn't be said with all the noise – I *did* like him, I wonder if I'll ever see him again.' De la Mare's love of the English naturalists was a marked thread throughout his life's reading; he loved Bewick (the *Memoirs* as much as the woodcuts) and Gilbert White and Izaak Walton. And, for him, Hudson was far and away the prince of these. He could not altogether share Thomas's enthusiasm for Richard Jefferies; the emotional mysticism Jefferies mixed with his observation of nature was much less to his taste than Hudson's curious penetrative poetry of the actual. In 1923 he wrote of Hudson: 'Nobody can love his work more than I do; and delight in it only deepens as one grows older. As for the style, it is as if all the birds and bells and water he had ever heard had each lent him their secret language and decoy.'[12]

That first summer of 1911, de la Mare and Naomi stole a long day alone together in Richmond Park that drew them close together – perilously close from his point of view. He asked her anxiously if she had thought the day together wicked, and he made light, a little ruefully, of having 'clutched the inviolable shade' under an arch somewhere. There was no happiness or peace of mind for either of them in stolen kisses, and from their letters it is clear that these were not frequent. There was no peace, either, in the endless analysing, probing and dissecting of their love which de la Mare could not resist, and which only exposed its frustration and sterility. As he grew gradually more unhappy, while the year wore on, he carried their relationship even more away from the sphere of real life, where they could see there could be no fulfilment – only, some day, some kind of end.

Constantly he addressed her as 'ghost', thought of her as inward companion, as his alter ego, as Idea. Again, as in the first flush of love for Elfie, he felt the death-wish as the only fit culmination of his intensified, almost exacerbated, sense of aliveness: 'And as I stood on the platform at Clapham Junc. & watched every train come pounding in that wasn't mine, I just longed to take the jump – simply because I was so crammed up with life. Do you understand that?'[13]

Quite often, in the distress and perplexity his thoughts about her brought him, he would turn for consolation to his youngest child: 'I have just been lying down with Colin. It is not a particularly martinettish proceeding; but we hold hands while he sighs himself off to sleep and it's always a very peaceful five minutes for me. He must be like the Scythian apple which "breathes out in the deserts of Arabia a faint and soporific odour at evening to comfort the hearts of the lost".'[14]

The usual Dene Cottage family holiday took place in August, and Hodgson turned up in the first few days and stayed for three of them. He and Thomas distinguished themselves during a cricket match on the lawn by mighty drives right over a nearby haystack. Hodgson took so particular a fancy to young Colin that he offered to adopt him, and later on quite seriously proposed that he should arrange for him to be trained as a billiard-marker – he was very keen on the game, and knew all the top players of his day. Naomi was another visitor at Dene Cottage; she came toward the end of August for a Saturday, after de la Mare had spent two or three weeks in a fever on her account, by day, and at night in guilty dreams of being executed or pursued. When she came, he was able to take her out to his hillside writing-places on Tarbury, under the huge beeches and the yew on the open slope that creaked in the wind.

He had been devoured by desperate craving before she arrived, and afterwards matters were worse. Elfie observed to him that his face 'went all thin in one evening' that day of Naomi's visit. She was not, of course, deluded. All three suffered, Elfie the most, though in the end Naomi's heart would ache the longest. De la Mare was overcome by all that both women felt – jealousy and longing – and he felt guilty and disloyal, although technically he was keeping the sixth commandment. If he had to mention Elfie, in a letter to Naomi, he never did so by name, but always as 'my wife', with a kind of stiff gaucherie that was unlike his free heart. He was not very successful in trying to treat this aspect of the liaison airily: 'Sometimes Conscience strikes the match and hastens the people out of church in the ashes,' he wrote to Naomi.

'Do you know him? He's a Grundy on his mother's side and some queer mixture of a Scotch elder and a gentleman on the other. And that, my dear, is a very officious stock.'[15]

He wrote the verses he later put into *Peacock Pie* called 'Bewitched', artificial in effect but biographical in their detail, for its fox and adder and 'beech boughs dusk and dim' belong to Tarbury. The poem goes on:

> I sit at my supper 'mid honest faces,
>   And crumble my crust and say
> Nought in the long-drawn drawl of the voices
>   Talking the hours away.

He used the phrase 'I crumble my crust' elsewhere, in a letter, to express the state of mind in which he would sit impotently wretched, not just in his own home, where the bewitchment of his infatuation had made him 'a stranger to my own kin', but also at Naomi's parties, where he watched her sparkling, ambitious, much in demand, flirting a little and, in spite of her real devotion to him, much more toughly constituted and self-confident than he was to stand the strain of their relationship.

Yet, along with the pain and unrest and the intensification of experience, hovering between vision and nightmare, he was also conscious of a real access of poetic force. 'I know it is You who are blowing up my poor smouldering ashes,' he told Naomi, and poems he sent her in September 1911 prove it: 'The Vision' ('O Starry face, bound in grave strands of hair'),[16] and 'When the Rose is Faded',[17] which rises out of the de la Mare minor into a major key of affirmation:

> 'Tis the immortal thought
>   Whose passion still
> Makes of the changing
>   The unchangeable.
>
> Oh, thus thy beauty,
>   Loveliest on earth to me,
> Dark with no sorrow, shines
>   And burns, with Thee.

To this more fruitful peace Naomi's physical absence undoubtedly contributed. His time without her at Dene Cottage was followed by a month she spent in Switzerland. He was really much more content with her when she was not there, and there were no jarring adjustments to make between the many-sided strong-willed woman of actuality and the 'You that no-one else knows of or shares – *our* You', which he did from time to time admit he had created, but held to be none the less real for that.

For her part, Naomi was writing him a voluminous journal-letter, of which she would show him instalments when they were alone. From now on the only letters she posted to his home were those that could do no harm if Elfie read them. There had been angry protests over this correspondence, and no doubt, besides whatever letters de la Mare showed Elfie, in the lame attempt to make her feel less excluded, she had chanced on something more intimate. Florence, twelve that year, and Dick, ten, were perfectly aware of the trouble and fiercely protective of their mother. They would try to take their father his letters before Elfie should be distressed by the sight of Naomi's writing on an envelope. Their blame and indignation naturally fell on her, the interloper. In fact Colin, aged six, was really the only one too small to be involved and disturbed. Even he could remember hearing doors slammed, raised voices, threats to leave home …

It flattered Naomi, naturally, to be so overwhelmingly the Muse. But she did not simply revel in it. 'I feel somehow as though I could be your *Gateway*,' she wrote in her private journal letter, 'that you could get through me and past me into a world I may never be able to realize – and if you could I think I could bear to be left behind.'[18] There was genuine insight in that: a more durable quality of realism than anything he felt for her. Her chief usefulness was the confidence she gave him. He had never before had the total sympathy and encouragement of a woman who was, though not his equal in imagination, certainly fully able to appreciate his own. She was quite his equal in knowledge and in nimbleness of wit. In learning she was even, at this stage, his superior.

Her exalted sense of mission towards him gave her greatly the advantage in peace of mind. Although she was fairly orthodox in Christian faith at that time, and later on became a Roman Catholic, she did not suffer at all from the guilt that fretted him. "It's a sort of religious feeling,' she wrote, 'and that is why I feel so justified – so sure that it is *good* to be with you.'[19] But her good did not extend to Elfie, for whom she had little respect or kindness; and like other lovers in similar cases she and de la Mare argued that, because they shared a part of his life that he could not in any case share with Elfie, their friendship therefore did not deprive her. The argument convinced Naomi, but de la Mare, living with the daily consequences of his double life, knew better. He clung obstinately to the one score on which his conscience acquitted him.

When Naomi was an old woman she told Eleanor Farjeon, by then a very close friend, that she had loved de la Mare 'in every way a woman does love a man'. If that were so, she behaved towards him most undemandingly and steadily, for at desperate moments she could most likely, had she so wished, have seduced him across the barriers which his deeper instincts demanded. Perhaps she divined that more than conscience was involved: a profound psychological reluctance, which to flout could only end for both of them in dismay.

10

'That Dungeon of Print'

Meanwhile, despite Newbolt's efforts, Arnold had turned down both de la Mare's new collections of verses. Finally, however in August 1911 Newbolt helped to place them at Constable, who from then on published all de la Mare's poetry until, after his son Dick had joined Faber, that firm took over all his books. In handing the two parcels of manuscript over to Constable, Newbolt's part as mentor and business intermediary in de la Mare's career was in fact over. Thanking him, de la Mare wrote: 'With those two it will make *six* leaking craft you have steered into harbour for me! Won't the B[ritish] P[ublic] *never* come down to the quay?'[1] For these two, at last, they would.

At about the same time a new way to make up essential income presented itself. When Heinemann mentioned one day to Spender that he needed a new reader of manuscripts, Spender recommended de la Mare. A little suspicious of Heinemann by reputation, he went for an interview and decided he did not seem 'very Gadarenish'. Naomi, though she disliked Heinemann personally, was enthusiastic about the job, and so was Newbolt, who wrote: 'The work of reading I have always found stimulating & encouraging – it has helped to clarify my judgement & make me both more tolerant of the individual & more ruthless about the art. It must I think be a good kind of work, for the best writers have many of them done it for years.'[2]

Newbolt could hardly have been more misguided, as things turned out. Heinemann would prove a master almost as hard as Oil, and de la Mare found the work had the deadliest mental effect. In any case he read much more slowly than Newbolt, whom few could rival for tearing out the heart of a book while standing with his back to the fire waiting for a dinner bell – and knowing that book thereafter with provoking thoroughness. De la Mare's appetite for reading was hearty, but he said he always mentally sounded the words to some extent, and this cannot possibly be done at the speed of the 'eye-reader' who registers the words subliminally.

While de la Mare stood (as it was to prove) on the brink of fame, Thomas wrote despairingly to him: 'My chief difficulty is having to write books which are costly & pay less than reviews. I have spent a quarter of the amount to be paid for my Icknield Way in travelling & books already. Only a direct & efficient interference from Providence can really improve things.'[3] In October 1911 he had one of his suicidal attacks, terrified Helen by taking his pistol out on his desperate rambles, and one day wrote miserably to say he could not bring himself to keep that evening's engagement at Anerley. 'There is nowhere I should so much like to be as your home now but I dare not come.'[4] He went away for two months to Llaugharne, to try the solitude cure that had helped him before at Dunwich, but wrote in November to say it had been rather too strong a dose. He who had enjoyed so respected and secure a position as the chief critic of the *Daily Chronicle*, in the days of de la Mare's total obscurity, now saw their positions reversed and de la Mare considerably the more successful, even in this field. Thomas's job had been curtailed when the *Chronicle* changed hands and policy, and now his income from hack books seemed to be drying up too. He tentatively hinted he would like work on the *Saturday Westminster*, but feared he would be cutting into de la Mare's corner by applying. De la Mare did what he could, praising his work loyally wherever possible in print, and, whatever Thomas later came to feel, did himself believe his praise had been of some practical service at the time. However, hurt remained, saddening for both men. Thomas was beginning to feel very isolated, and felt himself less supported by his friends than he deserved. 'Put not your trust in de la Mares,' he commented once to Janet Hooton.

In November 1911 came good news for de la Mare that must have made Thomas feel the contrast in their fortunes all the more keenly. Newbolt had been active in setting up an Academic Committee in the Royal Society of Literature, and this committee was now to award a new £100 prize, donated by the cultivated Princesse de Polignac, prominent social patroness of writers and artists. The prize was for the encouragement of style, to be awarded to a book published the preceding year and selected for promise, rather than to crown earlier successes. Newbolt began battling for *The Return*. It took all his tact and persuasion, for the committee were divided, and even though in the end they agreed to vote unanimously for the de la Mare novel, Newbolt felt that none of the others were really enthusiastic. However, he said, 'they thought it undeniably "promising" and thus the solid fact of the honour and the £100 which will fall into the De la Mare back garden like a huge rosy apple off a bare tree. When you consider it is 1/3 of their annual income and takes no grind to earn.'[5]

*

'What a drudge reading is,' de la Mare exclaimed to Newbolt after the first fortnight or so of work for Heinemann. 'One gets up after hours of it to find there is a real bird singing, or a real moon up in the dark – things one never so much as dreamed of in that dungeon of print.'[6] He soon discovered that the man before him in the job had spent almost the whole week toiling through manuscripts – which at this period were quite commonly in handwriting – in the office in Bedford Street. By February 1912 he was exasperated, and found the love stories the worst. 'This foolish reading galls me unbearably,' he wrote to Naomi. 'After all what is it? – spending one's time nearly all the week long in the company of frantic and garrulous and often nasty people – many of them out only to make money, without the least counting of the cost … Of course there are good books and clear brave imaginative minds among them. But I do so want to have a little quiet while to be and think in.'[7]

He never got to like Heinemann but felt in fairness to him (looking back in old age) that he had been an adventurous publisher, and though hard-headed had occasionally risked backing a book almost solely on its merits. He noted that Heinemann only adopted his reader's advice out of hand if it was damning; if publication were recommended, he always read the manuscript himself or got the backing of a second opinion.

One or two of de la Mare's reports survive. They show the care he would devote to a book, however bad, if there were any seeds of promise detectable. The absence of any superior attitude in his criticism, even where it is sharp, is even more conspicuous in these reports than in his reviewing. But from Heinemann's point of view he may have been almost too careful and noncommittal. He certainly did not have Newbolt's confidence and decisiveness, and had to compensate by taking more pains than he was paid for.

His work confronted him at once with the new movement towards realism and the erotic in fiction. One of the first things he had to handle was a novel of this kind by the American author Upton Sinclair, and very soon he had early works by D.H. Lawrence to consider. The problems with Sinclair's story *Love's Pilgrimage* caused him considerable worry. He thought the book perfectly sincere, and in many ways a beautiful piece of work, and suggested cuts with the aim

of saving it as much as possible from attack. Newbolt read it and
agreed with him; where he did pick on a fault it was not for indelicacy,
but because he thought Sinclair had introduced a passage of cruelty
and cowardice into the hero's behaviour without sufficient insight and
seriousness. And at another point, where the hero forces his young
wife's virginity, Newbolt's conclusion was that 'the author has gone too
far for decency and not far enough for realism'.[8] But in general
Newbolt was for publication, and de la Mare himself, though more
hesitant, carried the day with this support. Heinemann published, and
the book was promptly banned by Smith's Library. This made de la
Mare understandably the more nervous when faced soon after by the
manuscript (in its first form, as *Paul Morel*) of *Sons and Lovers*.

He had the usual difficulty for a critic not temperamentally
full-blooded and direct over sex – that is, he must deliberately discount
bias that might be a private prudery in himself, before he could obey
his own instincts and discrimination in the main concern –
imaginative truth. So he painstakingly earned the right to his final
opinion. This was that the 'un-human' part of D.H. Lawrence's work –
his uncanny imaginative insight into the beings of birds and beasts
and flowers, whether in prose or verse – was superior to his vision of
the human heart.

Since de la Mare's personal association with Lawrence was a slight
one, scattered over several years, and yet is of considerable interest, it
seems best to follow it through here, though this will anticipate a good
deal.

*

Lawrence was twenty-six when de la Mare became a publisher's
reader, and was just trying his second novel, *The Trespasser*, on
Heinemann – unsuccessfully. One of de la Mare's first tasks was to
read the manuscript of Lawrence's first volume of verse, later called
Love Poems and Others. Doubtful over some, but considering the rest
very good, he sent Lawrence his suggestions. But by then Lawrence
was absorbed in his next novel, and would not break off to work at the
verses. He and de la Mare only met once for discussion before
Lawrence eloped with Frieda von Richthofen to Germany.

De la Mare made a selection from the poems, still under debate, to
recommend to Heinemann for publication, and he read this new novel,
Paul Morel, when it arrived from Europe at midsummer. Heinemann
made up his mind over this manuscript much more smartly, and by the
beginning of July had rejected it as 'far too indecent'. He had burnt his

fingers with the public over the Sinclair novel, and was not in the mood for further and much greater risks. De la Mare evidently tried to conciliate Lawrence, who wrote scornfully to Edward Garnett: 'The other day I heard from de la Mare. He's a bit funky, as you said – sort of half apologetic ... He said he was taking my poems to W. H. [Heinemann] today. I hope the rotten little Jew won't have them. De la Mare says he'll recommend them strongly. Fancy de la Mare recommending anything strongly. Oh generation of tenderfeet.'[9]

De la Mare was meanwhile defending himself to Garnett: 'W. H. thinks the Libraries would ban the book as it stands ... Apart from this altogether, I don't feel that the book as a whole comes up to Lawrence's real mark. It seems to me to need pulling together: it is not of a piece. And the real theme of the story is not arrived at till half way through. This is of course only my own personal opinion and I should like to hear what you think. The best in it is of course extraordinarily good.'[10]

Sons and Lovers as published (by Duckworth in 1913) was obviously a good deal altered from the manuscript of *Paul Morel* which de la Mare had read. Garnett pressed de la Mare to review it, but he was reluctant: 'Unless Lawrence has considerably altered his novel I don't think I shall care very much for it. I read it in MS and thought – apart from the fineness of individual passages – that it was badly put together and a bit too violent here and there.'[11] Lawrence himself echoed this criticism when he told Garnett in December 1913 (by then he was halfway through his next novel): 'I shan't write in the same manner as *Sons and Lovers* again, I think – in that hard, violent style.'[12] In fact it is noticeable that all through their exchanges Lawrence kept two minds about de la Mare – a scornful irritation for what he thought timidity in his actions, but a respect he could not get away from for his critical discrimination. He very much wanted his approval and snarled if he did not get it. Considering their totally opposite approaches to art and life, this attitude on Lawrence's part is rather remarkable. It certainly shows how considerable a critic's reputation de la Mare was building for himself.

Though he disliked the novel, he had done his best to make amends over the poems, and also over Lawrence's *German Sketches*, which he liked very much and had recommended successfully to the *Westminster Gazette* (1912). Lawrence had already had a suggestion from Heinemann, which he knew originated with de la Mare, that he should make a book of these and give Heinemann the option on it. 'I s'll say yes (a lie),' he told Garnett.[13] Writing again a fortnight later he was more ready to concede that de la Mare had really, though in vain, strongly recommended the poems to Heinemann. 'De la Mare made the selection which is held in the clip,' he told Garnett. 'I think he has selected and arranged rather prettily – and with some care, I am sure. But perhaps you would like some of the others which he marked "doubtful" included.'[14] When *Love Poems and Others* was brought out by Duckworth in the spring of 1913, de la Mare's selection evidently remained its basis, though there were several additions by Garnett and his son David, which in Lawrence's opinion gave it an appeal to a more full-blooded and open-minded audience. It still remained, he felt, 'a bit exquisite, the collection – à la de la Mare – to convince the critics I was well brought up, so to speak.' Lawrence hoped that 'those who won't be pleased by one thing should find another they like. Whereas de la Mare in his choice only wanted to please the exquisite folk.'[15] There was some truth in this.

De la Mare reviewed the book for the *TLS*, and Lawrence, in suspense, set much store by what his verdict might be. After he had read the review, he only remarked: 'De la Mare was very cautious. I suppose he has to be.'[16] In fact, though the review is not written with the freedom of style de la Mare had when at ease with his subject, there is nothing ungenerous or oldmaidish in his response. Though partly critical, he distinctly declared that a remarkable new imagination had come on the scene. He found the poems 'clogged with excess of feeling. Nerves are on edge, the heart throbs heavily against its bars. Excess of all kinds is its weakness – even of vision, even of tenderness ... There are poems of sheer brutality, and passages almost without a vestige of restraint or reticence. But imagination, apprehension, economy of means, and often a delicate, ecstatic beauty are in this verse.'[17]

At this period, while abroad, Lawrence used de la Mare's friendly services over various manuscripts and contacts, as a kind of unofficial agent in England. It was de la Mare who put Eddie Marsh in touch when he wanted Lawrence's 'Snapdragon' for the first volume of *Georgian Poetry*. De la Mare singled this poem out as proof of the book's 'unquestionable seriousness' when he reviewed it; he showed he did not personally like the 'strong meat' it provided, but that he respected the evangelist of this kind of eroticism. He felt that 'the desire to possess life more abundantly' was the imaginative motive, although the result might be, for him, 'dense brooding desire that ... almost dazes and nauseates the reader with its desperate, naked excess'.[18]

Lawrence kept friendly feelings towards de la Mare, and wrote to him in the autumn of 1913 from Italy, describing the house he and Frieda were sharing on the Gulf of Spezia, and inviting de la Mare to visit them should he be in Italy: 'We have got a room you could have, and we would leave you alone. I think you might like it rather a lot.'[19] A visit to Italy was as far beyond de la Mare's purse as it was outside his wish. Nobody who loved traveller's tales so much could have had less actual wanderlust.

Lawrence's most ambitious novel, *The Rainbow*, rewritten over and over, came out in September 1915 – at once prosecuted for indecency and suppressed, not to win through till 1926. De la Mare wrote some review of it for the TLS, a 'long and largely favourable one' according to the account relayed by Lawrence's friend Catherine Carswell in her recollections, *The Savage Pilgrimage*. Apparently in proof when the prosecution came, the review too was suppressed. De la Mare wrote to Naomi, 19 October: 'I don't know why the Lawrence review hasn't gone in ... It's hardly worthwhile. J.D. B[eresford] told me the book has been banned as banned can be. On List I.A. *Ex.* and all sorts of things. What a naive world.' Not the comment of a prude.

Apparently the two men never met again after Lawrence removed his rejected works from Heinemann. Not that this was Lawrence's fault; he was much the more friendly of the two. When de la Mare was in Cornwall in 1916 Lawrence invited him to spend two nights at Zennor, where he and Frieda were then living. De la Mare made an excuse; he did not really like the idea of his own Cornwall, haunted and solitary, impinged on by Lawrence's insistent life-style. No doubt Lawrence made him feel uncomfortably respectable, rather prissy, 'a bit exquisite'. He was imaginatively quite at ease with a tramp or Davies's Supertramp, but was embarrassed by Lawrence – enough, anyway, to take no particular initiative to maintain the link, which had been mainly an offshoot of his much closer friendship with Edward Garnett.

This was a very different affair – an affectionate and lasting relationship, to which the great difference in personal taste and temperament in this case only added stimulus. Garnett was one of the most gifted and influential men in the publishing world of his day, and de la Mare, who had already benefited from his wholehearted backing of the *Mulgars*, was now to learn more from him than from anyone in his new trade of Reader. He and Garnett had known each other a year or two already when he arrived at Heinemann. They were fellow members of the Square Club, and by March 1911 Garnett was inviting de la Mare to join his particular circle who foregathered for Soho restaurant lunches on regular days, to discuss literature – among them Thomas, Norman Douglas, Masefield, Conrad, Belloc, Galsworthy and later J. D. Beresford. Garnett's mind was a very subtle one; prose fiction was the common ground between him and de la Mare, and they kept in close touch as new novels appeared, Garnett frequently pressing him (as in Lawrence's case) to review some new talent he had himself espoused with his usual wholehearted enthusiasm and promotion in all quarters. He had a high regard for de la Mare as a critic, while de la Mare found Garnett's opinions a most valuable touchstone for just that range of outspoken, realistic fiction where he felt most diffident and uncertain.

By the time they became friends – he was five years de la Mare's senior – Garnett had outlived the striking looks of his youth, variously described as those of an idealised romantic poet and a kitten on top of a may-pole. He filled out into a ponderous, wild-looking figure, very tall, with grey, jowled cheeks and thick-lensed glasses: a froglike face, or – as some young writers thought, watching his alarming approach at a literary party, every possible button undone – more like an outrageous great grizzly. But he would open discussion with delicious praise; the no less useful bullying came later. Prone to snort, to slop around in slippers, he remained as unconventional as ever into old age.

The quality of Garnett's mind was all expressed in his conversation; his written criticism is unreadably dull. When in 1922 he brought out a book of essays on his discoveries as a Reader, called *Friday Nights*, he wrote to thank de la Mare for his review: 'It was specially kind of you to tackle the book since I feel my temperament doesn't march with yours and in some respects is antithetic.' Antithetic, but never antipathetic – another feature of Garnett's electic genius for friendship. He had none of Lawrence's impatience with de la Mare's delicacy, and his nature was as affectionately loyal as de la Mare's own. When he died, at sixty-nine, his professional life and de la Mare's had drawn apart, but their rarer meetings had been still as warm as ever.

*

Once Newbolt saw de la Mare safely established at Heinemann and the extra income a material fact, he returned to a suspended attack about the need for the de la Mares to move from Worbeck Road, Anerley, which he and Ella considered an unhealthy house. Among well-wishers, he had already collected enough actual cash to pay for the move itself and to help furnish a new home. In the face of so much help offered, it seemed graceless to jib any longer especially as there was a tempting house available in the same neighbourhood. Six weeks later the family were installed in it.

The fifteen pounds extra in rent was still a serious matter, but 14

Thornsett Road, though not far off from Worbeck Road, was in a much less depressing quarter of Anerley – a trafficless neighbourhood, with groups of tranquil little shops on corners and hills up and down, the Crystal Palace glinting on the crest. The front windows of the house were set behind a stuccoed garden wall and a plot holding a chestnut and a birch. A pleasant old gas lamp stood at the edge of the pavement by the gate, and behind, the green open garden was spacious by comparison with all the family's former strips of ground. De la Mare found the quiet 'beyond price', and the space indoors (nearly double what they had before) permitted him at last 'my own jolly little room up out of the hurly burly'. Newbolt wanted to know why he had not yet received any bills to pay; so at last de la Mare and Elfie took heart, indulged their flair a little in the furniture sale-rooms and bought a Persian carpet.

Someone said of Cowper that he attracted presents as a buddleia attracts butterflies. De la Mare, though sensitively independent and resolute to make his own way in life, was also certainly a buddleia – in his case what he attracted was help, substantial and repeated. Not by any means all of the private benefactions he received over the years (and they were to continue) came at the instigation of the Newbolts and Coltmans, though a good many did. It seems more a kind of native good fortune. His personality combined a romantic appeal with the sterling good citizen. This odd mix aroused the wish to help, and at the same time gave confidence. Help, givers felt, would be put to sound use. He also had some kind of innocence of gratitude, which allowed him to receive blessedly (and later on when he was in a position to give, to do that as generously and acceptably). He neither forgot his many favours received, nor found the sense of obligation a burden, as men less humbly free-hearted frequently do. Artists of outstanding deserts have struggled on without any such luck, whether in their friends or in their native graces, and the difference this factor made is a conspicuous thread in de la Mare's fate.

In February 1912, on slight acquaintance, Edward Marsh invited him for the evening. On this very first occasion, in accepting, de la Mare contrived to make an ambiguous slip about the date concerned, and Marsh had to write again to be certain of his guest – a tiny contretemps between these two which would be repeated over and over in years to come. Something in Marsh's preciseness seemed perversely to affect de la Mare.

Marsh was his own age, an urbane man-of-the-world and a really able man of affairs, his broad shoulders at odds with his piping voice; impeccably dressed, full of small talk, a fastidious scholar with an unsleeping eye for the minutiae of form. 'He was a very genuine person,' Bruce Richmond once said of him, 'but everything about him – his high, affected voice – manner – appearance – conspired to make you think him just the opposite.'[20] The genuineness soon made itself apparent in his helpful, protective friendship for de la Mare, and his real enthusiasm for poetry – deep, if neither catholic nor adventurous. Siegfried Sassoon, looking back in old age, took a severer view of Marsh, but by then he was a lately converted Roman Catholic, and had come to see Marsh's undeniable lack of spiritual depth as an example of the man who 'discards sacredness'. He wrote to a friend: 'Dear old Eddie was hollow inside ... He did many good services to the arts; but was inwardly frivolous, and ended in despair – all his social world having collapsed.'[21]

De la Mare might have been quite as aware as Sassoon of Marsh's 'hollow inside' though his warm sense of gratitude would have kept him from phrasing the matter so dismissively. It did preclude intimate friendship; yet a considerable, lifelong bond was quickly established between them, and their lives were to be connected by an agreeable web of meetings and correspondence, discussion of projects and of de la Mare's work, through all the *Georgian Poetry* years and on into the 1920s.

As the most immediate effect of Marsh's entry into his affairs, de la Mare's social contacts with other poets rapidly multiplied, and his new house began to provide (for the first time in his life) somewhere adequate for modest hospitality. In February 1912, beside his first evening with Marsh, he spent his first at Edmund Gosse's house (more of this later) and was there introduced to Asquith, the Prime Minister. In fact he discovered in himself an appetite for sociability, and, since this did not prevent his working harder than ever, it seems clear that all this eager talk and company must have released more nervous energy than it consumed.

Yet to himself he seemed still doomed to helpless impotence, day by day, at the centre of his being, where Naomi's image was enthroned. A tremendous release of his powers and an acute frustration were going on in him at once. He seemed half-aware of it himself – that the romantic situation with Naomi was hopeless in human terms and yet that everything else he valued most was kindling from it. 'How many things have waited for their meaning till your coming' and 'Without our choice and even knowledge we somehow share a life and consciousness that to me was outside the expectation of experience'[22] – phrases from his letters to Naomi during 1912 – are sentiments that all lovers share to some extent. All artists who feel these things for a

woman fear that if they lose her this Vita Nuova of the imagination
will also abandon them. De la Mare was revealingly afraid that he
might lose Naomi, and the meaning of life's poetry with her, *from
within himself*, rather than by her own withdrawal. They had agreed
that the self he called 'Ann' or 'Nann' in her was someone he had in
part created – for he was quite ready to concede that 'we do create
those we love'.[23] If so, might he not one day do the reverse?

'I've said over page about your growing tired of me,' he wrote to her
from Netherhampton in May 1912. 'I suppose it's partly age that
makes the fear – & there flapped by a curlew wailing at the very sound
of the word! – but it's more still experience. I hate that treachery –
lukewarm or stone cold – to what one once held dear. – And there's the
curlew again & a poor cow on the hillside lowing for her calf. – It's one
of the horrors of being human: no wonder man turns to his heart for a
God in whom there is no shadow of turning. And yet I don't mean that
fidelity is the virtue most people think it. One changes from oneself &
every word & every action brings together or divides.'[24]

Already, at the beginning of the year, he had evidently told her
plainly (in the one letter she seems to have destroyed) that he would
not make her his mistress. Her reply does credit to the intelligence of
her love for him, and her readiness to be whatever he wished:

> I have read and re-read your letter. It is the plainest and clearest you
> ever wrote. At least I know what it means – and if you meant something
> else it can't be helped. You can only tell a person what they're able to
> understand. It's really what I've meant all along – and if I've seemed to
> *be* or to want something more tangible and less real it was only because I
> thought you did – only I couldn't say so. I could only tell myself that there
> had to be symbols and signs of realities so long as this muddy vesture of
> decay must needs stand between poor mortals an their sight of
> everlastingness.[25]

He wrote back to her from a much more divided and uneasy heart:

> Every beautiful thing changes with the eye that looks upon it. There it is,
> & the sense may be living or dead to it. I don't think you could ever have
> been to anybody more lovely & strange & unearthly than to *myself* you
> have always been to me. But simply because of that I have doubted &
> questioned & feared – only to keep my own … And I long for peace – to
> rest from this futile habit of thinking & picking to pieces & choosing the
> path I tread. What right had I to make you the friend you are, to want
> you to be mine & hate your having been anybody else's? Surely a man
> with a wife and four children has no justification for allowing *any* of his
> flock of selves to stray from the domestic fold. 'You ought to have stopped
> at the beginning.' *Was* there any? So the clatter & clash of conflicing
> views goes on … If I were never to see you again, the snail would creep

into its shell again & sour & rot … You won't be hurt if I say that it would be easier for you than for me. You would have lost nothing you cannot do without. You can speak of our having been friends as if it were a memory quite calmly & quietly. You have many real & live interests in life. And mine have got so few … It may sound devilishly hypocritical to say so, but if it hadn't been a real thing between us it would have been dead dozens of times over, & long ago – of my own fretting, of miserable talking. I can't think how you've stood it all, & the thought of it all. If I had been a Don Juan & you wildly in love with me could we have struck a harder bargain for the privilege? But sound sane peple respect Don Juan a thousand times more than a romantic acrobat.[26]

Comparing these letters, one must admit that her love gives her a good deal more human wisdom and honesty about him than his does about her. The natural atmosphere of her mind was quite unlike his: lower-pitched, combative, competitive, out in the light of common day; and, however much she loved to romance about her life (her friends all found her a great romancer), her instinct in any crisis was to face things bluntly – the opposite reaction to his. He did not romance about his own life, but he lived by a romantic reality he could discover in the commonplace and familiar. His imagination, of course, pierced far deeper than hers to a world of vision she quite humbly and straightforwardly recognised that she could only enter on his arm. But on the human level his love was more self-indulgent than hers. Only his four children kept the situation from breaking up his home life altogether.

Considering how sharp-tongued Naomi's circle of friends were, there was a marvellous absence of gossip about the affair, first to last. The discretion that the pair maintained – Naomi because de la Mare wished it (for she had nothing she personally felt much need to hide) – seems to have baffled or disarmed rumour remarkably well. There were some guesses, but they met no confidences, and Naomi, who loved attention and freely confessed it, showed herself very sensitive in this to de la Mare's feelings, content to be his Muse unrecognised.

Above all – supreme virtue in her position – she remained independent towards him, never a clutcher. She was also sharp, determined, that he should not write below his best. When he sent her in July 1912 *A Child's Day*, in the final stages before its long-delayed publication, he was already ashamed of 'this ghastly doggerel', and asked her to 'mark anything you think *must* be cut or altered'. She evidently agreed with his low opinion of it, and said so frankly, for he replied hoping she would never flinch from saying that his work was bad – 'as you never have'.

*

Meanwhile *The Listeners and Other Poems* came out in early May of 1912. Most or all of it had been written since de la Mare left Oil, during the three years in which his distinctive vision had matured, with the final impetus from Naomi. The book, with its nearly square red covers, only 5½ inches high, is enticing to modern eyes, but to de la Mare's resembled 'a provincial Sunday school prize'. By the time it appeared, the cumulative strains of his love, his Heinemann work and the usual reaction of depression when a book came out, had put him in a very low, flat mood. He hated the moment when his work was finally committed to the public and even he could do no more revising. Even a publisher's acceptance could produce the same unease and lowness. When he had told Ella the news that Constable had decided to take *The Listeners* and *Peacock Pie*, the previous August, he had written: 'I think I must feel something like the little boy who sees the poor rabbit he has petted & fed brought in smoking on a dish. I didn't want them killed & I wanted them much nicer!'[27]

He spent the Whit weekend of holiday in 1912 at Netherhampton, taking Florence. Cheering response to *The Listeners* began to reach him there. Reviews were full of praise. Edith Sichel urged him to send Edmund Gosse a copy, convinced that to have it from his own hand would give particular pleasure in that influential quarter. Gosse replied that he was 'charmed with the music and the fancy, and with the delicate, high, pure region of feeling in which your poetry moves'.[28]

Gosse's approval in those days was a kind of imprimatur for a young writer. He was now in his late sixties, and had long made it his business to become a personal friend of most of the best authors living. His standards were very high; a young writer must give solid proof of worth to attract an invitation to the house in Hanover Terrace, Regent's Park, for Gosse was touchy, and anxious that he should on no account lay himself open to looking foolish later on. It was a less fresh and generous approach to patronage than, say, Marsh's. But any newcomer in those last pre-war years, once welcomed at Hanover Terrace, was considered in a new light in the eyes of the world. So it was a definite feather in de la Mare's cap to have had his February invitation, and Gosse must have felt gratified to find that move so soon and safely ratified by this little book, which well outstripped all promise by de la Mare hitherto.

Thomas, in his straightforward, quiet way, put his finger on the secret of *The Listeners*, writing his own thanks: 'You might as well ask me to write a poem myself as to write about these. Each one takes me a little deeper into a world I seem to know just for the moment as well as you – only not really knowing it I cannot write. I think it is equal to *Songs of Childhood* & *Poems* together. It is as fresh as the first and it has the gray of the second book like gossamer over its blossom colours. I did not think one book could be so good. My favourite is "The Dwelling Place", if I dare commit myself.'[29]

Far more than is usual in a collection of short lyrics written over several years, *The Listeners* makes one whole. The poems in it gain much from one another, each taking the reader, as Thomas felt, a step deeper into their own world – one we seem intimately to recognise in the very moment of discovery. The attempt to use the fanciful to carry serious import is not very often made, or very seldom comes off. For de la Mare it was frequently (as it is sometimes in a Shakespeare song) the most natural and nearest way to communicate the most secret and inaccessible effects. Instinct had led him back from the statements and comments on life in *Poems 1906* (which he would tackle with more success later in life) to the old themes of *Songs of Childhood*: spells and witchcraft, lonely old houses, scenes of ruin and neglect and solitude. What is fantastic becomes, in these poems, all humanised and warm; what is human is all known as strange. The central experience of de la Mare's life speaks through every page; he alludes to it in a letter the previous year to Naomi: 'Now and again over one's mind comes the glamour of a kind of visionary world saturating this.'[30]

The mood of the book is wonder, aching with intensity but not so sad as in later volumes. There is relish and contentment and a great deal found acceptable, even in subjects that might have suggested lament – lonely old age, decay, transience. The more serious poems keep a beautiful equipoise between longing and affirmation. There was a voice in his mind which said, at this period of his life: 'My soul there *is* a country', and would again, when he was old.

The Listeners is also the most even of his collections. Many of the pieces in it became famous, but the rest are not much less good, and very few could be spared if one was gathering, out of his life's work, the key poems which show his two strengths, the original vision and the original music. This last had been mastered, as has been seen, by long, patient, arduous practice of an ear at first not at all perfect. By now, it had become one of the most faultless, subtle and inventive.

In the summer of 1912 Ella Coltman secured for the de la Mares a cottage at Cowden in Kent, belonging to her favourite doctor – that Dr Grey who had treated de la Mare in the last desperations of Oil. The local Rector sent round an invitation – he was another of Ella's old friends, W.R. Shaw-Stewart, and she had introduced them long ago. De la Mare duly went to tea, and was faced with an ordeal to be repeated over and over in years to come. He told Ella: 'Mr Shaw Stewart not only asked me to read "The Listeners" to him but Mrs Shaw Stewart asked me what it meant. I thought and thought and after a bit I began to see *a* meaning and I'm afraid I gave that. But was it better than none? – I just wonder.'

From the time the book appeared, he received frequent requests for the title-poem to be included in anthologies, and after a while he refused to grant permission any more. Apart from the fact that it grew hackneyed thereby, he perhaps felt (and if so, then truly) that for all its striking originality 'The Listeners' is something of a *tour de force*, less characteristic than some other pieces less famous. The never-ending requests to explain it were no less wearisome. Usually he would evade reply, saying that a poem means whatever the individual reader finds in it – or, carrying this further still, that at every individual encounter a poem is that particular experience and no other. He would say of poetry that *how* it is said is *what* it means. Once in the 1950s he told Laurence Whistler that 'The Listeners' was about '*a* man encountering *a* universe'. But once, to an old blind friend in Canada, he wrote in sudden surprising detail on the subject. This does not mean, with de la Mare, that the explanation he gave her then was the 'real' one for him. Indeed it is scarcely an explanation at all. It just means that on this occasion to this particular friend these were the hares 'The Listeners' started in his mind:

As to 'The Listeners' – I have frequently been asked to expound its meaning and in reply have usually suggested that the very kind enquirer should keep to any meaning he may himself have been able to find in it. As Lewis Carroll once said, [in] a letter in connection with something in the Alices, I fancy, 'Since words mean more than one means when one uses them, I shall be very pleased to accept whatever meanings you may have discovered' in mine, something to that effect. This, I know, is not much better than a getaway. Moreover (quite between ourselves, of course!), I am now a little vague concerning what *was* the intended meaning of those particular lines. Its rudiments, I think, were that the Traveller is a reincarnation revisiting this world beneath the glimpses of the moon, and there asking the same old unanswerable questions of the Listeners – only conceived but never embodied – who forever frequent, it would seem, this earthly existence, but then are even these rudiments definable – from the poem? Every poem, of course, to its last syllable *is* its meaning; to attempt any paraphrase of the poem is in some degree to change that meaning and its effect on the imagination, – and often disastrously. What the poem (or even a letter for that matter) means is inherent in its terms and (however wide their implications may be) that meaning is nothing less and nothing different. In the finest poems the meaning fairly fizzles and rays out in every direction, it is the primal cell capable of infinite subdivision and of innumerable potentialities. It is the expression of a sort of plastic individual truth immerged in beauty: whereas a scrap of science is for the time being a self-contained announcement of what is an ascertained fact – universally provable by those intelligent enough to comprehend it. You can't prove a poem; it proves you.

Well, well, I didn't intend to make such a fuss as all this.[31]

*

By the summer of 1912 he was again very badly exhausted. He wrote to Naomi at the beginning of August: 'What a relief it would be to have nothing to do that I didn't want to do, for a while. I have always hated writing – except rhymes: but it's not only that. It's to have a break from *reading* what one doesn't want to – and above all these love stories. It seems as if one were continually breathing a stale slightly nauseous air. I used to think reading could do very little harm, but I don't now. The awful thing is that even the sins of inferior people are inferior: & many of these MSS. are like cheap dingy photographs, not only of a mind, but of a whole inward world. Somehow or other I had hardly come across this kind of thing before I began work with Heinemann; it's the ghastly tameness that is so shocking. The heart knoweth its own rottenness – but to write about it & betray one's mind, I'd sooner chance being a Perfect Prig.'[32]

Not that he took much break when he did get away. The respite from Heinemann reading in another Cowden visit, merely allowed him to tackle one of the long composite articles for the *Edinburgh Review*, which he always found a peculiarly formidable task. Even Thomas and Hodgson, looking in, failed to cheer him. Breaks elsewhere – at much-loved Brighton and Netherhampton – left him equally burdened. The real obstacle to rest was that his position at Heinemann was repeating the old Oil pattern of exploitation: if he took a few days off, nobody deputised, and manuscripts simply piled up for double drudgery on return. Newbolt had at first declared exultantly that at Heinemann he was getting 'every kind of an education'. By the summer even he began to realise with anxiety the actual toll the readership was exacting.

But a more congenial source of income was about to begin.

11

Peacock Pie

Eddie Marsh wrote to de la Mare in September 1912 inviting him to the Moulin d'Or to meet Wilfrid Gibson, and to discuss a plan that had hatched a few evenings before, from a joking suggestion of Rupert Brooke's. He had been proposing a hoax to draw public attention to poetry – a book of poems all written by himself, issued as an anthology from a dozen promising writers. Marsh had replied that with less trouble they could easily find twelve genuine representative poets to promote. Brooke thought that Marsh, older and with more authority than himself, should edit it, and the notion rapidly crystallised into a practical scheme. The book, they felt, would demonstrate that a new era had begun.

As Newbolt had noticed when he tried to revive public interest in poetry with the *Monthly Review* in the early 1900s, there had been a long trough of public disregard since the Romantic movement, after the immense popularity of Tennyson and Browning had petered out in the shallows of the Nineties. In 1912 contemporary poets were still not widely read and discussed, apart from Masefield. Much talent, these friends felt, deserved a popular recognition it did not get. Marsh suggested 'Georgian' as the label for the new movement they hoped to launch, and they secured as publisher Harold Monro, who brought out *Poetry Review*. He and Marsh both backed the venture financially. By common consent the very first discussion on choice of poets to invite had included de la Mare's name, and he was one of the first they approached. All contributions were to be chosen by Marsh from recently published work.

At the dinner to discuss all this further de la Mare had his first meeting not with Gibson, who was unwell, but with Rupert Brooke. He found himself a great deal more attracted by the man than he had been by the early work of his in which Naomi had tried to interest him, and which he had felt had a 'too polished beauty'. Brooke was one of the many talents that Naomi's flair for promise had spotted at the outset. He was now twenty-five, but she had given him the prize in a *Westminster Gazette* competition for a sonnet sent in under a pseudonym while he was still in the Upper Sixth at Rugby, and he had continued to compete in her verse contests for several years afterwards. It was a winning article in another of her competitions (later in 1912) which led to Brooke's trip to America, beginning the following May, with a commission from the *Westminster* to write articles on his travels.

De la Mare was deeply impressed at the first meeting, as were most people, by Brooke's appearance and personality. He used to say that Brooke was the only *man* he had ever met whose looks distracted his attention from what was being said. As on the whole he rather disliked outstanding good looks in men, this was an unusual tribute. Nor for that matter is there any evidence that de la Mare was ever the least attracted physically by his own sex. He seemed in his talk to have a very uncomplicatedly old-fashioned heterosexuality, and showed little interest in the deviations of others. The sort of comment he would make, if the matter did cross his path, was his remark to Naomi in the summer of 1912 while bogged down in a review of the lesbian writer Vernon Lee: 'God bless her, I do so dislike that kind of woman. It *must* be important to be one's own sex. Is she?'[1]

But the first sight of Brooke was apt to take people aback whatever their age, sex or leanings; and de la Mare sat rather abstracted while *Georgian Poetry* was proposed, watching him. He put the recollection into print after Brooke died of 'that serenely eager, questing face, stilled, as it were, with the phantom of a smile that might have lingered in the countenance of the Sphinx in her younger days ... It was a face not in the least feminine ... but of the rarest beauty ... you silently surveyed with an interest and admiration as instinctive and unreserved as those you would bestow on the young Greeks and their immortal horses on the frieze of the Parthenon.'[2]

Brooke and he were not to know each other very long or very intimately; yet this not particularly well-off young man at the restaurant table was to become, almost fortuitously, one of de la Mare's chief benefactors through many years to come. Already there was some such unformed benevolent desire in Brooke's mind. After this occasion he wrote to Frances Cornford: 'I've been meeting a lot of poets in London, they *were* so nice: very simple, and very good-hearted. I felt I'd like, almost, to live with them always (and protect them).'[3]

Eddie Marsh has been scorned for concealing Brooke's flawed and vulnerable real self in a haze of romantic idealisation, and so beginning, by his Memoir, the golden legend too popular after Brooke died. It is worth noting that de la Mare, who was in general an independent judge of character and no fool, wholly subscribed to this view of Brooke, as did many of his other contemporaries. Evidently, for those not in the secret of his private troubles, Brooke's radiance in company completely concealed his inner lack of confidence and vulnerable character.

De la Mare soon had champions of his own to put forward for inclusion in the new anthology: Ralph Hodgson, John Freeman, and Vivian Locke-Ellis. But time was already short if the book were to catch the Christmas market, and Marsh did not know Hodgson's work at all, had never heard of Freeman, and was unimpressed by the 'long and very obscure' poem of Locke-Ellis's which Monro had recently sent him. He closed his list. The only one of the original caucus suggested who had refused his invitation was Housman, on the grounds that only a relative or a duchess could get poetry out of him, and Marsh was neither – 'Besides, I do not really belong to your "new era".'[4]

Nor did de la Mare, though he was Housman's junior by fifteen years. His formative time as a poet was only just over, but it was completely over. Neither his vision nor his style were modified by his association over the next six years with the Georgian movement. It was *The Listeners*, with *Peacock Pie*, which made his name during those years, further gilded by *Motley*. The great popular success of Marsh's volumes did not raise it higher, though they certainly helped enormously to widen his public. And as his star did not rise with the Georgians', neither did it decline when they fell into disfavour. The accusations against them of a too complacent and cosy view of life, and of a style copied from each other, both left him out. Those who found his poetry too little involved with contemporary life or with large human issues would have done so anyway: it was not as a Georgian they condemned him, but as a fanciful escapist, and as a stylist restricted by too 'beautiful' a vocabulary, drawn from a past that was already the past before the Georgians began.*

It was great good luck for *Georgian Poetry 1911–12* that its debut coincided with the opening of Monro's Poetry Bookshop at 35 Devonshire St, off Theobald's Rd, near Gray's Inn. It sold very well off Monro's shelves, and received excellent publicity through the readings held there. These Poetry Bookshop readings, originally intended to

---

* Such a criticism was there from the beginning among some of the Georgians themselves. Alida Monro recalled that her husband admired 'The Listeners' for its rhythm and its decorative quality, but thought that de la Mare took superficial and minor themes. Monro cared much more himself for 'engaged' poetry.

bring verse to a poor neighbourhood, became instead a popular literary social institution which brought the influential trooping from the West End. This helped many poets in the book to recognition.

Marsh had been afraid that 'Q's tiresome book', *The Oxford Book of Victorian Verse*, just out that autumn, would take a good deal of wind out of the Georgian sails.

Quiller-Couch's anthology, padded out with mediocrity, disappointed de la Mare. 'Just think, my child,' he wrote to Naomi, 'what Q might have done if he'd refused fatness, dared raging and tearing and simply frozen to *the* thing. His book is not only poor but such a wicked pity. It's extraordinary how the best refuses to shine when the sham moons are about ... We *must* do one.' So they would, each of them, and Naomi's slim *A Private Anthology* was good and unusual too, if not in the class of de la Mare's *Come Hither*. But when the time came, they made them separately.

Marsh had chosen his own collection of de la Mare pieces entirely from *The Listeners* – 'Arabia', 'The Sleeper', 'Winter Dusk' and 'Miss Loo', a representative choice which did de la Mare's sales good, for the success of *Georgian Poetry* was instant. If the printers had only got it out in time, Marsh reckoned he could have sold most of a second impression for Christmas presents, so rapidly did orders pour in, and customers to the Bookshop. Marsh generously paid royalties to his poets, rather than the usual fee for anthologies. He also saw to it that they should become each others' personal friends, and after several attempts he introduced de la Mare to Wilfrid Gibson, at the presentation of the Polignac Prize, which this time went to Masefield.* When he undertook a protegé, Marsh was very thorough. Besides de la Mare, he introduced Gibson that day to Gosse, Maurice Hewlett, Newbolt, Sturge Moore and Masefield himself, wondering whether anyone had ever been introduced to quite so many poets at once. But in all this bevy, it was with de la Mare that Gibson was to make the closest friendship. Gentle and unlucky, he himself best fitted Brooke's description of those good-hearted and simple and nice poets he wanted to protect.

Maurice Hewlett was a successful romantic novelist, and de la Mare had already come to know him through Ella and the Newbolts, as their Wiltshire neighbour. After he died, de la Mare wrote that he 'had admired him so much personally that I could imagine any young

---

* At the presentation, de la Mare came up to Marsh and said in a grieved voice, 'They've given him more than they gave me.' Marsh felt flabbergasted at the seeming bad taste of the remark, until de la Mare went on: 'They've given him an envelope.' E. Marsh/ R. Brooke 29 Nov. 1912, see C. Hassall, *Edward Marsh*, p.200.

woman falling in love with him – not an easy thing to imagine of a fellow man!' Yet there was something he once admitted he did not care for about Hewlett's *company* in his novels – just as he did not care for Meredith's. This was always one of the matters he set most store by when rating a book: the author's company counted ultimately for more than his literary gifts or failures.

Hewlett wrote to Marsh about *Georgian Poetry*: 'The truest poets you have are Brooke, Davies, de la Mare. Lawrence [who was represented by 'The Snapdragon'] will be good too, someday … There's a very high level – a tableland of art, with no cloud-kissing peaks.'[5]

Over the last part of a century since the book appeared, the ground has sunk considerably. Only the poems by Hewlett's favourites stand as they did. The major part of *Georgian Poetry 1911–12* consists of long poems or long excerpts, and it cannot be denied that they are stodgy. De la Mare had to review the book himself the following April in the *Edinburgh Review*, and it is noticeable that (in agreement with Percy Lubbock in the *TLS*) he singled out roughness and adventurousness as the characteristics of its poets. In fairness to this first volume, the accusations of caressive and complacent chirruping, for which the Georgian movement was later mocked, cannot be levelled against it. It did just what its originators hoped to do – demonstrate poetry breaking fresh ground, and claim for it, for several decades to come, a newly-awakened public. All that can dilute the poet into the mere literary man was now pouring into de la Mare's cup. Invitations multiplied – to join the English Association and the Omar Khayyam Club, to improve André Gide's conversational English, to lunch with Asquith at 10 Downing Street. Gosse had a hand in three out of four of this list. De la Mare accepted and accepted, whatever the Heinemann grind, and everywhere he was a great social success. Gide (recalled prematurely to France) bewailed himself to Edith Sichel, who had arranged the de la Mare coaching. At the one conversational session which had actually come off, he had taken to de la Mare so warmly that he kept him over tea till seven o'clock. At the Prime Minister's de la Mare lunched among the titled hostesses of literary salons, the grander critics and patrons and the more august poets – 'A.E.' and Yeats were present. Asquith's own interest in poetry, and in de la Mare himself, was genuine and personal.

Yeats and de la Mare had only met once before. They left Downing Street together and walked and walked, each confident that the other was leading him to the Tube. Eventually, circling Leicester Square again and again in the January afternoon and talking hard, it dawned upon them that they were going nowhere. Nor did that discussion, animated and absorbing enough for its moment, lead anywhere important in de la Mare's life either. Two years went by before Yeats made a move to renew the acquaintance, and then it was because a lady (possibly Katherine Tynan) who wanted to meet de la Mare, asked him to effect this. Later on they met quite often in Ottoline Morrell's circle, and Yeats came out to de la Mare's Taplow home in the heyday of his entertaining there. They had plenty to say to each other: perhaps inwardly some sense of rivalry: no impulse to communicate at any depth of feeling on either side. As a poet, Yeats felt a certain real admiration for de la Mare, its terms indicated in his remark to Newbolt about the Epitaph, 'Here lies a most beautiful lady': 'There is not an original sentence in this poem, yet it will live for centuries.'[6] De la Mare for his part, though he found the Celtic twilight rather a bore, did not underestimate Yeats's art. Respect for it was mixed, however, with a mild restiveness at some bogus and inflated elements in Yeats's notion of life's secrets. Looking back, he would poke gentle fun at the high-priestly airs. Though he himself worshipped poetry as something quite literally divine, miraculous and essential, his sturdy instinct was that poets themselves should wrestle and pray in the pews alongside the rest of the congregation, not get up behind the altar and wrap themelves in a cope. He was ready enough, each time opportunity offered, to sit at Yeats's feet while the brogue monologue chanted on, impressing on himself the while (so he said) 'This is *Yeats*: I must remember every word.'[7] But each time he got up to leave he found it was the same thing – alas, already nothing whatever remained! He cherished an occasion later at the Morrells when Yeats was holding forth about the occult. De la Mare presently stole a glance across the captive audience at the face of Virginia Woolf. She gave no other sign, just let her eyebrows go up – one tiny lift, expressing all.

With Yeats there is always the sense that he toyed with occult experience in order to exploit it, while one part of his intellect all the while disbelieved. He is like a man performing a conjuring trick and hoping to hoodwink himself into seeing it as a miracle. De la Mare was never trying to deceive himself; he was exploring, intent on a hidden country he was convinced was there. He never suspended his common-sense, and his speculations on the supra-normal avoid the tinge of silliness in Yeats's. Nor did he share the Irishman's eagerness to claim extra-sensory powers. Yeats would insist he had heard a spirit-warning rather than admit some passer-by might have whistled in the street. De la Mare, on the other hand, though so sensitive to atmosphere and often oppressed or alarmed in solitude by the presence of the uncanny, was extremely cautious in claiming more than a handful of psychic experiences of any definite and dramatic kind. He might experiment as an after-dinner game with ouija-board and table-turning, and closely speculate on the results, but he noticed and respected the instinctive aversion the normal self feels at a mediumistic séance, and that recoil seemed to him a warning signal against prostituting the powers of the spirit. Nor did he confuse psychic stimulus with spiritual value. He took life as it came, as sufficient marvel. It would not occur to him to do as Yeats did, and set about deliberately inducing 'profound states of the soul'.

After de la Mare parted from Yeats on that January day in 1913 he went on to tea with Ella Coltman, and there found Ezra Pound. He had already come across him once, at a Square Club dinner. On that occasion he and Edward Thomas had sat side by side, united in common hostility. This second meeting did nothing to change de la Mare's attitude and Ella found him very scathing afterwards about her guest. (She was always more philosophically amused than troubled when her heterogeneous acquaintance failed to get on.) She and her family had been seeing a good deal of Pound, then living nearby in Kensington on very little indeed, and she would stoke him on a solid afternoon spread. Once when after lunch Mrs Coltman offered him a second cup of coffee, 'Please, *seven!*' he fervently replied. Ella had observed that the young American, whom she herself found 'awfully sarcastic and hard to please', really liked and admired de la Mare, and was eager to pursue the acquaintance. But de la Mare rarely took such a determined dislike as he did here. Pound's posing, his bizarre style of dress, his flamboyant hair, all thoroughly confirmed the impression of sham his *Canzoni* had made on de la Mare when Naomi had sent the volume along for review two years before. 'What an unspeakable sixteenth he is,' he had written back then, 'with his patchoulied fallaleries.'[8] In his review he had castigated Pound's work, calling it 'too egotistic and not individual enough. By much the greater part of his volume is at least one remove from reality – from his own reality. And if there is one thing on earth and in man that is of the very essence of reality – that strange alliance between soul and sense – it is poetry.'[9]

But it was like de la Mare, when he and Pound were both old men and Pound a broken one, to take his part then and speak of him with compassion. He felt that Pound's broadcasts in the Fascist cause had not deserved such savage punishments as followed. But he never came to think any the better of Pound's poetry. There is nothing surprising in that: their notions of poetry, one would think, were quite incompatible. The odd thing is that Pound, on the contrary, should value de la Mare's. Indeed, one account of him affirms that 'He disliked equally all the Georgians with the solitary and surprising exception of Davies and Walter de la Mare'.[10] He certainly tried hard in the summer of 1913 to persuade de la Mare, through Ella, to come to see him in Kensington and to bring any poems he might have free for publication. Pound had 'hitched himself', so he told Ella, to an American magazine, and was very keen to get de la Mare to contribute. Would he dine, or suggest any other time? Ella relayed all this doubtfully; she evidently expected neither the lure of good pay nor of an American public would tempt de la Mare to have anything more to do with Pound. And she was right.

The previous autumn Katherine Mansfield and John Middleton Murry had agreed with de la Mare for verse contributions to *Rhythm*. Sending a January reminder, as nothing had arrived, brought them two from the *Peacock Pie* manuscript, then awaiting publication. Murry preferred 'The Song of the Mad Prince'; Katherine had 'a great weakness', she said, for 'The Mocking Fairy' ('Won't you look out of your window, Mrs Gill?'). The upshot was an invitation to tea in the *Rhythm* 'office' – in reality the one small room in Chancery Lane which was at that time their home. They were very hard up, though not still by then (as they had been) running the paper at a loss of ten pounds a month. Eddie Marsh had stepped in to shore up the spirited venture for a few months longer. De la Mare met the couple at lunch, with J. D. Beresford, a novelist, soon to become a close family friend. They took him home for the afternoon. 'And we talked – which somehow nobody could do at lunch,' de la Mare reported to Naomi. Katherine remembered one of the subjects that set them off – hedges. Naomi was out of town, and de la Mare described the occasion to her more vividly than usual, his gaze for a moment lifted from their own plight: 'Katherine told stories uncommonly well and shook her fuzz and curled herself up in an armchair à la Russe and said "Wasn't it, Tiger?" or "Don't you think so, Jack", and would I review Eddie in the March number and come twice a week to tea. Debauched with personality I stumbled downstairs again and turned to the *left* in Chancery Lane.'[11]

He got very lost on the way home; the talk had exhilarated him, and Katherine's personality had thrown a good deal more spell over him than he would think it politic to admit to Naomi. He and Katherine felt at once a very particular affinity. It was a bond of personality really much easier to recognise than whatever knitted him to Naomi, for Katherine's highly-keyed intuitive responses, and her valuing of the child-self, were a much more native match with de la Mare's own. Had fate thrown these two into a passionate friendship, there would not be the puzzle that persists, first to last, in his with Naomi. Here, however, there was no question of any such affair; both were fully involved elsewhere, and never even met more than two or three times. Yet the friendship was to be important – and equally so to both. Through Katherine's years of illness and exile ahead, de la Mare was to assume a curiously central place as inward companion and point of reference for her solitary life of thoughts.

For his part, her personality soon bewitched him completely. He never spoke of her again with the detachment of that first report. He thought she had genius, defended this opinion in print and talk with all his critical judgement, and never changed his mind. A strongly romantic personal feeling certainly coloured this judgement. He saw her in a glow of chivalry which was confirmed forever by her tragic early death.

*

At the end of March 1913 he and Thomas shared a few days together at Dillybrook Farm near Bath, where Thomas had put up before. De la Mare arrived ahead at Dillybrook, in a hailstorm, and found a grey flint house with rows of little white windows. The place had an atmosphere to please him that set the storyteller side of his mind to work, cataloguing the furnishings contentedly for Naomi. When Thomas turned up next day, wet through, on his bicycle – he had a commission to write an account of a West Country cycling tour, which he published as *In Pursuit of Spring* – the two sat out in the sun between downpours beside the flooded Frome, and watched it foaming over the long curved weir, talking of each other's work: 'E.T. was saying, none of the people I write about are quite solid, tangible. And how one writes is how one lives.'[12]

Thomas and he were not cheerful company for each other on this occasion: 'E.T. was kind and interested, as much as anyone could be but I think he was not sorry to be on his way again. People soon bore him: we were speculating today how many people one would welcome to reside within a radius of ten miles. "Three or four" was his guess: and that doesn't sound extravagantly misanthropic. But I suppose the fewer chosen, so much the more in a way it is a confession against one's self.'[13]

Thomas took himself off again on a 'warm cloudy morning that could do no wrong', as he put it in his book. He must have rather resembled a cranefly – that leisurely, tired persistence, lanky knees buckled at angles, the bicycle winging and whispering over the puddles. A small boy had noticed it, and yelled 'Longlegs!', a country name for that insect. This stuck in de la Mare's mind – perhaps Thomas joked about it – and so found its way into *Peacock Pie*.

De la Mare stayed on alone a day or two, fretting to Naomi, jealous and self-involved, guilty and fanciful. Yet before he too departed it is plain that solitude and country life had wonderfully pacified the fret into reverie. 'Did you persuade me to go away to bring me near? Did you know how everything would fall away into peace?'[14] he gratefully wondered to Naomi – then, revealingly: 'I hate coming back because I have you best down here.'[15]

His nature suffered badly simply from his lack of enough solitude. Neither Elfie nor Naomi would have found him so nervously on edge if he could more often have come to a solitary standstill by a weir in the West country, and felt his wits

> slipping away in the enormous roar of the falling water. I didn't want to *be* anything but *that*: it's in my head now, – with the light slowly draining out of the valley & Venus smooth & cold in the swerve of the stream. I just shut my eyes & there was nothing but darkness & the thousand voices & very curious, a little gold figure in the distance of the darkness. It was the third time I had gone there today. I climbed back over the hill again & the birds had all stopped singing – except a thrush on the other side of the hill. And owls instead were flitting up & down & hooting. I sat on a birch tree stretched across an opening into the wood & there was Orion & he had shot an arrow dropping clear through the dark blue towards bright Venus; & the Pleiades like scared birds flitting up from its flight, & Sirius barking at his heels.[16]

As a description of the actual scene, this, written to Naomi on the first day of April, could be dismissed as 'literary'. But it was not a finished product so much as a necessary stage of a fermenting process. While he idled out such decriptions to her (and he let himself go much more to her in this way than to any other friend) he was halfway between the impact of a real experience and the romantic verse incantation in which some elements of it would reappear as images – distilled probably almost out of recognition, and combined apparently at random just for the music's sake, yet in some curious way organised with one another by a logic of suggestion potent enough, though it is pedantry to analyse it. Naomi kept an early handwritten version of a poem called 'Dust to Dust' in a hand that suggests that de la Mare wrote it about now. He improved it with a few slight alterations, to appear in *Motlev* as this:

> Heavenly Archer, bend thy bow;
> Now the flame of life burns low,
> Youth is gone; I, too, would go.

Ever Fortune leads to this:
Harsh or kind, at last she is
Murderess of all ecstasies.

Yet the spirit, dark, alone,
Bound in sense, still hearkens on
For tidings of a bliss foregone.

Sleep is well for dreamless head,
At no breath astonishèd,
From the Gardens of the Dead.

I the immortal harps near ring,
By Babylon's river languishing.
Heavenly Archer, loose thy string.

Frome into Babylon's River; Orion over Dillybrook into the divine intervention of death; mere fancies embroidered for Naomi into whatever poetry is – one can see a little way into the chemistry.

The odd thing is that, sombre as Thomas had seemed, apparently cycling his way into yet another hack book, these very same things would provide for him also, a year later, in 1914, ingredients of the same chemistry: life-into-prose-into-poetry. And momentously for him, since the process had all his life till then stuck at the second stage.

Robert Frost's contention (when he persuaded Thomas over the brink into writing verse in 1914) was that Thomas had already created poetry as good as any man alive. To prove his point, Frost referred him to paragraphs of *In Pursuit of Spring* and told him to 'write it in verse form in exactly the same cadence'. It seems as if Thomas did just this. One passage of *In Pursuit of Spring* opens with a sentence so closely paralleling de la Mare's letter to Naomi it is obvious that it describes the same scene, possibly on the same evening. 'Venus, spiky with beams,' Thomas wrote, 'hung in the pale sky, and Orion stood up before us,* above the blue woods of the horizon.'[17]

He went on:

All the thrushes of England sang at that hour, and against that background of myriads I heard two or three singing their frank, clear notes in a mad eagerness to have all done before dark; for already the blackbirds were chinking and shifting places along the hedgerows. And presently it was dark, but for a lamp at an open door, and silent, but for a chained dog barking, and a pine tree moaning over the house. When the dog ceased, an owl hooted, and when the owl ceased I could just hear the river Frome roaring steadily over a weir far off.

* No actual companion is mentioned in *In Pursuit of Spring*, except here and there a kind of imaginary *Doppelgänger*.

A few months later, following Frost's advice, Thomas wrote the poem 'March':[18]

> What did the thrushes know? Rain, snow, sleet, hail,
> Had kept them quiet as the primroses.
> They had but an hour to sing. On boughs they sang,
> On gates, on ground; they sang while they changed perches
> And while they fought, if they remembered to fight:
> So earnest were they to pack into that hour
> Their unwilling hoard of song before the moon
> Grew brighter than the clouds ...

No question whose is the more living prose here: the mad eagerness of Thomas's thrushes, their 'frank clear notes', drop one straight into the freshness of the moment. But his verse is less sure – not yet inevitable. *How* the thing is said is not absolutely *what* it says, as de la Mare held that poetry must be. With de la Mare's letter and poem, by contrast, the *poem* feels the unerring thing, as it goes about its curious, remote business. What it says could be said no other way.

The spring of 1913 saw the beginning of de la Mare's acquaintance with someone who would become the closest work-friend of his next thirty years. Rather more than a year earlier he had received a note enclosing a presentation copy of a novel, *The Bracknels*:

> Dear Sir,
>   I hope you will accept this little tale which I venture to send you in token of my great admiration for your beautiful books.
>   Believe me
>   Yours very truly
>   Forrest Reid.[19]

The response must have been disappointing, for de la Mare (wondering incidentally if he were addressing a man or a woman) merely sent an acknowledgement. Reid, undaunted, seized the next opportunity, sending a letter and a review, both in praise of *The Listeners*. De la Mare replied warmly, hoping that they could meet, and adding: 'At present I am drudging as Reader to Heinemann & if you are not bound to any publisher and have a MS. awaiting publication I wonder if you would care to send it to me.' In fact Reid's next novel, *Following Darkness*, had already gone to Arnold, and it was a review rather than a Reader's report which de la Mare wrote of it in the autumn of 1912.

He confided to Reid: 'What I have read has been a kind of personal pleasure and recognition very difficult to put into words.'[20] It was a strong, curious shock of affinity he felt, more intimate, in this unknown Ulsterman's work, than he had ever felt before.

The recognition was mutual; Reid had discovered it, on his part, some years before, on a winter afternoon in Cambridge University Library, 'when I was prowling round the shelves upstairs and took down by the merest chance a thin pale-blue volume called *Songs of Childhood* by Walter Ramal. I had never heard of Walter Ramal and ... it was as if in the silence and fading light of that deserted library, I had, like some adventurer in the Middle Ages, sailed all unexpectedly into sight of an unknown and lovely shore.'[21]

When Reid next got over to England and could at last meet de la Mare, he was introduced to the St George's Café and to de la Mare's friends there – Thomas, Hodgson, Davies. Like Hodgson, Reid had a side quite distinct from the literary; they shared a passion for dogs and for games – though where Hodgson's was for bull-terriers and billiards, Reid's was for bulldogs and championship croquet. It was croquet just as much as his poet friendships that brought him over to England, generally once a year. He was two years younger and much of de la Mare's own middle height and figure, his clothes a little old-fashioned – usually a blue suit with baggy pockets. His face was both ugly and attractive, blunt-featured, with a square high forehead and an Ulsterman's long, sardonic upper lip. The eyes de la Mare remembered as 'greenish, scrutinising, unfaltering'; they were often lit with ironic mischief. Reid could be touchy and difficult, though de la Mare did not find him so. He loved an argument and pursued it with salty prejudice, restless eyebrows twitching. He valued goodness and affection above everything. His passion for small boys and boyhood had all shades of feeling involved in it, and inspired some of the best and worst of his individual and uneven novels; but there was a simplicity and directness in the way he steered his emotional nature, and he also possessed a streak of the visionary – something ingenous but also disciplined and pungent, that kept his personality in balance. He was a man entirely after de la Mare's heart.

They shared a common engrossing interest in the problems posed by the supernatural for the fiction-writer, and at their first talk Reid discovered that de la Mare had written short stories of this kind. At once he began to ferret these out for himself from the back-numbers of the *Cornhill* and *Monthly Review*, and from then on persistently urged de la Mare to publish a collection, laying by every old copy of his tales in periodicals he could put his hands on.

*

The strain of too much reading, too much writing, increased

oppressively. In June 1913 Edith Sichel gave de la Mare another opportunity of country quiet to alleviate matters, and he went to finish his long article for the *Edinburgh* alone in her house at Hambledon Hurst, to which he and Dick had once walked the ten miles from Dene Cottage. 'I could live happily here awhile,' he told Naomi, 'with no visitors, few letters and only a glimpse now and then – if that – of town, to give a renewed edge to its peace ... To have you, away in the country, in a house we'd found and made – just your free self – to make every beautiful thing more secret and every secret more real and every day a kind of gamble between the impossible and the unhoped-for. How long could it last? Would the blue devils quite go? It would be pretty near madness to possess anything quite so much.'[22]

One day she had observed with justice that, in his relationship with her and Elfie, he wanted both to have his cake and eat it. He could not forget that. 'And yet,' he excused himself, '– however we may look at it – what else is possible? And my dear it's the false advantages not the desperations of a so-called respectable course that suffocate heart and mind.' At night he had symptomatic dreams. 'I saw a kind of scorpion, but it was white, and crawling amidst an intense white-hot fire from which I wanted, but was too horrified, to save it. It didn't burn, but crawled with perplexed antennae, and presently broke at one of its joints, but without consuming ... And last night I dreamt I watched what appeared to be a mortal conflict between a lobster (?) and some other more horrible and (again) vaguer and forgotten thing. There was no stir – only intense hostility and each was busily feeding and feeding on the other's brain.' He was bone-weary yet shrewd enough to recognise that what he wanted was not really rest 'but life and reality – and then more Riddles'.[22]

Naomi had sensibly decided to divide her cake: to eat what she could, have what she could, and cut out complaint. 'I'll not vow to be faithful to you,' she had written to him at Dillybrook, 'but I'll *promise* not to blame you when you come to the end of me and go on to your next adventure. Shall we try to be at peace together while it is yet day? It is so splendid to have found each other at all and why should you fret because I will not set limits to my love. I *don't know*. If I vowed and promised you'd be bound too and you can't be. There we've got to stop. I can't bind myself to you because you can't take the responsibility. Don't you see that the only way you can have me at all is by leaving me free. It isn't fair to ask me for things you can't take.'[23]

Her clear-sightedness already included the possibility of her marrying someone else (though as yet she had nobody in mind). But when de la Mare died, Naomi (who indeed had gone on to marry, and was by now in her seventies) declared, coming away from his memorial service: 'You see, I am his widow!'[24] The old romancer's characteristic self-dramatisation was only ratifying what she had foreseen clearly enough as early as 1913. In March that year she wrote to him: 'No one else could possibly ever make any difference to the true fact that ... we've taken friendship as far as it *can* go, that I give you what I've never given anybody else, nor ever shall. You can't feel that way twice, there aren't two people alive like you. You are you, and you found me. But I'll not vow that I'll never love *at all* again, because I've loved and I still love other people.'[25]

*

Peacock Pie came out at midsummer 1913, 'done to a turn', as Edward Thomas had hoped it would be. The book met with such chorus of praise from friends and critics as perhaps no other did in all de la Mare's career. He had selected the rhymes directed at childhood, centred right inside a child's 'Now'; nearly all those with a remoter, sadder note he had put already into *The Listeners*. This makes *Peacock Pie* gayer, less wistful and less nostalgic than *Songs of Childhood*. It is full of bright, curious, fanciful small subjects intensely present, each casting a long shadow – bread and cherries and a dog's teeth 'like ships at sea' – the commonplace valued as a kind of 'good news' for the unstaled imagination. Abounding inventive verve keeps fancy almost always free from whimsy and the self-conscious.

Once, later on, de la Mare wrote to Naomi, about a happy mood: 'Sometimes quite bright ideas come one's way and so they did in childhood and sometimes there is a wonderful novelty, as there was then.'[26] Such moments of wonderful novelty are what he put in his pie, and for them he followed his own recipe: 'Get very tired first.' Like the early poems written late at night after days at Oil, many of these he wrote around midnight, after his 'Heinemannly drudge' was done for the day:

> 'Come!' said Old Shellover.
> 'What?' says Creep.
> 'The horny old Gardener's fast asleep;
> The fat cock Thrush
> To his nest has gone;
> And the dew shines bright
> In the rising Moon;
> Old Sallie Worm from her hole doth peep;
> Come!' said Old Shellover.
> 'Ay!' said Creep.[27]

Only one or two in *Peacock Pie* ('The Little Bird' is one) were pieces still left over from the Nineties; most that can be dated were from the decade since *Songs of Childhood*, and some, by de la Mare's own account, belonged to the year before the book's publication. Besides their far more skilled music (by now hard to match anywhere) he had acquired a new command of story, caught in part from the ballads he loved, but perhaps more directly from their Victorian fairy-tale descendants, 'Goblin Market', 'Up the Airy Mountain'. In his own best poem-stories – 'Berries', 'Off the Ground' – the note he masters is the old, kindly, grotesque, amused one of the English folk-tale classics.

Scattered between, are a few poems which might just as well have found their niche in *The Listeners*: 'The Truants', with its refrain of the children 'magic hath stolen away', which Newbolt loved; 'The Song of the Mad Prince', whose riddling enigmatic dialogue owes something perhaps to Mary Coleridge. It is almost a rune, its meaning condensed to the edge of musical nonsense, but catching the mind by the root.

Gosse wrote in warm congratulation; he liked best the 'Three Queer Tales' and the witches and fairies. Eddie Marsh, in response to de la Mare's direct request for criticism, decided that there were 'about 15 perfectly lovely and delicious things that won't pass through any sieve, however wide-meshed'.[28] But the letter it meant most to receive was from Edward Thomas. De la Mare put it away, with the envelope pencilled 'Very special precious'. Thomas had already read the book in manuscript, and wrote on 24 June 1913:

> My dear de la Mare,
>   Your book has caught me up on my travels. I shall cut it tomorrow night, I hope, at an inn at Salisbury. I promised it to myself as I should strawberries & cream, liver & bacon, or salad, Gruyère & home-made bread. And it is just as definite a pleasure. If I had to imagine a book to fit your title I should imagine your book; at least I should imagine something which only your book would embody. I love it & I think not the less because 'Magic hath stolen away' all of me that could feel such things without your help. Hudson's are the only other living man's books that give me such perfect pleasure, with its edge perhaps a little keener for the faintest touch of envy. I hope some paper will give me a chance of saying this in some more tedious & roundabout way.[29]

He signed off: 'Yours ever ET. Coo-ee', as if he 'yelled across the combe'. Ella too was concealed in the book as 'Poor "Miss 7"', a rhyme de la Mare wrote about her stay in some nursing-home. To Eleanor Farjeon Thomas said that *Peacock Pie* and Frost's *North of Boston* were the only two pure gold nuggets he had ever dug out of his poetry reviewing. And in talking once to David Garnett, he put Frost first and de la Mare second among all living poets.

Yet de la Mare had his private unease about the acclaim; for after all these were only his 'rhymes'. To Naomi, thanking her for her praise, he shows a twinge at so much success weighed on nursery scales:

> Of course if I *had* taken out the little that's any good in the book, the rest wouldn't have been worth bothering about at all. And I'm pretty sure there ain't going to be no 'considered' stuff from this Wallie. He's done. I never can help laughing at what a friend of Thomas's said to him at Oxford – 'oh yes, I like some of de la Mare's work pretty well, but then he isn't a *serious* poet, is he?' Something like that. It's true of course *and* modestly concealed in the [*Peacock Pie*] hotch-potch's motto –
>
>> I paid him a visit, still hoping to find
>> He'd done his small best (?) at *improving his mind*: –
>> He told me his dreams ...[30]

He admitted he winced at some accusation of hers about ' "superficial indolence". I don't think it was indolence – not superficial anyhow – but just reiterated incapacity and blindness, for I drudged and drudged even at the doggerel.'[30]

*

If de la Mare had had his way, the first edition of *Peacock Pie* would have been illustrated by Claud Lovat Fraser. He and Fraser had been introduced the previous summer by Hodgson. A big friendly youth of twenty-two with a long, full face and heavy-lidded eyes, Fraser spent much of his time in the theatre, and in collecting old street-ballad broadsheets. Under the influence of these, he formed his own distinctive style, using mainly a reed pen, and a thick black economical line of great verve and confidence. He worked in watercolours and inks, and loved bright juxtapositions of pure colour. At this first meeting his work was quite unknown to de la Mare, except for some verses which had come Naomi's way in manuscript, and in which (so he remembered) she had found 'the real thing'. It was Fraser's personality – endearing but already mature – and a playful turn of mind which jumped with his own, that attracted him; and they took to each other equally.

After Fraser married, four years later, his wife noticed the way in eager talk he and de la Mare would finish each other's sentences, and that Fraser, who liked to be read aloud to while he drew, would get de la Mare to do this from his own work. This congeniality made a strong, immediate impact; it was quite unlike de la Mare to show work of his own to a new acquaintance, nor at that first meeting did Fraser know anything of the children's rhymes that would be published a year afterwards. Yet only a week later de la Mare at tea in Fraser's studio, must have read or shown him some of them, for on an impulse he asked him to do a drawing for them. Fraser sat down at his drawing-board there and then, and drew one for 'Who said Peacock Pie?' – a negro page in a red coat carrying that dish, garnished with a sweep of plumes. This was the first of many occasions when de la Mare sat talking away at Fraser's elbow watching pictures 'positively leap into life on the paper' under that quick and unselfconscious hand.

That first July afternoon together in 1912, de la Mare came home from the studio afterwards and wrote off to Naomi: 'I don't think there's any doubt at all he's a *real* touch of genius.'[31] He was at once seized with a strong desire that Fraser should illustrate the whole book – a thing directly contrary to his usual attitude. Fraser at once agreed, though with a twinge of doubt; it seems that he was far from realising yet what a vogue could be introduced in this field, for he asked that the illustrations should appear anonymously, 'as it would never do to let my critics know that I had done quaint chapbook pictures'.[32] The fear cannot have bothered him much longer, for a few months later he launched on his public career with the *Flying Fame* designs – modern versions of the old chapbooks and street-ballad broadsheets. Perhaps his work on *Peacock Pie* ('embellishments' he called them) – and de la Mare's delight in them – helped dispel his doubts.

When the *Flying Fame* venture began – with Fraser himself, Hodgson and Holbrook Jackson each laying out a capital of five pounds to finance it – de la Mare was the first but one, outside their own partnership, from whom they invited an original poem for a broadsheet. (James Stephens was the first.) So de la Mare's poem 'The Old Men' came out to Fraser's attractive design, the rhyme-sheets printed and then hand-coloured by him or by Hodgson, whose own style of decoration became almost indistinguishably modelled upon Fraser's. Sometimes, to relieve the tedium for themselves, they would vary the colour-schemes. Results sold very well at tuppence plain, fourpence coloured, distributed from Fraser's studio. In all, meanwhile, Fraser did about fourteen *Peacock Pie* drawings, probably mostly in 1912, though at least one is in his later style of fine line and was quite likely added purely for his own pleasure, around 1920, by which time the project had been put aside.

In September 1912, after a gap, he wrote to de la Mare: 'Alas! when I took up my pen I found that the chapbook spirit had forsaken me and I could not draw a single stroke satisfactorily!'[33] But he was as keen as ever to finish the work, and it was a great disappointment to both men when Constable finally ruled out his designs as too expensive to reproduce. Soon after, they vetoed any illustrated edition, for the time being. With his usual generosity, Fraser handed over the rejected embellishments to de la Mare as 'your property please do treat them as such'.[34] De la Mare only succeeded in getting them published in a 1924 edition of *Peacock Pie*, by which time Fraser had already been dead three years.

In the interval, Heath Robinson had done line illustrations for an edition of 1916. *Peacock Pie* lent no handle to the marvellous crack-brained mechanical inventions from his comic side, and without this he had nothing. It is characteristic of Fraser's amiability that he only wrote to de la Mare about the coy and fustian production which resulted: 'It is very good but somehow not my idea of it.'[35]

Nor perhaps are Fraser's own embellishments quite one's idea of it either, but they are so vital in themselves that the difference in essential character between poet and illustrator is not fatal. The two joined hands on the side of the homely and grotesque, of childhood's vitality and oddity – and such magic as belongs to those qualities. But the text is drenched with another magic, too, which was quite aside from Fraser's range: the quality summed up for the little boy in the *Come Hither* introduction as 'Theeothaworldie'.

> Ere my heart beat too cold and faintly
>   To remember sad things, yet be gay,
> I would sing a brief song of the world's little children
>   Magic hath stolen away.[36]

Wisely, that was not a note Fraser attempted to echo.

Sketches for *Crossings* by Lovat Fraser, never used.

12

Ghosts and Shadows

In the summer of 1913 de la Mare went on from a few July days at Netherhampton to visit Beresford and his family at St Merryn, between Newquay and Padstow, where they had taken a cottage. So far all he had seen of Cornwall was Tintagel, some time long ago in boyhood with Poppy – but this was enough already to associate the region with pleasurable menace, for he had given the *Songs of Childhood* ogre, with his 'disastrous thumb', an unmistakably Cornish home, 'Trebarwith Vale'. Now, from the St Merryn visit on, Cornwall gripped his imagination as no other countryside would do. He actively disliked the rich red-earth luxury of South Devon scenery, and Naomi's alps were no need of his; what he wanted, and found in Cornwall, was landscape as nearly as possible a parable of inward solitude – and as such, alarming as well as blest. He was always slightly at stretch when west of the Tamar, more awake than usual – even literally, for he said he always slept very lightly there.

Altogether he had four substantial country breaks this summer, yet nothing seemed to relieve his tension and exhaustion. Edward Thomas was worried by his run-down and fine-drawn appearance, and his letters to Naomi from Cowden in Kent, where the family was again spending its holiday, are oppressed, even acid. He felt unreal, in continual worry of mind, and exasperated with distaste for the tasks his life was spent on, and for the way in which he could perform them. The friction in his marriage grew worse and worse in such conditions, and he would write now with dangerous desperation to Naomi of his longing for letters: 'Couldn't there be some way that only I could read? I always burn your letters. It isn't any wish to deceive anybody, there's little of that *essentially*. I don't tell lies when the question's a real one – only hold my tongue – another form perhaps.'[1]

He never once envisages in their letters any actual plan of their living together; it was just that the 'balancing-act', which he anyway despised, grew inexorably more impossible. To lose the children was unthinkable, and Naomi recognised in his home 'a whole part of your life over which I have no sort of claim'. But the need to ease things somehow this August drove them to desperate measures.

While the family were away at Cowden they apparently spent three days together in Naomi's room. Afterwards de la Mare wrote: 'The three days just gone are the first we've really had and there they will always be. I never knew before what peace it would mean without that ceaseless counting of minutes and you were the dearest and kindest Nann I never even imagined there was. And we've imagined a good many!'[2]

When she was old, Naomi categorically volunteered, when she knew that this biography was to be written: 'I was never de la Mare's mistress.'[3] She had in her own moral code no reason whatever to have hidden the matter had it been otherwise, and her natural wish to be recognised as his inspiration would have inclined her, now he was dead, to speak out. So also would the strong need she had by temperament to take the centre of the stage – that 'inveterate vanity' de la Mare was always teasing her for. And if this were not conclusive, Naomi's final confession to a close friend in her last years certainly would be: that they had never been lovers, and that she had wanted them to be.

If these three days did not break de la Mare's resolve, then it was plain nothing now would ever do so.

*

Edward Thomas descended that autumn once more into his private hell of depression. Ironically, he was struggling at the time with a book on Ecstasy. On 5 October (1913) he met Robert Frost at the St George's, introduced by Hodson. De la Mare seems also to have been at the café that day, but he and the American did not meet. Thomas's letter to him the next day shows he had been at one of his suicidal crises, and that their talk together in the evening had greatly relaxed his desperation: 'Thank you for what you said last night. I think I have now changed my mind though I have the Saviour in my pocket. The final argument was my mother who has received nearly all the other blows possible.'[4] The Saviour may have been the revolver that Helen Thomas so dreaded to see him take from his drawer when he flung off for black hours in the woods, leaving her sick with anxiety, listening for a shot. If not, it was some other means of self-despatch.

Thomas at any rate felt he may have owed his life to de la Mare's comfort and persuasion, on this occasion. When he chose, de la Mare did in fact have the gift of the confessor – unintrusive, even elusive, though he might usually appear. On such occasions, to meet some friend's great need, he could use a quite unexpectedly direct probe, questioning on, unembarrassed by emotion, even tears, so that whatever the trouble was – some sharp detail of a deathbed or some long-suppressed guilt – it could find release.

In January 1914 he went off to Netherhampton. Such mid-winter visits became a custom, for the winter aspect of the place suited him almost more than its idyllic summer one. He loved especially his solitude before sleep in the long, low bedroom, with fourposter, candles and a crackling fire. Outside, black tufts of trees topped the frozen slopes of the down, and the strangeness of life pressed in. Not that it needed to exert much pressure. 'Just then,' he wrote to Naomi, sitting up in bed before sleep, 'there was a steady increasing surge of wind through the bare branches of a huge elm beyond the window – but no – it was merely my evening coat slipping off the sofa! And yet that wave of wind will always faintly be.'[5]

At Netherhampton he intended to do some stories, and some 'Quantock letters'. He had constantly urged Naomi to write novels; he thought her reviewing (as he thought his own) essentially a waste, whatever the merits of the result, believing that criticism stole from its author – some of the grindstone wearing off into the meal. Now Naomi had persuaded him into a collaboration. The result, *John Fanning's Legacy*, was a novel in letter form, mainly written and directed by her, about a dead novelist, and his young secretary's attempt to write his biography. Much of it is satiric comedy of the literary world, taking off finally into murder melodrama. Its atmosphere is nowhere poetic, and the whole is rather crudely and shallowly clever. De la Mare's part was to write the letters of an elusive, whimsical friend of the dead man, called Nicholas Quantock. He strongly suspected, and objected to, portraits drawn from Naomi's acquaintance. 'The odd thing is that *all* my conceptions differ from yours,' he told her; 'they are real people to me but only in the sense that characters made up or discovered are real – more real in a way than life.' And again: 'I do so intensely dislike the using even of bits of people of fiction – though of course it's done everywhere. The people one invents have no restrictions but their reality. Besides, the talk!'[6] But when the book appeared, Naomi's less sensitive approach had won. By the time she finished and published the book, in 1927, her relationship with de la Mare had totally altered, and Quantock, a weak inset into a fiction never of the de la Mare cast, had become an embarrassment to him. He would not allow

Naomi to acknowledge the collaboration, and she had to write
Quantock's final letters herself.

His chief task during that Netherhampton break early in 1914, was
to write his first lecture, at the invitation of Michael Sadler,
Vice-Chancellor of Leeds. Rather than talk on Coleridge or read his
own poems, he had taken up Sadler's third suggestion: a lecture on
'Magic in Poetry'. The idea caught his fancy, though the actual
composition was a great labour. He groused to Naomi: 'Who wants to
write about magic. And I'm dead sick of the pomposities – of being
"us"-ish. The lecture is scraping along – but I'd sooner be planting
primroses on my own grave.' When he came to the end of the first
section he took the manuscript upstairs to practise his delivery in 'the
Ark', the longest room in the house. He had a ruthless audience:

> We stuck poor Delamare up at the other end [Newbolt wrote] and Celia
> and Ella and I sat by the fire and listened to the first bit of his lecture and
> two quotations read aloud from 'Dark Rosaleen' and Chr. Rossetti's
> 'Prince'. It was cruel of us, but cruel only to be kind. By some strange
> chance he is the most *prosaic* reader I have ever heard: when he reads
> prose he is almost unintelligible, so illogical in his accenting, but when
> he reads poetry he reads in a cold and excessively logical accent, as if
> *determined* to reduce all to the tone of common day. In fact he reminds
> me of a stage father (British) reading with cold angry contempt the
> poetical effusions of his own disappointing son – 'I suppose you consider
> that sort of thing very fine!' We mixed a good deal of cruelty with our
> kindness – it was no case for compromise – we simply roared and
> shouted. After two attempts the *lecture* came out more clearly but the
> poetry will take much more coaching.[7]

Poor de la Mare! In the year before he died he was describing that
scene and it still rankled. He had been reading aloud 'about ¾ of a
minute,' he said, 'When Harry burst out laughing and said "I don't
think I should do it quite that way Jack." I don't think I've ever really
forgiven him for that!'[8]

When the actual day came for delivering the lecture in Leeds, he had
completely lost his voice, and at the hall, after his whispered
explanation, it was decided that somebody else should read it for him if
he proved inaudible. 'I began – as clear and animating as a flageolet,
"Ladies and gentlemen"! Nothing was wrong with the vocal organs.
Only some wise self within had tried to circumvent so unwholesome,
unnatural and repulsive a performance.'

Into the lecture, he compressed much of his ponderings (on love, as
well as on poetry) of these last three years, when magic had been the
note of both. He conceived of magic as the sudden condensation of any
moment into intenser significance. Felicity in a line of poetry may

bring it about, or a chance mood of perception, but the surest way is love, and by that he meant very exactly and exclusively romantic love, a certain pitch of longing to which human fulfilment is more than irrelevant – an enemy.

This lecture written at the peak of his capacity for romantic poetry, was the nearest he ever came to describing the philosophy behind his poems, or to stating in public the theme scattered throughout the huge correspondence to Naomi. 'Love,' he declared, '… not only transforms this world but reveals the one sure truth that all experience is a conflict between realities.' The child growing up 'will learn that beauty need never perish in the mind, that self counts for nothing, compared with self's dream, that even Helen herself (or Susan) is a ghost, an embodiment of divinity. As the phantom in Mr Hardy's poem explains to the lover:

> O fatuous man, this truth infer,
> Brides are not what they seem;
> Thou lovest what thou *dreamest* her,
> *I* am thy very dream.

And he quoted from Traherne: "Tis not the object but the light that maketh heaven.' In the highest state that poetry can induce, he held that 'beauty – even earthly beauty – becomes only a promise or a memory, the symbol of a remote reality'.

No wonder he clung almost hysterically to his ideal in Naomi, imploring her to suppress, or better still abolish, the clever efficient woman of the newspaper office and the literary party. 'Ghosts and shadows – shadows and emanations' – these were what he valued most, just because to him they were not faint things but essence: the concentrated implication of all. It was not so much Naomi herself that he feared to lose, as his capacity through her for magic itself.

Just now that capacity was at strength. A few weeks after writing the lecture he sent Naomi a dated manuscript of a poem, 'The Blind Boy', and among the many undated ones which she kept pell-mell with his letters, is another so closely matched in format it seems likely they arrived together. If so, 'The Ghost', one lyric which puts him, if anything does, among the lasting English poets, belongs to this spring:[9]

> 'Who knocks?' 'I, who was beautiful,
>   Beyond all dreams to restore,
> I, from the roots of the dark thorn am hither,
>   And knock on the door.'

'Who speaks?' 'I – once was my speech
  Sweet as the bird's on the air,
When echo lurks by the waters to heed;
  'Tis I speak thee fair.'

'Dark is the hour!' 'Ay, and cold.'
  'Lone is my house.' 'Ah, but mine?'
'Sight, touch, lips, eyes yearned in vain.'
  'Long dead these to thine …'

Silence. Still faint on the porch
  Brake the flames of the stars.
In gloom groped a hope-wearied hand
  Over keys, bolts, and bars.

A face peered. All the grey night
  In chaos of vacancy shone;
Nought but vast sorrow was there –
  The sweet cheat gone.

In its trappings romantic enough, yet this is one of de la Mare's major, serious poems. Its pang of loss and longing penetrates to central human experience, and, by the paradox of beautiful expression, grief so voiced moves the reader inexplicably with consolation. It is the peculiar property of verbal beauty; nothing else will do it.

De la Mare could seldom be decoyed into discussing his own poems, technique apart. But once at the end of his life when this was mentioned as one of his best, he fended off the compliment with foolery ('You can't speak of my *best*, can you, though? There couldn't be a *best* among my poems') but then let a very brief admission escape: 'That's one of my favourites.'[10] At once his talk glanced off, escaping further comment.

*

Thomas had never struggled up very far from the previous autumn's despair. The letters of isolation and disappointment he wrote to Edward Garnett at this period caused de la Mare heartache when Garnett published them after Thomas died. Not that he himself was reproached in them, but Thomas did feel let down by his friends. All the same, by February 1914 he was getting some work from Naomi which he told Eleanor Farjeon was 'by de la Mare's intercession', and before August he mentioned to de la Mare doing at least one article for Richmond at the *TLS* Garnett tried to comfort de la Mare for the pain the letters from this period gave him: 'I daresay he over-estimated his chances. We know how extremely difficult it is to hook A on to B and I believe you did effect this juncture if not then, later. But E.T. was probably feeling bitterly isolated. I don't think I gauged the extent of this, myself, till later on.'[11]

Yet Thomas undoubtedly did feel that he had done more to put de la Mare in the public eye in the past than de la Mare was doing in return for him, now he was up and Thomas down. There was no work from Thomas yet that deserved praise in the terms he had used of *The Listeners* and *Peacock Pie*, and Thomas of all men would certainly not have praised hackwork if he had not felt honest admiration. As it was, de la Mare got smartly rapped by Gosse in 1916 for too much enthusiasm about Thomas's prose. Nor is there any review of de la Mare's of any work of Thomas's which does not commend. He lobbied hard too, through Newbolt and others, to get him a grant from public funds – and in February 1914 Thomas did receive £150 from the Royal Literary Fund. In 1915 de la Mare, campaigned to get him a Civil List Pension, or at least something from the Royal Bounty. In 1916 he turned to Marsh, then Secretary in charge of Civil List Pensions, who did secure a maintenance grant for Thomas of £300. After Thomas was killed, de la Mare gave Helen all the assistance he could, with letters of recommendation of all kinds, including one for the Civil List Pension, which was secured, bringing her considerable relief from worry.

*

In June 1914 Rupert Brooke returned from his year in America and the South Seas, and sought out de la Mare's company again. He had enquired from Marsh, writing from Tahiti, about a suitable London club to join when he got back:

> What do the jolly people all do? I want to belong to the same club as de la Mare. Where does de la Mare go? To Anerley S.E., I suppose.
>
>> There was once a metrist of Anerley,
>> Whose neighbours were mundane but mannerly.
>>> They don't cavil the least
>>> At a stray anapaest
>> But they *do* bar his spondees in Anerley.[12]

In fact de la Mare was by now feeling a certain satisfaction that he could hold his own at the glossy hem of the literary world, where smart society overlaps it. Human character fascinated him; he was very sociable, and what shyness he felt, avoided self-consciousness. He had mastered completely the knack of twitching conversation away from the small-talk shallows into the deeps of his own real interests.

Newbolt, in fact, noticed an 'even quite worldly' tinge appearing in his conversation. This took its brief colour from Naomi's set, and his position there.

They generated a rather more brittle and knowing social atmosphere than his other habitual companions. They were permissive and sharp-tongued, and often more ambitious than really distinguished. Through Naomi they helped spread de la Mare's reputation, and supplied some interesting and useful contacts, but not many of those abiding friendships which meant most to him originated at her parties. Her evenings required at least a veneer of Mr Worldly Wiseman, and de la Mare, who was a very successful guest, found himself at times with the misgivings his Midget felt, when she is taken up by the smart and clever in the West End drawing-rooms of Mrs Monnerie's set. Yet he could not help finding it pleasant that, though he sat quietly at Naomi's assemblies (never the centre of the stage nor in the habit of going up to accost others) yet the rest would seek him out; everyone wanted the chance to meet him. Naomi would make a social event of any new de la Mare poem the *Saturday Westminster* published. Someone would take the chair; a table was provided with pretentiously symbolic glass inkstand and quill pen, and, stationed behind this, some reader, usually Naomi herself, regal in aquamarine silk, would render the new poem, should de la Mare not be there for her to call on.

Elfie's health suffered this year. She was ill and worn and worried, yet strong-minded enough when de la Mare put the question to her in March (at Naomi's request) to answer, no, she did not wish him and Naomi to stop seeing each other. For her own part, Naomi was suffering more now than in the first year or two. She spent part of May 1914 with the Beresfords in Cornwall, and de la Mare went there alone in July with an article to write for the *TLS*, on maps. Cornwall kept for him all its old power to invade the seen with the unseen. But something was lost, something inexorably fretting out, parching out of life, turning its magic brown at the edges. He would not recognise it yet, dare not entertain the possibility for a moment; yet in the 'conflict between realities' it was romantic love that gradually lost ground, however ardently he still protested it.

Beresford had arranged, as if casually, that Naomi should occupy a cottage nearby for the latter part of de la Mare's stay. But when she came, all was as much fret and friction as ever. They had parted on a tiff in London, and Elfie had bitterly resented that Naomi was to follow him to Cornwall. Now they were together, they were helplessly irritable with each other. The only actual happiness their companionship brought de la Mare was that of memory when she had gone, and he could once more read her into the landscape at will, without a woman at his side who was as real, tired out, and short-tempered as himself.

The trouble in Cornwall was that they discovered, before Naomi left, that they had placed themselves in a false position by accepting Beresford's plan for them to be there together. It became plain they were assumed to be lovers. Beresford approved the liaison as he saw it, overriding the doubts his wife had for Elfie's sake. Beresford saw things as the majority of Naomi's set would have done: that an affair with someone intellectually worthy of de la Mare, would be good for him as a writer. Beresford would have thought scruples about adultery 'Victorian' and irrelevant. If he thought about Elfie at all, he probably assumed she need not know. Naomi's letter to de la Mare on her return to London shows she had felt it better, before she left Cornwall, despite the strong feelings she knew he would have against any such action, to speak out frankly to the Beresfords 'rather than by an iron discretion' to allow 'such definite and in a way plausible suspicions to flourish. As it is they are altogether cleared away and I do not think there need be any further discussion of the matter. A plain knowledge of the truth is never dangerous as misinterpretation of very hard facts can be. Please try to see it a little from my point. I had to clear myself *and* you and it was no use piling up lies when the truth was so simple and so clearing.'[13]

He detested this breach of their reserve and privacy. The definition of innocence so 'clearing' in Naomi's eyes was very little help to him. Technical marital fidelity can combine the highest cost with the minimum of real meaning, and this was one 'very hard fact' over which he did not deceive himself. Nor, whatever his own nervous exasperation at home, can he have liked the unlikeable hardness in Naomi towards Elfie. She dismissed her as silly, with the brisk contempt of a clever, strong-willed, liberated woman toward anyone of her own sex so utterly dependent, domesticated and self-deprecating. Subconsciously she probably stiffened herself against qualms with the dislike we all take up instinctively for anyone we are harming.

In later years the two women would make valiant efforts of forbearance, even achieving friendly relations with each other for de la Mare's sake. Their devotion to him was their only thing in common, and for both it finally overrode every other consideration. Meanwhile the Cornish episode increased his load of uneasy compunction towards them both.

Experience had given him good reason for the poem called 'Astray' that he had written long before he met Naomi, but did not publish until old age.[14] It expresses something he felt always – young, old, but most keenly of all in these middle years:

> This is not the place for thee;
> Never doubt it, thou hast come
> By some dark catastrophe
>   Far, far from home.
>
> Never one came loving thee;
> Never loved thou one, now gone;
> But some hapless memory
>   Was left – to live on.

*

He set off home from Cornwall on a morning that looked to him grey and threatening, but yet without any misgivings beyond his personal concerns. The shot the assassin had fired three weeks before at Sarajevo had awoken few ordinary Englishmen. But the day after he reached London the Austrian ultimatum to Serbia was announced, and a week or two later he was writing of the Cornish holiday as if across a chasm. As his intuition already seemed to hint, the days when he and Naomi would walk so closely, wrapped in a world-excluding private intensity, were gone: 'How queerly faraway look those two small folk walking to Treyarnon and in the darkness and the rain.'[15] Now they must turn to face outwards, and that in itself would give a fundamental shift to their fixed relation.

Looking back past yet another war, comparing notes with his own generation or describing the past to the young, he would always say that the 1914 war had completely carried away the world as he knew it till then. Success had come for him just in time to float him into those circles which had most of all enjoyed security till now. Civilisation as understood in the world of Eddie Marsh, the Newbolts and the more established writers he came across through Naomi and Gosse depended absolutely upon this Edwardian sense of security and leisure, built up over long years of peaceful Victorian supremacy and empire. Even the most struggling writers like Edward Thomas drew unconsciously on that huge reservoir of the unviolent tradition. Later generations of their kind have envied their privileged exemption from the sense of universal threat. This inborn confidence went with a kind of spiritual plenty, or at any rate the assumption that such a quality reigned in the world. Idealism, nobility, romance, value attached to great areas of human experience that, once crumbled and soured into disillusion, would not return.

De la Mare had a letter from Marsh, scribbled three days before war was declared, between bouts of work at the Admiralty, still gamely planning a second *Georgian Poetry* and asking for poems – anything written since 1912 – but adding, 'Isn't it strange what an air of unreality there is about very real things.' For himself, de la Mare found scribbling a review like writing with the pen of an automaton, his mind in a haze of the universal consciousness of anxiety, doubt and incredulity. And though rather ashamed of himself, he was busy laying in a hoard of flour and sugar before the family went, as planned, to Cowden, and anxiously urging Naomi to do likewise.

A few days later Heinemann dealt his blow: 'It simply amounted to this,' de la Mare told Naomi: 'that of his generosity he would give me two *or* three months at half salary and so save paying me in full for *one*. Somehow the obvious Jewiness of his proposal sticks in my throat – though just now he *may* be justified in ignoring an obligation.'[16] He refused Heinemann's proposed terms, ending his work for him this month. (Heinemann, on a recent visit to Germany, had seen the German arms stockpiled on the railway station platforms, and had no doubt of the war's outcome. He cut down his staff drastically at once, whatever their alternative prospects.)

At least de la Mare still had his reviewing, and he assured Marsh that his position was not as bad as someone had suggested – probably Naomi, who was extremely fussed on his behalf. She had already done her utmost to get him to accept fifty pounds from a fund she was helping to organise among literary people for writers in difficulty. He flatly refused – if for one reason only, he said: Heinemann was asked to subscribe! Naomi, exasperated, thought he was being wildly unpractical and foolish.

It was perhaps this fund which led to a story recorded by Marsh's biographer Christopher Hassall: that de la Mare 'glanced casually at a letter which had been sent to him in error, saw that it was a charitable appeal on behalf of some literary personage, overlooked the fact that it referred to himself, and sent it back with a pound note and an apology for the smallness of his contribution.'[17] Apocryphal as it may be, the story is in character.

Already his hopeful courage, always brightest when it was a question of enduring fate rather than attacking it, rose to meet the war. 'One thing, when all this is over – whatever "this" may mean, the air will be the sweeter and surely the earth a better place to be in if one be's at all,' he wrote to Naomi.[18] Newbolt's optimism, considering his sanguine nature, is less remarkable, but must have helped to keep up de la Mare's buoyancy – especially as, the moment he heard of

Heinemann's action, Newbolt wrote to renew his former guarantee that, as long as he was himself financially afloat, the de la Mare family should never sink. He offered open house to the whole family at Netherhampton, and help in finding de la Mare a temporary Civil Service job.

De la Mare, for his part, was particularly anxious about Thomas, and they kept in close touch by post in those first weeks. Thomas's letters mention the outward events, but nothing yet of the inward ones which were to make this summer's end so momentous for him. His family had settled in Herefordshire for the weeks of Robert Frost's company which were so radically to influence his life, and from Ledbury he wrote to de la Mare some time before the end of August. 'Being under half a mile from Frost's four children ours are provided for. We walk & cycle. I write what I can. But no publisher editor or public is concerned. The dribble of work has stopped … I hope you are all right. People aren't going to let you be anything else so far as they can provide, though I expect you don't feel that it is so.'[19]

Those words ('I write what I can. But no publisher editor or public is concerned') strongly suggest that Thomas may already have tried out Frost's advice and begun verse. But at first this was a secret shared only by Eleanor Farjeon, Frost and Helen Thomas; and Eleanor Farjeon herself, in her account of Thomas, did not recall poetry much before early October 1914.

Thomas wrote again on 30 August: 'If the War goes on I believe I shall find myself a sort of Englishman, tho neither poet nor soldier. If I could earn anything worth while as a soldier I think I should go.' De la Mare felt uneasy at being patriotic in an inkpot only. He could not even get himself signed on as a special constable at Cowden. The family's time there this year had been full of extravagant rumours, including the famous one of entrained Cossacks glimpsed on the way to the front with snow on their boots. A thunderstorm was enough to start a panic scare of air attack on London. All was conjecture, the mood almost superstitious; no one knew what to expect of the immediate future. Yet after all the first fatality in de la Mare's circle had nothing to do with the war. Edith Sichel died suddenly at the end of August, only a week after he had been dining with her.

Back in London he had enough on hand to occupy the present fully, and offers of more in plenty. An undistinguished patriotic poem by him, 'Happy England', came out in the *TLS*. He wrote also 'The Fool Rings His Bells', later called 'Motley' which gave the collection it appeared in its title. His war-poems are few, and very dreamy and remote the battle-horror looks through his fancy's eyes, in the light of the subsqent war-poetry trench life was to evoke:

> They are all at war! –
> Yes, yes, their bodies go
> 'Neath burning sun and icy star
> To chaunted songs of woe,
> Dragging cold cannon through a mire
> Of rain and blood and spouting fire,
> The new moon glinting hard on eyes
> Wide with insanities!

Yet even had he been a realist, actual conditions of the Front had been little reported in England as yet, and civilians had no idea how to picture the soldier's lot.

He was asked to write 20,000 words on Henry James, and exclaimed 'I'd rather dry the Atlantic with a mop!' He set to work on articles on A. C. Benson, Patriotic Ballads and a minor symbolist, wishing someone would instead employ him to write appeals for volunteers to enlist. He felt he could put some warmth into the subject. Marsh, meanwhile, remained worried about his financial position, not fully believing his assurances; very likely he discussed these anxieties with Rupert Brooke, for de la Mare and Lascelles Abercrombie were the two Marsh had most on his mind among his poets.

It must have been this summer, or the year before, that Brooke brought the young actress Cathleen Nesbitt out to Anerley for the day. Elfie was ill and it was an occasion when de la Mare seemed rather overrun with children and domesticity. On the way back in the bus Brooke wondered to Cathleen whether marriage, if it produced so many cares, was a 'good thing' for a poet. She felt that some memory of that day may have been lingering in his mind when, later, he half-jokingly asked her: 'Shall I leave my somewhat unlikely future wealth to *you* so that you can stop acting in bad plays – or to some poets so that they may have time to write good poems?' As his own royalties at the time (she gathered) only amounted to about fifty pounds, it cannot have seemed just then a very momentous decision either way.

In de la Mare's letters to Naomi, news of friends and discussion of the war now abruptly and entirely superseded the claustrophobic monotonous repetition of fret about their own relationship. Although he apologised for his 'obsession' about the war, the letters to her had in fact grown more buoyant. They do not read at all like those of a man descending into a nightmare, but rather as if he were shaking himself awake, roused from a trance.

Then came an illness, enforcing the first prolonged separation in their whole relationship, and serious enough to give his view of life a profound jolt. At the end of October he had an attack of appendicitis, and after this was allowed to work only two hours a day until the operation could be arranged. Newbolt took prompt action to raise the money for it among his friends, easily procuring a hundred pounds without exhausting the list of people willing to contribute, and getting as much again from the Royal Bounty. But from Naomi the news of the first appendix attack provoked an unfortunate reaction. Already exasperated by what she felt to be a quixotic obstinacy in de la Mare's earlier refusal of the money she had tried to press on him from her fund, her alarm at this fresh crisis now broke over his head in the form of many an angry 'I told you so!'. Elfie's solicitous sympathy must have been much more what he wanted, and there was (probably for the first time in a long while) peace between husband and wife.

De la Mare did not like Naomi at all in this managing and strident attitude. He scolded her for scolding, and called her Miss Tan Trums; there was an undercurrent of real antagonism in his resistance, and no chance to make up the quarrel before his hospital stay began. In itself the ruction would not perhaps have made a lasting difference, but with circumstances as they were, it was some kind of psychological last straw. Undramatic, it yet proved decisive. Much later, for *The Burning-Glass* (1945), de la Mare wrote a couplet in the quatrain 'Divided':

> Lovers may part for ever – the cause so small
> Not even a lynx could see a gap at all.

It would take lynx eyes to realise, for some time, that this gap had now opened; and naturally it would be Naomi who first discovered the fact, quite possibly before de la Mare was really aware himself that a fatal detachment had set in for him, 'beyond all dreams to restore'.

The appendix operation was successful, but exceptionally long and delicate. Dr Grey had advised a private ward in Guy's, and there de la Mare remained into early December. He took an absorbed interest in the experience, the nearest he had yet been to death. Writing to Laurence Binyon twenty-three years later, he still liked to dwell on the curiously 'pacifying and serene' remembrances he had kept of it. Once he woke in the night, rambling, to see the sister and night nurse, lantern in hand, at the foot of his bed, and assure them in solemn accents (so he remembered) that 'all Institutions were to be swept away'. The quiet smile he got in answer haunted him. The fact was he delighted in nurses; the relationship suited him perfectly, and they found him a beguiling patient. He even wheedled the sister, one night, into breaking her reserve to describe her childhood to him. One of his fellow-patients with whom he often talked, much mystified him with allusions to his horses, carriages and so forth. The day he left he revealed that he was an undertaker, having kept the fact dark all those weeks, out of delicacy, as long as his companions had any doubts about their manner of exit from the ward.

Elfie visited as often as she was allowed in, and wrote between: 'As soon as I leave you I only live to see you again.' Naomi came once, near the beginning, but after that they did not meet again for two whole months. Rupert Brooke, now in the Royal Naval Division and just back on leave after the Antwerp Expedition, paid him a visit in mid-November – a very stimulating hour. He was only just in time, for when he got back from Guy's that day he found a telegram posting him to Portsmouth, to the Nelson Battalion. The experience of seeing the refugees on the roads of Belgium had resolved the war for him to a clear issue, a cause to which he could wholly, gladly commit himself; this must have shown in his face and bearing as he talked at de la Mare's bedside, for when the news came next spring of his death, de la Mare told Elfie that at this last meeting Rupert had seemed to know it would be so, and was not sorry. Brooke wrote to explain why he would be unable to come to Guy's again:

> I wish I could have done so. I'm afraid that by the next time I pass through London you'll be quite well & out of reach. That's badly expressed, isn't it? But you catch the hang of it. I've several things about war I wanted to tell you. They'll keep. I wanted to say, too, that I loved your poem on the war in the Times in August. That & Masefield's, & Hardy's perhaps, & one other, were the only ones of the enormous crowd I thought good. Forgive my impudence.
>
> We're waiting here for the invasion – ready to go off at any hour of day or night. It's queer that the Admiralty seem so certain of it happening. I've a kind of horror at the idea of England being invaded, as of some virginity violated. But I'd enjoy fighting in England. How one could die![20]

Thomas, always specially considerate to Elfie, wrote to describe for her a visit of his own when he found de la Mare in good spirits, drawing an Eastern potentate with a pearly headdress on a sheet of *The Times*. Hodgson came sometimes also, and himself drew in a sketch book which de la Mare had with him; these drawings suggest they probably discussed their lapsed project for Hodgson to illustrate some of de la Mare's rhymes. Hodgson and Thomas coincided at the bedside at one moment, very awkwardly for them, for unknown to de la Mare they had just quarrelled about the war – so hotly on Hodgson's side that they were no longer on speaking terms. It was all because Thomas flatly declined to take any very hostile view of the Germans.

After this visit Thomas wrote to urge de la Mare to use his influence with Eddie Marsh to make the second *Georgian Poetry* more representative – not, as at present seemed to be the plan, 'a repetition of the first plus Hodgson only'. He wanted Marsh to include Locke-Ellis and Frost: 'He is probably not friendly to me or my opinion or I would write to him direct. He ought to see "Mowing" and "The Tuft of Flowers" in Frost's first book, *A Boy's Will*.'[21]

The patients' large sketch book in which Hodgson drew his nonsense pictures to amuse him, soon collected also some new poems. De la Mare wrote them out with dates attached; among them was one in his best vein, beginning

> For all the grief I have given with words
> May now a few clear flowers blow,
> In the dust, and the heat, and the silence of birds,
> Where the friendless go.[22]

Most of the other verses are convalescent pieces of no great energy; one, experimental, had an uncharacteristic broken modernist refrain:

> Alas, my loved one is gone,
> I am alone;
> It is Winter.[23]

In early December he was taken to convalesce at a copiously furnished and dark Victorian mansion in Harrington Gardens, belonging to the Shusters – Paula Shuster was one of the Coleridge and Coltman circle. He was cossetted, with a butler to valet him who was, he said, the nearest approach to a father he had had since he was three, and he was driven to the Park in an invalid landau to avoid the vibration of a motor-car. Time slipped by 'like water and the days like smoke … it seems rather impossible that I can ever be just the same old Frump I was or forget the enchantments of morphia, and the luxury of being dead.'[24] It had been a spiritual holiday, a deep rest, which he had needed. 'Between you and me,' he confessed to Naomi, 'I'm still in love with Jordan though I didn't ever get down to its green banks. It seems as if I was never so happy as then, just like childhood – something inside me: perhaps – but it's no good speculating.'[25] He was brisk about a poem she had sent him: 'I know it isn't finished – but judging from experience I don't believe *you* really know what downright *gruelling* at a poem means. This wants little, but wants that strong.'[26] When she was hurt at this, he wrote back tartly: 'You ought to be larned.'[27] He made no great haste for a meeting. When they did meet, due to some misunderstanding she thought he was an hour late. His letter afterwards is in the tone of plain, ordinary friendship, and talks of outward things – plans for his next book of poems.

Part III

The Hum of Noon

13

Professor

Convalescence from the appendix operation was slow. De la Mare's physical and emotional reserves had been severely taxed long before this illness, and the curious, rescuing halt it brought was too drastic. He had to pull himself back on to his feet with greatly reduced stamina, to face the deepening war-gloom, and he had now finally lost that romantic afflatus which had given his interior world, at forty, the intensity most poets lose with their first youth.

It would still occasionally revisit him – move him in other faces, and to individual poems as poignant. 'Mistress Fell',[1] for instance, as romantic a ballad of love and grief as any at the height of his passion for Naomi, would be written some time in the summer of 1915, and his next two collections, *Motley* (1918) and *The Veil* (1921) show little decline in that note from *The Listeners* – though this is partly because both include poems written before the war. But Magic would never again be the constant pitch of his inward life, as it had been for the past four years of infatuation. Among the poems left unpublished at his death was a comment of four lines on what Keats called 'the feel of not to feel it'. Whatever its immediate occasion, this was surely the point in his life when he felt its truth most bleakly:

> Even as the heart – how stark the cost! –
> May grieve that it grieves no more, in vain,
> So love, its inmost impulse lost,
>   Dies never to rise again.[2]

He went to Worthing, and peered moodily between lodging-house geraniums at recruits drilling in the persistent January downpour. He picked over poems for a new collection, without confidence – how could he feel his own verses to be other than thin and illusory when the very truth of the heart's imagination had just taken such a jar? He took a flat dislike to the Channel – a dingy thing, he thought, after the clear

Cornish billows. Later, further along at Weymouth, he wrote morosely to Naomi that even storm could not rouse it here to beauty – it would be only 'like a violent woman'. The metaphor was not chance-chosen. He dispatched reserved, moodless, bantering letters, adding to thanks for a visit 'and we didn't argufy much, did we?' When she reproached him with no longer caring, he denied it, phlegmatically, explaining that their quarrel of October was quite over – in terms that made its work irreversibly plain. 'I want to see you,' he declared, 'because I think the next time you won't *wrangle* so.'[3]

Netherhampton was some improvement on Worthing. He pottered by the rainy Nadder, thankful to be alone, or sat upstairs in the Ark scribbling rhymes for the book Hodgson had agreed to illustrate. The promise of this very congenial collaboration was something of a life-line. But even among the Newbolts he was sometimes seized by such a dread of talking and company he longed to run away and hide. Furse was in a bad depression after a breakdown, and de la Mare found it hard to know what to say to him – he fancied they deepened each other's gloom. Furse's son Ralph had married Celia Newbolt the previous summer, and he and Francis Newbolt were both soldiers now. Newbolt had been knighted; de la Mare found the title disconcerting, as if Harry had just grown a long black beard. The knight sat watching the convalescent from the other end of the Ark with amazement, for though de la Mare called himself stodgy and listless, and said he felt a lonely thing like some old minor maiden aunt out of an unread Dickens, yet he seemed visited by an odd, desperate facility. 'He goes on all day, covering sheets of paper with that small weird writing, I can't do it,' Newbolt protested.[4]

De la Mare soon had 'a large batch' finished. One of those he did for Hodgson, probably during this time, was 'Sam's Three Wishes: or, Life's Little Whirligig',[5] on the theme he had long ago overheard Colin pattering to himself in his three-year-old's daydream: 'When you be very old you will be a little boy again.' 'Same old every child's tradition,' de la Mare had commented then to Ella. Now he made of it one of his best stories in rhyme. Children do seize on the notion in it of life coming full circle, as if that answered to something vital in their own philosophy. They love, too, its intense relish of domestic bliss – Sam's kitchen glorified by the roasting goose his first wish brings:

> Copper and brass
> Winked back the winking of platter and glass.
> And a wonderful squeaking of mice went up
> At the smell of a Michaelmas supper to sup –
> Unctuous odours that wreathed and swirled

Where'er frisked a whisker or mouse-tail twirled,
While out of the chimney up into the night
That ne'er-to-be-snuffed-too-much smoke took flight.

This story was a particular favourite with Hodgson – 'Such fooling and such beauty have never come together in the world before,' he exclaimed. 'I wonder if you realise what you are setting my pencil to live up to.'

De la Mare had instinctively found the best tonic possible. Presently, however, what was intended as another short piece for Hodgson, ran away with him and he found himself embarked on an extremely long saga of an oriental King and his Queen Oo-Chee, which he later called 'Cathay'. He finished it in spate – seven hundred lines in five days. Then read it aloud – *very* loud, as Margaret Newbolt was going deaf – and his spirits sank again. He felt it was a failure, deplored the five days wasted, and in the end never published it.

Hodgson, enthusiastic though he was, found it difficult to get started on his own; he wanted de la Mare's actual company to support him, and the de la Mare children's too. His notions for the book's format show how completely he had absorbed Lovat Fraser's views: 'Crude raw stimulating colour – away with all *Tints*!'[6] But fortune favoured this venture no more than Fraser's proposed *Peacock Pie*. Again, only a few bright, engaging pages of illustration, exactly in the *Flying Fame* style, ever got done. Hodgson was jaded by his hours on the beat with the AAC Mobile, went for a while into hospital himself, was then taken up totally with the dying of his dog, and at last found he had lost all inspiration and interest.

The abandoned rhyme collection scattered itself, in time, into various other de la Mare volumes; several into *Stuff and Nonsense* (1927). Hodgson's personality, in the background of de la Mare's mind while he wrote, had called out a good deal in cheerfully ruthless comic vein – the Victorian Uncle rather than the Peacock Pieman. In 'Ann's Aunt and the Bear', one of those that Hodgson liked so much, the Aunt defends a wretched dancing bear, but no tears are to fall when the bear hugs her for it.[7] As for his wicked masters:

Had quite, quite base been either man,
They might have fed the bear on Ann.

Once back in London, de la Mare's spirits revived, and he began to catch up briskly on reviewing. But about now, at the exact middle of his life-span, he slipped into a way of talking of himself as old. Photographs taken three years later, in 1918, still show a glance and a

smooth skin remarkably youthful and attractive. His trick of
anticipating old age – as if he almost wished it on himself – half
alarmed and half exasperated Ella, who was about fifteen years older.
(It was still provoking her twenty years later.) Another sign stress had
left was his continuing burden of disturbed dreams. Perhaps they were
a vent for his perpetual unease at being a non-combatant in the war.
He felt his work was parasitic and irrelevant. Newbolt investigated
chances for him of something patriotic, in the Ministry of Food, but
nothing came of this yet. A. C. Benson, retiring from a Royal Society of
Literature Chair of Fiction, wrote hoping that de la Mare would
succeed him. De la Mare doubted: 'Did a Professor ever *ought* to have
piped up "Has anybody seen my Mopser?"' (one of the *Peacock Pie*
rhymes).[8] But Newbolt reassured him and a Professor he became and
remained for the next twenty-three years; also a director of the
children's magazine *Chatterbox*, attending its board meetings. Such
positions seemed to him a kind of masquerading, but no source of
income could be neglected that would help make good the gap left by
the Heinemann job. However, success now, at last, crowned Newbolt's
campaign for a Civil List Pension. By Gosse's intervention, a hundred
pounds a year for life was granted to de la Mare in March 1915.

*

Meanwhile Thomas had been secretly pouring out verse for several
months, showing it as yet to few besides Eleanor Farjeon. To her he
wrote in February: 'I am still hesitating about sending my verses to de
la Mare and others. It is too much like begging for compliments – I
shall wait.' Four weeks later he could wait no longer.

> My dear de la Mare,*
>   ... I am sending you some verses by a very young poet (not a young
> man) who desires to remain anonymous except to you and one or two
> other people. Don't mention them anywhere, as they are to be published
> (if at all) under a pseudonym. He is coming to town next week and hopes
> to see you and remains
>   Yours ever
>   E.T.
> Whatever (in reason) you think of the young poet.[9]

De la Mare must have been too pressed to make more than hurried
temporary acknowledgement, without detailed comment, for three
days later Thomas followed up:

---

* Thomas never used his Christian name, and de la Mare in return settled for an
affectionate 'E.T.'.

My dear de la Mare,

    The young poet must be much vainer or more touchy [?] than you are used to. He can't imagine how he will stand waiting a week or how then he can stand hearing he has gone wrong over metre sometimes & yet (apparently) not always. But he does think you may be right because he agrees with you in liking those 4. But then the poor fellow likes the others too. He wishes you could prepare him for the horrible truth (it must be horrible) beforehand …

    If I can get my ankle really mended I shall have to try to serve my country after all. The gardener next door has just been called up & when I heard him talking about it I felt worse than I have done yet.

Yours ever
E.T.[10]

When he did get de la Mare's full opinion on the poems, Thomas replied, in an undated letter:

Yours is the only interesting criticism I've had. But I think it is probably too fundamental, considering that I wrote (if anything) with a feeling that I did use the Morse Code. They all seemed speakable tho none chantable. However I can see you soon now.[11]

He then glances off to write of other matters, and, even allowing for his reserve and modesty and the fact that they would soon be together for a proper discussion, there seems a shade of disappointment in the letter, after his obviously intense impatience to know de la Mare's verdict. One would guess that de la Mare had suggested some further process, and it is the greatest pity that his letter to Thomas has been lost.

Thomas's sotto-voce poetry with its loose ends and deliberately conversational casualness – so much the opposite of his own art – perhaps seemed to de la Mare to lack definitiveness, to be only the notation for what he longed for Thomas to work out in full.

*

In mid-April de la Mare took Dick, who was convalescent too, to share a hotel holiday with the Coltmans in Weymouth. Elfie's present for his birthday was a pipe, for which he had conceived a sudden ardent whim. The letters between husband and wife while he was away on this visit have a note of comfortably affectionate lightheartedness long-absent – 'Well, here we are dear Mrs Fridy' – and contain romantic local legends and thumbnail sketches of the kind they had long ago delighted to exchange, for example, fellow-passengers in the train include: 'A large lady with a brazen voice discussing a Church tea or something or other of a pagan nature with another piece of brass.'[12] The contentment of sharing such morsels with her once more is plain. Not that he had ceased to share them with Naomi, but there was no longer the exclusion of the one by the other.

Dick and he scoured Portland Bill for convicts and quarries, 'and then suddenly we dipped in at a gate and were in a delicious old graveyard thick with green sleeping with old stones and lichenous cherubs and dreaming skulls (in stone). I think I must have been dead myself once – it seemed so homely.' Naomi questioned him on the reason for his love of graveyards. 'My mother has it,' he told her, 'and the very sight of a tombstone is to me like seeing something real in the midst of sham.'[13]

One morning he awoke from a dream of being shot through the eye, to papers full of a German despatch claiming attack on Ypres. The same day's post brought Ella a letter from Francis Newbolt, saying his trench was only sixty yards from the Germans. They knew he was dug in near Ypres, and Jack had him so vividly in his mind's eye he said he felt almost as if he could touch him on the arm to say 'Take care!' (Francis was in fact knocked unconscious and sent home after this with shell-shock.) For de la Mare it felt like 'playing cards in Church' to be in pleasant Weymouth while the war 'festered on the horizon'. He came to speak of it as a cancer. But the day after his forty-second birthday on 25 April, all this anxiety about the Ypres front was eclipsed. News arrived of Rupert Brooke's death, two days before, from blood-poisoning caused by a gnat-bite on his lip; he had died while in transit for Gallipoli. De la Mare read the news in *The Times*, and the same day came a letter about it from Naomi. A few days later, Eddie Marsh urged her to get de la Mare to write about Brooke. He complied with a heavy heart – 'There's a wretched feeling it will be a kind of sexton's work, but I think he would understand and that it's the little one *can* do.[14]

In fact his tribute in the *Westminster Gazette*, and the one from Henry James, were the most balanced and perceptive in the ensuing torrent of myth-making. He actually prophesied the myth: 'Once in a way Nature is as jealous of the individual as of the type. She gave Rupert Brooke youth, and may be, in these hyper-enlightened days, in so doing grafted a legend.' In this first article he called Brooke 'himself the happiest, most complex, and characteristic of his poems', dwelt on 'that happy shining impression that he might have come – that very moment – from another planet', and on poems of his that caught 'the sudden flowering miracle of the ordinary'.[15]

Three weeks after Brooke's death, Marsh wrote to de la Mare of his bitter grief, and thanked him for his 'beautiful writing about Rupert, which pleased me, I think, more than anything that has been said about him'. The day after this letter came one from Brooke's mother:

21 May 1915   24 Bilton Road
                                                      Rugby

Dear Mr De la Mare,

Among the papers of my late son Rupert which have come into my hands I find a letter from him to me which I treat as a private nature, but he mentions his wishes with regard to whatever property he might have & I am anxious to carry these out to the letter & am writing to tell you that he asks me to see that all the money he possessed at his death after his debts were paid, and all the money from the sale of his writings should be divided equally between you & Mr Wilfrid Gibson & Mr Lascelles Abercrombie. In his letter Rupert says that if he can set you free to any extent to write the plays & books & poetry you want to, his death will bring more gain than loss. He asks that Mr Eddie Marsh should look after the publication of his literary matters, & after consulting me, decide which of his writings, including if necessary letters should be published & how & when. The actual M.S.S. are to belong to me & I shall see to it that those which according to Rupert's wishes do not go to anyone else, will, after my death be in the hands of Mr Marsh.

To put me in a position to carry out Rupert's wishes I intend to take out letters of Administration to his Estate. I am afraid his total property must be under £500 & I understand that to get a grant of administration two Bondsmen have to enter into a Bond for the due administration of the estate. Will you become one of such bondsmen for me with Mr Wilfrid Gibson? I am quite sure that whatever interest my son Alfred might have, this will be relinquished to carry out Rupert's expressed wishes & there is nobody else concerned beyond myself in doing this.

I remain.
    Yours sincerely,
      M. R. Brooke.

I have written so far in a lawyer-like way in order to make the matter quite clear.

I should like to add four things.

1. that Rupert's death leaves his brother & myself quite well off & his brother ultimately better off than if he had lived.

2. That we have both of us *quite* enough.

3. That this isn't at all unexpected, though I didn't know who he would name.

4. It is one of the few bright gleams that are shining for me just now that I am able to do this.

                    M.R.B.

When she had settled Rupert's debts, she found enough money in hand to distribute £166 19s 8d to each of the three heirs, as a first instalment of an inheritance which would soon be exceeding wildest expectation.

She had barely wound up these financial affairs in mid-June 1915 when news came that her other son, Alfred, had been killed in France.

*

In June Brooke's collection *1914 and Other Poems* was published, edited by Marsh; it contained the famous war sonnets which he had been writing at the time when he and de la Mare had last met in Guys hospital. De la Mare reviewed it in the *TLS*, and stressed the large part that intellect played in Brooke's poetry – a theme he would develop in a later study. He spoke of thought and feeling as at conflict in Brooke, said he dwelt more in his mind than in his senses, and noted a 'perpetual interrogation of the unknowable' – the very quality in Brooke's mentality that Newbolt had found so like de la Mare's own. He described this poetry as 'the raid of a boy over the walls of the transitory into the orchards of beauty more than the harvest of a quiet eye'. Although he had himself sensed foreknowledge in Brooke, he partly discounted this now, remembering perhaps his own experience at times when death had seemed the only fit culmination, just because life was then 'pelting through the body'. Not too much stress,' he wrote, 'must be laid on his assurance that death could come early. It may be a symptom of unusual vitality.'[16]

Marsh finished his memoir of Brooke in July, and brought some of Brooke's last fragments of verse to discuss with de la Mare. Monro had persuaded him to take up again the idea of a second volume of *Georgian Poetry*, and he asked for de la Mare's 'When music sounds, gone is the earth I know'. But he was fussing still about its last line,

> The swift-winged hours, as I hasten along.

Not this time because of its extra beat, but because 'It seems so strange that you should be "hastening along" instead of stopping to listen to the music in the same hush and awe in which you've steeped all the surroundings.'[17] And in a later letter he returned to the attack:

> 'When the band began to play
> Hastened de la Mare away.'[18]

De la Mare was against his including 'Off the Ground' ('Three jolly Farmers / Once bet a pound') from *Peacock Pie*; he probably thought it too slight and childish for this setting. But Marsh was obstinately determined, marshalling support from the Gibsons, Abercrombie and Frances Cornford, and in the end getting his own way. It was a pity he did, for his choice* left out many things more original and imaginative, and merely emphasised de la Mare's whimsical side. After reading 'The Mocking Fairy', Frances Cornford had exclaimed: 'How does he *do* it'; Rupert Brooke had chipped in, justifiably, 'He does it too much.'[19]

De la Mare complained that Marsh was very fastidious in his choice of poets for the book, and still would not hear of Locke-Ellis or John Freeman, 'charm I never so wisely'. His 'charming' on poor Freeman's behalf met with so many rebuffs that he was finally reduced to slipping in only the first three letters of his friend's name among his other recommendations to Eddie: 'Fre ...?' Marsh eventually relented, in the third *Georgian Poetry*.

Critics greeted the second book with qualified praise; some were beginning to murmur that the simplicity of these poets was too easy. De la Mare himself was dissatisfied with the book's narrow scope. Deaf to many suggestions, Marsh had scarcely enlarged his list of poets at all, though the volume was fatter than the first. The public, however, continued to buy – it sold over 13,000 copies. The piece de la Mare admired most in it was perhaps Abercrombie's 'The End of the World', which he called 'its own comet.' He championed Abercrombie stoutly all his life, and remained convinced his work had always been much underrated.

For some weeks of August and September 1915 the de la Mares were lent a cottage on the slopes of Cumnor Hill outside Oxford – de la Mare had had quite enough of Cowden, miserably associated with strife and gloom. He did a little sightseeing in Oxford, but not much, remarking to Naomi: 'Don't tell anybody – I'm the least bit tired of this medieval city, though I haven't medievalled much about it yet.' There is an edge to his tongue about the University, as there was later on in remarks about Eton when grandsons began to go there – a touch of defiant independence from the boy who had had no privileged education: 'I'm not *very* sorry I never had a chance to dress in double blues – though backgrounds are useful and one never knows how much they enrich the past.' He addressed Naomi, in this letter, as 'Aunt Omniscientia', and signed himself 'Your loving nevvy'.[20]

One unexpected visitor at Cumnor was Bridges. De la Mare's letters, from the earliest days of his friendship with Ella, had shown the greatest admiration for his work, particularly the shorter lyrics (he had given them to Naomi as a special present in the first year of their love), and he kept his respect for him always, speaking of him

* The de la Mare poems in the second *Georgian Poetry* were 'Off the Ground', 'Wanderers', 'Melmillo', 'Alexander', 'Full Moon' and 'The Mocking Fairy'.

personally with something of the old-fashioned awe with which Ella and Mary Coleridge had, in their generation, regarded Tennyson and Browning. He did think him a great man, and an authority. He did not think him a great poet, but a very real one, sure to live, and held that he had one of the least usual of all artistic gifts: he knew how to write about happiness. So when Bridges's immensely tall figure came striding into the parlour unheralded, on a late September evening, attended by his wife and elder daughter, de la Mare felt honoured. No one was about except the children, who made a bolt for freedom. Colin, littlest and last, got caught making off through a window. Bridges's great hand descended on his curls, sat him captive between his feet, 'and the Lorreate' (de la Mare told Naomi) 'stretched himself along a little sofa and pulled Colin's hair and told him how to cut dolls' heads off, out of a long, beard-pointed, rather cavernous face, in a deep, rumbling voice.'

'About as unlike his verse as the husk of a chestnut is to the polished thing inside,' de la Mare's report continued. 'I suppose the husk's for living on the Surface with – protection against nibblers and munchers … That's the worst, and I suppose in a sense the best, of educated people. It takes such a time to get to the real wood. And even then you sometimes discover that by a curious freak it is the veneer that's *underneath*. The old boy was very gracious and talked – and he might not have been to a squab of a scribbler whom he didn't and couldn't care a 2d dash to see.'[21]

It was true that Bridges did not care for de la Mare's poetry, and this was a continual source of bewilderment to Newbolt – that one close friend of such judgement should be blind to the gift of the other. The next year, 1916, Bridges brought out his anthology *The Spirit of Man*, whose aim was to be a 'defence and stronghold' for readers in time of war, and whose pieces were chosen in the belief 'that spirituality is the basis of human life … rather than the apex or final attainment of it'. No line by de la Mare appeared in the book, and Newbolt was incredulous at Bridges's rejection – 'worse, scores it with his blue pencil, saying that in every poem there's a word or words that "can't pass"!' He reported that Bridges's wife 'copied out and took home for him 14 poems by D all suitable for his *Spirit of Man* – and R.B. refused them all, for the reason given. It will be a rude eye-opening for him when he gets to Parnassus.'[22]

In October 1915 Marsh sent the first payments out of Brooke's bequest, for the two volumes of his poems, and also a meticulous third of Brooke's share of the royalties of *Georgian Poetry*. Brooke's sales had begun to gather momentum, but no one as yet could have foreseen what was to come. Christopher Hassall, Brooke's biographer, says that by 1926 sales had reached about 300,000 copies, excluding those sold in America. It was this steady augmenting of his own income with money from the Brooke bequest, together with his Civil List pension, which accounts for the fact that de la Mare was able to maintain his family in spite of the war, and could later send Dick to Oxford, without ever again having to take a salaried post – and this even though success and fame never brought him outstanding sales himself.

14

America

Preparing lectures in the London Library reading-room in the autumn of 1915, de la Mare sighed to be writing poetry; 'But, if I had all day and every day I couldn't now. It's one of the blessedest joys of the whole thing that it's impossible even to turn out a nursery jingle unless *some* queer little door's ajar in one's mind, *some*body's peeping in at the window at one.' Then, just for a flourish, he ended this letter to Naomi: 'Fare ye well Nowe Dulcibelle   There's pinks and winesoppes blowing   And that Boye who loves ye well   A poison Darte is throwing!   See he smiles the Urchin Ladde   Laughing softe at his own graces   Nay how *canne* he strike thine harte   When his gaze on thy Sweete Face is!   Extempore 3.45   Amen.'[1]

There were Zeppelins over Croydon now, and, for a man so much the prey of private anxieties, de la Mare was surprisingly tough about such public alarms. He would run upstairs to get a good view, and half-welcomed the excitement of the raids and the sense of defying a threat.

On 9 November he spoke to the Royal Society of Literature on 'Ghosts in Fiction', his first important London lecture. Ella warned him to speak slow, and not to let the buttoned-up, unresponsive faces of polite society hurry his pace. In fact he had gained in confidence since those humiliating rehearsals in the Ark, and Newbolt reported a 'most charming and finished performance'. De la Mare never became a completely easy or entirely audible lecturer, but he was not a very nervous one, and was perfectly able to project his charm of personality. The knack of getting in touch with an audience had been his, after all, far back in Esperanza days. Among his other selves there was still tucked away the actor, who rather enjoyed an airing.

Longman wanted to bring out a revised second edition of *Songs of Childhood*, and for the past year or so de la Mare had turned over this idea, and had asked Thomas for suggestions over what to alter.

Thomas remained reluctant; indeed to revise poems so spontaneous and tender was a dubious undertaking for middle age. De la Mare held the thread of his childhood throughout life in a much more continuous way than most men do, yet his tone of voice was bound to have changed in fourteen years, and the artless, willow-wren charm of the *Songs* is not the same as the concentrated individuality of *Peacock Pie*. Later he was partly to repent the bold work of February 1916 when, besides revisions and rewritings,* whole poems for the *Songs* were omitted and new ones added. When he came to revise the book yet again for inclusion in *Collected Poems 1902–1919* his third thoughts on the matter were much closer to his first ones. Revision was for him an irresistible lifelong itch, and a great deal he published late in life had undergone repeated revisions, often years apart, when in its buzzard-like circlings his imagination came round again to the same vantage-point.

Florence's babyhood had done much to inspire the *Songs* in the first place. Now, to help de la Mare re-enter their world, he had another tiny girl on his knee at Netherhampton – Celia's firstborn, Jill. 'It seems very odd to be dandling a baby again,' Jack wrote to Ella, '– a glimpse, I shouldn't wonder, into the psychology of the Monthly Nurse. *My* first, *my* second and so on ad infinitum.'² Jill Furse had only a short life into which to cram poetry, beauty, and the art of the stage, and she began it with vivid haste, responding very early to de la Mare rhymes.

This edition had a new envoy, beginning:

> Child, do you love the flower
> Shining with colour and dew
> Lighting its transient hour?
> So I love you

Ella asked 'Was it written at Jill's request?' In a sense, it probably was; though all his poems were more truly addressed to 'Child' than to any Jack or Jill.†

---

* 'The Gnomies', for instance, reappeared very much altered, to Forrest Reid's regret, as 'Sleepyhead'. Reid later came to reprove the revisions very sharply for failure of sympathy with 'Walter Ramal's' innocence. On the other hand, one of the new additions, 'The Funeral', became a favourite of Reid's for just that quality, and for speaking from within the child's own attitude as perfectly as any of the early poems.

† He did write one rhyme expressly for Jill, that beginning 'Oh, yes, my dear you have a mother/And she, when young, was loved by another', perhaps with that 'ad infinitum' of his letter to Elfie in mind.

*

Henry James died at the end of February 1916, and de la Mare wrote a
memorial article for him for *The Living Age*. He still felt him to be a
very great man, but when James's letters were published in 1920 he
expressed to Eleanor Cecil very much the same shift of feeling he had
described over Poe:

> A few years ago I was one of the H.J. fanatics; and the worst of being a
> fanatic is that a sudden coolness may spring up. The letters are
> wonderful – though not exactly wonder-ful; but there is something in the
> younger H.J. which is not very endearing and actively present, and
> something in the elder that in spite of his enormous hospitality keeps me
> (I couldn't write the m small enough in these circumstances!) ill at ease. I
> doubt if there ever was before such an all-imaging consciousness and yet
> one with quite so active a blind spot in its inward eye. He has enormously
> increased the range, but has he really adjusted the focus ... To criticise
> him makes one feel uncomfortably humble and also invariably sets one
> imitating his style. But dare to be even more of a Philistine than ever I
> must; perhaps because the hush is oppressive: and yet one goes on
> gaping at his artistry.[2a]

Of the three writers who most affected him, Poe, James and Hardy, the
last was the only one he continued to hero-worship to the end.

He seems to have met James only twice, first at some lecture. James
had been much pleased by an unsigned review by de la Mare of one or
other of his early memoirs. De la Mare described a 'rather aghast'
encounter:

> I remember I wished he was still unshaven! but more acutely, his eyes.
> There was very little colour in them and as the orbs came round to assize
> one – this 'one' was instantaneously reminded of, say, a small fishing
> smack, any more or less nondescript vessel on the wide wide ocean ... He
> was urbane and perhaps even kind and I was rather amused at realizing
> how frequent an incident I was for him. He was portly and a trifle
> hieratic.[3]

Amplifying the same image in a letter of the 1930s, he said he felt
the grey eyes were not exactly pigeon-holing this new specimen, just
taking in that tiny vessel on the ocean. 'I wish I could have seen what
was in the mirror behind the eyes – nothing flattering I am afraid.'

The second meeting was a chance one. As de la Mare and Naomi
were walking one dark wintry day along the Embankment that portly
presence loomed suddenly out of the twilight mist. De la Mare felt
amused: 'with outrageous philistinism I clattered into a profound
reverie. I saw it in his eyes ...'[4] Naomi recollected listening for a pious

ten minutes to the conversation of 'two variously labyrinthine minds'. Not much real contact was achieved.

*

February 1916 was the month of Verdun, and lingering hopes of a quick end to the war faded out. The friendly letters de la Mare wrote to Naomi – as long, but much less frequent than of old – were full of descriptions of Netherhampton, where he was spending his usual winter break, of interest in her own concerns, and of all he planned himself. He was to sit for William Rothenstein, 'for a series of Bubbles and Babbles of the Day he is doing for Harold Monro'. Rothenstein's work suggests well the mobility and concentration of de la Mare's features. He caught a closer likeness in the several portrait-drawings he made during de la Mare's middle years than any other artist, and the two men and their families made friends.

Georgian Poetry II was making its way, and the months ahead were packed with settled tasks, plenty of journalism and engagements. Perhaps there were few such assignments he really relished, but it was the busy, secure routine of an established writer. To Naomi he showed some melancholy and harped on ageing, but he did rally against this the conviction that one 'grows younger in the sense of delighting in the real, simple and natural and therefore in being alone, in being inarticulate (and *not* a writing creature) and in looking about at things and life'.[5] He drugged himself with work against the nag of war. He felt low – and he counted his blessings.

It seems he made up his mind finally this spring to accept the essential loneliness his temperament spelled. That late and desperately-sustained attempt to unite his inward being with another's had ended for him in the least painful way it could: with disenchantment, but not with heartbreak or a rupture. Self-restraint had its reward now; the muse had evaporated, but a valued and useful friend remained in Naomi. It even became possible for him to refer smilingly and affectionately to their romantic past, as two old friends might sometimes turn over a photograph album together. For Naomi this cannot have been easy, but she saw it was the best way, and silently concurred. For some while after de la Mare's time in hospital such of her letters as survive show that she tried to ignore the change in him and bring him back to the old footing. But she was too intelligent to deceive herself long, and as she had before decided that half a loaf was much better than no bread, so she did again now. She knew herself valued by him, and rested in her unchallenged supremacy among his women friends. She was still the trusted critic and confidante of all his work in progress. There was relief also in the fact that he became a far less demanding companion, a thoughtful and considerate friend who watched over her.

Edward Thomas sensed the flatness in him, though he was not privy to the personal reason. He decided that the routine that success had shaped round de la Mare must be to blame. He wrote to Gordon Bottomley: 'De la Mare continues to wear himself out at reviewing and making more money than he really needs, except that he is committed like everyone else to some accidental standard of living.'[5a]

In the spiritual hiatus where de la Mare now found himself, busy but dulled in heart, and doubtful over a new collection of poems, without any particular new creative work in mind, this was a lucky moment for an adventure now proposed. It came his way as a result of Brooke's legacy. Brooke had been awarded posthumously the Howland prize, in the gift of Yale University, for *Poems 1914*. (The prize was awarded for the best work of idealistic tendency published in the previous year.) A lecture by the winner was a condition of the prize, and someone must take Brooke's place. Neither Abercrombie nor Gibson could go to America to do it, so Marsh approached de la Mare. He demurred, but then gave in to persuasion. 'I'm a stupidly shy bird that prefers its own small cage,'[5b] he wrote; but he felt under too great an obligation to Brooke's memory to refuse.

Marsh plied him with travel advice, and insisted he prepare a special lecture, which should give him the opportunity to bring in a passage about Brooke – some such subject as 'Poets who have died young'. In the end 'Youth and Poetry' seemed to offer the right scope.

He was to sail in the autumn. Meanwhile he went away again in July to the Beresfords in Cornwall, this time to Porthcothan, a farm standing alone above St Merryn's, to which they had migrated. The house was old, cool, roomy, and if not actually haunted held a touch of expectation of a ghost. The D. H. Lawrences had been there from December to March, and Lawrence loved it – (de la Mare rather wished he did not). Lawrence said it was 'like being at the window and looking out of England to the beyond'. De la Mare loved to sit outside in a basket chair while he contemplated the oval of night-scented stocks lying in a sort of draggled swoon in the noonday, 'the voices of chicken and bee and lark' the only sounds. He would wake almost every night of this Cornish visit and get up and peer out of the window at the mysterious seaward dark, the world 'very quiet and rather heavily bowed under its clouds', the garden a shallow pool of scent from the stocks revived by the midnight.

Crayon drawing of de la Mare by William Rothenstein, *c.* 1929.

James de la Mare (father), taken when ill of cancer.

Abraham de la Mare, elder brother of James.

Lucy de la Mare (mother),
young and old.

De la Mare's birthplace, 83 Maryon Road, Charlton, taken just before demolition in the 1960s. Photograph: Sidney W. Newbery.

Patty (Martha) Walstow.

Walter de la Mare as a choirboy.

De la Mare's boyhood home, 61 Bovill Road, Forest Hill. Photograph: Peter Newbolt.

Poppy de la Mare.

Bert de la Mare in 'Esperanza' days.

The Ingpen household: Roger, Poppy, Lucy de la Mare (seated).

Elfie Ingpen in 'Esperanza' days.

De la Mare as aesthete of the Nineties.

De la Mare, early 1900s.

Dock House, Billiter Street. An Esso photograph.

De la Mare family, 195 Mackenzie Road, probably summer 1905 before Colin was born.

De la Mare, probably taken on the same occasion as above.

De la Mare playing with
Florence and Jinnie, 195
Mackenzie Road.

195 Mackenzie Road.
Photograph: Peter Newbolt.

Florence and Dick visiting 23 Earl's Terrace. Photograph: Celia Newbolt.

Dick and Colin in school days.

Jinnie dancing.

Mary Coleridge aged twenty-two in 1883.

Ella Coltman, young and old.

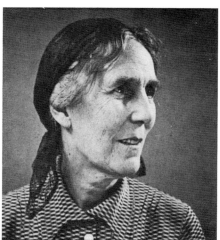

Netherhampton façade.

Henry and Margaret Newbolt in early Netherhampton days.

'The Ark', Netherhampton, where de la Mare wrote 'Fare Well'.

The kitchen garden, Netherhampton.

Naomi Royde-Smith, *c*. 1910.

Ralph Hodgson.

Florence aged about fourteen with her mother.

Colin and Florence outside 14 Thornsett Road, Anerley.

Dick and Florence, Colin and Jinnie on a cycling expedition.

A seaside day: Jinnie, Elfie, Florence, de la Mare and Colin.

De la Mare, *c.* 1924.

De la Mare in the 1920s.

De la Mare, probably late 1920s.

Playing pirates: Dick and Colin behind their father.

The de la Mares sightseeing with Colin to drive them, early 1930s.

De la Mare staying with J.D.
Beresford at The White House,
Claydon, summer 1920.

The de la Mares staying
with Percy Withers in the
1920s.

De la Mare with Rupert Thompson about the time of his marriage to Florence.

Julian Thompson at Penn in the 1940s.

Elfie in old age.

De la Mare in Taplow days. Captioned by him: 'Lager will out.'

'N' Saxton as de la Mare first knew her.

Convalescence at Penn: Florence, de la Mare, 'N', Elfie.

De la Mare with Forrest Reid at Penn.

De la Mare talking to Royalty
with Rupert Thompson behind.

South End House, Montpelier Row, Twickenham.

The Old Park, Penn.

Walter de la Mare at the end of his life. South End House, probably early 1956. Photograph: Allan Chappelow, MA, FRSA.

He came home the better for his holiday, and was silent on dark states of the mind in his letters – mainly because he felt ashamed to complain, in a time of universal suffering and with his own lot comparatively easy. Rupert Thompson, a young admirer of his writings who was by now often at Anerley, was in George Trevelyan's First British Ambulance Unit, and de la Mare now hoped to join it also, on the Italian front, but was turned down in July because he could not drive. There was profound relief at Netherhampton, for Newbolt had been indignant at the scheme – he felt de la Mare would either be kept behind the lines in safety, which would worry him and be no 'experience' to him as a writer, 'or he would be in the thick of it and go clean off his head with the horrors'. Nor was the work paid – how could his family live? As an alternative, a friend hoped to get him part-time Red Cross work in England, and in fact a temporary office job for three days a week, sending what crumbs of news could be gleaned to relatives of the missing, materialised for a while before he left for America.

*

October 1916 brought a hubbub of farewells and arrangements. Before he set off, de la Mare was given Marsh's manuscript of his memoir of Brooke to read. Mrs Brooke had by now vetoed its publication indefinitely, after months of battle, parley and mutual exasperation. It presented a view of Rupert which she thought false and distasteful. She certainly treated Marsh very harshly, and had she had her own way she would probably have turned the memoir into an unreadable garland of miscellaneous tributes. Yet it is impossible not to feel some sympathy for her, for there were real faults in what Marsh had written, and he did not know Rupert's private life fully enough to draw a comprehensive portrait of the flesh-and-blood young man who was so rapidly disappearing behind a marble national monument. De la Mare saw the two sides to the quarrel, and felt he might be able to take up some position of mediator. He wrote understandingly to Marsh, showing sympathy all round, but could make little difference. Interventions by third parties seldom do, in such painful clashes of the bereaved.

Thomas, who during the previous summer had quietly resolved his doubts and enlisted in the Artist's Rifles, had now transferred into the Artillery, whose widows got a bigger pension. His friends reacted uneasily – the higher pension was matched to the much greater risk of fatalities. If de la Mare, as he planned when he sailed, had returned to

England by Christmas 1916, Thomas would still have been there. But when he did come back it was February, and Thomas was already in France.

One of their final meetings must have been a tea together in August, with John Freeman and Roger Ingpen, when Roger discussed with Thomas his hope of bringing out, at Selwyn & Blount where he now worked, a volume of poems by 'Eastaway'. This hope was to materialise in 1917: a book of sixty-four poems, but too late for Thomas to see it.

Thomas wrote his farewell letter from the Trowbridge barracks on 29 October:

> My dear de la Mare,
>   I wish you luck & some surprises – for I don't suppose you expect anything very pleasant – & I hope you won't have to dive for them. I should like to be coming too. As I can't, give my love to Frost if you find you can see him. He is at Franconia, New Hampshire, but would come a long way to see you. Before you return I ought to be somewhere out of England. You never know. I think I would sooner go East than just to Flanders. I ought to have a commission next month, having passed my exams so far. I am only 4 or 5 from the bottom in a squad of 42, so I feel no great assurance yet. The great thing is not to hit your friends, & you are perhaps as well out of the danger zone. I wonder where Hodgson is?* I suppose either in Anti-Aircraft or Coast Defence. I hope I shall be preserved from Coast Defence. I want a far greater change than I have had so far. Goodbye. Give my love to your wife & all
>   Yours ever
>   (Cadet) Edward Thomas

That 'far greater change' was beginning to assume the hint of premonition Brooke had displayed. Thomas wrote in the next few days after his letter to de la Mare the valedictory poem 'Lights Out', the one which penetrates the wish for this deeply:

> There is not any book
> Or face of dearest look
> That I would not turn from now
> To go into the unknown
> I must enter, and leave, alone,
> I know not how.

It is a poem on Sleep that is a poem on Death, making his own, with grave, eager acceptance, the universal sense of surrender and farewell. In a lighter moment he made up a rhyme, to the tune of his favourite song 'Rio Grande', alluding to that bonfire (on his last leave) of the private letters in which de la Mare's probably perished:

---

* Hodgson joined up in the Navy, but later transferred to the Army.

I've burnt my letters and darned my socks
And I'm bound away for ever.

De la Mare sailed from Liverpool on 4 November 1916, on the SS *St Paul*. He had chosen an American ship for the Atlantic crossing, but by now this seemed only a dubious safeguard, and he took such a dislike to the boat during the next week or so that he flatly refused to make his return journey in her. They ran into rough weather almost at once, and she began to pitch and roll excessively. It was a vile passage, and the first time he had ever left England; he was very homesick, and looked with longing eyes on another American vessel, which they crossed the first evening, blazing like a Chinese junk on the dark sea, and on her way into Liverpool. The *St Paul*, too, travelled in the full glare of her own lights, specially trained on the stars and stripes, to advertise her neutrality.

De la Mare's lifelong dislike of strange surroundings was soon oppressing him. Even in a new place that he *liked*, such as the Cumnor cottage, he would write: 'I shall be glad to be back ... There's a kind of solitude only possible in the familiar. Once I were an animal in a burrow. A kind of ferment of the unusual keeps moving in one's mind.'[6] Now, walking along the decks, he had to fight down a claustrophobic horror of being tied to the ship, '*not able to get out*'. The best he could do to cheer himself up was an old childhood device: 'It may be a dream. But I'm going to sleep now so shall wake into reality.'

After two nights they ran into a gale wild enough to send everything sliding round the cabin; water came in through the porthole, and once he thought the ship might turn turtle. (His alarm was not unfounded – he heard later that the *St Paul* did capsize, in a calm sea, in New York harbour.) The third-class quarters shipped a sea and washed out the passengers, 'some of them half-drowned', he said. There is quite a reminiscence in these descriptions of Grandfather Browning writing to his little daughter Lucy and wallowing in the more horrific details of that storm off Brighton. De la Mare found it almost impossible to sleep, as he could only keep from sliding about by lying on his back and wedging knees and elbows against the sides of the berth. But the chief feature of the voyage was unbearable tedium. He declared he would as soon live in the Bon Marché at Brixton. The ship seemed like a genteel suburb, where the inhabitants *partially* dressed for dinner and dined too well, to horrible music and a horrible flare of lights (electricity itself was still an unpleasant novelty to him), the whole scene softly or wildly asway with the ship. Hunched in the storm-proof waistcoat Laura Coltman had given him, he clung to one very involved notion for comfort: 'Oh well I'm on my way back. You *must* go out of England to know how dear it is.'[7] One must admit he made a good deal of fuss.

Towards the American coast, the weather relented and the air grew clear as glass. When the skyscrapers finally took the horizon on a grey, cold Sunday morning, the Statue of Liberty looked as he had pictured that frigid lady – except that she was green, and just large enough to be hopelessly small for sea and sky. His arrival had none of the advance publicity often arranged for English *literati*, but when he was nearly through the customs and feeling uncommonly desolate ('I just crumbled down into my boots') a round-faced steward, beaming, pressed a card into his hand. It said he must look out for a lean six-foot-two figure, who had such another card stuck in his hat-band, and as soon as they had met, de la Mare was writing home: 'Russell Loines is IT', and 'a brick of the first water'. Only a few days later he was already pressing the Newbolts for Loines to stay at Netherhampton on his next English trip – sure sign of his feelings. Even Housman (not the easiest to please of the many English writers that Loines hospitably welcomed to the States) declared that Loines seemed to find friendship the only natural relation with anyone new. He was a very successful marine insurance lawyer, and a passionate amateur of poetry. Extremely sensitive, he somehow shed assurance and security all around him, and, best of all, he shared de la Mare's own insatiable curiosity. On arrival at any strange railroad station with five minutes to spare before the next train, Loines would suggest: 'Let's go and have a look at the town!' He took de la Mare under his wing as if he had unlimited leisure, though his professional life was exhausting and the habit of overwork led, in fact, to an early death.

He whirled de la Mare off, as soon as landed, to see the sights of New York. These proved an odd choice: a chrysanthemum show, an exhibition of fossils and dinosaurs at the Metropolitan Museum, and another of 'Birds in their Natural – fairly natural Harnts!' The New York crowds made a first impression that was to the Englishman's eyes curiously old-fashioned; the young women with white-stockinged legs, and the prosperous-looking gentlemen resuming their high silk hats as they came out of church, seemed, to his eyes, mid-Victorians.

The Loines home was on Staten Island, at Dongan Hills, and looked out on the island's wooded slopes; to de la Mare's relief it was a charming *English* house, with a 'charming quite as nice as English' mistress and two girls of nine and five, the sight of whom almost reduced him to tears. There was a bob-tailed Old English sheepdog – and tea! De la Mare wrote to Naomi: 'R.L. is first and last a dear of inexhaustible energy, interest, resource, enterprise, and sovereign kindness. So I ought to be vurry, vurry happy, which in snatches I am.'[8] But homesickness predominated in most letters. He was uneasy to find so little English news in American papers, and disconcerted that his lecture was fixed not for 21 November, as he had believed, but for 14 November, only three days off. He set to work hard to finish it; every now and then he would burst out of his room with anxious problems, but Loines could always provide whatever was wanted, from court breeches to criticism, returning to all requests the same peaceful 'Sure-ly.' Late into the night he and de la Mare talked and talked over the great log fire, raiding the cellar for Cox's Orange Pippins, which Loines had imported for his orchard.

When the day came, the audience was friendly and quite a small one, and the lecture well received, though the hall was so hot de la Mare said that at every full-stop he could feel, as it were, the marrow coursing down his spine. He was amazed by the American appetite for lecture-going; they seemed to enjoy them like Punch and Judy shows, and, following this first public appearance, he found that introductions and recommendations were soon creating a lecture-tour for him. After only a short while he reported that he had given eight lectures and readings in seventeen days. It was probably an exaggeration to say (as he did in old age) that he picked out his route with a pin, for the sound of the names of the towns, but he probably did do more travelling than a professionally-planned tour would have involved, returning betweenwhiles to the Loines home as base. He complained mildly of fatigue, and of feeling a little 'chastened and desperate', but he kept fit, and noticed with some surprise that he managed without ill effects a pace which would have brought him to collapse in England.

The New York winter climate exhilarated him, and so did the warmth and friendless he found everywhere. He was remarkably resilient to the usual pressures – to being photographed, glutted on private and public picture-collections, whisked up the Woolworth Tower, asked over and over again what was the meaning of 'The Listeners', and subjected to literary ladies in bevies. 'There are numbers of women over here,' he remarked sombrely to Elfie, '*numbers*.' In looks and charm of manner, as well as in the romantic character of his poetry, he appealed especially to the female American, and a large number of his invitations to lecture came from women's colleges and girls' schools. Spending a night at Wellesley, he noted that he and the night-watchman were the only males in a community of fifteen hundred; and to one quiet and luxurious girls' school, Westover, he returned twice, he found its atmosphere and its headmistress, Mary Hillard, so congenial. He was interviewed for the cultured *Boston*

Evening Transcript, and the journalist found the tables turned on him – de la Mare plied him with so many of his own absorbing questions about America and showed such beguiling and genuine enthusiasm for American writers (particularly Poe, Hawthorne and Henry James) that at the end the man had few notes to take away. Interviewed or interviewing, and in spite of his reticence about his personal affairs (which all Americans remarked on) he made a very warm impression. Everyone noticed the absence of English hauteur and condescension.

His own first impressions of the States gradually altered. At first he was mostly surprised at the likeness between the two nations – his Oil years had led him to expect a very alien outlook. The cultivated New Englanders he met seemed not only to talk much like Englishmen but to think like them. He met, in this milieu, no pro-Germans – though once, on being told he had the editor of *The Fatherland* in his audience, he read defiantly *at* him his own inoffensive praise of his motherland, 'The Englishman' from *Songs of Childhood*. But as time passed, subtler differences of outlook in his hosts made themselves apparent, until by the end it was the contrasts that stuck out most. One was that Americans 'seldom seem to *stop* to think, which, paradoxically, makes them go rather slow. They love to talk about, rather than into, a subject.'[9] For such a traditionalist, the feverishly contemporary – even extempore – character of the American scene was naturally conspicuous too. Among literary people he found 'the moment indescribably important', and wrote to Naomi: 'All's finished and has been finished for centuries, practically, in England. Here one is reminded again and again of a half-completed house-removal with packing cases and bundles and bits of furniture in unpicturesque disorder in the corridors and on the lawn. What will it all be in the end?'[10]

While he was at Boston in December he made friends with the eminent surgeon Harvey Cushing and his wife, and was allowed to watch a brain operation. He does not seem to have suffered from queasiness, and repeated the experience on another occasion at the London Hospital, where he was also allowed into the post-mortem room. He remembered the beauty of a dead child he saw there, and was struck by a student he saw doing a post-mortem on a woman; while he went on cutting into the heart he talked meanwhile to another student about the party they had been to the night before. There was a touch of old-fashioned sentiment in this regard for the heart as sacred, yet his fascination with medical mysteries also had an Arrott strain of genuine scientific curiosity, mixed with an unresting desire to come as close as possible to the frontiers between the physical envelope and the spirit's behaviour.

He saw a good deal of New York, mostly, he said, the 'best, highest, richest, hardest, noisiest parts'. His trips into the city were mainly to visit the Howlands, who gave him a close lifelong friendship, one of the best things the whole adventure brought him. Charles Howland had instituted, in memory of his father, the prize awarded to Brooke's poetry. He was four years older than de la Mare, a close friend of Loines, and, like him, a lawyer. He worked later on for the League of Nations, and finally became a Governor of Yale. Like Loines, he combined in unusual degree the scholar and man of affairs – a blend which gave both men that unaffected and original attitude to literature which de la Mare loved best. He valued Howland's fine critical judgement, and his frank, penetrating, disarming letters to de la Mare are a beautiful example of plain speaking from a friend.

Among other entertainments, the Howlands took him to a football match and a Shaw play. The Shaw he scorned – 'It's witty enough, but the squibs seemed a little damp and the whole thing is as badly and shallowly put together as the cheapest play he used to deride.' His pet hatred of Shaw went back at least to 1908, when he was trying to win Ella over to the *Autobiography of a Super-tramp*, but deplored the preface to it 'by that unspeakable man Shaw'; and it lasted with no less heat all his life. Not long before he died, he was talking with such vehemence on the subject that his exasperation lost him his balance, and the tirade came to an end in laughter, spread-eagled against the chest of drawers behind him. In the 1930s he grudgingly conceded once that 'G.B.S. is unquestionably a Grand Old Man, but he has done more harm in some ways than three of him put together. How many innocents do you suppose he has deceived into thinking themselves clever? It's bad enough to be it – but to think it!'[11] He hated arrogance of every kind, but worst of all he hated intellectual arrogance and this, combined, he felt, in Shaw with sheer conceit, made him boil over.

A visit to the opera to see *Lohengrin* met with no greater approval than the Shaw play: 'I'm old & blasé & the singing & acting bored me almost as much as the crowd. A remarkable lady, Spanish, Mrs Lydig, who is a Princess in New York & the patroness of a Spanish painter, just for the moment the talk of the art cliques (America is all "moments") was one of the party. She is remarkable in other respects than the fancy she has for completely whitening her face – apparently with chalk – pricking out her lips with vivid carmine, intensifying the slender bows of her eyebrows & greasing her eyelids.'[12] A certain wondering late-Victorian disapproval looks out of this; blasé was not really the apt word, for the truth was that artifice and sophistication in a woman always rather shocked him, as did any deliberate attempt to entice. Once, in England, he went to meet Florence for lunch in a big department store, and while waiting for her to join him he noticed a young lady sauntering between the tables and making as much of her sex-appeal as was humanly possible. 'She passed close by my table, and gave me – well, an eye so glad that I turned away. It was my only refuge, you see. After a bit, to my surprise, she came strolling back, and did exactly the same thing again! I thought: this *is* a fast little cat! Of course I had no idea she was only trying to sell the clothes she had on.'[13] Even then, in his manner of telling this tale, there lingered some reproof for the model's glances.

As engagements in America multiplied, he decided it would be a waste of dollars to return before Christmas. His sales there were rising, and by Boxing Day the lecture-tour agent Pond had approached him for engagements – sure sign of success. *Harper's* and the *New York Bookman* had asked for poems, the *Yale Review* for March was to publish 'Fare Well' and 'Nightfall', and John Cowper Powys, at an enormous luncheon, introduced him as 'the poet of the last two months'. He could not command the crowds or the pay of another of Pond's clients, Rabindranath Tagore, then on a tour of his own; nor was he the draw that Wilfrid Gibson would be when he arrived soon after. (Strangely enough, Gibson was by far the best-known of Marsh's Georgians in America at this period.) But de la Mare was certainly by now no longer the unheralded stranger who had landed in November.

Letters from home came at reassuring intervals, and de la Mare did not realise till afterwards how much agitation was caused there by the far more erratic mails in the other direction; sometimes Elfie went two or three weeks without a word. The Newbolts had wanted to get her to Netherhampton in December, but she had to refuse on account of a 'nervous heart' – a far from purely physical or passing condition. She who would worry wildly if Jack were half an hour late back from a day's work in town – and would then beg the children, directly his carefree figure came in sight, not to betray her – can scarcely have known a tranquil day this winter.

With the New Year arrived Gibson, 'under Pond's appalling wing. On the very docks it flapped and disclosed 5 (five) (v) reporters. I met G for a moment today. He whispered just 3 words into my ear. "Take me home!" ' Their paths crossed several times, and de la Mare described Gibson giving a poetry-reading in New York, standing on one leg and surrounded by the 'scenic horrors' of a stage rural cottage complete with 'geraniums on the chimney piece and a portrait of Granfer on the wall ... They're an odd folk.'[14]

On what seems to have been a separate occasion, a reading was organised for both poets in tandem, with an exchange of acidulated pleasantries between their introducer and Amy Lowell, 'as firm on her fourlegged chair as a Pyramid in the Sands of Egypt'. One of the most regular questions put to de la Mare in America was: 'What do you think of Amy Lowell?' Whatever he found to reply, in letters home he called her a phenomenon impossible to imagine arising in England – a formidable Amazon of letters who smoked a cigar.

On the last day of January 1917, just to complete Elfie's discomfiture, Germany announced unrestricted submarine warfare, and two days later America broke off diplomatic relations. De la Mare was determined to avoid the *St Paul* for his journey home, and would have preferred a Cunarder, but Elfie in a fever of anxieties (three cables from her arrived in rapid succession) clamoured for a Dutch or an American vessel. In the end de la Mare booked his passage on the SS *Lapland*, White Star Line.

But of all English news, the most important to him was that of Edward Thomas's departure. Expecting to be off before Christmas, Thomas had called in November to say goodbye to the de la Mares and found everybody out except Colin. He sat in his puttees by the window telling the boy about gunnery until he could wait no longer. But Elfie returned just in time to track him down at the Freemans. 'Very bright and awfully handsome,' she told de la Mare. 'He is expecting to go any day.' However, it was the end of January before embarkation orders came, and Thomas had time to walk over from camp one day to see for himself de la Mare's Netherhampton. He wrote to Elfie on 22 January: 'I went over to see Lady Newbolt and Mrs Furse on Sunday. They were very kind but I own I enjoyed most feeling quite near to Jack for a time. It seems impossible for me to see him. I may go any day after Wednesday.'

He had tramped the long miles contentedly that twenty-first of January, over Stockton Down and under Grovely Wood in freezing drizzle – white grass and icy roads – receptive to every low-keyed beauty of the morning; passing two families of vagrants roasting the corpse of some creature by a slow wood fire; remarking the milestones 'lichened as with battered gold and silver nails'. It was his very last long walk in England, and is described in the pocket diary which would turn, a few pages later, to laconic accounts of primrosing in shelled copses in France. He kept it on him, and it came back to England with its pages strangely crazed and creased from the blast of the shell that killed him.

When he fell, de la Mare would write that a mirror of England had been shattered and it is in Thomas's notes on such a walk as this – dry, but a poet's – that one realises what he meant. No soldier died more precisely 'for country'. Asked once why he would fight, Thomas picked up a handful of soil and said simply, as he crumbled it through his fingers: 'Literally for this.'

*

In October, Thomas had encouraged de la Mare to seek out Robert Frost. A meeting between these two close friends of his had somehow never come off all the while that Frost was in England. Frost's letter to Louis Untermeyer written from New Hampshire on 14 November 1916 explains why:

> I have been in no mood to meet De la Mare. He is one of the open questions with me like what to do with Mexico. He has only treated Edward Thomas, to whom he owes more than half, measurably well. Personally I am indifferent about him and have been these three years. Don't think I asked Harcourt to do The Listeners on De la Mare's account. The sum of it is that without much to go on I suspect that the man who rhymes with Delaware is a bit of a British snob and will bear fighting shy of. I shall *probably* have to invite him here, because my mother was so sure she had taught me manners and I shouldn't want her to be mistaken. But I'm almost sure he scorns America and has only come over for what he can get out of us and against us. And I have his poems to save. If he is half as bad as I am afraid he is, he might spoil the poems. You know how many poems you have lost by meeting the man who wrote them. My not meeting De la Mare in England was rather accidentally on purpose.[15]

Frost's Anglophobic prejudice at that period of his life was not confined to de la Mare in particular; he would suspect any English visitor of condescension, and resented the hospitable welcome accorded Gibson later that spring on exactly the same grounds – that he had failed to help Thomas at need.

Frost let a month of de la Mare's tour go by after that letter to Untermeyer, and then either 'manners' prevailed or perhaps some of those reports had filtered through to him which emphasised de la Mare's freedom from British snobbery. At any rate he wrote off with a good grace on 14 December:

> My dear Mr de la Mare,
>   Edward Thomas wrote that you were to be in this large country, but he failed to say just when or in what part of it. Is it all parts – as we might be led to believe from reports come in – and all parts at once? And am I not going to be able to put my fingers on you before you are gone back to the place from whence you came?

He suggested he should set out to look for de la Mare in New York in about ten days' time. 'I go to you first: and then if you can come to us, so much the better. I shall urge you to come.'

In this letter Frost did not mention the fact (not publicly announced till four days later) that he had just accepted a sudden offer from Amherst College, Massachusetts, to teach there the next semester, beginning in January. So whether they met in New York or not, it was in Robert and Elinor Frost's new home in Dana Street, Amherst, that de la Mare did finally spend a night, during his last circuit of lectures and readings. This was an evening when he had wearily delivered 'Magic in Poetry' yet again, this time to the girls of Smith College. He makes no comments on the Frosts in his letters to Naomi and Newbolt, just mentions his stay. And in a letter in March, Edward Thomas complained: 'I wish you had said more about Frost.' Perhaps the visit was not a great success. Frost, when suspicious, could be bearish, and he may well have displayed his animus against de la Mare when they discussed – as no doubt they did – Thomas's fortunes.

Safer ground in common was a discussion 'about your metrics', which Frost began in reference to 'The Listeners'. The strong, immediate impression this poem had made upon him – coming across it by chance, so he remembered, in a periodical lying open on someone's table – was still vivid to him when he was talking of de la Mare at London Airport in 1961. He was then in his eighties, on the point of going home for the last time, and died shortly after. He said on this occasion that it was his way 'occasionally to recognise the really good thing with immediate impact'. Elsewhere he wrote: 'The proof of a poem is not that we have never forgotten it, but that we know at sight that we could never forget it.'[16]

In writing prose Frost dispensed with much ordinary punctuation, relying on arrangement of words in the rhythm of speech to convey the pauses and emphases necessary for a lucid reading. His lifelong study was to match in verse, too, the natural cadence of the speaking voice, and those tones of emotion by which the gist of a dialogue may be gathered even through a wall which makes the words themselves inaudible. With such preoccupations, he would naturally find a special technical fascination in 'The Listeners'. It is so straighforward a poem to read aloud, yet its scansion defeats the prosodists, for its actual metric pattern will not fit their formulas. Although its effect is, of course, quite unlike Frost's colloquial flatness, yet of all de la Mare's poems (except the conversational ones of old age, much less remarkable) 'The Listeners' most closely bears out Frost's theory that a poet should write with his ear to the voice, so as to construct 'a

sentence of sound'. He held that a sentence does not interest just by
conveying a meaning of words: it must do more, conveying a meaning
by sound. This extra significance is what the cadences of 'The
Listeners' carry strikingly – the urgency of the Traveller's challenge,
lapsing profoundly into a silence charged with presences yet
obstinately taciturn. It is the original and memorable form of the poem
to the ear which moves us with man's predicament in an enigmatic
universe, far more than does the rather stock-property symbolism in
which it is dressed for the eye:

> And a bird flew up out of the turret
>   Above the Traveller's head:
> And he smote upon the door again a second time;
>   'Is there anybody there?' he said.

Frost said that metre had to do with beat, and that 'sound-posture' (his
term for that meaningful rhythmic pattern which so absorbed him)
had a definite relation as an alternative tone between the beats, the
two being one in creation but separate in analysis.

Although this was just the exercise of analysis de la Mare loved, and
although Frost evidently showed him how much he admired the poem,
it seems he did not succeed in drawing him out on this occasion.
Perhaps de la Mare was too modest, or not enough at ease, or had
really composed the poem too much by ear to be able to say how he had
conceived its form. At any rate the following year Frost declared: 'I
believe I don't know a single poet who knows any prosody, except
always Robert Bridges. I once asked De la Mare if he had noticed
anything queer about the verse in his own "The Listeners" and he
answered that he hadn't noticed anything at all about the verse in it
queer or unqueer.'[17]

The poem may well have been one of those whose rhythm de la Mare
had adapted by ear from some prose passage – where often, as he
pointed out – a metrical basis may lurk, all the more effective for being
unapparent: 'It is ... in fine prose rather than in fine verse that the poet
is likely to discover both novel and subtle rhythms which a little or
much delicate contriving will convert into the most promising and
seductive of metres.'[18]

It seems likely anyway, from his lifelong study of the Authorised
Version, that the effects peculiar to 'The Listeners' have a biblical
origin. Several very early poems of his Horn-Book period experiment
with long lines reminiscent of his favourite passage from *Ecclesiastes*,
the great lament of the golden bowl broken and the mourners that go
about the streets.

Whatever Frost might have thought, de la Mare was quite capable of analysing prosody, but it was the 'much delicate contriving' he mentions, and not prosodic theory, that was the basis of his original metres. And to arrive at these he relied, as much as Frost did, on those instinctive breaks, trembles, speeding or slowing, which the flow of emotion itself spontaneously dictates, and which best express it.

The only incident that seems to have stuck in de la Mare's mind from the Amherst visit, was that when Frost accompanied him to the station next morning 'it was raining in gushing fountains and waterbrooks ... and our "trolley car" ran into a poor old white cow that was scrambling up out of the wayside ditch. Poor thing, there it sat in the rain on the track patient and passive not for very long in this world as she'd broken a leg. Frost referred to Flanders and away we went again.'[19] Eleven years later they were still corresponding about it. Frost was still teasing de la Mare by letter because he could not forget 'that cow we killed'.

As time went on, though they were never very intimate, the two men warmed toward each other. When Frost was hoping to get to England in 1923, he was anxious to arrange a stay at an inn to be near the de la Mares in their summer holiday at Skrinkle for a day or two. He had to cancel that voyage, but when he did get over next, in 1928, de la Mare wrote warmly to invite him to his home and Frost spent a night there and had other meetings besides. He wrote affectionately again ten years later, in September 1938:

> You must know you have been one of my very few contemporary poets. I have tried many others and been found wanting or found them wanting. I remember I had been thinking how rarely the spirit of delight now came to me at thirty-five and beginning to think it would come no more when your first poem swam into my ken. The experience is among my cloudy trophies hung. So is our ride from Amherst in the rocking chariot that killed the cow, and our talk once about your metrics, and that hour with you reading epitaphs in a little church you took us to the last time we were in England. I wish we could see each other again. I may get up my courage to come over.[20]

By the time of his final half hour in England in 1961, summarising his friendship with de la Mare against the background roar of departing aircraft, Frost conceded that de la Mare had 'made public amends' to Edward Thomas after his death, yet stuck to his old opinion that he had done less at the time than he should to praise and encourage in Thomas's lifetime his prose-writings, which Frost himself much admired. On this account, Frost showed to the end a slight reservation in his warmth for de la Mare as a man. Not as a poet, though; here he had kept in old age his first estimate: 'He was one of those that I thought really *was* one', adding with a twinkle: 'I pretend that about some of them socially.'[21] De la Mare's prose, on the other hand, he thought much less of, and disapproved of what he felt to be 'an element of spiritualism' in the stories.

De la Mare for his part would speak in old age of Frost as 'a great friend'. He also had certain reservations, but on his side they were about the poet, not the man. He often spoke with admiration of Frost's work, which he had been one of the first reviewers to praise, when he wrote on *North of Boston* in 1914 for the *TLS*; but he could not to the end decide how high a place his art really took. In 1928 he said that Frost 'appeals to me much more than any other living American poet, and though such predictions are as vain as they are easy, I believe his work will live'.[22] He used three poems of Frost's in *Come Hither*, three in *Behold This Dreamer*, and two in *Love*, his favourite perhaps remaining 'Stopping by Woods on a Snowy Evening', which he chose twice over. To Russell Brain he later commended the Wordsworthian quality in Frost, and his 'oaten voice'. But to Leonard Clark in those same last years he confided his struggles to arrive at a just judgement, at the time when he had Frost's *Complete Poems* to review. He asked Clark's opinion: 'Did he really get the tops?' – and on that occasion anyway agreed he had 'just missed it'.[23]

*

De la Mare's final circuit of American lectures in January 1917 brought him a brush with another lady of letters (a cousin of Logan Pearsall Smith) almost as formidable as Amy Lowell. He seems to have come off, if not the victor, at least stoutly enough: 'I lectured at Bryn Mawr College on Thursday & stayed the night there. A Miss Thomas is the President & it seems I all but shook the foundation by remarking at dinner that intellect was not Woman's divinest prerogative.'[24]

He was no feminist, and on occasion could take a rather unexpectedly conventional masculine line on the supremacy of the male intellect. Though he accorded women the advantage in intuition, Miss Thomas was not at all placated: 'What, Mr de la Mare, do you mean by intuition?' As he developed his defence, the rest of the table, so he said (embroidering the story a little, no doubt) became hushed to listen to such audacity. They were mostly professors and their wives. He claimed that several of the professors crept into his room next morning to congratulate him. Time, justly, has not stayed on his side.

As the tour drew to its close, he began to tot up his gains. Financially

they were hardly spectacular; he reckoned he would return only thirty
to forty pounds to the good, though had he stayed in England in such
lean times he believed he would have been twenty or thirty pounds to
the bad. Gibson and he had compared notes and decided their
American pay was quite good – de la Mare seems to have received
around fifty dollars a lecture, and Gibson, promoted by Pond, rather
more – but this was offset by the very high cost of living. Since the
point of coming had been to discharge his debt of gratitude to Rupert
Brooke's memory, he felt the profit on his lectures and readings to be a
bonus, and was content enough. Yet he did remark mildly, on
presenting the expense account of £90 13s 0d (for which, as trustee,
Eddie Marsh was to reimburse him). '*Only* – now that it is all over, it
seems to me rather a heady arrangement that the recipient of a prize
for £300 should have to spend about £100 to fetch it. It *might* go to
Moscow next time.'[25]

   He was certainly the richer in friendships. Russell Loines, though he
hoped to follow him to England in a few weeks, wrote to Mrs Brooke
that he felt on parting as if he had lost a brother. The script of 'Magic in
Poetry' was in tatters – delivered so often that de la Mare was sick of
the sight of it, nearly always the one requested. He had hardly needed
to bring the lectures on 'Ghosts' or 'Truth to Life in Fiction'. Of the
kaleidoscopic experience itself, nothing probably struck very deep –
nothing, certainly, that altered or directly fructified his art. Nor, since
he left Oil, had he ever gone so long without touching a poem or a story.
Yet the prolonged 'detestable novelty' he had so dreaded had turned
out, in the end, to be something he could manage quite as competently
as any other Englishman abroad; indeed he had enjoyed the larger
part. Thankfully now he could turn home towards his small embattled
country –

> At which he fell a-musing,
>   And fixed his eye on me,
> As one alone 'twixt light and dark
>   A spirit thinks to see.
>
> 'England!' he whispers soft and harsh,
>   'England!' repeated he ...[26]

He sailed home (conscientiously shifting Brooke's gold medal from
pocket to pocket to make sure it never left his person) to find his family
had been on tenterhooks for days past. Postings about ships' arrivals
were very uncertain, and Elfie had been led to expect the *Lapland* a
week before. Newbolt was a little exasperated by the consequent
alarums ('Mrs D who's a feeble dithery creature about the war is of

course living on jumps and dumps');[27] yet if Russell Loines had had his way there would have been excuse enough, for he had tried to persuade de la Mare to stay on so that they might both book a passage on the following ship. She was the *Laconia*, and the Germans sank her. Luckily in the end Loines's affairs delayed him too long and de la Mare could not wait, so neither of them was on board. De la Mare reported to Marsh: 'There was just a chance that I might have been on the Laconia – and a Romantic.' A pity perhaps not to have had that glory, he mused from the safety of England. 'One must think of one's great grandchildren.'[28]

Within a few weeks, on 6 April 1917, America moved into the war. The day before, a full-scale bombardment began, before the attack at Arras. On 9 April, Easter Monday, Edward Thomas was killed at his forward observation post. The news reached Anerley during that week. Edward Garnett wrote to de la Mare to break it, saying: 'I fancy that you and I were his best friends';[29] but before the letter arrived Mrs Freeman had come round to the de la Mares, dressed dramatically in total black to bear the news.

For de la Mare it was the central loss of the war. Later he would come to exchange work in progress as closely again with another fellow-writer, when he and Forrest Reid drew together; but that was a friendship of older men, begun in middle age and on a different footing. No one else ever held over him the particular imaginative and moral sway that Thomas had held these past ten years, and was to keep in memory always. One notices that de la Mare, who wrote so very few personal poems apart from the love poems for Naomi, wrote two about Thomas after he died: a simple couple of stanzas of lament called 'To E.T.: 1917',[30] and a longer one, 'Sotto Voce', a vignette of some day that he and Thomas had spent together, probably at Steep or Harting, when they had overheard a low magical warbling – 'inmost pondering of birdlike self with self'. It had been the undersong of a nightingale at noonday, hidden in the hot, blazing gorse. The picture, when silence fell again, of de la Mare 'in ignorant wonderment' recalled from his day-dream of music on Prospero's Island, while Thomas the naturalist watched him, moving his great hand in a gesture of gentle amusement, beautifully renders their relationship.

De la Mare wrote of Thomas: 'Mere observation will detect the salient sharply enough; but only a passive, half-conscious reverie will at last win to and share in the life itself.'[31] It was 'the life itself' they had shared together, above all else – whether of a bird or a book; partly in talk, partly in a mutual solitude of that same reverie, at ease in one another's company. With de la Mare's grief was mixed a surmise shared by others who had watched Thomas's melancholy and frustration uncloud him so unexpectedly when he enlisted. Had he not discovered in death a culmination? – something at least partly desired? De la Mare at any rate felt that Death had lured him on:

> Your very quiet seems to say
> How longed-for a peace you have found.

And Thomas's own poem 'Rain' suggests it, where he speaks of the love of death:

> If love it be for what is perfect and
> Cannot, the tempest tells me, disappoint.

Whatever inadequacy de la Mare had felt on the score of expression when Thomas had first sent him his verses, all reservation now dissolved into grieving enthusiasm. Bereavement can, of course, put a false value on a friend's work, but quite as often it can act as a shock catalyst for indistinct, unformulated responses, producing revelation. The 'mirror of England', as de la Mare's foreword to Thomas's *Collected Poems* called him, he now held to be 'of so pure and true a crystal that a clearer and tenderer reflection of it can be found no other where than in these poems; neither in "Clare and Cobbett, Morland and Crome", nor among the living, to whom he was devoted – in Hardy, Hudson, Doughty.' There was no higher praise de la Mare could bestow than for him to put Thomas's work, in this respect, level with Hardy's.

In that foreword he voiced also the remorse which afflicts everyone in bereavement, but which he suffered more than most – his letters show it over and over at every loss, and the poems speak of it. But at no other friend's death did he feel self-condemnation to such a point of anguish. He declared that every friend of Thomas, reading this volume of poems, 'must be conscious – though none more desperately than I – of an inexpressible regret that so much more was his to give if richer opportunity had been taken and a more selfless receptivity had been that friend's to offer. Every remembrance of him brings back his company to me with a gladness never untinged by this remorse.'[32]

He threw himself into the efforts for Helen and the children already begun by Garnett and E.S.P. Haynes. Thomas had left little or nothing, and Helen was undone by the first onset of her grief – ill and shattered, her characteristic resilience for a while utterly forsaking her. Gosse wrote kindly enough, but discouragingly – had not a grant gone to Thomas too recently for another yet? Nor would he disguise that he held as low an opinion of his gifts as ever. In any case, with the fall of

Asquith, who had sympathised so much with 'the sorrows of scribbling men', Gosse had lost much of his influence. Undeterred, de la Mare, Garnett and Thomas's other friends went on actively and widely enlisting support, and by May, the month after Thomas's death, Newbolt could tell de la Mare that a two hundred pound grant had been approved, with the possibility of further help for the children.

*

From now on till the war ended, de la Mare once again sat at an office desk, with his own writing pushed into one corner of it, for just the odd half-hour of leisure. Submarine warfare had told hard on food supplies: bread cards had been brought in for a short while in February, and Lord Devonport had been given the newly-created office of Food Controller, with Beveridge under him, to devise a compulsory rationing scheme extending to meat, margarine and sugar. This last was put in the hands of Stephen Tallents from the Board of Trade. Alick McLaren, friend of the Coltmans, suggested de la Mare's name to Tallents when he began to need assistance, knowing that de la Mare was looking for war-work.

Among an odd assortment of amateurs, stiffened with only a sprinkling of civil servants, who occupied the incongruous Mayfair setting of Grosvenor House, he was in fact better qualified than most to tackle forms and files. Under Beveridge, and Tallents (who really ran the place), there was quite a collection of writers and wits: Edgar Jepson, the racy man-about-town of Square Club Days, E. V. Knox, future editor of *Punch*, Percy Greenbank, a writer of musical comedy lyrics, and for half a year Alfred Butt, a Drury Lane theatre magnate. There was a famous cricketer, Sir Percy Palmer, and even, briefly, Aldous Huxley, blinking like a noonday owl. Next door to de la Mare's department a group of publicity experts and poster artists busily diverted their skills of the entertainment world to slogans such as 'Liver and Lights are Good for You'. An elderly clubman, wanting to know if it would be patriotic to order sweetbreads for his luncheon, wandered in one day and told de la Mare's department that they were using his old nursery.

From this odd team and odd surroundings a surprising amount of hard, tedious and efficient work resulted in the first rationing England had ever known. The Grosvenor House men had to work out their own system, with very little precedent beyond the grubby, dog-eared ration cards discovered on German prisoners. The team had so little experience of catering that their first problem was that none of them had even the slightest idea how many lumps of sugar or cups of tea went to a pound of either. Beginning from such rudiments, they had to master the needs of every variety of catering establishment, and the intricate shuttle-system of supplies then practised between wholesalers and retailers. Also, while the rationing scheme was still in its voluntary stage, they must reply to a miscellaneous host of conscientious private inquiries.

Gradually the team worked out a programme, complete with timetable, for devising a multicoloured series of at least a dozen forms, with memoranda to explain their rules. Finally and worst of all the forms themselves had to be drawn up – and endlessly revised. De la Mare's minute writing riddled the margins as he constantly strove to reduce officialese to plain English. His writer's instinct rebelled even at such intractable terms as 'catering establishment' – there must be *some* livelier and more human synonym? He also brought to their drudgery his proof-corrector's sharp eye for slips, and the Oil man of eighteen years' experience had hot opinions over the correct way to keep files. Alick McLaren favoured adding correspondence to the bottom, and battle was joined between the bottomers and the toppers. De la Mare (a topper) was good at keeping the team to schedule with the printers, very neat and tidy, nimble with calculations. The mysterious habits of numbers had never lost a certain fascination to him for their own sakes; they appealed to his speculative ingenuity.

He kept an index of the endless mail, and tackled the boring job of answering it. They were plagued with zany enquiries – did they know that a certain Teutonic-looking gentleman had *two turkeys* delivered every week? A ponderous clergyman had a crisis of conscience over the school-children's tea to celebrate his wedding; what should he do? De la Mare wove a biblical blessing into his counsel to postpone, and perorated: 'Then, in the years to come, when your school-boys and girls are asked "What did *you* do in the Great War" they may truthfully and proudly reply "We did without our school tea when the Vicar was married." ' His superiors felt a little dubious, and the letter was shelved.

De la Mare made lifelong friends from this curious interlude, for, despite the dull routine, the atmosphere was refreshingly unlike the mercenary one of Oil. Out of hours all his colleagues shared kindred interests. McLaren, dry and shy, conscientious to a fault, was yet an ardent reader, a most affectionate and civilised companion. So was the lame young Quayle, a devotee of Beddoes and of dictionary-dipping. The pace slackened as the summer of 1917 drew on, with cuckoos calling from the Park nearby. Once the scheme was drafted there was a

hiatus before the hesitant government actually put it into practice, so
de la Mare took to helping and encouraging Stephen Tallents with his
verse and prose sketches, and sometimes took up his own poems again.
Passing his desk, Tallents would notice the dark head bent over a
scrap of paper, the fine nib tirelessly trying out alternative words, one
below the other. On a sheet stamped with the Ministry of Food crest, de
la Mare scribbled two complimentary stanzas to 'An Absent Duchess',
for he was by then working in what had been her mirror-hung
bathroom, and there were many childish jokes and limericks.

When sugar-rationing eventually came into force, the public and the
Ministry team were both agreeably surprised. It was efficient – queues
shortened, supplies were fairly shared. De la Mare felt a modest sense
of achievement to set against the year-and-a-half of writing lost – and,
like the Vicar's school-children, something to reply when asked 'What
did *you* do in the Great War?' Yet all the time he still cherished the
hope of some more active service, still debated whether to volunteer,
and was advised not to this summer by a captain, on the grounds that
the conscription age might so soon be raised to forty-five, and overtake
his wish.

*

His own career, though pushed into the margins of life, had not of
course stood still completely. For one thing, in the summer of 1917,
Marsh was getting together material for a third volume of *Georgian
Poetry*, urged on by Monro (by now in camp himself) who wished a
third to follow steadily in the series, 'to show as clearly as possible that
English poetry does not allow itself to be distracted by such a passing
event as a war'.[33]

Marsh did enlarge the rut into which his Georgian group was
settling, including, this time, some actual war poetry: some Sassoon
and some Rosenberg. But when Eliot's *Prufrock and Other Obervations*
came out this year it opened a range of bleaker, demanding responses
that were quite ignored in Georgian pages. Marsh continued to refuse
the poetry which reflected the fundamental change in human outlook
the war was bringing in its train. He would take scarcely any verse
that did not observe the old traditional rules of regularity. Although he
had earlier published D. H. Lawrence's 'The Snapdragon', when he
was offered a choice from Lawrence's *Look We Have Come Through* he
declined the lot. Nor would he take any of Edward Thomas's poems,
although de la Mare offered to stand down for him.

Marsh wanted de la Mare to arbitrate over a possible new candidate,

Charlotte Mew. So far there had been no Georgian ladies. A later volume did include Fredegond Shove, but never that far better poet Frances Cornford. Marsh told de la Mare that Monro was pressing him very hard to include Charlotte Mew's 'The Farmer's Bride'. Enclosing a copy, he said: 'I *simply* can't make up my mind about it ... You are so good-natured that if you don't think it quite worth putting in, you might dislike saying so and spoiling the poor lady's chances – against this I set your known loyalty to G.P!'.[34]

The epithet 'good-natured' evidently put de la Mare out; his reply is uncharacteristically forthright and cutting. 'Where should I be as a *Critick* if this charge of goodnature got about!' As to the poem, he allows that 'imaginatively there are one or two touches', but faults it for almost everything he can think of – rhyme, rhythm, technique, attitude, tone, expression and 'dramatic confusion', concluding: 'That's about all the damning I can do ... may the Lord have mercy on *my* Opera. Diplomatically, wouldn't it be a little dangerous to let just *one* female writer smile down from the grille: I feel pretty sure this poem could be paralleled during the last two years. It would be a dizzy pinnacle for Miss Mew ... What an awful thing if C[harlotte] M[ew] is an irradiate disguise of E[ddie] M[arsh]! If so I withdraw every word. Mere *sex* prejudice.'[35]

In his antagonism perhaps there *was* sex prejudice – unadmitted, not of the sort he referred to, not against Charlotte Mew for being a woman; but offended (subconsciously) by any woman writing any poem that is nakedly about sexual emotion.

Marsh replied at once to thank de la Mare for making up his mind for him, and, to Monro's disgust, 'The Farmer's Bride' was dropped forthwith. De la Mare's judgement here was bad and off-balance, and later it was to make him uneasy. The following July he dined with Monro at the Poetry Bookshop; his host – her firm champion from the start – had brought out Charlotte Mew's first collection in 1916 with the disputed poem as the title piece. He now gave his guest the volume, and de la Mare reported that 'a most horrid stab of remorse pierced me'. He maintained that he still did not feel this poem 'absolutely itself so to speak. But as one of many it is greatly enriched; and the last in the book is a lovely thing.'[36] This was, in that edition, 'Exspecto Resurrectionem', a tender little epitaph-like prayer for a child, which he might very well have written himself. In fact so close do the two run – in idea, expression, tune – that surely a four-line stanza of his own, included among verses he sent to Naomi, must have owed its origin to it?

Here lies, but seven years old, our little maid,
One of the darkness Oh, so sore afraid!
Light of the World – remember that small fear,
And when nor moon nor stars do shine, draw near![37]

This compliment of unconscious plagiarism is surely the sincerest form of amends he could have made to Charlotte Mew. He did make her further ones (besides later becoming a personal friend). He put 'The Changeling' into *Come Hither*, two more into *Behold This Dreamer*, and another two into his final anthology *Love*. One of them is that 'Exspecto' which had won him over, and which remained his favourite to the end.

*

During the lull in office work in early summer 1917, he revised his own new collection of verse for Constable. He was more doubtful and lacklustre about this one than any of its predecessors – 'far from satisfied with it, and don't much care to see it published'. He also mentioned 'wasting' the Whitsun break in trying to write short essay-stories.

Edward Thomas was much in his thoughts, and one of those essay-stories was probably 'The Vats'. He told Gerald Bullett in 1944 that it had its origin in a discussion with Thomas one day about Time, which had led to a promise exchanged that each should write a story on the subject. In de la Mare's story the narrator has a shadowy companion with whom, during a ramble, he chances on a cluster of great stone reservoirs. These, vast and mysterious, are what Time is stored in. Neither companion nor countryside are particularised, but the turf and flinty dust and downland shapes of the landscape they had shared at Dene Cottage and Steep are suggested, and Thomas would seem to be this friend with whom the narrator discusses 'The divine Abandoner' – the 'vacancy of His presence' fills the scene where they so strangely discover the Vats. The story ends:

We knew now and for ever that Time-pure *is*: that here – somewhere awaiting us and all forlorn mankind – lay hid the solace of our mortal longing: that doubtless the Seraph whose charge is the living waters will in the divine hour fetch down his iron key in his arms, and – well, Dives, rich man and crumb-waster that he was, pleaded out of the flames for but one drop of them. Neither my friend nor I was a Dives then, nor was ever likely to be. And now only I remain.

The reminiscence of Thomas extends to the conception too. Though much more fanciful and ornate than a Thomas piece, it is the kind of prose-poem he was often drawn to attempt. The potent symbol of the Vats themselves, however, came from something much further back; a link is plain with that water reservoir of de la Mare's childhood. 'The Vats' came out in the *Saturday Westminster* in June, and a poem, 'Nocturne', followed in July. After that all writing ceased, for office work was in spate again.

In January 1918 the de la Mares earned Wilfrid Gibson's gratitude by taking in his wife and baby daughter while they were in difficulties. Eddie Marsh had managed to organise Gibson's temporary removal from the Army on account of bad eyes, and it was this that had permitted him his American tour – as well as a short holiday in the Malvern hills which he and de la Mare shared in August 1917. But he was now back in khaki, billeted only a mile or so from Anerley, and he became a regular guest at Thornsett Road on his Saturday evenings off – welcome relief to him, for never did a private find his soldiering a harder skill to master. His was a gentle, innocent, endearing personality, always a little at a loss in practical matters. Bespectacled, fair, vague, limp of handshake, with a mouth that turned down at the corners, he always looked as if he were about to cry – so said the de la Mare children, who were protective. Dick would see him off after these 'khaki Saturdays' – quite often spent in heated argument about poetry. On the way to the bus, every time, there was the same water-hydrant to pass on the pavement; every time without fail 'Wibson' managed to bump into it.

His tastes and de la Mare's were not in total accord; Gibson, for instance, disliked Poe, and probably extended the same disapproval to what was Poe-esque in de la Mare's work. Nor did de la Mare for his part admire the colloquial, homespun realism for which Gibson (at first) received such applause. Gibson indeed nursed a certain touchiness on this point, referring to de la Mare's low opinion rather petulantly, both in letters to him and complaints to Marsh – 'He is quite out of sympathy with my work at any time.'[38] Yet they spent several holidays together, each welcoming the other to his own favourite haunts; and as time went by and troubles multiplied on Gibson's head (he seemed a magnet for accidents, persecution and tragedy) de la Mare's attitude towards his writing altered from that of resented critic to chief encourager, supporting his unlucky friend when his flow failed and reputation dwindled. On several occasions he even succeeded, by an evening's sympathy and stimulus, in getting Gibson's poetry to begin again, and by a kind review could send his low spirits soaring into fresh hope – for a while. He included Gibson poems in all his three major anthologies, picking out whatever had a gleam of mystery or strangeness – for he never came to like any better than at first, that dry-bread realism which had created, briefly, a vogue.

All in all, Gibson's was the saddest fate of any of the Georgians. Once acclaimed the promising leader of an exciting new movement, when that movement came into derision the critics found in him the epitome of its vices. Never of much vitality, his many personal troubles* sapped away what energy of mind he had, and he declined into an old age of low mist. After de la Mare's death, when asked (for this present book) about his memories of that long and affectionate friendship, he replied in two pathetic typed lines: 'I did know Walter de la Mare once but I cannot now remember anything about him.'

Work at the Ministry kept de la Mare from home till nine at night in January 1918, and when he did get back there were proofs to correct for the new book of poems, and a lecture to prepare for the Royal Society of Literature, on Emily Brontë. The subject was close to his heart. Her genius affected him as an artist more profoundly than did any of those other Romantics – Poe, Christina Rossetti and Coleridge – whose works most immediately resembled his. Emily Brontë's grandeur, rough manners, direct gaze, make the difference between them more immediately conspicuous than their affinity; but despite their totally different temperaments and range, they laid hold on the mysterious human soul by a kindred instinct. Both dealt in the pitiless dark dramas of the subconscious; both were ardently responsive to masculine and feminine, yet both left aside the implications of adult sexuality, their art operating always on planes where these do not – or need not – apply. Each had what one might call the 'wise child' view of human passions. De la Mare placed the same paramount value as she did on earliest experience, dreams, human communion with nature, death as an integral part of living, passionate family affections, the lures and the risks of 'the shadowy region'.

> Its unsustaining vastness waxes drear;
> And visions rising, legion after legion,
> Bring the unreal world too strangely near.[39]

These are lines of hers; they might be lines of his.

He learned directly from her poems – those hit-or-miss glories of 'a schoolgirl of genius'.

---

* These included the death of his young married daughter in a landslide. The Gibsons took the baby to live with them, and in the Second World War, suspicious neighbours threw stones after Gibson because the baby's father was a German.

When I lie where shades of darkness
Shall no more assail mine eyes,
Nor the rain make lamentation
    When the wind sighs;

That stanza of his 'Fare Well' is too close for coincidence to her lines in 'The Philosopher's Conclusion':

O for the time when I shall sleep
Without identity –
And never care how rain may steep
Or snow may cover me!

Besides these affinities, one must admit that there was no woman writer who failed to attract him romantically if only she would die young and tragically.

*

As the nightmare endlessness of the war continued, de la Mare would begin to see the cold finger of possibility stretching out even as far as his own son Dick, seventeen in June 1918 and patriotically eager to serve. Yet de la Mare himself, though he felt all the horror and waste with anguish, sustained the same straightforward patriotism, undisillusioned, with which he had set out in 1914. There was an unexpected but considerable dose of John Bull among the more rarefied elements in his make-up, and the war brought it to the top. This united with his consuming love of country, in which 'England' became almost identified with 'Poetry'. So the sense of remorse with which he suffered the oppressive privilege of remaining a civilian, never left him. It speaks out in the four lines which he wrote when old, and simply called 'England':[40]

All that is dearest to me thou didst give –
Loved faces, ways, stars, waters, language, sea;
Through two dark crises in thy Fate I have lived,
    But – never fought for thee.

Meanwhile younger writers volunteered or were drafted, and one by one were snuffed out. Even from the contents of the latest *Georgian Poetry* volume, two names were listed 'dead in battle' while their editor was still receiving congratulations. Dwarfed against so much misery, private ambitions seemed futile and paltry. It was in a far more depressed and listless mood than his customary diffidence that de la

Mare handed over to the publishers, at last, the thin volume, *Motley*, over which he had shilly-shallied so long.

Its contents, drawn from seven years' work, were very uneven, yet the good pieces are so outstanding he need not have had his doubts. Because of them, *Motley* remains a landmark comparable with *The Listeners* and *Peacock Pie*. Partly, this is due to the inclusion of love poems of 1911 and 1912, written in the first flush of his passion for Naomi, but held back because they were too revealing. Direct love poems form at least a fifth of the book, and the proportion is more like a quarter when one adds those that sprang indirectly from the climate of that love. Even now, there were yet more lyrics for Naomi from that passionate period that he did not publish. Some of considerable force only found a place in his very last collections of all, and a few remained unpublished to his death. Discretion apart, perhaps he felt unable to assess them objectively for a number of years, in that loss of self-confidence which follows the evaporation of any ruling passion. 'So It Would Seem' he kept back perhaps because, by Naomi's account, it had originally ended with her name, and that as a rhyme-word, clinching all. He may simply not have hit upon the substitute rhyme 'Sesame', with which it finally appeared in *O Lovely England* (1953).

Not by any means all the best of *Motley*, however, belongs early. De la Mare was much cheered that Newbolt seized on the final pages of the book for special praise, for here (he replied) were some of his latest pieces. Among these are 'The Scribe' and 'Fare Well', the very last two in the book, and they are among his finest ever.

'Fare Well' is in a major key, not his usual minor one; an affirmation, the nearest he came to a personal credo. He wrote it at Netherhampton, probably in February 1916 while he was revising *Songs of Childhood*, or possibly at the same time the year before, when his own brush with death and the onset of war would have brought the ideas behind the poem into sharp focus.

He recalled that he was walking with Newbolt through the entrance into the Netherhampton kitchen garden one day when the poem came to him 'in a flash, as it were'. Almost certainly he was looking at the garden on a winter's day – he seems to have paid no autumn visits there in those years. If so, the harvest imagery of the poem must have been conjured by its valedictory mood, not the other way round.

Seven years later Housman wrote 'Tell me not here, it needs not saying', also predominantly autumnal in its imagery, though written in April. Unconsciously, he must have been deeply influenced by the de la Mare poem, for the likenesses extend beyond similarities of metre and long stanza-forms to detailed echoes, too marked to be coincidences. Housman, most strikingly, has

> And traveller's joy beguiles in Autumn
> Hearts that have lost their own

where de la Mare wrote:

> May the rusting harvest hedgerow
> Still the Traveller's Joy entwine
> And as happy children gather
> Posies once mine.

We know that Housman read 'Fare Well' with concentration: his insight almost uncannily in sympathy with its writer. He came across it quoted in a newspaper review, somewhere, with 'the rusting harvest hedgerow' misprinted as 'rustling' – and was instantly sure of this mistake. When T. F. Higham told de la Mare about this in 1950, he commented in reply that such an insight was 'unusually keen' – adding 'but then he *was* unusually keen in these matters'.[41]

Yet all the striking links between the two poems throw up the more sharply a fundamental contrast. De la Mare expressed a serene acceptance of mortality, that rests on a faith implied. He surrenders his Traveller's Joy without self-pity, provided that other children as happy may enjoy in time to come what he had. He only pleads that beauty may prove to have objective validity – and some mode of permanence. His attention turns away from himself:

> How will fare the world whose wonder
> Was the very proof of me?
> Memory fades, must the remembered
> Perishing be?

Beside this, Housman's pessimism looks chilly and egotistical as he passes on his inheritance with a shrug:

> For nature, heartless, witless nature,
>   Will neither care nor know
> What stranger's feet may find the meadow
>   And trespass there and go,
> Nor ask amid the dews of morning
>   If they are mine or no.

*

Even before the war ended, when shortages were still acute and Sundays de la Mare's only leisure, the week at his Anerley home began to gravitate around hospitality on that day. To please him, Elfie

would take limitless pains. Once, after she had died, in a sad mood he
said she had so sunk her personality and life in his and the children's
that he felt, now she was gone, as if perhaps he had never really known
her. But though she effaced herself, guests remembered de la Mare as
particularly attentive to her – she was not left out.

She and the girls would commonly spend most of Saturday in
preparation and much of Monday clearing up. On the Sunday itself,
usually it was de la Mare who opened the door, greeting the guests
with solicitous questions; and at that moment he often seemed to
visitors to be shaking off, with conscious effort, a mood that had been
melancholy or withdrawn. Elfie hovered in the background – her soft,
rather husky voice welcoming but apologetic. Her manner, when a
guest turned to her, seemed to say 'How *kind* of you to take an
interest!'

The company always drew up to the table for tea, in a little room
rather dusky and crowded with its cherished furniture. Pretty china
and several kinds of cake loaded the table. De la Mare, talking rapidly
and lightly, would eat little or nothing, and push his cup to one side.
Quick to notice if anyone were shy, he would draw them in by name,
but his 'What do *you* think?' was unobtrusive, not that kind which only
makes more uncomfortably conspicuous the faltering object of
attention. He would get the other poets present talking about their
own poetry, never his. His totally absorbed sympathetic listening could
launch even the very diffident into discussing their own aims freely,
never mind what celebrities were around. He had his conversational
toys, and liked to set them out among the cups and watch his guests
take them up. Most had a literary slant in those days: – ' "Break break
break on thy cold grey stones, O Sea!" – where should the caesura come?'
– 'Which do you like *least*, gold, silver, or lead?' He liked to query what
kind of man one would hesitate to ask into one's home. For himself, he
decided 'I'd have a man with seven wives, but not a cruel man – if a
man was cruel I couldn't ask him.' He always maintained there was
something inherently horrible in physical cruelty that even mental
torture did not reach. (This shrinking made no difference to his avid
interest in murder cases, however brutal.)

Released from the tea-table, he would stand about afterwards
picking up the ornaments as he talked, and rearranging their positions
with minute precision. Elfie noticed – and was not irritated: 'Jack
always has to move everything.' Discussion never flagged and visitors
usually out-stayed their intentions, so that often an unplanned surplus
of supper-guests got included on the spur of the moment. More cold
beef was cut – more fruit salad arranged in segments on individual

plates (always in elaborate mosaics). Nothing seemed a trouble. Such impromptu informality was not customary at that period.

The younger de la Mares came and went among the guests with quietly free-and-easy manners – the two dark girls of nineteen and fourteen a romantic attraction to quite a few of the guests. They seemed to men such as David Cecil, Siegfried Sassoon and J. B. Priestley, in all the years before the girls married, very much the kind of daughters de la Mare might have invented – heroines for his own poems and stories. (They each remarked on this, when recollecting the two, in old age.) Plainly this was a particular charm of the romantic family atmosphere in which such guests saw their host at his happiest. He patently adored his daughters, wanting to have them always at home, paying them a homage he gave no one else. Florence was the equable and capable one; her father declared that to have her at home was like having the South Wind in the house. Jinnie's looks were the more striking; strongly built, she yet gave an impression of fairy vitality and enchantment – once seen, invariably remembered. She inherited all her father's artistic force and vulnerability, and had, besides, a dangerous, moody, innocent sensuousness. She had set her heart on dancing, from small childhood, and was to become an acrobatic dancer in cabaret, later on training under Massine. All this caused her parents intense misgivings, though they only showed it in solicitude and worry – they were not parents to forbid a child its bent.

In the summer of 1918, while drudging in the Ministry with the problems of Jam, de la Mare was pressing the poetry of a new protégée on Marsh – Ruth Manning-Sanders. Even before he met her, she offered to lend a house in Cornwall for the family holiday in August. They accepted, and explored the coast – Zennor, Pendeen, Land's End, Marazion, the Logan Rock, St Ives. At Zennor, consumed with curiosity, they crept up to the cottage from which suspicious neighbours had driven D. H. Lawrence and his German wife the October before. Peering through the windows, they discovered with fascination that all had remained for nearly a year just as the Lawrences had left it, fleeing after their last hasty breakfast, whose remains still stood on the table. Twenty years later, describing the scene, de la Mare said they actually broke in through a window left ajar, and found, besides the eggcup and eggshell on the table, a list of books on the floor. (He was exaggerating: they walked in at an unfastened door.) Another eight years later his account had sketched in a further touch – this time the list on the floor included *Peacock Pie*! From Zennor they walked across the small gaunt fields to the church, where he copied down for Naomi one of the epitaphs he loved best:

> Hope, fear, false joy and trouble
> Are those four winds which daily toss this Bubble:
> His breath's a vapour and his life a span:
> 'Tis glorious misery to be born a man.[42]

'That's a masterpiece God bless bless it – the author the famous Mr Anon. I wish I were Mr Anon. Unknown, beloved, perennial, ubiquitous, in that wide shady hat of his and dark dwelling eyes.' Two years later he would put Mr Anon into a story – as the lover of his Midget.

This was a very sociable holiday, full of laughter and huge picnics, and de la Mare's susceptible heart was a good deal engaged by the young poetess whose house he had borrowed. She and her badly-crippled husband, who liked to hurtle down the lanes in his donkey-cart, were established nearby at Sennen Cove with a family party of their own. 'The ladies have all mopped their hair,' de la Mare reported, 'copper, black and flax, and to see them stooping in the sunset is a legendary experience.'[43] He might pass off Ruth Manning-Sanders to Naomi as crop-headed, freckled, and rather abrupt, but in fact he was in a thoroughly romantic effervescence after the long drab flats of the past four years.

As usual, he was ingenuously unprepared to believe that an attraction which began (and largely remained) among things of the imagination, could cause anyone anxiety. Fired with enthusiasm for Ruth's verses and for her pictures, which were to be exhibited that autumn in London, he tried to promote both with Naomi (who did publish some verse in the *Saturday Westminster*) – also with Roger Ingpen, eager for him to publish a volume of them. He even went so far as to volunteer to pay a third of the costs himself. Meanwhile the two households spent long days together, and de la Mare asked for some days' extension of his holiday from the Ministry, so reluctant he felt to break up this idyll. For once he even abandoned his usual undercurrent of industry, and told Newbolt that writing had been 'out of the question'. No wonder poor Elfie felt that no sooner had one threat to her peace receded than another was taking its place. She even consulted Naomi, but Naomi scorned such alarm. She would not let herself be disturbed, and judged this attachment a thing that would pass – in which she was right; but there were storms in both households before it did.

*

Victory, when November 1918 brought it, found the de la Mares hardly able to attend to it, in the grip of the Spanish 'flu. Both boys soon had it, Colin (now aged eleven) falling very ill. Ruth Manning-Sanders and her husband had come for a visit of a night or two; they caught it, and had to remain a month. It was hardly likely that de la Mare could escape, and soon Elfie and her daughters alone were left on their feet, with five to nurse and no possibility of outside help – every house in the street had someone ill.

When the Armistice was signed, de la Mare wrote to Naomi that he could not digest the news: 'It's beyond the powers of the imagination; though one is conscious of the vacancy of Peace as it were in the universal air – *and* an astonishing justification of Shakespeare's Happy Endings.'[44] Convalescing he consoled himself with re-reading the *Anatomy of Melancholy* – 'invigoratingest of books'. Naomi also was convalescing, on doses of George Meredith, no tonic to de la Mare. 'I've *never* been able to read Richard Feverel once,' he told her. 'I arrived at where Richard chastises the butler à la Tom Jones, and washed out my mouth with a page or two of Hardy.' That was his panacea for many ills. And out of the blue a letter had just come from Hardy himself. He wrote on impulse – 'for what is hardly a reason', he said, having turned out a cupboardful of press cuttings from years before. And then, he had turned up

a most generous review, such as only a poet could write, by you of The Dynasts in The Bookman. Well: better late than never, & I send my thanks. If I saw it at all at the time it came out – ten years ago – your name did not convey to me as it does now any of those delightful sensations of moonlight & forests & haunted houses which I myself seem to have visited, curiously enough; & that may be why I had no recollection of the article.

Believe me, yours truly
(& not a stranger, though we have never met except at the ghostly places aforesaid)
Thomas Hardy.[45]

No letter from anyone alive could have given de la Mare more pleasure and excitement. What he had felt for Hardy for many years was the purest hero-worship, but he had been too modest to make any approach. How could he express his own debt?

November 6 1918   14 Thornsett Road, Anerley S.E.
Dear Mr Hardy,
    I wish I could tell you how much your letter means to me and how greatly I shall always prize it. Strangely enough, I have been on the point of writing to you these many weeks past, in the hope of expressing something of what your books have been to me. But such letters, I know,

may be only a burden. Your poems are another life to me. When I was in
America at the end of 1916, and rather homesick all the time, the little
collection used to be my good-night reading day after day ... The other
day I lunched with Bruce Richmond and we fired our own favourites at
one another across the table ... In 1914 I 'pilgrimed' to Egdon Heath from
Weymouth, and to Bere Regis, and went in a softly falling rain, when the
daffodils were out and the sheep were bleating, to peer in at the Trumpet
Major's windows. The shrill of a robin in the little gate-house still echoes
in my memory. You will forgive these crude ramblings – they are only an
attempt to say how the poems just know me by heart – if I may say it like
that and that I am indeed very gratefully and truly

Yours
Walter de la Mare.

It was a pleasant foundation for a friendship, one he would not
neglect; but he felt too diffident to follow it up at once. It was Siegfried
Sassoon, a new friend of this November, who helped bring them
together the next year by inviting de la Mare to join in the surprise he
was devising for Hardy's seventy-ninth birthday: a volume of fifty
holograph poems as a tribute from all the leading poets of the time.
Eddie Marsh had Sassoon staying with him when peace was declared,
and, wanting to introduce him to various Georgians whom he had not
yet met, arranged that Sassoon should come to Anerley. As long ago as
1912 he had written to de la Mare to express his admiration for 'such
exquisite poetry', and for *Henry Brocken*, and had sent some verses of
his own, but since that exchange there had been no further contact.

Sassoon was romantically ready to hero-worship de la Mare. He felt
that inaccessible and drab Anerley on a raw foggy November evening
was a very odd habitat for Brocken, but still he was expecting, when
the door opened in the dim little house, some 'immediate impression of
poetic genius', and in his host's expression 'some implication of ghostly
communings'.[46] It was a common mistake. He was taken aback, like
others, by the amiably unaffected welcome of a short city-clerkly
figure, whose unusually massive head only made its impression of
distinction a few moments later. Even then, the impression conveyed
was of 'ratiocinative concentration', nothing the least ghostly or
ethereal.

Sassoon does not seem to have taken very much to the other guests
asked to meet him that evening. Gibson was there, and Freeman, who
led the talk off into Coventry Patmore's experiments in prosody. This
was a scent de la Mare loved to hunt: he had a great admiration for
Patmore, and no niceties of prosody could be too nice for him. Sassoon,
sharing neither delight, sat silent, and felt his best card to be a recent
visit to Hardy. He must have been eagerly questioned on that, but felt

his own attempts to respond were lame and clumsy, soon forgotten in Freeman's 'modestly discriminative' opinions on the novels; though Sassoon knew he had scored when he caught de la Mare's meditative undertone of envy: 'Lucky you, to be inside Max Gate.' Talk turned next to Henry James, and Sassoon, who had read neither *What Maisie Knew* nor *The Awkward Age*, again sat mute and mystified; but when they branched off into the short stories – the one field of James's work for which de la Mare's long-ago enthusiasm had never faded – Sassoon was rewarded at last by a glimpse of the host he had hoped for. De la Mare was speaking of the terrific effect of that scene in 'The Turn of the Screw' when the governess looks down from the window at the little boy standing below in the moonlight. She sees that though he is facing her, his intent gaze is cast up above her, and suddenly she realises that the apparition of Quint must be looking out from the tower over her head. Sassooon remembered how 'de la Mare's face was half in shadow, and it was then that I saw the haunting and haunted presence of genius in his eyes'.[47]

Sassoon was immediately liked by the whole de la Mare family for his unaffected approach. There was much less of the professional writer about the abrupt, vivid sentences of his conversation than of the fox-hunting man, village cricketer, infantry officer and country-house individualist. His striking good looks were a curious mixture of the quintessentially English and the oriental. At this time he was in his early thirties, but to the de la Mares he seemed much younger; indeed he kept an engagingly youthful quality always, expressed even in old age in the active way he strode about or perched himself on a table corner, staring shyly up and off, while loosing a low, rapid volley of surprising disclosures. To the de la Mares he showed a steady affection, without the rubs and ruffles liable to interrupt many of his other friendships. His long, loose, athletic figure flung out a sudden gesture of warmth as he left them that first night, as if he had known them all a long time, and he burst out, turning back to them from the road, 'Well, bless you all!'

15

Memoirs of a Midget

At the very beginning of 1919 de la Mare left the Ministry for good. A fortnight after his freedom began, Ella Coltman took him to a children's play – a bad one, he reported, 'but it will be useful if I ever set about scribbling one myself'. The hint is cagey; in fact he was already committed to the attempt.

The hankering to write drama never slept in him for long; from *A Darling Old Villain*, for the rest of his life, it would from time to time drive him to take out his old plays, tinker with them, try a new one. But he was no dramatist. The cumulative use of detail, appropriate to his storyteller's gift of thickening atmosphere and building up a character by hints and suggestions, was cut off at a blow by the economies of the stage, and without this freedom his invention lost its touch and became melodramatic and sometimes comical. Yet the hope remained privately very dear, and now luck threw in his way the one species of drama within his range.

A young preparatory-school master, Armstrong Gibbs, had already set several de la Mare poems for pupils to sing. He was teaching English and music at the Wick School, Hove, delicate health having kept him out of the army. When the head, Thring, offered him a hundred pounds to produce an entertainment to mark his retirement, Gibbs, on a bold impulse, wrote off to de la Mare, without personal introduction, to ask if he would write a fairy play which he could provide with incidental music. Half expecting to be ignored or snubbed, he was overwhelmed by a ready acceptance.

Ideas for a play came fast, but, with his eye on a future commercial production in London, de la Mare was very secretive, and counselled Gibbs to be the same – a musical play for children (he felt) was an idea rich enough to be worth filching. Apart from *Peter Pan*, little was then staged for children except pantomime, and he hoped they might capture the market. He weighed up likely gains, seriously, to set

292

against time spent, for he assumed the writing would take him a considerable period. Things turned out otherwise; *Crossings* never made a penny for him on any stage – only as published in book form* – and in fact the writing of it took no time at all. To be precise, he spent eight February days on the first draft, took three days break, then spent another eight on the second.

The plot, almost fortuitous, but sufficient, is a kind of Midwinter Night's Dream for children. An isolated little manor-house in snowy woods is occupied by a houseparty of children, who are to manage on their own. They are assisted by the local butcher, baker and mysterious candlestick maker, haunted by the benevolent ghost of the old grandmother whose bequest has brought them there, and menaced by fairies who kidnap the youngest for a lock of her hair. The finale gives excuse for a 'transformation scene', which to de la Mare had always been the climax of any childhood Christmas pantomime.

His natural immediate anxiety was whether his play was too 'Barrie-esque'. (He had at the time seen nothing by Barrie, though of course he knew *Peter Pan*.) But *Crossings* owed neither virtues nor failings to Barrie's brand of fantasy. It never approaches *Peter Pan* in theatrical dexterity. The dramatic surprises of Barrie's cunning plot can keep children riveted while revolutions of fashion in sentiment pass over. Besides it, *Crossings* is little more than a masque. But Barrie's 'boy who never grew up' looks meretriciously sentimental against the tender magic of *Crossings*, whose only sentimentality is in the prattle of the child Ann (as de la Mare came to realise, with vexation). When he was an old man, Leonard Clark once asked him whether he liked *Peter Pan*. He answered: 'Now Barrie's in heaven, therefore Barrie's children are in heaven. I don't know if I shall go to heaven but I think my children will go. If they do, they will fight – and mine will win.'[1]

Armstrong Gibbs was enthusiastic, and wrote a score so apt that de la Mare was delighted. For the next term and a half the play became the centre of life at the school.

*

The next task was the lecture de la Mare was to give at Rugby on the eve of the unveiling of a Brooke memorial plaque. He called it 'Rupert Brooke and the Intellectual Imagination', and it is the best of all his criticism – the most interesting in central idea and the most incisively

---

* Three times, once illustrated by Gwen Raverat. A few sketches also exist for illustrations by Lovat Fraser, never completed; see p. 223.

expressed. Here he sets out in full his contention that in childhood the
most valuable human powers are at their height, from which
adolescence and adult maturity are a lamentable decline.

One could say that his *view* of childhood, in relation to the whole of
life, was exaggerated, and to that extent was partly distorted and
tinged with the sentimental; whereas his *vision* of it – childhood
considered in itself alone – is one of unsurpassed insight.

In his study of Brooke he divided poets into the childlike, the
divining and contemplative ones, and the boy-like, the active-natured
and analytical. It was with the latter – the poets of the intellectual
imagination – that he placed Brooke, and, so warm is the
discriminating praise which follows, one almost forgets that in so doing
he has put Brooke in the second rank. He roundly repeats his original
idealised view of Brooke as golden youth: 'Nothing could be clearer in
his poems, in his letters, and in himself, than his zest and happiness ...
He flung himself into the world – of men, of books, of thought and
affairs – as a wasp pounces into a cake-shop'.[2] He aligned himself
wholly with Churchill, D. H. Lawrence, Holbrook Jackson and Eddie
Marsh in his memoir, in helping to turn that vulnerable young man
'with voluble sarcastic lip', who thought himself a failure, into the glad
hero of a national sacrificial myth.

De la Mare posted off the lecture to Marsh before it was published.
So generally wideawake and active an impression had been given by
Brooke that de la Mare had ventured a doubt in his manuscript
whether the word 'dream' occurred anywhere in Brooke's poems.
Marsh's letter with the returned package crisply listed its occurrence
in fifteen. De la Mare replied with chastened gratitude – 'Years and
years – intolerable years – of reviewing' should have taught him (he
said) to search the poems through again before trusting to an
impression. In fact with de la Mare memory and imagination were
never very distinct faculties. His memory was richly stored and
detailed, but it was always 'working', a fermentation in process, and by
instinct was impressionistic, not factual. In view of this, it is
remarkable how seldom he left slips in his published work, considering
that this included a wider choice of quotation and literary illustrations
than almost any other writer of his time. He had in fact an extremely
conscientious regard for accuracy, and would go to immense pains to
verify details. Truthfulness mattered to him as much as to a scholar –
though from a rather different angle. Indeed he placed imagination so
high only because he considered it the one instrument of the mind
which cuts deeply and accurately enough to discover truth. A writer, he
felt, could not afford to be inaccurate over detail, without subtly

damaging the essential life of his whole imaginative intention.

Rupert Brooke's mother kept her thoughts on the lecture to herself, and de la Mare assumed, after a month's silence, that this meant she had disapproved. Marsh reassured him: 'I don't think you need take her silence for disapproval. She has a streak of ungraciousness perhaps that is not the word but certainly a want of graciousness, that would make it easily possible for her *not* to tell you she liked it.'[3] Frances Cornford once called her 'a lovely lion' – a direct, tall Victorian, her formidable face a mass of fine lines like the glaze of old china, quick to point an intolerant finger at any softness of moral fibre. 'A mollusc' would be her scornful dismissal of such a character. A friend of Rupert's as unsure of himself as 'Wibson' would find her asperities, uttered in a loud rapid voice without pause for second thoughts, a social ordeal – Rupert's own nickname for her was 'the Ranee'. But de la Mare was never scared by a 'character', and, luckier than Marsh, was in a position to relish her prejudices without needing to oppose them. Not that he was above reproof. He seems somehow to have omitted, after this first stay in her home at Rugby, a bread-and-butter letter. (Perhaps he had waited, hoping for that word about his lecture which did not come.) He had some occasion to write later, in June, and got a tart reminder: 'Many thanks for your letter. Are you aware that it is the first thing I have heard from you since you left here on March 29th?'[4]

From now on Mrs Brooke would organise a reunion with him once or twice a year, collecting him to meet anyone she felt worthy – 'a rather brilliant young person with no frills' was her kind of recommendation. Her tone is always rather peremptory, and she could be amiably caustic over his arrangements, liking life's laces briskly tied: 'You never sent me your new address, which was a great oversight' – and why had he not kept her up to date with his personal concerns? But a real affection shows through.

She made it clear that she did not keep a penny earned by Rupert's fame, and told Marsh she would like the half of the profits from the *Memoir* and the *Collected Poems*, besides that assigned to the three beneficiaries, to be administered as a fund for poets and painters. On hearing of this, de la Mare wanted to waive his own portion to add to her fund. Marsh, anxious about de la Mare's security, managed to parry this by pointing out that it would make things awkward for the other two (Abercrombie and Gibson), who were not well off. Even for de la Mare, the current two hundred and fifty a year from Brooke's legacy was a substantial part of his income.

When Mrs Brooke died in 1930, her partiality for de la Mare put

Marsh in a very difficult position. He had by then let himself believe that her rancour against him had died out. Yet in her will, dumbfounding everyone, she simply cut Marsh out, transferring all his functions to four trustees, de la Mare among them. He wrote to Marsh in high embarrassment, realising that no blow could be so cruel, and assuring him that the four trustees still looked on him 'as morally Brooke's executor'. But the legal position, which they could not alter, made this too anomalous to sustain for long, and four years later Marsh handed over all direction of Brooke's affairs to them.

*

In the spring of 1919, after the lecture, de la Mare went back to Cornwall once more, to Porthcothan. The first days were spent alone with Dick, and, though they had five bedrooms to choose from, the father and son found it more companionable to share a double bed and lie awake talking just as in the faraway days of Mackenzie Road.

De la Mare began a phase of story-writing, stirred up probably by the interest Roger Ingpen had expressed in republishing the old ones. Poems and stories tended always to come in clusters, breeding on each other. He would continue for some weeks living among his invented characters and scenes almost as if he were an actor identifying with them. Several stories might eventually result. Then, at some heightening of emotional pressure, he was drawn back again to poetry, and, in the same way as with the stories, one poem would spark off another – quite often he worked at two new poems on the same day. With the spring storms, Porthcothan seemed to have a thousand doors at night, all creaking and complaining, and the old house both oppressed and stimulated him, arousing in him a vitalising unease. He was competing, along with several friends (Naomi and Ruth Manning-Sanders among them) for a short-story prize in the periodical *Land and Water*. Abruptly abandoning one half written, he wrote a complete new tale in two days (one of which was his forty-sixth birthday). It was all bundled off to Naomi for typing, to reckon up the total of words and if necessary cut, and to send it in to *Land and Water* for him – and would she please ferret out a *mandrake* who had got in, he knew, somewhere among the story's seabirds, and substitute *razorbill*? He could still count on Naomi for a good deal.

The story was 'The Creatures', a fable into which he put all that Cornwall meant to him. The state that the narrator describes, 'half-comatose, yet vigilant', absorbing this countryside like a 'pilgrim chameleon', was his own. His belief was that nature resembles a veil over some further reality of which the imagination in its visionary moments seems to achieve a more direct evidence, and such evidence was always closest to hand in Cornwall. In this first spring after the war he was particularly affected by it: 'Perhaps the sea does not fascinate me quite so much as to look down and up this valley,' he wrote to Naomi. 'Surely Cornwall's unreality is the nearest thing to the idea of a terrestrial paradise – its colours, air, strangeness, quietness, in the world.'[5] Long letters to Naomi went every few days, and those to Elfie were just as communicative, fanciful, warm and teasing ('My dearest old Fridy ... you dear old duffer'). A hard-won equilibrium had been established, in which his friendship with Naomi enjoyed a kind of St Luke's summer – certainly its sunniest time for him.

She supplied him this spring with a 'peg for a story' about a parrot, which excited him, and it seems to have started him on 'Pretty Poll'.[6] He told of his joy in contributing to Hardy's seventy-ninth birthday present. For it, he wrote out 'The Song of the Mad Prince'. The old man, delighted with the recognition from younger poets which the gift implied, sat down to compose forty to fifty individual letters of thanks and appreciation. In thanking de la Mare Hardy seized upon 'The Song of the Mad Prince': 'My wife says that it is her favourite among all your poems, while to myself it has a meaning almost too intense to speak of.'[7]

The words are curiously strong for Hardy, who had plainly read some sharp answer for his own heart into the younger man's riddle:

> Who said, 'All Time's delight
> Hath she for narrow bed;
> Life's troubled bubble broken'?

Emma, his first wife, had died in November 1912, only a few months before the poem had first appeared in *Peacock Pie*.

*

De la Mare returned from Cornwall hankering to do another play, and a novel, but became waylaid by the social and public literary life that was a snare as peace-time society reorganised itself. He escaped to the Wick School for a fortnight's rehearsals of *Crossings*. The talent attracted made this a very unusual school production. For the final month Professor E. J. Dent took over the producing and undertook to find them a conductor. The young man he secured was Adrian Boult. It was rumoured that Vaughan Williams and the *Times* music critic would both be at the performance. De la Mare himself became totally

absorbed, coaching the boys in detail, and to exhaustion point. Beside
the professional standard of the music (scored for flute, strings and
piano) his own script seemed to him 'terribly thin stuff'. The
dress-rehearsal, 'with hearts bursting in our boots', left him plenty of
those memories endeared by the special charm of bygone disaster:
Dent using the flat of his palm for desperate emphasis ('*You–must–
speak–up!*') and bringing it down on an upturned tintack; and de la
Mare himself, making conversation to the very Victorian sister of the
headmaster, in charge of costumes. Where *could* she have discovered
such forbidding vestments for the part of the Bayswater Aunt? 'All
Aunt Agatha's clothes, Mr de la Mare, are out of my own wardrobe.'

On the night, the schoolroom's crammed auditorium and cramped
stage fell under that curious spell of faultlessness that sometimes will
seize an amateur company and carry it beyond professional
productions. After the starry charity performances seven years later,
when the whole Lyric Theatre crashed into applause for Ellen Terry,
there was still agreement between Armstrong Gibbs and de la Mare
that these had come nowhere near the poetic impact of that schoolboy
occasion. Their high hopes from the Wick success, of a commercial
London future, came to nothing, for no producer could be persuaded to
risk backing it; but it did directly open a happy and successful career
for Gibbs. Adrian Boult had been so much impressed that he
persuaded him to abandon schoolmastering and rely on his composing.
De la Mare remained on very friendly terms, and would not allow the
text of the play to be published without the score – he thought it
nothing without Gibbs's music.

*

His next work in the summer of 1919 also involved child talent. A little
girl of twelve from America, Pamela Bianco, was to have an exhibition
of her drawings at the Leicester Galleries, and her father wrote to de la
Mare asking if he would write an introduction to the catalogue. Instead
he sent a complimentary verse, and then Bianco suggested he should
write poems to accompany the collection of Pamela's drawings which
Heinemann was to bring out in the autumn.

It was an odd collaboration. The drawings were neither of de la
Mare's kind of imagination, nor even childlike at all. This likeable,
unassuming little girl with round cheeks and plaits had perfected a
highly mannered style, using line with an economy and artifice more
reminiscent of Art Nouveau than of anything naif or primitive. The
drawings were remarkable enough to pack the gallery; de la Mare

himself thought them 'wonderful work' quite apart from Pamela's youth, and he liked her very much, and her dry, witty father too. But before the book, called *Flora*, was done, it brought him a great deal of exasperation. He thought Heinemann stingy, and championed the little girl's rights with more indignation than he would have felt on his own account. Then some of the rhymes and pictures were incorrectly paired by the printer. (There are at least five variants of the book to tease the bibliophile.) With inveterate modesty, de la Mare thought his collection 'nothing *apart* from the drawings', but in fact neither pictures nor poems really depend upon or illustrate each other. Both are self-sufficient.

Flora inspired more from him than verse-to-order. Seven pieces from it found a place in his next major collection of new work, *The Veil* (1921), and one of these, 'The Moth', Marsh took for the final *Georgian Poetry*. He selected eight de la Mare pieces for this fourth Georgian volume, to be published late in 1919. De la Mare had his doubts about appearing in that company again – 'rather an old bird to be chirping in the new nest' was what he said. Did he also have private doubts too, by now, about the nest itself? But Marsh could not be gainsaid. Whoever else was in or not, for him the de la Mare contribution was an essential part of each volume. And when serious attack by Middleton Murry fell on the Georgian movement this year, de la Mare, with Davies and Lawrence, was explicitly exempted from his general censure of false simplicity and corporate flavour. De la Mare did not write the committed poetry Murry hoped young English writers would turn to, but Murry continued to feel him unassailable in the achievement peculiar to his own gift. There was, of course, some adverse criticism of him; when he sent Marsh the 'Flora' poems he quoted a diatribe he had come across: ' "Many of his poems are at best rococo vases of an eighteenth century artificiality, insisted on in our strenuous age though thrones go toppling down ... I sometimes wonder whether, for some of Mr de la Mare's admirers, his magic consists in his flourish of clichés ..." Eddie, this is Harriet Monroe in "Poetry" on *Motley*; every word of it molten truth I know; but can't you stop any more of those old thrones from toppling down – and just when the vases are going out second-hand!'[8]

Second-hand – that is, in the *Georgian Poetry* series – they were still going for a good price. The 1919 volume sold five thousand copies in its first month. Hassall records that, under the royalty system Marsh had devised, 'poets who had featured in more than one issue stood to make annually what in those days was almost enough for subsistence'. De la Mare had featured handsomely in every one, and succumbed again to

Marsh's importunacy for the final volume in 1922. By then, he had taken to rhyming his thanks for the punctual largesse Marsh distributed twice a year. There were at least four such epistles; one ended:

> A quagmire *began* Christian's pilgrimage harsh;
> This Shade's dearest hope is a Heavenly Marsh;
> And a Jordan of current so tranquil and steady
> He'll steer his dread course with but one gentle Eddie.

At this period Marsh stood very much in the relation of a mentor to de la Mare, who valued his precise intelligence as a kind of sounding-board, though he often disagreed with him. He relied a great deal on Marsh's judgement for the choice and arrangement of his collections, asking detailed advice of this kind for *Peacock Pie, Flora, Poems 1901–1918* and *The Veil*. A little later Marsh 'diabolised' (his own term for acting as devil's advocate for his writer friends) *The Memoirs of a Midget*, minutely combing through the manuscript at de la Mare's request, searching out ambiguities, dubious punctuation and any possible slip, as well, of course, as weightier issues. Such editing was invaluable, and de la Mare called Marsh his Argus, turning to him in these years as he had once turned to Newbolt. That friendship had not cooled at all, but Newbolt belonged to an older school of poets; Marsh was the natural doyen of the Georgian circles in which de la Mare's life now so much revolved.

If de la Mare had had his way, the selection Marsh took for the 1919 *Georgian Poetry*, which included 'Fare Well', would have had among it 'The Imagination's Pride', a poem that Newbolt and Naomi ranked among his best.[9] It is not quite that, for effects too romantically lush clog the force of the deep and curious personal experience it is witness to, and the reader is deceived into taking the poem's warnings partly as literary figures of speech. Yet the poem is a serious plea for the temperance and balance necessary to the creative imagination's health:

> Be not too wildly amorous of the far,
>   Nor lure thy fantasy to its utmost scope.
> Read by a taper when the needling star
>   Burns red with menace in heaven's midnight cope …

One guesses at a reminiscence of the Magnificat in the poem's title. This would have been a boyhood memory very deeply implanted, since he sang it at St Paul's day after day. Another phrase of his, central to his philosophy, also stems from that psalm:

He hath showed strength with his arm: he hath scattered the proud in
the imagination of their hearts.

                                    *

His major concern of 1920 was the 'long book' – begun in January,
finished in August – which had been his ambition since war ended. To
get leisure for it, he terminated his regular reviewing, and cut down
lecturing till the autumn. With the phenomenal sales of Brooke's
poems and *Georgian Poetry* he felt just secure enough financially to do
this. The novel he undertook instead grew almost twice as long as *The
Return*. It became his most personal work, *The Memoirs of a Midget*,
and established his prose reputation.

Naomi believed she had suggested the subject, but Poppy recalled de
la Mare's fascinated discussions about dwarfs right back in his
schooldays, when he saw midget performers at circus shows. Even
then, she said, he used to speculate whether dwarfs experience life in
the same way as the normal-sized. And *Gulliver*, too, with its
Lilliputians, had been in childhood the book that most impressed him.
A midget was in any case only another example of the particular hero
or heroine he was always seeking out: beings for whom some handicap
or peculiarity, isolating them from their fellows, had preserved the
innocent eye, and the 'homelessness' of the outsider in the accepted
order. Only such characters as these apparently found the familiar as
strange as he did himself, and so could be spokesmen for that exiled
state which he felt to be man's true predicament on earth. For his own
part, he constantly exercised the awareness of novelty, guarding
against ever growing used to the commonplace, always trying to
extend his own field of consciousness. He would set himself to imagine
what it is to be a house, a river, a blind man. This last he claimed to
have carried into literal experiment, groping around once for a day,
blindfolded.

After the *Midget*, in the early 1930s, he attempted two even bolder
departures from the normal hero, using the part-animal viewpoint
that Nod in the *Mulla-Mulgars* had prefigured. *Mr Brush* was to be a
novel about a fox who studies the farmer's skills, and presently takes
over his farm. De la Mare read up details of crop rotation and
agricultural life, but the theme required more country lore than he
possessed or could imaginatively make his own. Begun almost at the
same time, *Mr Cat* is a much more fascinating fragment, almost
three-quarters finished, which carries the humanising of animal
perception a leap further. Mr Cat is from the outset at once actual cat

and actual human, in the most curiously convincing duality, such as one accepts in dreams. He becomes involved socially in a sinister relationship with a Miss Finch, and the various endings de la Mare sketched suggest that a murder mystery would be the climax. But the difficulties of resolving such plots, bristling as they must be with problems of suspended disbelief and consistency, finally defeated him, and he never finished either book.

The Memoirs of a Midget was in fact – surprised and sorry as he would have been to guess it – his last novel. He never lacked schemes that envisaged full-length treatment, but the novel was a form really outside his true range, *The Return* being the notable exception. Even the *Midget* might have been more effective as a long short-story, original and rich though it is. The incessant, close focus on detail – what Luce Bonnerot has called its 'pointillisme'[10] – demands an unrelaxing mental vigilance from the reader that becomes tiring over so long a composition. No reader can be expected to see the world in *every* grain of sand.

De la Mare chose for it the loose episodic pattern of his favourite Victorian novelists, Dickens and the Brontës, and outwardly it is a realistic account by a midget of her first twenty-one years. She is not quite consistently sized but verges upon fairytale dimensions – a perfectly-formed 'pocket Venus' about two feet high. She has one foot in another world, and finally vanishes from this one; but she is perfectly circumstantial – a nineteenth-century young gentlewoman, well-educated, good-mannered, religious and sharp as a needle. We know the details of her day, how she manages her finances, how she negotiates a staircase. In letters, de la Mare stated that the story takes place about the period 1883–91, 'particularly the latter years' – in fact the years of his own adolescence. It became his own spiritual memoir.

'Inward companions' were a need of his, from childhood's 'Tatta' to those who haunt his deepest poetry, and his midget, Miss M., became one who suited his needs so well that he declared to Naomi he had not met 'anyone so innard to talk to for – you know how many years'. He always spoke of her as a real person, with her autonomous existence, as he never did quite of Lawford or any other character from his fiction. She was above all the one mouthpiece well-disguised enough for him to trust with his own experience of infatuated love – its bewilderment and disillusion. Writing of Miss M's passion for Fanny Bowater in some way settled his own past. Its focus altered for him once he had seen it through her eyes. He told Naomi: 'And curiously, she really has had an influence on me too. I'm years older for one thing and further "out of it".'[11]

Miss M's littleness, delicacy and finesse serve a symbolic purpose, for the book has a poetic core. Quoted on the flyleaf are words from Webster which give a clue to this:

> Didst thou ever see a lark in a cage? Such is the soul in the body: this world is like her little turf of grass; and the heaven o'er our heads, like her looking-glass, only gives us a miserable knowledge of the small compass of our prison.

Miss M, in her courage, epitomises the adventuring spirit of man, reaching for a valid relation with reality, but conscious of an essential puniness in himself which constantly thwarts this.

The physically miniature always absorbed de la Mare. He took the same satisfaction in tininess for its own sake that children have. If he were not caught by the farawayness, strangeness, or forsakenness of whatever horizon his eye rested on, the chances were they would fall on the miniature at his feet – shell, pimpernel, hairpin, raindrop, wren. The *Memoirs* gave delightful scope for such observation: garden weed seen as jungle, hardly perceptible noises, the life of insects (which feature a great deal in the book). This element of the story actually brought him, so he said, to like creeping things he had found repellent before. But the poetic and realistic in the story are not so well fused in this story as in *The Return*. Now one, now the other predominates. Most of the minor characters are Dickensian, but with something dreamlike where Dickens would have had caricature. Fanny Bowater's mother (of whom Forrest Reid acutely remarked that we see her ghost as well as her body) curiously brings to mind Rosinante, Henry Brocken's old mare. But Mr Anon, the Midget's dwarfish lover, is not of the same mind-stuff; he belongs to the visionary world, not that of dreams. He is an Emily Brontëan emanation of the desolate half-bewitched garden of Wanderslore, which almost too oddly abuts the Bowaters' Victorian neighbourhood of circumstantial villas and small tradesmen.

The core of the book is the Midget's passion for the full-sized Fanny, beautiful and false. De la Mare had contrived circumstances about as far removed from the autobiographical as he possibly could, but the condition itself is unmistakeably what he had known for Naomi. It is as passionate – and as little centred on sex: it can only very loosely be docketed with that portmanteau label 'lesbian'. Nor has Fanny herself any link with Naomi's personality. But this love involves the same wild persistent questioning of beauty's accident: *what does it mean?*

The very memory of her beauty, when I was alone, haunted me as intensely as if she were present. Yet in her actual company, it made her in a sense unreal. So, often, it was only the ghost of her with whom I sat and talked.

It is as though, I do think, what we love most in this life must of necessity share two worlds.

These observations by the Midget are direct autobiography – such convictions fill the letters to Naomi. In life he apparently closed a total reticence over the severe emotional disappointment that had followed. He seems to have confided in no one, but through the Midget he confesses it sidelong: 'Love, living or dying, even if it is not blind, cannot, I suppose, focus objects very precisely. It sees only itself or disillusionment.'

Apart from love, the Midget's reactions to life are so closely identified with de la Mare's own that she generally seems more middle-aged than youthful; she is his mature forty-seven-year-old self at its most analytical and least childlike – rapturous often, or alarmed, disgusted, amused, but never self-forgetful. He scatters the book with affectionate allusions to his own history: Miss M's birthplace is Kent, her blood part-French like his, she has business forebears in a paper-mill, as did his grandmother Eliza Browning, her father is many years older than his wife 'who could slip round and encircle him in person or mind while he was pondering whether or not to say Bo to a goose'. The books her mother read her diminutive daughter were the same 'books of knowledge' Lucy had used. In fact de la Mare himself features shadowily in the *Memoirs* as Miss M's bookish friend Walter Dadus Pollacke, who possesses a winged head of Hypnos, as de la Mare did. Even her godmother shares the name of his own, in faraway Charlton – Miss Fenne. And, for the final touch, the Midget vanishes from earth mysteriously, leaving a cryptic note ('I am called away') pinned to the carpet, on 25 April – his own birthday.

He wrote the book with great facility, and this time he read Naomi each section as he finished it. She recalled that he had not known from one scene to the next what was to follow. He judged it would take just the six months it did, and the first draft was finished by June 1920. He then set to work to copy it all in longhand. With him, this also meant the inevitable grind of massive rewriting. Usually he was reticent about work in progress, but in this case he read aloud excerpts widely, even in early stages – to the family circle, and once to the Beresfords while staying the weekend with them. To please Beresford, who worked for Collins, he placed the book with them – in any case he felt Constable had let his poems go out of print too often. (In his lifetime he pursued through an impressive list that author's mirage, the perfect publisher.)

Beresford's success in combining literature and London journalism with a home wherever he pleased, from Cornwall to the Cotswolds, made de la Mare regret his own lack of enterprise: 'It seems so absurd to be cooped up in this streeted suburb when I might almost as easily be in the country and no more out of reach of London than he. But such is Fate.'[12] There would certainly be nothing to spare for a move while Dick was at Oxford. Dick had been offered an excellent opening in the tea business by the father of Rupert Thompson, that friend who had come originally to Anerley as a young literary admirer, but remained because of Florence. He decided (while she was still at school) that he would marry her, and in due time, did. But when de la Mare found Dick eager for university rather than Tea, he was not the father to urge the immediate financial advantage; somehow, they would manage. With rosy optimism he hoped that a quick serialisation of the *Midget*, followed by publication before 1920 was out, might pay for Dick's first year at Keble. But no book was more unlucky. Muddle, broken promises, foundered ventures, strikes and delay were to be its lot.

The misadventures began with the serialisation. Lovat Fraser made an offer for it for a forthcoming magazine, *The New Monthly*, of which he was to be literary editor. But ill-luck dogged this just as with Fraser's hopes to illustrate *Peacock Pie* (and later, *Crossings*). Before the magazine even got into circulation, it collapsed. By then it was August, and de la Mare was dismayed, for Dick had missed a scholarship and was going up to Keble as a commoner in a year in which virtually nothing at all had been earned. Fifty pounds' compensation from the Oxford University Press (who would have published the *New Monthly*) was scarcely adequate, and by now it was too late to serialise elsewhere. In any case this was proving difficult: neither style nor construction of the book favoured publication in sections. Yet, clinging unwisely to that dwindling hope, de la Mare decided to postpone publication in book form. All to no purpose. In the end the *Midget* was never serialised, and, between incompetence and the fuel and transport strikes in early 1921, Collins did not get it out for a whole year after it was finished – in those days a very long delay.

*

The Athenaeum, under Middleton Murry's editorship, was always eager for de la Mare contributions. In the summer of 1920 Katherine Mansfield was invited out to Anerley to discuss what he might offer the paper, but she was already too unwell to go, and asked de la Mare instead to bring his family to see her at Hampstead. With Elfie and Florence he spent one midsummer Sunday afternoon and evening at the house she called The Elephant, with a fire lit up for her sake, while

> the summer light
> Lay fair upon ceiling and wall as the day took flight.
> Tranquil the room – with its colours and shadows wan,
> Cherries, and china, and flowers: and the hour slid on.
> Dark hair, dark eyes, slim fingers – you made the tea,
> Pausing with spoon uplifted, to speak to me.
> Lulled by our thoughts and our voices, how happy were we![13]

'You had only to see the way she held a spoon,' de la Mare would say as an old man, 'to see how wonderful she was.' They never met again, and the details of this Hampstead occasion became fixed in amber for him. The emotion was mutual; Katherine relaxed into her happiest and gentlest self, and de la Mare proposed one of his favourite mental games: 'Supposing I just say "Horse in a field" – what do you *see*?' Later on, ill and alone at Menton, Katherine reminded him by letter of this talk, and of the small chestnut horse *she* had seen. She continued:

> Oh, I have such a lovely quotation for my next book. It says all I want to say: 'But Reverence, that angel of the world ...' It is from Cymbeline ... Which brings me to Shakespeare and the strange fact that though I have scarce spoken of Shakespeare to you I have never opened my book after that afternoon, without remembering what we did say, in fact I've even made so bold (in case I don't succeed in keeping the coffin from the door) to leave you my Shakespeare. The notes in it are really the talks I've longed to have ... Do you feel too that there are certain speeches, certain moments in some of the plays when the voices sound as from another world – it is a kind of secret speech from the kingdom of the imagination. No, I can't go into this in a letter. And I am frightened of boring you.[14]

Writing to Murry in October 1920, to praise his review of de la Mare's *Poems 1901 to 1918* in the *Athenaeum*, she said:

> I love DelaMare, love the man who came to tea – with his wife sitting there by the fire and dark, young, lovely Florence. The memory of that afternoon is so precious. For one thing I felt that DelaMare *recognised* you – I mean a certain 'you' – I almost mean 'us' – but that he couldn't have known ... And that brings with it always a sense of Peace that endures.[15]

In fact de la Mare did have a deeply intuitive grasp of the bond between couples he loved, and they would find their love for each other clearer in the focus of his own response.

Although, as Katherine was soon sadly aware, she would never again 'come to tea except by letter', Murry would save up memories of any talk he had with de la Mare to retail to her. She was always eager for news, and, whenever she finished something new, for de la Mare's approval to seal it. When *Bliss* came out in December 1920, she asked for it to be offered him for review before anyone else, and he eagerly accepted. The copies she shared with Murry of *The Listeners, Poems 1901 to 1918* and *The Veil* went about with her in exile, and in 1922 de la Mare sent her another poem (unidentified) for her birthday. They had so significantly stepped into one another's minds that she wrote to him in January 1922: 'I can truly, faithfully say that not a day passes but I think of you.'[16]

Her letters to him are among her very best, though few. So when the *Midget* was finally published and sent to her, de la Mare was downcast to find months go by without a reply. Finally she had discovered he had never had a letter from her which she said she had posted to him – and to 'Miss M' – the day after the book had arrived:

> I was a little bit … sorry there came no reply. I saw her locking the letter away – saw that exquisite small hand turning the key and heard the sharp, small sound of the lock – But how did she look? Her face was in shadow … If my letter wounded her – forgive me – The moment that comes back and back to me is Miss M coming home late that night with Fanny – Fanny drifting, dancing, turning on the fallen leaves. One has the feeling of watching them – of listening from another star. It … haunts me.[17]

The mannerisms and whimsical tone (all the dots are her own) suggests Katherine's style when she was not quite at ease with her correspondent. Some slightly insincere note sounds here, quite different from the simple, forthright wording of her next words in the same letter – praise for *The Veil*: 'It is great happiness dear friend, to have your poems. But one cannot say a word about them, or rather *I* can't. I can only give thanks for them; they are read very often.' In fact during the summer that the *Midget* came out she had spoken to Hugh Walpole of it in very different terms, coupling it as a disappointment with Lawrence's *Women in Love* (in which she herself figured in thin disguise). Walpole recorded: 'K.M. says it [*Women in Love*] is a filthy rotten book and De la Mare's Midget no good either.'[18] Probably she had mixed feelings, but certainly even if Walpole's version is exaggerated she was less than perfectly honest with its author. Did she ever post that missing letter at all?

*

While de la Mare was at work steadily copying the *Midget* ('eating it with every slice of bread and butter') news came to him that his mother, aged eighty-two, was very ill. She died only two days later, and it was a heavy blow. To Newbolt he wrote a year afterward: 'In a sense one of the Springs of my life seems to have failed; and yet I am assured that other life continues.' The little old lady who looks out so fiercely from family snapshots under her high, square brow – the Browning chin as determined as ever – had kept all her wits, interest and spice to the end. She lived with Poppy and Roger from the beginning of their married life, and a grandchild would go up to her small room as to a royal levée. Her affectionate, formally phrased letters to Jack, scattered with pious quotations, are turned with an eighteenth-century pithiness. For him she had been the key to his central identity, the shaper and guardian of his childhood, and so of his chief treasure. To Naomi he confided, after her death: 'It seems just like beginning again: it was always like being a child in her company.'[19]

The family summer holiday of 1920 was spent at Fowey, with de la Mare toiling away, but 'feeling rather a derelict creature and can't forget there's no mother to see'. Nor was Fowey, by his standards, 'real' Cornwall, being so thronged that life was hardly less sociable than in London: Hugh Walpole to lunch, Rose Macaulay to coffee – and he must of course call on Quiller-Couch. De la Mare found him 'much more Foweyish, thank goodness, than littery or professorial',[20] and relished Q's crusty character, (a good deal resembling Badger in *The Wind in the Willows* by Q's great friend). Russell Loines and his family were over from New York, and he had the de la Mares boating, sailing and off to the regatta. Loines stumbled over a trunk in his bedroom, and a box of matches exploded in his hand. He was much too dazed by the fall to unclench his fingers, and burned them raw. De la Mare set off in frenzied search for a doctor, and got back an hour or so later – to find Loines calmly telling his nightly fairytale to his two small daughters. Another day de la Mare gave him some pages of manuscript to read, after a typical British Sunday luncheon; Loines, who never pretended, returned them at teatime saying that unfortunately he had fallen asleep in the middle of the first page – up to that, he had enjoyed it. De la Mare was dashed – who would not be? – but Loines only needed to smile and lift his faint eyebrows; it was impossible not to respond.

Crossings came out in a handsome limited edition; *Poems 1901 to 1918* appeared, and was very well received by the critics. The *TLS* gave de la Mare a front page of serious praise, treating him as a master, and Gosse paid tribute in the *Sunday Times*. Middleton Murry's enthusiasm in the *Athenaeum* carried double weight, for by now he was known as the spokesman of the anti-Georgians. *Poems 1901 to 1918* was in two volumes; they arrived for the Newbolts at Netherhampton, one inscribed from 'Jack' and the other from 'Walter D'. Harry thought this very suitable, 'for if ever anyone had 2 personalities ... And there he is, both of him, and more, in these volumes.' Yet Newbolt believed that *one* of de la Mare's personalities still had 'no poems to express him'.[21] He had watched from a distance the vagaries of his friend's impressionable heart, and had blamed the 'sirens' and 'robber ladies' involved – and also Beresford, for encouraging the perilous relationship with Naomi. But, though glad for Elfie's sake that matters had finally settled down, Newbolt took no very censorious line about de la Mare himself: 'Bless him – he has been a joy to *us*, anyhow, though I fear an anxiety to his wife.'

Meanwhile a fresh blow fell when the Inland Revenue discovered that the three Brooke beneficiaries had all this time, in blithe ignorance, omitted the bequest from their Income Tax returns. Gibson totted up his third share as £2,218, so something like four or five hundred pounds appeared to be owing by each. Marsh pressed on all three the balance from his 'Rupert money' as a contribution, and suggested they seek help from George Rostrevor Hamilton, then an Inspector of Taxes and himself a poet. He handled the case skilfully for them, pressing (as de la Mare begged him) both for a reduction in the demand and for latitude over the period of payment. In the end the Revenue discovered some allowances that could be set against the charge, and agreed to payment by instalments.

De la Mare took on every lecture he was offered at this time, to make ends meet – though he did find two in a day proved excessive. He went to Holland for a week's tour in January 1921, and came back more struck by a minute dwarf's night-shirt he had seen hanging beside the clothes of a nine-foot giant, than he was by the galleries of Rembrandts. His book seemed to put him in the way of such things: he was much impressed when one day on a bus two midgets climbed up to share the top deck with him. From the time the *Midget* came out, admirers constantly sent him miniature books and bibelots 'for Miss M', of which he gradually amassed enough to fill a large tallboy.

One set of *Midget* galleys was given to Marsh, who would pounce on de la Mare's weakness – punctuation – or on any bad grammar or awkward constructions, or those unconscious lapses into metre which set prose jingling, and are the besetting snare of poets when they tackle prose. Another set went to Forrest Reid in Ireland for criticism at quite another level – Reid's intuitive appreciation of de la Mare's deepest poetic aims. From now on these two would almost always exchange work before publication. Reid looked up to de la Mare, but gave criticism with stimulating forthrightness. The *Midget* was his favourite. 'Surely the quaintest, curiousest and most enticing romance ever imagined.'[22] The best thing in it, to his mind, was the character of Mr Anon, 'for whom I feel an extra affection somehow ... You found him in England, but I claim him as my kinsman; he is of my world.'[23] At his good suggestion de la Mare rewrote the final chapter. Reid had declared: 'There should be *nothing* but dramatic presentation here – no analysis, no reference to Herbals. You must keep your climax uncooled.'[24] Meanwhile Reid continued to batter at de la Mare's inertia over the neglected short stories; he would take no excuse, and it was plain he would win in the end.

There was division among de la Mare's advisers over whether Miss M's final disappearance, reported by Sir Walter Pollacke, should come in as introduction or epilogue. Reid and Marsh advised putting it first, and finally prevailed, against Beresford's opinion. The disadvantage is that readers may skip an introduction, and so overlook entirely Miss M's strangest adventure of all, in the light of which the rest is meant to be read. Yet in the end it is her mortal adventures which count for most; the book would be complete without any suggestion that Mr Anon returns from the dead to fetch her.

Confusion and delay at Collins over the book's publication continued for much of 1921. Beresford tried to keep the firm to their promises, but unsuccessfully, and his own replies to de la Mare's enquiries were not free of evasion and muddle. De la Mare maintained a tone of jocular patience in passing on such irritations to Naomi, but she thought his patience a weakness, and flew into one of her famous storms of wrath. He found her once again altogether too masterful. She personally lobbied publishers and influential people to get the private edition of the book subscribed; this particularly annoyed de la Mare, and her direct attacks on Beresford upset him worse. In old age, looking back ruefully but honestly, she felt that it was this episode which had spoiled her relationship with him for good. Interference over a *book* made for the first time a rift in their professional lives, the platonic bond of fellow-writers which that earlier jar of 1914 had left unassailed.

16

Thomas Hardy

May 1921 brought a most welcome invitation – to Thomas Hardy at Max Gate. Hardy had given his great friend Mrs Henniker a ticket for a lecture by de la Mare in Leeds on Keats – this was the centenary year of Keats's death. Unjust to Fanny Brawne, in the fashion of the day, de la Mare detested what he called her 'little hawkish nose and retreating forehead', and dismissed her as vain and shallow. Nor was the rest of the lecture very original. But Mrs Henniker was impressed, and when she spoke to him afterwards he mentioned his veneration for Hardy. She asked Hardy to receive de la Mare should the younger poet call at Max Gate. Soon after, Hardy invited him to stay. No doubt Elfie was included in the invitation, for Hardy was punctilious, but illness of Dick's kept her in Oxford, and from there she wrote to de la Mare one of her few surviving letters that show a gleam of her inner self, almost always hidden behind domesticity and conjugal cares: 'And how I envy you, ever since I was a girl the very name of Thomas Hardy has caused one of those curious and unexplainable emotions of wonderful pleasure and aloofness.'[1]

De la Mare wrote that the two days of that visit stood out of his life ever after 'with an extraordinary saliency', and he recorded his impressions both in a poem written very soon after, and in a much later broadcast in his old age. His memory by then was that a production of *Tess* in Dorchester had made it impossible to get a taxi, so Hardy had to meet him at the station on foot. *Tess*, however, was not produced by the Hardy Players until 1924; during the week of de la Mare's visit they were doing *The Mellstock Quire*. At all events Hardy did escort him home on foot that day, 16 June, compelling his guest, much the younger man, to surrender his bag. He showed 'a child's satisfaction', de la Mare said, 'a rare courtesy almost peculiar to himself'.[2]

Falling into easy talk at once, they left the road for the moss-quiet downland turf, and suddenly in the midst of their conversation de la Mare's ear was caught by a low, delightful trilling of birds. It seemed to come from a shallow hollow about thirty paces off. He lifted his hand and enquired what the birdsong was. Hardy came to a standstill by him, and eyed him with his characteristic tilted glance, which was, so de la Mare said, 'never penetrating, always divining and comprehending' – terms that well describe his own. Hardy replied that he had heard no birds. To de la Mare it seemed as if the old poet had magicked them into his mind. He told the story in a poem, adopting in compliment something of the Hardy manner:

> All Dorsetshire's larks for connivance of sweetness seemed trysting to
> greet
> Him in whose song the bodings of raven and nightingale meet.
>
> Stooping and smiling, he questioned, 'No birdnotes myself do I hear?
> Perhaps 'twas the talk of chance farers, abroad in the hush with us here
> In the dusk-light clear?'
> And there peered from his eyes, as I listened, a concourse of women and
> men,
> Whom his words had made living, long-suffering – they flocked to
> remembrance again;
> 'O Master,' I cried in my heart, 'lorn thy tidings, grievous thy song;
> Yet thine, too, this solacing music, as we earthfolk stumble along.'[3]

De la Mare was dissatisfied with the poem, and kept it back from collections till it found a place at last in *Memory*, in 1938. When a friend asked him for a manuscript copy, he said: 'It doesn't get its meaning out – that all the magic of nature is his as well as all the wisdom and compassion of human nature.'[4]

Max Gate, at the end of that inspiring walk, he found something of an anticlimax – 'not in the *least* like the House Beautiful'. The downright ugliness of the House, designed by Hardy himself, often gave this shock to the reverent newcomer. Hardy told him that the builders had chopped off the skull of a Roman skeleton in the course of their work, and in the garden he showed him a sepulchral stone with a Latin inscription – legionaries had been quartered there. Hardy thought it inauspicious, and had persuaded ivy to grow over the inscription.

De la Mare wrote to Elfie: 'T.H. is just what I always divined he was; and I love talking to him. We talked the whole morning … Now T.H. is going to take me to his favourite churchyard, in which he knows most of the company. So we share that hobby.'[5] Florence Hardy picked a bunch of white roses in the garden, for her predecessor's grave, and the three of them walked in bright hot sunlight across the dusty downs to

Stinsford. On the way they met two very tall strangers, a gentleman entirely in black and a nun. When they had passed and gone on a little, Hardy said that both were personal friends; his remarks about them and his manner in meeting them so fired de la Mare's curiosity that he bent down and pretended to tie his shoelace to get a better view of their retreating backs. To him, just sketched in by Hardy's casual conversation, they had become as fascinating as characters of Hardy's own. After this Max Gate visit, he would often say that to be with Hardy was to *become* a character in one of his novels and at this date actual Stansford was still essentially the Mellstock of Hardy's stories and poems, saturated with their life. On expeditions to it Hardy used to carry in his pocket a home-made tool for scraping the tombstone inscriptions clean – a little square of wood like a toy spade, which he had carved himself. On one of the last occasions he used it, tackling his family's tombs (very mossy because of the yew that grew over them), he mentioned to his wife that 'Walter de la Mare had told him that he preferred to see the gravestones green'.

Hardy showed de la Mare a poem he had lately been writing, 'Voices from Things Growing in a Churchyard'. The first verse runs:

> These flowers are I, poor Fanny Hurd,
>   Sir or Madam,
> A little girl here sepultured.
> Once I flit-fluttered like a bird
> Above the grass, as now I wave
> In daisy shapes above my grave
>   All day cheerily,
>   All night eerily!

Florence Hardy's *Life* of her husband relates that Fanny Hurd's real name was Hurden, and that she was a delicate child who went to school with him and who died when she was about eighteen; her grave is there in Stinsford churchyard.[6] It seems most likely that she was the same child whom Hardy grieved to have hurt one day, as de la Mare relates in *Early One Morning* (1935). Hardy told him how he had mischievously pushed this girl, one winter's morning, on to the schoolroom stove behind her, so that she burned her hand: 'He was then an old man ... but the time, the place and the child herself were still vividly present in his mind. He afterwards showed me not only her grave but also the manuscript of a poem in which he mentions her and, if poetry can, makes her ever lovable.'[7] Did Hardy's reminiscence recall a similar occasion to de la Mare, and so give rise to the little poem of compunction, 'The Playmate'? He certainly said it was about an actual incident long ago. It ends:

> Weep no more; how dark a face
> In thy hair! Oh, I shall see
> How many years, this silent place
> Where I was cruel to thee![8]

De la Mare said that Hardy had been stuck for a word in his lines about Fanny Hurd, and that he had been able to make some suggestion which helped – and that this encouraged Hardy to finish it. Hardy himself put it more strongly when Roger Ingpen visited Max Gate in 1927; Roger reported that Hardy 'told me that he took a walk with you and pointed out the grave of a girl on whom he had written two lines of a poem and no more. You said you liked them and wished he had finished the poem. And so, he said, it was owing to you that he had finished them.'[9] It was de la Mare who mentioned the poem to J. C. Squire, which led to its appearance in the *London Mercury*, where it was printed alongside de la Mare's own poem about that illusory birdsong on their first walk.

Hardy took de la Mare halfway up the great slopes of Bulbarrow, and sightseeing to Weymouth. They also went over some old house that had belonged to the same family since the Conquest. When ill at ease, Hardy could take refuge in a shell of commonplace responses, just as a working man may protect himself in similar social situations. It fended off clever, visiting probers, like Virginia Woolf, from his privacy. Plainly, by contrast, he felt markedly relaxed in de la Mare's company, habitually expressing to him the very self of his poems and novels. This ease of imagination when together was deeply enjoyable to both. When he left, Hardy lent him Lytton Strachey's life of Queen Victoria, just out, and a revolutionary change from the ponderously reverent biographies the public were used to. 'There's not a dull word in it,' de la Mare wrote, returning it, 'though I'm not sure whether this is *altogether* a compliment. The last few pages suggest somehow a vital essence that is absent from the rest, more or less. But what subtle writing.'[10] On 9 August, Hardy wrote to thank him for a copy of the *Midget*:

As you will be already overburdened with criticisms I shall not attempt to add greatly to them, except by saying (if that is criticism) that I have liked the story very much, & that I think some parts – innumerable parts – of the writing to have so subtle a beauty that it may possibly be wasted on the tribe of ordinary novel readers into whose hands it will fall. I don't see how you can help this waste, though you may avoid repeating it by saving up any such future inspirations to beauty for your poetry – to which remark you will mentally reply, I shall do as my inclination leads me.[11]

In saying this, Hardy was almost repeating advice given to himself which had very much struck him in the 1870s; Coventry Patmore, who had then just read *A Pair of Blue Eyes*, had 'regretted at almost every page that such unequalled beauty and power should not have assured themselves the immortality which would have been impressed upon them by the form of verse'.[12] The point also arose in conversation between Hardy and de la Mare, no doubt with reference to the style of the *Midget*. De la Mare cited in a lecture, 'Truth to Life', Hardy's view that a writer should 'purposely admit into his prose (and doubtless verse too) stretches of flattish narrative and so forth. How else can he reveal by comparison, when the need comes, its energy and impulse and tension!' And in his 1955 broadcast on Hardy he exclaimed: 'You must not make it continually as flawless as you can, as then it may become too much of a strain on the reader. How well I remember his saying that.' He reverted to the point so often that he must have recognised in himself this danger of over-writing, and strove continually to correct it. Two years before he died, he said again to a fellow-writer that the art of writing carefully must not show: 'It's like somebody walking delicately because he's in a rich house.'[13]

The praise in Hardy's letter about *The Midget* which meant more than any other to de la Mare was his comment on Fanny Bowater: 'The most real of the characters to me is Fanny. You can touch her with your hand almost.'[14]

*

Muddles over the *Midget* had gone on right up to publication day and, as a last straw, the expensive subscribed limited edition did not appear until two months after the standard one. But the novel was instantly successful; it went quickly out of print, for Collins were caught by surprise; and de la Mare's name became for once controversial.

It is difficult to recapture the temper of the period about the book's subject. Looking back, it appears very odd that the intelligentsia of the early 1920s, who had asborbed the frankness and realism of D. H. Lawrence and the horrors of the Western Front, should have boggled at a fictional study of a dwarf's physical abnormality – especially a lovely dwarf. Yet it was this which struck several of the most intelligent of de la Mare's circle, including Newbolt himself, who wrote to a friend: 'I suppose it's just the abnormal element that I would rather do without.'[15] One of the letters which pleased de la Mare particularly came from an Edinburgh children's specialist who wanted to know if he had had medical training, since the study of a dwarf's psychology was so accurate. It was not the only time that his insight and observation earned him corroboration from psychologists, who found that his stories illuminated the cases they had handled.

By the time the book had appeared, and he was with the family at Aldeburgh for the summer holiday, he felt disenchanted with it – it had receded far enough for praise only to emphasise for him his private sense of aims not mastered. The book's fame began to bring him a large number of new friends, and he was much in demand for weekend visits to country houses. These partly assuaged his claustrophobic discontent at his 'streeted suburb' life. Elfie now often accompanied him – a change which Newbolt noticed with approval, in view of past embroilments.

Another development was that the elder children now brought home many friends of their own generation – Dick from Oxford, Florence from the Royal College of Music. Dick's Oxford friend Leonard Rice-Oxley, a don at Keble, became very close to de la Mare, and Frank Morley, a young American Rhodes Scholar with no English home-base, was always welcome to stay or to share the family holidays. Henry Williamson, who relied on Dick (much his own age) as a steady anchor for his own impulsive and erratic personality, came to de la Mare for advice on his nature-writings. At Christmas 1921 de la Mare told him he would take five years to arrive – accurately enough, for it was in 1927 that *Tarka the Otter* brought fame.

Among young women who came out to Anerley was Storm Jameson, a protegé of Naomi's, shy and lately from the north. De la Mare would never let her go off alone from his door, but would escort her on the tram as far as the Crystal Palace. She used nervously to wonder what she would find to say to him on these homeward journeys, but once seated together on the tram it was never a problem, and he would talk all the way, plying her with questions about her writing, and with conundrums. How did she see her characters? Or people in memory? Life-size or tiny? Her answers would promote half a dozen nimble metaphysical explanations why this might be. And he would go home to sort his conclusions into a new lecture on 'Character in Fiction'.

His taste in friendship was omnivorous. He did not need close personal intimacy, or even a very distinguished mind, to stimulate his own. Genuineness and good nature counted for much more. He was more often at ease among the affectionate and enquiring than among the brilliant; in fact he noticeably sought out friends among humbler talents. If so, it was not that he needed such for a foil to shine against, but rather, perhaps, as protective colouring, a better background for the 'pilgrim chameleon'.

Charades were a favourite pastime at Anerley, with de la Mare usually taking the more sinister Bluebeard roles. Production was impromptu, though occasionally a more elaborate piece would be rehearsed beforehand. Another new friend of these years, the young J. B. Priestley, shone at these occasions, and found in the de la Mare home a warmth and informality he had missed since he left the north. Argument was another feature of family life which increased as the children grew up; Dick and Colin had the same liking for this as their father, and they would join him in marathon 'discussions' which grew very heated. Elfie and the girls, quietly despairing, would take refuge in talking among themselves. The subject under dispute hardly mattered – it might be the difference between cognition and precognition ('Why do we say "What is he *like*?" instead of "What is he?" '). One of their worst arguments was over whether marmalade could be classed as jam. Once, de la Mare and Dick attacked each other for an hour on the question of the subjectiveness or objectiveness of reality – what an apple '*is in itself*'. Finally de la Mare got up and went over to the apple in question, lying on the mantelpiece – and was enchanted to discover that it was a mock one made of soap!

Another type of friendship that he made without stint or caution during these years was the sort carried on entirely by post-bag. He was just as likely to begin a lifelong association by answering an admirer as by a personal encounter. This often trapped him into terrible labours (sycophants, neurotics and the suicidal battened on his good nature), but friendships he really valued sometimes came out of it – as, for instance, with a Scots Presbyterian minister, W. H. Hamilton, to whom he sent getting on for two hundred letters. Hamilton was gloomy and dry, but honest, loyal and affectionate, and de la Mare's replies, mostly on poetry but also condoling over the machinations of Presbyterian committees, are far from duty-letters. He was always as likely to launch into one of his most interesting themes to such correspondents as to intimates like Forrest Reid, or to someone of Hardy's exceptional quality.

By now he often had fifteen letters to answer a day, which made a secretary essential, and after a few months of the *Midget*'s good sales there was enough money to employ Lucy Rowley, his niece. Many succeeded her, but she remained a favourite, and without her the main labour of the following year would not have been feasible.

*

The Veil and Other Poems came out, applauded, in time for Christmas

1921, a collection which marks the end of de la Mare's most romantic
and lyrical period. After this, individual poems would break out again
with his distinctive, pure, strange quality of vision and music, here and
there in every volume, and none was quite without it. But after *The
Veil*, in the 1930s, the note grew sadder and the questions darker, and
then, as serenity returned, the mood grew increasingly reflective and
musing, the tone more often conversational.

Already in *The Veil* what Newbolt had called de la Mare's
Pre-Raphaelite quality – ecstatic intensity of pictorial detail – has
almost vanished. Brooding over and weighing more elusive subject-
matter (sometimes really obscure), the poet's mind seems to be
searching always further away from common experience, and, to
express this, seeking out ever more subtle modulations and metric
inventions. Alongside this overclouding, one notices some definite
returns to that sober self of *Poems 1906*, concerned to draw
conclusions.

Yet these changes are not very fundamental or striking ones: there is
no pronounced development in de la Mare. Unchanging in his vision,
he remained also almost unchanging in style, staying so sure of the
idiom he required that he might seem to have been oblivious (though
he was not) of the extraordinary stylistic changes going on around him.
Wordsworth's or Frost's theory of poetry as natural speech can never
have meant much to him. He did not think that poetic experience could
be tied down to the expressions a man would use for other matters:
each experience was unique, and should dictate its own utterance. It
did not worry him in the least that 'beautiful' words went out of
fashion, or that nobody else used Thee and Thou any more. The poets
who came after Eliot and the war seemed to cause him no doubts.
Other Georgians, like Robert Graves and Hodgson, might to some
extent, as they grew, follow the same graph as Yeats from a highly
wrought diction to dry, pithy modernism, shorn of ornament. But for
good and ill, de la Mare went on using any word he pleased, keeping to
the end his marked preference, acquired in the Nineties, for the
brocaded and arcane. He makes only minor concessions to the
colloquial, and, always when he does, they seem more recognisably
delaMarian than of the street.

However, most of the poems in *The Veil* had been written in the
three-year interval since *Motley*, so the slight perceptible change – the
overcasting of his mood – does bear some direct relation to his personal
life. His vision had now distinctly lost its rapture, but it was not
disillusioned. 'Where then the faith thou hast brought to seed?'
questions, with reply, *The Veil*'s poem, 'The Catechism',

'Where the sure hope thy soul would feign?'
'Never ebbed sweetness – even out of a weed –
    In vain.'

Unshakeable conviction in absolute value still made the enigma of life worth questioning, and questioning endlessly. He could go further, out of conviction that life *has* ultimate significance. He still kept a Shakespearian faith in man, always to him a 'piece of work' to wonder at, however often corrupted. Coming on some other weed underfoot (for this is a favourite motif)

> [Man] wheels his wondrous features to the sky;
> As if, transfigured by so small a grace,
> He sought Companion in earth's dwelling-place.

It is the Christian vision, Man in the divine image; even though the Divinity can only be grasped by heart-ache over His absence. De la Mare always seems surest of his God when thinking of Him as the Creator. When he turns from the beauty of created earth to the invisible world of spirits, he is not so sure. Nor is God apparently ever beside him as a personal friend – unless that taciturn and enigmatic 'inward companion' who figures so often *is* this divine friend, disguised. Indeed one guesses he does in part correspond to what the indwelling Holy Spirit is for the Christian, or, more nearly, what Inwit is for Langland.

Katherine Mansfield, who loved *The Veil* particularly, found in 'Awake!' (a lament for missed opportunity, for failure of awareness) the piece that spoke most sharply to her own experience:

> Why hath the rose faded and fallen, yet these eyes have not seen?
> Why hath the bird sung shrill in the tree – and this mind deaf and cold?
> Why have the rains of summer veiled her flowers with their sheen
>   And this black heart untold?

Fashions change, and the poem has faded and fallen with them, but one can see why she loved it. For her, as for de la Mare, to sustain *awareness* at the highest pitch from moment to moment was the most important thing in life.

After *The Veil* came a long period chiefly of prose – there was no further collection of new poems for eleven years. Forrest Reid had at last prevailed on de la Mare to collect his old stories in earnest, and revision of these started him upon new ones. They include 'Lispet, Lispett, and Vaine', which originated, so Naomi said, from the question her sister asked de la Mare one day; 'Who made the Midget's gloves?'

He spun an extravaganza, partly symbolic, about a firm of silk merchants and their downfall. (His Huguenot forebears had traded in silk.) The story is rather thin and mannered; a much better symbolic tale on a similar theme (the challenge made to materialism by the 'uselessly' beautiful) was 'The Tree', one particularly admired by Chesterton. De la Mare also finished 'Out of the Deep', a wonderful study of the imagery of the subconscious. But none of these have quite the poetry of the earlier symbolic stories; their inventions are nowhere so suggestive as that enigmatic chest in 'The Riddle', or the strange crying bird of 'The Bird of Travel'. Yet perhaps his best symbolic tale was just ahead. It came in by a characteristic side-step or knight's move. That is, he framed it to set out (in terms of poetic fable instead of those of a discourse) why he was making 'for the young of all ages' his innovative anthology: *Come Hither*. The story is the Introduction.

17

Come Hither

The conception of *Come Hither* had been in de la Mare's mind for some while. He wanted it to transcend the ordinary anthology, to have real unity, and to be a true introduction to poetry. The result was, in its time, a completely original kind of book, personal and creative – pervaded by his own *company*, throughout.

The relation between childhood and poetry that the book posits is at once serious and radiantly spontaneous, and can have an effect for life on those who meet it young. Auden, in his inaugural lecture as Professor of Poetry at Oxford in 1956, spoke of it as a prime influence on his own boyhood. The variety in it, 'unofficial poetry', such as counting-out rhymes, appearing on terms of equality alongside Keats's Odes, had opened his eyes as an adolescent to the fact 'that poetry does not need to be great or even serious to be good' – a very liberating lesson for Auden's own gift.

Lucy Rowley helped her uncle as secretary throughout, and her recollection was that he built the anthology around the story which forms its introduction, not the other way about. Certainly the story was written very early on in the collecting of material. It is more specifically an allegory than anything else he wrote – in general he shunned that form for the strait-jacket it tends to impose. Here he quite avoids this drawback. The narrative is beautiful and sufficient in itself, and anagrammatic names fingerpost its other level of meaning without restricting the subtle range of references on many planes.

A little boy, Simon, finds on his rambles the old house Thrae ('Earth'), whose absent master is Nahum Taroone ('Human Nature'). Nahum's aunt, Miss Taroone (or perhaps she is his mother) welcomes Simon, and allows him the freedom of Nahum's round tower-room, crammed with books and the souvenirs of his adventures. On his last night there, the little boy sits up to transcribe, as companionship for his own adventure into life, the poems he has most come to love in an old volume he has discovered there, whose title he reads as *Theeothaworldie*. Miss Taroone is no tepid, abstract Mother Nature, but a being as much herself in her own right as Miss Loo or Old Susan, and the atmosphere of Thrae recaptures the particular wonder and awe of early de la Mare poetry – his prose fable seemed to provide a key to an Edenic vision his verse could not, at this period, unlock.

The whole book takes its unity and atmosphere from the marvellously clear fresh wisdom of the story. De la Mare included contemporary verse in it, and the choice from his friends (allowing for the limits his envisaged audience imposed) shows a remarkably just and steady sifting of what is valuable in the Georgians' verses. He had no precedent for this original conception of an anthology, though he may have taken some hints from William Allingham's *Nightingale Valley* (1862), his own old shabby copy of which he had lent to Naomi in the first days of their courtship, as a precious thing. Allingham had included light verse, though he was not so bold as de la Mare with 'unofficial poetry'.

Some of this ingredient was so very personal that Forrest Reid taxed him with slipping in work of his own under the signature 'Anon'. De la Mare admitted that there were one or two 'bits of rhymes' of his own in the book – also a word or two that he had altered in the wonderful old children's game-rhyme 'The Key of the Kingdom', and possibly some scraps of prose passed off as quotations among the notes. The notes also included a poem of Florence's, signed 'Elizabeth Ramal', and in the main body of the book a very good nonsense song, 'Tony-O', by Colin, signed 'Colin Francis', of which his father was inordinately proud. The notes to the book, originally meant to be a brief gloss, turned into a whole extra anthology, a kind of ruminating, discursive conglomerate – much as later on *Desert Islands* developed by incrustation out of a lecture on *Robinson Crusoe*.

The labour of *Come Hither* far exceeded de la Mare's original expectation; yet it went ahead without weariness, and when he finally sent Celia Furse a copy he said he did not think he had ever enjoyed doing any book as much. Collecting permission for so many entries still under copyright was itself a formidable task; all the correspondence to do with this lay spread over the floor, and Lucy Rowley, picking her way among the piles, competently took over all the business side.

In all, de la Mare spent only a year on *Come Hither*, and one in which he also lectured a great deal and was much occupied with stories. Before Lucy's day he had always sent manuscripts out to be typed; now he found he could save himself untold labour by dictating his stories. It was, after all, much like making up stories and telling them to her when she was small, and he could soon compose fluently like this, walking up and down the room as he spoke. Even stories built up very delicately of suggestion, such as 'Missing', were composed in this way. Lucy would be drawn in. 'What shall we do today, Lu?' he would ask, and when he came to an amusing passage he would burst out laughing to enjoy it with her. She did not get the impression he had worked it out in his head beforehand. He seldom composed a whole story on end; he would work at it for about a week and leave it to settle. What she typed during his afternoon break from work he would correct that evening and return to her thickly smothered in revisions.

*

A task that cost him little trouble during 1922 was a volume for the American market, *Down-Adown-Derry: a Book of Fairy Poems*, in collaboration with an American illustrator, Dorothy P. Lathrop, who specialised in fairy drawings. One of her pictures gave him the idea for 'The Fairy in Winter', a poem Naomi much admired and Forrest Reid equally disliked. He disapproved of de la Mare's fanciful and decorative side rather as Thomas had done. De la Mare wrote to him: 'I am sorry you dislike "The Fairy in Winter" so much; simply because it gave me rather unusual pleasure to write it. Anyhow, she is still there in the snow-fields of my imagination. Of course, she would melt in another climate. What I do feel is that *all* such beings may share one world, living their own strange lives, and yet more or less unperceived by the denizens of a different density, so to speak. We must have this all out some time. As soon as the word "belief" is mentioned, mists begin to rise in every valley.'[1]

Did he 'believe in fairies'? It is impossible to say firmly (whimsical moods aside) that he did *not*. He certainly did not feel that the nature of reality, with its infinite variety of levels, definitely excluded them. The fairy world was at least a better explanation than any other for certain kinds of experience for which he felt the evidence too genuine to ignore, and which must somehow be related to the rest of life.

Reid lectured him a good deal on the need for simplicity: 'Be as subtle as you like in your thought but cling to simplicity of expression.'[2] He thought this, with some justice, de la Mare's greatest temptation, and condemned his inversions as a growing mannerism. Marsh had warned about this as long ago as *Peacock Pie*. De la Mare defended himself rather vaguely on the grounds that inversion either came off or it didn't, and could not be defended or attacked on principle. He doubted anyway 'whether ordinary talk is necesarily the best or most forcible or most attractive form of expression'.[3]

   Apart from its obtrusiveness, inversion in an uninflected language
such as English may leave the reader uncertain which noun is the
subject and which the object. Poetry can seldom afford ambiguous
grammar, though perhaps the lines in 'Fare Well' that run this danger,
do manage to hold their alternative meanings together 'in solution', as
it were:

> Since that all things thou wouldst praise
> Beauty took from those that loved them
> In other days.

When T. F. Higham, then Public Orator at Oxford, wished to weave
this quotation into his Latin oration on de la Mare, he had to ask him
to be specific – was Beauty the subject, or object? As he suspected, de la
Mare had been using inversion; Beauty was the object.

                              *

In the spring of 1922, de la Mare met J. M. Barrie for the first time,
and later continued the acquaintance on visits to Cynthia Asquith at
Stanway in Gloucestershire, where she played hostess for Barrie's
house-parties. Barrie made a strong impression on him, though they
never became intimate. He described the first encounter to
W. H. Hamilton:

> I met Barrie for the first time at dinner a month or 2 ago, and brought
> away an extremely vivid and, in a sort of way, massive impression. There
> are some men who remind one of quite rich and tastefully decorated shop
> windows. You are less conscious of what may be in warehouse, so to
> speak. In others, the exhibits are fewer, and a ghostly warehouse with its
> contents is very clearly brought to mind.[4]

That he meant Barrie was of the latter kind, he makes plain to
Hamilton in a letter of 1928:

> Apart from the qualities of his writing which no one disputes, I have
> sometimes wondered whether Barrie has ever set down his inmost
> feelings and conclusions about this complicated existence of ours. There
> is that opening act to 'Brutus' – which suggests that if he really tackled a
> tragedy there would be some deadly dark clouds in it whatever silver
> linings might appear. Being in his company one feels that – his steady
> listening and the little he says. Not that an artist is bound to tell
> everything, or that he should not definitely choose to hold his tongue
> when he thinks that loosening it will be of no service in what he is most
> intent on. Still – I wonder what you feel?[5]

One worry in 1922 was the plight of Ivor Gurney, the gifted young poet-composer, whose nervous stability had been wrecked by active service in France and whose best verse was to come to him in a mental asylum, where he died. His appalling misery in care vented itself in incoherent letters to writer and musician friends. Those that reached de la Mare distressed him desperately; Gurney would rave that he was 'denied the mercy of crucifixion'. Before sanity completely gave way de la Mare had enlisted Marsh's help to try to get Gurney a suitable job or a pension. Marsh did supply some money from a fund he kept for such uses, and Gurney had secured with this the lowly job in Gloucester he had wanted; but soon suicidal depression forced him into the asylum, never to recover.

After all these years it was only this May that Elfie was finally coaxed out of her retiring habits into paying her very first visit with de la Mare to Netherhampton. As for him, pushing aside his notes to *Come Hither*, spread on the table in the Ark, he launched out with gusto into the old talks with Newbolt, and these Newbolt's rational mind found as tantalising as ever. But it did not matter; going nowhere in de la Mare's company was a pleasure – like walking in a good maze, where all the paths are culs de sac, or else go in the opposite direction to the apparent one. 'We kept hailing each other across the tops of hedges,' Newbolt wrote of one such talk, 'and found ourselves very often quite close together – for ½ a second, and then off again ever so far – not differing but diverging.'[6]

One evening they talked international politics till midnight. Newbolt found de la Mare 'a very random thinker on that subject – never follows any argument, and hits at every ball like a girl at cricket standing anyhow from moment to moment'.[7] De la Mare's politics remained throughout his life this erratic, highly prejudiced, and emotional affair. His interest in the subject at all was only intermittent, but once roused, fierce.

The year 1922 closed once again with a *Georgian Poetry* volume, and this time Marsh had to exert all his powers of appeal against de la Mare's wish to stand down for younger contributors. Marsh pleaded that he always wanted to make a quarter of the book de la Mare, and that, though it had gone too far to suppress, he would really wish that the volume could be given up altogether if de la Mare persisted in his threat to withdraw. 'Your things are almost the only ones of the last 3 years that I am *sure* are *really* good and without them the book wd be a wilderness.'[8] De la Mare had to give in. Alongside his 'Moth', the volume contained Lawrence's wonderful 'Snake', Graves's 'Pier Glass', and Blunden's 'Almswomen'. But the rest of the collection was insipid stuff, and this time there would be no successor.

*

Reviewers were enthusiastic about *The Riddle*, the 1923 collection of short stories made at Forrest Reid's insistence. De la Mare's old editor, St Loe Strachey, wrote to say he had never altered his opinion about the early *Cornhill* tales, but de la Mare had decided in the end that these would not do in his collection – though he left 'The Moon's Miracle' on the list of contents till the eleventh hour. He and Roger Ingpen decided they would next gather up, for Selwyn & Blount to publish the following year, three 'essay stories' woven round invented epitaphs, under the title *Ding Dong Bell*. The earliest of these, 'De Mortuis', figures in that original list of work that Roger had sent in 1901 to James Pinker, now dead.

De la Mare's books were selling well, both in Britain and America. In November 1923, he wrote to Eric Pinker, the son who had taken his father's place, asking him to keep £1,600 credited to his account, and to send on the balance. This shows how very considerable *earned* royalties had become, quite apart from the *Georgian Poetry* and the Brooke money and the Civil List Pension. Dick was out in the world now, working as a publisher at Selwyn & Blount, and Jinnie was studying under Massine, and considered very promising.

During 1923 de la Mare was invited, among much other lecturing, to give the Clark Lectures at Cambridge, a course of a dozen on 'The Art of Fiction' – the most important academic assignment of his career. King's College and Trinity became familiar haunts, though he never felt he quite belonged there, sleeping in an enormous bed in Vernon Harcourt's room at Trinity, surrounded by the whiskered features of bygone wranglers, and by Harcourt's forbidding collection of gigantic oriental jars. Moreover he never got used to talking in a hall where he could hardly see over the lectern. Screens were arranged at the back of the audience, which he declared crept steadily forward as the course proceeded and attendance dwindled.

The old Universities always made him feel defensive, and lectures had remained generally an ordeal – he complained that they 'obliterate one's core so to speak'. Never confident enough to speak only from notes, he always read, and rather inaudibly. Yet, screens or no, he drew good audiences in Cambridge; and, though unassertive, he was not really timid as a lecturer. Once, in Hull, when the audience rustled too long, he broke off his introduction to settle them sharply: 'If you can't be bothered to listen to me, I can't be bothered to talk to you.'

He succeeded in thawing Housman, of whom he saw a good deal
while at Cambridge: 'We sometimes sat together at High Table. He
could ... easily stay mum through a whole meal if he felt that way
inclined (as we all must sometimes); but he could also be uncommonly
good company. I remember what seemed to me to be a pretty ironical
little compliment he paid me once. He'd come to one of the lectures, and
with a dry little smile remarked: "You seem to have caught the knack."
Caught the knack!! – and I have always abominated the job; as one
must I suppose if one can't extemporise richly and eloquently ... I
never could get a lecture short enough.'[9]

In May 1923 he was at Max Gate again, taking Elfie, but he left no
record of this as distinct from the first visit. Next month Hardy gave
him moral support over his bent for dark fiction. Jack Squire had
eagerly taken for the March 1922 number of the *London Mercury* that
much-rejected masterpiece 'Seaton's Aunt', which had found no place
for itself since it was first written in 1909. Several of de la Mare's
friends still disliked the story intensely. Hardy wrote:

> As to what friends say about 'Seaton's Aunt' – well, I shouldn't listen to
> them. It is a *splendidly gruesome* story: & I always feel that a man
> should write what he can write best: if you have a bass voice they must
> accept bass from you, & not be perpetually wanting you to sing treble.
> That's my plan, anyhow.[9a]

He added in a postscript that Masefield, on whom the Hardys had
called at Boar's Hill, had '*a haunted house* immediately opposite him!'
Hardy liked to slip in news of haunted houses to de la Mare whenever
he could. When he had thanked him for personal birthday greetings in
1919, before the holograph anthology of poems arrived, he had
continued: 'We sometimes look for that old haunted house of your
poems when we go hither & thither: but though I have one or two of my
own they don't seem so interesting as yours: so we shall go on
hunting.'[10] Certainly there is something in common between a
haunted house in Hardy and one in de la Mare, but also one notable
difference. Whenever Hardy describes an old house, every detail
speaks of *History*; it is the past which is numinous – oppressing Tess in
the old house to which Angel Clare takes her after their wedding, and
making memorable every physical detail of Poxwell Hall in *The
Trumpet Major*. But from de la Mare's work, history, as such, is
curiously absent. Nor did it figure much in his conversation. In what he
writes, he is uninterested in the past except as a quality of the present.
The ghostly presences that haunt his houses do not have their
imaginative source in a real bygone age. They exist timelessly,

emanating from the place where they are, and from its quality, not from what had happened there. His invisible world is without period.

From Max Gate, Jack and Elfie went on to a Pembrokeshire farm which had much attracted them when glimpsed in an otherwise dismal holiday the year before. Skrinkle was remote enough to have no road to it at all, and in all directions round it there spread that rather austere coastal beauty de la Mare was always most moved by. It was a worthy successor to the Cornwall he had loved and Skrinkle farmhouse had points in common with Porthcothan. Solid, slate-roofed, its plain stone face whitewashed yearly, it looked out through a gabled porch at the treeless, wind-scoured fields of the headland. The children of Prothero, the Welsh farmer, noticed how de la Mare would take his chair and 'squat anywhere' to write, the paper spread on his knees, often surrounded by his family and their guests. Leonard Rice-Oxley, a very favourite guest at Skrinkle, found it a mystery how much work got done under such conditions.

From Cwm Praesipe (pronounced 'Preesip'), so steeply tucked under the headland close to the farm that the path down was almost imperceptible from above, the view opens past Skrinkle Bay to the Lydstep Caves, with Caldey Island far out. Two great caves run up at the far end of Skrinkle Bay, and a way lies right through them into an enclosed inner bay beyond. The place affected those who spent holidays with the de la Mares there. Middleton Murry, who was among these, underwent an experience of paralysing terror while climbing on the cliffs there with de la Mare, on the family's second visit to Skrinkle in August 1923. Next day a landslide carried that whole portion of the cliff onto the beach. This incident was surely in de la Mare's mind when inexplicable terror seizes the narrator on the cliff-walk, in the story 'Mr Kempe' – though this tale owes its chief suggestion to a Porlock visit, the following year, and to Culbone's minute church up in the woods there.

De la Mare liked at Skrinkle the old childish occupations for his leisure; once he built an enormous sand-volcano, which (by means of careful ignition within) could be made to smoke satisfactorily. Frank Morley, the young American they took under their wing for holidays, helped Jinnie practise her 'lifts' and acrobatic turns on the sand, and Siegfried Sassoon held a brief wild rodeo on a yearling who shied him into the hedge. Manorbier Castle, where the vicar one year persuaded de la Mare to judge an Eisteddfod, became the setting of his fairy story 'A Penny a Day'. His imagination had been caught by the dwelling-house built within the walled courtyard of the castle itself. A cottage inside a castle wall, 'on the coast of West Wales', became the romantic home of the heroine, Griselda.

In December 1923 de la Mare met Charlotte Mew for the first time. He had already, the year before, done what he could to atone for past unkindness about 'The Farmer's Bride' by joining his name to Masefield's and Hardy's in appealing for a Civil List Pension for her. The sum granted was small – only seventy-eight pounds a year – but it meant a great deal to her. Sydney Cockerell, a friend of de la Mare's for several years past, arranged a restaurant lunch party for her, and de la Mare was completely captivated by her personality and liveliness. Four years older than him, tiny, with a long thin face and an upswept shock of fine white hair, she would stalk into a room defiantly, dressed mannishly. Deeply ashamed of her poverty, she could be defensive and strident when socially ill at ease; but at the luncheon she enjoyed herself and relaxed, showing the very attractive gaiety so many melancholy natures have when a lucky occasion releases them. Possibly de la Mare's gradual alteration of opinion about her work had been influenced by Hardy, who rated her the best woman poet of her day. They certainly made friends, enough for her to write to him of the occasion: 'There is to me something timeless about delightful things – so I don't quite think of it as over.'[11]

*

1924 began with the offer of a knighthood. Sassoon was deputed to sound de la Mare's feelings. Among the multitude of letters from Sassoon, his ingenuity contrived never to address de la Mare twice alike. This one opened:

Dear Taroone
  (This ought to be written by 'E.M.' [Marsh]; but I am using red ink to show that it is an unusual affair.) A humble intermediary between greatness and Official Recognition, I merely inform you that a Civil Serviceable friend of mine (not 'E.M.') asked me (the recent New Year's List having been assailed on account of the absence of names allied to the Arts) to take soundings in the ocean of your intellect as to your willingness to become Sir Walter. Well; well; 'baint that a danged queer message from Tufton St? 'Lone for an end' cried Knight to steed ...
  (And Mister did remain.)
  But as all poets of true metal are Knights of the Holy Ghost, and you are one of them – why *not* Sir W? It has a crusading cadence, I think. And you know how we all adore you. But I am impinging on your independence. So merely remain
                                    S
                                    S
Your primeval* letter to me enclosed. Please return it with your 'feelings in the matter'.[12]

* i.e. from the Prime Minister's office.

De la Mare did decide Mister to remain – and wisely, surely; poets are meant for the green bay, not for rank and consequence, and when one succumbs to a knighthood, somehow original new poetry is less expected from his pen. (The offer was repeated in 1931 and again refused.)

Replying to this first refusal, Sassoon began, of course, 'Dear Mister', and admitted to relief at the decision. He went on: 'In 1950 I will arrive with a deputation and hand you the OM, which you already possess as far as I am concerned, so there's an end of it.'[13] He would have been only three years too early.

Ralph Hodgson was leaving England, to de la Mare's sorrow, to take up a post in Japan at Sendai University. He lived in Japan until two years before the next war, and was never much in England again, finally settling in Ohio. It was strange, self-imposed exile for a man who loved his native land so dearly, and de la Mare remained convinced that Hodgson could have written 'a superlatively good book on Englishness'. Natural indolence, however, was proof against such encouragement. Once, so de la Mare heard, a rumour got about at Sendai that Hodgson was actually writing poetry. Promptly the Principal and the Professor of English waited on him, 'and assured him that he was to ignore entirely all his academic responsibilities until the visit of the Muse was over'. But, de la Mare continued, 'the lamentable – the miserable fact being either that She had never peeped in (which I don't believe) or that he wouldn't look at her. You know his favourite line of English poetry? "I fear some work before me lies*." ' [14]

Sassoon and he had gone to the station to see Hodgson off for Japan, and the conversation somehow turned upon nuns. De la Mare was bold enough to assert he had known merry ones; Hodgson violently disapproved of religious profession, and, oblivious that the time for long farewell had come, the three became involved in a hot dispute. (According to Sassoon, Hodgson was not an agnostic but that rarer thing, an actual atheist.) The very last that Sassoon and de la Mare heard from him as his boat-train drew out was a defiant parting shot from the window, snapping his fingers: 'I don't care *that* for your old thug Jehovah!'[15]

George Moore's *Conversations in Ebury Street* came out in the spring of 1924, and de la Mare figured twice in them, on both occasions with John Freeman as fellow-guest. He left no comment on this maundering

---

* Hodgson maintained that this was a line of Falstaff's, but where he found it remains a mystery.

and superficial work of semi-fiction, beyond a passing mention of it to Naomi at the time: 'And did you recognise the Charum, the veevacity, the Range?' She did not; she wrathfully attempted (in vain) to get an opportunity to slash at the book in review, on the grounds that de la Mare was 'dreadfully misrepresented', as he was. Indeed it is difficult to see why the book ever had any reputation. Both *Esther Waters* and *The Brook Kerith* (which de la Mare had reviewed with such sympathy that Moore asked Naomi who had written the article) were works of real originality. But the *Conversations* present a view of life fatuously complacent, mandarin and edgeless. Among other things quite uncharacteristic of de la Mare, he is presented as quoting poetry by heart at enormous length, and is allowed only a very brief defence of Thomas Hardy in a long attack on him by Moore. Hardy himself must have been unusually stirred by this, for in his notebooks he recorded his displeasure (a rare reaction from him) and also the names of those 'disciples' to whom Moore purported to have related these opinions – de la Mare among them.

De la Mare's celebrity was in fact reaching the pitch where he had to contend with the public parade of his own thoughts and personality, in various degrees of distortion, or at least with an eroded privacy, in the works of other writers. In this same year appeared a full-length critical study of his work by R. L. Mégroz[16] – rather to the indignation of Forrest Reid, who had longed to do it himself, and had so far met with only vague and postponing half-assents from de la Mare. Mégroz wrote the book against time, and was often in financial difficulties. De la Mare helped him more than once, and no doubt his kind heart hoped to further Mégroz's career by letting him do the book. But he drew the line at answering a long questionnaire brought to Skrinkle, where the family had invited Mégroz for the discussions he wanted. He found de la Mare an adept, patient stone-waller; Rice-Oxley remembered an imperturbably kindly 'I have no idea' returned countless times to such queries as how did he write his poetry, and what in his opinion was his best work? Nor was de la Mare pleased by such biographical snippets as appeared in the book. He was always flatly against publicity that invaded the privacy of any living writer, and indeed extended this to the dead (as his story 'The Revenant' shows). When a newspaper telegraphed to ask his opinion whether newly discovered love-letters of Browning and Elizabeth Barrett should be published, he sent the pre-paid form back with the simple answer 'No'.

A 'merry nun' such as he had mentioned to Hodgson came into his life this year, because of his lectures in Glasgow, and remained a close friend and voluminous correspondent for the rest of his days – Sister

Frances de Chantal, who spent all fifty-eight of her years as a religious at the Roman Catholic convent of Notre Dame at Dowanhill, Glasgow, an active community which ran a teacher-training college. They met soon after her first letter to him, on one of her visits to London, and he several times stayed at the Glasgow convent, reading his poems in their classrooms (where one twelve-year-old was disgusted by his Sassenach delivery: 'Jist spiled his own poitry, he did').

Sister de Chantal, a cheerful, intelligent woman with several distinguished men among her friends, hoped in a quite open and guileless way to convert this one. In her time she was instructress to almost six hundred converts who turned to Rome, and once, addressing a meeting on 'hobbies', declared roundly that making converts was hers. Her method with de la Mare was to assume agreement unless definitely checked, speaking of her faith as if he shared it already. She put her trust in a busy, practical round of pieties, relics and schedules of novenas, constructing of these a brisk, orderly defence against the world's evil. De la Mare gently returned the relic of St Thérèse of Lisieux she had pressed on him. Yet he read the copies she sent him of the *Universe* with more than mere courteous interest, and later embarked on Aquinas. On her side, she struggled with *The Return*, considerably baffled, and fell back on discussing it in professional terms, with reference to exorcism.

There were times in de la Mare's life when he really did seem attracted to Roman Catholicism, so much that even his children wondered if he would embrace it. Yet, with his total refusal of dogma and his ingrained dislike of self-committal, he can never have been really near it. Plainly what attracted him was the seductive major poetry of a central tradition, and still more the visibly radiant effect of faith on people who possessed it to the degree of this endearing friend.

He loved Sister de Chantal's letters, which took to beginning 'Very dear Mr de la Mare', a compliment he returned. She prayed every day for a blessing on him, and after Chesterton died she got his widow to agree to offer prayers for de la Mare's conversion. When she heard he was dangerously ill in 1927 she told him briskly that in that case she would 'step on the gas' with her prayers – she was learning to drive a car at the time. He told her: 'I treasure your good wishes and everything else you do for me as much as only a *very* good poem could say.' Her serene definiteness about dogma never riled him, as it would certainly have done had she been a man, particularly a priest.

Another lifelong friendship which began at about the same time probably had more influence on his attraction to the Catholic view of life than even Sister de Chantal – R.N. Green-Armytage, most warm and humanly delightful of bookmen and collectors. He had wanted to be an actor but instead became the youngest barrister in England when called to the bar. He left the law during the war to take over an old bell-foundry and engineering firm in Bristol, to make munitions. But his central interest was literature, and in his long years spent in Bath, he became, in an unassuming, friendly way, the sage of that city. Writing as a stranger to invite de la Mare to lecture to a Bath society, he stressed the strong appeal his poetry had for 'papists' like himself, such a sympathy as they generally only felt (he thought) for writers of their own faith: 'The thing is psychic and has something to do with TRUTH (in Nature and Art and Philosophy) as we see it. You get it quite clearly in Francis Thompson's wonderful poem "In No Strange Land" every line and word of which reeks with the same truth that, to us, seems implicit in the *whole* of *Motley* (especially the title poem, "The Scribe", "Fare Well", etc.) not so strong in *The Veil* perhaps, but bursting through all three sections of *Come Hither*, which is a glorious book.'[17] During the next thirty-three years these two men exchanged easily a thousand letters. Green-Armytage's were usually long, always comforting and reviving. He understood de la Mare's spirit much better than did Sister de Chantal, with whom Green-Armytage also corresponded – he told her she would never make a convert here. In his own frequent discussions with de la Mare about faith, he was very unassuming, sharing news of his own personal journey, not making claims to inside knowledge of salvation. An eager bibliophile, by the time he died he had assembled a complete collection of de la Mare, almost down to the last elusive pamphlet – and de la Mare must have been more republished in his own lifetime than almost anyone of his generation.

After a visit in June 1924 to St Andrews, for his first honorary degree (proposed by W. H. Hamilton) and a Skrinkle holiday in August, de la Mare went once again to lecture in America, this time by invitation of Johns Hopkins University, Baltimore. It needs little description here for it repeated much he had experienced last time, but with the difference that he was now a well-known figure in the States. The *Midget*'s success there had led to the publication of American editions of his earlier books, and a much greater American public for his poems. (On the voyage out, once other passengers discovered his identity, he was kept busy signing autographs.) He had Frank Morley for pleasant companion, and together they watched the sudden apparition of Newfoundland through the captain's telescope. He wrote a slight story, 'Cape Race', round this incident and that of the tiny landbird they discovered fluttering inside a high window of the ship's lounge. He delivered his first lecture only seven hours after landing, and from then on was in demand – giving about forty more before he came back in December. There were many old friends to visit, and he renewed contact with Frost. He enjoyed each turn of the kaleidoscope as it came, but no longer looked about him with Columbus eyes. The only memories that sank deep, this time, were of the obsessive hush and vacancy of the decaying South. Here, he found his own brand of neglected, watchful house; and Jim McLane, one of the young men who had stayed at Skrinkle, took him to the Maryland home of a childless aunt and uncle. They rambled through the fields of pumpkins and maize near an inlet of Chesapeake Bay, enjoying together the curious melancholy, and visited a churchyard on a hilltop as night was falling. De la Mare put this region into the only story of his to have an American setting, 'The Lost Track', written soon after. The track in it was a real deserted railway line he had found himself, which in his story leads to a house as remote and brooding as Jim's uncle's and aunt's – 'mute with its own story'. The windows were shuttered, a creeper brilliantly dyed in the colours of Fall, clung in wisps across it, and in front were the wild morning glories which de la Mare had discovered with delight, 'a living mat of myriad tiny silent trumpets; bright blue, red, purple, slashed, striped, parti-coloured. A ravishing sight to see.'[18]

Thankfully he climbed into his bunk at last, and slept away most of the voyage home. No sooner had he set foot on his 'all-beloved, unparalleled, ever-remembered sweet green ENGLAND'[19] than he was met by the family at 4 p.m., who told him they had not an hour to spare, for they had given notice to quit Thornsett Road, and after that many houses, as Newbolt put it, had been 'killed under them'. Now a sudden chance had come up of a Georgian one at Taplow in Buckinghamshire, the property of Lord Desborough. De la Mare was sent off to clinch the matter there and then. He and Lord Desborough got on very well – and talked more about King Aella than about terms. But the agreement was signed, and the new home secured.

18

Hill House

De la Mare was very glad to say farewell to cramped quarters, and above all to Anerley. He had lived a curiously long time in so inappropriate a setting. Real shortage of money had of course held him there, but also that old instinct for enduring the known rather than risking a venture, which had kept him eighteen years in Oil.

Elfie was ordered to rest just at the time of the move, for fear of a spot on the lung, and was sent away for some weeks. Dick, Florence and their father struggled with the hoards of papers he had accumulated – he kept virtually every postcard he received, not very methodically, but roughly stuffed into files of the year. He also retained almost every draft and scribble of unfinished work. His squirrelling instinct went further, and up to eight unopened copies of *Punch* might be found round the house at a time. Several would already have acquired draft lines of poetry scrawled around their wrapper bands. There would come a point when one of the family asked 'Can I open *Punch*?' and grudgingly he would say 'I suppose so, if you *really* want to'; but he did not like it.

Hill House, Taplow, was tall, standing up a steep path graced by a fine arbutus, in the nose of a road-fork on the outskirts of Taplow village. The main rooms on the south-west corner each had a bay window looking away to Windsor Castle on the skyline. It was a pleasantly odd building, with a large number of rooms, two staircases and a 'ladderish back-stairs' as well. A long dining-room, opening on to the garden, was often lit for parties just by the firelight and candles, and here de la Mare would arrange elaborate flower-pieces in the alcove. There was a sort of 'No Man's Room' they called 'Duff', and next to it one which de la Mare claimed was haunted. Altogether it was a far more suitable setting than any he had yet inhabited; yet his feelings about it were mixed. Years later, after they had left it, he was often homesick for it, yet he once remarked that he had never been really happy there. The only house he loved wholeheartedly was the one he spent his last years in.

Yet the Hill House years were ones of contentment, the happiest for Elfie, and the only ones in which she need not overwork. A little later in this era they could even afford several servants, including a 'houseparlourman', an unusual genus they found much preferable to the female kind. De la Mare was much amused when this faithful person, named Liggins, was referred to as 'the butler'. Liggins was a student of form; Ascot was not far off, and he would report the winners in the last event when he came in to draw the curtains. De la Mare took to putting half a crown on a horse now and then, though he did not bother to go to the races.

He got on particularly well with his landlord, Lord Desborough, who had pleasant hobby-horses, such as belief in the need for a fixed date for Easter. Lady Desborough's style was flowery and intense; she was in the habit of sending across pencil notes: 'Dearest Friend – put one syllable in the exquisite handwriting on a postcard ... How *learned* you are, how do I ever dare speak to you???' She was determined that the resident genius at the gates should not be missed by the brilliant and blue-blooded who crowded Taplow Court for her Saturday-to-Monday houseparties. Nor was it easy for him to plead excuse, when his comings and goings were almost under her eye, and when her invitations, so pressing and so frequent, always offered a flock of alternative dates. To sing for one's *breakfast* is beyond most men, and these Sunday mornings when he had to set out unfortified to meet the titled and sophisticated, just down from their beds, were an ordeal.

In Hill House itself the round of hospitality increased, and since the burden of entertaining no longer fell directly on Elfie she had leisure for her own friendships at last among de la Mare's acquaintances – particularly with Lady Ottoline Morrell, to whom she and de la Mare came to feel loyal attachment. They were unembarrassed by her eccentricity, though the Taplow villagers would gather at the road-fork to see the carriage roll up and watch the fantastic figure alight, tall, gorgeously and exotically dressed, with marmalade-coloured hair, long face powdered dead white, and mouth painted blood-red. But her intense, elaborate manner never bothered the de la Mares, who took her simply for herself; and in her letters to de la Mare she would often drop the defences of mannerism and talk quietly of what she really cared for. She came a great deal to Taplow, and de la Mare went to her weekly 'At Homes' in London, which were almost exclusively literary. In the new home a spate of story-writing began, for which suggestions were welcomed. Someone proposed a second-hand bookshop for a background, and accordingly de la Mare wrote 'The Green Room'. During the summer of 1925, the first at Taplow, he wrote most of the stories for his first collection for children, called *Broomsticks*, and several for the next adult collection, *The Connoisseur*. His business letters to Roger Ingpen at this period became full of complaints, even sharp in tone. Selwyn & Blount were in difficulties, and Roger was not the most businesslike and punctual of correspondents. The two men had gradually changed places – nowadays it was Jack who wrote in the tone of the elder and more experienced man of affairs, keeping Roger up to the mark; very different from the sensitive beginner Roger had been so tender to shield, twenty-five years ago. But their mutual affection did not suffer.

Everyone wanted to visit the new home. Harry Newbolt came in July, and reported it was just as if the whole family had gone to Heaven and he had visited them there; but when he returned in December he was aghast to count eighty-nine signatures in the visitors' book during the interval and wrote crossly to a friend about the bills the de la Mares must be running up (hardly his affair by now). 'They are devoured by ghouls.' Although there was more room than before, Hill House was not at all grand, and often became as crammed as Thornsett Road. Those who came to tea would stay on and swell the supper-party in proportion; one evening they sat down to it a more or less impromptu twenty-two.

Newbolt also complained with the same nannyish asperity, that de la Mare was descending to potboilers, and that his tales had lost their purity of magic – they no longer made him 'wonder where they came from'. Perhaps this was said in a fit of the megrims, for when most of the stories de la Mare was writing that year came out in volume form, in May 1926, as *The Connoisseur and Other Stories*, Newbolt was far more delighted than he had been over the *Midget*, and said de la Mare had surpassed himself. Hardy was of a contrary opinion; according to Virginia Woolf's Diary they discussed *The Connoisseur* when she visited Max Gate soon after. Her entry mocks Hardy's conversation with deliberate malice of the trite. She had not succeeded in drawing him out, so is paying him out.

> Then there was de la Mare. His last book of stories seemed to them such a pity. Hardy liked some of his poems very much. People said he must be a sinister man to write such stories. But he is a very nice man – a very nice man indeed. He said to a friend who begged him not to give up poetry, 'I'm afraid poetry is giving up me.' The trouble is he is a very kind man and sees anyone who wants to see him. He has sixteen people for the day sometimes. 'Do you think one can't write poetry if one sees people?' I asked. 'One might be able to – I don't see why not. It's a question of physical strength,' said Hardy. But clearly he preferred solitude himself.[1]

For whatever reason, it was true enough that poetry, for the moment, had deserted de la Mare. But the change in his style of life – the crowded sociability, the access of comforts and financial ease – may just as likely have been a compensation for this loss, as a cause of it. The condition he called 'fiftiness' (he was now fifty-two) was probably at the root of it. No amount of solitude could have cured that – though, of all curious medicines, old age and another war were to do so.

*

During the first summer at Taplow, Florence told her father she was engaged to Rupert Thompson. A few years earlier, de la Mare had written with foreboding to Newbolt, whose son Francis had then just got engaged: 'Oddly enough, I feel that a daughter-in-law would be another (however distant) kind of daughter. It's the prospective son-in-law (may he long remain prospective) that sets me squinting. But I practise holding two cold hands together under phantasmal coat-tails in front of the fire, and looking over my spectacles at the pirate.'[2] The event, when it actually happened, cannot have been really unforeseen, and de la Mare had nothing against Rupert, who had been their friend for years. Yet he could not rise to the occasion, he said, and blurted out 'I am sorry to hear it!'

It was no more than the truth. Life was re-playing 'A Darling Old Villain'. Always possessive about the women he loved, he felt Florence – equable, capable, responsive – particularly essential to his well-being. How was he to imagine his future without her? Hers was to be a very happy marriage, but throughout the August and September of her engagement he was plunged in gloom. Jinnie, too, had fallen in love, but the 'pirate' in her case had gone abroad for three years, and she was waiting faithfully for him; otherwise de la Mare would have lost her too by now, for she never lacked wooers.

Florence was married on 26 September, with a hundred and fifty guests at Hill House. Her father was still a little dazed by the calamity; he wrote plaintively to Florence after the ceremony: 'Of all the things I ever knew this is the most unexpected *still*.' They had looked through the hymn book together to make a choice, and were charmed to chance on that verse which completely met their case:

> Be present, awful Father,
> To give away this Bride.

When the actual moment came, bride and father had become so deeply immersed in discussion about something else that they very nearly forgot to set off in time.

*

In November 1925 *Crossings* at last reached London, with two matinée performances for charity at the Lyric Theatre, Hammersmith.[3] Ellen Terry came out of her retirement to play the ghost of Susan Wildersham, a silent part – no lines for her to forget. Angela Baddeley gave a beautiful performance as Sally, and Jinnie danced the Queen of the Fairies. Ellen Terry was in her late seventies; Clemence Dane's impression of her a few years earlier had been already of 'Ariel shut up in the tree'. To those who had never seen her act, she now seemed only a dear old lady, rather deaf and blind, unable to concentrate for more than a few moments. But her performance in *Crossings* belied all this, Her biographers, Edith Craig and Christopher St John, at the dress-rehearsal, described her first entrance: 'The vision of this fragile creature, far advanced in years, yet somehow not old, tremulously gliding across the stage with loving arms outstretched, the spirit of beauty, rather than beauty itself, filled the spectators with a strange awe. A long sighing "Oh!" arose from them all ... a more wonderful tribute than any applause.'[4] On the opening day, de la Mare said that 'the roof came down' at that first entry. Later on, as she turned to go off, he could catch her murmur to the child who played Anne, pleading to be told where and how to make her exit from the darkened stage.

The Connoisseur got a more mixed welcome than the general favour which had become usual for each new de la Mare book since 1912, when fame arrived. Many people found the title-story far too obscure, and the tales in general too elaborate. All the same, the book contains three of his best sinister stories, 'Mr Kempe', 'All Hallows' and 'Missing'. The last, he said, 'concerned a stranger (*not* a nice man) whom I chanced to sit near to in a teashop years ago'. 'All Hallows', he told Forrest Reid, sprang from a sentence in a guide book describing the siting of St David's Cathedral, by the sea. From this phrase or two, he had spun a richly decorative tale, in which the Cathedral is the central character – its verger tells the visiting narrator that it is being taken over and rebuilt by demons; the very statues on the roof have mysteriously altered to a fiendish outline and aspect. On his way to Tenby a year or so back, de la Mare had spent 'one or two queer hours', so he said, on the top of the Abbey at Tewkesbury, forcing himself to crawl up to touch a mast that rose out of the lead roof on the tower. For a thickset man in his fifties, not at all daring or athletic, it was an odd exploit, suggesting a strong whim of the imagination set on having the experience, to store up for use, whether consciously at the time or not. De la Mare set the most powerful scene of his story on the rooftop of his Cathedral, All Hallows. He had needed to frighten himself a bit, it seems, up on top of Tewkesbury leads, for that.

In any case churches to him were often more sinister than other buildings, and he would be more at ease rambling about outside, among the dead in the graveyard, than within doors. Graham Greene noted that throughout the stories, churches figure more as the stone memorials of a dead religion than as sanctuaries of a living faith. It is noticeable also that they are never once in his work the scene of a wedding or indeed of any comforting or celebrating – nor (as in Hardy) of comic relief.

When he visited St David's for the first time in July 1926, shortly after the story was published, he found it less impressive by far than fancy had painted it. As he strolled about it with Colin, he was amused that a cleric taking round a party, glanced at his face and enquired 'Was he, too, *one of the Cloth?*'

Rambles by car to distant appointments, chauffered by Colin, were a new pleasure. De la Mare had bought a 'Wessex' cheap off Charles Howland at Christmas 1925, and the long sightseeing saunters in Colin's company greatly lightened the burden of lecturing, which in other respects galled him more and more. He said the word LECTURE would be found, after he died, imprinted on his spleen, and whittled down such engagements as much as he dared. Colin had followed a year of work in the studio of Alec Buckels, the artist who decorated the first edition of *Come Hither*, by a brief ambition for the stage. His father did not oppose this, but helped it to lapse. He confided privately to Green-Armytage that his own convictions were steadily against the theatre as a profession, particularly for a man, and that he and Bert had both been very glad they had gone no further with their own bent for it in youth. If he had twinges of conscience about keeping Colin at home instead of urging a career upon him, he quieted them by reflecting that Colin's health had not been strong at school, and that one day he would surely become a writer … Such parenting did nothing to develop enterprise in Colin and he (delightful company that he was) showed little of his own. Meanwhile, only too enjoyably, they explored England together, discussing everything under the sun as they went. Among other plans, they made a pact together, half-serious, that whichever died first should make every possible effort to return and pass a hint to the survivor about what was on the other side.

After much pressure the Newbolts and Ella Coltman prevailed on de

la Mare and Elfie to come with them in August 1926 on their annual
trip to the Alps, where they joined a party of friends. To Newbolt, this
was 'Alauda Maxima', the greatest lark, and afterwards he asserted
defensively 'They enjoyed themselves. They did! They did!' But de la
Mare would tell how he and Elfie fell into each other's arms when the
green fields of England once more trailed past their train window on
their return. All the same, he did enjoy a good deal of it and was a
lively companion, though nothing he did or saw abroad inspired any
writing. Newbolt, like Naomi before him, had confidently predicted
that mountain scenery would inspire de la Mare poetry; but all de la
Mare's creativeness had been fostered by the need to transform the
circumscribed – the emerald slit of world seen through a keyhole into a
suburban garden was what he required, not sublimity at all. At
Tesserete he did, in fact, find himself a keyhole, and was more excited
by what he could see through that than by all the vista of peaks.
Peering through the lock of a long-deserted, weed-grown church, he
spied a mysteriously rich interior, with two tall *new* candles. What
could be the explanation? Here stirred a story or a poem, perhaps, but
the mentions of scenery in his other letters strike no such spark.
Newbolt talked with him all day long, but found 'he remains as elusive
as ever – has even turned into something else. I expected to find him
more English, by contrast, but he seems on the contrary to fall into the
European background and become Southern and French.'[5] Ruefully he
recorded that though the de la Mares had 'done' Lugano, Como and
Maggiore at the rate of a day apiece, 'he and his wife really like best to
go down to Lugano town and buy chocolate and picture postcards. Such
is humanity, such are the Great Poets.'[6]

The success of *Crossings* at the Lyric had of course revived de la
Mare's play-writing ambitions. Some while ago he had laid plans to
collaborate with Rice-Oxley ('R-O' as he was known to the de la Mare
family) on a melodrama; there was to be a doctor in it, and de la Mare
thought the scene should be Brighton. 'I know the doctor – what he is
like, but I don't know what he'll *do* – Can you find some more people?'
he asked R-O, more as if he were engaging a cast of actors than writing
their parts. Nothing came of the collaboration, but by October 1926 de
la Mare had written the piece himself – 'a sort of shudder play' in three
acts, called sometimes *Dr Fleet*, sometimes *The Lady Killer*. He took it
quite seriously, and suggested to Eric Pinker that he should procure an
introduction to the producer, Basil Dean. Green-Armytage, who had
once wanted to be an actor, still took a close interest in the stage. He
advised de la Mare that the doctor's victim, the elderly Mrs Fleet, was
too physically unattractive to hold an audience's sympathy. De la Mare

was argumentative: 'I think her very unattractiveness in person makes the situation more tragic and isn't that tantamount to saying more dramatic?'[7] It was a rather naive view of stagecraft. Another play, *Consolation*, which Pinker sent for an expert reader's opinion, fared no better; the expert damned it (not enough story, characters unattractive, dialogue uninteresting) and thought it too sordid for a music-hall audience. De la Mare was piqued – he had not thought *that* possible. In old age he had a final try at staging his work, sending some of his little one-act early plays to Joyce Grenfell, hoping she might use them as sketches. Honesty compelled her to say that they were unsuitable – poor technically, and too diffuse. At the end of 1926 Naomi finally closed a chapter (so long finished on de la Mare's side) by her marriage to the actor Ernest Milton. This took her away from literary London altogether. By now she had for some years turned in earnest to novel-writing, and de la Mare had helped her constantly with advice on her early fiction. She became very prolific, producing over forty novels in all, and deserving well enough the ready public she found in her day, but in spite of a good style, intelligence and frequent touches of truth to character, her novels have no great imagination. Too often the romantic parts suffer from wish-fulfilment studies in masculine Genius that remind one uneasily of many inferior passages in her letters to de la Mare.

From her marriage on, living by her books, she followed Milton wherever his stage career made it convenient to settle. She broke off many of her old social ties, and became, like her husband, a Roman Catholic. Deliberately, in every way, she set her face towards a completely different path. She and Milton achieved together a long and successful marriage, oddly assorted in some respects, but devoted, even particularly touching – a triumph over unlikeliness by the strong-minded, romantic woman she was, and the histrionic, highly-strung, generous-minded actor. He placed her, for life, on a pedestal of admiration, though not by temperament drawn to her sex. If he minded the place de la Mare had had in her affections, he showed only generosity toward his memory.

Her contact with de la Mare virtually ceased. She came to tea once when he was old, but saw he was not at ease, and so she let matters rest thereafter. For her, sadness inevitably remained.

1927 very nearly marked the end of de la Mare's life. The year began with the usual bouts of illness, put down to influenza, and before a serious infection took hold of him under this disguise, he was busy retelling traditional fairytales for a Blackwell volume, *Told Again*. The infection took a real grip about the beginning of March, and before it was rightly diagnosed, he became very ill indeed. In April a specialist recommended a London nursing home; he hated this, and was thankful to be moved by Florence into her own home in Sussex Place. He was not a good patient; if he wanted anything he must have it, and Florence and Rupert combed London frantically one hot Sunday evening for blocks of ice to put in a tin bath under his bed.

At the beginning of May he had six teeth out under local anaesthetic, and later another five. Dental infection may have been the cause of the more serious trouble which followed an operation on the prostate gland at the end of that month. The physical enemy after this was bacillus coli, but it set up a nervous distress which told against him quite as dangerously as the infection itself. Only the unusual personal influence of the surgeon, Frank Kidd, prevented spiritual malaise from completely vanquishing de la Mare's stamina. He declined into a state of alarming weakness – the will to live seemed paralysed. Jinnie, visiting him at this time, asked if he would like some fruit or flowers. The whisper (impossible for him to resist it) came back: 'Too late for fruit – too soon for flowers.'

One relapse followed another, and Kidd, who loved poetry and deeply admired his patient, grew very anxious. Gradually, however, he gained an ascendancy over the sick man with his own strange personality. Once, when old, asking a friend if he had ever met anyone quite unique and unlike anybody else, a true genius, de la Mare cited Kidd: 'Fancy being a hero-worshipper at 54/5! Anyhow what I owe him only the Scribes Elsewhere could tell.'[8]

Kidd was something of a dandy, a slight figure, with hooded lids over his striking blue eyes, and an autocratic temperament, highly-keyed. He played the violin very well with his small skilful hands: he could wear his wife's French gloves (size 6¼). Many well-known people came under his scalpel, and he was always deeply interested in the workings of their personalities. It was this strong personal sympathy which saved de la Mare from his own apprehensions and depression, perhaps further burdened with an irrational sense of guilt. (He let drop a remark suggesting this was so to Sister de Chantal: 'I believe, somehow, that we are to a very large extent personally responsible for all illness.'[9])

The prostate operation was carried out in the house, because de le Mare pleaded for this. Knowing how alarmed he was, Kidd broke his otherwise invariable rule of avoiding contact with the patient just before an operation (because he himself was always then so strung-up) and went to sit with him until the anaesthetist arrived. To distract him, Kidd plunged into discussion of Hardy's *Dynasts*, and de la Mare forgot everything in sharing this enthusiasm – for himself, he thought it was the finest single poetic achievement of the age, and Kidd was in lively agreement. Next Christmas Kidd (who found de la Mare, so his wife said, the most grateful patient he ever had) received a fine edition of *The Dynasts*, for which de la Mare had even begged from Hardy a line in his own handwriting as inscription.

One day when things were at their worst, Kidd, needing to be absent awhile, peremptorily exacted a promise de la Mare would stay alive until he returned in the morning. De la Mare made an effort of will all through the night – and was aggrieved because Kidd did not arrive before breakfast to see if he had kept his word! To Sister de Chantal he said that one burden of the night hours was the curious belief which took hold of him then 'that one ascends to midnight or one a.m., and then gently descends till dawn. That semi-conscious climb to midnight was a dreadful burden, and I simply can't tell you how interminable the night could seem to be. I'd look at my watch at three, spend a brief lifetime, look at it again, and find it was twenty past. I wonder what our natural [illeg] norm of time really represents.'9 Kidd found an answer to his problem of insomnia in an eccentric Irish hypnotist called Leahy, who had a hot temper and a false leg, which proved a disadvantage. Climbing to his patient's room, sporting a Leander tie and a little drunk, he would succeed in inducing slumber, and would then descend – step, *thump*, step, *thump*. Before he had reached the ground floor the nurse was speeding down to recall him. 'The bloody man!' he would explode, and rushed up again, bursting in on the patient: 'You bloody well go to sleep!'

Soon de la Mare had another and very serious relapse. Word was sent to his children by Ottoline Morrell that they should return at once from Cornwall, where they were taking a respite. When Kidd discovered that they had arrived back in London, that evening, he was much put out: the anxiety of this very anxious family was, he thought, the worst possible thing de la Mare could have about him at this moment – the very fact that he had been considered ill enough to cause this family return would be dangerous. It must be concealed. Accordingly Kidd flatly forbade them to go near him, and they had to speak in whispers while they were in the house at all. Nor did this satisfy Kidd; one of them must return at once, so that letters should arrive from Cornwall to deceive the patient into believing that they were all still tranquilly there. Nobody could say no to Kidd, so Dick returned obediently later that same evening, by rail. He arrived at Newquay at six in the morning, and walked across the fields to St Cubert, where they had been staying. There he found a telegram:

'*DADDY SINKS WE RETURN TOMORROW*.' Horrified, he turned
straight back in his tracks yet again. On the walk back to the station,
the extreme of emotion and fatigue led him to a mystical conviction of
an after-life which supported him through the miserable journey to
London, wondering if he would arrive in time to see his father alive. He
got there to find him – better! The telegram should have read '*DADDY
THINKS WE RETURN TOMORROW*'.

To Elfie this illness was a time of desperate strain, inclined as she
was to expect the worst whenever de la Mare was even the least
indisposed. Sometimes he wilfully played up to her – 'Come further
into the room,' his weak voice would plead, 'I can't quite see you.' Once,
waking from an over-vivid dream of the bottom half of a jar of mixed
pickles, he alarmed her dreadfully by insisting on getting out of bed to
look for the other half. She got out as well – to hide his razor! His
children, as children will, early grew cynically wise to his so-called
delicate health and recognised it for what it was – Elfie never.

Yet it is curious that his interest in *death* shared none of the
negative, morbid tinge there was to his obsession with symptoms. Once
he had come through his Nineties adolescence into the adulthood
brought by marriage and fatherhood, personal survival seems never
again to have been seriously in doubt. He did not seem anxious
personally about dying, from then on, only consumed by desire to probe
the mystery. *Evidence* of an afterlife seemed to him positively to crowd
into this one as life went on – though of its *nature* he was less sure; it
might have its own great dangers. But towards these, and the passage
of death itself, he showed only intense interest – no dread whatever.

His imagination was very active during his illness. A night-nurse
(one he intensely disliked) came to Kidd in real concern about his
sanity, because he insisted he saw a red-bearded intruder creeping
along on the balcony outside the window. He stoutly maintained
afterwards 'He was not in the *least* a hallucination.' It did not need
illness to project such visible visitors from the subconscious. He was
fond of telling how once in quiet mood he became aware of a tiny man's
figure, very actual indeed, in the room. They confronted each other for
a considerable moment of intensity, in broad daylight; then gradually
the visitor began to insinuate his outlines into the polished
convolutions of the grain round a knot in some piece of furniture, and
so gradually abstracted himself altogether into it. He went back no
doubt whither he had originated, that is, among those symbols the
undermind throws up to embody its workings, and which a chance
passivity of sense and will may suddenly attach to the outside world,
as vividly as Blake's Ghost of a Flea.

In this 1927 illness, as before, de la Mare kept close note of the changes of consciousness dangerous disease may produce. Once again, as in 1914, he believed that his whole mental outlook had taken a profound new turn – something utterly unexpected. 'If all the scanty intuition I am possessed of had done its utmost, it couldn't have foreseen for me a fraction of what that experience [the illness] would be – mind and body,' he wrote to Sister de Chantal. 'Taking just trivial things, for example: one's powers of observation become so much more acute. You seem to be able to read the fleeting expressions on a face as quickly as you fall in love with a field of buttercups.'[10] He spoke also, as he had to Naomi after his stay in Guy's, about a curious inward happiness the illness brought, clear as a fountain. Kidd peremptorily declared, since the high temperature and lassitude continued, that his patient must go to Brighton – there he would get well, here in London he would not. As de la Mare was being driven there at speed in an ambulance, he noticed how changed ordinary people looked as they flew past the window – 'like foreigners in a strange country: *and* just a twinge of Traherne'.

Brighton was to de la Mare all his life a kind of talisman – 'Dr Brighton', the health-bringer – ever since his mother had told him about her childhood there. No doubt Kidd took this into account. Sure enough, as soon as he was ensconced in a Hove nursing home, he began to mend, and by the end of September was at last allowed home. Not until he was recovering did the question of Kidd's fee arise at all, and even then it was de la Mare who raised it, not the surgeon who had come to see his patient almost every day during the crisis. The reply was: 'If it would cause you anxiety or difficulty, there isn't any.' Even when de la Mare reassured him, Kidd left it to him to decide the amount. As it happened, the illness does not seem to have brought any severe financial anxiety; de la Mare was well-off enough at this period to bear even the loss of the best part of a year's work, which is what in all it cost him.

Even during that blank stretch he contrived from time to time a trickle of industry. A suggestion of Dick's set him upon a more ambitious task than retelling fairytales: a book of Old Testament stories in his own prose. And when he could not work at all he could still make up stories, and tell them to a niece. He told her about a scrabbling old man who haunted Hill House with a herd of exotic animals, and about another old man whose skin slipped its position, so that his nose protruded into his hat, and his mouth functioned in the region of his elbow. He wondered, meanwhile, if he would ever get back his powers of fiction: 'Perhaps little tea-party tales; and of how the squire's daughter nearly fell into the river, and the curate is not really sallow and narrow, but the son of a baronet Big Game Slaughterer.'[11] The original and subtle tales hurrying from his brain just before the bacillus had struck him down seemed hopelessly out of reach. Misfortune had cut off the most prolific season of good storytelling he had every enjoyed, and his despondent instinct was near the mark. He was not to recover anything like that fertility and pace for more than a decade.

19

The Mundane Thirties

1928 was a year of tedious convalescence. By November de la Mare was telling Newbolt that the whole scene had changed for good – the landmarks were so altered. Not only by his own health, or deaths such as Gosse's and Ellen Terry's. Hardy, so central a figure for him, died in January, while de la Mare himself was suffering a setback, and the *Times* announcement of his death mentioned that among the last things read aloud to him had been 'some de la Mare poems'. Sydney Cockerell, Hardy's close friend and executor, confirmed that a few days before the end, in the middle of the night, Hardy had asked his wife to read him 'The Listeners', and afterwards he said, 'That is possibly the finest poem of the century.'[1]

Ill as he was, de la Mare insisted on attending the packed burial service at Westminster Abbey. He told Naomi: 'I don't want to be more of a snob than necessary, but there certainly were rather odd people there – I couldn't for the life of me, I mean, find any link whatever between them and T.H. One little ferret-like old man as soon as I stood up for a hymn, mounted my chair. There was a wall of such people in front of us, though as I hadn't gone to *see* anything it was not of very much consequence. Only – well, such things don't remind one of the first chapter of *The Return of the Native*.'[2] 'I am sorry with you,' de la Mare wrote to Green-Armytage, 'that he was not buried where he wished to be; still, I have heard that in his will there was a statement that he should be buried there [Stinsford] unless it was publicly desired otherwise. Something to that effect. I remember his actually saying to me, when we were in Stinsford Churchyard together, "That is where I shall be." And he said it as one might refer to going to bed, and looking forward to resuming a book for an hour or two before sleeping, and the same old familiar dreams. Or perhaps he meant simply that he would be glad to get to sleep.'[3] Later on, when asked to do Hardy's life for an 'English Men of Letters' series, de la Mare refused, giving his reason in a curious, revealing phrase – he had 'known Hardy too well'.

In his debilitated state, Dick's suggestion that he should try versions of his beloved Old Testament stories must have seemed to offer a ladder back to his own story-writing; otherwise it is odd that he should have taken up the idea, for he generally held all modernisations of the Bible in utmost scorn – the exact wording of the Authorised Version was almost mystically sacrosanct to him. Yet here he was, attempting his own paraphrase, and in the outcome he steered a rather dull course, losing the immediacy of biblical narrative and yet too hobbled by reverence to say things his own way. Worse, a prudery totally foreign to the Bible creeps into the story of Joseph, falsifying the issue and ruining the drama. De la Mare simply leaves out the sexual motive of Potiphar's wife, together with all mention of Joseph's escape from her clutches, leaving his clothing (that fatal evidence) in her grasp. So her persecution of him is just vaguely ascribed to malice, and Potiphar is given no circumstantial reason to doubt Joseph's good faith. One object of de la Mare's, as he said in his introduction to the book, was to send children of twelve and thirteen to discover the stories for themselves. If so, it was surely unnecessary and foolish, even allowing for the customs of the day in children's reading, to bowdlerise to this extreme, especially as he had, in his own boyhood reading, taken the Bible whole, without a quiver. Forrest Reid regretted the bowdlerising of 'Joseph', but thought it acceptable. Naomi with flat honesty replied to de la Mare's gift of the book: 'I already had the Bible stories and I don't like them – any more than I like the talkie film *The Flood* – but I like to have a copy of them from you.'[4]

Stories from the Bible (1929) was the first of de la Mare's books to be published by Faber's, which Dick had joined in 1927; from now on he was to handle for them almost all his father's prose works, and later, when copyright arrangements with de la Mare's earlier publishers permitted, the poetry. He and his father kept so closely in touch over work that letters hardly had to pass between them. It was a happiness to de la Mare to have a son and publisher so enthusiastic about his work, and a characteristic note from Dick would accompany a manuscript to the printer, asking for a little extra attention, as he was anxious to produce it 'as near as possible to perfection'. Equally characteristic were apologies for 'my father's corrections and dear me what a mess he has made of the proofs!' Infinite patience was needed. If asked to cut, de la Mare would do so, but would almost invariably make so many alterations that he ended by adding still more.

*

In June 1928 his first grandchild was born, Florence's son Nicholas. 'Positive novelties in life,' de la Mare wrote, 'are very rare. I never even faintly realised what a pacifying experience it is to become a grandfather. It is a sort of coming into port, though the why of it lies rather too deep perhaps to be able to show itself.'[5] In July Jinnie became engaged to Donald Ringwood, the young engineer who had sailed away three years before. Her father found it no easier to bear than when Florence had made the same fell announcement; he almost broke down and could hardly utter a word that he should. Jinnie was dancing that August in Deauville, with her mother for chaperone; but marriage would end her dancing days.

Forrest Reid was now at work on the full-length critical study of de la Mare's work he had so long coveted. But it still made de la Mare uneasy that 'F.R.' should be wasting time (as he felt) that ought to be spent upon his own odd, original fiction. However he willingly supplied all the biographical detail asked for, and took a great interest in Reid's critical findings. As far as his own work was concerned, 1929 found him still very low in energies; *Desert Islands* came to completion, and a handful of good short stories, but little else. He wrote little or no poetry, seldom went to London and complained of a sense of sluggishness and drudging. When Newbolt saw him in February he was horrified at the corpulence now framing and spoiling his features, though he 'seemed cheery and well in manner'. It was a phase that passed when full health returned, but at the time his looks put Newbolt in mind (unkindly image) of the tough British matrons who used to run bathing machines in Leech's drawings.

Going through the proofs of Reid's book proved some stimulant, however, and soon after de la Mare was at work on 'Crewe', masterpiece of all his ghost stories. Also, he wrote 'Willows', very good in his Jamesian vein – elaborate, but sure, the account of a visit by a student, writing a thesis, to the home of his subject, an author thought by the world to be dead. Almost the whole story is taken up by the student's conversation with the poet's mother, a formidable woman with 'a slightly mannish and astringent voice', who demolishes the biographical passages in an article written by a friend of the student. (Perhaps the shade of Mrs Brooke stands behind her?) By chance, as he is leaving, vanquished, the visitor meets an old man wandering, simple-minded, in the grounds, who presses a scrap of unintelligible poetry into his hand. The tragedy after all has been a survival, not a death.

After an excursion to Holland, the de la Mares took their 1929 holiday at Instow in Devon, where Rice-Oxley joined them. He was, as ever, a delightfully congenial companion, welcome to all the family, and one of the very few with whom de la Mare would share *silence* as well as talk. They would lean against a wall together looking at a house, without a word, while long tranquil tracts of time went by. Then de la Mare would begin to ask: 'What sort of a person do you think lives in that room?', the idea of a story rising in his mind. Perhaps it was a room with shutters: any little individual detail was enough. Rice-Oxley's humorous, responsive, unaffected attitude was very conducive to imagination, whether de la Mare needed to wind up or unwind.

On a very hot day in September Jinnie was married and he had to walk up the aisle at Taplow to give her away. He wrote about this wedding with grieving, and a kind of unconscious foreboding: 'I am less used to the thought of it now than I was before it occurred, and as is the curious way with humanity I seem to miss her right on into the future, even though there is no possibility, at present at any rate, of her being far away.'[6] Jinnie's marriage led in fact to tragedy, so this time his haunted mood was to have justification, but not at once.

Meanwhile the 1930s were a prosperous, sociable, but somehow tepid decade, de la Mare's best powers only sporadically active, though from time to time he would produce another of his best stories or a good poem. Of course, he kept very busy – some editing, a little selective lecturing, far too many introductions to other men's books, and some adjudicating at poetry-reading competitions – the kind of active, popular literary figure in his late fifties and early sixties of whom the world might well assume that his significant contribution as an artist was over. Yet both this bustle and this fading of creativeness were deceptive.

He was still, at the core, contending with the damage done by that nearly mortal illness, but also he was still recuperating.

*

J.B. Priestley, looking back (the time when he knew de la Mare best was in the 1920s and 1930s), said he did not himself believe in reincarnation, but, supposing he had, de la Mare struck him as how a very great man might appear while resting in some interim span, between two lives of major achievement.[7]

Several close friends of de la Mare's old age variously corroborated this – they might love his work, but the dominant personal impression remained of a man far larger in his own nature – more central, more catholic and more profound – than he ever put into the sum of his work.

Certainly this was true in the 1930s, and in this part of his life a man of morning and evening shades struggles to keep his focus sharp in the flat light of afternoon. The real spring of his art was not in the end aesthetic beauty but spiritual life, and the blight of a dry period is, for such a nature, hardly escapable somewhere in mid-journey.

F.R. Leavis, in *New Bearings in English Poetry* (1932), declared that de la Mare had written himself out, and professed to discover in *The Veil* that the 'unwholesomeness of the fantasy-habit' was implicitly and explicitly admitted at last, and that for this very good reason no further collection of poetry had been forthcoming. 'The magic has ceased to work for Mr de la Mare,' he said, and predicted that he would probably 'not produce much more good poetry'. However, next year, 1933, *The Fleeting and Other Poems* came out; no negligible collection, and there were many more to follow, with some memorable new poetry in every one. Though the drying-up of his verse to a trickle during these middle years depressed de la Mare, he sensibly made the best of what creative energies he had, spending them largely on essays, such as his fine study in May 1930 of Lewis Carroll.

In June 1930 Dick married Catherine Donaldson, in style, at Holy Trinity, Sloane Street. 'From a social point of view,' Newbolt reported, 'it was regarded as a remarkable achievement – a sort of apotheosis of the Delamare family; who could possible have foreseen it in the days when he was floundering in Oil like a survivor of a U-boat crew, and knew nobody West of Croydon, SE? His old diffidence flounders still – before the service began I sat next to him and talked of Islands – told him that M[argaret] and I were married in an island church – and he said "I wish I were in an island church now, a desert island for choice." What his imagination boggled at was the prospect of arming the Lady Albinia Donaldson, the bride's mother, and a lady of some presence, down the aisle at the end of the ceremony. He was lost in astonished admiration of his son's confidence. "Isn't it a most mysterious thing – to see your own son displaying a quality that you know is no part of yourself?" '[8]

Two months after the wedding, fire broke out in the Taplow house, and though the damage was eventually confined to three rooms, it was thought for a time that the whole building might go. It was 7.30 on a Sunday morning, and amidst all, the relieved thought flitted across de la Mare's mind that anyway on this occasion he was excused Lady Desborough's aristocratic breakfast! After the fire he remarked to Rice-Oxley that he was in a way 'rather glad' – it was a change; everything had been going too well. His feeling was not the superstitious one of propitiating Nemesis, but rather a sense of the balance of justice, from his puritan side. No one took freedom from care less for granted; Rice-Oxley, remembering this talk, felt in de la Mare an unusually marked capacity for accepting what went wrong. Early struggles certainly did not make him cling to good fortune once it came. He sat light to it, preferred to remain a bit detached.

A new book of stories came out in September 1930, with a title that would suit any one of his works: *On the Edge*. The stories in it were all of recent years, except the finally rewritten and much revised 'An Ideal Craftsman', held back from both *The Riddle* and *The Connoisseur* because de la Mare had continued to feel dissatisfied with it as too raw, and the woman drawn too crudely and lumpishly – he told Forrest Reid: 'I am not sure she is quite the kind of person Jacobs would have chosen to be murdered by.'[9] The eight stories in this book are much longer than of old, taking up more pages than do fifteen in *The Riddle*. Symbolic tales, already fewer in *The Connoisseur*, have here disappeared completely. Their element lay very close to that of the poems, and they had arisen in the seasons of de la Mare's life when poetry also was frequent. These longer stories, more prosaic but very good of their own kind, have no touch of 'Theeothaworldie'; only three even deal in the supernatural. Violent death by suicide or murder is noticeably a growing preoccupation. When the supernatural does break in, Poe-esque conditions are no longer necessary; the ghost in 'Crewe' needs no background of demon-haunted Cathedral or ruined, romantic Wanderslore – it stalks the broad August daylight of a cornfield, dressed as a scarecrow. The story is entirely narrated in a station waiting-room, purely to supply an ingredient in atmospheric effect. Naomi had laughed at de la Mare long ago for his obsession with railways, rivalling even churchyards as settings for stories. Railways became to him, in fact, what ships were to Conrad or country roads to Hardy: symbols of man's fate, of his mortal transit, thrown among strangers. He spent a great deal of time himself in trains throughout his professional life, and gaunt waiting rooms, deserted country halts, the curve of vanishing rails – uneasy, expectant, open to the unknown, symbols of hiatus – were at once in poetry and in oppressiveness, natural breeding-grounds for his inventive moods.

The other ghost story in *On the Edge* is 'The Green Room', the one set in a second-hand bookshop. The narrator, in an act of kindness, has arranged for a dead girl's poems to be published – but her shade shows its contempt by bringing the plaster ceiling down upon the newly-minted volumes. Nobody else's ghosts come back for quite de la Mare's purpose – that is, not to alarm the living so much as to test them, to show up the shallowness of human daily life against an enigmatic, intenser reality beyond it.

The girl had committed suicide, killing herself with strychnine, and the old bookseller says ' "It isn't exactly the poison I myself should choose for the purpose. It erects up the body like an arch, sir. So." With a gesture of his small square hand Mr Elliott pictured the effect in the air.' This is a repetition, almost word for word, of that description de la Mare had overhead at the age of five. His lifelong interest in murder cases engrossed him to the point of obsession at this period. Several of his friends shared it, notably Forrest Reid and E.H.W. Meyerstein. Reid sent him many accounts of trials from the collection lately bequeathed him by A.L. Lewis, a fellow-Ulsterman, eccentric father of C.S. Lewis, who had shared Reid's own passion for criminology. Lewis senior had been plagued for years by dreaming that he had committed a murder, and the problem was how to dispose of the body. De la Mare himself had several such dreams; in one, brooding in agony over what he had done, he started up, hoping that his crime (perpetrated on someone he loved dearly – in one of his accounts, a sister) might prove to be 'only a dream'. Going upstairs to a chest of drawers, he pushed in a hand among the clothes he had been wearing on the fatal day, only to feel the thick tweed of a jacket clotted and sticky with blood. A psychologist might see in such dreams the expression of impulses particularly suppressed by so very tender-hearted a daylight self. They also have a bearing, perhaps, on an irrational sense of personal responsibility he suffered, voiced in a remark put into the mouth of the Midget, who says she holds herself mysteriously responsible not just for what she does, but in some sense for the whole of her world.

Meyerstein, another of de la Mare's murder-addict cronies, had been in Roger Ingpen's and John Freeman's circle from early days. Versatile and very well-informed, whether on murder, music or metre, he was also captious and difficult, with a trying passion for reading his own poems aloud. (Once, asking his audience if they heard them better with his false teeth in or out, he instantly demonstrated the alternatives.) De la Mare was ready to put up with almost anything for Meyerstein's talk – 'rich as a plum pudding' – but his malice could wound badly. Once, in 1946, he wrote to de la Mare out of pure mischief-making, in snide praise of his 'unconscious and instinctive' tactics in evasiveness. He chose for cruel illustration some story that Edward Thomas (whom Meyerstein had never met) had told of de la Mare 'that when he talked to you he felt that he was talking to someone the other side of a gate. And, the other day when I read your preface to a posthumous collection of his verses, a very charming preface, by the way, I registered 'the

gate is removed BECAUSE THOMAS IS DEAD.'[10] De la Mare's
protesting reply shows how this hurt, for there was nobody alive now
who could take away the sting of the suspicion, once again, that
Thomas had found him less of a bosom friend than he had needed, or
than he himself had so eagerly desired to be. He begged Meyerstein not
to hint, but to tell him what the occasion was: 'E.T. and I were very
close friends and in looking back I am conscious of no obstruction of
that kind in the talks we had.'[11] His reply is of unusual length, and
Meyerstein, who had an adroit intuition for placing a barb, must have
delighted in his success.

*

Instead of accepting the knighthood again offered in 1931, he
had the more congenial honour of presenting, in his turn, a silver
medal* to Sassoon, who wrote him a satirical verse-letter describing
how long de la Mare's speech would be, so that finally the audience
would rebel and cry

> 'What's more we think it best you should
> Withhold that silver disc. We've found
> That S. Sassoon's no bloody good …
> Now, what price Ruby Ports all round?'[12]

Sassoon was still as agreeably schoolboyish as ever. This year driving
near Taplow one evening with Edmund Blunden, who also knew de la
Mare, though not so well, Sassoon suggested they should call, but that
as it was already late they had best reconnoitre first. Just as if they
were back on the Western Front, they skulked more or less on all fours
by way of the garden, to reach up and peer over the windowsill. Seeing
the family within, standing about by the fireplace, plainly preparing to
go to bed, they crept away again, still doubled up, by the way they had
come, and said nothing of the matter.

The marriages of the three elder children had proved no such
devastating chasm as de la Mare had feared – they still came home
often. Jinnie and Donald, and the three still living in Hill House (de la
Mare, Elfie and Colin) all went to Paris and then Deauville for a
summer fortnight. They did little conventional sightseeing. What de la
Mare liked best was to loaf by the Seine watching, say, the professional
dog-washer at work, with his sulphur bright on the dog's back. The
more conspicuous sights of Paris rather bored him. Only the French

---

* The A.C. Benson Medal, given by the Royal Society of Literature.

countryside had any great appeal – the leagues of lanes between quiet harvest fields and woods, 'on the sane side of Deauville'.

Months of 1932 went by with little to mark them but country-house visits and lectures. Forrest Reid applied his old cures for writer's block – why not send him what chapters of *Mr Brush* (the fox novel) did exist, and see if any comments he could make might re-start the flow? But de la Mare jibbed. He spoke of two other schemes jigging about in his skull; but there they too remained. One idle day he tried his hand at a diary. Headed 'A Day's Information August 4th', it ran to several closely-written pages on one uneventful day's doings. He did not try a second entry.

A week or two later, he went off for a second visit to Stanway. Barrie and Cynthia Asquith agreed in finding him the 'most undisappointing' of all poets to meet in the flesh. Chesterton was there too, and de la Mare observed to Green-Armytage: 'Apart from the head, Barrie is a sort of Chesterton *in parvo*, of all but the same angle of rotundity, and to watch them together gladdens the eye. I love talking to Barrie. He is always full of the crispest and most sagacious reminiscences, and I always feel that he has never yet written his *own* book. *Circumspice*, and tell me who has.'[13]

There was warm admiration and affection between him and Chesterton, who published a good many de la Mare stories and poems in his *Weekly* during the 1920s, and praised him highly several times in print. After one meeting with him, de la Mare wrote to Green-Armytage: 'It is the *substance* of everything that he does that is so astonishing, quite apart from his urbanity and humour.' When Chesterton died in 1936, he left de la Mare grieving 'with a kind of incredulity', and de la Mare wrote him a verse-epitaph calling him a 'Knight of the Holy Ghost'. (Sassoon's phrase, when the knighthood was offered to de la Mare – 'all poets of true metal are Knights of the Holy Ghost' – must have got stored away.)

At Stanway, a very beautiful house, de la Mare was enchanted, looking out early from his window, to see a little woman in black in the graveyard close by, scrubbing her husband's tombstone – just as once, years before, he had looked into Bemerton Church near Netherhampton and glimpsed a tiny woman kneeling up on the altar to polish the brass candlesticks and had thought how much George Herbert would have liked to see her there. Now, he wrote about the scrubbing widow of Stanway the stanzas called 'Beneath a Motionless Yew'.[14]

That poem had a handful of companions: 'The Railway Junction', 'The Slum Child', 'The Spark' – the first cluster of verses for a very long time. He sent them to Forrest Reid, telling him despondently that even the lecture he had been at work on was impossible to finish – an old one on 'Craftsmanship' he was enlarging, and for which notes and drafts survive in piles (he had half a mind to make a book of it). Reid pounced on the poems with pleasure, and gave some blunt advice:

> I think you are far better scribbling your rhymes than doing your craftsmanship stuff ... The passage you read to me, about words, did not interest me. There you have it quite plainly; but that doesn't mean the rest wouldn't. Only I don't see why you shouldn't leave that kind of thing to the professors. Your job is something a great deal more human – which they can't do.[15]

Perhaps this influenced de la Mare; certainly his interest in publishing another collection of poems revived a little. He told Reid he had about thirty old ones, and a few new pieces, enough for a small book. One of the new ones was 'The Owl',[16] and he turned to his Roman Catholic friends for judgement, as it introduced the figure of Christ. The story was based on the old legend Hamlet refers to – 'They say the owl was a baker's daughter.' Christ appears as a wandering beggar turned from her door by the girl, who is thereupon changed into an owl, outcast of the shades. The de la Mare poem suggests that she shows pique because the stranger will not respond to her advances. Sister de Chantal was shocked by this suggestion that the Lord could be attractive sexually. Nonplussed, de la Mare left Green-Armytage to arbitrate. He soothed the nun and defended the poet, and 'The Owl' was duly published.

He worked at the new collection of poems during the early part of 1933, through his usual spring 'flu. During his second bout of it, his son-in-law Rupert Thompson took his place and read a lecture for him. Ten minutes before time was up, as he ploughed on through page after page, his horrified eye fell upon a notice blocked out in large capitals, at the foot of the next: HALF TIME! In March, when de la Mare had to speak at Eton, the same thing happened. He had been extemporising for once, outlining the story that introduced *Come Hither*. He had nowhere near finished when he saw there were only ten minutes left, so wound up with the pithy peroration 'Well, that's that!', and read poems for the final minutes.

He was probably writing 'The Feckless Dinner Party',[17] one of the new collection's most striking poems, during these weeks, for he sent it out in March for magazine publication. It is perhaps the sole recognition in all his verse of Eliot's existence in the living world of poetry around him: a piece consisting almost entirely of snatches of modern conversation, satirically caught, much as in 'The Waste Land'.

Eight guests are paired to go down to dinner, and the fragments of dialogue in which each character is sketched display a sharpness of ear reminiscent of Katherine Mansfield. But the butler who leads them astray is called Toomes, and the party are swallowed in the underworld, leaving the house (perhaps it is Earth after Man has come and gone) to the sunbeams, with all the smart, vain chatter hushed. It is a thirties variant on his old theme of the world left emptied, after mankind. In 'The Listeners' he had treated it as romance:

> 'We wake and whisper awhile,
>   But, the day gone by,
> Silence and sleep like fields
>   Of amaranth lie.'[18]

Very few poems in the new collection, *The Fleeting* (1933), are inspired by happiness or joyful wonder; few refer to childhood, though a good number are compositions of a long while back – including that early 'Robin' Mary Coleridge had taken exception to. The general tone is much more pessimistic, and the critics all noticed this; one heading went so far as to run 'A Poet Loses Faith'. Melancholy, remorse, the lost past, life's cheating and disillusion are the main themes. That said, one may pick out one or two poems as perfectly child-eyed as 'Tom's Angel', or 'Comfort', with its philosophic cat on the warm hearthstone. Laurence Binyon wrote in sympathy as always, impressed by de la Mare's 'power and subtlety of epithet – true sign of the poet', but he admitted (apologetically) that he could not make out what happened to the feckless diners, and put in a warning, too, against taking Hardy's manner and themes: 'I like better the poems where you are most you.'[19] He seems to have felt that Hardy's influence must be behind the deepening pessimism. Nor did he like *The Fleeting*'s longer poems – and apart from 'The Owl' they are indeed the weakest in the book.

At Netherhampton in May, as de la Mare and Newbolt paced up and down the walled garden, they wondered what was the truth of the rumours from Europe. The unfamiliar name of Hitler cropped up. But while they were together the two took the old happiness in the old way together, not guessing it was for the last time. They played bowls once again, and talked not by the hour but by the three hours together, – de la Mare speculating at a moment's notice on Blake, on Jeans's astronomy, on telepathy, on Yeats – Newbolt feeling 'rather like Alice in Wonderland talking with a Dabchick – you can imagine her, or me, asking an intelligent question or making a rather high-class allusion or quip – but instead of answering it the Dabchick goes down "Bob" and comes up again forty yards away flirting his tail.'[20] Just as it always had been.

They had barely taken their opportunity in time. Directly after de la Mare left, the weather turned thundery, and on the very hot June 6, Newbolt, rehearsing for a local George Herbert pageant, seemed as if shattered by the sultriness, very ill, even astray in his memory. This illness, so unheralded and never certainly diagnosed, soon cut him off from active life by a curious detachment. A pane of glass seemed to slide between; his mind remained perfectly clear behind it, but lost all impulse to respond. In his last few years, spent in Ella Coltman's house on Campden Hill, he became a parchment shadow of himself.

To visit him was a sad ordeal, and de la Mare shrank from it. Perhaps the overthrow of the inner citadel in a personality he had revered and depended upon was a particularly cruel blow to his own sense of security. He was conspicuously ill at ease in the same way around this time when visiting his admired surgeon Kidd in the melancholic decline which preceded his death. De la Mare could not lose his self-concern in sympathy on either occasion, could not throw off constraint and personal dismay with his accustomed outgoing warmth. Margaret Newbolt was very understanding; she told de la Mare, after one of his very few visits, that she knew what it cost him 'to see Harry and not to see him'. All the same, these were situations he did not manage at all well.

In October 1933 his last collection of new children's stories came out, *The Lord Fish* – by far his best. Unlike his stories for adults, where from first to last the best and worst came along erratically intermixed, his children's tales had developed steadily in excellence. This time, too, there was a genuine affinity between the imagination of the illustrator, Rex Whistler, and his own. Though de la Mare did protest a little at the portrait medallion included in the jacket design, because it 'gave him a nose like Hosea'.)

He took up again the abandoned novel *Mr Cat* but by the end of February 1934 he had embarked on a new book, which rapidly blossomed.

It sprang (in the fashion of *Desert Islands*) from a superabundance of material he had amassed over the past year and a half just for a lecture on 'Children and Writing'. He now planned the book as another anthology with an essay-introduction, but it soon developed into a full-length disquisition, profusely illustrated by long extracts from the juvenilia of notable men and the early chapters of autobiographies. The three major anthologies (*Come Hither, Behold This Dreamer* and *Love*) together with *Desert Islands* and this book, *Early One Morning*, all composed between 1921 and 1942, form one distinct genre in his work; for the prose studies are so nearly anthologies, and the anthologies each such a comprehensive survey of one theme, assembled in mosaic. He collected no random miscellanies. The mosaic of other men's words remained strongly expressive of his own mind and personality: subtle, specific, digressive: suspicious of abstraction, formula, and generalisation: deeply romantic and yet energetically rational as well. Truth presented itself to him as linked and held in balance by so many filaments of association that he found it less easily distorted if these were laid side by side, not trimmed too tidily by the systematic intellect. The great forerunner of the kind of book he evolved to answer these needs is Burton's *Anatomy of Melancholy*, such a favourite of Edward Thomas's, who had introduced him to it in early days.

This second attempt at a prose *Anatomy* was much better designed than *Desert Islands*. Both cost him great effort, and *Early One Morning* the most. He and his secretary, now Olive Jones (an indispensable helper for a decade), read enormous numbers of autobiographies in search of material. De la Mare spent most of 1934 on this task, laying aside stories and poems almost completely. When he first decided to make a book of the material, he already had so much that he expected to bring it out by September; but as time went on he extended his aims, wanting to include everything of any note in the childhoods of all English writers. He said the affair had become like that tree in Arizona which grew so tall it took two men and a boy to see to the top. By the time the year was out and the book in proof, he was exhausted. The autobiography of his own early days, which Forrest Reid had so often urged on him, is really here in *Early One Morning*, floating in fragments between those of other men. Many of the memories most significant for him find a nook here, and a scatter of anecdotes also about his own children – such as that shrill indignant voice (Jinnie's probably) 'expostulating from an upper room into the silence of the universe: "Daddy, *can* you cuddle God?" '[21]

The full social life of Taplow continued, Colin still at home, but Elfie often ill and needing rest. Though very few outsiders knew it, she was seventy-two this year, and the bustle of activity still natural to de la Mare at sixty-one was telling on her. Jinnie and her husband had moved and were living in Lincoln; she found domestic life in a provincial town lonely and monotonous, and began to be unhappy. This small cloud of distress, which was gradually to encroach on and destroy her marriage, was already a threat on de la Mare's horizon. For a long while it would remain something he perhaps unconsciously refused to face. But at present he and Elfie only looked forward eagerly to the birth of another grandchild – Jinnie was expecting a baby next spring. (The child, Stephen, was born after a very difficult labour, and she never had another.)

Florence and Rupert Thompson had moved to Penn in Buckinghamshire, a large, comfortable, contented home where de la Mare spent, this year, a particularly happy Christmas. Five months later, he reverted to the matter:

> My particularly dear Babbie [his pet name for Florence from childhood]
> ... And now, dearest heart, I have got you at my mercy, I must tell you what a lovely time I had at Christmas. It is true I came away a little hungry – considering the Season; and regretted that everyone was so quarrelsome and the dear children so – childish. On the other hand I definitely (as they say) enjoy those I love having nicer presents than (e.g. rather *weighty* dictionaries) are bestowed by my dear ones on *me*. It's so difficult to be really kind and considerate to the aged; and you made, and your noble husband made so many many disjointed efforts.[22]

And so on and so on. This style of foolery was the usual way of the overflowing affection between them, winding up abruptly 'All blessings, my own dear; I'm longing to see you again', and signed: D. 'D' was beginning to stand for 'Danda', his grandchildren's version of 'Grandfather', rather than for 'Daddy'. The grandchildren had already noticed that one thing made him unlike other elders of their acquaintance. Tillie, Dick's little daughter, was overheard enquiring of a small friend, 'Have you a *laughing* Danda, like mine?' That pleased him very much.

*

After the toil of *Early One Morning*, de la Mare had to deliver to the Royal Society of Literature a lecture on *A Midsummer Night's Dream*, presenting his theory (based on internal evidence) that it is of mixed authorship, a rather brave venture (and his only one) into controversial textual criticism. Moreover, it earned high professional praise.[23] The Shakespearian scholar Dover Wilson had already claimed that the discrepancy in the play between the jingling lines, wooden and end-stopped (especially in the lovers' dialogue), and the fine ones mixed with them, must be due to a later revision of an early draft; he confessed in the *Tribute* for de la Mare's seventy-fifth birthday that, had he had the courage, he too would have claimed that this poor and inexpressive early version was not by Shakespeare at all.

The next task was to prepare a new 'Collected Poems', from de la

Mare's output since 1919. But how was he to interpret the word
'Collected' with work so miscellaneous? What about his comic
collection *Stuff and Nonsense* (1927)? Could the Nonsense be included
as having links with the child-poetry, and the Stuff – the merely
humorous verses – be left out? He soon discovered that no two advisers
agreed which was which. In the end, *Poems 1919 to 1934* included the
songs from *Crossings*, rhymes from the *Mulgars*, almost all *Flora* and a
few more childish pieces, but nothing from *Stuff and Nonsense* or *A
Child's Day*, nor the *Ding Dong Bell* epitaphs.

   Meanwhile Forrest Reid still pleaded for *Mr Cat* – could he not read
it as it stood, however bad de la Mare thought it? But he was too late.
De la Mare was absorbed in a new long short story, one of his finest,
'The Trumpet', about two small boys of the sort of age Reid was
describing in his novel *The Retreat*. Very likely reading Reid's
manuscript had brought the subject of boyhood to the front of de la
Mare's mind. In his own tale, one boy, dared by the other, climbs up to
the carved angel, who is blowing the last trump, standing on a high
tomb in the church where they have trespassed by night. He falls to his
death. The story cost de la Mare much labour, and left him finally still
dissatisfied.

   In mid-January 1936, Roger Ingpen, now sixty-seven, fell suddenly
ill, and a week later was dead. The shock to Elfie who had already been
ill, at the year's end, with bronchitis, needing a nurse, was
overwhelming. It was a hard blow for de la Mare himself. Roger had
been prolific in his quiet career, and had become a respected Shelley
scholar, but he had only a hundred and twenty-eight pounds in the
world to leave wife and daughter. Sharp worry and a press of business
for them (when he was quite unfit for it) compounded de la Mare's
grief. So did the usual gloom after 'flu, and so did deaths of other
friends. He longed for the anodyne of work, but exhausted himself
whenever he tried it, continuing to run a high temperature. If he
worked at all, Elfie became overwrought; she could not control her
anxieties for his health. They were thoroughly bad for each other, and
the atmosphere of dismay in the home was oppressive.

   Then providence took a hand. The very day after Roger died, Elfie's
nurse (who had already demanded a salary rise) now requested a day
off to see the King's funeral procession. The Middlesex Hospital was
rung up for a replacement, and the nurse who chanced to be on call at
that moment was a Sister Nathalie Saxton. Directly she arrived, she
had a wonderful effect on the gloom and disarray of the household,
shedding reassurance on all, de la Mare included. 'N', as she very soon
became known to the family, was a born nurse, tireless, devoted, with

clever hands and heart. Much later on de la Mare told her (and it suited her) that she was like a mandarin duck, cheerfully riding out the waters of any trouble. Very capable, she was quite without the usual unattractive side-effects of efficiency. In her nursing she always put the patient's wishes and contentment before routine. On this first occasion she stayed about two months, long enough for de la Mare to come to rely on her so much that he did not want her to leave. But by then Elfie and he were so much recovered, N felt that she should go on to patients in more urgent need.

She will be so important in de la Mare's story that she needs here some fuller introduction. She came of Welsh and Gloucestershire country stock, and had caught typhoid from a child patient in her first months as a nurse. She continued at work, with a temperature of 105, only admitting to a headache; after the illness was diagnosed she was away a year. As soon as she returned, she caught diphtheria, and was away for another six months, warned that one more disaster would mean giving up the profession. In later life dogged by bronchitis and asthma, she became very slight and pale. Almost anyone else would have owned themselves beaten. She had other qualities as well; her family went in for a good deal of ardent amateur painting and crafts, and anything skilfully-made caught her eye. She had very little formal education, but possessed an inborn taste, and a sense of poetry in living. She was now in her twenties. De la Mare became at once very much attached to her.

Meanwhile Sister de Chantal had become disturbed about his spiritual safety, by a review of *Poems 1919 to 1934* which claimed that he entrenched himself in faery lands and looked out on a spectre of Nothingness which he had to exorcise by a spell of words. De la Mare turned as always to Green-Armytage for comfort, who stoutly defended the freedom to doubt, and observed: 'Very few of us get much further in the Creed than "Credo in unum Deum, Patrem Omnipotentum, factorem coeli et terrae". *After* that (for the man is mentally deficient who can't go even that distance) we all begin to wobble.'[23a] De la Mare said he agreed entirely, and in his reply came as near as he ever did to a definition of his own position:

It isn't just mouthing and quibbling and seeking cover that makes one cautious at last concerning the meaning of one's terms. I learnt that lesson long ago in fumbling over lectures. I entirely agree with you about that first sentence, for example: Credo in unum Deum; yet even at that should still speculate (on my own account) as to what I meant by maker, earth, heaven.

A lot of qualifying follows, after which he continues:

> To all of which no doubt the plain man would say, 'you mean you find it
> impossible to say what you do believe?' And to that I should say Yes;
> except in the degree you mention. And I couldn't do that even a fraction
> as well as you can. In brief, what we believe is inherent in the state and
> attitude of our spirit and being, however impracticable it may be to
> express it in reason, & however far we may fail to remain faithful to it
> and to its implications. This of course is wholly between ourselves.[24]

It was a tribute to Green-Armytage that he would 'speak out' at all on
such a subject.

Rosalind, Roger's daughter, had fallen in love with a young naval
officer, Raymond Hawkins, soon after her father died, and they very
quickly became engaged; de la Mare, highly alarmed, felt himself
responsible for her in Roger's place, and called for a speedy interview
in order to grill the interloper thoroughly on his character, prospects
and intentions. The two men were closeted a long while together, and
Rosalind waited nervously with the rest of the family for the verdict.
When the door opened the two came out, obviously on the best of terms,
laughing and talking. Asked how the young man had managed so
easily to satisfy every practical anxiety, de la Mare revealed that he
had never put any of his prepared questions at all; something had
sidetracked him at once into discussing what it would be like to run a
fish-and-chip shop, and that is all they had, in fact, discussed. It
seemed to have disposed of the situation.

*

A new volume of stories, *The Wind Blows Over*, came out in October
1936, and won high praise from Grahame Greene and Edwin Muir. It
returns to a vein more poetic and visionary than *On the Edge*, but still
below *The Riddle* (except perhaps in 'The Trumpet'). One tender,
domestic story, 'Physic', is interesting biographically because the
interior sketched is plainly suggested by Anerley, on such an evening
as Elfie and Colin must often have passed when he was little, with
childish illnesses causing exaggerated anxiety, and the threat of a
break-up of the marriage hanging in the air. The tenderness in the
portrait of the wife (through whose eyes all is seen) gives striking proof
of reconciliation. Obviously de la Mare understood intimately just
what Elfie had gone through on his account.

A poorly-adapted broadcast of *Henry Brocken* in February 1937
stimulated him to write something specifically for radio – the story
'Odd Shop', chiefly a dialogue between a customer and a shopkeeper

who sells nothing but *sounds*. They come packed in little separate boxes: a cricket, a gale near St David's, milk dropping from a teaspoon, the whisper an evening primrose makes when its petals 'first gradually, then, as if its very being had so decided, unfurl in the cool of the evening'. Towards the end the customer is directed to turn the knob on a box not for sale. The shopkeeper says it is precious to him – 'It cost a friend of mine his son.' the customer repeats what he hears, a low, cold, small, unfaltering voice: 'No, no it can't be done. It can't be done. No, no, not even for him ... It can't, it can't be done' – the voice of conscience, the shopkeeper tells him. 'And yet I am still a little uncertain that it wasn't the voice of what they call the ego, Sir.' Finally, as a present, he presses into the customer's hand the box that holds, barely articulate, the voice of advancing age. It is a very suggestive and fascinating little story, perfectly adapted to the medium.

Troubles continued – in fact worsened. De la Mare and Elfie fell ill again; he had three weeks of bronchitis, there was no secretary. Olive Jones had broken down herself and had to leave. There was no parlourmaid nor 'parlourman'. De la Mare, much harassed, resorted to easy work, writing rhymes to the pictures for children of the young illustrator Harold Jones. He enjoyed doing *This Year: Next Year* – any work was a relief from worry – but the rhymes keep too close an eye to the mannered pictures, and seldom take off into his own world.

He took his low spirits and Elfie's alarmingly failing vitality to Brighton. Acrimonious references to rich hotel-haunting Jews abound in his letters from there. Such remarks were normal among Englishmen before the war and the horrors of Hitler's Final solution sealed the lips of their generation, and in the 1930s jokes about money were pinned on Jew or Scotsman interchangeably, by mere convention. All the same, de la Mare's grumbles are noticeably frequent, and are part of a bundle of not very serious but quite definite personal prejudices – he did not love dogs as a race, nor the Japanese, nor the Americans (much as he loved individual American friends). On this level of feeling, he did not like Jews either.

He launched his 1938 volume of verses, *Memory and Other Poems*, without so much heartsearching as of old. Humble and straightforward, he worked on simply, following the impulse just as far as it led, grateful for its recurrence at all. He assumed it was November or December with him now (prematurely, as it proved), but still, whether the new poems were good or not, it was best to 'Sing while you can'. If the songs were shorter and sadder, that was part of the changing season, and to be accepted as such. Forrest Reid had frankly said he did not think the new collection, shown him in manuscript for his selection, up to de la Mare's highest standard. 'Your best poetry was, I think, always more narrative than reflective, though in a sense the two were combined. But it was the pictures, the stories, that most had the little shock of strangeness in their beauty. Anyhow, of course, we want these new things, and there isn't the slightest reason why you should be dubious about them.'[25]

An older voice of counsel had fallen silent, would not utter a word of praise of the new collection. On 19 April 1938 Harry Newbolt's long fading ended quietly, in Ella's house, with Margaret watching over him by night and Ella by day. Writing to Margaret, de la Mare affirmed again his sense, as always after the death of a friend, 'that he is at least as close then in presence, as he ever was in life'.[26] It is more than many a committed Christian believer can claim.

He wrote a tribute in *The Times*, and later the entry on Newbolt in the *Dictionary of National Biography*, over which he took endless pains. But his deepest feelings he put into a brief memoir, next to another by Ralph Furse, in a little volume of Newbolt's later poems, collected by Margaret, who called it by the title of one of them, *A Perpetual Memory*. Fashion had long left Newbolt aside, and this collection is scarcely known, but it contains poems better deserving preservation than most of those rousing sea songs which had made their splash in the Nineties. De la Mare was right to claim: 'his deepest, quietest, most precious poems came later.'[27]

De la Mare dedicated his own *Memory and Other Poems* to Poppy and Roger, and there is a poem in it, 'Brother and Sister', surely written with Poppy in mind – hers, 'old, now', the 'eager clear blue eyes, / And lines of laughter along the cheek.' The book's title was apt enough; the poems dwelt much on the past – as far back as his own earliest childhood 'down by the full-bosomed river'. Looking back, his view of life was bathed in gratitude, so that though the sadness Forrest Reid noticed, and the thought of death, are certainly there, they are not disturbing, as they were in *The Fleeting*, when it was the predicament of present and future that still obsessed him. There is less questioning altogether, less ghostliness, more a thoughtful telling-over of small familiar beauties of common day. With this resigned mood came clearer expression; many of these poems are lovely for their lapidary brevity, such as 'Swallows Flown':

> Whence comes that small continuous silence
> 　Haunting the livelong day?
> This void, where a sweetness, so seldom heeded,

Once ravished my heart away?
As if a loved one, too little valued,
Had vanished – could not stay?

As usual, there are some poems in the book of much earlier date;
'Courage' may go as far back as the 1914 war, and 'Dry August Burned'
belongs to the Dene Cottage days of Florence's small girlhood.

Green-Armytage now urged a collection of the *Times Literary
Supplement* reviews, and in August 1938 de la Mare began collecting
for this; but it was soon obvious that lectures and reviews together
would provide enough for three books at least. He calculated that the
TLS had published at least 300,000 words from his inkpot – still the
same one his headmaster had handed him when he left St Paul's. He
decided when putting together *Pleasures and Speculations*, during the
next two years, to confine the book to essays based only on his lectures.
He kept the reviews for the much later volume *Private View*. He had
resigned his Professorship at the Royal Society of Literature, deciding
to cut out lecturing almost completely this year, and the car was taken
out of retirement and sold. Colin in any case was no longer available as
driver and companion to sweeten lecture-travel. He had been at work
the past four years at the Book Society.

Most of de la Mare's energy was absorbed now by his new anthology,
on dreams, which he was rapidly assembling. So much reading and
brooding on the subject of dreaming stirred up the dreamer in himself,
and gave him restless nights; but he was pleased to find that faculty
still active. Some expert had worried him by pronouncing dreams to be
uncommon after the age of sixty, and he had feared the withdrawal of
what had always been one of his greatest pleasures. After the actual
collecting for the book, there remained the introductory essay, and he
confided to Forrest Reid, once embarked on it: 'I doubt if I have ever
found anything so deadly.' It was a complicated theme, for he had
extended his brief from a study of dreaming proper to an exploration of
the whole nature of imagination. Yet work, however exacting, was
some antidote to the menace in the news, as August advanced. The
scope of the book stretched out to examine any kind of consciousness
known to man, and its effect on imagination – whether asleep, awake,
or in the guessed-at state of death. De la Mare seemed to be intent,
once and for all, against the threat of war, to affirm and illustrate his
case for imagination as the supreme activity of man. Later, when the
war was at its height, he made another such deliberate gesture with
his final anthology, celebrating Love.

Meanwhile, as the tension continued, he broke out to Green-
Armytage: 'When, and in what, is this atrocious crisis going to end?

Imagine merely the waste of spirit *only* it is the cause of.'[28] Throughout, he was Chamberlain's man, and he would argue for an hour together with Rupert Thompson on the telephone about this. He was still stoutly maintaining in November: 'I don't think myself that Neville Chamberlain could have done anything else than ensure peace at Munich, knowing as he did the state of France etc.' He remained obstinately of the same conviction, and would never admit in after years that he had been mistaken.

He suggested to Lord Desborough that he might give up the tenancy of Hill House next Lady Day – it was much too big for them now, with Elfie's health grown so precarious and servants hard to come by. A London flat might be a better home. But the Desboroughs would not hear of it, and, perhaps in deference to their wishes, no immediate further action was taken. Next year, fate would take the matter into its own hands. Meanwhile, to the guests who still flocked there, the hospitality at Hill House went on just as ever. Edith Sitwell came, and was much struck by the magical arbutus at the door. She told de la Mare that he and Yeats had been the two inspirations of her youth. (However, on another occasion she dismissed his work as charming but slight.)

For a while after the Munich tension was over, life resumed its old pattern. Ralph Hodgson came and went for the last time in November, descending out of the blue for an evening in his old fashion. He seemed in excellent spirits, and told de la Mare about his new poem, 'The Muse and the Mastiff'. De la Mare was intensely interested, and thought it sounded the best thing Hodgson had done. He had almost finished it in Japan, but in fact he never did bring himself to complete it. And alas, when de la Mare finally saw it, privately printed, in 1942, he hardly knew how to reply to Hodgson. He wrote to Sassoon: 'I can't make head or tail of it – and as it's about a dog the latter has importance ... Why publish it like this in fragments with no gloss; a few words might have sufficed.'[29] Over the years to come, whenever news of Hodgson came to de la Mare or Sasson, they would exchange it, eagerly and regretfully, and de la Mare and Hodgson corresponded with all the old affection to the end. But Hodgson himself he never saw again, with all his moods – the saturnine, the choleric, and the delightfully genial.

Rice-Oxley came the Christmas after Munich, partly as an emissary from Keble College to offer an honorary fellowship, something that gave de la Mare particular pleasure, as the precedent had been Hardy, similarly honoured by Queen's. At the end of January, Yeats died. Though of late years he and de la Mare had met quite often, they had never become, as men, closer than friendly acquaintance, and as artists they had continued to regard each other with a mutual mixture of interest, admiration and considerable reservation. Yeats's death left de la Mare the sole genuine heir of the Romantic Movement alive. There is no question which poet had the greater range of vital talents, yet arguably it is de la Mare who had the profounder insight into what so occupied them both – Mystery. David Cecil once remarked that de la Mare's, though the smaller window, looked on a farther horizon; and that does justice to them both.

*

In February 1939 de la Mare consented to join the Athenaeum, as had been repeatedly urged on him in bygone years by Newbolt; Max Beerbohm had added his persuasion, but de la Mare had always jibbed. Once he accepted, it became a convenient place for meeting friends. A fellow-member whom he now began to see a good deal was Owen Barfield, one of that close-knit group of friends which embraced so many of the most interesting symbolist imaginations of the day, including C.S. Lewis, Charles Williams and Tolkien. He made Barfield's acquaintance through the latter's scholarly study *Poetic Diction*; Barfield's theories on words attracted and interested him deeply, and they also had long discussions on anthroposophy and the life-work of Rudolf Steiner, of whom Barfield was an ardent adherent.

When the proofs of *Behold This Dreamer* arrived, de la Mare sighed to Florence that it was like having a dead horse in the house. After they were all sent off, fatigue swept over him. He wrote to Green-Armytage, who himself was in a state of aridity, pressing his usual panacea – *write* something.

He went on:

> I wish there could be any consolation in saying how often I share the experience of 'that wave of utter dulness', leagues different from anything in the nature of boredom, and as if life's tide had gone out, leaving nothing but a waste of arid sand ... there is this tide – didn't Alice Meynell speak of it? – & it ebbs, & flows again, as mysteriously and inexplicably. There is too that state of mind when everything, one feels, is there (however minute the everything) *underneath*, but there is nothing in sight: like a rabbit warren & not a single rabbit. One can't express anything then; but it may be worth trying to do so ... It is one way, if only for the time being, out of 'the dark'. I am convinced that poetry is of incalculable value, beyond what is even imagined of it. One may ignore it for a time, & then go back. *Itself* will have taken a new life meanwhile.[30]

Many Englishmen would remember the final springtime of peace for its beauty. 'Even in this lovely Spring,' de la Mare wrote in May, 'I find one self almost weeping for delight in it, & another less aware of it than a mole in its hermitage.'[30] Everyone's thoughts were tending again with foreboding towards the autumn – spring season for wars – or so, at that period, was generally believed. De La Mare was corresponding with Forrest Reid over the second volume of Reid's autobiography, *Private Road*, and was himself making a collection of retold stories about animals, for children – mostly animals of folk tale. Reid was also helping him over *Pleasures and Speculations*. He longed for Reid to come over on one of his old summer visits, but the chance passed, and, separated by the war, they were never to see each other again.

When the long suspense ended in September, de la Mare, like many others, felt the actual declaration of war a relief. Within a fortnight, Hill House was filled to capacity. Poppy, Rosalind, Jinnie and her child, Stephen, (all London dwellers by now) moved in for comparative safety, and with two little evacuee girls as well. De la Mare felt they could not possibly stay on much longer in Hill House under these conditions, but he could make no plans. He kept at work, finding the strength of that habit odd in the face of such upheaval. But September had not yet done with him; and when he wrote a few weeks later that 'the War ... seems to have disorganised one's complete mental mechanism, a whole system of notions',[31] it was not only war but desperate personal anxiety that preyed on him.

On the twentieth of the month, the day before the two servants left, Elfie, beset by troubles, bent down to pick up a book and felt the sudden pain of a pulmonary thrombosis, due to a clot of blood in a muscle affecting the arteries. The cook and parlourmaid left, as they had planned, just the same (they had made themselves such pests that nobody grieved). Two nurses had to be installed at once and the London children sent elsewhere. At first Elfie rallied encouragingly. Plans were endlessly discussed, but it was difficult to come to any decision – beyond that of leaving Taplow, probably before Christmas. But first a home must also be found for Poppy and Rosalind.

In the midst of all the household confusion and cares of Elfie's illness, and with ironically idyllic autumn weather at the windows, de la Mare worked on. He could still make notes for Reid's *Private Road*, and immerse himself for an hour in speculation on the past, and on dreams. He wrote to another friend about the dogged panacea: 'Don't you find writing anything (why are letters the most difficult things now?) is in itself a temporary lifeline.'[32] It was a time to speak out, with 'this fatuous and inescapable War' hanging over everything, shortening opportunity, which anyway at sixty-six had begun to feel too short, with 'so much friendship still to share'. Yet this war was not for him, in the sense the first had been, a total change; the peace between had always worn something of the temporary air of an armistice, and the old Victorian and Edwardian sense of security had never been regained. Certainly de la Mare took the second war with more equanimity; for one thing, age exempted him this time from the gnawing sense that he ought to be fighting. Nor did he need to justify his daily work: Elfie so ill, needing nurses, required every penny he could earn. His duty was obvious: to provide, and to keep fit himself. His vitality seemed to come up to meet these necessities. Once again he spent long hours at his table, and he was not going to lower anyone's morale by complaints or doubts. During the first war he had admired Newbolt's optimism; now he equalled it himself. But with him this brave front was an act of faith; he was by temperament as apprehensive as Newbolt had been sanguine. 'I feel confident that things will come out right in the end,' he wrote to Sister de Chantal, and early on he took up a Churchillian contempt towards Hitler and his 'gangsters'.

Florence and Rupert had already invited him to bring Elfie to be nursed in their home at Penn, and in November, when it became plain that recovery must be a matter of months not weeks, they left Hill House for 'an indefinite stay' at Penn, leaving the house for the time being locked up as it was. 'Practically everything is still there except ourselves,' de la Mare wrote to Sister de Chantal, 'and it is the house that now seems a ghost, although perhaps our spectres still stir about in it.' He felt that 'we shall never come back, I think'.[33] The decision was soon confirmed: in mid-December, Elfie had a setback. Only Florence's tireless, gentle efficiency made peace for work at all possible for her father. The invalid slept badly and could do little to occupy herself through the long tedium of night and day, and there was the constant effort of living with the nurses. De la Mare spread his books and papers in a study comfortable, quiet, but not his own, and worked away stubbornly, rewriting 'Poetry in Prose' for his book of essays. This year he confessed to Cynthia Asquith that he hated Christmas, the beloved feast. It came and went like a ghost. He was very homesick and remained so.

Yet the interior tides of the contemplative – most of all those of the contemplative artist – often run quite inexplicably counter to outward prospects, as de la Mare had noted. So it was to be with him. The dull, rather mundane Thirties gave way to Forties and Fifties which – in spite of old age, war and all – were to call from him, though indistinctly and secretly at first, a curiously different, far more inspiriting tune.

Part IV

A Citadel More Central

20

Twickenham

De la Mare laid hopeful plans for Elfie's recovery, and for a flat in London that she would be able to manage. Dick heard of one, and his father secured it, in South End House at Twickenham, which dated from 1726 and stood secluded, the tall end one of a row of smaller, graceful old houses, facing the west side of the park of Marble Hill House. The two upper floors provided de la Mare with two suites of beautiful panelled rooms. The house, embowered in other trees, stood beside so huge a plane that even his fourth-floor windows only looked out into its green waist.

The furniture went off to Twickenham, though Elfie and de la Mare stayed on at Penn for the time being. Through the spring of 1940 he struggled with Florence to strip Hill House of the accumulations of fifteen years. The greater part of the manuscript of *Songs of Childhood* turned up among rubbish the charwoman was about to throw away. (Next year it was acquired by the Library of Congress.) And, one morning, with a blue sky and his bonfire blazing away, de la Mare was sorting through a jumble of old papers and letters, left in a large Tate & Lyle sugar box (probably ever since the 1925 move from Thornsett Road). A faded photograph – choirboy in surplice – made him pause. Deeper in, he lit upon an old black commonplace book, whose existence he had utterly forgotten. At least twenty-two pages were crammed, top to bottom and side to side in his old thrifty fashion, several columns abreast, with verses from his early thirties, many dated 1905, and the rest (he thought) not later than 1906. Some had been marked 'copied'; a few had later appeared in print. Some had gone no further than pencil drafts, and some (he told Forrest Reid) were 'complete' such as

> When I am dead, O think no more of me
> 'Twill be a task of transient difficulty.[1]

But the greater part lay just as the young man had put them aside, in

Mackenzie Road days, before Colin was born.

It was a happy find, providing at one blow the main material for a new book of poems and rhymes for next year. Still better for his spirits, it set him writing more of them. Preparation of this new poetry book helped him through the drag of the first year of war as no prose task could have done. He called it *Bells and Grass*, not realising till it was in print that he had been quoting from Hodgson's poem, 'Eve'.

*

A particular pleasure, now visitors had abruptly become rarities, arose from the determined pilgrimages to Penn, begun this spring, by a new and special friend, Dr Martin Johnson. Johnson was a distinguished physicist whose main interest was astronomy, but his nature was a Nahum Taroone one, widely inquiring. He held that every university student should study something of the arts if he was reading science, and vice versa. His mind was fresh, warm and humble, and he himself wrote equally knowledgeably on the sculptures of Chartres, Beethoven's late Quartets and the mathematicians of ancient Baghdad. He was classicial scholar enough to try his hand at a prose translation of the *Odyssey*, and it was a passage from this that de la Mare chose when he put the touching death of Odysseus's hound, Argos, into his anthology *Love*.

To introduce himself, Johnson had sent de la Mare a paper of critical appreciation, and from the start it was a particular pleasure that such praise should come from a scientist. De la Mare went on in his last years to make other scientific friends, among them Russell Brain, the neurologist, and Professor Andrade, another physicist. All these were scientists enthusiastic about poetry in their leisure hours. De la Mare still felt that there were two orders of truth; still holding that of poetry and faith to be immeasurably superior to the truth of scientific reasoning. (One notices that whenever he contrasts poetry with science, he speaks as if faith and poetry were indistinguishably one.) But he had outgrown, by the time Martin Johnson entered his life, the conventional condescension of his youth, when he had seen 'Sweet Poetry turn troubled eyes / On Shaggy Science nosing in the grass'.[2] The change came not just by maturity, nor the great widening of his own range of interests, but was partly also due to the enormous development in science itself during his lifetime – most of all in physics. Where once among scientists only the naturalists had seemed to him to preserve a sense of wonder, now, by the time he wrote (in 1944) an introduction to Johnson's *Art and Scientific Thought*, mystery had once more flooded the entire field of physics. He could at last thankfully acknowledge this: 'we can only be grateful for release from the nightmare of a knowledge so complete as to be uninteresting.'[3] That oppression of the late nineteenth century – the prospect that science, given time, would inevitably *explain away* the miracle of existence – had appeared even more spirit-killing to the young de la Mare than religious dogma, but by now he had outlived the hold of both tyrannies on the society of his time.

A most unexpected person had introduced Johnson to de la Mare's poems, while they were friends as young men – F.R. Leavis, later of so very different a mind about them. For Johnson, de la Mare's poetry had at once and permanently become a passion, linked closely with his search for the common base of insight that art and science could share (he was sure) if only the right attitude could be defined and cultivated. His own approach to science kept a Renaissance, adventurous width of view, the disciplines of experimental method only intensifying his sense of marvel. Poetry he would discuss tentatively, as a very humble outsider, but he was nevertheless one of the not very great number to whom de la Mare found it useful to show unpublished poems – and he got frank comments back.

On his visits to Penn (he was a Birmingham University don, very overworked and delicate) it was Johnson's own field, quite as much as de la Mare's, that they discussed – the habits of nebulae, the White Dwarfs of Sirius, and the Aurora Borealis. These laborious trips to Penn entailed setting off at daybreak from Birmingham on a cross-country mixture of local trains and buses, crowded and unheated, to arrive about ten thirty in the morning, leaving after tea for four-and-a-half hours of changes and delays to get home. But the effort for Johnson, and the loss of a working day for de la Mare, was to each equally worthwhile. They kept on regular close terms for the remaining sixteen years of de la Mare's life – devoted, yet without ever becoming intimate at all about their personal affairs (in the way de la Mare was with, say, Green-Armytage). His friendships with men, in fact, could be equally valued and nourishing to him over a very wide spectrum from the confidential to the reticent – his sense of close sharing quite at ease in either mode, since *the ideas* to be pooled were so consumingly the point of it all.

By July Colin and Rupert were in the Local Defence Volunteers (not yet called the Home Guard). Jinnie was on Air Raid Duty, and de la Mare, at Twickenham, lying awake and knowing her beat would pass nearby, hurried out one night in waterproof and bedroom slippers, and accompanied her on her rounds (which was against the rules). His anxieties about her increased; her husband Donald's absence, and the war, had unsettled her. She was depressed and unwell. Towards September the Battle of Britain accelerated; when de la Mare visited the Twickenham flat there were often three alarms in a night. Absorbed alone in study and writing, as dark fell, he was not the most methodical householder about blackout; he got official reprimands, and (so his landlord remembered) the police once even rowed across the river to tell him his high upper windows were beaconing to the further bank.

The doctor had by now given up all hope of recovery for Elfie, diagnosing Parkinson's Disease on top of her other maladies. Her brother and sisters, worn out and one of them ailing, came to swell the family, sheltering in Florence's care. Poppy's flat at Bedford Park took a direct hit, and Donald, there on leave, was buried for three hours under the rubble before he was rescued. Through December 1940, Elfie grew worse; she could scarcely walk at all. Meanwhile, among other bad new coming in from friends, Green-Armytage's foundry at Bristol was obliterated, and he lost a great deal of money, though none of his capacity for warm supportive letters, interested in everything. They continued to arrive with cheering frequency and helped de la Mare's spirits considerably. For his own part he found the present moment good whenever he could, relishing any lovely day in his own letters: 'a William Blake sun stationed exactly midway of my windows', the Old Park rooks 'creaking in a leafless tree'.[4] But at times he felt caged and frustrated and once burst out that in many ways he should prefer a hen-house to a home from home. He wrote to Ella: 'The supreme ordeal is still to come: according to all the signs. And my Bones tell me that England will outface it.'[5]

He had enough now for his *Bells and Grass*, and was writing more poems for adults. Also, he was collecting, as his personal antidote to hatred, all the most individual affirmations of love he could discover in poetry and prose, asking Forrest Reid and Green-Armytage and other friends to send in whatever they personally treasured.

By mid-January 1941 Colin, as his parents had dreaded, was gone – into detested army camp at Oswestry. De la Mare struggled with his own exhaustions – 'there's so much enervastation [sic] to get through nowadays before any imp within can come alive'[6] – and he had, for good measure, a corneal ulcer in the eye. All the same it is noticeable that he managed not to get ill – he missed out, this year, even his regular seasonal bout of 'flu' – now that so much was at stake all dependant on his keeping going. Then came a gleam of real joy – Colin's engagement to Lilias Awdry, who had been a Taplow neighbour, and whom de la Mare dearly loved. She came to see him, and he wrote to Colin: 'I loved to watch her talking and almost to hear her heart singing underneath. Unfortunately it must be many months (if ever) before an advance copy of the Love Anthology is available. But I don't think this is positively essential for the time being.'[7] Lilias, beautiful and gentle, was everything he wished for Colin. They were married a month later, Colin uncertain, even two days before the date fixed for the wedding, whether he would be given leave in time to be there.

Pattie, beloved figure of de la Mare's youth, died at this time. Writing sadly to Bert (himself ill) de la Mare said he could not recall, in all those years, the slightest shadow ever having come between them and that if anyone would find themselves instantly at home in Paradise, surely *she* would! He knew Bert would share what he was feeling. Right back to the afternoon story-tellings 'in the hazel glen' they had been Pattie's boys together, listening to her voice, glad of her charm, her competence, her love surrounding the six children and their mother, following the fortunes of all.

Elfie by now no longer distinguished dream from reality. It grew more and more a wearing difficulty to procure the nurses she needed night and day. Rupert, struggling with difficulties at the office, after bomb-damage, had begun, ominously, to need again the X-ray treatment he had had in the 1930s. Yet in spite of all that Florence had to shoulder in the house, and although at nearly forty-two she was carrying another child, not intended and long after his brother and sister, she still contrived her hospitality toward any of de la Mare's friends who could come to them, as well as the large circle of Rupert's and her own.

Towards the end of July, sitting in the garden, de la Mare heard from the window above him the first exclamation of her new-born son. What did it express, he wondered, greatly moved – astonishment? delight? anger? reproach? He was enthralled to watch another child so intimately again from its first hour. He gave this most beloved of all the eleven grandchildren such absorbed attention that the bond between them (for Julian was a special and unusual small boy) became one of the strongest he had with anyone over the next twelve years.

He was reading widely round his anthology, and in general more and more ranging outside literature itself, delving into the sources of human behaviour – a study of sex and the moon, William Cyph's *The Process of Human Experience*, Ribot's *Psychology of the Emotions* – such were the sort of books that littered his table from now on, though never displacing the editions of the poets. To Binyon he wrote: 'For me

the War and all the word implies has only increased and intensified my
old delight in poetry: the citadel seems even a little more central.'[8]

He realised he could only use half of what he had collected for the
anthology. But because of paper-shortages, Dick, as his publisher, was
obliged to ask him to cut that by half again. Even so, the book ran to
over 700 tightly-printed paged. 'To surrender one after another my
love children after they have been adopted is a reiterated wrench,'[9] de
la Mare complained to Green-Armytage, who had lately sent him the
most wonderful *trouvaille* in the book, the brief, authentic letter of a
dying factory girl, discovered by him quoted in a newspaper cutting as
an example of love worth most of the contents of the book under review.
De la Mare was looking especially for such out-of-the-way instances,
not basing his choices solely on literary work. When at length he got
the bulky package off to Faber, there was a week of alarm and
suspense while it lay lost in the wartime registered post. The prospect
of having to repeat such a task was almost impossible to contemplate.

He was undertaking very few public engagements now – a broadcast
or two in 1941 – a poetry reading with Edith Evans – otherwise he
worked steadily at Penn, taking up a little work now and then for a day
or so of solitude at the flat. This summer he told W.H. Hamilton he was
working about fifty hours a week; and on top of this came the
inevitable chore of answering letters, mostly in longhand. Nor were
they ever very brief. It was no idle retirement for a man of sixty-eight.

Bells and Grass came out in November 1941. It had an early
freshness about it, partly belonging, as it did, between *Songs of
Childhood* and *Peacock Pie*, and it was well received by a public that
had never been so hungry for books, especially ones like this, offering
complete distraction from the war. It was illustrated by Rowland
Emmett – his first attempt (so he told de la Mare) at book illustration.
His fancy, humorously extravagant, goes much better with the poems
than does that of most of de la Mare's verse illustrators, but the
Emmett grotesqueries, though sympathetic to the poems, go off at a
tangent on their own – more gremlin than faery. The fact that de la
Mare's poetry is essentially unsuitable for illustration at all shows the
more plainly when taken on by artists really gifted in their own line, as
Lovat Fraser and Emmett were. The moment the page is turned, the
reader goes back to inward notions less distinct but more suggestive.

De la Mare ticked off the passage of the war in his letters in
stout-hearted certainty of a limit to its suffering, rather like a boy at
school – two years already 'which won't have to be repeated'. Looking
back, it was safe now to admit that 'from May to September of last year
was absolutely touch and go' (he was writing to Colin). 'I doubt if any

intelligent observer outside England (and possibly the Empire) believed we had a dog's chance. And now, what would you give in hard cash for Hitler's?'[10]

Dorothy Collins had become a friend through G.K. Chesterton, to whom she had been secretary. Finding that de la Mare had never met Belloc, except once on a bus, she arranged for this, while Belloc was staying with her for help over his own work. De la Mare asked him (as he had long ago asked Chesterton) if the idea of a previous life on earth were heretical? Chesterton had replied doubtfully: 'Not heretical but much disapproved of.' Belloc promptly dismissed the notion as rank heresy. De la Mare then asked him if, given the opportunity, he would himself welcome a return to earth? Belloc paused – he was dressed rather theatrically in black (or so de la Mare described him to Ella in later recollections) then – 'Come back? *No – thank you.'* Miss Collins thought her tea-party was going quite well, but, tea over, Belloc at once rose, excused himself in his most gallant manner, and went into the next room shutting the dividing doors. De la Mare asked if she thought he had bored Mr Belloc? She did her best, saying probably Belloc wanted to work, but inwardly suspecting that Belloc had discomfited them both as a gesture, liking to have her to himself. He had done this kind of thing before and could be a most embarrassing guest. She looked anxiously for signs of offence, but de la Mare stayed on, serenely talking, until seven. He may have stayed extra long on purpose to reassure her – it would have been in character.

He found himself depressed and irked by the narrowing-in of human concerns the war induced: the dull round of topics in conversation – rations and prices, weather and food. America and Japan entering the conflict seemed to him only to pinch in the outlook still further; it was like being, he felt, in the third volume of one of the old-fashioned novels, of which one had hopelessly mislaid the other two. If it were not so Satanically actual, how unreal it would be. The hypocrisy of propaganda on both sides, the 'third-rate pulpiteering', lies and humbug, constantly disgusted him. But the great popularity of poetry was one cheering feature. Publishers had never known such sales, and his own verse was doing well. A one-volume *Collected Poems* appeared, on the scarce and flimsy war-time paper, off-white and flecked like the 'austerity' bread, and was snapped up. It was the choice of the Book Society for March 1941. The *Midget* received a similar spur to its sales in America through the Reader's Club.

For his Midget's collection, the Rostrevor Hamiltons sent him a minuscule copy of Gray's Elegy. 'I think,' he wrote back, 'it is a most engaging and *elegant* piece, a little sententious perhaps, and though its

theme might well have been less doleful and sepulchral and I deplore
its tendency – not pronounced of course – toward the socialistic, it may
well survive much that is now *in* the mode. If it is a first effort, then
surely it shows a perceptible promise.'[11] Gray's Elegy was always a
target for digs. Later on, he amused himself by 'improving' the poem,
cutting out all adjective and superfluous trimmings, so that it read at a
brisk trot:

> The curfew tolls the knell of day
>   The herd winds o'er the lea
> The ploughman homeward plods his way
>   And leaves the world – to me!

He was impenitently philistine over the Augustans, and would not be
persuaded to appreciate their virtues on any account.

He needed more and more acutely the outlet of meetings and talk,
and used the Twickenham flat increasingly. Most weeks now he would
come up for two nights, glad to wake early among his own possessons,
throw back the blackout, and let in the sun and the hand-shadows of
the plane-leaves in summer, or of its dangling, meditative finger-bones
in winter. He had only about an hour and a half of house-help a week,
and spent a great deal of his own time polishing, keeping the brass and
furniture as carefully as Elfie would have done. He liked to watch from
his high window the cricketers and tennis-players and the allotment
gardeners 'curling their kale', or to go up to see the gulls taking the
sunset on their wings, from his flat-topped roof. He was glad of the
easing solitude, to relax from placating difficult nurses, and from the
need to be punctual for his host's meals; yet towards evening the
tree-shaded rooms seemed to deepen their atmosphere of expectancy to
an oppressive degree. Visitors noticed that when he greeted them at the
foot of his private staircase, hung with samplers, at tea-time, he was
somewhat at stretch after the long hours of brooding and working
alone, and very glad to turn to company. He admitted that it could get
'unignorably silent' around nine o'clock, and would sometimes resort to
another hour of housework then, before bed, to rally his spirits.

One of his refreshments was to meet 'N', his former nurse, during
these trips to London. She was essential to him throughout the strain
of Elfie's illness and withdrawal. He could trust her completely, and
her quite different life and background, outside his literary world,
refreshed him. On his part he could show her a world of poetry she had
not had opportunity to find for herself, and it was a happiness to him to
share it with someone to whom it came so fresh, and for whom it need
not be analysed. He plied her with endless questions on medicine,

treatment, symptoms, and still more on out-of-the-way characters and dramas she had come across in her profession: tyrants, alcoholics, love-children, the pitiful and the peculiar. N could relate such things very well for him, in her compassionate and detached way. She was straightforward and candid and talkative (which he liked), but also loyal beyond ordinary professional rectitude. She took his own delight in outings and simple pleasures, and they would often spend her day off pottering round antique shops, looking for bargains. They would pick up a blue Chinese pot, for a lampstand, perhaps, or spot a delicate handle-less porcelain cup only flawed by a hair-crack. Then they would go to sit and talk on the seat in front of one of the two churches islanded in the busy torrent of the Strand. They might slip inside the church for shelter, and kneel down for a moment together in its peace. In her company he need not strain to question belief; they did not discuss religion, she said. Plainly, alongside her, he could just take the comfort of sharing its observances as he had in childhood. It was a rest.

Sometimes he would take her to talk in St Paul's Churchyard, where he had loved to spend spare moments as a boy. In the evenings after such happy days, they would stroll across the Park singing 'Now the day is over', he in his pleasant baritone, growing a little gravelly with age, she in a deep, true, unselfconscious alto which he loved to hear. With him, she said, 'It seemed a perfectly natural thing to be doing in such a place.' He could be completely spontaneous with her. She would enter into his webs of make-believe and was a good listener, delighted by his jokes, so they shared a lot of laughter. Responsive as she was to him, she exacted nothing in return, except that she would not let him become too dependent. At the day's end her slight figure walked away briskly to her duties, nor must he spare long from his. 'It's dreary being so perpetually pressed with urgent work,' he admitted. 'Still, I can't work too much.'

There was more to these meetings, however, than her rectitude would allow to surface. She had become very dear to his susceptible heart in the misery of Elfie's decline. Not that she had romantic looks. Ill health had pinched her small, thin frame, and hard times in childhood had ruled out any such extras as help for teeth that stuck out. Her dark hair, high cheekbones and dark expressive eyes appealed to de la Mare, but they won him by the same straightforward charms of loveability and helpfulness that had made Pattie beautiful to his childhood eyes. Other nurses at N's place of work began to notice the very distinctive handwriting that turned up so frequently in her post. 'You *are* a dark horse, Saxton', was remarked. Presently N's mother, soul of old-fashioned contrywoman's honour, became uneasy and she and N, whose Christian conscience was equally tender, talked things over. N, suppressing her own feelings, put a brake on the relationship. She burnt de la Mare's precious letters, steered the friendship steadily away from dangerous currents, but continued her support, paddling gamely on like the mandarin duck she reminded him of.

Elfie, somehow, even with a nurse at hand, fell from a sitting position right out of bed in May 1942, probably causing an impacted fracture of the thigh. But it seemed pointless to put her through the ordeal of an X-ray, as the treatment could only be the same whatever the verdict. She rallied from the shock, but for fear septicaemia might follow, the less expensive 'nurse-companion' with whom they had lately made shift, had to be replaced by one fully qualified, rather formidable and very expensive. De la Mare needed a weekly income of sixteen pounds to make ends meet, and this meant what he called constant 'hugger-muggering'.

He was too anxious this summer to take the week's holiday Lady Desborough had planned for him, with Cynthia Asquith, at Panshanger in Hertfordshire. (He had taken none whatever since the war began.) But he kept fit: in August 1942 he told Cynthia Asquith he had been working hard from seven in the morning till ten p.m. the last week or two, in a race against time, and felt none the worse for it. The introduction he was writing for *Love* was, all the same, an exhausting task, and this time the weariness got into the prose and hazed the essay over. There are some vivid passages in it, the best one describes his new grandson Julian (who could now crawl 'as fast as a hedgehog') falling asleep with a saffron crocus-bud in his hand, holding it so carefully that when Florence looked in on him later in the evening, it had come into bloom. That seemed to de la Mare a symbol of love which better expressed his thoughts than all the definitions he was toiling to articulate, and he was right. The essay is too voluminous: the ramble he took through its argument too haphazard. And when all was said, one major field had been left poorly represented and very sketchily discussed – the whole subject of sexuality. There was a section labelled 'Eros' and some Donne – but even Donne in snippets, and his great directly sensual poems omitted. Imaginative love predominated; bodily love is merely peripheral.

It gives the book a most curious imbalance. He knew he had not fully succeeded, and told Forrest Reid that the introduction had given him so much trouble that he had never been so quickly and completely cut away from a book before. 'Sleeping Beauty was not more thornily hedged in than this subject is, and the hardiest bramble is sex.'[12]

In November 1942 Colin had leave, giving treasured opportunity for talk, to store against the dreaded time ahead when he would be posted abroad. 'When you do go,' de la Mare wrote to him, 'I do hope it won't be for long and not very far. And all the time you will be having two lovely things to look forward to, as well as peace.'[13] By the second of the two he meant the child Lilias had conceived. It was lucky, as he wrote, that he could not know how far and how long Colin's absence would prove. He was in North Africa and then Italy for much of the campaign, and therefore never saw this unborn child, Julia, until she was two and a half.

Meanwhile November passed in dread, from day to day, about this posting overseas. The years had modified the old, intensely protective parental feelings less towards Colin than towards any of the other three. For both parents, Colin had always been the Benjamin – very specifically so, for de la Mare's unabashed passion of paternal tenderness belongs more to the world of the Old Testament, in note, than to twentieth century English family sentiment, however devoted.

*

Now and then he would scribble again in a diary – things that might suggest a story, or a poem, taken from small events of the day; the kind he himself attracted and a little unlike those which occupied most Londoners, ploughing through the drab third winter of the war.

> *Friday*. I put the kettle which had been simmering on my bedroom electric stove (lighted to take the damp out of the room). Above the minute musical whispering arose a peculiar Gregorian chaunting so deceptive that for a time I suppose [sic] it came from the wireless: but it was 11.30 and the moment the simmering stopped the monastery became silent.[14]

And another time:

> Dense fog. Hauntings. A thin paper bag rustled off the table in the kitchen as I turned to leave the room. I looked back sharply over my shoulder. Supposing one found after the destruction of the paper bag – bound up indirectly with something else and important – *still* one heard the rustle and then of course visualized the bag itself. And that once, after walking in one's sleep, one found oneself reading a message upon it – say a significant baker's name and address …[15]

*

1943 began with the death of Laurence Binyon. Though they could not often meet, de la Mare had valued his friendship more and more, and grieved to feel, now, that Binyon, gentle and totally unassuming, had probably never guessed how much. De la Mare had been deeply interested by Binyon's master-work, the remarkable feat of translating Dante into English *terza rima*, and he had cared for his melancholy, reflective lyrics, that were so true to his quiet outlook and his cultivation. Binyon tended to post him one, ahead of a visit, calling it 'the kind of thing you do so much better than I or anybody else', and saying 'You can tell me if you like it and how to improve it when we come over.'[16]

In spite of 'nightmare weeks of difficulty' to supply home-nursing for Elfie this spring, Rupert and Florence went to great lengths to prepare a surprise supper-party for de la Mare's seventieth birthday, at Penn. Seven old friends, all men (Wilfrid Gibson among them), were somehow assembled, though war and illness put many out of reach. It was a lovely party; Martin Johnson noticed that as the evening wore on and he himself grew tireder and tireder, de la Mare became brighter and brighter, and began to bait him: 'Why do you scientists keep pressing the importance of size? Size doesn't mean a thing.' He would go so far on occasion, Johnson said, as to deny even the objective value of scientific observation at all, claiming that the nebulae of Andromeda were only interesting in so far as they affected 'Mrs Smith, my charwoman'. The party broke up very late, and when de la Mare got to bed, sharing a room with Dick as they had loved to do long ago, he talked him to sleep about two a.m.

His vitality could still stand a good deal. Only a week before this party he had performed at a charity poetry reading at the Aeolian Hall, with cocktails and a rehearsal beforehand, royalty present, a packed audience, a dinner afterwards, speeches, delightful reunions with friends he seldom had a chance to meet, such as Gordon Bottomley – and after all was over, he arrived at Waterloo at ten-thirty to find there would be no train to Richmond until after midnight. When at last he reached Richmond, he had to walk the rest of the way by the wail of the siren under the moon, and as it was useless to go to bed until the All Clear sounded, did housework and made his breakfast porridge, which he was awake again to eat at six o'clock, after only four hours' sleep. He seemed to have recovered at seventy the vigour and zest for life lost in 1927, when he had been fifty-four.

This spring he was reading C.S. Lewis's latest book, *The Screwtape Letters*, at Green-Armytage's suggestion. Words could hardly express how repellent he found these letters of spiritual direction from a senior devil to a junior tempter in charge of a particular 'case'. He would refer to the book as 'The Tapeworm Letters'. He had a lively admiration for Lewis's philosophical study *The Problem of Pain*, and for his allegorical space-novel *Perelandra*. But this excellent, uncomfortable work of Christian morality riled and disgusted him. Lewis's attitude to the Tempter has not a scrap of the reverence with which, irrationally enough, human recognition often dignifies his figure. To de la Mare, sensible though he was, the fiendish 'Thrones, Dominations, Princedoms, ... Powers' remained in *all* aspects always to some extent poetic. Satan for him was always one who 'where he glanced a gloom pervaded space', more than the meanly ugly, odious intimate of the daily human heart. It is perfectly logical that a devil should only be able to talk of Christ, as Screwtape does, with the vulgarity of total incomprehension; but de la Mare could not stomach that vulgarity. In this connection one notices, later on, something of the same reaction of personal outrage about his loathing of Ronald Searle's satirically-drawn cartoons of schoolgirls. Searle's work was plainly disliked by him because it had desecrated the shrine of childhood; and to that extent it was a sentimental dislike. In theory he would have allowed that an artist may make use of whatever material he pleases, but in practice he treated Searle's satire of adult folly and vice as a blasphemy, because it used pigtail terms to make its point.

As summer 1943 came de la Mare began to write despairingly to Green-Armytage that the task of caring for Elfie at home was finally getting beyond them – Florence could not carry on much longer. The supply of nurses de la Mare endlessly applied for and interviewed, as his share of the responsibility, was running out completely. Crises and scenes the more difficult nurses provoked, became unbearably exhausting, and now Elfie was subject to frequent minor heart-attacks. A nursing home became unavoidable. They found one not far off, but it was a dejecting decision for all of them.

De la Mare was very cast down; he became afraid of going aground altogether, and losing the capacity to work. Yet besides the resolutely good face he always put on things in letters (only admitting the strain to Green-Armytage) his private jottings show how he could still, just as he had learned to do in the eighteen years of Oil, take any open-hearted relief the passing moment offered. Weather itself became once again in old age (as it had been in those brief moments out of doors, coming and going from the City) a vital source of change and refreshment. He never went to bed without looking out to see what kind of night it was. Waking early at Twickenham he noted:

May 29th. Went up to the roof about 5.30 (double summer time). The dawn was beginning to colour the sky – thin fleecy cloud (which later wisped into silver white plumes and feathers against the flattened pale blue of the sky) and low in the East was the last half-quarter (the de-crescent) of the moon, of a rich corn-colour. I don't remember ever before to have seen this so early in a summer's morning; have seldom seen it at any season. Birds *beneath* me in the trees were singing matins; the house seemed to be in a shallow dish as it were of this strange bubbling and babbling music.[17]

The voice and spirit of such an entry might just as well be those of fifty years before, taking from the skies above Wandsworth something – anything – to arm him against the day in Billiter Street, and at the same time to put away small, novel, precise grains of detail for future use.

He dwelt more and more on events of nature in his letters: the rainbow that once lasted an hour over Twickenham; some bright particular planet. And he mentioned his plane-tree – more in terms of a familiar than of an object in the view – as often as he would give news about acquaintances. Sometimes, of course, he might be writing fancifully, yet his attention to his tree was not at all a whimsy. He took this huge, living creature of London as a very real companion, and never tired of debating what degree and kind of consciousness it might have. He would refer to its life, alongside his, in much the same terms as he might have used for speculating on some taciturn but prized relationship with a neighbour who intrigued him.

The hated day came when Elfie was taken off. But the helpless sadness of visting her, exiled, was mercifully short, less than three weeks. She died on 11 July 1943. Reaction of utter dejection set in, now that the long strain was ended. De la Mare felt as if he could hardly remember her happy (as she certainly was in Hill House days) before this illness began. Once, later on, he remarked sadly to Leonard Clark: 'I have a feeling that I didn't really know her, because she hid herself in us.' The one comfort was that so over-anxious a heart had met death finally without apprehensions.

*

Nervous exhaustion gripped him; and there were more than a hundred and thirty letters of condolence to answer, a task nobody could have persuaded him to delegate or omit. Most had to be done by hand, on top of his other work. He took a little holiday at last, with Florence and Rupert and their children – the first time (so he wrote to Bert) he had been free of his inkpot since early 1938. But even in this dead-end lassitude the germ of a new work was stirring. By mid-August he mentioned to Martin Johnson, a fellow-devotee of Time conundrums, that he had been making 'a brief screed in verse with Clocks for nucleus'. It would turn out, in fact, not brief, but the longest piece of verse he had ever written, a sustained and individual new departure.

21

Widower and Traveller

Love came out in September. It had conflicting reviews. He found he did not mind very much; in fact he had never been over-sensitive to published criticism, though praise from any quarter he valued had been a great stimulant when he was younger. He would rely on chance or hearsay to bring reviews to his notice, and did not bother to use a press-cutting agency. But sales of *Love* were good, and before the end of November the first edition had sold out.

He was spending more time at the flat now, but found its solitude increasingly oppressive, and began regular weekday hospitality for visitors, baking batches of rock-cakes. American friends sent him food-parcels throughout the war, and somehow the tea-table was always well spread.

In November, coming home in the blackout, he misjudged, jumped from the Twickenham bus before it had stopped, and fell flat on his face on the pavement. He trudged home with a black eye and probably slight concussion, bound himself up, alone and dazzled by the bright kitchen light, finished making his macaroni pudding, and went to bed. Next day he went back to Florence and was kept at Penn for three weeks. By the time he opened his oven door again he was intrigued to observe the delicate forest of mould his macaroni had put up. The misadventure made the family, and N, very anxious about his solitary flat-dwelling; yet he obviously needed more and more the independence of his own home. something would have to be done. Meanwhile, as always, he was intensely interested in the symptoms and after-effects of his injuries. The accident, he noticed, though it had slowed him up physically, was mentally stimulating; he felt as if he had upset a hive of bees while having hardly anyone to share the honey with.

*

'Nothing much happens outside,' he wrote to Forrest Reid in June 1944, 'but a good deal inside: more at times than I can manage to get even with. Is that your experience too? The rhymes and stories I *don't* shock the Paper Controller with. There are almost enough (rhymes) for a new collection ...'[1]

Now, in his widower seventies, came resurgence of wonder and energy in the heart, and with it a press of poetry such as he had not experienced since the early 1920s. This next year or two would be the most sustained period of poetry-writing in his whole career – almost exclusively devoted to this, and producing, amongst lyrics, his two most ambitious long works: *The Traveller* and *Winged Chariot*, neither of a kind he had tried before.

The Traveller is philosophic, a kind of waking dream or dry-land *Ancient Mariner*, illustrating a personal conclusion about life. *Winged Chariot*, which grew out of that 'brief screed of Clocks', is a conversational meditation or sequence, composed rather like a musical suite. It is sprinkled with lyric passages, loosely embroidered on a disquisition.

Neither work was planned to be a long poem. *The Traveller* he originally expected to become just one of the new collection, already half gathered together. As it outgrew all possibility of such inclusion, he called it a white elephant intent upon occupying its own howdah. But though the form was a new venture, the horseman on a quest, for hero, had always been a favourite in poems, and turned up too in the poetic novels – *Henry Brocken* and the *Mulgars*. It was as ready a device for suggesting the human predicament in the poetry, as railways provided for him in the short stories – modern in setting, but equally concerned with man's lonely transit and uncertain destination.

His Traveller had forerunners, casting shadows of the same theme, right back to the horseman who knocks at the Listener's door, and the knight in the 'Song of Finis' in *Peacock Pie* who flings a last challenge to the universe and urges his steed into space. Other wanderer-figures illustrate 'The mockless victory defeat can be'.[2] This article of faith crops up as the defiant slogan, writing to Elfie: 'Defeat is Victory', and ends the poem of the same early, struggling period: 'Dare to defeated be.'

Now the tragic, dogged wayfarer came up to stir his imagination again. Grappling as he was with the attritions of wartime and a personal desolation, the impulse behind it carried this time a much greater and graver force. His maturity backs it, the traveller-figure is less romantic and decorative, facing the fate that baffles him. He is closer in.

Also a quite new and curious preoccupation shapes the story. Taking up the idea of Earth as a sentient being, de la Mare invented a sombre fable of a man travelling across the huge Eye of Earth to the pupil, where at last he meets its gaze looking back at him. The concept of sentience in the heavenly bodies had been in his mind a good deal in the last three years, in his discussions with Martin Johnson. In fact their constant talk of astronomy and the nature of the universe probably had a good deal to do with his choice of such a story. Later this year, when he came to write an introduction for Johnson's *Art and Scientific Thought*, he said: 'How many times, I wonder, did I attempt to compel him to concede that no Universe of *any* dimensions can be of much account without a comprehensive consciousness capable of the completest appreciation of it in every detail.' Longer ago he must often have discussed with Newbolt (whose favourite belief it was, consoling him for transience) the theory of 'anima mundi', the great world-memory in which all that we love and lose is retained. At one time de la Mare thought of using 'Anima Mundi' for the title of the poem, but Johnson was against it, sensibly.

The Traveller's symbolic journey is toward Life's resolution, the ultimate point where 'Life with death / Brings all to an issue'[3] – in this poem a dark one. Childhood to the grave, life is a battle lost from the outset. Salvation lies only in the stoic and benedictory spirit with which it can be fought. The Traveller's adventures are those of a soul in the Dark Night of the mystic, undergoing *kenôsis*, but without ultimate certainty of any heaven. The poem marks the same kind of personal experience, perhaps, in de la Mare's career that 'The Waste Land' had in Eliot's. It arose out of the bitter experience of the past few years – personal ageing, the endurance of an inescapable personal trial with no possible happy outcome, and, in the course of that (and of the war), disillusion, remorse, grief and the deepening sense of loneliness which his letters of the early 1940s increasingly mention. Yet evidently such unhappy origins were not at all in the forefront of his mind. Probably the poem's deepest drive was to assimilate and accept such experience, and it did achieve a self-healing. At any rate de la Mare himself was surprised, when *The Traveller* was read by old friends such as Ella, and by the general public, that they should take it as darkly as they did.

It is a partial failure, on a grander scale than anything else he wrote; it remains fascinating, though its archaic, bookish diction and fantastic accidentals hamper his ability (never strong) to give convincing body to sustained philosophic ideas; and the ideas behind the symbols matter so much here. Also, the severe *via negativa* of the theme is rather oddly served by so thoroughly romantic a fable. The narrative is hypnotically interior, hard to make out. But the vivid landscape of the Eye itself, well suggested in John Piper's coloured drawings for the poem, stands out unforgettably; so does the spirit of marvelling compassion, the consuming concern with the ultimate enigma, and the instinct that to face stark privation with blessing and endurance is the only act that no doubts whatever can make meaningless.

Once again, though, de la Mare does not commit himself. Ambiguity closes all, and one is left in doubt whether he intends triumph or tragedy by the Traveller's end. Whichever it is for him, his companion the horse is certainly left to perish, abandoned and in terror. Whatever the horse represents – the mortal self, or the body – her end is annihilation, although she is both beautiful and faithful. (De la Mare admitted he got very fond of this horse in the course of writing the poem.) Yet, though it does not fully succeed, *The Traveller* adds a new note of gravitas to de la Mare's voice. Here, as an old man, he seems to be grappling with something at the centre of his humanity. If he had been the escapist his detractors label him, he would never have made this ambitious attempt at all. It occupied him almost exclusively during 1944, up to August, except for some other poems and a little work toward *Winged Chariot*, still just called 'Clocks'.

Outwardly very little indicated or accounted for this unexpected intensifying of the poetry impulse: his letters during these months speak much of loneliness and depression: the current ran underground, counter to circumstance, counter even to mood, but strongly.

*

For a period he had no domestic help at all at Twickenham, and would blacklead his own grates and clean the many windows – twelve panes to each – outside and in. Raids still disturbed the nights. Meanwhile he was finding old age an interesting experience in itself, not merely a curtailment of former ones. He wrote to a friend in September 1944:

> My own impression is that one of the least expected things in life is the self etc., that awaits one towards the end of it, not necessarily that it is any better than the self that made its journey thither but it is at least a little different and novel. I think I even read differently from what I used to – looking through the window of the words rather more intently and closely; and there is a tendency to attend spontaneously not only to what is said but to more than one of the meanings of what is said. One is less likely to rest in B after leaving A than to wish to go on to C, and this is equally true of outside things, people, etc. I wonder if you agree. It is

difficult to see how this comes about: *not*, I think, merely gradually. One seems to inherit it – a pleasant little legacy from a hitherto unheard-of aunt. But is there any really satisfactory book on the subject of old age, and at what year would you fix the 'old'? *De Senectute* is the only one that ever came my way but this was a bit too early, when I was about fourteen. I cannot remember a single syllable Cicero said. There is of course a queerly intense sense of being old when one is about twenty. I can actually recall sitting in a railway carriage, gloomy oil lamp overhead, and realising that I resembled Atlas.[4]

To Ella he mentioned that 'I have been reading T.H.'s novels, Henry James's long-short stories and Wilkie Collins's *No Name* (turn and turn about) and am sure it is the company of the story-teller that is (even though one may be hardly conscious of it) my chief delight – or the reverse. Even a novelist's characters are looking-glasses, at various angles.'[5] He liked to read books in clusters – he was in the habit most of his life of keeping several going together, and using them, as in this instance, for a kind of commentary-by-comparison, to illuminate each other. The 'company' of the author, in James's case, was not always to his liking, and he complained that James squeezed his 'orange' so dry of every possible suggestion and implication that there was nothing left for the reader to extract for himself – which left a vague disappointment: 'After the story is finished, it is *all* over.' In Hardy, on the other hand, he could enjoy, for the sake of his beloved 'company', even the bad parts and the unbelievable coincidences. Wilkie Collins had been a lifelong fascination and he amassed from time to time a quantity of notes, yet never brought all his study of his work to publication.

With age, he took to asking advice before publication much more widely. The poems for his next collection, *The Burning-Glass*, were sent round to be sifted by Rice-Oxley, Green-Armytage, Forrest Reid, Martin Johnson – even by a very new friend, one he had not met and never was to meet, and whose name he had only known since she had first written to him this May.

She was Elizabeth Myers, a Roman Catholic novelist in her early thirties, already ill of the tuberculosis she died of three years later, and lately married to the elderly Littleton Powys, brother of the three novelists. De la Mare fell in love with her a little – at first letter. She had written impulsively to thank him for what his work had meant to her. In May 1944 her chances of living much longer seemed precarious, and she felt she must speak out to de la Mare, who had been her favourite poet since her poor and wretched childhood in Manchester. Once, aged eleven, she had run across the city after school to hear him recite his poems in the Town Hall, but was turned away because she did not possess the shilling for a seat.

De la Mare was moved and touched by all this, and by Elizabeth's warm, rather boyish directness. She was particularly drawn to friendship with men much older than herself, and, driven by the sense of short time ahead, she wasted none. The tuberculosis itself heightened her responses and her religious faith gave her gaiety.

A correspondence of long letters, exchanged every week, sprang up immediately. De la Mare marvelled at her – the freedom from self-pity, the courage, industry, ardour. She reawoke in him the chivalrous homage he had felt for Katherine Mansfield, her plight giving her a kindred glamour. He was a little dazzled by this into over-rating her actual gifts as a writer and overlooking a touch of spiritual inflation, of conscious attitude, that made her brave creed of love and joy, to some tastes, a touch ingenuous and high-pitched.

She published three novels, designed ambitiously for a cycle of four allegories, but died halfway through writing the last. Throughout their course de la Mare took the most serious and admiring interest in her progress. He believed intensely in her poetic vision, and minded very little the naive psychology, improbability and melodrama that flawed its erratic gleam. He wrote her some of his best and longest letters, was very soon deferring to her judgement on his work before that of anyone else, and received her praise with a franker delight than he usually admitted to.

A fire of suggestions and counter-suggestions from his friends continued all autumn 1944 over *The Traveller*. Among so many, opinions naturally conflicted. His uncharacteristically vacillating deference to these, suggests that de la Mare suspected the task he had set himself was beyond his proper range, and it is doubtful whether the poem benefited from all their involvement. If a poet's own concept cannot make his philosophic theme lucidly organic to its imagery, an advisory committee will never make up the defect. But de la Mare felt free enough of the work now to take some brief holidays – one very happy one at Bournemouth, staying with Bert, whom he had not seen for five years. He still hankered after writing another novel, but began to realise that if the sustained energy for this had failed him for the past twenty-one years, it was not likely to come again now.

After a stroke his sister, Flo, died in November 1944, and he mourned her as 'the most loving heart and gentlest mind of anyone I have ever known'. He was also bitterly grieved at the end of this month to hear of the death, a few days after the birth of her second child, of Laurence Whistler's young wife Jill, Newbolt's grand-daughter. He wrote to Ella: 'Life goes on much the same as usual, and one goes on with it; but there is something within that keeps on returning to this tragic enigma, the life come, the life gone.'[6] And to Margaret Newbolt:

> Self-centred creature though I am, I often think of dearest Jill – in that way too that brings life to a remembrance, to such a degree at times that it resembles an hallucination, and one all but draws back one's head – but I cannot be really reconciled to these things. To think of the innumerable brave or desperate partings during these last years – and the no return! Each is unique and has no mention in the bitter tale. How minute a fraction of it all would be fatal to one individual consciousness; as I suppose there is a maximum of grief as there is of pain which the human body and spirit can endure.[7]

The deaths of so many he loved had made him no more inured to that enigma, and never would.

*

One of the Twickenham guests was Owen Barfield, who wisely urged that the central ideas of *The Traveller* be made more explicit, and the passage towards the end, in which the landscape traversed is actually *stated* to be the very Eye of Earth resulted, at any rate partly, from Barfield's suggestion.* Barfield also got him more than just politely interested in anthroposophy. De la Mare was finding that *ideas*, of all kinds, absorbed him more the older he grew. In the early morning he would find so many conclusions or 'footprints of steps forward' (he said) littering his mind that he could hardly keep pace with them. One of the worst deprivations of the war had been the rationing of talk; he needed other people much more as an outlet than for stimulus. Alone, he did not stagnate so much as ferment, like yeast in a corked bottle.

When Martin Johnson came to see him at Penn in April 1945, they had a battle royal on imagination versus logic, which began, to de la Mare's later penitence, with searching questions even before Johnson had had a cup of tea after his journey! Johnson sent him a paper on physics, logic and the imaginative significance of time. Such exchanges were immediately fertilising to the ideas formulating all this while for

---

* Barfield even pinned de la Mare down once (as hardly anyone could) to explaining the meaning of one of his earlier poems, 'The Changeling' in *Peacock Pie*. De la Mare said the word 'changeling' had for him the association of the beautiful and the heartless – the 'Belle Dame' figures of poetry and fiction, like George Eliot's Hetty Sorel, creatures of seduction, fatal to those who listened to their spell. another 'changeling' of his own poetry is the lady of 'Bewitched' in *Peacock Pie*, and the scene with Cryseyde and the boat at the end of *Henry Brocken* comes very close to the story suggested in 'The Changeling' itself.

Winged Chariot, and de la Mare liked to play the same kind of counterpoint with current companions as with current reading, ranging the ideas of one friend in front of another – Johnson against Barfield – and so testing out some theme running in his own mind.

He and Barfield exchanged their favourite lines in de la Mare's most beloved Wordsworth poem, 'Poor Susan'. He loved Barfield's choice: 'Bright volumes of vapour down Lothbury glide', but felt it carried a *slight* suggestion of washing-day. He stuck to his own prizewinner: 'In the silence of morning the song of a bird.' Simplicity, in good poetry, was to him inexhaustibly interesting: how, for instance, was one made aware beyond doubt that Susan was good and lovable? True simplicity was for him the release of profound and subtle levels of association, which the complexity and obscurity of modernist verse, on the contrary, actually inhibited. This was his chief objection to difficult poetry: that it does not achieve its own aim of including more meaning, but instead fatally shallows and limits our responses. He surmised that some modern obscurities – say in Dylan Thomas – were due to indolence and not fundamentally necessary. 'Poor Susan', along with 'Rio Grande', 'We'll go no more a-roving' and the 'Phantom Horsewoman' were among the indispensibles he once suggested in a discussion of 'what you'd take across Lethe'.

*

During recent months Jinnie's failing marriage had collapsed into divorce proceedings brought against her by Donald, who was awarded custody of the little boy. As life had darkened for her, Jinnie had become irreversibly alcoholic. Her father refused to recognise the addiction until much too late. N felt that if he had come to terms with the fact sooner, his influence might have persuaded Jinnie into taking treatment in time. But he could not bring himself to believe in a disaster so horrible in its inroads on personality for the daughter he had loved with such passionate, romantic solicitude. Angry protectiveness made him take her part very bitterly against Donald in the miseries their divorce entailed at that date.

Whatever he felt about the actions Donald felt forced to take, it is sad that de la Mare would not see the little boy much after this – he could only be brought to do so at all by the persuasions of N and of his niece Rosalind, who had kept her own friendship with Donald. The coldness toward the small grandson is one bleak failure of charity in a life so conspicuous for that grace. De la Mare's misery for Jinnie never found relief or healing, since her life's wreck was to go on down. Certainly his own life never brought him any worse or more confounding anguish.

*

On 6 May 1945 he wrote to Margaret Newbolt:

> I somehow cannot quite believe that Summer is still to come, & after that lovely burst of Spring, surely a matchless one, of all my 72. Nor is it possible to 'believe' that the War is over and in this welter of vileness and horror. But I do earnestly believe and realise that England has crowned herself with her greenest laurels and thank Heaven for that. The resolution, the audacity, the endurance, the unflagging intelligence – well, there we are.

The 'vileness and horror' he speaks of were those of the German concentration camps, as each, one by one, over-run and liberated from April onwards, gave up its secrets. De la Mare, appalled, felt such inhumanity could only be explained as a temporary mass 'possession' by the Devil. By June the European war was already becoming the past. Looking back, what had been five years of every kind of emotional and mental extreme looked to him now like a dream, 'or rather a deadly and prolonged vacuum of being'.

Then on 6 August the first atomic bomb was dropped on Japan, and suddenly the horrors of Belsen and Auschwitz seemed by comparison a lighter thing to bear, for this further horror carried acute moral distress. De la Mare could not here comfort himself by telling over 'England's greenest laurels'; she had connived at a crime, so he felt, and this struck at the roots of his patriotism. To Colin by letter, and to close friends at Twickenham in constant unhappy discussions of the ethics of the bomb attack, he betrayed what an appallingly ironic blow final victory had dealt him. He remained convinced that the bomb should have been demonstrated harmlessly as a threat. For many like him, that August day was a shattering Judgement Day in which they suddenly shed for good the upholding sense of innocence on the Allies' side.

Other dubious and dark issues that had been settled out of hand in the course of the struggle – such as the saturation bombing of Germany – only came to general knowledge in any detail, for the civilian population, later on. But when the atom bomb was dropped all public perspectives altered; a huge unease, both of conscience and of menace for the future, was thrown up to hang in the air and not to disperse. Ralph Hodgson was one whose spirits and belief in the future never recovered. De la Mare was too resilient for this kind of despair, but the strength of his feeling showed still in a letter of November 1945 to Gerald Bullett: 'The world is in a dreadful state, face to face with an unforeseen and desperate disappointment and disillusionment, and, in most that matters most, in supreme danger.'[8]

During this uneasy aftermath, he wrote no more poetry for a while. *The Burning-Glass* was much praised – the review he cared for most was by Elizabeth Myers – but one by Naomi in *Time and Tide* called attention to the sadness of these poems, and to Elizabeth he defended himself more than was usual for him:

> I haven't yet seen Naomi Royde-Smith's review of the 'B-G': she has always been most generous to me. There is no doubt too much of the melancholic in the poems; but if 'sad' is their effect, then they have failed (as they should not have done) to produce their own antidote. No true work of art is merely sad: e.g. Dürer's Melencolia – or Tennyson's 'Break' or 'The poplars are felled', or the Scottish ballads etc. etc. This is true even of a letter. Did you ever happen to see one in *Love* beginning 'Dear Alf'? It has the keenest pathos, is tragic and final – and yet what it leaves at its close is an inward radiance and reconciliation. Apart from grizzling and lamentation and self-pity and canker, much depends on what a poem is sorrowful about; and somehow even the blackest with remorse or despair may be redeemed by its form. 'Nihilistic' is quite another matter. Not – to come back – that any of this is intended to be a vindication. A writer, I fancy, is an animal that should very seldom defend itself, however sharp its claws: not even against the openly unfair; and I am quite sure N.R.S. wasn't that.[9]

He wrote one story, in October 1945, and a good one too – 'An Anniversary', which he called 'a zinc-edged story with a coldly odious hero'; a black ghost story for a black season. His secretary of this time, Violet Barton, was so much affected by its hero that she could hardly bring herself to finish typing it – an involuntary tribute that pleased him very much.

*

Peace, too, proved a very disillusioning affair, and de la Mare began to blame the politicians for it. The first post-war election appeared to him a souring exhibition of self-seeking and ingratitude. He was disgruntled by the success of Labour and angry at the fall of Churchill. On the subject of politics, he took to expending the most exhausting partisan heat, displaying cast-iron prejudice that assorted comically with his marked open-mindedness and detachment on other issues. Even mild Gerald Bullett, with whom he generally talked poetry, found himself, when he came to tea and supper in April 1947, spending the entire evening in political argument – and Bullett (as he explained afterwards, attempting to mollify his host) was not a 'hundred per cent socialist', merely against the Tory line – for himself he would prefer a radical Liberal government. It was very unexpected to see de la Mare on these occasions brushing aside all speculation, and laying down the law, fulminating in sweeping True Blue terms. However, the phase of political acrimony did not last more than a year or two. Otherwise he showed little sign of further ageing. He would still go out to the Savile Club to meet a friend for lunch, go to a play with Alick McLaren, perhaps, or to a Boat Race party at the Rostrevor Hamiltons; nor did he suffer afterwards when he had taken a six-thirty morning train to Plymouth but found its luncheon places already booked up (shortages were in many ways worse now than during the fighting), so that he had to deliver his afternoon lecture with only a glass of milk inside him.

He sent Elizabeth Myers a description of one of those waking dreams which reinforced his theory of a continuous dream-activity, merely inhibited by daytime's conscious attention. Sassoon had became prone in old age to similar experiences – he decided his were 'hypnagogic visions' – and they discussed these a good deal in letters of the early 1950s. This is de la Mare's account to Elizabeth:

> I'll tell you of one of my waking scenes – though it's nothing in comparison with yours asleep. I was at a public tea & an instrumental quartette was being played. I thought I would try to get away, then waited. First I saw a stream of pellucid greenish water flowing in shallow concavity above its bank, rapidly, and as if impelled by some other impulse than that of gravitation. Its smoothness began to form itself into watery furrowings & the ridges of these to interweave & intertwine: at which I realised that this was caused by the *hair* they contained; it had begun plaiting itself. I let my attention – not my sight – as it were travel up-stream & discovered a gigantic figure – marmoreal but living, & all of this in the loveliest colour – lying supine in the translucent depths of the water whose hair was streaming over his brow and face from the back of his head. He seemed to be asleep. And that is all. There have been two or three similar experiences, one of them when I found the company and din of the Tube rather oppressive. None has been horrifying; and all have been of a singular and unusual beauty. I am certainly not (I should say) even on the verge of sleep and the onset is quite different from mere imagining or making-up.[10]

Another example is told in the introduction to *Behold This Dreamer*. That time the waking vision was a continuation of an interrupted sleep-dream. De la Mare had jumped out of bed on waking and rushed to his window, because it had been so vivid – an allegorical procession of Spring, advancing up his Anerley street. He then saw his dream continue, printed on the actual roadway below. His entrancing

Primavera, with attendants, was being drawn towards him on a magnified toy-cart with clumsy wheels like gigantic cotton-reels. After standing there absorbed to see her go by, he went back to bed and remembered nothing more.

Evidently, though he could sometimes summon up such scenes when deliberately looking for a mental escape from an actual situation, others occurred sporadically through adult life, in miscellaneous states of health or mood and very varying degrees of the voluntary. All such waking scenes, whether he wrote them down or talked about them, he would mention in the same tone – that is, not at all impressed by possessing the faculty – always very much impressed and blessed by the result – and at the same time keen to investigate and analyse rationally, as far as seemed worthwhile.

*

In May 1946 he invited T.S. Eliot to tea, and Owen Barfield to meet him. The talk turned on Social Credit and some book on the subject Eliot was currently interested by. Barfield noticed that de la Mare was quite able to hold his own in this field. He was himself much struck by the 'aura of unhappiness' Eliot carried about him. De la Mare agreed, adding: 'And did you notice – of course you did – his very unusual eyes. They reminded me, but to their advantage – of Henry James's. One feels, too, that the unhappiness, if there, offers no way in. I wonder.' No way in at any rate for him; he and Eliot never got closer to each other than courtesies. He found Eliot a little humourless – at least he felt that humour was a quality Eliot 'thought rather small beer of' – and went on to wonder: 'Is a really hospitable imagination practicable without it?'[11]

He felt, as he had done with Yeats, a suggestion of the pundit, and was restive at Eliot taking himself quite so seriously as a poet. They were probably most at ease with each other when acting together to help someone in difficulty, as on an occasion when Eliot had enlisted de la Mare's help for George Barker. (He would do so again in 1948 for Ezra Pound, and de la Mare readily agreed to sign a letter attesting Pound's services to literature.)

Neither Eliot nor de la Mare could be expected to have great admiration for the other's poetry, but on occasion they exchanged gifts of it. When de la Mare gave him *The Traveller* for Christmas 1946 (into which he had written a sonnet from fifty-one years before), Eliot replied: 'I am very proud to possess this inscription. And it is an astonishing poem. I hope I may retain my powers as you have, but I am always a prey to apprehensions.'[12] He contributed a complimentary poem to the Faber 'Tribute' for de la Mare's seventy-fifth birthday. His final assessment was probably summed up in his introductory words at the memorial reading of de la Mare's poems held soon after he died by the Arts Council. Eliot said he always thought of de la Mare's poetry as chamber music – but the best kind of chamber music.

Eliot's letters in the early 1920s, when he was very eager to meet de la Mare, are much more free and warm in tone than the later ones. He had been very anxious to get him to contribute to the *Criterion*, and when he sent him the passage in *Ash Wednesday*, beginning 'Because I do not hope to turn again', was delighted by de la Mare's praise, writing back: 'I have not received any comments on that little poem which have given me more pleasure than yours, and I shall treasure your reply among a small collection of autograph letters.'[13] But that last phrase, though kindly meant, would have jarred a little on de la Mare. It was not the way he would want or expect a letter of his to be prized; and there seems to be an unconscious condescension in the compliment – it appears to confer a flattering distinction: admission to a choice collection.

The cordiality of those early letters suggests that Eliot had a stronger interest in de la Mare's work and mind when he was young than when he had matured into his own utterly different aims and methods. De la Mare for his part confessed in 1950 that he had never read *Four Quartets* (admitting at the same time that he had not read *Paradise Lost* right through either – 'not nearly!'). In 1951 he told Laurence Whistler, when talking about allegory and his own resistance to its bonds: 'What I have against T.S.E. is that in *The Waste Land* he felt it necessary to give precise meanings and correspondences.'

In his attitude to Eliot there was perhaps a touch of envy for a reputation that he felt a bit overrated. Whistler described to him a device set up in the Lion and Unicorn Pavilion of the Festival of Britain, with a display of a small handful of the greatest names in English poetry, and mentioned that alone among all moderns, Eliot's was included. De la Mare showed astonishment at what, in such select company, seemed an exaggerated compliment: 'What! Our Tom?'[14] When Whistler mentioned that Eliot was said to have modestly protested, de la Mare merely remarked quietly: 'I imagine he could have forbidden it absolutely, couldn't he?'

*

He found himself coming more and more under the spell of

Twickenham. His envy in the early 1920s of country-dwellers had been little more really than a wearying of Anerley. It was not at all essential to him to live deep among fields and woods, provided he had some greenness and beauty in his immediate surroundings. A suburb of Twickenham's age and beauty was the almost perfect environment for him – a fringe-world being, as from childhood, his natural habitat. Colin, Lilias and their child Julia were living for a while in the downstairs flat while house-hunting for their first home together. De la Mare would come up after the weekend at Penn, and spend a summer Monday afternoon in great content, shopping for provisions, loitering on the way back in the sun through the old alleys by the river, to watch the ferry from the steps of the White Swan, and children bathing where a high tide had flooded the banks, and to look across to Eel Pie Island, beautifully wooded. He liked to pick himself haws to taste, and share a joke about stealing them with passing boys, and get home to join Lilias, on the old Hill House garden seat, under the plane-tree, before going in to cook his milk jelly and plums. That was for him a very pleasant day. What N said of him was perfectly true: he did not ask much from life to be happy.

She would quite often come out now for the day to Twickenham, or stay longer if he was not well. Her health had forced her to retire from professional nursing, and he took her with him on holiday to Hove, where friends equally fond of them both, the Duffins, found them rooms in a small hotel. This was one of those companionable friendships which made de la Mare very contented all his life, however much his more remarkable friends might sigh, finding such people dull. H.C. Duffin had written a critical book on de la Mare's poetry.[15] Mrs Duffin provided equal affection and excellent sandwiches indoors, or a picnic to share, the four of them, in Preston Park, followed by a Western at the cinema. With N, he pottered about the Brighton Lanes for antique trifles, spending far too much on some Regency candlestick with blissfully guilty satisfaction. Some years before, when he gave up smoking cigarettes, he had begun collecting silver, rather at random, with the small consequent savings. None of this collection was exceptional, but he took great pleasure in his pieces.

The Traveller was out in time for Christmas 1946. John Betjeman praised it as de la Mare's 'strangest and loveliest poem',[16] but on the whole it fell rather flat. Not many critics discussed its ideas seriously, until Vita Sackville-West's persuasive and interesting Warton Lecture seven years later.* Curiously enough, that central notion of the Eye of

---

* Cf. also her essay for de la Mare's seventy-fifth birthday tribute.

the Earth, which de la Mare had feared might prove altogether too startling, she did not think important enough to the poem's philosophy to bring into her discussion at all.

Ella received the book with de la Mare's blessings and good wishes at Christmas. She shook her head over this, finding the poem the darkest he had ever sent her, an ironic present to accompany traditional wishes for 'peace and joy'.

*

The bitter winter of 1947, with London shivering under shortages of coal, gas and electricity, brought deaths of several old friends, but all other bereavements were eclipsed by the loss of Forrest Reid. 'One says lost,' de la Mare noted, 'but the loss continues and may deepen.' His grief had a misery in it, too, for it seemed clear that had Reid had better food (he died of tuberculosis of the stomach) and more attention sooner, he might have been saved. De la Mare was tormented by the thought that if only he had known more, he might have been able to rescue him. These two had exchanged work in progress for half their working lives; no critic came so close to de la Mare's own aims and nature, and could be so outspoken. Nobody writing alongside prized innocence, moral sensitivity, childhood, with quite Reid's humorous, instinctive purity. A favourite saying of his, 'intelligence is a moral quality', had expressed de la Mare's own ethic with a fellow-feeling he missed now wherever he turned.

At about this time Colin's family moved out from the lower floor of de la Mare's Twickenham flat, after the birth of their second child, Charmian; and loneliness weighed on him. He turned more than ever to N. She came to nurse him through 'flu and they would in any case meet about twice a week.

He was working on *Winged Chariot* and also had an unusual commission from Dick – to write an introduction to the volume on the painter Chardin in the Faber Gallery paperback series edited by Roy Wilenski. To Elizabeth Myers in 1945 he had listed his favourite painters as Rembrandt, Velasquez, Piero della Francesca, Goya, Degas, Holbein, Gainsborough, Sickert, Breughel, and Chardin. The list points up his marked preference for painters of human character rather than landscape and the absence of all moderns. Velasquez was probably his earliest passion, haunting his mind and his poems at the period of *Songs of Childhood*. But there is a mention of Chardin painting a black-green bottle and an onion 'in a kind of stagnant ecstasy' as early as 1919, and Chardin's still-life studies were a permanent enthusiasm; there is an old-age poem on one in *The Burning-Glass*. Faber's had secured scholarly experts for their introductions, among whom de la Mare knew himself to be a complete amateur, so he took great pains and made no pretence of other than a literary appreciation.

Chardin had, he thought, the perfectly balanced nature: true man of science and supreme artist. The skills of emphasis in his compositions fascinated de la Mare – 'that crucial cork' in the 'Cellar Boy': how did it acquire such intense significance? – the play of infinitely varied and related whites – the 'almost dazzling' effect his memory kept of Chardin's overturned cauldron, in fact no more than suggested by relation to the cellar-maid's white apron and surroundings. Poppy particularly remembered how, even as a small boy, he had been unusually sensitive to colour. Now he was noticing that its hold on his attention had strengthened with age. But what preoccupied him most in Chardin's work was the question *why* a painted loaf should so affect the whole spirit of the onlooker – the old riddle of the two-way relation between work of art and beholder which endlessly intrigued him between poem and reader. Chardin summed up what *he* meant by a realist: one who revealed the essential self of the bread, the knife, the overturned cauldron, as opposed to the 'actualist' whose legerdemain makes you 'stoop to pick up the cauldron'.

He had only lost Forrest Reid three months when Elizabeth Myers died too. She had travelled, in a last gallant bid for recovery, with her elderly husband to Arizona. In the desert climate she appeared to rally and wrote on with as much optimistic zest as ever. But at the end of the voyage home, instead of the May warmth she had hoped for, a bitter east wind met her. She overtired herself, strained her heart, and died very shortly after. De la Mare grieved for her as if it had been Katherine Mansfield's death over again. His brother Bert and Lettie fell ill together and N went off to nurse them, and came back only to nurse de la Mare himself with bronchitis and an antrum that had to be punctured. He was ill all through weeks of beautiful summer weather, and in risk of pneumonia. But as soon as he could, he resumed visits to keep an eye on Bert at Bournemouth and began working hard again. Even if he came over to Pinner to visit N and her mother briefly his duffle-bag came too, stuffed with papers. The load of correspondence, the frequent journeys, anxieties, were all building up throughout late summer of 1947: a much more taxing life than he had led for years, and bound for catastrophe.

His old blind Canadian friend, Miss Simes, had come over to England the September before and visited him; now he had a

manuscript of hers for which he was to write an introduction. Francis
Meynell was enlisting his help over the centenary for his mother Alice
– de la Mare agreed to open an exhibition in her honour at the National
Book League and to broadcast on her work. Meanwhile Bert suddenly
took a turn for the worse and he posted off again urgently to
Bournemouth, then shortly afterwards for two days to Bath, where
Ella and Margaret Newbolt had lately moved. Laura Lodge, last of the
homes they shared, was a small house after his own heart, with a
secretive garden where a fountain played behind high walls, above the
great sweep of the city. Margaret's hearing-aids were both out of order,
a frequent mishap, for when either of them protested at her brusque
handling and emitted weird yells and whistles, she would set about
curing it with vigorous thumps on the table edge. Without such aids
she was by now stone deaf, but she and de la Mare still managed
conversations of two hours at a stretch, for she was always deep in
some fresh enthusiasm whenever a visitor arrived, and asked the most
ranging and comprehensive questions – de la Mare scribbling his
replies rapidly on her notepad, rather wishing she did not put them
away so carefully afterwards, to be shared (as he rightly suspected)
with the next beloved visitor.

He asked her one of his own favourite questions about old age: 'How
often does the unique occur to you? – what you cannot remember to
have seen before?' and leapt to his usual plea at her replies: 'I think
you should put those into writing.' He was always urging Ella too to
write her own *De Senectute*. He thought it a most neglected field,
generally only written about by people who could not yet know what
they were talking of. Ella sat in the background with Florence and
Rupert, nodding with energetic approval to see de la Mare and
Margaret once again hard at it in the old Netherhampton way.

Back from Bath, he read a paper to a society meeting in London and
returned to Penn that night. Two days later he was due to be lecturing
again, and anxiety over Bert (after the first relief at his rally, from an
operation) had begun once more to sharpen. De la Mare had just
written to George Rostrevor Hamilton: 'I can hardly breathe in the
mélange of things to get done ... In about a fortnight I hope (unless it
has proved mortal) to be in quieter waters.'[16a] But mortal it nearly did
prove.

At the end of October, 1947, about to set off to London for his lecture,
he was getting ready upstairs at Penn when the blow fell. Afterwards
he vividly recalled sitting with his head cupped in his hands – it had
suddenly (it seemed to him) turned into a ball of ice: 'I can remember
nothing colder in effect.' It was a severe coronary thrombosis. Later he

said it felt more as if he had been shot than the onset of an illness. For three weeks his life was in danger.

Lying there, in the first desperate hour, it still tickled him to observe his son-in-law come in and tidily shut a drawer that hung open. N rushed to be with him and nursed him day and night, Florence once more taking on the whole household burden of so critical an illness, and Rupert dealt with his correspondence. As Rupert sifted through clamouring requests for criticism of bulky manuscripts, bids for sympathy from the neurotic, the suicidal and the purely egotistical, as well as the sincere requests for help of all kinds, he realised just how impossible this drain on de la Mare had become.

N tried to keep her patient's restless brain quiet and contented. She said it was the worst possible illness for his temperament, since he was forbidden to talk – a more or less mental and physical impossibility to obey. As November began, his progress was good, but the attacks of breathlessness were distressing. Some time went by before N took any sleep at nights; even then she woke at two and four a.m. to make him cups of tea. By December danger faded; it became simply an ordeal of patience.

He grumbled to find himself falling asleep so often – even between mouthfuls – and when at last he could be levered out of bed for the first time, his legs felt like cricket stumps. A worse bore was the tedium of his dreams. They seemed full of 'morbidly ordinary' acquaintances. What a waste of the blissful dark to spend it in the study of a congested genealogy of Mr and Mrs Abraham Lincoln, which had no documentary evidence in support of the data, and which his dream-self knew to be a tissue of fake and falsification. Yet he repeated now what he had said in 1927: that he would not have missed any of his serious illnesses for worlds – the mind became so clear, the whole experience was so interesting. It seemed to him not static but more resembling a journey. By January 1948 he began to share it with friends in letters again, dwelling, with a fascination too innocent of invalid's egotism to be boring, on the light shed by his symptoms on the mechanics of thought. He noticed that, like Dr Johnson after his 'severe stroke of the palsy', his hand made wrong letters, and he asked his own Dr Johnson, 'M.J.', whether 'the full *consciousness* of an inability to spell correctly – a seemingly brain-directed manual ability – is any substantial evidence that one has a mind as well as a brain?'[17] He had mirrors arranged so that he could see from his bed the birds coming to feed in the snow. 'Isn't it a scarcely credible joy to know we are only a very few weeks from the first snowdrop?' But he still had to live 'like an old housecat', his walks confined to the upper corridor. There was no possibility of

reaching Bert, now facing the prospect of more operations, except by
letter:

> Well, my dear old Man, I'd dearly love to see you and you know I'd come if
> I possibly could. There is so much I think about when I'm alone that I
> wish to share with you. *Not* unhappy things; and there's never a day goes
> by that I don't think of you and share a prayer with you …
> Your lifelong old
> J.[18]

He was even composing again – but not on paper – probably stories.
One of his greatest solaces was the company of Julian, now seven and a
half, who had taught himself more or less to read and spell by ear, in
an individual but perfectly logical way, evolving in the process such
usages as 'vallyerbull', 'supearyer', and, on the dark side of life,
expressions of 'hora'. De la Mare had always loved to have him around,
giving him sheets of paper to write on under his table while he himself
was working, and had so encouraged him that Julian was writing
easily at four, even before he could read. They kept up serial games of
make-believe such as de la Mare had played with his own children, and
N, too, took part. The force of his grandfather's imagination was
sometimes too much for the boy, and make-believe played quite so well
could tilt alarmingly into a reality of its own. Julian liked to pretend
there was a crook hiding in the fringe of trees along the Penn
shrubbery, but when 'Danda' told him the mounted police had come for
this character, and were waiting at the end of the drive, Julian became
frightened and they had to stop – no wonder, for de la Mare was
visualising as he spoke: 'Of course I could see them as plainly as
anything. I could hear their stirrup leathers creaking.' And he noted:
'If with children one pretends to be a Bear, they love it, but if then one
pretends to one's *self* to be a Bear they do not.'[19]
Once he could begin to walk out of doors, a visit to Hove was
planned; but he caught gastric 'flu soon after arriving there and was a
month making up the lost ground. All the same he felt well enough to
receive the eight grand-children (Jinnie's Stephen was included on this
occasion) for a seventy-fifth birthday lunch at Hove, also a hundred
and a fifty letters of good wishes. He revelled in his published birthday
Tribute, secretly organised by his bibliophile friend Dr Brett, and kept
from him by Faber's, as a perfect surprise, until the book was out.
There were about forty contributions – prose, verse, portraits and a
Max Beerbohm caricature.
He began to go outdoors in a wheelchair, and by mid-May was fit
enough to leave Hove for Penn, where the family celebration of his

birthday had been saved up for his return. He was in excellent spirits at the party, and afterwards, remembering the laughter, wondered how he could have had no warning from within. Only a few hours before, Bert, after some days' unconsciousness, had died at Bournemouth. Lettie had specially begged that he should not be told till after his party. 'It had always seemed strange to me,' he said, 'that we *can* so remain unaware of any such ordeals endured by those who are nearest and dearest to us. With him I have shared as it were the whole of my life ...'[20] They had been able to meet very little in latter years, but 'How sharply and reiteratedly one misses the possible company, even, of those who are gone.'[21]

An offer came of the Companion of Honour, to de la Mare's total surprise. He wondered if acceptance had any political overtones – would people think he favoured socialism if he accepted it from a Labour government? Rupert disabused him, and the honour certainly pleased him very much.

Ella was dying; de la Mare wrote to her sister Anna, who had described for him her mental wanderings: 'That wild nonsense about the moon and stars, & hills & valleys, & that lovely humorous, happy smile on her face – how vividly I see it! means, don't you think, how much life & self & imagination is burning on.'[22] But the very day he wrote this, she died, and with her was gone the longest friendship of all his writing days.

*

The Twickenham flat had been locked up nearly nine months when he was driven home for a few days as an experiment, with N, and gave his first tea-party, and attended (on 18 July 1948) a special audience with the King to receive his C.H. Quite as ardent a royalist as his mother, he revelled in the occasion; they sat at a little table together and talked away for twenty minutes, the King informal and easily amused. Back at Penn, the Thompsons entertained a visitor from Nigeria, the Oni of Ife, 'a Christian ruler', so de la Mare described him, 'affable, wideawake, vain, sagacious and enquiring',[23] with five wives and forty children. He would burst into a soprano hoot of laughter from pure pleasure and surprise when de la Mare's pianist grand-daughter Shirley played Schubert for them or when watching Julian through the wrong end of a pair of binoculars. There was a Victorian paternalism in de la Mare's descriptions, though it would never have shown in his manners. N had come to take care of him permanently now, and accompanied him on any visits away. Visitors to Twickenham, though gradually thickening in numbers once more, would often find themselves alone with the two of them, and sometimes de la Mare was ready, after tea and much talk, still to prolong the occasion with a stroll down to the riverside, sometimes even with dinner after it in a small Italian restaurant, Vacheri's, at Richmond. It was a favourite of his for many years, and once, asking the waiter what had become of the usual one, Joseph, was told he was ill. What was wrong with him? 'Well, sir, heart, liver *and* kidneys – regular mixed grill as you might say, sir!' This appealed to him a great deal.

The close friends who came often, usually appreciated N's real position of friendship in his life, but she was so self-effacing that she never showed the slightest offence if others less sensitive treated her as just a 'companion', paid to officiate behind the great man's teapot. Now and then she even undertook, for love of de la Mare, to receive those he could not face. Sometimes Meyerstein, with his malicious moods, was more than he could bear, and he would beg N to entertain him; once she was even made to take him out to dinner alone at Vacheri's, which she found very alarming, because he 'would say such awful things about people'. 'W.J.', as she and most of his friends now called de la Mare (the older generation who had known him as 'Jack' rapidly thinning away) exacted a good deal of her, taking an expert's interest in her housework, and pursuing her in her busy day with the impatient question: 'How long will you be?' He had perhaps taken a fancy to get at a piece of polishing together, or of rearrangement, and would not wait for her attention – 'Oh, let's change all the pictures round!' Very often N would not feel like doing this at all – but did! To please him, she would lay down anything else, break her much-needed rest, hurry back from an outing – he did not really like her to be gone from his side at all. And, once embarked, 'W.J.' would direct the rehanging of the pictures with wholehearted zest: 'I should be writing, but I *do* love this!'

No one lived more in his possessions. The pictures were all so many gates to other modes of life, of whose secret nature he never tired. There was his watercolour of York Minster, beloved since childhood; it had been his mother's, and he and Bert, as boys, had cracked its glass when they fired the brass knob of a bedstead, filled with gunpowder, in through the window. De la Mare was forever daydreaming about the invisible interior of that cathedral, making up stories about small figures painted going in and out.

Opposite the foot of his bed hung a dusky green watercolour of a small mysterious white house deep in a wood, a slot of window showing near one corner. He loved to conjure up a shadowy figure, on the edge between fact and fancy, that his eye could catch creeping round the foot of that wall, if he were half-attending. 'I could haunt that picture,' he said. 'How curious it would be to find oneself haunting a picture!'

Polishing was a matter on which he had dogmatic views. He would take a mop, boil the kettle, and put the mop in the steam in preparation for an attack on the beautiful old cupboard on the landing. 'Now, N, I'll show you what *I* do. Like *this*, both hands rubbing up and down.'

His favourite old pieces had nicknames – 'Tiger', 'Nannie Crack' (which held the collection of Midget books and objects), and 'Susanna'. This last was a wall clock, still cherished though it would not go, with a handsome plain face from which he had learned to read the time as a child. It finds a place in *Winged Chariot*:

> To me, one cracked old dial is most dear;
> My boyhood's go-to-bed, its Chanticleer;
> Whose tick, alas, no more enchants my ear.
>
> Dumb on the wall it hangs, its hands at noon;
> Its face as vacant as a full-blown moon;
> The mainspring broken, and its wheels run down –
>
> A kitchen chattel. No fit theme for rhyme;
> That case encrusted with a century's grime.
> And yet, it taught me 'how to tell the time'.

After he died, N sad to discover it had been disposed of casually, managed to retrieve it, even to get it repaired so that it ticked on for her with the voice out of his childhood. N was quite often now torn between care of him and her mother's need of her, left alone at Pinner. To solve this, sometimes Margaret Saxton would be brought over to Twickenham, so that both could be under N's wing together. Mrs Saxton shared many of her daughter's qualities and de la Mare got on with her comfortably and affectionately. She, too, was quite ready to enter into his own amusements. One afternoon she was to sit with him while N attended a hospital reunion. On return, N asked how they had passed the time. They had been browsing together in encyclopaedias for odd scraps of information. W.J. had said: 'Lady Cynthia Asquith is coming to tea tomorrow. I want to get one over her. We'll hand one up to her! – *"Do you know how many kinds of acacia tree there are?"* ' (He and Margaret had just hit on a reference to twenty-three species.) After Cynthia Asquith's visit, N enquired how did things go? De la Mare was regretful: 'I did mention it, but she just shook it off. I couldn't make use of it at all!'

London University gave him a DCL in December, and he was fussed about about the possibility of an anginal attack in public, hating the idea of being conspicuous, and relieved to have doctor's orders to miss out the dinner beforehand. At the ceremony he sat next to Winston Churchill, also being honoured, who kept murmuring to him out of the corner of his mouth: 'Lovely scene, lovely scene.'

1948 had been full of griefs and illness, yet his mood was not dark. At Christmas he gave N a manual on needlework, with a rhyme, one of a series of little valentines and *billets doux* he made for her, just as he had done for those he had loved as a young man. Private piffling is excellent for declaring love (as Swift used it to Stella) and probably, for this purpose, the worse the better – wit and finesse don't do half as well. So the doggerel about N's needlework dashed along, couplet after couplet, with execrable puns, high spirits, no literary pretensions whatever – attesting as only such headlong rubbish could to so central a tenderness. Naturally, the final flourish took the most brazen plunge of all:

> *And* what never slattern dreams
> Clothes are often what they *seams*.

Winged Chariot

N's cherishing, and his own exceptional stamina, had wonderfully restored his vigour. Although the coronary had been a severe one, he made a remarkably more resilient recovery from this, in his mid-seventies, than he had in his prime from the illness of 1927. By the spring of 1949 he was full of energy for work and friends. Invitations went out on all side for the delicious teas and lunches N would cook.

Sometimes now four or five would be invited for tea at a time, and if so, the company was usually heterogeneous – young and old, the unknown, the celebrities and the commonplace all mixed together; de la Mare was not only without snobbery, whether of success or rank, but quite without the habit of grouping and classifying people. Conciliatory too by nature, he developed no effective social technique against the pressing or the pretentious; those who pushed their way into his hospitality were seldom snubbed, with the result that a fair number of mere acquaintances plumed themselves on close friendship without grounds for it.

He made his own atmosphere at his parties, and whoever was there it was always their host that each guest most wanted to talk to and hear. Tea was always eaten sitting up to the dining-room table, as of old at Anerley and Hill House – the same lavish spread, of which de la Mare accepted at once one token morsel, which generally remained uneaten on his plate till he was ready to rise. Then he would move the party into the comfortable smaller sitting-room, where his china cat lay inside the fender, like the cat in his poem 'Comfort', 'on the warm hearthstone'. N sensibly insisted that he should have help with the letters that attended all this sociability. He did nothing about it, but she herself managed to secure a good young typist for two hours or so, three days a week.

As he looked down in early March 1949 to see the floods over the allotments skinned with ice, Twickenham seemed to him a place of enchantment in the sun. His home suited him perfectly and all was harmony in it under N's reign. Among the poems he gave her in manuscript from time to time was one he revised and published the next year as 'The Changeling'.[1] In her version he called it 'At Last', and the mood of its final stanza suggests his present contentment:

> Old now; only with thee
> My homesick heart can be
> Stilled in like mystery;
> Long did life's day conceal
> Thy tender dream and spell
> Now all is well.

His lifelong interests ramified around him. All he cared about most – for his pleasures had never depended on much bodily activity – were still within his scope and reach, and he found himself still as full of appetite for living as ever. Best of all, he was busy – contentedly able to say, 'I am up to my eyes in ink.' This was because he had begun to write poetry again, 'and after so long an interval I am very anxious to get on with it. Things stale, too, in one's mind, particularly if verse has anything to do with it.' And in another letter: 'The tap-root of Habit how deep it goes and there are very few things in this world the love of which survives so effortlessly as that for poetry.'[2]

Certainly the excitement of real work again and the 'head' of eager talk that rose on top of that private activity were more tax on his physique than in the past; he overtired himself with his enthusiasm, and N had to take him away to Hove in May 1949. All the same he was eager to invite friends down there too, for the day, and she would indulge him. Her care was never fussy, never bossy; she followed the rhythm of his inclinations and vitality, and when close friends on a happy evening looked across to see if, by a head-shake, she would indicate that they were tiring him and ought to be leaving, they would meet only her expression of happiness in his pleasure. If he did overtire himself on some occasion which he had enjoyed, she was quite content to take that in her stride, and repair the lost energy by special care the next day. In fact she would defend the life of impulse with professional seriousness, holding that the body makes better use of food and rest when work is finished and the mind inclined for them. Or that some prolonged session of talk and laughter can be better than any benefit of rigid routine.

This Spring Laurence Whistler was commissioned by de la Mare to engrave a decanter for him to give to the Warden and Fellows of Keble College. Whistler asked for a poem, so as to compose a design round it, and chose 'Day' from some gathered for the next collection. Florence, Rupert, and their children had given de la Mare an engraved goblet for his seventy-fifth birthday, the year before, and on the back of that Whistler had included a forgery of the familiar signature 'WJdlM' in a crown of stars. This time, going further, he persuaded de la Mare to use the engraving tool himself to sign his own name – a little shakily. But it took a great deal more persuasion of his modesty to allow a further small work this year, on which Whistler had set his heart – an engraving of the last verse of 'Fare Well' on the window-pane of the end closet in the flat, known as 'Bray Minima'.* The lines would hang there, in transparency, between whoever looked out and the screen of Twickenham treetops which by now epitomised for de la Mare

> 'the world whose wonder
> Was the very proof of me.'

This engraving, too, he initialled, when he finally gave in.

He worked hard once more on *Winged Chariot*, so long dormant. Bit by bit it grew more individual in scope and ambition, until by degrees it came to embody all his pet lifelong theories upon the nature of Time. When Owen Barfield came to Hove at the end of May 1949, de la Mare had some of it ready to read to him in typescript. This work cost him much pains, but very happy ones. The stuff of it was all to hand, alive in his imagination; it was only hard to find it a form. He evolved one that mingled casual conversational passages and lyrical flights, including at times colloquial terms and modern 'props' – his Yale lock, his telephone with its Speaking Clock service – and from these modulating easily into romantic and archaic diction without any break in tone; for this was natural to the character of his own thoughts, where homeliness and romantic strangeness habitually rubbed shoulders. Perhaps to help orchestrate his ideas, he adopted the device of marginal glosses which Coleridge had used for *The Ancient Mariner*; both have their precedents in Purchas. De la Mare's marginalia, however, are not narrative, but suggestive comments at a tangent. They are all arranged to look like quotations, but he admitted a good many were made up by himself.

Sometimes he would get N to take down a sudden idea for a stanza late at night when he was awake and very lively, and when she, almost too sleepy to scrawl, had got up to make him a cup of tea. A jotting like

---

* Ever since Anerley, the family sitting room in each house had been called 'Bray', from some obscure joke compounded of the Vicar of Bray and the volume of talk (braying). The Twickenham flat had three Brays, each opening out of the other – Magna, Parva and Minima.

this might be only the barest sketch of garbled sense, almost gibberish and defectively rhymed; it would be just enough to hook into his memory till he could work it out in the morning. Sometimes he would dictate actual composed passages of stories to N like this, too, beginning anywhere and just stopping when the impulse flagged – sometimes even in the middle of a sentence. Slices of actual story were likely to be dictated after lunch, before he went to rest, or after tea; whereas the seeds of stories more often sprang whole into his mind in the nocturnal sessions. Here is one such:

> Capsized boat in water tub – Visitors finds this when revisiting a flame of years ago, whom he intends to ask again to marry him hearing she is out when he calls he returns into the garden and thinking perhaps the toy ship belongs to garden [sic] son, he puts it away carefully out of sight on top of tarred shed when he returns to house the lady has come in rejoices to see him but is intensely changed; touches mourning in her dress, suggest that this is due to death but realises that the boat belonged to her little boy whose loss she has never recovered from.[3]

As a rule he would get N to write on alternate lines to leave him plenty of space for insertions. There is even one such scrap which more suggests her own style than his, as if he were borrowing not only her hand to write it down but her own straightforward flow of thought, as a kind of familiar mental shorthand for the scene in his mind, and the girl (rather resembling N) whose thoughts, alone by the river, he is imagining.

Informal though it was in tone, the Time poem was formally rhymed, in triplets (and sometimes even quadruplets): no very easy task to carry through without monotony for about four hundred stanzas. It set de la Mare leafing through his rhyming dictionary till it nearly came apart. The poem rambled and grew like the long talks over tea, bringing in similar pleasures and subjects. He described the beloved plane-tree in it, and South End House, brought in some childhood memories, and branched off to tell a short fairytale about a cat. As he had said of Forrest Reid's last novel, 'It just easies along', an odd creation, very much an old man's poem, with the particular virtues and characteristics of an old man's company. One cannot imagine a young one devising it – nor many old men either, for few poets write specifically out of the *happiness* of old age.

*

Poppy came to stay with him from time to time at Twickenham; with

Bert gone they depended on each other more and more for the reviving of the loved past, and Poppy could look after him if N had to be away. He directed her: 'You wash and wipe and I'll put (the comestibles) away! That seems fair enough.' When he sent her a cheque as a present – Poppy never had much to spend – he used the traditional formula from their childhood pretending game of 'Bankers' with Bert: 'Here is a piece of paper, if you don't write on it you won't be able to change it h'm *h'm*.' When she was present the flat can seldom have been silent. As de la Mare said, 'There's a good deal to talk about when you have shared this world with anyone for about 75 years', and since both liked to *do* the talking they spent a good deal of pains, with much amusement on his side, fencing for an opening. 'Her conversation,' as he said affectionately, 'is not what you might call *of the first water*.' Poppy's defence against interruption of her monologue was to throw out, as defiant bridge across any forced pause for breath the two words – 'And *so* ...!' They argued aggressively and enjoyably, tucked into N's cookery, swapped memories of Forest Hill, and nonsense, and laughed a great deal. Poppy, who survived him, said they never went more than three weeks or so without a meeting, all their lives.

Owen Barfield was gently pumping de la Mare, as ever, for elucidations of his poems. He got a surprisingly matter-of-fact one about little Louisa of 'The Keys of Morning' in *The Listeners*. He had wondered (like other readers) what was the significance of Death's smaller key:

> Both were of gold, but one was small,
> And with this last did he
> Wag in the air, as if to say,
> 'Come hither, child, to me!'

De la Mare wrote back: 'The two "keys" – one was for Death's big door, the other for the little – like the Irishman who cut two exits in his chicken-run (a) for hens, (b) for chicks.'[3a] Laurence Whistler, asking the same question on another occasion, queried whether the little key was to go in by and the big key suggestive of a way out the other end of death. De la Mare smiled and said that, if it meant anything, it was that Death had a sense of humour, and confessed he had nothing so mysterious as Whistler's symbolism in mind. All the same, he was taken by the notion and decided: 'Well, I shall always say that now.' In the same conversation he resisted another suggestion – this time that the introduction to *Come Hither* was more of a precise, decipherable allegory than anything else he had written. Surely it is; but de la Mare did not want to think so. He would not agree, and protested that you could 'say Sure Vine was the Universe, Mis Taroone Nature, and Nahum her imperfectly understood son who is more than Nahum, but that is mere sermonising ... The correspondence *must* be left loose.'

Snow fell to bury 1949. He looked back on the year: 'I can't remember to have "worked" harder than during this past year: trying but a great treat.'[4] The note of happiness is very plain; he knew and hugged his good fortune, and creative energy continued high through most of 1950. In January he was writing away at his 'screed in verse' in the small hours, and that spring coveys of fresh poems for the new collection went out in the old style to periodicals. Looking back at midsummer, the past half-year seemed to him busier than ever. 'It's curious that so much should have come to be done at this somewhat advanced stage.'

Simon Asquith brought Augustus John to make a chalk drawing of his head, and it was completed in forty minutes. 'I sat down in the nearest chair, he leaned his drawing-board against another, sat down himself, and set to work without the minutest preamble, merely asking me to turn my chin a little more to the West – the direction indeed in which it is normally bound. We had a delicious talk ...' But even so it was some effort. 'Why "sitting" and talking should be so much more tiring than merely sitting and talking is something of a mystery.'[5]

De la Mare sent off ninety poems to Martin Johnson for his choice – the book was planned to hold about eighty – and at Johnson's criticism he left out one he had recently written about the atom bomb, a subject that emotionally involved him to a degree he could never handle successfully in verse. His similar verse-attacks on materialism or scientific arrogance often read naively. Irony of a very subtle lambency played over all his talk, but curiously, in his verse, as Johnson candidly told him, he was downright bad at irony. Nor does his diction help: 'dullard' and 'popinjay' are epithets that carry no charge of anger to a twentieth-century ear.

Johnson also made some criticism of the new poems on the grounds of obscurity; and he was not the only reader to nettle de la Mare by asking what some of them were really *about*. De la Mare considered modernist obscurity mostly due to mere laziness, but his own very careful verse could become quite as obscure through the opposite fault: a too-conscious art spent on avoiding the obvious, to such an extreme that direct statement, altogether eliminated, leaves only a tenuously-linked succession of hints, floating on music.

Among several old poems revised (some, de la Mare said, in their first versions more than a half century old) one called 'A Daydream' attracted particular praise in a review by Edmund Blunden. It had been, in fact, among those Mary Coleridge looked through (in its earlier form) for *Poems 1906*. Another, 'The Vision', written for Naomi nearly forty years before, was cited by Duffin in an article in the *Spectator* as an example of de la Mare's unique retention of lyric inspiration into old age. De la Mare does not appear to have felt any need to disavow praise received under such slightly false colours. Perhaps he felt it of little relevance to a poem that readers should know when the first impulse to write it had come. Certainly he never arranged his poems, within any particular mixed collection, according to chronology.

Inward Companion (1950) is one of the most varied of all these collections, and most unequal. Yet its prevailing mood is more serene than most; faith in God the good creator seems surer, and the infinitely varied and marvellous potential of nature is to de la Mare, more than ever in old age, the proof of the sovereignty of imagination, compassion and beneficence. The old anguish is there – at transience, at corruption, at the impossibility of knowing whether the replies that experience seems to make to our longings have objective validity, or are merely subjective, conditioned by our own temperaments. The difference is that de la Mare now seems less tortured than he was by this predicament, and by the doubts it raises. He seems to accept it, looking it gravely but more briefly in the face, and then passing on – or turning back – to the direct response, as in childhood, trusting himself once more gently and simply to the evidence of the senses and the instinctive movements of the heart. That he depended on a strong spiritual faith, whatever its precise grounds, could not be doubted by anyone reading the poems of his old age – as readers of (say) *The Fleeting* might well have doubted. Never explicit, such faith has become everywhere implied, and carries the unsentimental tenderness and authority of suffering fully faced.

*

Directly *Inward Companion* was off to the printers, he turned to a choice of English sonnets to go, with an essay, into the current *Saturday Book*, and to toil at what was now the fifth revision of *Winged Chariot*. When it had been despatched to Dick in typescript, de la Mare reckoned that this version was nearly a thousand lines long. To add to his own task, he had just decided to make the extra lines in certain stanzas all end throughout on the same rhyme as the rest – though he called this *felo de se*. In practice it occasionally meant five or even six successive rhymes to the same word.

Sonnets were interesting him a good deal just now, and he became deeply absorbed in a theory on the relation between beat in verse and the natural bodily rhythms of breathing and pulse – and between these again and the rhythm of sea-waves breaking on the shore. When seized with such enquiries he became quite obsessed. N was questioned on the normal rate of pulse, and when she replied that 68 to 72 would be normal per minute for a young person (the pulse tending to get slower with age), he set her to count the number of waves, minute by minute, day by day, as they broke on the Hove pebbles. His findings – with a proposition that might have appealed to Sir Thomas Browne – he added tentatively at the end of his essay on the sonnet, in which he tried to account for the enduring popularity of this difficult verse-form. He reckoned that a sonnet takes about a minute to read aloud – the best way to read it.

> During that minute the heart beats normally about seventy times –
> diastole and systole. One double pulsation to every two syllables. And no
> less regularly we breathe. So beat the breakers of the sea on rock or
> shingle, as do the ripples even of a puddle ... Can it be that this
> minute-full of heart-beats, welling over with the sensuous, imaginative,
> and intellectual experience recorded in what we read, has in itself a
> half-secret influence on one's innermost self ...?[6]

For relaxation he kept his 'window-watch' on the Twickenham seasons, finding the spring of his seventy-seventh birthday (1950) still a 'strange and utterly astonishing Event – really, of course, an infinitely gradual succession of events exquisitely minute. It marvels me more and more: and how I do detest the quasi-scientific elucidations of all such phenomena.'[7] His other current enthusiasm was a fat volume of Audubon's *Birds of America* which he pored over, a very few plates at a time, to spin out the delight as long as possible. Each Audubon study he found 'magical in its variety and design, and in the living presence of what he seems to have loved so intensely that he inhabited each one in turn *and* its surroundings.'[8] It was Green-Armytage he was writing to – the closest left to him now of all his contemporaries, and the one who most shared his zest for the *present*. When he talked of the past there very seldom crept in to de la Mare's tone sadness because it was behind him; he had so very strong a faculty for re-living, for plunging heart and imagination wholly into the experience recalled, that this gave his reminiscing unusual freshness, variety and haphazardness. He did not repeat himself as much as old men usually do, nor did the memories follow set grooves; whatever he dredged up nearly always bore the stamp of rediscovery, and was memory in that live yeast condition which impels poet and artist to *make* with what is remembered. Perhaps also his continuing curiosity and fertile new speculations upon all he recalled also kept the past 'potential', as it were. He did in one respect repeat himself, of course – in trying out the same gambit upon a succession of friends; but this he had always done – for the deliberate pleasure of collecting comparisons, seldom by mistake.

Frances Cornford came in the spring of 1950, and with her he spent a long happy session reviving their old mutual joy over Rupert Brooke's company. There were few others left now of such early Georgian friendships, but Margaret Newbolt, herself still ardently alive in mind, was living in London again, and came (in the charge of the nieces who cared for her now) to see him. They continued the same long, eager discussions as of old, though she now no longer even attempted to use any hearing-machine, and the little pad (partly inscribed already by other friends) came out at once. But this time de la Mare was determined not to allow his replies immortality; he was sitting close enough to a drawer to slide each page into it surreptitiously as he wrote the next, distracting Margaret's attention the while, and she had to leave when the hired car arrived, puzzled but unable to trace her vanished hoard.

This summer two loved friends from the far-off days of his American travels, Florence Lamont and Virginia Howland, also visited him, and the latter, who had not seen him for twenty-five years, described him as 'deeper, richer, warmer, more sure of what really matters and counts, *blessedly* older'.[9] He radiated so much energy of mind on these occasions – often recharging from his own store the sense of vitality in his visitor – that it would seem incongruous at the end of the talk to hear him excuse himself on doctor's orders from coming downstairs. Nor did he yet look his age. But what most distinguished him from others of his years was that one felt the passing moment was still uniquely precious to him. What he would mainly seize on to discuss was likely to be some train of enquiry arising out of immediate things – the startling effect of a bright interior caught across two dark interconnecting rooms in the mirror hung beyond them, or the great complex of the plane tree's dangling mottled arms – how did they manage never to get in each other's way? Or perhaps it would be some oddity of his own mental processes which he had recently noticed, some poetry reading he had lately listened to on the radio, and found 'too perfect', and must analyse exactly why that should be displeasing and inappropriate.

He would come into the room from his afternoon rest already beginning to say, before the threshold was crossed, 'Don't you agree ...?' or 'Isn't it a curious thing that ...?' He still read very widely, and keenly debated controversies and puzzles of the day – Hoyle's theories of astronomy, Leslie Hotson's researches into the identity of 'Mr W.H.' of the Shakespeare sonnets. He spoke more often now of fatigue, and was becoming very much wearied by any journeys, yet still found it worth incurring this cost in exhaustion to gain the stimulus which meetings for discussion gave him. He would still rejoice too in those fresh landscapes it tired him out to reach, as when he visited Lettie again in Dorset, and saw once more the open sea, the sunset river, and the wonderful skyline of Purbeck with the ruins of Corfe Castle.

A new great friendship began when, in the summer of 1950, T.F. Higham the Oxford Public Orator wrote to him about translating the quotation from 'Fare Well' for his speech when de la Mare was to be given an Honorary D.Litt. by the University. De la Mare was not fit enough to attend the June Encaenia, and his presentation, to receive the degree, was postponed to the following February, but meanwhile a very happy bond, mostly through letters, grew up between him and Higham, who had a rich field of his own interests to share.

When *Inward Companion* came out in November, it was welcomed – the warmer serenity of these poems of old age were a comfort to many. In any case de la Mare had well passed that stage when, at any rate in England, a well-known man begins to be popular on account of his age itself. Yet even allowing for this advantage, the praise from Stephen Spender, Blunden and many others of discrimination gave him very great pleasure, and kept up the writer's energy in him. But he was harrassed by correspondence, and was suffering from piles, an old complaint. He did not feel well enough to spend the usual family Christmas at Penn. In addition to his own minor health-worries, far worse anxiety was deepening about Rupert, and in January 1951 the family learnt it was cancer that lay behind all his variety of ills.

*

De la Mare got to Oxford for his honorary degree in February 1951, which gave him great pleasure; he loved the ceremonial in Wren's Sheldonian, the black and grey robes in the land-locked pool of graduands, the reunions with Rice-Oxley, David Cecil and his three grandsons (Dick's boys) at the Dragon School; also a meeting at last with Higham, over tea in his house. Higham was a sensitive translator of the Greek and Latin poets, so they had many subtle minutiae to exchange about the problems of persuading mind-stuff into words.

There was also Higham's notable collection of shells from all over the world to examine engrossed. On later occasions he gave de la Mare two from it, a Lyra Imperialis and a Precious Wentletrap, prized exhibits ever after to visitors at Twickenham, their intricate convolutions and ornaments stirring him to endless speculation. 'How delicate a problem it is,' he wrote, 'that the occupants of self-erected edifices of such beauty and artifice and strangeness should never gain an outside view. But isn't that possibly true to *some* extent also of W.S.?'[10]

It was a very hot summer, and N and de la Mare spent many of the baking mid-days down by the river at Twickenham. He loved to watch the cargo boats. N would fill flasks, help him down the wide, cool staircase to the ground floor, and wheel him in a chair to the riverbank under the trees, until the sun began to slacken. One day, by the time they turned home, a high tide had brought the water creeping over the path. A couple of boys with untidy, pleasant faces helped N push the chair up by another route; de la Mare tipped them half-a-crown each and they ran off, delighted and surprised. When the two came indoors, happy and content with such an outing, he would begin to coax: 'Now while I rest, Enny, you write it down – you describe what you saw this afternoon.' He never tired of persuading her to try his own craft on the impressions and pleasures they shared. Obediently she would set to work, prompt and unselfconscious as in all she did, and pour out upon paper the details of their happy day – the willows, the fishermen, the bargee-family's clothes hung out to dry – all those small things they had relished together. She would wonder how he could take such interest in her thoughts and company, feeling herself of no account beside him, not well-educated, not clever. 'Don't you see, it's because you are *you!*'

Neither had anything the least childish about them: the small, straight, briskly-moving nurse, her hair parted and drawn back (because he would have it so) in a rather Victorian smooth severity; and the old man she wheeled before her, with his impressive head and unusual, vivid glance. But the secret of their charm for each other was that, with both, the wholehearted interest and pleasure of childhood, fresh to every impulse, had never staled.

*

Reviews of *Winged Chariot* began to come in. Desmond MacCarthy said: 'He has written poems for half a century and never at any date did they seem to his readers either modern or old-fashioned.'[11] He thought the theme well-suited to de la Mare's 'dragonfly attention', but put his finger on the obvious weakness of this longest and most discursive of all de la Mare's poems: a lack of that unifying power to arrange its ideas which a Pope or a Fitzgerald would have commanded. Others took up the question whether de la Mare could be considered a 'Modern', for the poem had made its own terms with prevailing fashion, adopting contemporary informality of tone while yet retaining, alongside this, de la Mare's usual highly-mannered literary diction. The weakness in unity MacCarthy faulted was, of course, one that had cost de la Mare great pains to try to overcome; but without either narrative or sustained philosophic argument he could only offer the slenderest logical pretext for the dartings of the dragonfly. And he apologised to Eddie Marsh: 'I'm pretty certain there is no positive "train of thought" in it: not much more at any rate than a light engine and a guard's van.'[12]

About this time Robert Speaight, the actor, introduced de la Mare to Jean Mambrino, a young Jesuit and gifted poet. The Frenchman's vivacity, spiritual insight and warmth, made this another special friendship, mainly postal. Answering Mambrino's first letter of admiration, in the summer of 1951, de la Mare said that it had brought 'that inmost happiness of mind and heart which I fancy only poets can share to the full, because, in this, spirit and the imagination communicate one with the other and in two minds'.[13] Pausing there, he was amused to see he had slipped, for the first time he could at that moment remember, into claiming consciously to *be* a poet. It was a noticeable fact that he always spoke, and without false humility, merely of his own 'verses' or 'rhymes'. He had long ago argued to Naomi that, even should one write an indisputable *poem*, the claim to *be* a poet stopped the moment its last line had been finished – it was a gift of good fortune which might well never come that writer's way again. His advice to a young beginner was emphatic: never think of 'being' a poet, or of becoming one; *just write*. Like Hodgson, he held the calling and title of poet the highest honour possible, and went on to Mambrino: 'If one has an all but lifelong yet inexpressible idea of the true meaning of the word, that [i.e. his hesitation to claim it himself] is easily understood. You might indeed perhaps agree that it w'd be safer in general to denominate nothing positively as "poetry" until it was, say, a hundred years old.'[14]

When inviting the Frenchman to Twickenham, he added: 'In a very real sense we have *already* met.' Mambrino came with a manuscript notebook of his own poems, in September 1951, and read aloud his own translations from *Peacock Pie*. He and de la Mare continued a lively exchange of books, articles and poems, though de la Mare felt at a disadvantage with his imperfect spoken French, so they would talk in English. (He confessed that on his own brief visit to France he had 'never said a word'). They met seldom but Mambrino had an unusual gift for intimacy, and they visited, as de la Mare said, 'by heart'. He even spoke, diffidently but confidingly, to Mambrino of spiritual things – the peace that escapes workaday living, but which was there for him in any glance out of his many-windowed home at bird, tree, cloud, raindrops on the glass, or the very light itself – and just now and then when a piece of writing went well.

In August 1951 Sir Russell Brain, the distinguished neurologist, became one of several visitors so fascinated by de la Mare's conversation that he began the habit of keeping notes of their talks. He later published his record as a book, *Tea with Walter de la Mare* (1957), an indication worth having of de la Mare's table talk, but which remains an indication only. As Brain pointed out, de la Mare was no monologuist, for all his talkativeness, but a very responsive listener also. Unfortunately modesty led Brain to suppress almost all his own contributions, presenting de la Mare's remarks on their own, separated from the context of interchange, which shallows and disjoints them, exaggerating his 'knight's move' leaps of association to a grasshopper fidget at all not the same thing. The prismatic flexibility of de la Mare's humour and irony, on the one hand, and the strength of his seriousness on the other, both suffer. Also, the defect he had noted, writing of fiction, that a long conversation of short parts tends to wash thin the scene where it takes place, applies with real damage here. Some men so lose themselves in intense discussion that while it lasts they are quite oblivious of everything external. But with de la Mare the *setting*, the complete passing moment, with all its subtle adjuncts of time and place and light and sounds from the fire or the street, was an integral part of what was passing between their two minds whenever he talked closely with a friend. At South End House, the home which best fitted him, everything contributed to impress this – *the moment* – strongly on consciousness, while the talk flowed. The district itself, so secluded, romantic and unexpected to a visitor arriving from the middle of London, gave the effect of coming physically into a delaMarian region of the mind. Then, the prodigious 'guardian tree', the rooms in which every picture and curious ornament was important to his inner life – from the Dürer 'Melencolia' which had meant so much to him from early Anerley days, to the head of Hypnos he had introduced into the *Midget*, and that big coloured print of Breughel's 'Winter' which has a poem to itself in *Memory* – every detail added its own emphasis to the atmosphere. It was not a case of possessions arranged with studied deliberation to project a certain impression, but simply that, accumulated with love over long years, they had become so much a part of their owner that they were now an extension of his identity as personal as the shell of the Lyra Imperialis to its animal inside. They created an 'envelope' for whatever passed in talk, which tended to keep its presence felt, occupying part of the visitor's conscious attention all the while. Also, de la Mare was a conversationalist comfortably at ease with pauses: he liked to drop into them as part of the relaxed companionship of the talk, like rests in a musical score.

Robbed of all this rapport, his oblique verbal flashes stiffen into staccato *mots*. And with it vanishes the satisfying, intimate, contemplative quality such talks always had, unless de la Mare were particularly tired-out and restless. Brain had a just phrase for the idiosyncrasy of his conversation at its best: 'a soliloquy for two'; but it was for two plus the unique scene and that particular meeting.

*

In September 1951 Rupert finally died, nursed at home. De la Mare, thankful that so much suffering was over, grieved bitterly for Florence's heartbroken desolation – she and Rupert had been a very united couple. Her father cancelled social engagements, work was the only relief – serious consideration now of a book of his old reviews, though he was uncertain if he had enough time and energy left to carry it through.

A sad time, one would have thought, and so it was in much; and yet to Laurence Whistler, visiting him that September, sadness did not seem uppermost in de la Mare's mind. It was an afternoon of warm wind, tossing the great plane and scattering pieces of sun across the green leaves of Marble Hill. De la Mare had been unable to sleep during his much-needed afternoon rest, and came into the room tired out; yet the impression was of some inner serenity that increasingly supervened. He talked continuously and happily that day: of fiction, poetry, the meaning of life – and also of a big boxing-match in New York between Turpin and Robinson, over which he had eagerly taken sides. Writing down his impressions of a long and fascinating talk after he came home that day, Whistler felt:

> Though he is weaker, the beloved, than a year or two ago, he seems to me *less* haunted than then, and the ache of impermanence seems less acute.

I do hope he may move out of that still further before the day when he
must go, or definitely foresee going.[15]

It was noticeably a clearer mood than, say, when these two had stood
on an earlier occasion at the window, the Marble Hill cuckoo calling in
the delicious evening, watching together the young chestnut leaves at
the moment when they looked, they agreed, like bright handkerchiefs
plucked up into a point in the middle. De la Mare said he couldn't bear
to see them, 'because it will never happen again' – lightly, to mean
ostensibly that *this* spring would never happen again; but that was not
all he meant. Or, on another evening, saying goodbye: 'Well, we've had
an A.1 talk – and now I'll excuse you from coming to my funeral.'

Joyce Grenfell, who had first known him many years earlier, came in
the spring of 1952, and they rediscovered each other. She thought he
seemed far better than when she had seen him last, ten years before
during the war, at Penn – with Elfie down for tea, 'there and not there',
a shadow in the background with her kind parchment face and velvet
dress. Joyce Grenfell noticed how merry 'W.J.'s glance was now, how
young his skin looked. They watched from the window the heads and
shoulders of a rowing eight swing their way levelly across the green
outlook, the river itself invisible. De la Mare would exclaim as they
went by: 'The prettiest sight on earth!' and claim theirs was the most
beautiful of man-made movements, except for an expert rider's.

With lady guests, de la Mare really preferred to have each to himself
– and certainly they did too. The *tête-à-tête* was always his happiest
form of conversation, and besides, he liked to flirt a little. When he had
to ask several close female friends on the same day he would try to
placate by such little compromises as spacing their invitations out by
quarter-of-an-hour intervals. Cynthia Asquith brought a kind of
cooking-clock or egg-timer to remind her not to stay too long and tire
her host; she set it firmly on the tea-table, where its officious tick was
not appreciated by her fellow-guests – nor by her host, though he was
not one to show his irritation. Cynthia Asquith's talk in general
company was astringent, forceful and amusing, and she still had
striking good looks. De la Mare was braced by her company, and they
were old and close friends; but when he was alone with Joyce Grenfell
he could relax into random reminiscences and giggles over absurdities.
They laughed a great deal, and he would keep her talking till seven
o'clock, behaving like a beau; and he really did not like her to say
goodbye, reverting to his old lover's trick of sudden baseless anxiety:
'Take *great* care of yourself!' When she protested, he would turn it off
with a flourish of gallantry: 'If you see the Koh-i-Nor diamond sitting

on a plate, you naturally say "Do take care of it." ' On the telephone he would play up to her: 'I'll die if you don't come.'[16]

Long gone were the days when he had found communication by telephone a constraint. He could make ten or twenty minutes by telephone as rewarding as a visit, and sometimes would extend it almost to an hour. Such talks would be close, even if the other person had to contend with the whistles and shunts behind a Paddington station phone – intimate, amusing, quite at ease, de la Mare wasted no time at all on the shallows the instrument encourages. As far as he was concerned, visualising away, the friend was *there*, the cork out, ideas free to flow between.

He enjoyed the invisibility too, the chance for impersonations, a kind of 'Mr Waterman' game. He rang Whistler one day to inform him he was wanted by Scotland Yard; and another assumed voice, with a slight foreign accent, pouring out a tale of woe from a stranger who had broken his leg, once deceived even N so successfully that she became most sympathetically concerned, and was passing the receiver to her own doctor, who happened to be in the house, before it dawned on her who was speaking.

He was hard at work, and on projects still ambitious – selecting from essays and reviews, with a *two*-volume work in mind – embarking on the second half of a lengthy story in rhyme: 'Poor Jeremiah', from long ago. Plans like these had to be abandoned in the end, but in 1952 they were still the centre of the day's activity – sometimes for spells of the night too. He told Martin Johnson:

> I am being stupidly busy, and shall probably die of it in the next few weeks. I keep on shilly-shallying about my epitaph. I don't want a costly tombstone, so mustn't indulge in anything even remotely epical. What do you feel about just a simple statement:
>
> > It was Ink
> > I think.
>
> Is this sufficiently informative. There is an alternative:
>
> > Too many a quarto
> > That he hadn't ought to.
>
> Or does this style encourage slovenliness.[17]

On 7 September 1952 the *Sunday Times* published a beautiful and powerful new poem by him, 'We Who Have *Watched*' on the sense of responsibility the individual somehow obscurely bears for general evil, something that had always been for de la Mare one of the inescapable conditions of a full, thinking human state. Instinctively he felt in tune with the religious mystics who declared 'Sin is a Lump', 'No man is an island' and 'Who is not weak and I am not weak?' The enigma of why this responsibility exists, if it does, de la Mare nowhere defines – to do so would have led him into regions of philosophic definition or religious dogma, alien to his truth. But where he did recognise truth for himself, it is noticeable that there is no question whatever of escapism. The responsibility, however anguished and totally obscure, was something he just faced, and shouldered. Hints at this conviction come in letters and poems, and in that passage where the Midget considers it, but he had never voiced this notion of the mutuality of man, that we are 'members of another' with such direct force:

> We who have witnessed beauty fade,
> And faces once divine with light
> In narrow abject darkness laid,
> Consigned with busy heedless spade
> To clay from mortal sound and sight –
> Where look we for delight?[18]

The poem ends 'What mercy dream *we* of? Even the italicised verb *Watched* in the title emphasises the emotional charge: the weight of guilt. He himself had watched, especially in the years since 1939, such losses happen very near to him – of the young, the gifted, the innocent, by death, by error, and worst of all 'by wanton sickliness defiled', from inside themselves. The dismay in 'We Who Have *Watched*' runs parallel to Blunden's 'Report on Experience', and to the bitter, moving quiet of that poem's comment: 'This is not what we were formerly told.' De la Mare's experience had none of the horrific circumstance that give Blunden's poem such authority, and the poem does not compare in power, but it is of the same seriousness.

The *Sunday Times* publication of it raised a rather absurd small flurry of protest. A sentimental public could not bear their charming old poet to speak out like this; he was not expected to deal in anguish so nakedly personal and so committed. Several letters were printed in reprimand, and there were some in defence. One of de la Mare's American lady correspondents wrote demanding that he should at once write another poem refuting the first, and someone else actually did that – it was printed in the next week's issue. De la Mare commented to Cynthia Asquith:

It's curious that the moment there's a tinkle of controversy in a poem, people who I am sure don't really care much for poems, or rather poetry (a very different matter) immediately begin to take interest ... There is a little oddity perhaps in controversing about any piece of writing that consists solely of questions, and the only answer that occurred to me was, is the miserable bard legitimately entitled to write a poem on Sunday beginning Humpty Dumpty sat on a wall, and to follow it up on Monday with another poem beginning Humpty Dumpty had a great fall.[19]

There was a broadcast that same week by George Rylands on 'The Speaking of Poetry', using records of the voices of Yeats, Eliot, Newbolt and de la Mare, and one critic, curiously, noticed an unexpected affinity between Newbolt's style of reading and de la Mare's – both meditative without any striving for effect. It is possible there was more than chance in this resemblance, and that de la Mare had kept some inflections and techniques ever since his earliest coaching in this art, up in the Ark at Netherhampton. He read much better for the microphone than in a public hall; the resonance and variety of tone in his voice showed in their beauty when the voice need not be raised. For an instrument close to him he could 'think aloud', as if in privacy, gaining by this an impromptu, intimate, 'throw-away' delivery that lets the reader efface himself.

Bronchitis lengthened out his Autumn stay at Penn. While N was away, he wrote (as usual) impatient for her return: 'Tomorrow! It has seemed nineteen ages and I'm in *no* shape alas. Dr R. said Oh law, I *am* wurried about you! You're ageing very rapid, and what about the Toom?'[20] Even when he did reach Twickenham, he kept his bed another month; visitors were discouraged, in December the doctor forbade him to answer letters. Another thrombosis threatened, only injections staved it off. Yet he had lately managed to accomplish his recorded part in a composite broadcast on 'The Experience of Age'. He was the junior in a foursome of Laurence Housman (87), Gilbert Murray (86), and Bertrand Russell (80), interviewed in turn. 'From *a* point of view,' de la Mare commented, 'the exposition might be covered in three words – Look up Moonshine! Look up Moonshine! [sic].'[21] But the result was an interesting programme, and Viola Garvin wrote to him that it had 'a sort of condensed glow of happiness'.

Some visitors were not banned. Whistler, invited three times in one week, found him cheerful, saying he was writing a lot of verse. Asked about rhyming, he remarked that he often had to run through the alphabet to find a rhyme, or use a rhyming dictionary – he had lately acquired a new American one. His mind would limber up by running idly into nonsense-rhyme, rather like draughtsman embellishing a margin with doodles while thinking his way into a design. Getting up from his rest that afternoon, a toilsome process now, de la Mare had made up several, which he quoted. One, which had other versions, ran:

> I think of the sunny mountains
> Where once my cousin dwelt.
> They were sold to a firm of accountants
> And now have been overbuilt.[22]

He had a way of drawing his hand over his face as if to smooth the laughter off it, and then would begin at once on a quite different topic.

He had lately discovered a new enthusiasm, for books of ecclesiastical architecture – substitute for those actual churches and churchyards he had never been able to resist whenever he passed one. He sat up in bed surrounded by parish churches, French and English cathedrals – 'Absolutely inexhaustible,' he declared, 'any time and anywhere a real solace. I'm not very good company (all the time I mean) for myself just now – so celestially active a mind! and so hebetudinous an old body.'[23]

He *was* good company, all the same, for any visitor allowed in to tea – full of absurd little jokes and desultory memories. And sometimes even now the disputers like Whistler could get betrayed by lively discussions into the old cut-and-thrust of argument, which at this date was really much too tiring. It could begin so easily, and de la Mare never hesitated to advance the most illogical propositions, so that the listener, to counter them, would feel obliged to use such very obvious banalities of reason or commonsense he would heartily wish he could take flight himself into de la Mare's own tactic of absurdity. One such 'discussion' got de la Mare nettled enough to mention it afterwards in a letter. It had begun with his pronounced prejudice against the modern world of machine-made things; uniqueness was the essential element in beauty, he claimed, and that afternoon he would not allow that a mass-produced or even reduplicated thing could be beautiful. Nor would he even admit that the beauty (and uniqueness) may lie in the design – as for example in a beautiful type-face, which is the work of an artist, and unique and surely not less valuable (Whistler argued) because reproduced thousands upon thousands of times in a book. Still ruffled two days later, de la Mare wrote to another friend: 'And, would you believe it we disagreed very gently but persistently, whether of the two was the more beautiful, a four-in-hand, either minus or plus the horses, or an Exquisite Rolls Royce. Between you and me it passes my comprehension that such a conversation should be possible, but it was elaborated about 20 years or so ago when Colin and Dick were two to one. Why, bless my heart, even a perambulator is lovelier than, say, a gazelle.'[24]

At the new year he complained gently: 'I have been in bed more or less the last five weeks and yet find it difficult really to rest.' His doctor,

who was a good psychologist in this, ordered him doses of brandy on
early waking, and to eat 'Crunchies', a crisp chocolate-covered bar. It
amused him to be prescribed small treats as medicine and find they did
him good.

In February 1953 Whistler found him still in bed, pale and talking
perhaps with less animation than on the last occasion, but with a mind
clearly as active, acute and imaginative as at any time in these last
three years. It was running on his early days as a reviewer, because he
had been finishing *Private View*, the collection of criticism. He had
wanted to write, instead of the preface just done, a proper introduction
to the book which would discuss what reviewing is at root – a question
that interested him a great deal. As he pointed out, nobody has a good
word to say for the critic, yet criticism is constantly applied whenever
we experience any work of art. But he had had to abandon writing any
such essay, admitting simply: 'I'm worn out.'

In the re-reading of his old reviews he had sometimes felt, he said, a
touch of patronage towards this vanished self. More often, he was
subdued by finding him 'less wandery, more securely based, and more
confident in the expression not only of his convictions but of his
"views" '[45] than the self re-reading them forty years on.

In the preface, he paid a warm tribute of gratitude to Naomi's help,
as his editor in the *Saturday Westminster* days. They had not met since
the Taplow years, and very seldom corresponded now, but she had
lately helped him by lending a huge bound volume of *Westminster*
back-numbers.

Some of his *Times Literary Supplement* notices he could not accept
were his till their office records proved it. On the other hand there was
one piece he had been confident of, but the *TLS* told him it was by
Virginia Woolf. 'That was a bit conceited of me, wasn't it?' he
murmured.

The prescribed half hour of conversation was soon up, but as
Whistler made to leave, de la Mare detained him, declaring he should
talk to N now – he himself would just listen. This meant, of course, that
Whistler and N exchanged two sentences each about a performance of
Macbeth she had lately seen, before de la Mare's resolution broke
down. In the end he talked on for another hour, discussing the case of
Bentley, the young man recently executed despite some extreme
protests and a last-minute attempt to get a reprieve from the Home
Secretary. The victim, a policeman, was not actually killed by Bentley,
but by his accomplice, a boy too young for the death sentence. Bentley,
it was claimed, had urged him to shoot. De la Mare spoke firmly in
favour of the execution, though when they went on to touch on the

horrors of carrying out such a sentence he said that capital punishment should be abolished. Then he added that nevertheless there was no point in keeping such a fellow alive – 'He has to die some time, and he is of no conceivable value in this world.'[26] His advocacy of the death sentence was not merely a passing one; when the abolition of capital punishment became a national issue, Lord Altrincham approached him to seek his signature for a petition for abolition. De la Mare's typist remembered that he dictated straight on to the machine very lucid and fluent reasons for taking the opposite standpoint.

23

'Sing while you can'

As soon as he seemed fit for it he resumed work – 'Like a mouse sniffing cheese after an endless diet of sawdust' – but it was not yet really within his reach. He began to nibble in earnest at a scheme for an autobiography, envisaged by him as a record of highlights only ('When you get into dinner-parties, you're damned, aren't you?'). Nothing came of it, and he found it difficult to put his mind to any job. When Dick proposed a pocket selection of his poems, he turned this over to Green-Armytage to choose them and write the introduction. He now felt very tired all the time; the work he needed for peace of mind itself harassed him, and the contentment of 1950 and 1951 at 'being so very busy' failed him; he spoke of his lot in the spring of 1953 as 'Endless work and desperate toil'. The completion of *Private View* had drained him; it had been reduced finally to a not very lengthy single volume, but the sifting process had been extremely taxing.

A visit to Hove was tried, but with no great effect; he spent most of his stay in bed. He felt apprehensive as his eightieth birthday drew near and he began to be pestered for interviews, and he realised with a sinking heart that the day was bound to bring a flood of extra correspondence. In the event he was forbidden to deal with this at all, and Olive Jones came to Hove, where he spent the birthday, and acknowledged all his birthday congratulations for him. It was just as well: there were over eighty telegrams alone. Tributes were printed, a big portrait photograph covered the front of the *Listener*, the *Times* bore another with the caption 'Genius in our Midst', and the *Sunday Times* commissioned a special portrait drawing for which he had to sit. Amongst all the rest came a long narrow white envelope containing the Queen's offer of the Order of Merit. He was one of the very few people of his time besides Churchill to receive the O.M. as well as the C.H., and the only writer.

*

Florence was moving to a smaller home, at Henfield near Brighton, so de la Mare drove over from Hove for his last long visit to Penn. A recorded reading of his poems, made at Hove, was broadcast during Coronation week, and by substituting the name 'Elizabeth', he published a rhyme which had started: 'Victoria is my Queen!' written in 1897, the year of the Diamond Jubilee, and put in the first Horn Book for the Rowley small children. His investiture with the O.M. stirred his romantic heart, and made him more passionately and sentimentally a royalist than ever. He sat all by himself to listen to the whole of the Coronation on the radio, visualising it so intensely that it seemed to him afterwards that he had been there. After his audience with the Queen, he told Margaret Newbolt: 'H.M. is a marvel and I worship her – to such a barbarous degree that I quite forgot not to talk too much.'[1] He was well that day, on the top of his form.

Private View came out the same month, and had its own share of congratulations. The larger part of the reviews which made up the book were studies of recognised masters, written to mark collected editions, centenaries, and the like. Wisely, de la Mare gave the major space to his early pieces, which show his critical appreciation at its best – crisper and briefer than his later essay-style. It was all a poet's criticism, magnetising out of other authors' work such metals as corresponded to his own.

He felt doubts about producing yet another book of poems, but Dick was firmly for it, and de la Mare left the choice a good deal to him – at any rate over early verses, as he explains in his Author's Note to the book, which speaks apologetically of 'these relics'. The book was to consist of those pieces printed in magazines since *Inward Companion* had appeared (quite a large number), together with a few recent ones, and a proportion (this time larger than ever) of revised versions of early work that had escaped previous siftings, either by design or from random magpie storage. Among them appeared the last of his love-poems to Naomi that he himself would ever publish, 'So It Would Seem'.

There was also the tender poem, 'The Disguise', given earlier to N and surely about her, although for publication he removed the portrait's individuality. Her version had begun:

> Dream-haunted face,
> High cheeks, and dark clear eyes,
> So natural and sweet,
> Few may perceive how wise.[2]

It is a pity that he substituted, for those 'high cheeks' 'still lips' – something of a de la Mare cliché, reducing the particular woman to just another of his many dark-eyed Anonymas, charming but alike as peas.

O Lovely England (1953) is the slightest of all his collections, and adds little new in kind, though the skill and flexibility of his music remain. The book was a not unworthy final sheaf, and as such it was praised. It was chosen in March 1954 as Foyle's Book of the Year, a distinction that carried a £250 prize. It seems strange that an early poem so beautiful as 'Astray' should have escaped all former volumes. However, the strongest poem 'We Who Have *Watched*', was one of the latest written, and another of the best, 'All Gone', mocks the depressing platitudes current about old age.

He had found it quite different, and not at all a depressing experience – only in certain details. To be kept to time for instance was harder. 'Dickie Dragonheart ... doesn't hesitate to ask even nowadays if he may have revised proofs back in 10 days (And I know it all comes from kindness).' One of the people who could screw up his resolution to get a piece of work done, without worrying on at it for ever, was a young married typist, Mona Tait, first called in when one of his regular Twickenham secretaries fell ill. Her previous work had been commercial rather than literary, but de la Mare took to her a great deal, and she was often able to help him wind up his lagging vitality. He was haunted by the fear that if his habit of industry were once to snap he might break down completely in will for all creative writing, and never get going again: the ultimate misery. Mona Tait had the kind of dark, attractive looks and delicate features to which he had always been susceptible; also a quality of brisk elusiveness. She could argue, and she could detach herself, and was not in awe of him. He spoke of her 'gentle but formidable heart'. His long words foxed her; she would dispute them, and out would come the big Oxford Dictionary and she would of course find he was right. He probably rather liked the fact that she was a little surprised at this outcome.

He acquired a Smith's 'timer' – not unlike the device that Cynthia Asquith had brought to tea – and would set it for an hour. It became difficult to get him to continue with any task that wearied him, once its bell had rung. He would talk all the time the typewriter was tapping, and interrupt; and there were the occasional miserable mornings when he would sit with his clip of unanswered letters, unable to dictate one sentence. As he always tackled his letter-chores first, that meant no creative work either. Long years ago he had said that on a day without work he felt like an angler without bait; now it was downright torment. But such occasions were few. His memory remained to the end

surprisingly good for what was in the current clip, and he seldom
needed to read his correspondence over again before dictating the reply
already clear in his mind. Later on Mona Tait learned to imitate his
turn of phrase and he would gleefully sign some small forgery. When
dictating stories, he was as fluent as of old, 'telling them aloud' straight
ahead in the old style, without notes or hesitation; if he did break off
and start again, he would go on to a completely different slant.

He varied a great deal in energy now, but not so very much in mood.
Asked if she had thought him happy, Mona Tait said she had felt he
was lonely – that essential condition he spoke of as one of the things
increasing with age: something really little affected by outward
circumstances, for he felt closely surrounded by those dearest to him
and realised the blessing of that. It was just that the essential human
condition being a solitude, this becomes more salient as time goes on.
'Almost invincible' he called this substratum of loneliness now.

One of his resumed amusements at this time was in singing and
whistling. He would greet N with a whistle in the morning, to show he
was awake (by now, of course, she slept near him on the same floor),
and when alone they would still break into song together. In the cold
winter of 1955 he made up a rhyme and a tune for it –

> Bury me in a snowdrift
> Whate'er the month may be
> And when the Spring buds break again
> Just float me out to sea

– and they would belt this out, very early in the morning, in voices as
deep as they could reach, until laughter dissolved the duet. 'There's a
touch of genius in that second line,' he remarked. He discovered that N
had a repertoire from childhood of temperance songs and hymns, and
at tea-parties now he loved to show her off. She would oblige, in her
very pleasant alto, with the greatest simplicity and naturalness,
sitting behind the teapot to render 'Who'd Be A Drunkard?' or 'Father,
dear Father, come home' – (the old parlour song of the little girl trying
to drag her father from the public house while her small brother lies
dying at home). De la Mare delighted in these, partly for their good
tunes, partly for the flavour they recalled of his boyhood. He would
have liked N to revive such recollections in her dress also, but here she
was not quite so biddable. Though readily falling in with his wish for a
demure Victorian hair-style, she let him sigh on in vain: 'Why *don't* you
wear a bonnet, N? I *wish* you'd get a bonnet with cherries on it.'

For that matter, he had not quite lost his interest in his own clothes
and appearance. He was gently vain of his neat hands and feet

(especially the latter) and would ask N, could she not find *any* reason, while visitors were present, for him to remove his socks? She thought the best plan would be to wear sandals; then he need only turn up his toes while talking to draw admiration discreetly downwards. He liked her sometimes to get out, for close friends, a sheaf of photographs of him taken by professionals at various times. He gave them mocking titles as they lay strewn on the floor – 'Myself at Scotland Yard', 'The Soul's Awakening', 'What is that Smell?', 'The Dotage' – but would pretend some indignation when these were greeted with derisory agreement, working his shoulders a little like a sparring boxer and expostulating: 'Look here!' In fact they very seldom did him justice; so mobile an expression generally seems uncharacteristic in a 'still'. Most of the photographs looked like an actor in various roles, each slightly a caricature of his real self.

Other musical entertainments at the tea-parties developed out of N's performances. Joan Hassall the wood-engraver, a familiar visitor of later years (de la Mare greatly admired her art), often came with Joyce Grenfell, and would set up a small table-harp and play to Joyce's singing, 'Glory to Thee my God this night'. De la Mare wrote afterwards that while they were singing the evening hymn, somehow 'it was early morning in June, or May, and a lovely morning ... Have you indeed ever come across anyone who could simply at call sing so small (rhyme) and in perfect association with the little harp?'[3] They sang Elizabethan songs, carols, folk songs, and then all together Tallis's Canon. Joan Hassall had a substantial figure, and de la Mare noticed how her tongue would unconsciously and endearingly stick out a little between her lips with the effort of concentration, like a small girl's, while she dextrously twanged the strings. These singing parties were a continuing pleasure. In 1954, in bed in winter, he got Joyce Grenfell to sing him 'O Mr du Maurier', and not to be outdone, replied with a Maurice Chevalier number.

By this time, when acquaintances pressed him to let them bring their children too, this had become, very naturally, quite often a secret burden. The modern child who picked up de la Mare's precious ornaments without asking, hailed him casually as 'Walter', and roamed around the room unchecked behind parents deep in talk, was a trial.

Too courteous to show his irritation, de la Mare suffered in silence – or rather, in a flow of talk on other things, while N anxiously did her tactful best to distract the unruly in the background.

Nor was he, as a matter of fact, particularly good with any child-visitor who was shy – in spite of his passionate love of children and of observing them, and his intimate relationship with some, above all with Julian. He liked children to be forthcoming. A boy scarcely out of childhood might get searching general questions to answer, such as 'What character in a book is most real to you?' De la Mare never stopped to think, for one thing, that his fame might produce awe. From his point of view, he was speaking to an equal. Once at Penn, after a volley of his difficult queries had met with very shy replies from a young godson (expected to speak up in the presence of a listening circle of de la Mare grandchildren and family), his 'Well, what *are* you interested in, then?' came with crushing effect, though he had not meant to snub. Even an adult among his friends – some writer not well-known – would feel confused at times when approached on such *very* level terms over technique.

At this late date, after so many years of apparently total burial and oblivion, even the years in Oil came back acceptably to memory, and he would reminisce about them quite often. He seldom criticised any of those for whom he had worked; indeed he rarely spoke of anyone with direct asperity, and once said: 'What an intolerable burden it is to really dislike any fellow creature',[4] referring to one of the very few he really did. But he did once get on to the subject of unsolicited visitors with some sharpness: 'The worst experience you can have is the American bore.' One gentleman from Texas had furnished him with details of the size, population and political history of that state, *ad nauseam*. 'After a while,' de la Mare said, 'I told him I had to leave the room. It wasn't for the normal reason! I merely went out for a *rest* – about five minutes.'[5]

*

By early 1954 the demands of caring for him were telling heavily on N's health. She was at times desperately tired and asthmatic, but hid the exhaustion as best she could and carried on. So did he. In January the BBC's van called to record a story, 'Bad Company'. He was in fact 'hard at work as can be' on a new book of stories, many of which remained only half done at his death. 'Reading them over,' he said, 'I was struck by a certain insistence on old Mors as if being old one could not but sit with one's eyes fixed on the further bank. And then I came across a MS. of about 1900 also full of Mors, so it seems to have been an inveterate habit.'[6] The bent was probably inborn; though double family bereavement when he was three – painful death for his father so soon after sudden death for Uncle Abraham – may have had something to do with it. Certainly, though not from gloom, his work had questioned death persistently and the clue it withheld was as vital to him now as ever.

In February 1954 he had a fall in his bedroom against the live electric fire, but escaped with a singed dressing-gown and a fright for N. His balance was becoming unsteady; he described himself as 'loosely bed-bound'. His day was usually spent in bed until tea-time. But he had plenty of work in view; besides the book of stories, he had decided on a volume of his collected lectures, as urged long ago by Green-Armytage. The revision this kind of book would entail would obviously be even more taxing than *Private View*; all the same, he worked at several of the lectures over and over, and had a good deal of the book prepared before his death.*

He had to shuffle, leaning on N's arm. Making an entry like this, slowly and laboriously, he would distract the visitor's attention by commenting on something in the room or beyond the window that could form a peg for a conundrum. He fell again – much more seriously – in the bathroom, hitting his head, and slight concussion followed. After this his writing became extremely crooked and feeble for several weeks. Lucidly and intensely interested in the mental symptoms the fall produced, he seized the opportunity to pursue at first hand the light such effects could throw on the precise relation between brain and mind and discussed with complete detachment and rationality his mental aberrations, referring to them as 'delusions' – which drew gentle expostulations from N: 'I don't think you need call them that, dear.' He retorted: 'There's no reason why one should avoid speaking of a delusion, any more than a corn.' He told Russell Brain, who paid him several professional visits, that he had not at first felt he was in his own house but in another, called 'Grosvenor Cottages'. His room itself seemed to vary in size, or change its shape, and he found it impossible to visualise what was behind him. He said he thought of the brain as a kind of mosaic; if it received a jolt, the myriad pieces 'don't quite settle in the same places'.

N brought a mirror, and propped it against the bookcase at the foot of his bed, so that he could see for himself the view through the window behind him, the cottage and stable of Marble Hill. Another fall – out of bed this time – toppled the bedside books with a crash, and the doctor wanted the legs of the bed sawn short to lessen risks.

Stimulated by the revisions he had been doing these past months, de la Mare said his head was full of ideas for new stories that fascinated

* Unpublished.

him and he could not stop writing them. He remarked on the way the characters in them arrived whole – to talk about 'making them up' was not correct at all. 'You couldn't just invent a button on – it would have to be sewn on properly.'

Sometimes he would invite a friend to 'lap-supper' by his bedside, or would have one in, even later, for Cointreau and coffee by the fire. Once, as soon as Whistler sat down on one such late visit, ending near midnight, he began: 'Women – what do you like in a woman? I ask because I am hoping to get on in the world by asking the right questions. And so I am trying them out on you first.'

He spoke that evening of at least ten unfinished stories, some of which he thought better than anything in *A Beginning*, the new collection whose contents were now nearly ready. Asked if he could take up any unfinished story on any day and go on with it, he said yes. He claimed he could do much the same with poems even, 'but that is not so certain'. He asked what great poet Whistler would have liked to be; Whistler hesitated, saying it would depend how much one was prepared for what it would involve – their lives were apt to have a great deal of suffering. 'One might say,' de la Mare replied, 'that in a *real* sense the best lives are the ones which have a great deal of suffering', but added that the torment of the last year of Keats's life was almost unbearable. He agreed in the end with his visitor's choice: 'Yes, I should like to have been Vaughan.' They talked of 'My soul, there is a country', and de la Mare recalled Bridges saying to him: 'I don't see anything in it. What is the point of the winged sentry?' De la Mare could only stare in amazement.

Late on a December evening, he told various dreams – one of walking downhill towards a little town at the bottom. 'You couldn't describe it as a village, it was too sophisticated and evil.' All was brilliantly lit up, he did not know how. He had to cross water to get to the main street, and the noise of the water alarmed him. The houses were of a Tudor sort, with overhanging upper stories. Everyone was watching him at the windows – 'Evil faces of bewitching beauty'. Bewitching, he added, in the real sense: sinister. The whole place was evil. It was in the atmosphere, 'like oxygen', but as an element that made it difficult to breathe. He also spoke of a story – probably a fragment of a very early one – which he hoped to include in *A Beginning*, but never finished, about two evil characters who *invented* a third – 'But do you know, that character was, to me, the reallest thing in all those stories.'

Sometimes Poppy was there at these late sessions of talk. Her conversation might not be 'of the first water', but it enjoyed running in similar channels. She loved telling ghost-stories at first (or very nearly first) hand, and while de la Mare and his visitor were discussing sinister dreams, she could be heard, in the background, talking to N about condemned cells and other enjoyable horrors.

A long, quite new story by de la Mare, 'The Cartouche', came out in December 1954 in *Encounter*. It is so allusive in narrative that the point dissolves in a mist of asides. He would ask visitors if they understood what happened in it, and was really put out if they honestly replied 'No'. Although he was not oversensitive to criticism, he did always hope his latest work might be praised above the early, and felt rueful at someone picking out a recent and rather slight poem in *Time and Tide*, 'The Sleepwalker', as his best. 'It was one in the eye for me', he said, for the poem belonged to Florence's childhood, when she used to sleep-walk at Mackenzie Road. Green-Armytage had a very early poem, 'The Morrow', printed for him as a pamphlet to give away to friends. Resigned to being 'usually horizontal', making up yet more doggerel epitaphs for himself, he would mention, without complaint, that it had been months since he last went downstairs, and then add in the next sentence: 'What's particularly lovely up here is that you look down on the birds' backs as they fly, wings outspread.' N caught bad 'flu and her mother came to help. By now, N very seldom had a clear night without going to de la Mare's bedside, and was nearly always bronchial or asthmatic or with aching head; she became thin and light as a child. It did not matter to her; they were so happy together that there was no burden. When they were both in trouble, she with a high temperature and he with a fall on to the footpiece of his wheelchair, she sat up in bed, keeping old friends like Green-Armytage, too considerate to bother de la Mare himself, up to date with news about him: 'W.J. is now only able to move about the house in a wheelchair' but adding that she was laying plans for getting the friendly park keepers to carry him down to his rooms below, that he pined to see again.

When they went to the sea in April 1955 (as much for N's sake as his own, for she was barely convalescent) he had to be carried in at the back door of the hotel by a porter, and the wind and rain nearly volleyed them into the sea. They had had to give up their favourite Hove hotel and go to Brighton, to get a suitable ground-floor room – a change de la Mare hated. The hotel was 'a massive pile ... of a very substantial character', and he detested it. When they came home, N gave him (for his eighty-second birthday) a blue budgerigar, a bird that pleased him by something of the character he had always liked (and used in poems and stories) of a parrot. The expression of its 'blackberry sphere of eye' reminded him of his choirboy glimpses of Gladstone. At first he was against teaching it to talk, but later on it came to mutter, in its small grating chuckle, 'Pretty boy'. Its company provided him with inexhaustible lines of speculation.

A *Beginning* was in proof, and Colin very much pleased his father by supposing that the title story, which was his favourite, had been a recent one – when actually it belonged to the time of 'The Almond Tree'. Work for the lecture book continued.

There was a second mirror beyond the bedroom, placed so that it reflected into the one at the foot of the bed – the old device used in his 1947 illness – in this way he could still see the plane-tree. In July he happened to be looking its way during a thunderstorm when, to his mixed horror and fascination, the tree was actually struck by lightning, in a fork where there was a hole. Leaves that had piled up inside were set alight; the smoke-puff was an odd coffee-colour, he noticed, as it spiralled up. The bark slipped down round the limbs ('like a woman's frilly-frillies', so he described it), and the park keepers told him that the giant, supposed to be over three hundred years old, older than South End House itself, must be doomed. Experts found a crack in the trunk from apex to base. De la Mare was greatly distressed and shaken, even quoted from the burial service: 'We brought nothing into this world and it is certain we can carry nothing out.' He did feel the tree's existence bound up with his own, something as real to him – though his feeling was simply strong attachment, not superstitious terror – as the old bedridden cottager feels in Hardy's *Woodlanders*.

Yet the tree did survive, and stands to this day, though much tree-surgery has shortened it and the magnificence he knew has gone. Sometimes he would pass time in trying to find a name suitable to its personality – some word bearing a sense, in the sound, of the forbidding, as the word 'Ichabod' does. The right one should be many-syllabled, and begin with an A, he thought, but he could not hit upon it. He often instinctively spoke of it as 'he'. 'My Green Goliath is so still in every tendril you'd think he was shamming dead or gone to dreamland,' and he would pursue its riddle. 'If one imagined it to have a consciousness, one falters a little. It would be rather like entering into the chill for a moment, say, of St Paul's. I suppose animals, birds, trees etc., are much more *plus* their surroundings than human beings usually are. That is why Wordsworth presumably had sometimes to touch his gate-post to make sure that it was real.'[7]

He wondered whether we see an actual tree or a sign for a tree – the Idea of a tree, which is perhaps the reality. Was the so-called 'real' tree the counterfeit? Certainly he suspected some clue lay in *this* tree to the nature of the real beyond the actual, that might give at last, to enquiry, or dreaming, if persistent enough.

*

One day in July 1955, as Joyce Grenfell was leaving, he said: 'Come again soon. I won't like this year to be over. My days are getting shorter. But there is more and more magic. More than in all poetry. Everything is increasingly wonderful and beautiful.'[8]

It was a sweltering August, and he was having pain in his swollen ankles still from the fall in the spring. He wore his dark dressing-gown all day now, deciding he was unlikely to return to the palaver of getting dressed any more, it was too great an effort. But he fretted to see his downstairs rooms 'before it becomes really impossible. Again and again I have suggested sliding down the banisters but my medical Advisors seem opposed to the idea.'[9] In October several of his closest friends saw him, Naomi among them. They had not met for twenty-two years and she went away depressed, feeling he had little pleasure in her coming.

Leonard Clark, one of the younger poets who had become a friend in recent years, began to hatch plans for a De la Mare Exhibition at the National Book League to mark his next birthday, and he took a pleased interest in this. It was also cheering to have *A Beginning* come out in October 1955 to a good welcome – it was even called one of his best collections. A letter from David Cecil, whose criticism he admired so highly, came saying: 'You never fail to make me see the familiar in a new, strange, delightful way. You rejuvenate experience for me, as no other living writer does. I expect I have said all this to you before in a letter. May I say it again.'[10]

When Whistler came in December, de la Mare mentioned again an old projected allegorical story 'The Aunts', one Naomi had in old days tried hard to get him down to. He described it now in some detail, as if he still wanted to write it. It was to have been about a little boy who lives in a country house with three aunts – the World, the Flesh, and the Devil – who have odd ethical ideas, while another aunt (the Church) lives on the outskirts of the big estate. The boy likes her and visits her. He knows that something terrible once happened in the orchard (the Crucifixion). Whistler urged him to do it still. 'My dear Laurie, I haven't the time now. One can't write more than two thousand words a week, do you think?' Whistler protested that it surely need be no longer than the story-introduction to *Come Hither*; curiously, this seemed never to have occurred to de la Mare, who had always envisaged it 'as long as the Midget or longer,' and he seemed attracted by the idea of trying it as a short story. But the effort of recasting it was too great. An early story, 'The Miller's Tale' (on Pinker's list in 1901) came out in *Time and Tide*, and a poem appeared here and there.

Anxieties about Jinnie went on growing darker. It was difficult to keep track of her address, heartrending not to know what to do to help her best, or how to ensure her any financial security in the future. De la Mare never mentioned her name now except to those closest of all.

As 1955 ended he wrote to Herbert Howells: 'I am not so much alive as once, and that mainly means that although the supply of material seems to increase I get so much more quickly tired of persuading it into words.'[10a] Yet in spite of anxieties and pains and declining energy, the best gift in fate did still persist – that 'supply of material'.

*

His engagement book for January 1956, kept by N, has scarcely a blank page, though the visitors were most often now the family. A new story began to grow in his mind, and he wrote to tell Mona Tait: 'The chief character, a very fair blonde with old-fashioned Victorian ringlets, is called Estling, but I'm not yet sure about her first name.' By March he said the more he got into the story, the more it was coming alive, though he had had no chance yet of getting anything on to paper. Miss Estling's surname was a characteristic composite, he had made her up out of the second halves of 'dearest' and 'darling'. She inhabited his mind in a restless fashion throughout the spring, though by May he realised he might not get her out on to paper at all – a pity, as nothing but the physical energy was lacking, for that.

He worked on at revising the lectures – a stiffer, dryer task than weaving stories. He felt low; his speech grew slower, and moving between bed and chair more of an effort. The doctors tried so many new medicines that even de la Mare, who loved to have a battery of bottles at his bedside, was wearied. They were trying to discover why he no longer had the full use of his left arm; X-rays showed arthritis: there was some ulcerous trouble. Cortisone brought some relief. Joyce Grenfell gave him a gramophone to cheer him, and he told her of the loud Bach and Beethoven he used to play on the one at Hill House – 'I like it so loud that it frightens me.' 'Come on in and have a bath of Beethoven,' was how he had welcomed his godson Nick Furse at Hill House front door long ago, when the boy had ridden over from Eton on his bicycle.

As April began he felt harried. 'Precious Heaven I *must* soon finish the copy for this blessed new book.' The BBC had prepared programmes for his eighty-third birthday on the 25th, and the Exhibition was to open on the 19th. He could not attempt to be present, but he recorded (an ordeal now) a message for the occasion. It began: 'It must have been well before my teens when I was warned for the first

time ... against making what was called an exhibition of myself.'
Leonard Clark had done his labour of love well, presenting a collection
of over half a century's work, including some of the early notebooks and
many manuscripts. The National Book League had never before held
an exhibition of this kind for a living author.

After the birthday de la Mare was in splendid looks and spirits; he
wrote to Sister de Chantal: 'To turn 83 and not to die of it – *that* has
been the crucial problem of my last few days.' And to Gerald Bullett: 'I
think there are drifts in the mind, and that they vary in their degree
and kind of felicity; and one of mine is unmistakably and unreasonably
– well, Up Jenkins!'[11] It was a beautiful and prolonged spring. The
robin that perched outside his window sang (to his ear) 'Won't you
come home, Bill Bailey?' But it was hardly a quiet life. He told Higham:
'I have practically decided not to have a great many more birthdays.'
He gave an interview to Boris Ford for the *Journal of Education*, and
became engrossed in talk, sitting in Bray Minima in his wheelchair as
it was a lovely afternoon – enjoying himself at several knight's moves
away from education.[12] N brought them brandy and whisky, and they
discussed characters in fiction, de la Mare querying the usual claim for
Shakespeare as the creator of a whole world of characters: 'You can't
call Macbeth a character. He's more like a walking shadow,' and
quoted 'tale told by an idiot signifying nothing', which he took to mean
not that life had no significance, but that it signified 'nothing,
nothingness, a world of nothing'. Tea had no chance to begin until
six-thirty, when N had to prise them away from a discussion that had
now moved via the current attempt to exterminate wild rabbits by
myxamatosis (which de la Mare found incomprehensibly cruel) to the
issue of capital punishment, on which Ford, an abolitionist, found him
unexpectedly challenging. Their talk did not end till seven-fifteen; not
till then had de la Mare given Ford any chance to leave. He had paid no
attention to the reels of tape that had whispered their way through the
conversation; they induced no self-consciousness, and as it happened,
the machine, wrongly adjusted, had left them completely blank.

Tea-parties continued as usual, and on 20 June de la Mare wrote to a
friend of the midsummer leaf and blossom: 'One looks at it partly with
amazed delight and partly with anticipatory regret at its transito-
riness.'[13] But he had no more need to fear that. Nothing he looked out
at this evening would fade, for him.

He had been very well all day, and sat on in Bray Minima, almost all
made of its two windows, south and east. When N suggested bed at
last, he said: 'I don't think I will yet'; but then he did. At about
nine-thirty he exclaimed: 'Oh, N, I do feel seedy!' One glance at him

was enough. He was in a cold sweat and his face grey. It was another coronary thrombosis. He did not want N to leave the room, but she had to call the doctor instantly. An injection was given, and oxygen sent for. De la Mare hated the mask, and kept taking it off. Dick and Colin came, then Florence and Jinnie, and all four spent the night there. N, disciplined to the last, wrote her professional, impersonal notes on the case for the doctor: 'Patient very restless – difficult and irregular breathing – did not sleep – very talkative.' All possible remedies were tried, and oxygen given almost continuously. Towards dawn he slept about an hour. His pulse had been imperceptible all night, and when he woke he was worse. He was quiet through the day – the longest day of the year – and slept now and then. Sometimes he was sick, and when Russell Brain, who had been told that he was dying and invited to see him, came into the room, de la Mare apologised for his lack of party manners. Yet he was bright, happy even, and joked: 'I think we shall cheat them yet.'

N wanted to do everything for him herself, but Florence insisted she should have some help, and a nurse was engaged for the night. De la Mare was certainly aware by now that he was dying. At one moment he spoke to Brain of 'onlookers'; to the pretty nurse he murmured drowsily: 'It's a long time since we met – you must have come out of a dream.' He spoke tenderly of N, repeated for Dick his 'Fare Well' – needing some prompting. The longest day drew in quietly, and the short night fell. N had gone out of the room for a brief rest. The nurse who had taken her place tucked him in – it was 2 a.m. – and bent over him. She asked if he was quite comfortable. 'Yes, I'm perfectly all right,' he answered – then he caught his breath in one gasp and died. There was no time to fetch N or the others. The nurse could only wake them and tell them he had gone.

*

His ashes were buried in the crypt of St Paul's, and his memorial tablet stands near neighbour there to Canon Scott-Holland's. At the crowded burial service, the Dean spoke of him as a 'child of Paule's'. The Bach Toccata and Fugue in D Minor that he had loved to hear at volume on his gramophone, rolled out from the organ as loud as he would have wished. His will, after the bequests, went on to say: 'For the love and devotion of my children and in special my daughter Florence, and the affection of friends, priceless blessings in a life divinely generous of blessings, I should strive in vain to express my perpetual gratitude.'

Miss Taroone, in the *Come Hither* story, advises the little boy:

'sleeping, waking; waking, sleeping, Simon, sing while you can.' Keats thought 'a man's life of any worth is a continuing allegory.' If that is so, de la Mare's life kept remarkably close to this one, of his own writing. His departure also, it would seem, was much like Simon's, after the child's long night spent in writing out the poems he liked best, in the top room of Miss Taroone's house:

'With a kind of grief that was yet rapture in my mind, I stood looking out over the cold lichen-crusted shingled roof of Thrae – towards the East and towards those far horizons. Yet again the apprehension (that was almost a hope) drew over me that at any moment wall and chimney-shaft might thin softly away, and the Transformation Scene begin. I was but just awake: and so too was the world itself, and ever is. And somewhere – Wall or no Wall – was my mother's East Dene ...'[14]

References

Abbreviations

EC   Ella Coltman
EdlM   Elfrida de la Mare (E. Ingpen)
EM   Edward Marsh
EOM   *Early One Morning* (1935)
ET   Edward Thomas
FR   Forrest Reid
HN   Henry Newbolt
MEC   Mary Coleridge
NR-S   Naomi Royde-Smith
REI   Roger Ingpen
RNG-A   R.N. Green-Armytage
Square brackets indicate dating by internal evidence.

Part I. Industrious Apprentice

Chapter 1. Origins

1. Flo Rowley/WdlM 24 April 1927.
2. Colin Arrott Browning, *The Convict Ship* (1847), Preface.
3. Ibid., p. 358.
4. C.A. Browning/Lucy Browning, 20 May 1846.
5. S.T. Coleridge, *Biographia Literaria*, Ch. 4.
6. Cf. *EOM*, pp. 555-6.
7. Cf. ibid., pp. 169-70.
8. Ibid., pp. 282-3.
9. *The Return* (1910), p. 6.
10. Ibid., p. 7.
11. *Winged Chariot* (1951), p. 16.
12. WdlM conversation with L. Whistler.
13. *Winged Chariot*, pp. 16-17.
14. *EOM*, p. 93.
15. Mss fragment (see also *EOM*, p. 212).
16. *EOM*, pp. 278-9.
17. Ibid., pp. 289-90.
18. Ibid., p. 335.
19. Russell Brain, *Tea with Walter de la Mare* (1957), p. 118.
20. *Henry Brocken* (1904), p. 11.
21. WdlM/W.H. Hamilton, 19 February 1940.
22. *Memoirs of a Midget* (1921), p. 16.
23. WdlM/HN, 18 February 1905.

Chapter 2. Schooldays

1. W.R. Matthews and W.M. Atkins, *A History of St Paul's Cathedral* (1957), p. 254.
2. *Hornbook No. 4* [probably Christmas 1898].
3. G.L. Prestige, *St Paul's in its Glory* (1955), p. 211.
4. Note by WdlM included in brochure of record of St Paul's Choir tour (Columbia Artists Inc.), 24 June 1953.
5. Thomas Browne, *Religio Medici* sect. 9.
6. WdlM/NR-S, 26 May 1911.
7. *A Quiet Life*, Lecture on Reading, Royal Society of Literature.
8. WdlM/Clarice Eedy, 26 February 1944.
9. Mss: *How I Became an Author*.
10. Henry Scott-Holland/WdlM, pmk 24 April 1883.
11. *William Russell*, WdlM mss.
12. *Memoirs of a Midget*, p. 16.
13. Note for brochure for St Paul's Choir recording, 24 June 1953.
14. Mss: *William Russell*.

Chapter 3. 'Floundering in oil'

1. Scott-Holland/WdlM, 6 April 1890.
2. Ibid. [August 1890].
3. WdlM/E. Ingpen, 25 January 1895.
4. Mss: *How I Became an Author*.

Chapter 4. Elfland

1. WdlM/E. Ingpen, pmk 11 April 1894.
2. Ibid., 13 April 1894.
3. Ibid., 18 April 1894.
4. Ibid., 20 April 1894.
5. Arthur Symons, *The Symbolist Movement* (1899).
6. WdlM/E. Ingpen, undated [April 1894].
7. *EOM*, p. 583.
8. *Private View* (1953), p. 73.
9. WdlM/E. Ingpen, 24 November 1894.
10. Peter Green, *Kenneth Grahame* (1959), p. 125.
11. Mss: *How I Became an Author*.
12. Editor's introduction to *The Eighteen Eighties*, Royal Society of Literature essays.
13. *Winged Chariot* (1951), p. 38.
14. WdlM/E. Ingpen, 15 March 1895.
15. James Payn/REI, 9 April 1895.
16. WdlM/E. Ingpen, 24 May 1895.

Chapter 5. 'Walter Ramal'

1. WdlM/E. Ingpen [? August 1895].
2. Ibid., 23 October 1895.
3. Ibid., 23 November 1895.
4. Ibid., 7 December 1895.
5. Russell Brain, *Tea with Walter de la Mare* (1957), p. 104.
6. WdlM/E. Ingpen, undated.
7. John St Loe Strachey, *The Adventure of Living* (1922), pp. 211-17.
8. WdlM/E. Ingpen, 26 May 1896.
9. Ibid., 9 October 1896.
10. Ibid., 19 November [1896].
11. Ibid., 24 April 1897.
12. Ibid., 12 April 1897.
13. WdlM/Ian Donnelly, 24 February 1955.
14. WdlM/E. Ingpen, 29 September 1897.
15. E. Ingpen/WdlM, 29 September 1897.
16. Notes by WdlM for Checklist of *Walter de la Mare*, Exhibition by

National Book League (1953).
17. Edward Wageknecht, *Walter de la Mare's The Riddle: A Note on the Teaching of Literature with Allegorical Tendencies. College of English*, XI, November 1949, pp. 72-80.
18. Forrest Reid, *Walter de la Mare. A Critical Study* (1929).
19. Conversion of King Edwin by

Paulinus: Bede's *Ecclesiastical History*, II. 13.
20. Guy Halkett, Assistant Editor/ WdlM, undated.
21. WdlM/REI, 22 December 1899.
22. Ibid., 28 January 1900.
23. Possibly an early version of 'Renunciation', *The Fleeting* (1933).

Chapter 6. Pinker

1. REI/WdlM, 1 July 1900.
2. J. Pinker/REI, 16 July 1900.
3. WdlM/Pinker, 21 July 1900.
4. WdlM/Lucy dlM, 26 April 1901.
5. WdlM/REI, pmk 27 April 1901.
6. Scott-Holland/WdlM, 2 June [1901].
7. WdlM/Pinker, 18 July 1901.
8. Chopin, *Ballade*, 111, Op, 4.
9. WdlM/REI, 19 November 1901.
10. Richard Doyle watercolour, C. Longman/J. Pinker. quoted Pinker/ WdlM, 25 November 1901.
11. WdlM/S. de Chantal [1937].
12. WdlM/HN, 7 February 1902.
13. Henry Newbolt, *My World As In My Time* (1932), p. 279.
14. Ibid., p. 280.
15. Ibid., p. 281.
16. WdlM Memoir in Henry Newbolt, *A Perpetual Memory and Other Poems* (1939).
17. Ibid., Ralph Furse Memoir.
18. Scott-Holland/WdlM, 11 April [1902].
19. WdlM/HN, 14 November 1902.
20. WdlM/W.H. Hamilton, 13 May

1944.
21. ET/Gordon Bottomley 26 July 1906: George Thomas (ed.) (1968), *Letters from Edward Thomas to Gordon Bottomley*.
22. ET review of *Songs of Childhood, Daily Chronicle*, 14 August 1902.
23. ET review of *Poems 1906, Daily Chronicle*, 9 November 1906.
24. Alice Meynell/WdlM, 26 September 1902.
25. WdlM/Alice Meynell, 30 September 1902.
26. WdlM/REI, 15 June 1903.
27. *Henry Brocken* (1904), pp. 128-9.
28. Ibid., p. 158.
29. WdlM/REI, 17 December 1903.
30. *Henry Brocken*, pp. 147-8.
31. Ibid., p. 80.
32. *Poems 1906*.
33. *Poems 1906*.
34. WdlM conversation with the author.
35. *Academy*, 26 March 1904.
36. WdlM/Pinker, 3 November 1904.
37. WdlM/HN, 20 November 1905.
38. WdlM/HN, undated.

Chapter 7. Edward Thomas

1. WdlM/HN, 11 April 1904.
2. *Poems 1906*.
3. MEC/WdlM, 7 October 1906.
4. Enclosed by HN, 30 January 1906.
5. *The Fleeting* (1933).
6. WdlM/HN, 29 March 1906.
7. WdlM/EdlM, pmk September 1906.
8. WdlM/HN undated [September

1906].
9. Alice Meynell/WdlM, 23 October 1906.
10. ET/WdlM, 31 October 1906.
11. Ibid., 14 November 1906.
12. Ibid., 27 August 1906.
13. MEC/HN, 30 December 1906. Quoted in Henry Newbolt, *Later Life*

and Letters (1942), p. 105.
14. ET/Gordon Bottomley, 22 April 1907, *Letters from Edward Thomas to Gordon Bottomley*, p. 137.
15. Walter de la Mare, Introduction to John Freeman's *Letters* (1924).
16. Editor, The *Cornhill*/WdlM, 29 July 1907.
17. WdlM/EC, undated.
18. EdlM/WdlM, 21 August 1907.
19. MEC/?EC, 8 June 1907.
20. WdlM '*Mary Coleridge: An Appreciation*', *The Guardian*, 11 September 1907.
21. WdlM/EC, 27 August 1907.
22. EC/HN, 17 September 1907.

23. WdlM/EC, undated [November 1907].
24. Ibid., 13 March 1907.
25. Ibid., October 1907.
26. HN/WdlM, 2 February 1908.
27. WdlM/HN, draft, undated [early 1908].
28. HN/WdlM, 5 February 1908.
29. EC/WdlM, 23 April 1908.
30. WdlM/EC, 17 June 1908.
31. Ibid., 9 July 1908.
32. WdlM/EdlM, 20 July 1908.
33. Ibid., 26 July 1908.
34. John Usmar/WdlM, 6 October 1908.

Chapter 8. The Newbolt Circle

1. WdlM/EC, 4 February 1908.
2. Ibid., October 1908.
3. WdlM/HN [late October 1908].
4. ET/WdlM, 4 November 1908.
5. 'Nod', *The Listeners, and Other Poems*, 1912.
6. WdlM/HN, 11 November 1909.
7. Forrest Reid, *Walter de la Mare: A Critical Study* (1929), p. 128.
8. WdlM/EC, 3 November 1909.
9. Ibid., November 1909.
10. *Private View*, WdlM, 1953, p. 195.
11. Bruce Richmond, conversation with the author.
12. WdlM/EC undated [July 1909].
13. ET/WdlM, 18 January 1909.
14. Ibid., 18 January 1909.
15. Ibid., 1 February 1909.
16. WdlM review *An Annual of New Poetry. Saturday Westminster Gazette* 28 April 1917. *Private View*, p. 117.
17. ET/Gordon Bottomley, 14 December 1909. *Letters from Edward Thomas to Gordon Bottomley* (1968), p. 196.
18. Edgar Jepson, *Memories of an Edwardian* (1937), p. 135.
19. *The Listeners*.
20. EC/WdlM, 13 May 1909.
21. Ibid., 13 May 1909.

22. WdlM/EC, 20 May 1909.
23. 'All That's Past', *The Listeners*.
24. Conversation with the author.
25. ET/WdlM, 8 June 1909.
26. 'Old Susan', *The Listeners*.
27. ET/WdlM, 8 June 1909.
28. HN/WdlM, 7 April 1909.
29. WdlM/Pinker, 9 June 1909.
30. Ibid., 17 June 1909.
31. 'Seaton's Aunt', *The Riddle* (1923), p. 127.
32. WdlM conversation with L. Whistler.
33. WdlM/EC, 12 October 1909.
34. ET/WdlM, 9 October 1909.
35. HN/WdlM, 10 November 1909.
36. HN/EC, 25 October 1909.
37. EC/WdlM, 7 April 1910.
38. WdlM/EC, 12 May 1910.
39. WdlM/HN, 2 July 1910.
40. WdlM/L. Hockey, 1 October 1945.
41. Janet Hooton, conversation with the author.
42. WdlM/NR-S, 15 November 1915.
43. HN/WdlM, 22 July 1910.
44. *Memory and Other Poems* (1938).
45. WdlM/EC, July 1910.
46. Ibid., 10 September 1910.
47. ET/WdlM, 28 October 1910.
48. NR-S/WdlM, 1 October 1910.

Part II. Romantic Acrobat

Chapter 9. Naomi Royde-Smith

1. *John O'London's Weekly*, 24 April 1953.
2. NR-S, undated [early 1911].
3. WdlM/NR-S, 11 April 1911.
4. *The Listeners*.
5. WdlM/NR-S, pmk 8 April 1911.
6. Ibid., 19 March 1911.
7. *Motley and Other Poems* (1918).
8. WdlM/NR-S, 24 April 1911.
9. EC/HN, undated [1911].
10. WdlM/NR-S, 22 July 1911.
11. Ibid., 30 June 1911.
12. WdlM/Edward Garnett, 4 December 1923.
13. WdlM/NR-S, 24 July 1911.
14. Ibid., pmk 19 July 1911.
15. Ibid., undated [mid-August 1911].
16. *The Burning-Glass and Other Poems* (1945).
17. *The Listeners*.
18. NR-S/WdlM, 16 September 1911.
19. Ibid., 16 September 1911.

Chapter 10. 'That dungeon of print'

1. WdlM/HN, undated [early August 1911].
2. HN/WdlM, 1 October 1911.
3. ET/WdlM, undated [October 1911].
4. Ibid., 23 October 1911.
5. HN/?Alice Hylton, 18 October 1911.
6. WdlM/HN, undated [January 1911].
7. WdlM/NR-S, 17 February 1912.
8. HN/WdlM, 28 January 1912.
9. D.H. Lawrence/E. Garnett quoted in C.G. Heilbrun, *The Garnett Family*, pp. 142-62 [date not given].
10. WdlM/E. Garnett, undated [summer 1912].
11. Ibid., 27 May 1913.
12. D.H. Lawrence/E. Garnett, 30 December 1913, Aldous Huxley (ed.), *The Letters of D.H. Lawrence* (1932), p. 172.
13. D.H. Lawrence/E. Garnett, 4 August 1912, *Letters*, p. 48.
14. Ibid., 22 August 1912, *Letters*, pp. 50-1.
15. D.H. Lawrence/A.W. McLeod, undated, *Letters*, p. 60.
16. D.H. Lawrence/E. Garnett, 22 March 1913. Quoted in *The Garnett Family*.
17. Review by de la Mare of D.H. Lawrence, *Love Poems and Others*, *Times Literary Supplement*, 13 March 1913.
18. Review of *Georgian Poetry 1911-12* by de la Mare, *Edinburgh Review*, April 1913, *Private View* (1953), p. 127.
19. D.H. Lawrence/WdlM [Autumn 1913].
20. Conversation with the author.
21. S. Sassoon/Dame Felicitas Corrigan, 28 July 1965, *Poet's Pilgrimage* (1973), p. 66.
22. WdlM/NR-S, 6 July 1912.
23. Ibid., 28 June 1912.
24. Ibid., pmk 22 May 1912.
25. NR-S/WdlM, undated [before 20 January 1912].
26. WdlM/NR-S, 20 January 1912.
27. WdlM/EC, August 1911.
28. E. Gosse/WdlM, 18 May 1912.
29. ET/WdlM, 15 May 1912.
30. WdlM/NR-S, 8 August 1911.
31. WdlM/Georgina Sime, 7 February 1944.
32. WdlM/NR-S, 5 August 1912.

Chapter 11. Peacock Pie

1. WdlM/NR-S, 8 June 1912.
2. 'Rupert Brooke and the Intellectual Imagination', *Pleasures and Speculations* (1940), p. 193.
3. Christopher Hassall, *Rupert Brooke: A biography* (1964), p. 360 [date not given].
4. Christopher Hassall, *Edward Marsh: A biography* (1959). A.E. Housman/Edward Marsh, 1 October 1912.
5. M. Hewlett/EM quoted in Christopher Hassall, *Edward Marsh*, p. 205.
6. Quoted by HN/Alice Hylton, 4 June 1914.
7. WdlM, conversation with the author.
8. WdlM/NR-S, 9 July 1911.
9. *Saturday Westminster Gazette*, 19 August 1911.
10. John Gould Fletcher, *Life is my Song* (1937), quoted in Charles Norman, *Ezra Pound* (1960), p. 103.
11. WdlM/NR-S, 4 February 1913.
12. Ibid., 30 March 1913.
13. Ibid., 1 April 1913.
14. Ibid., pmk 30 March 1913.
15. Ibid., 2 April 1913.
16. Ibid., 1 April 1913.
17. Edward Thomas, *In Pursuit of Spring* (1914), p. 178.
18. I owe the connection between the passage from *In Pursuit of Spring* and the poem 'March', concerning Robert Frost's advice, to W. Cooke, *Edward Thomas: a critical biography* (1970), pp. 184-5.
19. FR/WdlM, undated [probably early 1912].
20. WdlM/FR [undated].
21. Forrest Reid, *Walter de la Mare: A Critical Study*, pp. 37-8.
22. WdlM/NR-S, 1 June 1913.
23. NR-S/WdlM, 26 March 1913.
24. Private information.
25. NR-S/WdlM, 26 March 1913.
26. WdlM/NR-S, 7 February 1916.
27. *Peacock Pie: A book of rhymes* (1913).
28. EM/WdlM, 29 July 1913.
29. ET/WdlM, pmk 24 June 1913.
30. WdlM/NR-S, 28 June 1913.
31. WdlM/NR-S, undated [after 11 July 1912].
32. L. Fraser/WdlM, 29 July 1912.
33. Ibid., 2 September 1912.
34. Ibid., 24 November 1912.
35. Ibid., 2 March 1917.
36. 'The Truants', *Peacock Pie*.

Chapter 12. Ghosts and Shadows

1. WdlM/NR-S, pmk 25 August 1913.
2. Ibid., 23 August 1913.
3. NR-S, conversation with L. Whistler.
4. ET/WdlM, pmk 6 October 1913.
5. WdlM/NR-S, undated [January 1914].
6. Ibid, pmk 6 December 1913; ibid. undated [May 1914].
7. WdlM/NR-S, 26 Jan. 1914; HN/ Alice Hylton, 24 Jan. 1914.
8. WdlM, conversation with L. Whistler.
9. *Motley and Other Poems* (1918).
10. Conversation with L. Whistler.
11. E. Garnett/WdlM, 29 April [1920].
12. *Collected Poems of Rupert Brooke*, with a Memoir by Edward March (1918).
13. NR-S/WdlM, undated [July 1914].
14. *O Lovely England and Other Poems* (1953).
15. WdlM/NR-S, undated [August 1914].
16. WdlM/NR-S, undated [August 1914].
17. C. Hassall, *Edward Marsh*, p. 300.

18. WdlM/NR-S, undated [August 1914].
19. ET/WdlM, undated [August 1914].
20. R. Brooke/WdlM, 20 Nov. 1914.
21. ET/WdlM, 30 November 1914.
22. 'For All the Grief', *Motley*.
23. 'Alone', *Motley*.
24. WdlM/NR-S, pmk 7 December 1914.
25. Ibid., pmk 14 Dec. 1914.
26. Ibid.
27. Ibid., 19 Dec. 1914.

Part III. The Hum of Noon

Chapter 13. Professor

1. *Motley*.
2. Unpublished until *Complete Poems* (1969).
3. WdlM/NR-S, pmk 21 January 1915.
4. HN/Alice Hylton, 20 January 1915.
5. *Story and Rhyme* (1921).
6. Ralph Hodgson/WdlM, undated [early 1915].
7. *Stuff and Nonsense* (1927).
8. WdlM/HN, 3 March 1915.
9. ET/WdlM, 21 March 1915.
10. Ibid., 24 March 1915.
11. WdlM/EdlM, pmk 24 April 1915.
12. WdlM/LucydlM, undated.
13. WdlM/NR-S, 25 April 1915.
14. WdlM/NR-S, 28 April 1915.
15. WdlM on Brooke, 8 May 1915, *Westminster Gazette*.
16. *Times Lit. Sup.* review by de la Mare of Rupert Brooke, *1914 and other Poems*, 22 July 1915.
17. EM/WdlM, 20 September 1915.
18. Ibid., 25 September 1915.
19. Christopher Hassall, *Rupert Brooke* (1964), p. 457.
20. WdlM/NR-S, 7 September 1915.
21. Ibid., 31 September 1915.
22. HN/EC, 15 February 1924.

Chapter 14. America

1. WdlM/NR-S, undated [October 1915].
2. WdlM/EC, undated [February 1916].
2a. WdlM/E. Cecil, 12 May 1920.
3. Mss of a lecture 'Life and the Novel'.
4. WdlM/Frank Nicholson, undated.
5. WdlM/NR-S, 7 February 1916.
5a. ET/Gordon Bottomley, 11 February 1916, *Letters from Edward Thomas to Gordon Bottomley*, p.259.
5b. WdlM/EM, 6 October 1916.
6. WdlM/NR-S, 3 September 1915.
7. WdlM/EdlM, pmk 14 November 1916.
8. WdlM/NR-S, 23 November 1916.
9. WdlM/Poppy Ingpen, 7 December 1916.
10. WdlM/NR-S, pmk 2 December 1916.
11. WdlM/RNG-A, 2 February 1933.
12. WdlM/EdlM, 23 January 1917.
13. Conversation with L. Whistler.
14. WdlM/HN, 16 January 1917.
15. Robert Frost/Louis Untermeyer, 14 November 1916, *The Letters of Robert Frost to Louis Untermeyer* (1964), p. 45.
16. Robert Frost memorial article: 'The Poetry of Amy Lowell', *Christian Science Monitor*, 16 May 1925. Quoted in Lawrance Thompson, *The Years of Triumph 1915-1938* (1971), p. 277.
17. Robert Frost/C.L. Young, 7 December 1917 (see *The Years of Triumph*, p. 118).

18. 'Prose in Poetry', *Pleasures and Speculations*, p. 103.
19. WdlM/NR-S, 17 January [1917].
20. R. Frost/WdlM, 22 September 1938.
21. Conversation with L. Whistler, 1961.
22. WdlM/S. de Chantal, 30 Oct. 1928.
23. Private information.
24. WdlM/EdlM, pmk 23 Jan. 1917.
25. WdlM/EM, 7 March 1917.
26. *Songs of Childhood* (1902).
27. HN/Alice Hylton, 21 February 1917.
28. WdlM/EM, undated [mid February 1917].
29. E. Garnett/WdlM, 18 April 1917.
30. *Motley*.
31. 'Edward Thomas', *Private View*, p. 118.
32. Foreword, *Collected Poems by Edward Thomas* (1920).
33. H. Monro/EM, June 1917 (quoted in Christopher Hassall, *Edward Marsh*, p. 412.
34. EM/WdlM, 1 September 1917.
35. WdlM/EM, 3 September 1917.

36. Ibid., 28 July 1918.
37. 'Afraid', *Poems 1919-1934*, also *Inward Companion: Poems* (1950).
38. W. Gibson/EM [summer 1917], see C. Hassall, *Edward Marsh*, p. 423.
39. 'Often rebuked, yet always back returning', Philip Henderson (ed.), *The Complete Poems of Emily Brontë* (1951).
40. *O Lovely England and Other Poems* (1953).
41. WdlM/T.F. Higham, 2 June 1950.
42. In fact by Francis Quarles.
43. WdlM/EC, 7 September 1918.
44. WdlM/NR-S, pmk 13 November 1918.
45. Thomas Hardy/WdlM, 1 November 1918, review in *The Bookman*, June 1908. See R.L. Purdy and Michael Millgate (eds), *Collected Letters of Thomas Hardy*, vol. 6, p. 201.
46. S. Sassoon, *Siegfried's Journey* (1945), pp. 106-7.
47. *Siegfried's Journey*, p. 107.

Chapter 15. Memoirs of a Midget

1. L. Clark, conversation with the author.
2. 'Rupert Brooke and the Intellectual Imagination', *Pleasures and Speculations* (1940), p. 195.
3. EM/WdlM, 11 April 1919.
4. Mrs Brooke/WdlM, 15 June 1919.
5. WdlM/NR-S, 12 May 1919.
6. *The Connoisseur* (1926).
7. Thomas Hardy/WdlM, 15 October 1919. *Collected Letters of Thomas Hardy*, vol. 5.
8. WdlM/EM, 12 September 1919.
9. *The Veil and Other Poems* (1921).
10. Professeur Luce Bonnerot, *L'Oeuvre de Walter de la Mare* (1969).
11. WdlM/NR-S, 16 August 1920.
12. Ibid., 12 May 1920.

13. 'To K.M.' *The Fleeting and Other Poems* (1933).
14. Katherine Mansfield/WdlM, 2 May 1921.
15. K. Mansfield/J. Middleton Murry, *The Letters of Katherine Mansfield to John Middleton Murry* (1954).
16. K. Mansfield/WdlM, pmk 21 January 1922.
17. Ibid.
18. See Frank Swinnerton, *Figures in the Foreground* (1963), p. 102.
19. WdlM/NR-S, 13 July 1920.
20. Ibid., 16 August 1920.
21. HN/Alice Hylton, 14 October 1920.
22. FR/WdlM, 3 March 1921.
23. Ibid., 11 March 1921.
24. Ibid.

Chapter 16. Thomas Hardy

1. EdlM/WdlM, 18 June 1921.
2. *BBC Broadcast 28 April 1955, A Meeting with Thomas Hardy*, Recording Lib. No. X21770.
3. 'Thomas Hardy', *Memory and Other Poems* (1938).
4. WdlM/Percy Withers, 4 October 1921.
5. WdlM/EdlM, undated.
6. Florence Emily Hardy, *The Life of Thomas Hardy* (1962), pp. 413-14.
7. *EOM*, p. 213.
8. *Bells and Grass: A book of rhymes* (1941).
9. REI/WdlM, 19 August 1927.
10. WdlM/Thomas Hardy, 5 July 1921. *Collected Letters of Thomas Hardy*, vol. 6.
11. Thomas Hardy/WdlM, 9 August 1921. *Collected Letters of Thomas Hardy*, vol. 6.
12. *The Life of Thomas Hardy*, pp. 104-5.
13. Conversation with L. Whistler, 1954.
14. Thomas Hardy/WdlM, 9 August 1921. *Collected Letters of Thomas Hardy*, vol. 6.
15. HN/Alice Hylton, 21 August 1921.

Chapter 17. Come Hither

1. WdlM/FR, 6 January 1922.
2. FR/WdlM, 13 December 1922.
3. WdlM/FR, 6 January 1922.
4. WdlM/W.H. Hamilton, 2 May 1922.
5. Ibid., 9 March 1928.
6. HN/Alice Hylton, 15 December 1922.
7. Ibid., 10 May 1922.
8. EM/WdlM, 15 June 1922.
9. WdlM/M. Morant, 26 May 1952.
9a. Thomas Hardy/WdlM, 28 June 1923. *Collected Letters of Thomas Hardy*, vol. 6.
10. Thomas Hardy/WdlM, 6 June 1919. *Collected Letters of Thomas Hardy*, vol. 5.
11. Charlotte Mew/WdlM, 6 January 1924.
12. S. Sassoon/WdlM, 8 January 1924.
13. Ibid., 31 January 1924.
14. WdlM/RNG-A, 16 February 1931.
15. S. Sassoon, conversation with the author.
16. R.L. Mégroz, *Walter de la Mare* (1924).
17. RNG-A/WdlM, 15 November 1923.
18. 'The Lost Track', *The Connoisseur*, p. 322.
19. WdlM/P. Ingpen 14 Dec. 1924.

Chapter 18. Hill House

1. Virginia Woolf, *A Writer's Diary* (1953), pp. 92-3.
2. WdlM/HN, 20 January 1922.
3. 19, 20 November 1925, Lyric Theatre, Hammersmith in aid of King Edward Hospital Fund.
4. Edith Craig & Christopher St John, *Ellen Terry's Memoirs* (1933), p. 300.
5. HN/EC, 26 September 1926.
6. HN/Alice Hylton, 4 August 1926.
7. WdlM/RNG-A, 17 November 1926.
8. WdlM/Florence Thompson, 20 July 1927.
9. WdlM/S. de Chantal, 21 September 1927.
10. Ibid., 21 September 1927.
11. WdlM/Florence Thompson, 10 August 1927.

Chapter 19. The Mundane Thirties

1. Sydney Cockerell, conversation with the author.
2. WdlM/NR-S, 6 February 1928.
3. WdlM/RNG-A, 23 January 1928.
4. NR-S/WdlM, undated.
5. EdlM/Percy Withers, 11 June 1928.
6. WdlM/Eleanor Doorly, September 1928.
7. J.B. Priestley, conversation with the author.
8. HN/Alice Hylton, 6 June 1930.
9. EdlM/FR, 12 March 1929.
10. E. Meyerstein/WdlM, 9 October 1946.
11. WdlM/E. Meyerstein, 27 October 1946.
12. S. Sassoon/WdlM, 11 February 1931.
13. WdlM/RNG-A, 1 September 1932.
14. *The Fleeting*.
15. FR/WdlM, 1 September 1932.
16. *The Fleeting*.
17. Ibid.
18. 'All That's Past', *The Listeners*.
19. Laurence Binyon/WdlM, 13 June 1933.
20. HN/Alice Hylton, 13 May 1933.
21. *EOM*, p. 246.
22. WdlM/Florence Thompson, 29 May 1936.
23. Scholar's Library edn. of *A Midsummer Night's Dream* (1936), *Pleasures and Speculations*, p. 305.
23a. RNG-A/WdlM, 7 April 1936.
24. WdlM/RNG-A, 9 April 1936.
25. FR/WdlM, 10 October 1937.
26. WdlM/Margaret Newbolt, 7 May 1938.
27. WdlM Memoir. *A Perpetual Memory*, p. vii.
28. WdlM/RNG-A, 5 September 1938.
29. WdlM/S. Sassoon, 5 January 1943.
30. WdlM/RNG-A, 9 May 1939.
31. WdlM/Winifred Gill, 30 October 1939.
32. WdlM/Irene de Selincourt.
33. WdlM/S. de Chantal, 5 December 1939.

Part IV. A Citadel More Central

Chapter 20. Twickenham

1. WdlM/FR, undated [1940].
2. 'The Happy Encounter', *Poems 1906*.
3. Introduction, M. Johnson, *Art and Scientific Thought* (1944).
4. WdlM/Eleanor Doorly, 19 December 1940.
5. WdlM/EC, 13 December 1940.
6. WdlM/E. Doorly, 19 December 1940.
7. WdlM/Colin dlM, 5 March 1941.
8. WdlM/L. Binyon, 16 June 1941.
9. WdlM/RNG-A, 18 August 1941.
10. WdlM/Colin dlM, 27 September 1941.
11. WdlM/G.R. Hamilton, 8 February 1942.
12. WdlM/FR, 2 November 1943.
13. WdlM/Colin dlM, 4 November 1942.
14. MSS diary entry, 13 November 1942.
15. MSS diary entry, 11 November 1942.
16. Laurence Binyon/WdlM, 8 September 1938.
17. MSS diary entry [marked only '29 May'].

Chapter 21. Widower and Traveller

1. WdlM/Fr, 2 June 1944.
2. 'The Defeat', *Memory and Other Poems* (1938).
3. 'Away', ibid.
4. WdlM/F.C. Nicholson, 18 September 1944.
5. WdlM/EC, 28 August 1944.
6. Ibid., 9 December 1944.
7. WdlM/Margaret Newbolt, 11 March 1945.
8. WdlM/Gerald Bullett, 11 November 1945.
9. WdlM/E. Myers, 12 February 1946.
10. Ibid., 13 May 1946.
11. WdlM/RNG-A, 13 October 1945.
12. T.S. Eliot/WdlM, 23 January 1947.
13. Ibid., 22 August 1927. The poem 'Because I do not hope to turn again'

was quoted in *Desert Islands* (1930), pp. 272-3.
14. Conversation with L. Whistler.
15. Henry Charles Duffin, *Walter de la Mare. A Study of his Poetry* (1949).
16. John Betjeman, *Daily Herald*, 1 December 1946.
16a. WdlM/G. Rostrevor Hamilton, 20 October 1947.
17. WdlM/Martin Johnson, 18 January 1948.
18. WdlM/Herbert dlM, 24 February 1948.
19. Conversation with L. Whistler.
20. WdlM/Colin dlM, 1 June 1948.
21. WdlM/RNG-A, 3 August 1948.
22. WdlM/Anna Coltman, 30 June 1948.
23. WdlM/M. Johnson, 26 July 1948.

Chapter 22. Winged Chariot

1. *Inward Companion: Poems* (1950).
2. WdlM/Arthur Donelly, 15 February 1949.
3. MSS fragment.
3a. WdlM/O. Barfield, 16 November 1949.
4. WdlM/F.C. Nicholson, 27 December 1949.
5. WdlM/Rupert Thompson, 1 February 1950.
6. Introduction to 'Sweet as Roses', Leonard Russell (ed.), *The Saturday Book, Tenth Year* (1950), p. 136.
7. WdlM/RNG-A, 23 April 1950.
8. Ibid., 23 April 1950.
9. Virginia Howland introducing a reading in USA, July 1950.
10. WdlM/Alison Uttley, 2 March 1951.
11. Desmond MacCarthy, *Sunday Times*, 24 June 1951.
12. WdlM/EM, 8 October 1951.

13. WdlM/J. Mambrino, 23 August 1951.
14. Ibid., 23 August 1951.
15. Notes of conversations by L. Whistler.
16. Joyce Grenfell, conversation with the author.
17. WdlM/M. Johnson, 7 May 1952.
18. *O Lovely England* (1953).
19. WdlM/C. Asquith, 22 September 1952.
20. WdlM/N. Saxton, 23 September 1952.
21. WdlM/RNG-A, 17 September 1952.
22. Conversation with L. Whistler.
23. WdlM/RNG-A, 19 December 1952.
24. WdlM/Morchard Bishop, 22 December 1952.
25. Author's preface, *Private View*, p. xi.
26. Conversation with L. Whistler.

Chapter 23. *'Sing while you can'*

1. WdlM/Margaret Newbolt, 10 July 1953.
2. *O Lovely England*.
3. WdlM/Joan Hassall, 29 September 1953.
4. Conversation with L. Whistler.
5. Ibid.
6. WdlM/Ian Donelly, 19 February 1954.
7. WdlM/Rupert Thompson, 9 October 1948.
8. Joyce Grenfell, diary entry, 25 July 1954.
9. WdlM/G. Rostrevor Hamilton, 10 November 1955.
10. David Cecil/WdlM, 19 October 1955.
10a WdlM/Herbert Howells, 2 December 1955.
11. WdlM/Gerald Bullett, 30 April 1956.
12. Boris Ford, 'The Rest was Silence: Walter de la Mare's Last Interview', *Encounter*, September 1956.
13. WdlM/Sara Jackson, 20 June 1956.
14. 'The Story of This Book': *Come Hither*.

Index

Works by Walter de la Mare (WdlM) appear under title; other works under the names of the authors.

Henfield (Sussex), 434

Henley, W.E., 72

Henniker, Florence, 311

Henry Brocken (WdlM; novel), 96, 100, 109-12; publication and reception, 113, 115-16; broadcast, 364; and changelings, 395n

Henry, Leonard, 177

Herbert, George, 356, 359

Hewlett, Maurice, 208-9

Higham, T.F., 285, 324, 421-2, 445

Hill House *see* Taplow

Hillard, Mary, 263

Hitchman, Mrs (singing teacher), 25

Hitler, Adolf, 358, 365, 371, 381

Hodgson, Ralph: friendship with Freeman, 128; WdlM praises, 151; at Hootons, 169; character, 171-2; friendship with WdlM, 171-2, 185; and *Georgian Poetry*, 207, 239; and Reid, 217; and Fraser's *Flying Fame*, 222; illustrations and sketches, 238-9, 244-5; and WdlM's poetry, 245; war service, 260; style, 318; lives abroad, 330; visits WdlM at Hill House, 368; and atom bomb, 397; on being a poet, 423; 'Eve', 376; 'The Muse and the Mastiff', 368; 'To Deck a Woman', 171

Holland: WdlM visits, 309

Holman Hunt, William *see* Hunt, William Holman

Hooton, Janet, 169, 171, 190

Horn Book, The (magazine), 83, 85, 87-8

Horton, W.J., 69-70, 76

Hotson, Leslie, 421

Housman, A.E., 207, 262, 327; 'Tell me not here', 284-5

Housman, Laurence, 429

Hove, 292, 297-8, 402, 407, 413-14, 433-4

'How I Became an Author' (WdlM; article), 50

Howells, Herbert, 444

Howland, Charles, 265, 340

Howland, Virginia, 420

Hoyle, Fred, 421

Hudson, W.H., 16, 184, 220

Hueffer, Ford Maddox (Ford), 164

Hunt, William Holman, 42

Hutchinson (publishing house), 142

Huxley, Aldous, 276

'Ideal Craftsman, An' (WdlM; short story), 93, 117, 147, 353

'Idealists, The' (WdlM; short story), 96

Ife, Oni of, 408

'Imagination's Pride, The' (WdlM; poem), 300

Ingpen, Ada Mary Frances (*née* Delamare; WdlM's sister; 'Poppy'): on sister Florence, 5; family life, 6, 18-20, 49, 76; character, 6; relations with WdlM, 19; at St Paul's, 34; on WdlM's self-education, 50; amateur acting, 53-4; WdlM describes, 88; marriage, 95; and *Henry Brocken*, 111; and WdlM's *Memoirs of a Midget*, 301; Lucy lives with, 308; WdlM dedicates *Memory and Other Poems* to, 366; at Hill House in war, 370; flat bombed, 378; on WdlM's colour sense, 404; visits WdlM at Twickenham, 415-16, 440

Ingpen, Alfred and Constance (Elfie's parents), 55

Ingpen, Alfred (Elfie's brother; 'Dom'), 55

Ingpen, Elfrida *see* de la Mare, Elfrida

Ingpen, Roger (Elfie's brother): relations with Elfie and family background, 55-6; WdlM's letters to, 63; chaperones Elfie, 64; sees WdlM's manuscripts, 65; and Horton, 69-70; encourages WdlM's writings, 73, 77, 90-1, 93-4, 118; at *Cornhill*, 78; WdlM describes, 88; and birth of WdlM's daughter Florence, 90-1, 93; marriage, 95; and publication of WdlM's *Songs of Childhood*, 99; lends money to WdlM, 108; and WdlM's *Henry Brocken*, 111; at Hutchinson's, 142; depicted in *The Return*, 166; and Edward Thomas's poems, 260;

Henry and Mary Ponsonby:
Life at the Court of Queen Victoria
William M. Kuhn   £9.99 Paperback   07156 3230 2

Henry Ponsonby served as Queen Victoria's private secretary for a quarter of a century and his wife Mary collaborated with him in his work. The Ponsonbys met and married at court; they raised their family in Windsor Castle; they lived and died in the corridors where prime ministers and princes passed as they went back and forth to see the queen. Under attack from republicans at the beginning of the Ponsonbys' time in office, their solution to these various problems left the Victorian monarchy in a position of unparalleled strength. The issues which they advised on have particular resonance today when the monarchy's future is once more in question.

'This is history writing at its brightest and most bold.'

Kathryn Hughes, *Books of the Year, The Sunday Telegraph*

'Throws a fascinating new light on the closing quarter-century of the Queen's reign.'   A.N Wilson, *Critic's Choice, Daily Mail*

Siegfried Sassoon: The Making of a War Poet
Jean Moorcroft Wilson   £9.99 Paperback   0 7156 3121 7

The first volume of Jean Moorcroft Wilson's magnificent biography of one of the twentieth century's finest poets, published in conjunction with the eagerly awaited second volume. Wilson traces the origins both of Sassoon's patriotism and of his anti-war stance that culminated in a statement that was read out in Parliament and a spell in a convalescent home, covering his life up until the end of the Great War.

'A story in which the roots are as interesting as the core ... invaluable to historians of the period.'   Andrew Motion, *The Times*

'Thorough and perceptive'   Jeremy Lewis, *Observer*

ORDER FORM (BLOCK CAPITALS PLEASE)

SURNAME_____ FIRST NAME_____

ADDRESS_____

_____ POSTCODE_____

METHOD OF PAYMENT (PLEASE TICK AS APPROPRIATE)

Invoice to my Grantham Book Services account
By cheque (payable to Duckworth Publishers)
Please send account opening details (trade customers only)
By credit card (Access/ Visa / Mastercard / Amex)

Card no:

Expiry date: /   /   Authorising Signature: _____

POSTAGE (Private customers) Please note that the following postage and packing charges should be added to your order:

UK deliveries: £4 on orders up to £20; £5 on orders over £20
Export surface: £5 for first book + £1 for each additional book
Export airmail: £9 for the first book + £2 for each additional book

QTY	ISBN	TITLE	PRICE	TOTAL
__	_____	_____	£_____	£_____
__	_____	_____	£_____	£_____
__	_____	_____	£_____	£_____
__	_____	_____	£_____	£_____
__	_____	_____	£_____	£_____
			POSTAGE £_____	
			TOTAL £_____	

To: Sales Dept, Duckworth, 90-93 Cowcross Street, London EC1M 6BF
Tel: 020 7490 7300 Fax: 020 7490 0080
Heidi@duckworth-publishers.co.uk